DISCARD

Reader Series
in Library and Information Science

Published *Readers* in the series are:

Reader in Library Administration, 1969.
Paul Wasserman and Mary Lee Bundy.

Reader in Research Methods for Librarianship. 1970.
Mary Lee Bundy and Paul Wasserman.

Reader in the Academic Library. 1970.
Michael M. Reynolds.

Reader in Library Services and the Computer. 1971.
Louis Kaplan.

Reader in American Library History. 1971.
Michael H. Harris.

Reader in Classification and Descriptive Cataloging. 1972.
Ann F. Painter.

Reader in Technical Services. 1973.
Edward L. Applebaum.

Reader in Medical Librarianship. 1973.
Winifred Sewell.

Reader in Government Documents. 1973.
Frederic J. O'Hara.

Reader in Science Information. 1973.
John Sherrod and Alfred Hodina.

Reader in Library Cooperation. 1973.
Michael M. Reynolds.

Reader in Music Librarianship. 1973.
Carol June Bradley.

Reader in Documents of International Organizations. 1974
Robert D. Stevens and Helen C. Stevens.

Reader in Library and Information Services. 1974.
Michael M. Reynolds and Evelyn H. Daniel.

Reader in Library Systems Analysis. 1975.
John Lubans, Jr. and Edward A. Chapman.

Reader in Media, Technology and Libraries. 1975.
Margaret Chisholm.

Reader in Library Technology. 1975.
Shirley Gray Adamovich.

Reader on the Library Building. 1975.
Hal B. Schell.

Reader in Social Science Documentation. 1976
Christopher D. Needham.

Reader in Operations Research for Libraries. 1976
Peter Brophy, Michael Buckland and Anthony Hindle.

Reader in Operations Research for Libraries

Edited by

Peter Brophy,
Michael K. Buckland
and
Anthony Hindle

1976

Information Handling Services
Library and Education Division
An Indian Head Company   Formerly Microcard Editions

Published by Information Handling Services
Library and Education Division
P. O. Box 1154
Englewood, Colorado 80110

Printed in the United States of America

Foreword

Unlike many other academic disciplines, librarianship has not yet begun to exploit the contributions of the several disciplines toward the study of its own issues. Yet the literature abounds with material germane to its concerns. Too frequently the task of identifying, correlating, and bringing together material from innumerable sources is burdensome, time consuming or simply impossible. For a field whose stock in trade is organizing knowledge, it is clear that the job of synthesizing the most essential contributions from the elusive sources in which they are contained is overdue. This then is the rationale for the series, *Readers in Library and Information Science*.

The Readers in Library and Information Science will include books concerned with various broad aspects of the field's interests. Each volume will be prepared by a recognized student of the topic covered, and the content will embrace material from the many different sources from the traditional literature of librarianship as well as from outside the field in which the most salient contributions have appeared. The objectives of the series will be to bring together in convenient form the key elements required for a current and comprehensive view of the subject matter. In this way it is hoped that the core of knowledge, essential as the intellectual basis for study and understanding, will be drawn into focus and thereby contribute to the furtherance of professional education and professional practice in the field.

Paul Wasserman
Series Editor

Contents

V

THE EVALUATION OF POLICY

VI

THE USER

VII

AN OVERVIEW

Introduction

One of the most striking features of libraries is the enormous growth in their size and complexity during the past century. It is not simply a matter of their individually doubling in size every 16 years, as shown by Fremont Rider, but also the development in networks linking individual libraries in larger and larger information systems, which makes library growth seem certain to continue. Furthermore, the worldwide expansion of education, research and leisure seem certain to guarantee a steadily increasing demand for library and information services. To all this should be added the widening diversity afforded by modern technology. Sound recordings and microfilms are already accepted library materials. Typewriters and telephones have become normal features of library technology. Computers, ultra-micro-reduction and other technological advances are bringing further variety to library and information services.

Change of any kind except straightforward expansion poses real difficulties for the conscientious library director. Some of these problems are likely to arise in any non-profit, service organization. Since the organization exists to serve its users, their satisfaction should be dominant and thus ultimately, the users have a substantial amount of control. Also, there are different constituencies with differing demands. This is very clearly seen in a university where there are competing claims for the library's resources both by subject (humanities versus science) and by function (teaching versus research).

It follows that any significant change is likely to involve changes in the way in which service is provided to particular groups and reallocation of the relative distribution of resources. Given the intangible nature of library use and the difficulty of establishing benefits, and given the influence often exercised by library committees and trustees, it is clear that effective public relations and political skills can be important. The prospect however, of a more objective approach to policies and planning, with as much measurement as possible, does hold advantages for the library administrator. It means, in particular, a more formal style of management with a more explicit assessment of who is served and how well. This should raise the level of debate on library policies by shifting to objective fact some of the reliance hitherto placed on subjective opinion.

Another advantage is that, as the formal analysis and modelling of library systems becomes slowly more complete, it should be possible for library policies to become progressively more internally consistent and more efficient as the relationships between the parts become more precisely understood.

There is little prospect of subjective judgment being eliminated from library planning, but there are good prospects of shifting some of the bases of judgment from opinion to observation. This is important because it ought to lead to better library provision. It is also important that it be done carefully and well and this implies that librarians should be actively involved in doing it - and using all the help they can get.

The mission of this book is to provide some timely and relevant help by presenting one of the most powerful developments of post-war management studies: Operations Research - the use of models to aid managerial judgment in complex situations. It cannot be claimed that non-profit making services such as libraries and information services are especially amenable to the operations research approach and its application to libraries is only just emerging from the research and development stage. A library is basically a very simple concept, but the sheer diversity of its users and of their needs, the rather intangible nature of the services it provides, and the difficulties in assessing the benefits derived from these services make policy-making complex and problematical.

Nevertheless it is already clear that operations research has much to offer to library administrators and its use in developing library and information services seems certain to increase in a cost-conscious world. This book has been designed to explain the nature and purpose of operations research to those concerned with the planning and management of libraries and information services. The education and training of librarians is usually weak in quantitative studies and methods. Consequently, a major factor in the selection of each paper has been the lucidity of exposition and the relatively low level of mathematical knowledge required to understand the basic arguments presented. Although some papers do contain mathematical reasoning, all materials presenting "university level" mathematics (even some concerned with libraries) have been rigorously excluded.

Nevertheless, the following pages may contain some mathematical symbols and concepts which are unfamiliar to some. This is an unfortunately necessary situation because there are distinct limitations to the extent to which quantitative (or any other) concepts can be presented efficiently without some reliance on the terminology and notation appropriate to the concepts concerned. Readers who have difficulty in understanding the mathematical portions are urged to start by concentrating on the ideas involved, relying on the narrative and taking equations and computations on trust. However, it is also suggested that they do not hesitate to seek the assistance of someone with a background in university level mathematics. It is likely to be the notation which is difficult rather than the underlying concepts. Once these are grasped, the notation will seem far less formidable.

Some of the papers are specifically concerned with library problems, but many are not. More library-oriented material could have been included, but this would have conflicted with our basic aim. This book has not been designed as a technical state-of-the-art review of library operations research for specialists. Neither will it turn librarians into O.R. specialists overnight. However, the inclusion of a specially prepared and up-to-date bibliography will help those who wish to read further. In keeping with the full title of this series, a few papers are concerned with information systems other than libraries as such. Finally, we would stress that this volume is closely related and indeed deliberately complementary to the *Reader in Library Administration* edited by Paul Wasserman and Mary Lee Bundy which inaugurated this series. All interested in effective library and information services are urged to examine both volumes.

A special acknowledgement is due to A. Graham Mackenzie, Librarian of the University of Lancaster. It was through his leadership as Director of the Library Research Unit that all three editors had the opportunity and the environment for serious work in the application of operations research to library problems.

Peter Brophy
Glasgow, Scotland

Michael K. Buckland
West Lafayette, Indiana, U.S.A.

Anthony Hindle
Lancaster, England

Reader in
Operations Research
for Libraries

I

THE METHODOLOGY OF OPERATIONS RESEARCH

These days virtually every librarian and library school student has heard of "operations research" although many may have but a hazy notion of what it implies for the library profession. In the first Chapter of this Reader we consider the philosophy, methodology, and technology of the discipline and whether the application of operations research to libraries can be justified. We consider whether we can expect useful results from the expenditure of effort in this direction.

Firstly, however, it is necessary to explain, in non-technical terms, the techniques of our chosen approach. Operations researchers have sometimes justifiably been reproached for their tendency to blind their non-mathematical audience with mathematics, and the editors, in writing the first paper of this Chapter have kept the mathematics as simple as possible and have taken pains to ensure that their explanations of such techniques as "linear programming", "queueing theory", and so on, are couched in terms which can be followed by the layman.

In the following papers, consideration is given to the application of this type of methodology to library problems, and to the general problems of the application of scientific methodologies to complex organizations. The discussion includes most of the key problems such as "qualitative versus quantitative" approaches; the problems of handling the human element; the role of mathematics; the concept and value of "systems thinking" and so on.

The Techniques of Operations Research: A Tutorial

Anthony Hindle, Michael K. Buckland and Peter Brophy

In this first paper, written by the editors, the fundamental techniques of operations research are outlined. Beginning with a definition of the discipline, the authors go on to isolate its characteristic features and to explain the twin processes of model building and model solution. A serious attempt has been made to use language which non-mathematicians can understand and the paper is aimed specifically at those librarians who, although they have no formal scientific training, would like to know more about the seemingly esoteric activities of operations researchers. The concepts behind such techniques as "linear programming", "queueing theory", "statistical decision analysis", and so on, are all basically straightforward, and this is the way in which they have been treated in this paper.

A. Introduction
B. Scientific Decision Making
C. Model Building
    C.1. Queueing models
    C.2. Simulation models
    C.3. Statistical models
D. Model Solution
    D.1. Mathematical programming
    D.2. Statistical decision analysis
E. Review

A. INTRODUCTION

Operations research has been defined as "the attack of modern science on complex problems in the direction and management of large systems of men, machines, materials and money in industry, business, government and defence. The distinctive approach is to develop a scientific model, incorporating measurements of factors, such as chance and risk, with which to compare the outcomes of alternative decisions, strategies or controls. The purpose is to help management determine its policy and actions scientifically"[1]. The discipline of O. R. is now firmly established in military, industrial and academic contexts in all the developed countries of the world.

The majority of operations researchers are employed in industry in a wide variety of companies. It is recognized that O. R. pays dividends. Most of the remainder are in the defence area or in academic institutions. O. R. in public administration (in both national and local contexts) is, as yet, at an embryo stage. However a very rapid expansion is envisaged in this area of application over the next few years.

A certain amount of O. R. has found its way into libraries and information services, and some of these applications will be described in other papers of this Reader. In this paper, however, we shall concentrate on the techniques of O.R., taking examples from libraries and also from other contexts.

B. SCIENTIFIC DECISION MAKING

It is clear from the definition of O.R., given above, that it is very much concerned with improving the quality of decision making by subjecting the decision problem to rigorous and objective scientific analysis. Before we can fully appreciate the implications of this approach it is necessary to describe the general nature of decision making. Consider, as an illustration, the following decision situation.

A patient enters a clinic complaining of a spot on the end of his nose. The doctor immediately decides that this is a symptom of one of three possible diseases, which he refers to as d_0, d_1, or d_2.

d_0 is a psychosomatic disorder. Both the patient and doctor are imagining the spot on the end of the patient's nose. Or, more realistically, the patient is demonstrating a symptom of diseases d_1 and d_2 but, in fact is suffering from neither.

d_1 is a common, non-serious, and non-costly disease. It is, by far, the most likely cause of the patient's symptoms. It can be successfully treated by applying a treatment referred to as t_1. If not treated in this way the patient will recover but only after a period of discomfort and time away from employment.

d_2 is a relatively rare and quite serious disorder. It requires a fairly expensive treatment, referred to as t_2, which will cure it very quickly indeed. It will also respond, to some extent, to the other treatment referred to as t_1, although the patient will take a long time to recover. If untreated the disease can be very persistent although the patient normally shakes it off eventually.

The doctor has available to him a test or examination, referred to as E, which will detect, with considerable reliability the presence or absence of disease d_2. The test is, however, expensive.

The society in which the doctor works is cost conscious about medical treatment. It would like the doctor to minimize the expected total cost of treating the patient. It identifies the following costs:

i) The cost, in lost productivity, of disease d_1 if untreated.
ii) The cost, in lost productivity, of disease d_1 if treated by treatment t_1.
iii) The cost, in lost productivity, of disease d_1 if treated by treatment t_2.

A similar cost table can be produced for diseases d_0 and d_2. Other costs are as follows:

iv) The cost of treatment t_1.
v) The cost of treatment t_2.

vi) The cost of examination E.

It is assumed, for simplicity, that the doctor has to carry out his diagnosis, examination and treatment on this one occasion only. In other words, he cannot review the case at a later date.

What should the doctor do?

The decision described above is one which we will attempt to solve later in this Chapter. However, for the moment let us note that it contains two features common to all decision problems:

a) An *assessment* of the consequences of taking (or failing to take various possible actions. For example, the doctor needs to know the consequences of deciding not to treat the patient who has the particular symptom in question.
b) A *valuation* of the various consequences in order that the 'best' action might be identified.

For example, the doctor needs to know the value to be attached to "lost productivity". Also, it is necessary that all the consequences of each action be measured in the same units: for example in monetary units.

It should be noted that, in this problem as in most real life problems, the doctor's 'values' are to some extent, imposed upon him. This is clear from the statement that society " . . . would like the doctor to minimize the expected total cost of treating the patient". In other words, there is some purpose or *objective* to be attained by the taking of a decision, by the making of a choice.

Thus decisions are taken in order that objectives might be attained. This requires the assessment of the consequences of alternative choices and the valuation of these consequences in relation to the objective sought. Already we have posed questions which will normally prove very difficult to answer.

What is, or should be, the objective to be sought?
What possible actions are available?
What are the consequences of these actions?
How can these consequences be measured on a common scale?
How can the best solution be deduced?

In order to help in the answering of questions like these, O.R. indulges in three primary sorts of activity as follows:

(i) Model Building

This refers to the attempt to write down, often in mathematical form, an explanation of the reasons certain consequences will follow from certain actions. A simple verbal model of part of the doctor's problem described above might be the following:

"If the doctor administers the test (E) to patients with spots on the ends of their nose then there will be a positive reaction if, and only if, the patient has disease d_2."

One well-known mathematical model is represented by the following equation:

$$P \times V = K$$
where
P denotes Pressure
V denotes Volume
K denotes a Constant

This is Boyle's Law which states that the measurement of pressure multiplied by the measurement of volume, with reference to certain sorts of physical entitites, remains a 'constant' (some fixed number). In other words if you had some gas under pressure in a cylinder and were to transfer it to a larger cylinder, the extra space would result in a lower pressure. Conversely, transferring it into a smaller cylinder with less space would necessitate a higher pressure. The equation not only reflects the nature of the relationship but permits one to compute precisely what the changed pressures would be, provided that the volume, the initial pressure, and the constant were known.

(ii) Model Solution

The second primary activity can be termed "model solution". A model or set of models is useless unless something can be done to it in order to obtain answers to the questions in which the decision maker is interested. Let us say we have a model of the following form:

$$M = a \times a^2 + b \times x + c$$

where M is the measure of performance (e.g., total treatment cost in our example); x refers to the variable under the de-cision-makers control (e.g., number of injections of pencillin); and a, b, and c are constants.

In other words, we know precisely how performance is affected by alternative decisions concerning x (in this illustration the number of shots of penicillin). The decision-maker's interest is in knowing the value of x to choose in order to minimize (or maximize) the performance measure (M). It is necessary to be able to "solve" the model. In this particular case we should need to use elementary calculus to compute the optimal solution mathematically, but, having plotted the model on a graph, the "minimum" (lowest cost) point is obvious and the value of "x" can be read off the X-axis. (See Figure 1.) Very often, however, mathematical models are so complex that solution is very difficult or can only be partially achieved by either graphical or mathematical techniques.

(iii) Derivation of "Measure of Effectiveness"

Very often as in our doctor's problem, one of the most significant difficulties is that of deriving a single measure for all the diverse consequences of an action. For example, there are treatment costs directly related to the price of the drugs and other resources, costs associated with loss of productivity, costs associated with obtaining information, the value of the doctor's time, and so on. In order to obtain a single variable to maximize all these diverse "costs" they must be assessed and related to a common scale of measurement (made "commensurable"). This is seldom completely attainable.

In addition to these primary activities there are other aspects to a complete O.R. investigation such as data collection, data processing, the design of a system to handle revised procedures, and the implementation of changes, and so on. However, these activities are common to all management services functions whereas the characteristic feature of O.R. is its direct attack on decision problems using scientific modeling and associated measure of effectiveness.

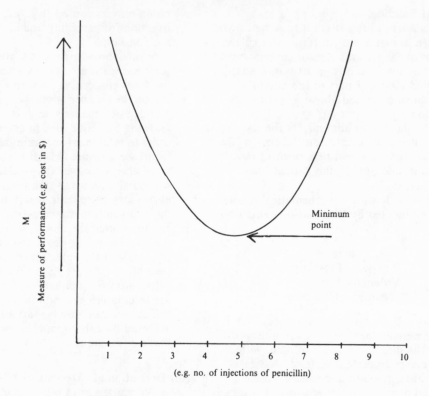

FIG. 1   GRAPH OF M = a X x² + b X x + c

C. MODEL BUILDING

What are the consequences of a particular course of action likely to be? What will happen if we open a new reading-room? How will the staff react to a new organizational structure? These questions require predictions to be made by the planners. The way O.R. can help is by building a scientific model of the situation under consideration from which predictions and forecasts can be drawn.

In this section we will attempt to build several models, some of which will illustrate an approach to library problems, while others will show the use of an O.R. model in other service industries. These models will include:

Queueing models
Simulation models
Statistical models

It is not intended, of course, to give a complete coverage, but merely to illustrate the concepts and principles involved in model development.

C.1. Queueing Models

Let us say that the provider of a service has a problem: the customers' average waiting time for service is regarded as being too long. Although, if the customer is lucky, he may arrive and find the service point unoccupied, if he is unlucky he may find himself at the back of a long queue. The administrator of the service considers that long waiting times cost money — either because he feels responsible for the loss of money incurred by the customers (e.g., he may be responsible for ensuring that highly-paid researchers are not kept waiting for service) or because he feels that the expectation of being kept waiting inhibits custom. His problem is to decide whether or not to provide an extra service point which would also lead to costs due to extra wages. Although there are many facets to a problem of this type, one is the prediction of what the customers' average waiting time would be if an extra service point were to be provided. In order to estimate this we require a mathematical model of the situation.

Taking the simple case where there is, at

present, only one service point, we need an equation giving the expected waiting time, assuming that the customers arrive in no discernable pattern — "at random" — and that the time taken to provide them with service is variable but has a measurable average value. Scientific research has resulted in the derivation of a set of equations for this and related problems. They are known as *queueing models*. The reader is recommended to take such formulae on trust for the time being. Anybody wishing to examine how they were derived is referred to standard texts[2]. The basic equation in queueing theory is:

$$\text{Expected waiting time} = \frac{\text{arrival rate}}{\text{service rate} \times (\text{service rate minus arrival rate})}$$

If we denote the expected waiting time for the single service point system as E_1, the arrival rate as λ*, and the service rate as μ, then we can express this equation in the form:

$$E_1 = \frac{\lambda}{\mu(\mu-\lambda)} \tag{1}$$

Other measures which are of interest are the chance** of not having to wait at all, denoted by P_0, and the average queue length, denoted by L. These are given by:

$$P_0 = 1 - \frac{\lambda}{\mu} \tag{2}$$

$$L = \frac{\lambda^2}{\mu(\mu-\lambda)} \tag{3}$$

In a situation where more than one service point is provided a customer has a choice; if one service point is occupied he can go to another. The equations for a system containing two service points are as follows:

$$E_2 = \frac{\lambda^2}{\mu(4\mu^2 - \lambda^2)} \tag{4}$$

$$P_0 = \frac{2\mu - \lambda}{2\mu + \lambda} \tag{5}$$

$$L = \frac{\lambda^3}{\mu(4\mu^2 - \lambda^2)} \tag{6}$$

Using these two sets of equations we are in a position to compute comparisons between the two alternatives (one service point or two) and to make predictions which should help the service manager to make his decision.

Clearly there are many situations in libraries where customers (library users) are liable to have to queue. In many ways the problem of having to wait for service could be claimed to be one of the main sources of friction between the library and its users. (For example, without this problem there would be hardly any need for a reservations system and libraries could rely more extensively on interlibrary loan than they do at present.)

Let us consider a hypothetical library problem involving queueing. A university library has created a small collection of undergraduate text-books, held on closed-access so that the potential borrower has to make a request for the book at the service desk. Books can be borrowed for only very short periods of time (say, 4 hours) and heavy fines are charged to ensure that books are returned on time. Requests for books are treated on a "first-come, first-served" basis, but the present policy of providing only one member of staff to service these requests has, on occasion, resulted in large queues. The librarian would like to

---

*The liking of mathematians for using Greek letters as symbols is too deep-rooted to be resisted. It can result, as here with *lambda* and *mu* in queueing theory formulae, in a notation which has become internationally standard and 'correct' for the presentation of particular concepts. Fighting standard practice by substituting a less alien notation is conducive to confusion, both among those who are already accustomed to λ and μ and also among those who are not, who would be hindered in relating what they learn here to future encounters with queueing theory which are certain to use λ and μ. If this is unpalatable, please blame the foibles of the scientific community, not the authors of this paper.

**The concepts of chance, likelihood and probability permeate scientific research of all kinds and neither library science nor management science can avoid them. The notation used, however, deserves comment. In everyday speech one tends to refer to likelihood in terms of averages on a scale from zero to ten, e.g., He is late for work nine times out of ten. One degree more refined is the use of a percentage which is in terms of a scale from zero to one hundred, e.g., 90% of the time he arrives late for work. A third approach, much used in scientific research, is to use a scale from 0 to 1, e.g., there is a 0.9 chance that he will be late for work. All three mean the same thing, but the last form, which is used in this paper, may seem unfamiliar at first.

know whether, if he were to provide an extra member of staff, worthwhile reductions in the average length of queues and the average time that a user has to wait for service would result. Let us build a model of this situation.

We shall assume that demands for books in the reserve collection occur at random throughout the time period in which we are interested (say, the normal working day). We define the requests as arriving at a rate of λ requests per hour, and the maximum number of requests that one assistant, working as hard as possible, can serve in the same time period is defined as μ. Obviously, if λ is greater than μ for any length of time the situation becomes unstable, the queue builds up continually, and either the pressure of requests, λ, must be decreased (e.g. by turning users away) or the ability to cope with them, μ, must be increased (e.g. by employing extra staff). We shall assume that the situation in our reserve collection is not as bad as this and that the level of staffing is, on the whole, sufficient to handle the traffic*. However the queue occasionally builds up, because requests arrive randomly (and, therefore, sometimes arrive in "bursts").

We have already presented equations for each of the two systems which we wish to consider (i.e. either one assistant (equations (1) to (3) above) or two assistants (equations (4) to (6)). The next step is, of course, to collect data with which we can proceed to check the validity of our model and to make predictions.

Let us assume that observing the service desk and its immediate neighborhood has led us to conclude that, on average, a user has to wait one minute before being served. Furthermore, we have determined that the assistant can serve 75 requests per hour and that the average request rate is 41 requests per hour.

Then we have the following data:

The service rate, μ, is 75 per hour.
The arrival rate, λ, is 41 per hour.
The observed average waiting time, E_{obs}, is one minute.

Calculations concerning one assistant

Substituting the above values into equations (1) to (3) above, we can compute as follows:
The expected waiting time with one assistant, E_1, which is given as

$$E_1 = \frac{\lambda}{\mu(\mu-\lambda)}$$

in equation (1) becomes, on substituting the values specified above:

$$E_1 = \frac{41}{75(75-41)} \text{ hours}$$
$$= \frac{41}{75 \times 34} \text{ hours}$$
$$= \frac{41}{2550} \text{ hours}$$
$$= 0.016 \text{ hours}$$
$$= 0.96 \text{ minutes}$$

The expected time, 0.96 minutes is close enough to the observed time, 1 minute, for us to be confident in our model. The chance of a user not having to wait at all, P_0, which is given as

$$P_0 = 1 - \frac{\lambda}{\mu}$$

in equation (2) becomes, on substituing the values specified above:

$$P_0 = 1 - \frac{41}{75}$$
$$= 1 - 0.55$$
$$= 0.45$$

The average queue length, L, which is given as

$$L = \frac{\lambda^2}{\mu(\mu-\lambda)}$$

in equation (3) becomes, on subsituting the values specified above:

$$L = \frac{(41)^2}{75 \times (75-41)} \text{ persons}$$
$$= \frac{41 \times 41}{75 \times 34} \text{ persons}$$
$$= \frac{1681}{2550} \text{ persons}$$
$$= 0.66 \text{ persons}$$

Calculations concerning two assistants

The expected waiting time, E_2, which is given as

---

*In terms of the notation, that λ is equal to or less than μ or, in mathematical notation, $\lambda \leq \mu$.

$$E_2 = \frac{\lambda^2}{\mu(4\mu^2 - \lambda^2)}$$

in equation (4) becomes, on substituting the values specified above:

$$E_2 = \frac{(41)^2}{75 \times (4(75)^2 - (41)^2)} \quad \text{hours}$$

$$= \frac{41 \times 41}{75 \times (4(75 \times 75) - (41 \times 41))} \quad \text{hours}$$

$$= \frac{1681}{75 \times (4 \times 5625 - 1681)} \quad \text{hours}$$

$$= \frac{1681}{75 \times (22500 - 1681)} \quad \text{hours}$$

$$= \frac{1681}{75 \times 20819} \quad \text{hours}$$

$$= \frac{1681}{1561425} \quad \text{hours}$$

$$= \text{approx. } 0.001 \text{ hours}$$

$$= \text{approx. } 0.064 \text{ minutes}$$

$$= \text{nearly 4 seconds}$$

The chance of a user not having to wait at all, P_0, which is given as

$$P_0 = \frac{2\mu - \lambda}{2\mu + \lambda} \quad \text{in equation (5)}$$

becomes, on substituting the values specified above:

$$P_0 = \frac{2 \times 75 - 41}{2 \times 75 + 41}$$

$$= \frac{150 - 41}{150 + 41}$$

$$= \frac{109}{191}$$

$$= \text{approx. } 0.57$$

The average queue length, L, which is given as

$$L = \frac{\lambda^3}{\mu(4\mu^2 - \lambda^2)} \quad \text{in equation (6)}$$

becomes, on substituting the values specified above:

$$L = \frac{(41)^3}{75 \times [4(75)^2 - (41)^2]} \quad \text{Persons}$$

$$= \frac{41 \times 41 \times 41}{75 \times [4(75 \times 75) - (41 \times 41)]} \quad \text{Persons}$$

$$= \frac{68921}{75 \times (4 \times 5625 - 1681)} \quad \text{Persons}$$

$$= \frac{68921}{75 \times (22500 - 1681)} \quad \text{Persons}$$

$$= \frac{68921}{75 \times 20819} \quad \text{Persons}$$

$$= \frac{68921}{1561425} \quad \text{Persons}$$

= approx. 0.04 persons

Our model and our calculations upon them have, therefore, been able to tell us that what could be expected to happen if the librarian were to provide an extra member of staff at the service desk. Our prediction is that the users would have to wait for an average time of less than 4 seconds before being served (as opposed to one minute at present) and the average length of the queue will be drastically reduced from 0.66 persons to about 0.04 persons.

This is not the only type of problem in libraries which is amenable to being approached in terms of queues. Let us consider the use of this approach to produce a model which will help us with the following decision problem[3]:

How Long Should the Loan Period Be for a Particular Book?

Consider one book. The occurrence of requests for it may follow no discernable patterns and be — in statistical terminology — at random. Alternatively there may be some kind of pattern but, as an initial assumption, it may be acceptable to assume that the occurrence of requests is at random during a given period of time. Making this assumption we can use another equation developed by Operations Research scientists. The reader is again urged to accept the formula on trust for the time being and its derivation, which is available in standard texts, will not be reprinted here. The equation can be used by formulating the problem in the following terms:

We know that there are, on average, λ demands for the book in each time period. In this situation, the likelihood, referred to as P(n), of a given number of requests for the book (let us denote this as n requests) occuring is given by the formula:

$$P(n) = \frac{e^{-\lambda}(\lambda)^n}{n!}$$

where e is a constant, whose value is approximately 2.718, and n! means the amount produced by multiplying n by all the numbers less than n down to 1. (e.g., 4! = 4 $\times$ 3 $\times$ 2 $\times$ 1 = 24) (Note: 4! is pronounced "four factorial")

For example, let us suppose that, for this book, it is found that, *on average*, 8 requests are made in any year. We can calculate, from the above formula, the likelihood of any particular number of requests occurring. If, for example, we are interested in the likelihood of 10 requests occurring then we can take the equation, substitute the values of 8 and 10 for λ and n respectively and compute the answer, thus:

$$P(n) = \frac{e^{-\lambda}(\lambda)^n}{n!}$$

becomes

$$P(10) = \frac{e^{-8}(8)^{10}}{10!}$$

which, after a good deal of calculation, produces a value of approximately 0.1. We have, therefore, computed a forecast which can be phrased as follows:

If a book is requested, on average, eight times per annum, then the chances are one in ten (*or* 10% chance *or* a probability of 0.1) that it will be requested ten times in any single year.

Let us also assume, in order to simplify the problem, that the average length of time for which books are borrowed corresponds to the length of the official loan period. (There is some empirical evidence for this[4] and, even if the assumption is accepted reluctantly, it is good practice to start by using assumptions which make the problem more tractable. Later one returns to the assumptions and, if deemed appropriate, checks on the evidence behind the assumptions or explores the impact on the calculations of the assumptions being invalid. In this paper we are more concerned with describing an approach than computing actual predictions for a particular

library.) Since a book which is borrowed generally becomes unavailable to the rest of the user population until the end of the loan period, we should be able to predict the average availability of books which are subject to a given frequency demand.

Before we build this model, it is important for us to realize that many libraries provide two or more copies of books believed or expected to be in heavy demand. If one were to think of this situation as an analogy of providing additional staff at a service desk one could conceptualize it in terms of providing two or more "channels of service" for demand on the book. We shall use the symbol c to denote the number of copies of the book. Furthermore, we shall endeavor to make our model widely applicable by using the official loan period as the unit of time in our calculations instead of specifying actual hours or days.

If the number of requests in a given loan period is equal to or less than the number of copies available, then all requests will be satisfied. We can express this more formally by saying that if n copies are available then all the requests for all of the books in all of the loan periods in which the number of requests, n, was 0, 1, 2, 3, ... up to an including the periods in which the number of requests, n, equal the number of copies, c, will be satisfied. Strictly speaking, perhaps it ought to be stated that none of the requests in these categories will go *unsatisfied* since, by definition, there are no requests in the time period when n = 0.

In mathematical notation, the sum of the requests in these categories would be written:

$$\text{No. of satisfied requests} = \sum_{n=0}^{n=c} n \times P(n) \text{ for } n \leq c$$

This means that the number of requests, n, multiplied by the probability of there being that number of requests, P (n), when the value of n is zero is added to the number of requests multiplied by the probability of there being that number of requests, P(n), when the value of n is 1, which is added to the same form of multiplication of n and P(n) for each value of n on through 2, 3, ..., up to and including the case when n is equal to c, the number of copies.

On the other hand if the number of requests exceeds the number of copies and if we assume that no copy can be borrowed more than once during the loan period; then the number of satisfied requests cannot exceed the number of copies and is, therefore, limited to the number of copies available. In mathematical notation, the sum of the satisfied requests in these categories would be written:

$$\text{No. of satisfied requests} = \sum_{n=c+1}^{n=\infty} c \times P(n) \quad \text{for} \quad n > c.$$

This is similar to the preceding equation and means that we consider all values of n from c + 1 upwards (mathematically: to infinity, ∞) and add together as we go the results of multiplying the number of copies, c, by the probability that the number of demands, n, would have that value.

Let us now summarize our formulation of the satisfaction of requests. Having made our assumptions we assert that if the number of requests for a book is less than or equal to the number of copies available (in mathematical notation, $n \leq c$) then all of the requests made will be satisfied. In other words the number of satisfied requests will be the same as the number of requests (already defined as n). If the number of requests is greater than the number of copies (mathematically: $n > c$), then the number of satisfied requests will be limited to the number of copies available (c).

Adding the two components of *satisfied* requests (when $n \leq c$ and when $n > c$) together, we can divide the combined total by the total number of requests to compute the *proportion* of requests satisfied. Expressed as a percentage, this is expressed mathematically thus:

$$\% \text{ of requests satisfied} = \frac{\left\{ \sum_{n=0}^{n=c} n \times P(n) + \sum_{n=c+1}^{n=\infty} c \times P(n) \right\} \times 100}{\text{Total number of requests}}$$

For example, in one study[3] this formula was used to show that if we have, on average, one request per loan period, and if the library holds one copy of the book, then one should expect about 63% of requests to be satisfied.

If we wish to calculate the overall availability of the books in the library we could proceed by defining a number of different levels of demand, e.g., once a year, twice a year, once a week, and so on. We would then estimate the proportion (or percentage) of requests likely to be satisfied by a book at each combination of level of demand and number of copies. The model just described could be used for this. Then we examine the library concerned to estimate the number of books at each combination of level of demand and number of copies. Combining these data we could produce an estimate of the overall proportion of requests satisfied in the library as a whole.

If the present proportion of requests being satisfied is considered to be inadequate, we would use the formula above to predict the effect of buying more duplicates and, thereby, increasing the values of c or shortening the loan period (in effect, reducing the number of demands per time period).[4] Either of these strategies and any combination of them would result in an increase in the availability of the books in the library.

C.2. Simulation Models

O.R. specialists increasingly make use of computers in order to produce a 'simulation' of the real situation. In order to illustrate this approach a hypothetical library problem will be considered. A year ago, the Librarian decided to create a 'pool' of 10 clerical assistants under the direction of the superintendant of the service desk. Whenever one of the library's departments required clerical assistance, a request would be sent to the service desk superintendant and he would send the required number of assistants to the department concerned. However, work on the service desk was to have priority in the demands for clerical labor, and the superintendant was to be responsible for ensuring that enough assistants were at the desk to deal with any queues which might occur. Assistants were allocated for periods of slightly less than two hours (in fact a schedule based on four periods of 100 minutes each per day was used), but the decision concerning how many assistants to allocate to the service desk in each time period was taken at the beginning of each day. Once the assignment of an assistant had been made, the assistant could not be recalled until the end of the time period. In the event of the assistant being "spare", (neither assigned to the service desk nor requested by a department) additional work could always be found in the departments.

One of the problems which had been found was that demand at the service desk was highly variable, so that the service desk superintendant had to "insure" against there being insufficient staff at the desk by retaining a larger number of assistants than might otherwise have been required. One unfortunate result of this policy had been that the assistants at the desk spent some of their time unoccupied, while the other library departments have found that they had been unable to keep up-to-date with their routine clerical tasks because an insufficient number of assistants had been made available to them. The service desk superintendant regarded this situation as inevitable given the present staffing level. If no "insurance factor" were allowed for the possibility of peaks of very heavy demand, queues occasionally built up and complaints were received from users. The Superintendant suggested that two extra clerical assistants should be employed. This, he felt would alleviate the problem. He would also be interested in seeing if the time spent idle by assistants at the service desk could be reduced.

One part of an Operations Research approach to this problem is to predict the consequences for the library of an increase in the number of clerical staff employed and to determine the effect of reducing the "insurance factor". Obviously it would be possible to use a "trial and error" approach: one could recruit two extra assistants and see what happened. However, it would be quicker and more convenient if one could construct a model which could "simulate" the change. How do we build a simulation model of this situation?

We already know that sufficient staff must be kept at the service desk to deal with any level of demand which might reasonably be expected to occur. The system of employing a pool of assistants which is at least adequate for the highest peaks at the service desk and then assigning a varying number of assistants to the departments can be regarded as a control system designed to permit flexibility in the level of staffing at the service desk and also efficient utilization of labor by assigning "surplus" assistants to work elsewhere.

The next step requires the collection of some data relating to the system. Clearly we need to know many facts before we can build a valid simulation model: we need to know about demands, about staffing, about the interaction between user demands and staff, and also about decisions. Some of this data has already been given. The rest will be presented below.

TABLE 1.
ARRIVAL PATTERN OF DEMANDS AT THE SERVICE DESK.

A count was made of the number of demands made at the service desk during each time period on each working day Monday through Friday for twenty weeks. This gave 100 observations for each time period. The table should be read as follows: On 2 days out of 100, the number of demands at the service desk during the first time period was in the range of 0-49.

NUMBER OF DEMANDS	TIME PERIOD			
	I	II	III	IV
0- 49	2	0	0	0
50- 99	6	2	0	4
100-149	11	3	1	6
150-199	14	5	2	13
200-249	20	9	4	14
250-299	20	11	6	12
300-349	8	14	7	10
350-399	7	14	10	9
400-449	6	10	13	7
450-499	3	8	15	7
500-549	2	7	15	6
550-599	1	6	12	4
600-649	0	5	8	2
650-699	0	3	4	2
700-749	0	2	2	2
750-799	0	1	1	1
800-849	0	0	0	0

Table I shows the arrival pattern of demands at the service desk in each of four periods into which the day is divided — it shows the number of time periods during which zero, fifty, hundred, etc., demands (i.e. requests for a book to be issued, to be discharged, to be reserved, and so on) were received at the service desk. If we assume that these data are typical we can treat them as representing the *probability* of a given number of requests occurring. We need to convert the data. Two occurances out of 100 can be described as a probability of 2% if percentages are used or, using the scale from 0 to 1, this is a probability of 0.02. These probabilities can be presented in the form of a histogram representing the probability of a particular number of demands arriving at the service desk in a given period of time. Figure 2 shows the histogram for time period I.

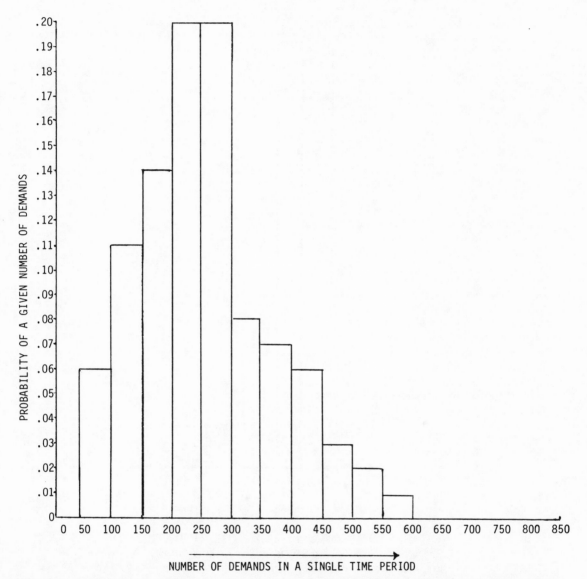

FIGURE 2. HISTOGRAM OF THE PROBABILITIES OF GIVEN NUMBERS OF DEMANDS AT THE SERVICE DESK DURING TIME PERIOD I. *This figure should be read: there is a probability of 0.02 that the number of requests at the service desk during time period I will be in the range 0-49.*

Figure 3 shows a further histogram, representing the probability of an assistant being occupied for a particular number of minutes by one demand at the service desk. Assistants allocated to library departments are assumed to be occupied for the whole time period.

The service desk superintendant has, over the past year, kept a record of the number of assistants he allocated to the service desk in each time period. He has calculated that, on average, 3.1 assistants were at the desk during period I, 5.3 during period II, 6.2 during period III, and 3.7 during period IV.

The decision rule is quite simple: In the beginning of each time period, the number of staff available for release to departments is the number of assistants available in the "pool" minus those needed at the service desk. Mathematically this can be written:

$N = p - d$

where N is the number of assistants to be released to departments.

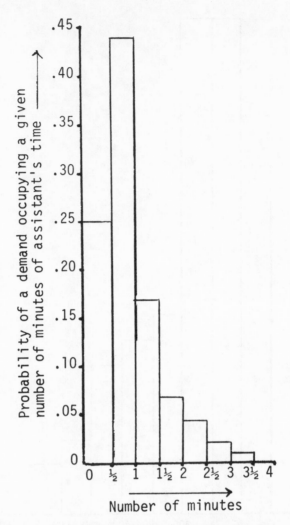

FIGURE 3. HISTOGRAM FOR THE DURATION OF A DEMAND. *This histogram should be read as follows: the probability of a demand occupying between ½ and 1 minute is 0.44 (or, a 44% chance).*

p is the number of assistants available in the "pool".

d is the number of assistants available for service desk duty during the time period.

The service desk superintendant examines the requests for assistants from departments before each time period begins and decides the number of assistants to be released as reflected in the decision rule above. The decision on the number of staff to be kept at the service desk during each time period of the day, however, is taken at the beginning of the day.*

We are now in a position to build an accurate simulation model of the system described above. Firstly we draw a Flow Diagram — a *logic diagram* which will later be translated into the series of instructions which constitute the computer program. Figure 4 illustrates this diagram. The diamond shapes represent decisions to be answered "Yes" or "No", and the boxes represent "sub-routines" (i.e. courses of action to be followed each time they are encountered).

*This example has some similarity to an actual service desk but has been simplified for the sake of exposition.

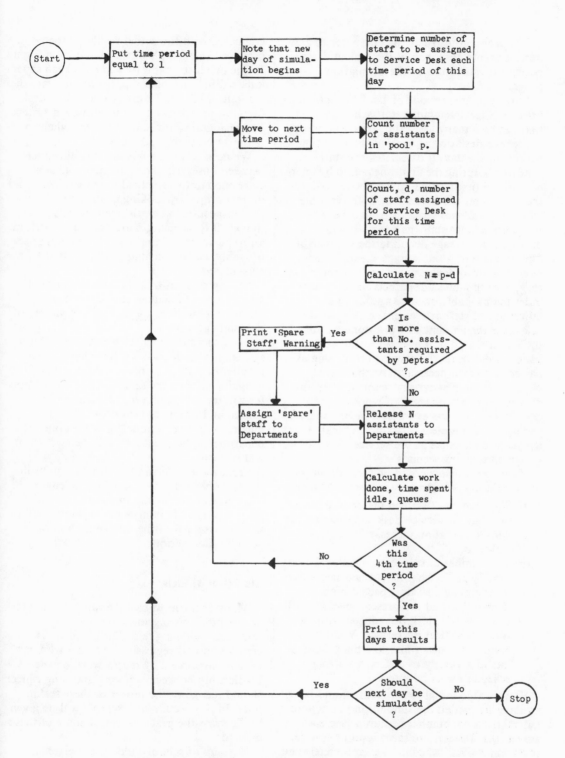

FIG. 4.   FLOW DIAGRAM FOR SIMULATION OF SERVICE DESK STAFFING.

The program instructs the computer to act out the events described in the logic diagram, noting various results as the simulation progresses.

Moving to time period I of day 1, the computer uses the Superintendant's staff schedule to find out how many assistants are required on the service desk during each of the four time periods of the day. It calculates the staff availability during the first time period by reference to the first formula given above, and then compares the number of staff available with the number of requests from departments. If there are more staff than requests, it prints out a message detailing the number of "spare" assistants and assigns them. It then releases staff to departments and, by means of the queueing models described above, computes the probable queues, waiting and utilization of staff at the service desk. It then calculates the amount of work done by all staff from the pool, moves on to the next time period and repeats the process for as long as has been deemed necessary. At the end of the simulation, a summary report concerning queues, idle time, amount of work done for departments, frequency of staff being "spare", and so on. Computers operate so quickly that ten years' experience at the service desk can be generated in a few seconds.

Many experiments could be carried out with our simulation. We can vary at least two factors:

  (i) The number of staff in the pool. Remember that the service desk superintendant considers that an increase in staff is called for.

 (ii) The number of staff employed at the service desk. To what extent is it necessary to ensure against unexpected high demand? Could the present level of staff at the service desk be reduced without too much effect on service? What could happen to queues and idle time if any one of a variety of different staffing schedules were adopted?

However the initial experiment should be to validate the model: the simulation is run with exactly the same number of staff as there are at present (i.e. 10) and the same level of service at current staffing schedule is used to determine the number of assistants to be assigned to the service desk in each time period. The results of running the simulation in this form can be compared with the actual results observed in practice. An example of this is shown in Figure 5. The two histograms (which have been superimposed for ease of comparison) illustrate the amount of idle staff time at the service desk found in practice and in the simulated system. The histograms are similar but not identical. Is the agreement good enough?

We need to decide whether the agreement between observed and simulated results is close enough for practical purposes. We could do this simply by looking at the simularity ("by inspection" as statisticians would say), though O.R. specialists may prefer to perform a formal statistical analysis of the comparison, probably using a technique known as the chi-squared test.

Having decided that the simulation model seems to be of adequate accuracy to permit further exploration, we engage in a variety of new simulations.

The experiments which follow would vary systematically the two key variables — the number of staff in pool and the schedule for assigning staff to the service desk. The computer will try out whatever combinations are chosen and produces results in terms of queues, idle time, amount of work done for departments, frequency of staff being "spare" and so forth.

From these, and similar, simulation results, the researcher is able to predict the consequences of employing two extra clerical assistants and of changes in the number of assistants assigned to the service desk in one or more time periods.

Statistical Models

Many of the most useful approaches in O.R. and in other management sciences involve statistical modeling techniques known as correlation and regression. Anyone who has become convinced by recent work on the relationship between smoking and lung cancer should recognize the power of these techniques. In this section an example will be given to illustrate the practical use of some of these methods.

A group of school children are given an intelligence test and several years later the same children take a test in mathematics during secondary school.

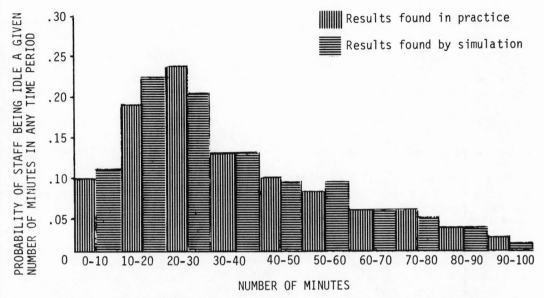

FIG. 5. HISTOGRAM FOR TIME SPENT IDLE IN ANY TIME PERIOD.

TABLE 2.
MATHEMATICS AND INTELLIGENCE
TEST RESULTS FOR 20 CHILDREN.
The range of scores for the Mathematics Test is zero to 30 and for the Intelligence Test zero to 160. This table should be read: child number 1 scored 12 out of 30 in the Mathematics Test and 80 out of 160 in the Intelligence Test Score.

Children	Mathematics Score	Intelligence Test Score
1	12	80
2	18	80
3	28	110
4	26	110
5	8	50
6	8	60
7	16	70
8	20	100
9	18	110
10	26	130
11	10	90
12	8	70
13	26	120
14	20	90
15	22	100
16	6	60
17	10	60
18	24	100
19	24	120
20	16	90

Table 2 gives the children's scores on the two tests. Let us explore these data to see whether these scores are related to each other. Let us plot a graph of these scores with intelligence on the horizontal scale ("x-axis") and mathematical achievement on the vertical scale ("y-axis"). The result is shown in Figure 6.

It is clear by inspection that the two variables do relate to each other to some extent because the data tend to be clustered along line a.* This level of "correlation" suggests that children with high intelligence tend to get high marks in the mathematics examination.

The slope of the line (a) in Figure 6 seems to "fit" the data best. One could draw a variety of lines and pick the one which seemed to be the "best-fitting" line, but, here again, a statistician would rely on computing mathematically what the "best-fitting" line would be.**

In Figure 6 line a, which symbolizes the general relationship between the test scores in mathematics and the scores in the intelligence test, can be used to make a variety of specific statements. For example, what would be a reasonable score in mathematics for a child scoring 80 in the intelligence test? By inspection one

---

*This simple graphical example of correlation suffices for present purposes. However, some reference needs to be made to the use by statisticians of a measure (or "co-efficient") of correlation. Stated briefly, this measure varies between minus one and plus one. Both of these extremes imply that the points fall on a straight line. If, in Figure 6, all the points fell exactly on line a, then this would mean that the two variables under consideration (in this case the two sets of test

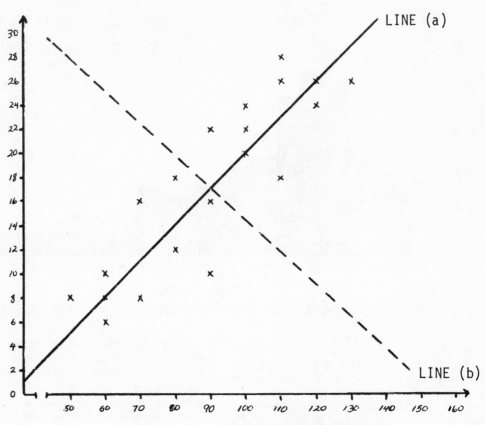

FIG. 6.   THE RELATION BETWEEN INTELLIGENCE
AND MATHEMATICS SCORES

can find 80 on horizontal x-axis, mark the point on the line which corresponds to the 80, then read of the point on the vertical y-axis which corresponds to this point: 14. The inference is that a score of 14 on the mathematical test would be a reasonable or typical achievement for a child who scored 80 on the intelligence test. It does not imply that all children scoring 80 in the intelligence test *will necessarily* score 14 in mathematics: 14 is the *most likely* value. This is because the relationship between the two tests is not perfect. Indeed in the data presented two such children actually scored 12 and 18.

Graphical methods like this can be very effective and require very little training. However it should be recognized that as problems become more complex, purely graphical approaches are liable to become unmanageable. Mathematical methods then become unavoidable and, indeed, scientists tend to prefer them anyway. The terminology and notation

scores) correlated perfectly and positively, i.e., an increase in one is associated with an increase in the other. The correlation co-efficient would be plus 1, usually written with a positive sign to avoid confusion, thus + 1. At the other extreme, the points on the graph might all fall on line b. This is also a perfect correlation but a negative one reflecting an inverse relationship between the two variables. In this case, an increase in one variable is associated with a decrease in the other and vice-versa. The correlation co-efficient is minus one (-1). Where no relationship of correlation can be detected the correlation co-efficient is zero. Therefore, the value of the coefficient indicates the amount of relationship in two ways. The larger the value between 0 and 1 the greater the correlation and, where a relationship does exist, the positive sign or the negative sign indicates the nature of the correlation. The correlation co-efficient for the data in Figure 6 is + 0.8 which reflects the fairly close fit.

**The technique used is called the "least square" method. A selection of lines are considered and for each line the distance between each point and the line is measured. The distance is squared and the squared distances are added together. The line for which the sum of the squared distances is least is considered to be the best fitting.

used in the example of the test scores is likely to be as follows. The relationship between the variable on the vertical y-axis and the horizontal x-axis, which is symbolized by the line a on the graph, is described in terms of y "being a function of" x. In mathematical notation this is written:

$$y = f(x)$$

The f( ) is simply a vague statement to the effect that there is some relationship such that the value of y depends on (or can be deduced from) x.

Mathematically the line a can be written

$$y = 0.3 \, x - 10$$

This can be confirmed by trying a few values of x or y. For example, in our example of a child who had scored 80 in the intelligence test, we subsitute 80 for x and can compute the most likely mathematics score (y), thus:

$$y = 0.3 \times 80 - 10$$
$$= 24 - 10$$
$$= 14$$

A word of caution is necessary here. A correlation of this type could have occured by chance: a freak result which might not reappear if a further 20 children had been selected. The best method of guarding against this possibility is to choose children in the sample at random and to make the sample large enough to produce meaningful results. This problem is a major preoccupation of statisticians and powerful statistical techniques have been developed to ensure that the sample is representative of the group ("population") as a whole, but we need not consider this matter any further here.

Another warning is also necessary concerning correlation is that the *existence* of a correlation between two variables does not *prove* that one variable *caused* the other. It may often be reasonable to assume that a change in one does cause the change in the other but a statistical correlation does not prove causality.

So far, we have concentrated on a simple "straight-line" correlation. It has to be admitted that it is more common for relationships to be more complex than this. In terms of a graph, the relationship may follow a curved line rather than a straight one. Conceptually this is little different. In practice it means that

drawing lines on graphs becomes a good deal more difficult and, in practice, a mathematical technique known as regression analysis is used instead of the "least squares" method to determine the precise formulation of the relationship.

D. MODEL SOLUTION

In this section we will discuss some techniques which can be used to derive solutions from mathematical models. Initially we will cover methods which are particularly appropriate where the consequences of each possible action are known with confidence and our objective is clear. This is then followed by a discourse on the solving of problems when many of the important factors are clouded in uncertainty: where cause and effect may only be hazily perceived.

D. 1. Mathematical Programming

Which action from a set of possible actions should we choose? Firstly let us assume that we know the consequences of each action with certainty. Let us further assume that we know what we want to achieve by the decision. Choice should be easy. But is it? Consider the following problem:

You are the managing director of a steel works which can buy three different grades of coal (A, B, and C). However the different grades are not all the same price, and their composition is not identical. In fact they contain two main impurities (phosphorus which we shall call P, and ash which we shall call X) in various proportions. These data can be summarized as:

Coal Type	%P	%X	Price
A	.06	2.0	£10 per ton
B	.04	4.0	£10 per ton
C	.02	3.0	£15 per ton

The research division of the steel works reports that, ideally, the coal should contain between 0.02 and 0.03% of impurity P, and between 2.0 and 3.25% of X. They have been accustomed to buying coal of grade C even though it is a little low on the proportion of impurity P. However, the price of this grade is high. The trouble with A is that there is too much P and only just enough X, whereas grade B contains too much P and too much X. It has been suggested that the steel works should buy some coal of each grade, and that the grades should then be mixed together to produce a fuel with the ideal constituents. The resultant mixture should be such that the total cost per ton is minimized. What proportions of grades A, B, and C should be bought?

In this problem the objective has been precisely stated in quantitative terms and the consequences, in terms of composition and price, of any action can be determined with certainty. It is clearly a mathematical problem and, in fact, can be solved using a technique known as "Linear Programming". Linear Programming and its variants are the most widely used (and useful) techniques in Operations Research for computing solutions.

Let us solve the coal purchasing problem using this method. Consider that we have one ton of coal which has been produced from a mixture of various amounts of grades A, B, and C. Clearly we can calculate the composition of the mixture and the price as follows:

Let a, b, and c represent the amounts of grades A, B, and C respectively, in the one ton mixture. Therefore, the percentage of impurity P in the mixture equals,

    0.06 X a (the amount of grade A)
plus
    0.04 X b (the amount of grade B)
plus
    0.02 X c (the amount of grade C)

i.e. Percentage of impurity P = 0.06 X a
    + 0.04 X b + 0.02 X c

By a similar process:

Percentage of impurity X = 2 X a + 4 X b + 3 X c
The cost of this ton of coal is easily calculated as follows:

    Cost (in £) = 10 X a + 10 X b + 15 X c

Since the cost and composition of any mixture can be calculated you could experiment with different mixtures and note the results. With a simple problem like the above you will probably find the best answer before long. However, if you had hundreds of impurities to deal with, many different grades of coal to choose from and many other properties of the mixture to consider, possibly resulting in hundreds of equations, the trial and error approach would require an astronomical number of calculations.

Let us pursue the mathematics a little further. Firstly we need to represent in the form of an equation the statement "the proportion of impurity P should be between 0.02 and 0.03 percent". From the proportions of P in the original grades of coal it is clear that the proportion of this impurity cannot fall below 0.02 percent (it would be equal to 0.02% if we used only grade C coal; if any other grade coal is added, the proportion of P increases). Therefore, we need only state that the proportion of P should be less than or equal to 0.03 percent. This gives us the following equation:

$$0.06 \text{ X } a + 0.04 \text{ X } b + 0.02 \text{ X } c \leq 0.03$$

By similar arguments the equation for the statement "the percentage of element X must be between 2.0 and 3.25 percent" is:

$$2 \text{ X } a + 4 \text{ X } b + 3 \text{ X } c \leq 3.25$$

A further equation is required. viz.:

$$a + b + c = 1$$

This simply states that the units of quantity are proportions which must add up to one ton of the mixture.

Also, for completeness, we need to state that the proportions (a, b, and c) cannot be negative amounts. We can only have a zero proportion (no grade A) or a positive proportion (some grade A). Each proportion must be greater than or equal to zero. This is written as follows:

$$a \geq 0$$
$$b \geq 0$$
$$c \geq 0$$

Let us write the full set of required equations down:
(for element P)
$$0.06 \text{ X } a + 0.04 \text{ X } b + 0.02 \text{ X } c \leq 0.03 \quad (7)$$
(for element X)
$$2 \text{ X } a + 4 \text{ X } b + 3 \text{ X } c \leq 3.25 \quad (8)$$
total
$$a + b + c = 1 \quad (9)$$
$$a \geq 0; b \geq 0; c \geq 0 \quad (10)$$
cost
$$C = 10 \text{ X } a + 10 \text{ X } b + 15 \text{ X } c \quad (11)$$

The problem can be stated as follows:

"Determine a, b, and c such that they satisfy equations (7) through (10) and lead to the minimum cost as calculated from equation (11)".

Solution

There are several methods for the solution of the problem but we shall use the graphical method.

Firstly we can eliminate c by using equation (9) above which states that

$$a + b + c = 1$$

By rearrangement we get

$$c = 1 - a - b$$

We can therefore substitute (1-a-b) in the place of c in place of equation (7), thus obtaining:

```
0.06 X a + 0.04 X b + 0.02 X (1-a-b) ≤ 0.03
```
Therefore
```
6 X a + 4 X b + 2 X (1-a-b) ≤ 3
```
Therefore
```
6 X a + 4 X b + 2 - 2 X a - 2 X b ≤ 3
```
Therefore
```
4 X a + 2 X b ≤ 1                          (12)
```

For equation (8)
```
2 X a + 4 X b + 3 X (1-a-b) ≤ 3.25
```
Therefore
```
2·X a + 4 X b + 3 - 3 X a - 3 X b ≤ 3.25
```
Therefore
```
b - a + 3 ≤ 3.25
```
Therefore
```
b - a ≤ 0.25
```
Therefore
```
4 X b - 4 X a ≤ 1                          (13)
```
For equation (11)
```
C = 10 X a + 10 X b + 15 X (1-a-b)
```
Therefore
```
C = 10 X a + 10 X b + 15 - 15 X a - 15 X b
```
Therefore
```
C = 15 - 5 X a - 5 x b                     (14)
```

We can now draw the graph shown in Figure 7.

The graph is drawn with a on the vertical axis and b on the horizontal axis. Taking equation 12 we know that the eventual solution must be such that 4 X a plus 2 X a must not exceed 1. We therefore draw the line which represents

$$4 X b + 2 X a = 1$$

and know that the solution must be on or below that line.

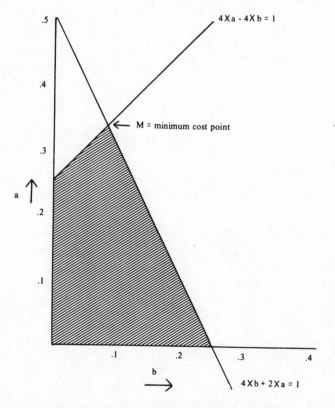

FIG. 7   COAL MIXTURE SOLUTION

Similarly we know from equation 13 that $4 \times a$ minus $4 \times b$ must not exceed 1. We therefore draw the line which represents

$$4 \times b - 4 \times a = 1$$

and know that the solution must be on or below that line.

The area of the graph which meets *both* these conditions has been shaded. The optimal solution must be in the shaded area. Where?

Coal of type C is substantially more expensive than coal of grades A and B: £15 as opposed to £10. Therefore, we should seek to minimize the proportion of C and maximize the amount of A and B. Inspection of the graph shows that the largest combination of a and b within the shaded area is M where we have .33 of a and .083 of b giving .413. Any other point within the shaded area gives a smaller proportion of A and B and, therefore, a larger proportion of the more expensive C. Point M, therefore, represents the least expensive solution within the shaded area.

Any point outside the shaded area would not give the desired blend of impurites.

Clearly then, the cost is minimized by taking a and b at point M. Thus a = 0.083, b = 0.33, c = 0.587 (from equation (9)) and the minimum cost £12.935 per ton (from equation (14)). Hence the steel works purchase the different grades of coal in the following proportions:

Coal Grade	Proportion as a percent
A	8.3%
B	33.0%
C	58.7%

This will cost approximately £13 per ton as against £15 per ton with the present policy of buying just Grade C. The mixture will be to ideal specifications.

The techniques of mathematical programming are designed for the solution of problems where a blending (or mixing) is required. They can, for example, be used to determine an optimal blend of resources for an organization and they can be used to suggest an optimal purchasing policy for raw materials in industry, and in problems of a similar nature.

In libraries, there have, as yet, been few successful applications. However it is tempting to think that potential applications are wide-spread: determining optimal staffing ratios, allocation of staff between departments, book purchasing and lending policies, and so on.

D. 2.   Statistical Decision Analysis

In many problems of decision the issues are clouded with uncertainty. One can never be sure, for example, under English weather conditions, whether a cricket match will survive a forecast rain shower; one can rarely feel confident in predicting the outcome of a foot-ball game; a librarian can rarely predict the number of users who will enter his library during the next day.

It is to deal with problems of this type that statistical decision analysis has been developed. Consider a simple game with playing cards. A gambler shuffles 52 cards and places three cards face downwards in front of you.* He suggests that you pay him 10 cents if they are *not all red*, and that he will pay you one dollar if they are *all red cards*. He further suggests that the game should continue for one hundred plays, i.e., he will shuffle and deal one hundred times. Should you play this game? How much do you expect to gain or lose?

This is a decision situation in which the only certain feature is the uncertainty of the outcome. Nevertheless, modeling techniques can again assist us. Firstly we need to know the likelihood or probability, P (red), that a single card, selected from a pack of cards, is red. This is given by the following equation:

$$P(red) = \frac{\text{Number of red cards}}{\text{Total number of cards}} = \frac{26}{52} = 0.5$$

What is the probability that all three are red? Here,

$$P(\text{all red}) = \frac{\text{Number of "all red" threesomes}}{\text{Total number of possible threesomes}}$$

The following threesomes are possible and equally likely to occur (R = red, B = black):

RRR
RRB
RBR
RBB
BRR
BRB
BBR
BBB

---

* To simplify the calculations we are assuming that each card is replaced and that the cards are reshuffled before the next card is drawn.

Thus there are eight possible types of three-somes in terms of "black" and "red" cards and therefore, since only one of these sets is "all red":

$$P \text{ (all red)} = \tfrac{1}{8} = \underline{0.125}$$

Clearly, by a similar argument, the probability, P (not all red), that a set of three cards is not "all red" is given as follows:

$$P \text{ (not all red)} = \tfrac{7}{8} = \underline{0.875}$$

What do these probabilities mean? They mean that if the gambler properly shuffles the pack between card selections and deals three cards honestly, one in every eight selections *on average* will be "all red" cards. It does not mean that you will necessarily obtain one set of all red cards in *every* eight selections, only that this is the long term average.

We now need a way of deciding whether to play this particular game and we do this by calculating the *expected value* (V) of the game. This is given by the following equation:

V = (Probability of winning x value of winning)
   + (Probability of losing x value of losing)
Therefore,
V = (0.125 X 100 cents) + (0.875 X -10 cents)
  = 3.75 cents per game

Thus by playing the game you will on average gain at the rate of 3.75 cents per game and you can expect to win approximately 3.75 dollars in one hundred plays. Again this does not mean that you will necessarily win this amount, or even win at all, but that this is the *long term* expected payoff.

What is the most that you would be prepared to pay him for playing this game?

Statistical decision analysis forms the basis for the solution of the problem faced by the doctor treating spots on the ends of noses outlined earlier in this paper.

However before we proceed to solve that problem we need to introduce a further important concept. This is the idea of a *subjective probability*.

When we talked about the probability of three cards being *all red*, we were talking about *objective* probabilities. If a pack of cards is shuffled properly and three cards selected and this process continued indefinitely, then the proportion of "all red" threesomes will converge on 1 in 8. This is an objective fact. However, in asking the question "What propor-

tion of patients having spots on the ends of their nose have disease d_1?" we may have no more evidence than the experience of the doctor concerned. If we then use this probability in further statistical analysis in exactly the same manner as an objective probability we become "Bayesian statisticians". The term derives from the work of the Reverend Thomas Bayes who wrote a paper in 1763 entiled "An essay toward solving a problem in the doctrine of chance"[5] in which he suggested, that probability judgments based on mere hunches could be used in the analysis of decision problems. In general, Bayesians are "sub-jectivists" and are happy to introduce intuitive judgments and feelings into the formal analysis of the decision problem if relevant objective data cannot be found.

We can now attempt to solve the doctor's problem.

Data

Clearly it is necessary to have some probability statements in relation to the problem. These will no doubt have to be supplied by the doctor on the basis of his experience in treating patients with spots on the ends of their nose. Also, of course, we will need the "costs" referred to earlier. Let us list the costs first of all. These are shown in Table 3.

TABLE 3

		Treatment		
		t_0	t_1	t_2
	d_0	5	20	40
Disease	d_1	70	20	50
	d_2	150	100	20

This table should be read as follows:

The cost, in terms of treatment cost *and* the loss of the patient's earnings, of disease d_1, treated by treatment t_0, (i.e., no treatment) is 70 units. If treated by treatment t_1 the total cost is reduced to 20 units.

The cost of disease d_2 if untreated is 150 units. If it is treated by t_2 this cost is reduced to 20 units.

Notice that even d_0 can be a costly disorder especially if the patient is treated as though he was suffering from diseases d_1 or d_2. This is due to the cost of the treatments and certain side-effects.

The cost of the examination (E) to detect the presence of disease d_2 is 15 units.

What probability assessments do we require?

First of all we need to know the likelihoods that a patient with a spot on the end of his nose has diseases d_0, d_1 or d_2. Maybe the medical literature will tell us. However it is more likely that the doctor, on the basis of his experience will have to tell us. Hence, we must be "Bayesians". Let us assume that the doctor states the following:

"It is unlikely that the patient is suffering from a psychosomatic disorder. I would expect him to be suffering from either d_1 or d_2 of which the former is by far the most likely".

After further questioning he agrees to the following probabilities, which, of course, add up to unity.

$$d_0 = .1$$
$$d_1 = .7$$
$$d_2 = .2$$

Secondly, by a similar process, it is necessary to obtain information about the examination (E). The examination is supposed to give a positive result if, and only if, the patient has disease d_2. But it may not be infallible. Let us assume that Table 4 represents the best available information about the test.

TABLE 4

	d_0	d_1	d_2
Positive reaction	Zero	.1	1.0
Negative reaction	1.0	.9	Zero

This table indicates that the test works well: no-one with disease d_0 will give a positive sign and everyone with d_2 will show "positive". However, although 90 percent of patients with d_1 give a negative result, 10 percent give a positive sign. Thus the test is not quite infallible.

We now have all the basic data required to solve the doctor's problem. What should he do?

Should he treat the patient with treatment t_1 because disease d_1 is the most likely? Should he, on the other hand offer treatment t_2 because disease d_2 is the most serious and costly? Should he test for d_2 using examina-

tion E before deciding on a treatment?

Below an answer based on Bayesian statistics is given.

Analysis

The technique of analysis used is called "decision tree" analysis. The first choice that the doctor has to make is whether or not to use examination E. In a decision tree a choice between alternatives is represented as follows:

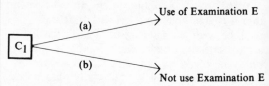

In other words, at choice point C_1, a decision is made as to whether to go along branch (a) of the tree and use examination E, or branch (b) and not use it.

Other choices are not under the doctor's control. For example, the patient may have disease d_0, disease d_1, disease d_2. This is outside the doctor's control. It can be referred to as a "chance point" and represented as follows:

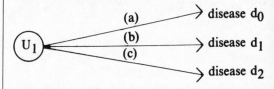

In other words at the chance point (U_1), represented by a circle, we might proceed along branch (a), i.e., the patient has disease d_0 or branches (b) or (c). Which branch is chosen is not under anyone's control.

In general a decision tree looks like the diagram in Figure 8.

There is a sequence of "choice points" and "chance points" and at the ends of the decision tree, in the rectangles, are the consequences of following a particular path. In our example, the consequences will be in terms of a "cost", i.e., one of the costs indicated in Table 3.

Obviously the purpose of the decision tree is to provide the information to the decision maker as to the choices he "ought" to make at the various "choice points".

The decision-tree for the doctors problem is shown in Figure 9. At the end of every branch there is a cost consequence — and it is this cost we wish to minimize. There are

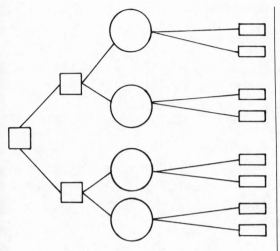

FIG. 8   A DECISION TREE

four choice points, labelled 1 to 4 in the rectangles. Let us proceed through the tree.

Let us first of all examine the consequences of not carrying out the examination E at choice point (1). This leads us to choice point (4). At this point we decide on treatment (t_0; t_1; t_2). Let us choose t_0. This leads to chance point (h) — the patient may be suffering from disease d_0, d_1, or d_2 with likelihoods 10 percent, 70 percent and 20 percent respectively. What is the expected cost of choosing t_0?

This is calculated by adding the results of multiplying the cost of each outcome by the probability of that outcome:

$$\text{Expected cost} = (.1) \times (5) + (.7) \times (70) + (.2) \times (150)$$
$$= \mathbf{79.5}$$

In other words this is calculated in exactly the same way as in our card game which we discussed earlier. This "expected cost" is written above chance point (h) in the diagram. The expected costs of the other choices is written above the chance points (i) and (j) viz. 36 and 43 units respectively. Obviously if we reached choice point (4) we would choose treatment t_1. Therefore branches t_0 and t_2 are blocked off with a double line viz. / /. However, the question remains should we be at choice point (4) at all? Should we have gone down the other branch at choice point 1? Let us examine this possibility.

The first thing that happens along the "experiment" branch is that we have to pay 15 units to carry out the "test" (E) represented in the diagram by a toll gate, thus $\frac{1}{1}$

We then reach the chance point (a): the

test may give a positive sign or a negative sign. What are the likelihoods or probabilities? These can be calculated as follows:

Imagine a thousand patients being given the test — they all have spots on their noses. What will be the result? First of all on the basis of the doctor's experience we expect that there will be 100 d_0's, 700 d_1's and 200 d_2's. All the d_0's will give negative signs: giving 100 negatives so far. Ninety percent of the d_1's will give negative signs viz. 630 negatives. Finally none of the d_2's will show negative. Therefore we expect 730 negatives and thus we get 270 positives. These probabilities (0.73 and 0.27) are shown on the branches from chance point (a).

Let us say we are now at choice point (2) and again in a position to choose a treatment. Going along t_0 we reach chance point (b). The disease may be d_0, d_1, or d_2. But having carried out test (E) and obtained a positive sign the probabilities are now different from those associated with the diseases along the "no examination" branch. In fact the probability of it being d_0 is "zero" in that d_0's always give a negative sign on test (E). The probability of d_1 can be readily calculated as follows:

Only 10 percent of d_1's shows a positive sign on test (E) and d_1's represent 70 percent of the patient population. We want the probability that a patient is d_1 given that he gives a positive sign. The formula is:

$$\frac{\text{probability of having disease } d_1 \text{ and giving a positive sign}}{\text{probability of giving a positive sign}}$$
$$(.1) \times (.7) \ / \ .27 = .26$$

The appropriate probabilities, calculated in the above manner, are shown over all the branches from chance points (b) to (j). We can now calculate the expected costs at these points. For example at chance point (d) the expected cost of choosing treatment t_2 is:

$$\text{(Zero)} \times (40) + (.26) \times (50) + (.74) \times (20)$$
$$= 28 \text{ units (approx.)}$$

The "expected costs" at the chance points (b) to (j) have been written in and best choices at choice points (2) and (3) added to our knowledge about choice point (4). At choice point (2) we should choose treatment t_2 with an expected cost of 28 units. At choice point (3) we should choose treatment t_1 with an expected cost of 20 units.

We now need the expected cost at chance point (a). This is given by:

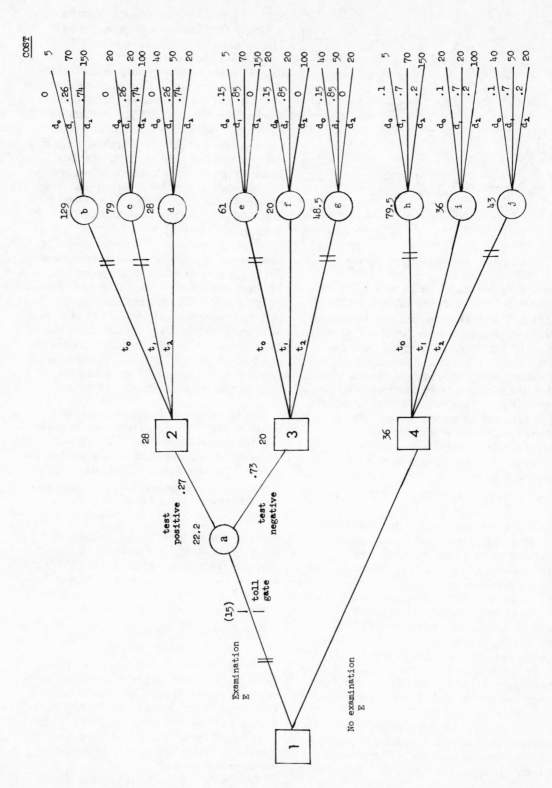

FIG. 9.   THE DECISION TREE FOR THE DOCTOR'S PROBLEM

$$(.27) \times (28) + (.73) \times (20) = 22 \text{ units (approx.)}$$

Our problem is now solved: the doctor should not carry out test (E) but should immediately offer treatment t_1. The expected cost is *36 units*. The expected cost, if test (E) is carried out, is 15 units (the cost of the test) plus 22 units (the expected treatment cost); giving *37 units* in all. Of course, if the cost of giving the test (E) could be reduced to 10 units then the doctor should always offer the test; offering treatment t_1 if the test result is negative and treatment t_2 if the test result is positive.

One of the more valuable outcomes of an analysis of this sort is that it gives a measure of the value of test (E) viz.

The cost of not giving the test minus the cost (excluding the direct cost of the test) of giving the test.

In our case 36 minus 22 = *14 units*.

How helpful is this approach? Clearly it is based on many assumptions and oversimplifies the doctor's problem. Also he may feel that "expected cost" is not an appropriate criterion. He may feel that he would rather minimize the regret, i.e., reduce the risk of the more serious consequences. However the approach can provide guidelines for doctors and throw light on the key problems of diagnosis and treatment in the health services.

E.   REVIEW

This tutorial has attempted to lay out the basic ingredients of operations research. The crucial first stage is to recognize that O.R. is concerned with taking (or at least trying to take) a more rational and quantitative approach to decision-making. This requires the careful analysis of the factors involved, the possible and probable outcomes of alternative decisions and the derivation of one or more measures of effectiveness with which to assess comparatively the alternative outcomes.

Analysis of the situation about which the decision has to be made is known as "model building" and examples are presented of three key types: queueing models, simulation models and statistical models.

Deriving the best solution (decision) or, frequently, the solution which, according to the available information, is probably the best, is referred to as "model solution". Two examples of this were presented. Linear programming, which is one of a class of mathematical programming techniques, is widely used to compute optimal solutions. However, where uncertainties are involved, recourse has to be had to statistical decision analysis as exemplified by the doctor with a pimply problem.

In a tutorial of this type it is not possible to examine all the ramifications of the techniques mentioned. Fortunately there are numerous textbooks on operations research to which the interested reader can turn for further details. However, the librarian who has grasped the concepts and techniques oulined above and who has an interest in the analysis of library problems will be well on the path of library operations research.

NOTES

[1] This definition appears on the front of every issue of the *Operational Research Quarterly* (the journal of the British Operational Research Society).

[2] Those interested in the derivation of this and other equations describing the behaviour of queues are recommended to consult Chapter 6 of Sasieni, M., Yaspan, A., and Friedman, L. *Operations Research — Methods and Problems.* New York: John Wiley and Sons Inc., (1959), or any other standard textbook of O.R.

[3] For much of the substance of this and the following paragraphs the authors are indebted to Ian Woodburn, who worked on this model with Michael Buckland and Tony Hindle. The results of this work have been reported in a variety of publications, including Buckland, M. K. and Woodburn, I. "An analytical approach to duplication and availability" *Information Storage and Retrieval*, vol. 5, 1969, pp. 69-79, and Buckland, M. K., *et al. Systems Analysis of a University Library; Final Report on a Research Project.* Lancaster: University of Lancaster Library Occasional Papers, No. 4, 1970. (sbn 901699 02 0) (ED 044 153)

[4] Readers interested in this approach are recommended to consult Buckland, M. K. "An Operations Research Study of a Variable Loan and Duplication Policy at the University of Lancaster" *The Library Quarterly* 42 (1) Jan. 1972, pp. 97-106, or either of the publications cited in Footnote (3) above. A more detailed treatment is in preparation: Buckland, M. K. *Book Availability and the Library User.* New York, Pergamon Press. Forthcoming.

[5] Bayes, Thomas. An essay toward solving a problem in the doctrine of chances. *Phil. Trans. Royal Soc.* 53 (1763), 370-418. Reprinted in: Bayes, Thomas. *Facsimiles of two papers by Bayes.* New York, Hafner Publishing Co., 1963.

ABOUT THE AUTHORS

Tony Hindle has been Research Director of the Unit for Operational Research in the Health Services, Department of Operational Research, University of Lancaster, since 1971. He took a B.A. in Psychology and Statistics at the University of Liverpool in 1961, and a Diploma in Industrial Psychology at the same University in 1962. In 1966 he gained his Ph.D. at the University of Nottingham (while sponsored by British Leyland), after spending three years at Loughborough University of Technology as a Research Fellow. From 1966-71 he was a Lecturer in the Department of Operational Research of the University of Lancaster. For some time his principal private consulting interest has been in the field of library management and planning, and he has acted as a consultant for a number of projects undertaken by the University of Lancaster Library Research Unit.

Michael K. Buckland has had a conventional career as a librarian sandwiched around five years involvement in the application of operations research approaches to some of the problems of library administrators.
He entered library work as a trainee in the Bodleian Library of Oxford University, after studying history at that university. After taking a diploma in librarianship from the University of Sheffield he joined the library staff of the University of Lancaster. In 1967 he became Assistant Librarian for Research and a series of studies were undertaken with colleagues concerning book availability and library management gaming. Meanwhile he received a Ph.D. from the Division of Economic Analysis and the Postgraduate School of Librarianship at the University of Sheffield in 1972.
Moving to the United States, he became Assistant Director of Libraries for Technical Services at Purdue University in 1972. His publications include various technical reports and papers on bibliometrics and aspects of library management, and a forthcoming book on Book Availability and the Library User.

Peter Brophy took his first degree in Information Studies at University College London, graduating in 1971. He then went to the University of Lancaster Library Research Unit as a Research Associate, and worked on a project which investigated the use of mathematical models for use in education for library management. In 1973 he moved to the University of Strathclyde, Glasgow, as Library Systems Officer, and helped to develop a number of automated library systems. He is currently Section Librarian (Science) at Teeside Polytechnic, Cleveland, England.

The Application of Scientific Research to Librarianship

Herbert Goldhor

In this extract Goldhor questions whether the scientific method can or ought to be applied to librarianship and also considers the sort of results which can be expected from scientific research in this field. Emphasis is placed on the need for "interpretation and theory" in addition to the collection of data.

THE APPLICATION OF SCIENTIFIC RESEARCH TO LIBRARIANSHIP

The application of scientific research to librarianship demands a consideration of some basic criticisms or objections. Inevitably then one also needs to look, at least in a general way, at the record of research in librarianship so far. And finally in this chapter are some suggestions for choosing a topic for research in librarianship.

IS SCIENTIFIC RESEARCH IN LIBRARIANSHIP POSSIBLE?

It is possible that the scientific method of inquiry, in the form of research studies, is not applicable to librarianship. For one thing the subject matter of the social sciences in general and of librarianship in particular may be too complex. The phenomena of librarianship however are intrinsically no more complex or difficult to understand than are natural or physical phenomena, e.g., human physiology or the atom. All events in nature are individualized and every moment is different from every other, but science is concerned only with those aspects or features of things which repeat themselves indefinitely. Perturbations occur in almost all fields, but in the case of the natural sciences we can generally measure the effect of disturbing forces; and to ascertain invariant relations we must isolate the factors involved and vary only one at a time. In librarianship, the extraneous factors are not easily isolated or measured, and what is usually needed is greater knowledge and understanding of more and different examples of the situation in question.

A second possible difficulty is that research in librarianship cannot be successful because it is studying the work of man and is subject to prejudice and bias, and because the act of observing may influence the phenomenon in question. This is certainly a problem in all social science research and is more critical in some areas (e.g., psychology and sociology) than in librarianship. As noted above, one of the assumptions in the use of the scientific method in the social sciences is that man can study himself while controlling or correcting the disturbing influence of his observation of what is happening. Making this assumption explicit means that the researcher must guard against the danger in question. It is certainly true that bias has crept into much social science research, e.g., interviewer bias in choosing respondents for a quota sample but corrective efforts have been successfully devised to counteract it, viz., the use of a probability sample and repeated callbacks.

Social science research is undoubtedly subject to prejudice and bias on the part of the researchers, the persons observed, the readers of the resulting report, the people who allot research funds, and the general public. This would come out clearly in any research study which might seek to ascertain the superiority in specified ways of communism over democracy.

SOURCE: Reprinted from *An Introduction to Scientific Research in Librarianship. Final Report, Project 7-1217.* Washington, D.C.: U.S. Department of Health, Education and Welfare (July 1969) pp. 25-33.

But note that natural science too has similar difficulties to face when it touches sensitive areas, e.g., vivisection, birth control, sex, and artificial insemination for eugenic control of human reproduction; and the history of science shows many topics to have been highly sensitive when the method of scientific inquiry was first applied to them. The answer lies not in withdrawal from that field of study but the conscious application of the best available measures to prevent such prejudice from effecting the results. In the last analysis, the method of science produces only tentative results always subject to further testing for confirmation or correction.

Similarly when social scientists predict election results from public opinion polls, they are possibly contributing to a bandwagon effect. This then becomes a factor to be studied. Medical researchers too may have an influence on the prevalence of cigarette smoking or of breast examination in the detection of cancer, by the announcement of the results of their studies, and such results constitute one more factor to be taken into account in future studies of the incidence and types of cancer. In physics the attempts to record the path of atomic particles by photography have led to a recognition that such measures distorted the actual path followed. The point is not that such interaction is desirable, but that often it is inevitable and must therefore be identified and recognized, and if possible measured.

A third objection which might be leveled against the application of research to librarianship is that there is no possibility to conduct experiments. But experimentation is only one way by which to gather data, and is not necessarily used in all fields of natural and physical science (e.g., astronomy). Experimentation is not the essence of the scientific method so much as is observation leading to generalizations tested by repeated observation (as in the case of Darwin's work) and by logical and mathematical checks.

Furthermore we underestimate the value of the results we can get from the approximations to the experimental method which are available to librarianship. Every time a library introduces a new method or a new device or a new policy, the situation approximates an experiment, usually without controls or data collection measures by which properly to evaluate the new factor. But such controls and such measures can be introduced. Such experiments typically take longer, and it is less easy to control irrelevant variables or to measure the results accurately than in the case of experiments in the laboratory. Though it is difficult (but not impossible) to duplicate an experiment in librarianship, verification of the results of a given research study can be approximated by a critical analysis of the methodology used. For this reason and because we in librarianship are still trying to find the most appropriate research methods, it is necessary and important that we study the scientific method self-consciously — unlike the researchers in physical and natural science who absorb what they need to know about method from their study and from laboratory experience with their teachers and experienced researchers.

Finally, the question of experimentation is less relevant in librarianship than in some other subject fields, because truth in librarianship (as in the study of any social institution) is in part a function of history. That is to say, we must know the past in order to understand the present and to predict the future. Historical studies in librarianship may be either collections of facts or they can be research in the narrow sense of using facts to establish the accuracy of guessed-at relationships. In a figurative sense, history is in part the record of previous experiments. In this book, historical research is treated as an equally valid and equally important method of ascertaining truth as is any other.

The net result of these various difficulties (the complexity of social science subject matter, the greater exposure to prejudice, and the difficulty of performing closely controlled experiments) is that we cannot expect to derive mechanical laws of universal and invariant connections which can be verified by a crucial experiment. Instead we must content ourselves with statistical laws which assert frequencies or probabilities but cannot be verified by a single crucial experiment or disproven by a single exception.

In any case, the question of whether librarianship is susceptible to scientific research can only be answered in time and after serious attempts have been made to apply the method of science to this field of study. If principles are found which survive all possible tests, the answer is clear. If such principles are not found, either the method was not applied correctly or indeed it is inapplicable. The alternative is to assume that there are not general principles in librarianship, and that art and skill are the main roads for achieving mastery over the phenomena with which we are concerned.

It would appear however that the method of science is applicable within broad limits, whenever men will obey its rules. The pattern of science, as a method by which new knowledge is gained, consists in essence of accurate observation, valid classification, generalization by hypothesis, testing or verification, and the formulation of predictive generalizations which ideally are applicable to a given situation in all times and places. Social science phenomena are natural phenomena too, and can be studied by the same general method of science which has been found so useful in the natural and physical sciences. Since we are now at a much more elementary level of knowledge about the subjects of interest to us in social science and librarianship than we are concerning the physical world, we need to develop the underpinnings of a science of librarianship, in regard to the elemental relationships between basic variables. If we seek a way by which to transmute base metals into gold, after the manner of the alchemists, we shall assuredly fail; if we are prepared to seek the answers to our present problems by the long road of science, and in the process almost certainly acquire even more valuable knowledge, we may very well succeed.

In this process it is useful to recognize levels of knowledge of a given phenomenon, and the achievement of each in turn is usually prerequisite to a mastery of the next. The first and most elementary is that of description and identification of the activity in question, in sufficient detail and based on enough cases and a wide enough variety of cases that we can feel reasonably sure we know the typical example. The second is that of explanation or understanding as to why or now the phenomenon occurs or happens, and how it is related logically to other events. The third level is that of prediction, in which we can specify what will happen to one variable when we introduce or modify another. And finally there is the level of control by which is meant "the process of manipulating certain of the essential conditions that determine an event so as to make the event happen or prevent it from occuring."[1] Thus, speaking of educational research, Mouly says "Our task, then, is to discover the uniformities underlying social phenomena so that they can be integrated into a meaningful structure which will eventually permit the prediction and control of consequences . . . predictability and control . . . are the ultimate purposes and goals of science."[2]

A CLASSIFICATION OF LIBRARY LITERATURE WITH REGARD TO RESEARCH

It is assumed here that librarianship is at least capable of becoming a science, in that there are universal, invariant relationships to be detected between various elemental factors under specified conditions. It is assumed that librarianship is at least in part more than an art, or a skill, or a field of practice in which all that we know or do is either because of agreed-upon conventions, generalizations from experience, philosophical assumption, or administrative judgments. As stated, these are assumptions and if they are false then the rest of this book is irrelevant to librarianship. But others have considered these assumptions to be true, and have done some studies which deserve varying amounts of consideration.

There is a relatively small body of published research in librarianship, in the narrow sense of research. Ennis and Fryden's study of public library circulation in a steel town, during a strike, is one example[3]; Norman Stevens' analysis of three information storage and retrieval systems (a card catalog, IBM punched cards, and a handbook printout of those cards) is another.[4] Incidentally both served mainly to discredit relationships which had been thought to exist; this is a necessary and useful stage of development in any field of study in which research is only beginning. Berelson's analysis of all studies in the previous seventeen years of the use of public libraries resulted in generalizations which apparently were universal but may or may not vary as other circumstances change; in this case the data collection method was basically that of using measurements taken by others in many separate studies.[5] We are even beginning to see the outline of broad generalizations which have been tested and confirmed, such as Bradford's law of scattering [6], and the conclusion of the Chicago school of readers' interest studies in the 1930's that accessibility is more important than subject interest in determining what will be read. Incidentally other and older fields of study are said to be no further advanced, e.g., business research is lacking in hypotheses and conceptual framework but rich in descriptions of current practices. [7]

In the second place, there is a larger amount of published and unpublished service studies or applied research in librarianship which are useful, interesting and valuable for practical purposes, but which involve no hypothesis or generalization. Most library school master's theses (and not a few doctoral dissertations) belong here, as to such studies as the Fry report on circulation systems [8], most bibliographies, many historical investigations in librarianship, almost all library surveys, and other sub-types. Some of these were not even thought of by their authors as research, and collecting them in this second category is not meant to deny them their place and value. But it is meant to indicate that these are not the kind of study with which this book is primarily concerned.

In the third place, there is an even larger literature in librarianship which consists of reports or descriptions of specific situations, or simply the opinions of the individual author with or without supporting evidence.

A fourth category consists of original data, either alone or with some statistical analysis, e..g., state library annual publications of collected data on the libraries of their respective states. Though we have an impressive amount of such data, they are often unreliable and non-comparable. Furthermore, the data which typically are collected and published are those which are easiest to secure (e.g., most libraries publish their annual circulation totals, but less than half ever record the number of reference questions received). In addition, libraries have new experiences each year in many cases, and new circumstances arise for which we so often have no or inadequate data. The result is that almost any investigator in librarianship must expect to go out and collect from the beginning what data he needs, and this is usually expensive, time-consuming and difficult. In fact, one good way by which to arrive at a topic for a research study is to ponder the data already collected and available and judged to be reliable.

Not only is there need for more and continuing compilations of data for research purposes, but it would be a great help if such data could be published or otherwise made available (as on IBM punched cards) so as to incorporate or allow statistical analysis, e.g., averages, breakdowns by various categories, or other comparisons (as with the previous year). Even the table headings used can result in more or less helpful classifications. The ideal to be sought in the field of public librarianship, for example, is a volume, possibly entitled *The Fact Book of the American Public Library*, which would be reissued every few years in a revised edition and would summarize all available data on all aspects of public libraries, classified or analyzed from all main points of view, and with further special analysis available from some central agency. Such a publication would be a great contribution to research in librarianship, just as in all the major fields of science there are handbooks of tables, values, constants, and other measurements which have been verified and recorded and are now available equally to any of a large number of different researchers.

We need to capture and record all available data of the past and to maintain continuing access to them; we also need to record in an organized fashion the data arising from the changes which are sure to occur in the future. But the collection, analysis, and publication of data do not constitute research as here defined, but only one desirable antecedent or precondition for it. "The gathering of facts is at the heart of scientific research; but, if it is unrelated to interpretation and theory, it is trivial and confusing."[9]

REFERENCES

[1] Deobold B. Van Dalen, *Understanding Educational Research: An Introduction* (enl., rev.; McGraw-Hill, 1966) p. 43.

[2] George J. Mouly, *The Science of Educational Research* American Book Co., 1963, pp. 8, 29.

[3] Philip H. Ennis and Floyd N. Fryden, "The Library in the Community: Use Studies Revisited," *Library Quarterly* 30 (1960) pp. 253-65.

[4] Norman D. Stevens, *A Comparative Study of Three Systems of Information Retrieval* Graduate School of Library Service, Rutgers — The State University, 1961, p. 149.

[5] Bernard Berelson, *The Library's Public* (A Report of the Public Library Inquiry) Columbia University Press, 1949, p. 174.

⁶ B.C. Brookes, "The Derivation and Application of the Bradford-Zipf Distribution" *Journal of Documentation* 24 (December 1968) pp. 247-65.
⁷ Paul H. Rigby, *Conceptual Foundations of Business Research* (Wiley, 1965) p. viii.
⁸ George Fry and Associates, Inc., *Study of Circulation Control Systems; Public Libraries, Colleges and University Libraries, Special Libraries* (LTP Publication No. 1; ALA, 1961) p. 138.
⁹ Lawrence A. Kimpton, "The Social Sciences Today," in Leonard D. White, ed., *The State of the Social Sciences* (University of Chicago Press, 1956) p. 351.

ABOUT THE AUTHOR

Herbert Goldhor was born in Newark, New Jersey and graduated from Dana College in 1935. He took his B.S.L.S. at Columbia and his Ph.D. at the University of Chicago. After a spell as Assistant (later Associate) Professor at the University of Illinois library school he spent 10 years as Chief Librarian of Evansville (Indiana) Public Libraries. In 1962 he took up an appointment as Associate Director of the Graduate School of Library Science at the University of Illinois (Urbana) and in 1963 he became Director of the School. He has been Editor of both Library Trends and Public Library Abstracts. His principal professional interests are research in librarianship, public library administration and education for librarianship.

Library Effectiveness: An Introduction to the Systems Approach

Philip M. Morse

This extract from Morse's "Library Effectiveness" introduces the need for long term planning in order to provide an effective and efficient library service. It is of vital importance to the librarian that he knows what is happening within his library, and he should therefore collect data. Equally, he should be able to predict what will happen in the future should he implement any selected policy, and he should therefore have an understanding of the way in which his library works. The need for data and theory, as complements of each other, is stressed.

Whether or not it ever were so run, the modern library certainly cannot now be operated as though it were a passive repository for printed material. The opposed requirements of storing an increasing collection and of maintaining easy access to the most-used part of it can only be balanced by active and discriminatory planning. Whether the material be stored on shelves, in microfiles, or magnetically, the exponential increase in publication makes it uneconomical, and even undesirable, to have all items equally accessible. In spite of this, however, the library must be operated so that the majority of its users can find their way to the items of information they need, with a minimum of delay and frustration. To achieve a balance between these opposing requirements, the manager of an existing library or the planner of a new one must know in some detail how the user of the library will act, how often he will use a catalogue or other reference material, for example, what books or periodicals he will refer to and how long he will need to use each item. As with any other organization in these rapidly changing times, the librarian should know, as accurately as possible, what now is going on and should be able to predict what probably will be going on in the future.

This is particularly true of science libraries. As D.J. de Solla Price[1] has indicated, most reference material in the sciences has a very short useful life; about one-third of the citations in the scientific research literature are to material published in the previous 10 years and the references to earlier material are mostly to a relatively small group of "classic papers," with more than half of the earlier papers ignored completely. In physics, for instance, most books published 20 years ago are out of date and a not inconsiderable fraction contain erroneous or misleading material, in the light of later findings. Surely such volumes do not deserve accessibility equal to the most recent publications. Since the first year of the average physics book's life constitutes roughly 20 per cent of its total utility, it certainly is worth staff effort to get these books bought, catalogued, and shelved before half their first year has elapsed and to spot quickly the more popular of them so additional copies or reserve arrangements can ensure multiple access during their most useful period.

POLICY DECISIONS

Administrative decisions, both major and minor, regarding all aspects of library planning and operation, can be wisely reached only in the light of knowledge of present library use

SOURCE: Reprinted from *Library Effectiveness* by P.M. Morse by permission of the M.I.T. Press, Cambridge, Massachusetts.

and by the help of careful estimates of future use. Here are some typical administrative questions that must be answered, either actively or by default, often or occasionally, by every librarian or library board:

1. What fraction of the yearly budget should be allocated to the purchase of books; to the purchase of periodicals? How should this be allocated among the various fields covered by the collection? How does one decide which books (or periodicals) within a covered field should be purchased? How and when does one decide to buy a duplicate? How can one evaluate alternative decision procedures?

2. How should books (periodicals, etc.) be placed in regard to accessibility? Which items should be put on open shelves, which in stacks, which on reserve shelves, to be used only in the library, and so on? Can the amount of use of a book be predicted, so that one can estimate the fraction of users who will be frustrated or delayed by reducing the book's accessibility? Can this be compared with the relative cost of moving books to a less accessible region individually or collectively? With a popular book, what fraction of prospective users will find the book has been borrowed by another user? How high must this fraction be before a duplicate should be bought or the book be put on the reserve shelves?

3. How much is the usefulness of a book (or periodical) reduced if its use is restricted to the library reading room? Can the reduction be expressed in dollars and cents or in any other measure allowing comparison with other methods of ensuring multiple access (such as purchase of duplicate books)?

4. What is the relative value of "browsing"? How much easier is it to browse in an open-shelf collection than in a stack library, or than from a card catalogue? Is it better to ensure that a popular book always be on the shelf, available for browsing, or should it be allowed to circulate, thus being unavailable for browsing part of the time? Should different books be treated differently in this respect? Will any of the proposed automated systems for information retrieval, using electronic computers, permit browsing? Can they be modified to do so? How important would this modification be?

5. Can a measure be devised for the loss of utility produced when a book (or periodical) is missing from the collection for a period, either because "it is being rebound" or because it has been mislaid or stolen? How can this measure be compared with the cost of a guard or of more speedy rebinding or of occasional inventories to discover which books are lost so as to forestall the frustration of the next potential user?

6. What should be done when there are more books than accessible shelf space? Are there less accessible but more compact ways of storing some of the less-used books? If so, which books should be relegated to such "cold storage"? Are there ways of estimating how many users would be discommoded by this action?

7. In the case of a university library, which has priority (in service, in book choices, etc.) the student or the faculty? Does the library use by the faculty differ enough from that by the student, so that there should be libraries (or collections or rooms) for each separately?

8. Should there be one central library for the whole university or should there be many branch libraries? What would the difference in cost be? Would this difference be "worth it" in some measurable sense, and how much duplication of books would be required to stock adequately a set of departmental (or school) libraries (in other words, how many physics books does a geologist or a psychologist frequently use, and vice versa)?

Questions of this sort are being answered all the time, either consciously or by implication, by librarians or by their governing boards. Much of the time the operating decisions, which should be based on an explicit analysis of such questions and their answers, are implicitly based on a reluctance to change past practices or a desire to emulate some other library, though it should be apparent that the answers may differ appreciably from library to library and even from time to time in the same library. Occasionally attempts are made to arrive at answers by "market surveys" of a sample of users. Experience is showing the dangers of such opinion surveys, unless they are very carefully worded and unless they are quantitatively checked against the actual behavior of the same users. Too often has the questionee persuaded both himself and the questioner that he would use some proposed new service, only to find that he seldom gets around to using it, once installed.

THE NEED FOR DATA

For some time to come many of the questions listed above will have to be answered on the basis of the librarian's experience and intuition. Some of them may always have to be so answered. But surely a greater quantitative knowledge about library use can assist in getting answers and will make it easier to determine when conditions have changed enough to warrant changes in operation and wherein procedures in one library should differ from those in another. Data on some or all of the following questions would be of value in this respect:

What services (chance to sit down, chance to look at a book, chance to take a book home, chance to look at the catalogue or to talk to the reference librarian, etc.) does the library attendee use and how often does he use them each visit? How do different attendees differ in their use patterns?

What is the pattern of visits by various attendees (users) of the library? Is there an hourly, weekly, or seasonal periodicity in attendance? How long do they stay; what is the distribution of lengths of stay? Is there a correlation between length of stay and the attendee's use pattern?

What is the pattern of book (periodical, etc.) use? With a freely circulating book, what is the ratio between use in the reading room and borrowing to take home? What fraction of the collection is not used at all during a year? How do these use factors change with the age of the book? Is there a correlation between the use factors for successive years? How do the use factors differ for different classes of books (field of specialty, foreign language, text, periodical, report, and so on)? Is there any correlation between the use factor of a book and the way the library was persuaded to buy the book (request from faculty, decision of librarian, decision based on list of new publications or on book advertisements, etc.)?

Data on all of these items can be obtained. Most of them are not gathered by most libraries. Expense and lack of librarian's time are the usual excuses given for the neglect. Certainly any of the data mentioned costs time and therefore money to gather; to answer all the listed questions in detail each year would overburden any library's budget. It is the thesis of this monograph that librarians must learn, just as managers of industrial, mercantile, and military operations are learning, to gather and use data of this kind. As use patterns change and publication increases, lack of data may lead to wastage and loss of utility; expenditure of time and money in gathering some of the data mentioned could save more than this in improved utility. In the near future, the introduction of data-processing equipment in library operations will make it easier to amass the data; librarians should experiment with such data gathering before mechanizing, comparing the various methods of data gathering and the value of the various kinds of data in assisting policy decisions, so the data-processing equipment can be designed to produce the effective data most efficiently. In the end it will be better to buy fewer books, for the time being, in order to collect the data.

It is also the thesis of this report that the application of modern techniques in the theory of probability makes it possible to reduce greatly the cost and time involved in keeping a running record of much of the data listed earlier. By developing and testing out (at 10- or 20-year intervals) a number of probabilistic models of the operation, the models can be kept current in the intervening years by the gathering of a relatively small amount of data. From the models the other details, which would be more expensive to gather regularly, can be reconstituted with a good degree of expected accuracy. Prediction of next year's operation thus consists of extrapolation of the few items of gathered data; the models then provide the details of the prediction. (The use of experimentally checked theories to predict the behavior of some system is, of course, the usual method of physical science and of engineering.)

THE NEED FOR THEORY

Thus an effective and efficient procedure for determining how well a library is satisfying the needs of its users involves both data gathering and data analysis. The two aspects are complementary: analysis, particularly the use of probabilistic models, can drastically reduce the amount of data required; on the other hand analysis without enough data may lead to erroneous predictions and decisions.

Both aspects deserve more detailed study than they have hitherto received; only an introductory and somewhat fragmented discussion can be attempted in the present monograph.

Contrary to usual practice, this book will concentrate first on the theoretical or analytic aspect, partly because it is less familiar to librarians and partly because the choice of predictive model determines, to a considerable degree, the nature and amount of the data required. The concept of feedback control must be introduced and illustrated early in the discussion to emphasize that the data are gathered and analyzed, not for historical reasons, but to ensure that the library operation is in fact carrying out the policy determined by management and that these policies do in fact satisy the needs of the library users.

Another dichotomy, orthogonal to the separation between measurement and theory, involves the concentration on one or another part of the system. One can study, for example, the library user, what he does, what books he uses, and the like; or one can focus on the items in the library's collection, the books, periodicals, and reports, and ask who uses a particular item, how often it is used and the like. Both aspects must be studied to attain an adequate evaluation of library operation.

It will be amply apparent, as the reader progresses, that the examples discovered here will indicate only a few of the ways in which the techniques of operations research can assist the librarian in his operational decisions and his planning for the future. The whole subject of acquisition and cataloguing, the functions of the reference librarian, and other activities of considerable importance in library operations will hardly be touched on. All the author can hope to do, with a subject as undeveloped as this, is to give a few examples of the method in some detail and hope that others, with a more intimate knowledge of library operation, can extend the theoretical models and develop others, to correspond to those aspects which have been perforce omitted in this monograph.

REFERENCE

[1] D.J. de Solla Price "Networks of Scientific Papers" *Science* 149 (July 30th 1965) p. 510.

ABOUT THE AUTHOR

Philip M. Morse gained his A.M. and Ph.D. from Princeton University where he was Instructor in Physics from 1929-30. In 1931 he was appointed Assistant Professor of Physics at M.I.T., and in 1937 he became Professor. In 1958 he became Director of the Operations Research Center at M.I.T., whilst retaining the chair of Physics. He has been a prolific contributor to the literature of physics and of operations research, and his "Library Effectiveness", although published only four years ago, has already established itself as a classic of library science.

Research Methodology in the Management Sciences: Formalism or Empiricism

Aharon G. Beged-Dov and Thomas A. Klein

It is extremely important that operations research should not be uncritically accepted. It is a powerful methodology deriving from the traditions of the scientific method. However there are important differences between the physical, social, and decision sciences and the authors of this paper examine these differences in a clear but comprehensive manner. They also touch on other "issues" surrounding science in management such as optimization versus expediency, the role of mathematical deduction, and so on. They recommend the increased use of simulation and gaming methods in order that O.R. models and managers might communicate more effectively.

The successful development of any idea is largely dependent upon wisdom and insights received from others who have taught and written. Whatever substance is in this effort is due to Russell Ackoff, Ernest Dale, William Gomberg, C. West Churchman and William Morris. The rest is our own.

The common factor in all deliberate inquiries, regardless of subject matter or criteria employed to judge the results, is the use of the scientific method: which compares the problem, constructing a model of the system under study, deriving a solution from the model, testing the model and the solution derived from it, establishing control over the solution, and, finally, putting the solution into practice.[1] The thoughtful application of the scientific method to solve difficult business problems is presumed to be the outstanding characteristic of the management sciences. Yet, unlike the natural sciences, where exacting research procedures and evaluation standards exist, in business research the problems of choice of research methods, the selection of evaluation criteria, evaluating the importance of various characteristics of alternative solutions and the availability of means for implementing the chosen solution are still unresolved.

Is the methodology of the management sciences essentially identical to the natural sciences? Should the means available to carry out research influence the methods used? Is formal analysis superior to the verbal interpretation of the experienced manager? These are some of the questions that require close examination, ideally within a validated conceptual framework. But such a framework is missing in the management sciences and, in the absence of established operational guidelines, a person intending to study a complex business problem must attempt to perceive and assess those serious methodological issues which are likely to arise in his work.

This paper will argue that the circumstances which permit progress in the natural sciences rarely hold in business or other organized enterprises. It will further argue that the methods of inquiry and standards of evaluation proper in the physical sciences must not be applied without modification in solving even the most structured managerial problems. Indeed,

"The differences in scientific questions make it necessary to employ varying methods. . . . In some branches . . . the most fruitful work may be that of careful, patient description. . . . In others, it may be possible to develop already a theory in strict manner, and for that purpose the use of mathematics may be required."[2]

SOURCE: Reprinted from the *Operational Research Quarterly* 21 (3) Sept. 1970 pp. 311-326, by permission of the authors and publishers.

This position is not meant to argue with the necessity for objectivity in the management sciences. Rather it recognizes that economic and temporal considerations are regular components of problem solving and that organizational objectives are determined by people. Management science has academic meaning only in the absence of real-world managerial problems. Operations research should be operational.

METHODOLOGY IN THE PHYSICAL SCIENCES

According to Ackoff, "the products of scientific inquiry . . . are (1) a body of information and knowledge that enables us better to control the environment in which we live, and (2) a body of procedures which enables us better to add to this body of information and knowledge".[3] The principal objective of the scientist is to crystallize the essence of the causal relationship suggested by evidence from a limited number of experiments. Under certain conditions, such a relationship may be used for predicting the behaviour of the phenomenon it seeks to explain. Then it may be accorded the status of a law. Ackoff has further observed that "the less general a statement, the more fact-like it is; the more general a statement, the more law-like it is. Hence, facts and laws represent ranges along the scale of generality".[4]

Theory is even more general; it must explain the laws it implies "in the sense of introducing ideas which are more familiar, or in some way more acceptable than those of the laws".[5] For example, Newton's theory of gravitation is an explanation of Kepler's three laws and of Galileo's law.[6]

Scientists are able to discover natural laws and build on the discoveries of other scientists because of one remarkable and immensely significant fact, a physical phenomenon is always the same if the conditions are the same whenever it is observed (temporal homogeneity); a physical phenomenon is always the same if conditions are the same wherever it is observed (spatial homogeneity). If it were not for these two properties of physical phenomena, one physicist has commented, ". . . it would be useless to conduct scientific research and attempt to cognize the world".[7]

Somewhat analogous to the way theorems are derived in geometry, the physicist begins with a set of idealized assumption from which, using rigorous logical procedures, he deduces consequences. Depending on how well the consequences correspond to the physical event being studied, he may accept, modify or reject the derivation. The methodology of physics is not completely analogous to that of pure mathematics (although the methods of some individual physicists may be a close approximation). Physical laws need not be completely based on logic if they are consistent with empirical evidence.

The analytical process operating here is involved and circular, rather than simple and direct. The simplest fragment of evidence must be established within the confines of a given conceptual framework, but the validation of natural laws requires experimental verification. Progress in physics depends ". . . on guiding speculations by experience and on frequent comparison between deductions . . . and the observed behavior of objects".[8] In this manner, the physicist ". . . arrives at the same conclusions about the real world by two different routes; one by experiment, and the other by logical arguments".[9]

There appear to be two mutually exclusive elementary hypotheses which colour the work of theoretical physical scientists. The first holds that every single act in the universe follows from some ultimate causal necessity which eventually will be uncovered. The other is that, at some level, nature is merely a random assembly of unrelated phenomena. But the everyday work of the physical scientist is not the deliberate exploration of the verity or falsity of one or the other of these hypotheses.[2] Rather, he is most likely to be concerned with specialized, refined problems of how a given material reacts to specified conditions. On the other hand, the engineer's chief concern is in the application of this knowledge in the design of operational systems. For this reason, any fundamental progress toward explaining physical phenomena in terms of physical laws is likely to be the product of work by physical scientists, not by engineers.[10]

POSITIVISM IN THE SOCIAL SCIENCES

Except for the work of some of the most abstract and theoretical practitioners, the methodology of the physical sciences is largely positivistic in the sense conveyed by Auguste Comte in the nineteenth century. Comte's thesis was that relevant intellectual activity was concerned with deriving natural laws from observations of physical and social phenomena. Such a position replaced the more primitive, as he viewed them, deductive methodologies of theology and metaphysics, although he recognized the necessity of ". . . the natural opening afforded by theological conceptions".[11]

Comte felt that social phenomena have distinctive empirical properties linked by general relations which are subject to principles of determinism similar to those of the natural sciences. But he conceived "social physics" as having two major functions: (1) the forging of a distinct discipline founded on careful observations and relentless critical analysis of its theories until they are consistent with the data; (2) to establish guides for conduct. There is, thus, a subtle but important difference between the positivism of the natural sciences and that of the social sciences in terms of the relative emphasis on deductive and inductive approaches to understanding data and their implications. While it may be argued that this variation in emphases is due to differences in the stage of development of the two areas, whether in the context of the mid-nineteenth century or the mid-twentieth century, the more valid reason seems to be the seeming tran-science of social data. (An even sager view may be that the stage of development of any discipline is a function of the extent to which the data attended exhibit phenomenological constancy.)

The role of mathematics in this scheme is of central importance. That the social sciences have become highly quantitative can scarcely be doubted, although the degree to which mathematics is a pre-requisite discipline does vary from economics to psychology to political science to sociology, etc. Comte argued that mathematics is ". . . the most powerful instrument that the human mind can employ in the investigation of the laws of natural phenomena".[12] His whole exposition, however, treats mathematics as a tool, as measurer and as analogizer, not as doctrine.[13] He further recognized that mathematical methodology had limitations in terms of the phenomena of various disciplines[14], e.g.

the social sciences, but pointed out that these limitations were not intrinsic but " . . . in our intelligence, . . . restricted in proportion as phenomena, in becoming special, become complex".[15] None the less, he concludes that mathematics provides both the origin and the method of positivism, a logical universality for the study of all manner of phenomena, although full-blown mathematical treatment of "the most difficult sciences" must await better understanding of their phenomena, ". . . in the character and relations in which they present themselves to us".[16]

This guarded optimism regarding the role of mathematics in the social sciences is not shared by such more recent authors as C. Wright Mills and F. A. Hayek. Although no devotee of medieval scholasticism, Mills felt the need to breathe life and relevance into his studies and into his data. His critical review of the Warner-Lunt "Yankee City" social stratification study indicates his impatience with data so classified and quantified as to lose meaning.[17] Hayek opines:

> "The blind transfer of the striving for quantitative measurements to a field in which the specific conditions are not present which give it its basic importance in the natural sciences is the result of an entirely unfounded prejudice. It is probably responsible for the worst aberrations and absurdities produced by scientism in the social sciences."[18]

These and countless other demurrers deal with misuses of mathematics in the social sciences. The validity of analysis is a question of methodology, not of rigour. Doctrinaire prediction of social events from untested mathematical statements is questionable practice, however rigorous, in a mathematical sense, such derivations might be. Elementary quantitative treatment of data, which has no yield in terms of insights leading to larger generalizations, as suggested by Mills, is also questionable. Rigorous empirical testing of mathematically stated hypotheses avoids both of these misuses and, depending on the richness of the hypothetical generalization, the adequacy of data, and the care of analysis, may generate a fundamental contribution to knowledge and understanding.

The central argument of social positivism questions the value of the axiomatic method as a formal deductive system in the social sciences. A formal axiomatic system may be viewed as a game consisting of a set of symbols, devoid of any meaning, and a set of rules which prescribe how the symbols may be manipulated. (Abstract mathematics, Comte's conceptualization of algebra and calculus, provides an example of such a system.) Though the rules and symbols can be established at will, once prescribed, they must be observed in the strictest manner.

Beyond mathematics, the value of a deductive system depends entirely on the rules and one's ability to assign meaning to the symbols; the derivations should not only serve the relatively unimportant function of summarizing a body of evidence, but should also yield an understanding of the phenomenon under study. Minimally, the method must provide the same insight that can be obtained from common sense. Thereafter, it should yield results which extend well beyond those which common sense would produce.

> "When this happens, some of the new results may be translatable into ordinary language, but still for others, this will become impossible. They will remain in mathematical symbols. When this point has been passed, a higher state in the development of a science has been reached."[19]

The power of the axiomatic method stems from the following attributes: (1) Conceptual clarity. The necessity to state ideas explicitly leads to the identification of contradictions, omissions, repetitions and confusions. This in turn fosters clear statements, explicit definitions and clear logical sequences; (2) Conceptual relevance. Formalization identifies those aspects of a theory which are affected by particular data by making explicit which theorems follow from which postulates. This, in turn, makes it possible to reason which theorems and postulates are affected by a particular experimental result; (3) Identification of equivalent theories and theorems. If theorems are explicitly stated in two or more theories, it is possible to see in what respects they are the same, i.e. lead to the same consequences, and in what respects they differ.

Despite these advantages of the axiomatic method, demanding conditions must prevail for it to be a valid predictor or interpreter of real world data. For example, Lord Robbins has stated:

> "Economic laws describe inevitable implications. If the data they postulate are given, then the consequences they predict necessarily follow. If, in a given situation, the facts are of a certain order, we are warranted in deducing with complete certainty that other facts which it enables us to describe are also present. Granted the correspondence [of the analytical] . . . assumptions and the facts, . . . conclusions are inevitable and inescapable."[20]

Because such conditions are seldom met in other fields, the valid application of the axiomatic method has largely been restricted to some areas of theoretical physics. Its application in other fields has not been marked with success.

In economics, the tradition of inquiry which produces results deductively derived from a set of assumptions is as old as the discipline. Unlike Robbins, however, few economists have presumed that the assumptions must be realistic. A rational decision-maker, intent on maximizing some presupposed criterion of utility and in possession of full knowledge about the available courses of action and their consequences, has been the central, albeit typically fictional, figure in classical economics.

This paradigm was probably conceived in the desire to rationalize, in economic terms, a liberal political philosophy. But it has survived almost two centuries of professional scrutiny because of the necessity to simplify and abstract the immensely complex behaviour of the market place, not for the purpose of policy. Economic facts are limitless in number. "To bring some order among them, detect their causal sequence or mere interdependence so that we may interpret real world occurrences is the task of analytic study."[21] To reach this objective requires the ability to look beyond, rather than into the facts. Facts may be the building blocks of science, but abstraction makes possible the "systematization of the given facts by means of general connections".[22] To solve a practical problem, the careful sifting of data may be essential. However, theory cannot be developed while insisting upon a close correspondence between the assumptions of the theory and the facts. For there is no way to reject or accept a theory which "works", unless its assumptions strictly hold in the real world. The richness of reality cannot be captured. If it could, the economist's dilemma would no longer be critical.

For the economist, reality is a complex of conditions which never stand still either in an absolute sense or in relation to one another. Patient scholarship and empirical effort result in an explanation of history, not a plan for the future. The evolution of an economic theory which takes all of reality into consideration, even if there were agreement as to what constitutes reality, is descriptively and predictively accurate, is but a hope. Meanwhile, economic theory can be no more than

"a highly simplified and schematized portrayal of certain aspects of the world in which we live. A theory is realistic not in proportion to how fully it incorporates the richness, variety, and complexity of the world at large (that is a task for works of art) but in proportion to how skillfully it exposes the workings of a few of the phenomena that comprise experience and renders them intelligible. If you want realism, look at the world around you; if you want understanding look at theories."[23]

How should such theory be tested? According to Friedman, " . . . as a body of substantive hypotheses, [economic] theory is to be judged by its predictive power for the class of phenomena which it is intended to explain".[24] In other words, only a theory which can be rejected or tentatively accepted on the basis of experimental evidence is meaningful in economics.

The question regarding what constitutes sufficient correspondence between predicted and actual results remains. What magnitude of error in predicted sales or gross national product is permissible for a theoretical proposition to be accepted? What magnitude of error is not acceptable? The common reliance on statistical acceptance criteria may or may not be appropriate. In this situation, as in other scientific endeavours, informed judgment must be applied — a decision which is not strictly scientific must be made. The more fundamental issues would, otherwise, be obscured forever.

POSITIVISM IN THE
MANAGEMENT SCIENCES

Morris has espoused the alternate confrontation of theoretical model and data as the way to understanding management systems.[25] Research efforts which lead to policy formulation or to discrete decisions, the purview of the management scientist, present slightly different problems than inquiry, the congenial end of which is an understanding of phenomena and their inter-relationships. Whatever conclusions or implications for policy

may be drawn by a sociologist or economist, he tends to be primarily interested in their historical validity.

The management scientist, on the other hand, is explicitly concerned, however queasily, with the future validity of his findings. While this queasiness may be reduced when the phenomena under study display significant short-run stability, short-run problems do not often afford the analyst the leisure of reaching the boundaries of his discipline.[26] However confidently the patrolman in Williams' Squad Car Game may contemplate the plight of the fugitive computing his oddments and pay-offs,[27] the management scientist in real life rarely confronts a process which does anything but grind inexorably on, often seemingly capriciously.

Thus, determining when to substitute informed judgement for the long run potency of a positivistic approach and, indeed, what constitutes informed judgement are more critical, more frequently confronted issues for the management scientist than for his hind-sighted colleague in economics or sociology. Nor does the development of Bayesian approaches to these questions provide easy solutions to these questions. Pure positivism in the management sciences, therefore, must undergo considerable judgmental adulteration in the interests of operationality and of meeting the inevitable deadlines. In business research, depth of understanding is but an instrumental end, rarely justifying an accumulation of data or conceptualization sufficient to fully satisfy the scholar.

ALTERNATIVE 1:
SYSTEM OPTIMIZATION

Improving organizational efficiency has probably been a concern of managers since the formation of the first human organizations. The disciplined study of management problems, however, is a product of this century, particularly of the past few decades[28]. Frederick Taylor attempted to solve industrial problems through the strict use of time, technical perfection of production methods, carefully planned incentives and rational factory organization based on work assignments structured to accomplish efficiently the main tasks of the firm.[29] Such an approach tended to distil out the human factors in organization.

Further developments in management thought and theory have focused on incorporating these human factors[30]. Consideration of motivation and the experiences of public officials, army officers, church leaders as well as business managers produced a tentative structure which still prevails. Economists, marketers and other social scientists have provided a disciplined picture of the organizational environment which constrains management.

One characteristic of much of the management literature is the lack of scientific pretentiousness. Principles, guidelines and general tendencies, rather than laws or theories, are the dominant terms. In the last few decades, these have evolved into concepts which, in their totality, make up a systems philosophy.

Stripped to its essentials, a system may be viewed as an orderly collection of cells which are interconnected by various channels of communication and control for the purpose of attaining a desired objective. Nature contributes many examples of systems which seem to operate satisfactorily, for the most part, without visible guidance and control. The solar system is one. The human body is another. (Although one may argue that the practice of hygienics and medicine constitutes a control mechanism, the principal function of these professions is to assist the human body in coping with its environment; outright control is reserved for fairly extreme situations.) On the other hand, social systems are notorious for incongruities of a kind and magnitude which biological systems would not long endure. But social systems are the product of man's ingenuity or, occasionally, lack thereof. Hence, man has the power to modify them or adapt to them or to choose some combinatorial way of resolving system incongruities.

The reduction of factions and conflicts in the internal workings of a system in the interest of increasing system performance is among the principal objectives of operations research and systems engineering. The function of system engineering may be summarized:

"Systems engineering recognizes each system is an integrated whole even though composed of diverse, specialized structures and subfunctions. It further recognizes that any system has a number of objectives and that the balance between them may differ widely from system to system. The method seeks to optimize the overall system functions according to the weighted objectives and to achieve maximum compatibility of its parts."[31]

With respect to business and industrial enterprises and, to some extent, any social system, the systems concept implies

(1) Solutions which do not explicitly consider the economic aspects of outcomes are not viable.
(2) Organizations are engaged in purposeful activities which can be controlled.
(3) Man is capable of understanding causes and effects and has significant latitude in choosing courses of action; and
(4) Important operating elements are interdependent parts of a larger system having special properties — design of the whole system can provide greater efficiency than the "bits and pieces" approach.[32]

The systems approach implies that problems are defined in molar terms, rather than that the whole results from an accidental summation of structures and processes of its parts. None the less, the rational decision-maker will, where necessary, factor a complex system into a number of more manageable subsystems. Babbage long ago enunciated the principle of factoring in a manufacturering context:

"That the master manufacturer, by dividing the work to be executed into different processes, each requiring different degrees of skills or of force, can purchase exactly that precise quantity of both which is necessary for each process; whereas, if the whole work were executed by one workman, that person must possess sufficient strength to execute the most laborious of the operations into which the art is divided."[33]

Of critical importance in the systems concept, however, is that factoring is based upon deliberate analysis of the whole task or organization, i.e., is not a given initial condition.

The systems concept and the factoring process permit the analysis and efficient management of large-scale projects and of the institutions engaged in them. The value of this approach to decision-oriented research is, by now, well established. Not so well established is the matter of appropriate procedures and performance standards. The degree of rigour and precisions imposed in prescriptive models is an important example. The simplex algorithm as an approximate, rather than precise, optimization procedure would probably have been a less important device than it has. On the other hand,

"Theory has been carried to a degree of mathematical sophistication in some areas which is not fruitful in the light of the crudeness of the date . . . From a realistic point of view it seems desirable for the theory to move in the direction of including other aspects of systems rather than to become oversophisticated on one area and to ignore others."[34]

The stripping of a complex question to its essentials, expressing these in quantitative terms, and formulating mathematical relations consistent with the problem is a process which requires more than mathematical expertise. Though considerable insight can be gained by analytical techniques, because business problems usually involve a large number of parameters and variables, it is rarely possible to justify an analysis leading to closed-form optimization techniques. Nearly all mathematical formulations of business problems are founded on assumptions and idealizations whose effect upon the final result cannot be readily be assessed. This makes it difficult to determine the accuracy of the solution relative to the problem it seeks to involve, not relative to the formulation. Even the simplest linear regression model assumes homoscedaciticity and the lack of intercorrelation. But the usual least-squares procedure does not include a built-in check of these assumptions. A rigorous check is such an involved task, it is rarely employed. (On the other hand, a simple plot of the residuals against the predicted values can provide a valuable insight.)

When one couples this aspect of business research with the problem known as the "human element", the insistence upon strict scientific standards in business research becomes even less plausible. As any experienced manager will agree, in proposing an important solution, one must consider not only the technical ability, but also the likely attitude of the people which may become affected by the proposal. The reason business is not analogous to meteorology is that the "prediction" of the researcher, no matter how well substantiated it may be, will prove wrong rather than right if some people would so decide. Similarly, objectively faulty predictions may match results because of their motivating effect.

ALTERNATIVE 2:
COMPUTERIZED HEURISTICS

Many business problems are so involved, that it is often impossible to conceptualize, let alone express analytically, even some of their more distinct components. To further compound the difficulty, problems are typically interdependent. For this reason, the firm has been described as a "system of systems" managed "by thinkers whose main productive output is responsible decisions".[35] With the advent of the computer it has become possible to cope with some of these problems in a satisfactory manner. That computers can process only so much data as man is able to supply, and that the validity of their output can be only as good as the data originally entered is well known. Perhaps because this aspect is often being over-emphasized, less appreciated has become the possibility that, by taking over the routine functions of data acquisition, data reduction and data processing, by pretesting proposed solutions and by performing numerous other administrative routines, the computer can free man to concentrate on the analytical and intellectual tasks that suit his interest, challenge his imagination and tax his talent.

What permits man to solve problems is his ability to select, abstract and classify information from the environment in which he is immersed and then recall, as the need arises, impressions from past experience which will enable him to solve a problem of current concern. This human trait, when coupled with the data-handling and computation capabilities of computers, makes it possible to build many machine systems which are well suited to handle complex problem-solving assignments. To attempt, without computer assistance, to solve a problem involving a few hundred variables and parameters is clearly not practical. To so distil such a problem that it is susceptible to solution by one of the standard optimization procedures, however edifying the distillation may be, is unlikely to produce valid results. Thus, simulation and heuristic techniques appear to provide the only alternative to pure intuition in many instances.

Simulation allows one to capture system detail and to take up problems which clearly cannot be attacked by standard optimization procedures. Alternative strategies can then be tested for efficacy on the synthetic system. Simulation is an appropriate technique for dealing with classes of problems which are too complex to be summarized in compressed mathematical form and, because of costs and difficulties of achieving satisfactory controls, cannot be attacked empirically. For sizeable problems, however, simulation is a costly procedure in terms of model design, debugging and estimating parameters which are ignored in standard procedures. In a decision-making context, these costs must be weighed against the marginal value of sharpened estimates of outcomes. Moreover, the difficulties in estimating parameters present questions of model validity that may be only slightly less serious than for standard procedures. The principal value of simulation, in such cases, may be limited to the understanding of system interrelationships and nuances forced upon the analyst.

Heuristic techniques represent an attempt to simulate processes engaged by man in unaided problem solving. The capacity of a computer for data storage and rapid computation presumably exceeds that of man. Such processes as search, comparison, elimination of less promising solution space and search truncation, common to man's problem-solving efforts, can also be programmed. These several processes, according to Simon, represent the core of human problem solving.[33] Enlistment of computer assistance in the more habitual and routine of these processes relieves the decision-maker for more humane pursuits, expanding the scope and number of problems he can confront.

It is difficult to conceive a realistic business situation not requiring the use of gross strategies, simplifying rules and educated guesses. Consider a manager confronted with a non-trivial problem. Aware that it soon becomes economically infeasible to study all available information, and that he will reduce his understanding of the problem by considering every relevant variable, the manager will settle for reasonable evidence.

A more specific example is afforded by the elusive relationship between advertising effort and sales. It is generally assumed that an increase in the former "causes" an increase in the latter. It is further recognized that increases in advertising (A) are not always followed by increases in sales (S) because certain identifiable conditions $(c_1, c_2, \ldots, c_k)$ may be present which impede the action of A on S. The problem is further compounded by the fact that changes in S may take place which have no apparent relationship to any corresponding changes in A. Should A be considered a "cause" and $c_1, c_2, \ldots, c_k$ as only secondary factors?

It may be argued that A is not at all different from $c_1, c_2, \ldots, c_k$. When they are stable, increases in S do not occur without an increase in A. Similarly, when A is stable, increases in S do not occur without some change in one or more of the conditions. The resolution of this issue lies in the statistical principle of concomitant variation as progressively developed by John Stuart Mill, Roland Fisher and Russell Ackoff.[37] To establish an increase in A as a critical cause of an increase in S, the following must hold:

(1) Increases in S are always preceded by relative increases in A, given $c_1, c_2, \ldots, c_k$;

(2) Within the limits set by A, S does not vary (in a statistically significant sense) as the conditions, taken in any possible combination, vary;

(3) Within the limits set by the conditions, S varies as A varies.

The difficulty in establishing these propositions and the potential existence of significant variables other than $c_1, c_2, \ldots, c_k$ reduce the likelihood of ever positively establishing the A→S casual relationship — or of refuting it — is obvious. The marketing scientist concerned with this formulation of the problem thus faces an impasse. The decision-maker, on the other hand, confronted with A as an available controllable variable and the bulk of available evidence, is likely to conclude that increases in A are necessary if increases in S are to be realized. Except that this discussion has avoided the shape of the S, A function, this conclusion is the essence of heuristics.

Ledley distinguished between "semantic" heuristics, exemplified by the decision-making process employed by a chess player contemplating his future moves, and "syntactic" heuristics, which reduce the search space while maintaining the solution space virtually intact.[98] An example of syntactic heuristics is a linear programming problem which, though solvable with an available code, would require many hours of computation because the matrix of coefficients is extremely large. One procedure is to select, according to some criterion, a small number of columns from the original matrix and then solve with the available code.

Semantic heuristics carry the automation of problem solving a step further than syntactic heuristics. Such processes are best described as preselecting a search strategy as well as a solution strategy, whereas, in syntactic heuristics, the search procedure remains under man's continuous control. This subtlety may be exemplified by a chess game. Conceivably, the opening player should be able to list each of the different ways in which the opponent could respond to any move he makes, then his own countermoves, and so on, for as many moves as are sufficient to win. In practice, this is completely infeasible because to trace out forty moves, the duration of a typical game, one needs to evaluate about 10^{120} possibilities. A machine that can make one million computations each second will need at least 10^{90} years to do the job. Two alternatives immediately suggest themselves: (1) to limit the search to several specific opening moves and follow these for only four or five steps (syntactic heuristics) instead of forty, or (2) to choose, in advance, a particular selection strategy and then proceed to examine it in depth (semantic heuristics). Both procedures are now practical for a programmed game.

If one were to observe a series of games pitting a gifted chess player against an heuristically programmed computer, as one might expect, the computer may lose. The reason is that the mechanical combatant, given its radically pruned search tree, will occasionally discard some desirable alternative which its more perceptive and flexible opponent could consider, thus leading to machine defeat.

SUMMARY AND CONCLUSIONS

The similarities and differences among the physical, social and decision sciences have been examined for methodological implications. Physical data and physical relationships exhibit a degree of constancy far greater than that to be observed in social data or social relationships. The role of the physical and social scientist is to describe and explain empirical data and to establish causal and associative relationships which may be used for predicting or controlling future events. The management scientist, too, must draw upon and, frequently, generate information like that of social and physical scientists in gaining an understanding of the system he assists in controlling. But the criterion of his performance is the efficiency with which control is exerted, not the validity of his findings about system inter-relationships.

Several dimensions of research methodology have been explored in light of their implications in the above three categories of intellectual endeavour. The validity of deductive formalism is dependent upon how well-observed results match logically derived results. To the extent that the basic premises and axioms are based on conceptualizations of the real world, their validity as a basis for prediction is determined by the spatial and temporal homogeneity of the phenomena with which they deal. For this reason, in general, axiomatic methods are more suited to the physical sciences than to the social or management sciences. But even the physical scientist is called upon for empirical verification of his derived findings. Scientists dealing with phenomena displaying significant instability may use deductive procedures as a means to gain understanding of critical relationships. Even where quantitative symbolism is employed, however, the real meaning of their findings is likely to be limited to the quantitative sphere. The ability to predict in quantitative terms and, thus, to provide the basis for control is severely limited. Deductive formalism for the social scientist and for the decision scientist, therefore, must be regarded as generating approximations and tendencies at best.

Inferential empiricism is a necessary ingredient of all but the most "pure" of intellectual pursuits. The necessity of verifying conclusions and predictions by observation, while, as previously suggested, a function of the stability of relationships under consideration, is well established in both the physical and social sciences. Given the demands placed upon the management scientist by temporal and economic considerations, however, the rigour he must employ in establishing the validity or generality of an hypothesis must be weighed in the balance of cost and value of such verification, i.e. is subject to the Bayesian concept of the value of additional information. While physical and social scientists should not parade conclusions as precise and definitive which are, in fact, but approximate, the decision scientist may be excused for this, if only he recognizes the limitations of his methods.

The question of mathematical as opposed

to verbal or other symbolic representations of real-world relationships has been investigated. The power of mathematical formulations to force clear definitions of concepts, to quantify them, and, through their own logic, to provide definitive conclusions and predictions, is well established. Outside of the intersection of clarity and quantifiability, however, lay many concepts which are one or the other, but not both, or which are neither. And these non-mathematical concepts have meaning to persons who would operate within or control their implications. If concepts and relationships which have meaning for such persons can be set in mathematical terms, mathematical approaches are definitely indicated. But for mathematically oriented scientists to coin conceptualizations for their own use which have no external meaning or to so distil important conceptualizations that their meaning is radically changed (not merely refined) serves little useful purpose. This dictum is especially pertinent for the management scientist whose output is immediate input for managerial decision-makers. This does not, however, remove a responsibility to assist decision-makers in clarifying problems and in quantifying relevant variables.

Within the context, the roles of closed-form optimization models, simulation and heuristics have been examined. Holistic approaches to problem-solving are recommended. Although large-scale organizations and tasks need to be factored into more manageable subsystems, important inter-component relationships should not be ignored. In the employment of standard optimization procedures, such as linear programming and inventory models, the temptation for unrealistic closure is strong; internal validity may be served, but at the expense of external validity. On the other hand, to the extent that analysis is intended to assist in decision-making, operationality and, hence, closure may be justified. None the less, along the ratch-like continuum of problem-solving methods ranging from the most informal to the most formal, it is suggested that the notches identified with the most commonly used operations research techniques are overly worn in proportion to the kinds of problems they are most efficient at solving. The

oft-cited caricature of the operations researcher as a mechanic who knows how to use a screwdriver and who frequently files slots in bolts rather than locate another tool is probably more frequently true than professionally tolerable.

Moreover, the strict adherence to the performance criteria of the classical economics tradition, those criteria typically employed in operations research models, probably does not characterize the utility functions of managerial decision-makers. Long-run profit maximization is not an operational concept to the real-world problem-solver. In addition, the desire for short-run profits is mitigated by such humane criteria as power, self-esteem and ease of implementation, as well as the consideration of costs incurred in locating the optimum as opposed to some satisfactory expectation. Without sullying the academic value of the further development of these formal models or its indirect potential for improving managerial efficiency, the present state of the arts appears to call for methods which approximate optimality and which build in criteria more difficult to quantify but which may be more meaningful in an actual managerial context.

This calls for interest in "satisfaction" rather than the "optimality" of classical analysis. It calls for decision-making procedures based on simplifying strategies. While the notion of satisfying, being ill defined and particular, cannot match the intellectual appeal of optimality, it must be remembered that a solution is defined as "optimal" only in the sense that no better alternative is available. The internal optimality of an artificial model is not the same as optimality in the system the model purports to represent. The former is merely a special kind of sub-optimization.

Thus, the increased utilization of simulation and heuristics, where appropriate in terms of previously noted external factors, is suggested. Such a step calls for an even greater reliance on computer technology for tasks presently done by men than presently contemplated by all but the most visionary seers. Man's hesitance to take this step, his tradition-oriented dichotomization between humane and mechanical activities, is, we feel, understandably based on his conceptualization of a conflict between man and machine. Within the context of the present paper, however, man enlists the aid of the machine, rather than opposing it. In this relationship, the machine places certain demands upon man regarding clarity of instructions, but man remains in control of both the machine and of the system

he is managing. Recognition of the value of this arrangement has brought us economic and social progress and freed us from mechanical tasks to engage in more humane intellection. In an efficient man/machine system, the best attributes of men and machines are brought to bear in problem-solving.

REFERENCES

[1] R. L. Ackoff (1962) *Scientific Method: Optimizing Applied Research Decisions*, John Wiley, New York. p. 26.
[2] J. von Neumann and O. Morgenstern (1964) *The Theory of Games and Economic Behaviour*, John Wiley, New York. p. 2.
[3] Ackoff, *op. cit.* p. 5.
[4] Ackoff, *op. cit.* p. 21.
[5] N. R. Campbell (1952) *What is Science?* Dover, New York. p. 89.
[6] A. Wolf (1928) *Essentials of Scientific Method*, George Allen & Unwin, London. pp. 126, 127.
[7] V. Ivanov (1965) *Contemporary Physics*, Peace Publishers, Moscow. p. 7.
[8] H. J. J. Bradick (1956) *The Physics of Experimental Method*, John Wiley, New York. p. 1.
[9] E. H. Coombs, H. Raiffa and R. M. Thrall (1954) "Some views on mathematical models and measurement theory." In *Decision Processes* (R. M. Thrall, E. H. Coombs and R. L. Davis, Eds.), John Wiley, New York, p. 23.
[10] E. F. MacNichol, Jr. (1967) "A discussion of the contributions that systems engineering can make to our understanding of living organisms." 1967 Institute of Electrical and Electronics Engineers International Convention Digest, p. 272.
[11] H. Martineau (1896) *The Positive Philosophy of Auguste Comte*, George Bell, London, Vol. 1. pp. 2-4.
[12] Coombs, Raiffa and Thrall, *op. cit.* p. 34.
[13] Coombs, Raiffa and Thrall, *op. cit.* pp. 36-43.
[14] Coombs, Raiffa and Thrall, *op. cit.* p. 49.
[15] Coombs, Raiffa and Thrall, *op. cit.* p. 46.
[16] Coombs, Raiffa and Thrall, *op. cit.* p. 49.
[17] C. Wright Mills (1942) "The social life of a modern community." *Am. Sociol. Rev.* 7, 263.
[18] F. A. Hayek (1952) *The Counter-revolution of Science*, The Free Press, New York. p. 51.
[19] O. Morgenstern (1963) "Limits to the uses of mathematics in economics." In *Mathematics and the Social Sciences.* The American Academy of Political and Social Science, Philadelphia. pp. 22-23.
[20] L. Robbins (1949) *On the Nature and Significance of Economic* Science, Macmillan, London. pp. 121, 122.
[21] S. Weintraub (1964) *Intermediate Price Theory*, Chilton Books, Philadelphia. p. 5.
[22] V. L. Bertalanffy (1962) *Modern Theories of Development: An Introduction to Theoretical Biology*, Harper, New York. p. 19.
[23] R. Dorfman (1964) *The Price System*, Prentice-Hall, Englewood Cliffs, N. J. pp. 10-11.
[24] M. Friedman (1953) *Essays in Positive Economics*, University of Chicago Press, Chicago. p. 8.
[25] W. T. Morris (1967) "On the art of modeling." *Mgmt. Sci.* 13, B-709. For a more expansive exposition see Morris (1965) *Management Science in Action*, R. D. Irwin. Homewood, Illinois. pp. 83-124.
[26] W. T. Morris (1964) *The Analysis of Management Decisions*, R. D. Irwin, Homewood, Illinois. pp. 470-484.
[27] J. D. Williams (1954) *The Compleat Strategyst*, RAND Series. McGraw-Hill, New York. pp. 57-60.
[28] H. Koontz (1961) "The management theory jungle." *J. acad. Mgmt.* 4, 174.
[29] F. Taylor (1911) *Shop Management*, Harper and Brothers, New York pp. 17-65.
[30] E. Mayo (1945) "The Human Problems of an Industrial Civilization," Viking Press, New York. pp. 157, 158.
[31] J. A. Morton (1959) "Integration of systems engineering with component development." *Electrical Manufacturing*, 64, 85.
[32] D. C. Feingenbaum (1963) "Systems engineering - A major new technology." *Industrial Quality Control*, 20, 9.
[33] C. Babbage (1846) *On the Economy of Machinery and Manufacturing*, 4th ed. John Murray, London. p. 175.
[34] F. Hannsman (1961) "A survey of inventory theory from the operations research point of view." In *Progress in Operations Research* (R. L. Ackoff, Ed.), John Wiley, New York. vol. 1, pp. 95, 96.
[35] H. Thompson (1965) *Joint Man/Machine Decisions: The Phase beyond Data Processing and Operations Research*, Systems and Procedures Association, Cleveland, Ohio. p. 123.
[36] H. A. Simon (1965) *The Shape of Automation for Men and Management* Harper and Row, New York. pp. 76-92.
[37] The first three of Mills' five "Canons of Induction" enunciated in *A System of Logic* (London: Parker, Son and Bowen, 1866) represent the first systematic effort to define causality. The fifth of these canons defines statistical correlation in qualitative terms. Fisher's *Statistical Methods for Research Workers* (Edinburgh: Oliver & Boyd, 1948) and *The Design of Experiments* (Edinburgh: Oliver & Boyd, 1949) provided the framework for the quantitative analysis of causation or its absence. Chapter 10 of Ackoff's *Scientific Method: Optimizing Applied Research Decisions* (New York: John Wiley, 1962) reformulates Mill's canons and integrates them with Fisher's theory of experiments to provide a general framework for the determination and measurement of cause and effect.
[38] R. S. Ledley (1962) *Programming and Utilizing Digital Computers* McGraw Hill, New York. pp. 352-354.

ABOUT THE AUTHORS

Aharon G. Beged-Dov received a B. S. degree in mechanical engineering from the University of Toledo, and an M. S. degree in industrial engineering from the same university. He received his Ph. D. from the University of Pennsylvania in 1967. In the same year he became Associate Professor in the College of Business of the University of Toledo, and he is currently Professor of Operations Research in the Department of Operations Research and Planning of the University of Ottawa. His research interests include mathematical programming and operations research methodology.

Thomas A. Klein has been Director of the Business Research Center of the University of Toledo, Ohio since 1967. He gained his Ph. D. from Ohio State University in 1964 and in the same year he joined the faculty of the University of Toledo as an Assistant Professor. In 1971 he became Professor of Marketing. He has written numerous articles and monographs on research methodology, on public policy in marketing and on related subjects.

Applied Organization Change in Industry: Structural, Technical, and Human Approaches

Harold J. Leavitt

A keynote of all management science and of operations research in particular is the concept of change. An O.R. study which does not contribute toward effective change is of little or no value. Leavitt, in this extract, makes it clear that there are many perspectives on organisational change and the various viewpoints may on occasion be in conflict. He places O.R. in his category labelled "technological approaches to organisational change" and he is critical of its handling of the human side of the enterprise. His warning is important in that the successful O.R. study is one which <u>does</u> take into account the feasibility in human terms of the proposed solution.

This is a mapping paper. It is part of a search for perspective on complex organizations, in this instance, through consideration of several classes of efforts to change ongoing organizations. Approaches to change provide a kind of sharp caricature of underlying beliefs and prejudices about the important dimensions of organizations. Thereby, perhaps, they provide some insights into areas of real or apparent difference among perspectives on organization theory.

To classify several major approaches to change, I have found it useful, first, to view organizations as multivariate systems, in which at least four interacting variables loom especially large: the variables of task, structure, technology, and actors (usually people) (Figure 1).

Roughly speaking, task refers to organizational raisons d'etre — manufacturing, servicing, etc., including the large numbers of different, but operationally meaningful, subtasks which may exist in complex organizations.

By actors I mean mostly people, but with the qualification that acts usually executed by people need not remain exclusively in the human domain.

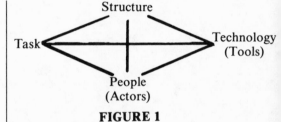

FIGURE 1

By technology, I mean technical tools — problem-solving inventions like work measurement, computers, or drill presses. Note that I include both machines and programs in this category, but with some uncertainty about the line between structure and technology.

Finally by structure, I mean systems of communication, systems of authority (or other roles), and systems of work flow.

These four are highly interdependent, so that change in any one will most probably result in compensatory (or retaliatory) change in others. In discussing organizational change, therefore, I shall assume that it is one or more of these variables that we seek to change. Sometimes we may aim to change one of these as an end in itself, sometimes as a mechanism for effecting some changes in one or more of the others.

SOURCE: Reprinted from W.W. Cooper, H.J. Leavitt and M.W. Shelly II (eds.), *New Perspectives in Organization Research* New York: John Wiley and Sons, 1964, (Chapter 4. "Applied Organization Change in Industry: Structural, Technical, and Human Approaches" by Harold J. Leavitt) by permission of the publishers.

Thus, for example, structural change toward, say, decentralization should change the performance of certain organizational tasks (indeed, even the selection of tasks), the technology that is brought to bear (e.g., changes in accounting procedures), and the nature, numbers and/or motivation and attitudes of people in the organization. Any of these changes could presumably be consciously intended; or they could occur as unforeseen and often troublesome outcomes of efforts to change only one or two of the variables.

Similarly, the introduction of new technological tools — computers, for example — may effect changes in structure (e.g., in the communication system or decision map of the organization), changes in people (their numbers, skills, attitudes, and activities), and changes in task performance or even task definition, since some tasks may now become feasible of accomplishment for the first time.

Changes in the people and task variables could presumably branch out through the system to cause similar changes in other variables.

We can turn now to the central focus of this paper, namely, a categorization and evaluation of several approaches to organizational change — approaches that differ markedly in their degree of emphasis and their ordering of these four variables.

Clearly most efforts to effect change, whether they take off from people, technology, structure or task, soon must deal with the others. Human relators must invent technical devices for implementing their ideas, and they must evaluate alternative sturctures, classing some as consonant and some as dissonant with their views of the world. Structuralists must take stands on the kinds of human interaction that are supportive of their position, and the kinds that threaten to undermine it, etc.

Although I differentiate structural from technical from human approaches to organizational tasks, the differentiation is in points of origin, relative weightings, and underlying conceptions and values, not in the exclusion of all other variables.

This categorization must be further complicated by the fact that the objectives of the several approaches to organizational change are not uniform. All of them do share a considerable interest in improved solutions to tasks. But while some of the technical approaches focus almost exclusively on task

solutions, that is, on the *quality* of decisions, some of the people approaches are at least as interested in performance of task subsequent to decisions. Although improved task solution serves as a common goal for all of these approaches, several carry other associated objectives that weigh almost as heavily in the eyes of their proponents. Thus some of the early structural approaches were almost as concerned with maintaining a power status quo as with improving task performance, and some of the current people approaches are at least as interested in providing organizations that fulfill human needs as they are in efficacious performance of tasks.

The several approaches are still further complicated by variations in the causal chains by which they are supposed to bring about their intended changes. Some of the structural approaches, for example are not aimed directly at task but at people as mediating intervening variables. In these approaches, one changes structure to change people to improve task performance. Similarly, some of the people approaches seek to change people in order to change structure and tools, to change task performance, and also to make life more fulfilling for people. We can turn now to the several varieties of efforts themselves.

THE STRUCTURAL APPROACHES

Applied efforts to change organizations by changing structure seem to fall into four classes. First, structural change has been the major mechanism of the "classical" organization theorist. Out of the deduction, logical, largely military-based thinking of early nonempirical organization theory, there evolved the whole set of now familiar "principles" for optimizing organizational performance by optimizing structure. These are deductive approaches carrying out their analyses from task backwards to appropriate divisions of labor and appropriate systems of authority. These early structural approaches almost always mediated their activities through people to task. One improves task performance by clarifying and defining the jobs of people and setting up appropriate relationships among these jobs. Operationally one worried about modifying spans of control, defining nonoverlapping areas of responsibility and authority, and logically defining necessary functions.

In retrospect, most of us think of these early approaches as abstractions, formal and legalistic, and poorly anchored in emphirical data. They were also almost incredibly naive in their assumptions about human behavior. In fact, almost the only assumptions that were made were legalistic and moralistic ones: that people, having contracted to work, would then carry out the terms of their contract; that people assigned responsibility would necessarily accept that responsibility; that people when informed of the organization's goals would strive wholeheartedly to achieve those goals.

The values underlying these early approaches were thus probably more authoritarian and puritanical than anything else. Order, discipline, system, and acceptance of authority seemed to be dominant values. The objective, of course, was optimal task performance, but within the constraints imposed by the hierarchy of authority.

In one variation or another, such structural approaches are still widely applied. It is still commonplace for consultants or organization planning departments to try to solve organizational problems by redefining areas of responsibility and authority, enforcing the chain of command, and so on.

A second widespread approach to structural change, allied to the first, somewhat more modern and sophisticated and somewhat narrower, too, is the idea of decentralization. The idea of changing organizations by decentralizing their structure was probably more an invention of the accounting profession than anyone else, though it has been widely endorsed by structuralists and by human relators too. Almost nobody is against it. Not too long ago, I heard the senior officers of one of the nation's largest consulting firms remind his large staff of young consultants that their firm was founded on the "bedrock principle of decentralization."

Decentralization affects the performance of tasks partially through its intervening effects on people. By creating profit centers, one presumably increases the motivation and goal-oriented behavior of local managers. One also adds flexibility so that variations in technology appropriate to the different tasks of different decentralized units now become more possible; so do subvariations in structure, and local variations in the use of people.

Decentralization can be thought of as a mechanism for changing organizations at a meta level, providing local autonomy for further change. Thus, within limits, decentralized units may further change themselves through the use of any one of the many alternatives available, and perhaps for this reason no group has questioned it, at least until the last couple of years.

Recently, two other structural approaches have shown up, but they have not yet reached a widespread level of application. One of them is best represented by Chapple and Sayles[1]. Theirs is a form of social engineering aimed at task, but via people. They seek to modify the behavior of people in order to improve task performance, but they do it by modifying structure, in this case, the flow of work. Out of the tradition of applied anthropology, they argue that planning of work flows and groupings of specialties will directly affect the morale, behavior, and output of employees. One of the failings of earlier structural models, in their view, is that the design of work was almost entirely determined by task and technical variables, and failed to take account of human social variables. They provide illustrative cases to show that appropriate redesigning of work, in a social engineering sense, affects both human attitudes and output.

I cannot overlook in this discussion of structure the implications of a second approach — the research on communication networks[2]. I know of no direct application of this laboratory research to the real world, though it has had some indirect influence on structural planning. In that research, variations in communication nets affect both routine and novel task performance rather significantly. The results suggest that appropriate communication structures might vary considerably within a complex organization, depending upon the type of task that any subunit of the organization undertakes. Thus far highly programmed repetitive tasks, highly centralized communication structures seem to operate most efficiently, but with some human costs. For more novel, ill-structured tasks, more wide-open communication nets with larger numbers of channels and less differentiation among members seem to work more effectively.

TECHNOLOGICAL APPROACHES TO ORGANIZATIONAL CHANGE

My first entry in this technological category is Taylor's *Scientific Management*[3]. Its birth date was around 1910, its father, Frederick W. Taylor. Its tools were work measurement tools. It bore none of the abstract deductive flavor of the structural approaches. From the classic programming of the labors of Schmidt, the immigrant pig-iron handler at Bethlehem, on to the more sophisticated forms of work measurement and analysis of succeeding decades, Taylorism has constituted a significant force in influencing task performance in American organizations.

Scientific Management, almost from its inception, took a position outside of the task, not of it. Taylor created a new technical skill — industrial engineering — and a new class of specialized practitioners — the industrial engineers. Theirs was a staff skill, a planning skill. They were the organizers and designers of work. The Schmidts were the doers.

Like the early structural approaches, Scientific Management was thus to a great extent ahuman, perhaps even inhuman. For in creating the separate planning specialist, it removed planning from its old location — the head of the doer of work. Many observers, both contemporary and subsequent, saw this phase of scientific management as downright demeaning of mankind. Taylor put his foot deeply into his mouth by saying things like this: "Now one of the very first requirements for a man who is fit to handle pig iron . . . is that he shall be so stupid and so phlegmatic that he more nearly resembles . . . the ox than any other type. . . . He must consequently be trained by a man more intelligent than himself."[4]

But despite the flurry of Congressional investigations and active counterattack by Taylor's contemporaries, Scientific Management grew and prospered, and radically changed structure, people, and the ways jobs got done. Indeed, it spread and flourished until no self-respecting manufacturing firm was without time-study men, methods engineers, work standards, piece rates, and job classification schemes.

The range of Scientific Management, however, was limited by its relatively simple tools largely to the programming of eye-hand and muscle jobs. Though Taylor and his fellows were ready to generalize their methods to almost any organizational problem, the methods themselves fell pretty short when applied to judgment and think-type jobs.

If one asks why Scientific Management flourished, several reasonable answers appear. The environment of the day, despite counterattacks by Upton Sinclair and others, was probably supportive. It was an environment of growth, expansiveness, and muscle flexing. Work in associated disciplines was supportive, too. Psychology, for example, was physiologically oriented, concerned with individual differences and anxious to be treated as a science. Hence it too, was measurement happy.[5] Finger dexterity tests meshed neatly with Taylor's motion study.

But most of all, Taylorism, like many other ideas, seemed to be carried by its own operational gimmicks — by its cheap, workable, easily taught techniques and methods.

Scientific Management receded into a relatively stable and undramatic background in the late 1930's and 1940's and has never made a real comeback in its original form. But the technological approaches were by no means dead. The development of operations research and the more or less contemporaneous invention and exploitation of computers have more than revived them.

I submit that operational operations research methods for changing organizational problem solving can be reasonably placed in the same category with Scientific Management. They have both developed a body of technical methods for solving work problems. They both are usually external in their approach, essentially separating the planning of problem-solving programs from the routine acting out of solutions. Operations research, too, is quickly developing in its operational form, a new class of hot-shot staff specialists, in many ways analogous to the earlier staff efficiency man. What is clearly different, of course, is the nature of the techniques, although there may be larger differences that are not yet so clear.

The operations research and information processing techniques are turning out to be, if not more general, at least applicable to large classes of tasks that Scientific Management could not touch (Schultz and Whisler[6]). Now armed with linear programming methods, one can approach a task like media selection in an advertising agency, though it would have been nonsense to time study it.

But note the over-all similarity: Change the setting of the movie from Bethlehem, Pa., to Madison Avenue; the time from 1910 to 1962: the costuming from overalls to gray flannel suits; and the tasks from simple muscular labor to complex judgmental decisions. Turn worried laborer Schmidt into worried media executive Jones. Then replace Taylor with Charnes and Cooper and supplant the stopwatch with the computer. It is the same old theme either way — the conflict between technology and humanity.

A distinction needs to be drawn, of course, between operational operations research and other computer-based information-processing approaches, although they are often closely allied. "Management Science" hopefully will mean more than highly operational applications of specific techniques, and organizations are also being changed by simulation techniques and by heuristic problem-solving methods. Their impact has not yet been felt in anything like full force; but tasks, people, and structures are already being rather radically modified by them. In fact, one wonders if these task-directed efforts will not end up having at least as radical an impact on structure and on the role of humans as on task solutions themselves. For out of new information-processing methods we now begin to reconsider the bedrock issue of decentralization and to reconsider the permanency and primacy of human judgments for making certain classes of decisions. All the way round the organization, visible changes are being generated out of technical innovations.

Without delving further into the substance of these more recent technological approaches, it may be worth pointing up one other characteristic that they share with many of their predecessors — a kind of faith in the ultimate victory of better problem solutions over less good ones. This faith is often perceived by people-oriented practitioners of change as sheer naivete about the nature of man. They ascribe it to a pre-Freudian fixation on rationality; to a failure to realize that human acceptance of ideas is the real carrier of change; and that emotional human resistance is the real road block. They can point, in evidence, to a monotonously long list of cases in which technological innovations, methods changes, or operations research techniques have fallen short because they ignored the human side of the enterprise. It is not the logically better solutions that get adopted, this argument runs, but the more humanly acceptable, more

feasible ones. Unless the new technologist wises up, he may end up a miserable social isolate, like his predecessor, the unhappy industrial engineer.

Often this argument fits the facts. Operations research people can be incredibly naive in their insensitivity to human feelings. But in another, more gracious sense, one can say that the technological approaches have simply taken a more macroscopic, longer view of the world than the people approaches. Better solutions do get accepted in the long run, because deeper forces in the economy press them upon the individual organization — competitive forces, mainly. Macroscopically these ahuman or people-last approaches may encounter bumps and grinds in the microcosms of the individual firm; but sooner or later, in the aggregate, human resistances will be allayed or displaced or overcome, and the steam drill must inevitably defeat John Henry.

The technological approaches assume some communication among firms, and between firms and the world; and they assume further that the demonstration of more economic solutions will eventually result in their adoption though the road may be rough.

The technological approaches seem not only to predict the victory of cleaner, more logical, and more parsimonious solutions but also to value them. Failure of human beings to search for or use more efficient solutions is a sign, from this perspective, of human weakness and inadequacy. People must be teased or educated into greater logic, greater rationality. Resistance to better solutions is proof only of the poverty of our educational system; certainly it is not in any way an indication that "optimal" solutions are less than optimal.

THE PEOPLE APPROACHES

The people approaches try to change the organizational world by changing the behavior of actors in the organization. By changing people, it is argued, one can cause the creative invention of new tools, or one can cause modifications in structure (especially power structure). By one or another of these means, changing people will cause changes in solutions to tasks and performance of tasks as well as changes in human growth and fulfillment.

In surveying the people approaches, one is

immediately struck by the fact that the literature dealing directly with organizational change is almost all people-oriented. Just in the last four or five years, for example, several volumes specifically concerned with organizational change have been published. All of them are people-type books. They include Lippitt, Watson, and Westley's *The Dynamics of Planned Change*[7]; Lawrence's *The Changing of Organizational Behavior Patterns*[8]; Ginsberg and Reilly's *Effecting Change in Large Organizations*[9]; Bennis, Benne, and Chin's *The Planning of Change*[10]; and Guest's *Organizational Change*[11].

This tendency to focus on the process of change itself constitutes one of the major distinguishing features of the people approaches. The technological and structural approaches tend to focus on problem-solving, sliding past the microprocesses by which new problem-solving techniques are generated and adopted.

Historically, the people approaches have moved through at least two phases: The first was essentially manipulative, responsive to the primitive and seductive question, "How can we get people to do what we want them to do?"

Although most of us identify such questions with borderline workers like Dale Carnegie, much of the early work (immediately post-World War II) by social scientists on "overcoming resistance to change" dealt with the same issues.

Carnegie's How to Win Friends and Influence People[12] was first published in 1936, a few years ahead of most of what we now regard as psychological work in the same area. Like the social scientists that followed, Carnegie's model for change focused on the relationship between changer and changee, pointing out that changes in feelings and attitudes were prerequisites to voluntary changes in overt behavior. Carnegie proposes that one changes others first by developing a valuable (to the other person) relationship, and then using that relationship as a lever for bringing about the change one seeks. One does not attack with logic and criticism and advice. A offers B support, approval, a permissive atmosphere; and having thus established warm, affective bonds (invariably "sincere" bonds, too), A then requests of B that he change in the way A wishes, while A holds the relationship as collateral.

Though social scientists have tended to reject it out of hand, current research on influence processes suggests that the Carnegie model is not technically foolish at all, although we have disavowed it as manipulative, slick, and of questionable honesty.

The Carnegie model, moreover, has some current social scientific parallels. Thus Martin and Sims[13], for example, directly attack the issue of how to be a successful power politician in industrial organizations. They argue that dramatic skill, capacity to withhold certain kinds of information, the appearance of decisiveness, and a variety of other calculatedly strategic behaviors, appear to be effective in influencing behavior in organizational hierarchies.

In fact, Carnegie-like interest in face-to-face influence has finally became a respectable area of social scientific research. Several works of Hovland et al.[14] on influence and persuasion provide experimental support for the efficacy of certain behavioral techniques of influence over others.

But if we move over into the traditionally more "legitimate" spheres of social science, we find that much of the work after World War II on "overcoming resistance to change" was still responsive to the same manipulative question. Consider, for example, the now classic work by Kurt Lewin[15]; and his associates on changing food habits, or the later industrial work by Coch and French[16]. In both cases, A sets out to bring about a predetermined change in the behavior of B. Lewin sets out to cause housewives to purchase and consume more variety meats — a selling problem. Coch and French set out to gain acceptance of a preplanned methods change by hourly workers in a factory. In both cases the methodology included large elements of indirection, with less than full information available to the changees.

But whereas Dale Carnegie built warm personal relationships and then bargained with them, neither Lewin nor Coch and French are centrally concerned about intimate relationships between changer and changee. Their concern is much more with warming up the interrelationships among changees.

Thus 32% of Lewin's test housewives exposed to a group-decision method served new variety meats, as against only 3% of the women exposed to lectures. Lewin accounts for these results by calling upon two concepts: "involvement" and "group pressure." Lectures leave their audiences passive and unpressed by the group, whereas discussions are both active and pressing. Similarly, Coch and French, causing the girls in a pajama factory to accept a methods change, emphasize group methods, seeing resistance to change as partially a function of individual frustration, and partially of strong group-generated forces. Their methodology, therefore, is to provide opportunities for need satisfaction and quietly to corner the group forces and redirect them toward the desired change.

But it is this slight thread of stealth that was the soft spot (both ethically and methodologically) of these early people approaches to change, and this is the reason I classify them as manipulative. For surely no bright student has ever read the Coch and French piece without wondering a little bit about what would have happened if the change being urged by management just did not seem like a good idea to the "smaller, more intimate," work groups of Coch and French's "total participation" condition.

One might say that these early studies wrestled rather effectively with questions of affect and involvement, but ducked a key variable — power. Coch and French modified behavior by manipulating participation while trying to hold power constant. In so doing, the artistry of the "discussion leader" remained an important but only vaguely controlled variable, causing difficulties in replicating results and generating widespread discomfort among other social scientists.

Other contemporary and subsequent people approaches also avoided the power problem and encountered similar soft spots. The Western Electric counseling program (Roethlisberger and Dickson[17]) that emerged out of the Hawthorne researches sought for change through catharsis, with a specific prohibition against any follow-up action by counselors — a "power-free" but eminently human approach. Later, users of morale and attitude surveys sought to effect change by feeding back anonymous aggregate data so that the power groups might then modify their own behavior. But the very anonymity of the process represented an acceptance of the power status quo.

It was to be expected, then, that the next moves in the development of people approaches would be toward working out the power variable. It was obvious, too, that the direction would be toward power equalization rather than toward power differentiation. The theoretical underpinnings, the prevalent values, and the initial research results all pointed that way.

But though this is what happened, it happened in a complicated and mostly implicit way. Most of the push has come from work on individuals and small groups, and has then been largely extrapolated to organizations. Client-centered therapy (Rogers[18]) and applied group dynamics (Miles[19]) have been prime movers. In both of those cases, theory and technique explicitly aimed at allocating at least equal power to the changee(s), a fact of considerable importance in later development of dicta for organizational change.

Thus Carl Rogers describes his approach to counseling and therapy:

> This newer approach differs from the older one in that has a genuinely different goal. It aims directly toward the greater independence and integration of the individual rather than hoping that such results will accrue if the counsellor assists in solving the problem. The individual and not the problem is the focus. The aim is not to solve one particular problem, but to assist the individual to grow ([20], pp. 28-29).

At the group level, a comparable development was occurring, namely, the development of the T (for training) group (or sensitivity training or development group). The T-group the core tool of programs aimed at teaching people how to lead and change groups. It has also become a core tool for effecting organizational change. T-group leaders try to bring about changes in their groups by taking extremely permissive, extremely nonauthoritarian, sometimes utterly nonparticipative roles, thus encouraging group members not only to solve their own problems but also to define them. The T-group leader becomes, in the language of the profession, a "resource person," not consciously trying to cause a substantive set of changes but only changes in group processes, which would then, in turn generate substantive changes.

Though the T-group is a tool, a piece of technology, an invention, I include it in the people rather than the tool approaches, for it evolved out of those approaches as a mechanism specifically designed for effecting change in people.

In contrast to earlier group discussing tools the T-group deals with the power variable directly. Thus Bennis and Shepard[21] comment

The core of the theory of group development is that the principle obstacles to the development of valid communication are to be found in the orientations toward authority and intimacy that members bring to the group. Rebelliousness, submissiveness or withdrawal as the characteristic responses to authority figures . . . prevent consensual validation of experience. The behaviors determined by these orientations are directed toward enslavement of the other in the service of the self, enslavement of the self in the service of the other, or disintegration of the situation. Hence, they prevent the setting, clarification of, and movement toward, group shared goals.

I offer these quotes to show the extent to which the moral and methodological soft spots of the early manipulative models were being dealt with directly in group training situations. These are not wishy-washy positions. They deal directly with the power variable. Their objective is to transfer more power to the client or the group.

But these are both nonorganizational situations. For the therapist, the relationship with the individual client bounds the world. For the T-group trainer, the group is the world. They can both deal more easily with the power variable than change agents working in a time-constrained and work-flow-constrained organizational setting.

At the organizational level, things therefore are a little more vague. The direction is there, in the form of movement toward power equalization, but roadblocks are many and maps are somewhat sketchy and undetailed. McGregor's[22] development of participative Theory Y to replace authoritarian Theory X is a case in point. McGregor's whole conception of Theory Y very clearly implies a shift from an all powerful superior dealing with impotent subordinates to something much more like a balance of power:

People today are accustomed to being directed and manipulated and controlled in industrial organizations and to finding satisfaction for their social, egoistic and self-fulfillment needs away from the job. This is true of much of management as well as of workers. Genuine "industrial citizenship" — to borrow a term from Drucker — is a remote and unrealistic idea, the meaning of which has not even been considered by most members of industrial organizations.

Another way of saying this is that Theory "X" places exclusive reliance upon external control of human behavior, while Theory "Y" (the theory McGregor exposits) relies heavily on self-control and self-direction. It is worth noting that this difference is the difference between treating people as children and treating them as mature adults[23].

Bennis, Benne, and Chin[24] specifically set out power equalization (PE) as one of the distinguishing features of the deliberate collaborative process they define as planned change: "A power distribution in which the client and change agent have equal, or almost equal, opportunities to influence" is part of their definition.

In any case, power equalization has become a key idea in the prevalent people approaches, a first step in the theoretical causal chain leading toward organizational change. It has served as an initial subgoal, a necessary predecessor to creative change in structure, technology, task solving, and task implementation. Although the distances are not marked, there is no unclarity about direction — a more egalitarian power distribution is better.

It is worth pointing out that the techniques for causing redistribution of powers in these models are themselves power-equalization techniques — techniques like counseling and T-group training. Thus both Lippitt et al.[25] and Bennis et al.[26] lay great emphasis on the need for collaboration between changer and changee in order for change to take place. But it is understandable that neither those writers nor most other workers in power equalization seriously investigate the possibility that power may be redistributed unilaterally or authoritatively (e.g., by the creation of profit centers in a large business firm or by coercion).

If we examine some of the major variables of organizational behavior, we will see rather quickly that the power-equalization approaches yields outcomes that are very different from those produced by the structural or technolocial approaches.

Thus in the PE models, communication is something to be maximized. The more channels the better, the less filtering the better, the more feedback the better. All these because power will be more equally distributed, validity of information greater, and commitment to organizational goals more intense.

Contrast these views with the earlier structural models which argued for clear but limited communication lines, never to be circumvented; and which disallowed the transmission of affective and therefore task-irrelevant information. They stand in sharp contrast, too, to some current technical views which search for optimal information flows that may be far less than maximum flows.

The PE models also focus much of their

attention on issues of group pressure, cohesiveness, and conformity. The more cohesiveness the better, for cohesiveness causes commitment. The broader the group standards, the better. The more supportive the group, the freer the individual to express his individuality.

These, of course, are issues of much current popular debate. But as factors in effecting change, they are almost entirely ignored by the technical and most of the structural models. In their faith that best solutions will be recognized and in their more macroscopic outlook, until very recently at least, the technical and structural models did not concern themselves with questions of human emotionality and irrationality. If these were treated at all, they were treated as petty sources of interference with the emergence of Truth.

Evidence on this last question — the question of whether or not truth is obscured or enhanced by group pressures — is not yet perfectly clear. On the one hand, Asch[27] has shown in his classic experiments that group pressures may indeed cause individuals to deny their own sense data. On the other hand, Asch[28] himself has warned against interpreting this denial as an entirely emotional noncognitive process. When ten good men and true announce that line A is longer than line B, and when the eleventh man, still seeking truth, but himself seeing B as longer than A, still goes along with the group, he may do so not because he is overwhelmed by emotional pressure but because "rationally" he decides that ten other good sets of eyes are more likely to be right than his own.

Moreover, some data from some recent experiments being conducted at Carnegie Tech and elsewhere[29] suggest that in-fighting and debate will cease rather rapidly within a group when a solution that is prominently better than other alternatives is put forth. This is to say that people use their heads as well as their guts; though at times in our history we have vociferously denied either one or the other.

Consider next the decision-making variable. Decision making, from the perspective of power equalization, is viewed not from a cognitive perspective, nor substantively, but as a problem in achieving committed agreement. The much discussed issues are commitment and consensual validation, and means for lowering and spreading decision-making opportunities.

Contrast this with the technical emphasis on working out optimal decision rules, and with the structuralist's emphasis on locating precise decision points and assigning decision-making responsibility always to individuals.

SUMMARY

If we view organizations as systems of inter-action among task, structural, technical, and human variables, several different classes of efforts to change organizational behavior can be grossly mapped.

Such a view provides several entry points for efforts to effect change. One can try to change aspects of task solution, task definition, or task performance by introducing new tools, new structures, or new or modified people or machines. On occasion we have tried to manipulate only one of these variables and discovered that all the others move in unforeseen and often costly directions.

We have more than once been caught short by this failing. The Scientific Management move ment, for example, enamored of its measurement techniques, worked out efficient task solutions only to have many of them backfire because the same methods were also evoking human resistance and hostility. The human relations movement, I submit, is only now bumping into some of the unforeseen costs of building a theory of organization exclusively of human bricks, only to find that technological advances may obviate large chunks of human relations problems by obviating large chunks of humans or by reducing the need for "consensual validation" by programming areas formerly reserved to uncheckable human judgment.

Approaches with strong structural foci have also on occasion fallen into the one-track trap, changing structure to facilitate task solution, only then to find that humans do not fit the cubby holes or technology does not adapt to the new structure.

On the positive side, however, one can put up a strong argument that there is progress in the world; that by pushing structural or human or technical buttons to see what lights up, we are beginning gropingly to understand some of the interdependencies among the several variables.

What we still lack is a good yardstick for comparing the relative costs and advantages of one kind of effort or another. We need, as Likert[30] has suggested, an economics of organizational change.

If we had one, we could more effectively evaluate the costs of movement in one direction or another. Likert urges an economics of change because he believes the presently unmeasured costs of human resistance, if measured, would demonstrate the economic utility of organizational designs based on PE models. But such an economics might also pinpoint some of the as yet unmeasured costs of PE-based models. For the present state of unaccountability provides a protective jungle that offers quick cover to the proponents of any current approach to organizational change.

If I man conclude with a speculation, I will bet long odds that, as we develop such an economics, as we learn to weigh costs and advantages, and to predict second and third order changes, we will not move uniformly toward one of these approaches or another, even within the firm. We will move instead toward a melange, toward differentiated organizations in which the nature of changes becomes largely dependent on the nature of task. We have progressed, I submit; we have not just oscillated. We have learned about people, about structure, about technology; and we will learn to use what we know about all three to change the shape of future organizations.

AUTHOR'S NOTE

Many of the ideas in this paper are expanded and restated in the author's chapter in J.G. March (Ed.) *Handbook of Organisations*, Chicago: Rand-McNally, 1964.

REFERENCES

[1] Chapple, E. D. and L. R. Sayles, *The Measure of Management* New York: The Macmillan Co., 1961.

[2] Glanzer, M. and R. Glaser, "Techniques for the Study of Group Structure and Behaviour," Psychological Bulletin, 58 (1), January 1961, pp. 1-27.

[3] Taylor, F. W. *Scientific Management*. New York: Harper, 1947.

[4] Quoted from Taylor, F. W. *Op. cit.*

[5] See for example Bendix's account (in Bendix, R. *Work and Authority in Industry*. New York: John Wiley & Sons, 1956) of the early enthusiasm of industrial psychologists. He quotes Hugo Munsterberg appraising the promise of industrial psychology in 1913:

. . . . still more important than the valued commercial profit on both sides is the cultural gain which will come to the total economic life of the nation, as soon as everyone can be brought to the place where his best energies may be unfolded and his greatest personal satisfaction secured. The economic experimental psychology offers no more inspiring idea than this adjustment of work and psyche by which mental dissatisfaction with the work, mental depression and discouragement, may be replaced in our social community by overflowing joy and perfect inner harmony.

[6] Schultz, G. P. and T. L. Whisler (eds), *Management Organization and the Computer*. Glencoe, Ill.: The Free Press, 1960.

[7] Lippitt, R., J. Watson and B. Westley, *The Dynamics of Planned Change*. New York: Harcourt, Brace, 1958.

[8] Lawrence, P. R. *The Changing of Organizational Behaviour Patterns*. Boston: Harvard University, Graduate School of Business Administration, Division of Research, 1958.

[9] Ginzberg, E. and E. Reilley, *Effecting Change in Large Organizations*. New York: Columbia University Press, 1957.

[10] Bennis, W. G., K. D. Benne and R. Chin (eds), *The Planning of Change*, New York: Holt, Rinehart and Winston, 1961.

[11] Guest, R. H. *Organizational Change: The Effect of Successful Leadership*. Homewood, Ill.:, The Dorsey Press, 1962.

[12] Carnegie, Dale, *How to win friends and influence people*, New York: Simon and Schuster, 1936.

[13] Martin, N. H. and J. R. Sims, "The Problem of Power", in W. L. Warner and N. H. Martin (eds), *Industrial Man*. New York: Harper, 1959.

[14] Hovland, C. E., I. L. Janis and H. H. Kelley, *Communication and Persuasion*. New Haven: Yale University Press, 1953.

[15] Lewin, K., "Group Decision and Social Change", in Swanson, G. E., T. M. Newcomb and E. L. Hartley (eds), *Readings in Social Psychology*, 2nd ed. New York: Holt, 1952.

[16] Coch, L. and J. R. P. French, "Overcoming Resistance to Change", *Human Relations*, 1 (4), 1948, pp. 512-532.

[17] Roethlisberger, F. J. and W. J. Dickson, *Management and the Worker*. Cambridge, Mass.: Harvard University Press, 1944.

[18] Rogers, C. R. *Counseling and Psychotherapy*. Boston: Houghton Mifflin Co., 1942.

[19] Miles, M. B. *Learning to Work in Groups*. New York: Bureau of Publications, Teachers College, Columbia Uni-

versity, 1959.

[20] Rogers, C. R. *op. cit.*

[21] Bennis, W. G. and H. A. Shepard, "A Theory of Group Development", in W. G. Bennis, K. D. Benne, and R. Chin (eds), *op. cit.*

[22] McGregor, D. *The Human Side of Enterprise*. New York: McGraw-Hill Book Co., 1960.

[23] McGregor, D. *op. cit.*

[24] Bennis, W. G., K. D. Benne and R. Chin (eds), *op. cit.*

[25] Lippitt, R., J. Watson and B. Westley, *op. cit.*

[26] Bennis, W. G., K. D. Benne and R. Chin (eds), *op. cit.*

[27] Asch, S. E., *Social Psychology*. New York. Prentice-Hall, 1952.

[28] Asch, S. E., "Issues in the Study of Social Influences on Judgment", in I. A. Berg and B. M. Bass (eds), *Conformity and Deviation*. New York: Harper, 1961.

[29] As reported in a personal communication from T. C. Schelling, 1961.

[30] Likert, R., *New Patterns of Management*. New York: McGraw-Hill Book Co., 1961.

ABOUT THE AUTHOR

Harold J. Leavitt was born in Lynn, Massachusetts. He took his B.A. at Harvard and his Ph.D at M.I.T. From 1958-67 he was professor of industrial administration and psychology at the Carnegie Institute of Technology, and since 1967 he has been Kilpatrick Professor of Organizational Behavior and Psychology at the Graduate School of Business, Stanford. In 1950-60 he was vice-president of the Institute of Management Sciences. He has made many significant contributions to research in Behavior in Organisations and Organizational Psychology.

Systems Analysis of a University Library

A. Graham MacKenzie

The Library Research Unit at the University of Lancaster, England, was set up to perform operations research studies in the field of librarianship. In this paper the University Librarian describes his reasons for setting up a centre for such studies under his own direction, and also describes the general philosophy behind the work being carried out at Lancaster. In an Appendix a simple O.R. model is presented as an illustration of the method.

In presenting some account of the work being done at Lancaster on the systems analysis of a university library, I wish to make it quite clear at the beginning what I do not mean. We are not concerned with "scientific management" as defined in the recent book by Dougherty and Heinritz[1] — time and motion study, work measurement or work simplification, the re-design of forms and stationery, and all the other paraphernalia of low-level industrial or commercial management. These admittedly have their place, but only a minor one: it profits a library little if its procedures are all perfect, but all directed to the wrong ends.

We are not at this stage concerned with information retrieval on the grand scale for two reasons; first, we do not believe that it can ever be an economic possibility for individual large general libraries to do this — apart from anything else, the problem of input is immense; secondly, we do not believe that it would fulfil all of our needs: it is possible to set up a simplified model of a library as a store of discrete bits of information, each bit being identifiable by one or several index-entries or "addresses". The user is assumed to approach the store knowing what he wants, and the problem considered is how to deliver to him what he wants quickly, cheaply and with certainty. We might conceive as a future possibility the establishment of some vast central store of information, computer controlled, accessible by coded instructions passing over telephone lines from any part of the country or of the world, and deliver-

ing information by some teleprinter or television technique. In a limited field, such a study has been done; the Library of Congress report[2] recommends an expenditure of some $70 million for the complete transfer to computers of its catalogue and internal processes. This is excellent news for all concerned with information retrieval, "conventional" librarians and information officers alike, but to my mind it is putting the cart before the horse: it seems risky to spend sums of money of this order on work which does not go to the root of the problem of library use.

We agree that it may become economic to use the computer-controlled central store to deal with the accelerating increase in the mass of discrete items of information; but such a store would fulfil only part (and perhaps only a small part) of the functions of a library. Some people — perhaps as many as half of the total[3] — come to a library with a precise question: "What was the value of British imports of bananas in 1962?" But many others come with a more general kind of question: — "Has anything been written about banana imports which may throw light on my theory of commodity trade?" They browse, they leaf quickly through a book to see if it may help them, they follow up footnote references from one book to another; they are interested in ideas or methods of presentation as well as gobbets of information. There are strong indications that successful library use at times depends on serendipity — or lucky discovery — rather than on painstaking

SOURCE: Reprinted from *Library Systems and Information Services* (Crosby Lockwood, 1970) pp. 35-43, by permission of the author and publishers.

directed search. It is not clear that computer-controlled information stores have any relevance to this more general type of library use; in spite of Project MAC and Project INTREX[4] you cannot yet readily browse in the memory of a computer. Much of the work on scientific documentation — indexing and retrieval, abstracting, the information needs of scientists, the improvement of scientific journals, fundamental work on the nature of communication through language, and on coding and translation — seems to us to have in mind the simplified model of the library as an information store to which precise questions are addressed. But library policy should be based on what people actually need from libraries. Comparatively little work has been done on this question; there have been many attempts to find out what the library user actually uses, but what he uses and what he needs are not necessarily the same things[5] — [7]. The consideration of actual needs may imply a complete rethinking of the technical methods which are appropriate and economic. On the face of it, indeed, the printed book which can be held in the hand is well adapted to the needs of those who seek answers to questions which are general and not precise. But it is not easy to transmit, without introducing delay or inconvenience, and the mass of printed knowledge is too great, and growing too fast, to make it possible to assemble fully adequate collections in (say) 60 university insitutions in the United Kingdom. This is the dilemma: and it is not answered by dealing only with the problem of retrieving and transmitting precisely identified factual information.

The methods of use-study commonly employed have only a limited relevance to the problem stated here: they may be able to state with some accuracy what happens at present, and analyse the scholar's (rather than "scientists", because we must consider the humanist as well) own evaluation of what he believes he needs; but this is only a subjective judgment, and will usually be made without a full knowledge of either the current situation or of potential developments. In information work it has often been shown in the past that the supply of a facility very rapidly creates a previously unthought-of demand, and the field has become so specialised that few practising scholars are in a position to understand the present, let alone forecast the future.

For these reasons, the University of Lancas-ter has in mind a long-term programme for the investigation of the research worker in relation to his sources of information and the interaction between them. This undoubtedly varies from subject to subject, and probably even from person to person. If a specific question cannot be answered immediately, is there a penalty in wasted time whilst the answer is obtained from another library? This will depend on the researcher's methods and whether he works on more than one project or aspect of a project at the same time. How does the penalty vary with the delay? Is there a cumulative effect so that the researcher becomes semi-frustrated and uses the library less frequently than he might? If he does, then is the problem of duplication of research severe and does the quality suffer? Is the quality of research reduced when browsing is restricted? Is there a limit to the amount of browsing which a man will do? Could the browsing be done at intervals in a regional library instead of in the local library? All these questions must be answered in a quantitative form. Once some generalisations such as these have been established, it would then be possible to derive optimisations for such variables as the size, function and location of individual libraries.

For example, should an individual library purchase obscure books and journals if they are unlikely to be used frequently or by more than one man? Should there be a potential minimum usage for single books or should all the books on a topic be considered together? The results of such a study might be used to design a hierarchy of libraries, for which a balance would be struck between wasting money on purchasing "unnecessary" books and causing frequent duplication between libraries on the one hand, and wasting researchers' time and causing duplication of research on the other hand.

Such an investigation, however, still lies in the future; it is undoubtedly the most important section of the whole problem, but initially the University has restricted itself to a more immediate object, namely the study of a library system as it is. Little or nothing is known, in objective mathematical terms, of how exisiting libraries operate, and what has been published[8] — [10] is based on experience in the U.S.A., where budgets are much more lavish and operating conditions and users' needs are very different. In addition most of this work has been conceived as a necessary prelude to some form of partial or total mechanisation of the domestic economy of a library, rather than as a tool to aid management in decision-making — an example of this attitude is contained in the excellent pioneer study of the University of Illinois by Schultheiss[11], which analyses in extreme detail the technical processes involved in acquiring, cataloguing and issuing books, but ignores almost completely the purposes behind all these activities. This limited sense of systems analysis does not satisfy us; it needs to be done if we are eventually to mechanise our processes, but in a different and more restricted — even although a more detailed — way.

What we mean by systems analysis is much more far-reaching in its effects — in a few words, it is the use of scientific method to study the effects of managerial decisions in large-scale, complex situations. A librarian, like any other administrator, has to make many decisions in his routine work: generally at present these are the resultant of many conscious or unconscious forces — his previous training and experience, his innate prejudices, the internal politics of his organisation, even sometimes the state of his liver! Now the ecological system formed by a library and its readers is complex, delicately balanced and expensive; therefore decisions taken without full knowledge of the facts, and of the probable consequences of any given line of action, are likely to result not merely in trial and error, but in trial and disaster.

We need considerable justification for experimenting in vivo with a library system which has achieved a reasonable balance; the potential dangers are great. On the other hand, there is no such thing as the perfect library. How can we improve, then, without risking damage to the system? Obviously it is possible to tinker with small sections of a system — to redesign a form here, change a loan period or a rate of fine there — but the effects on some other segment of the library may be quite unexpected. Modern techniques of operational research are at our disposal, including the one essential tool of the mathematical model, which bears the same relationship to the object of study — in our case the library — as does an engineer's force diagram to the girders of a bridge he is designing.

How can we set about an operational research or systems analysis of a library? The normal procedure for such an investigation, let us say in a large industrial concern, is fourfold: first, to define the objectives of the company (perhaps maximum long-term profit within certain constraints such as the law of the land); second, to flow-chart all the processes which form the company, in whatever detail is required; third, to construct a mathematical model, using appropriate equations to describe each process or operation; and lastly, to use this model to optimise the company's operation so that the highest possible proportion of each of its stated objectives is attained.

Unfortunately, most O.R. studies are conducted in terms of profitability, where it is relatively simple to determine the objectives; but an academic library is a service organisation, and cannot look at its operations in this light. It is, of course, fairly easy to arrive at a first approximation of a library's purpose — the tentative definition which we have adopted is "to assist in the identification, provision and use of the document or piece of information which would best help a user in his study, teaching or research, at the optimal combination of cost and elapsed time", but unfortunately this raises many more questions than it solves. For example, bibliographical training of students will result in increased library use, and thus in higher operating costs in book purchases or inter-library loans; and yet this training itself is also expensive in terms of salaries. If the sole criterion were financial, obviously we ought not to try to increase library use — but we should then be producing inferior students. Similarly, to invent an extreme example, we might interpret "at the optimal . . . elapsed time" in the definition of our objectives as meaning that we should maintain a helicopter and pilot to fly to the National Lending Library four times a day to collect loans for our scientists; the delay would thus be minimised, but at a cost which might prevent us from buying any books at all, and which in any case would far outweigh the value to the university of the readers' time which has been saved.

One solution to this problem which has been suggested is quite ingenious, and is in fact also being studied by a parallel investigation in the University of Durham: various aspects of a library's services (additional book purchase, improved inter-library loan service, improved reference service, SDI, free photocopying, extended opening hours, etc.) are assigned prices which, although nominal, bear some relationship to the true costs. Members of the university are then asked to imagine that they have at their disposal a certain fixed amount of money and to declare how they would wish to spend this on varying combinations of the proposed benefits. Although this is a standard technique in marketing operations, we see certain objections to its use in a library situation, in particular, that those asked are unlikely to be able to visualise in any detail the results, good or bad, which would come from these additional services if they were provided.

It is becoming clear to us that there are serious difficulties in formulating an academic library's objectives in relation to its research readers, and hence in optimising its performance, unless we can find out more about the function and performance of the research worker himself, as outlined earlier in this paper. We are therefore trying to proceed to the second and third stages of the analysis, by flow-charting and by constructing a simplified model which can be made more sophisticated as our knowledge grows.

A few of the equations for the construction of this dynamically balanced model have already been formulated, and a start has been made on quantifying some of the variables which will have to be built into it. It is our expectation that when the model is complete, even in its simplified state, we shall be able to inject into it any number of differing managerial decisions and investigate how these will affect the system with the passage of time. (It would, of course, be equally possible to inject existing decisions to see whether they are likely in the long run to have the intended effect — the aim of this type of model is to simulate either backwards from the optimal end-state or forwards from any set of decisions, provided that the model itself and its associated computer programmes are sufficiently sophisticated and initially represent all the required inputs and outputs.) An example of the basic structure of one part of the model is given in the appendix, although since the project is still in its early stages this must be regarded as highly provisional and unsophisticated — for example we have not built in the space requirements for storage, staff and readers, on the financial implications of different grades of workers.

Simultaneously with the investigation of the technical processes of a theoretical model of a library we are looking at the actual provision of textbooks for students at Lancaster. We are perhaps in an unusually favourable posi-

tion to do this, since there is a collection of over 2,000 volumes representing material which departments consider to be essential reading for undergraduates' lectures, essays, and seminars. This collection is stored on closed-access shelving, and books are issued for periods of up to four hours or overnight; we can therefore easily analyse the use made of it (as a library which merely has a "reference" collection of this type of material cannot do) and, equally important, we can study with complete accuracy what we call the frustration factor — the proportion of enquirers who do not get the book they want at the first attempt. To our surprise, during two weeks just before an examination period, this proportion averaged only 11%, indicating that the system was working reasonably well. We have plans to correlate the use of this short-loan collection with a record of lecturers' recommendations to students, and hope eventually to be able to predict with some accuracy the number of copies of a title which would guarantee a given availability rate in any particular set of circumstances; and it should also be possible to extend this theory to the provision of all books required by undergraduates, although data collection is much more difficult in an open-access collection. This type of experiment demonstrates that quantification which is originally undertaken for the sake of model-building has an immediate relevance to the routine operation of a real library — our subjective impression had been that the average frustration factor was about twice as great as the figures demonstrate.

This exercise in data collection also suggests a possible index of a library's performance, and hence a quantifiable set of objectives, which might be difficult to specify in any other way. If we assume a constraint imposed on the system by the maximum financial support available to the library, and specify levels of availability of printed materials for different classes of users, it should be reasonably easy to predict from the model what the results are likely to be in terms of the system as a whole, and by managerial decision to adjust frustration factors to optimal levels. We do not believe that this is the complete answer to the problem of defining objectives, but it is certainly an improvement on the hit-and-miss method of reaching decisions which is currently followed.

A further valuable result of model-building is that it will inevitably draw attention to areas where further research is needed, and thus aid us in formulating more precisely the major investigation into the total dynamic ecological balance between information and its users; we realise that we are only at the beginning of a project which may take many years, and that it may not be possible to achieve the results which I have optimistically foreshadowed in this paper. Nevertheless, we belive that the exercise is well worth while; the mere process of analysing in detail what we do from day to day must bring a deeper understanding of our eventual objectives, and this in itself will help to smooth the channels through which information flows.

APPENDIX

Simple model of some consecutive technical processes with a built in optional decision rule.

The system is represented as a number of stages through which material passes for processing. We assume that the time scale is divided up into intervals of time (e.g. hour or week) referred to as slots during which the flows of work and labour are constant.

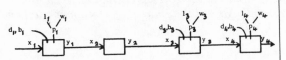

x = input rate (items per slot)
l = labour allocated (manhours per slot)
w = processing rate (items per manhour)
p = processing capacity (items per slot)
b = backlog at end of slot
d = delay to next item assuming serial processing (slots)
y = output rate (items per slot)

Consider the system in time slot (t).
Decision rule allocates just enough labour to clear backlog in one time slot.

1 Ordering

If decision rule then $l_1(t) = \dfrac{b_1(t-1) + x_1(t)}{w_1(t)}$.

otherwise $l_2(t)$ given.

$P_1(t) = l_1(t) \, w_1(t)$

$y_1(t) = p_1(t)$ if $b_1(t-1) + x_1(t) \geq p_1(t)$

$y_1(t) = b_1(t-1) + x_1(t)$ otherwise

[Because input rate might be less than processing capacity.]

$b_1(t) = b_1(t-1) + x_1(t) - y_1(t)$

$d_1(t) = b_1(t)/p_1(t)$

2 Bookseller

Assume distribution of supply times.
f (i) = fraction of books supplied during the i th slot since order despatched.

$x_2(t) \qquad y_1(t)$

$y_2(t) = \displaystyle\sum_{i=0}^{i=\infty} f(i)\, x_2(t-i)$

3 Accessioning

X_{31} input rate of purchased material (items per slot)

X_{32} input rate of donated material (items per slot)

$x_{31}(t) = y_2(t)$

$x_3(t) = x_{31}(t) + x_{32}(t)$

If decision rule than $l_3(t) = \dfrac{b_3(t-1) + x_3(t)}{w_3(t)}$

otherwise $l_3(t)$ given.

$P_3(t) = l_3(t) \, w_3(t)$

$y_3(t) = p_3(t)$ if $b_3(t-1) + x_3(t) \geq p_3(t)$

$y_3(t) = b_3(t-1) + x_3(t)$ otherwise

$b_3(t) = b_3(t-1) + x_3(t) - y_3(t)$

$d_3(t) = b_3(t)/p_3(t)$

4 Cataloguing

$x_4(t) = y_3(t)$

If decision rule then $l_4(t) = \dfrac{b_4(t-1) + x_4(t)}{w_4(t)}$

otherwise $l_4(t)$ given.

$p_4(t) = l_4(t) \, w_4(t)$

$y_4(t) = p_4(t)$ if $b_4(t-1) + x_4(t) \geq p_4(t)$

$y_4(t) + b_4(t-1) + x_4(t)$ otherwise

$b_4(t) = b_4(t-1) + x_4(t) - y_4(t)$

$d_4(t) = b_4(t)/p_4(t)$

REFERENCES

[1] Dougherty, R. M. and Heinritz, F. J. *Scientific management of library operations*. New York, Scraecrow Press. 1966.

[2] Automation and the Library of Congress: a survey sponsored by the Council on Library Resources. Library of Congress, 1963.

[3] Hanson, C. W. "Research on user's needs: where is it getting us?" *Aslib Proceedings*, 16, ii, 1964, 64-78.

[4] Overhage, C. F. J. and Harman, R. J. (eds). INTREX: report of a planning conference on information transfer experiments. Cambridge, M.I.T. Press. 1965.

[5] Information methods of research workers in the social sciences: proceedings of a conference . . . . edited by J. M. Harvey. Library Association, 1961.

[6] Science, government and information: Report of the President's Science Advisory Committee, U.S.G.P.O., 1963.

[7] Menzel, H. "The information needs of current scientific research." *Library Quarterly*, 34, i, 1964, 4-9.

[8] Becker, J. "System Analysis - prelude to library data processing," *ALA Bulletin*, April 1965, 293-296.

[9] Leimkuhler, F. F. *Operations Research in the Purdue Libraries in Automation in the library, when where and how*. Purdue University, 1965, 82-89.

[10] Leimkuhler, F. F. "Systems analysis in university libraries." *College and Research Libraries*, 27, i, 1966, 13-18.

[11] Schultheiss, L. A. Culbertson, D. S. and Heiliger, A. M. *Advanced data processing in the university library*. New York, Scarecrow Press. 1962.

ABOUT THE AUTHOR

A. Graham Mackenzie graduated in classics from the University of Glasgow in 1950 and, after service in the Royal Air Force, became Keeper of Science Books at the University of Durham, England.

In 1963 he became the first Librarian of the new University of Lancaster and had the challenging opportunity of creating a university library at a time when the foundation of several new universities in Britain produced a climate receptive to innovation.

One theme of Mackenzie's administration is the need for clarification of the theoretical and quantitative understanding of library systems and their use. This resulted in the founding, in 1967, of a Library Research Unit which has concentrated on operations research studies.

Mackenzie has served as chairman of the editorial board of the Journal of Documentation and as a consultant on missions for UNESCO and OECD.

II

PRACTICAL OPERATIONS RESEARCH: SIMPLE CASE STUDIES

In this Chapter the reader is brought down to earth and presented with a selection of successful case studies which illustrate the sort of tactical problems frequently tackled by the Operations Researcher. Five case studies are presented, some concerned with libraries and information services but others describing applications in other areas, ranging from industrial production to community nursing. They illustrate a number of the standard techniques of O.R. in a nontechnical fashion. The librarian should compare the problems dealt with in these papers with the problems which he faces in his own library. He should try to recognize the similarity of form and structure even if the content of the problem is quite different. We believe that in the context of actual studies of real problems it is possible for the librarian to see how the methodology of O.R. is brought to bear on problems which are very similar in form to many of the problems which he himself has to face.

Towards an Adaptive Loan and Duplication Policy for a University Library

A. Hindle and M. K. Buckland

The preceding paper by Mackenzie revealed the rationale for undertaking research into library problems. The following paper describes what is, to date, the most successful piece of work by the group established by Mackenzie. It is concerned with the basic library problem of making and keeping books available. In order to do this, it is necessary to relate conceptually and then numerically the different factors which, in interaction, affect availability.
- *the pattern of demand*
- *the length of loan*
- *the amount of duplication.*

In this paper there is an emphasis on the importance of making systems adaptive so that they respond and adapt to changing pressures and circumstances. Although originally designed to introduce library O.R. to O.R. specialists, the paper is equally successful as an introduction to O.R. techniques for librarians.

The work described in this paper was supported by the Office for Scientific and Technical Information who have actively encouraged the library research at Lancaster. Acknowledgement is also made to the University Librarian, Mr. A. G. Mackenzie, without whom the work would have remained a merely academic exercise.

THE PROBLEM

In common with most community services, the basic criterion of success is the level of satisfaction felt by the community as a result of the service provided. Symptoms of dissatisfaction generally appear in the form of complaints directed at the Librarian or members of his staff. Although no explicit quantification of "level of satisfaction" was attempted, the Librarian felt (towards the end of 1968) that something had to be done to stem the rising tide of complaint about the low availability of materials.

The Librarian initiated an Operational Research investigation with the brief that the team were to formulate alternative methods for increasing document availability, evaluate these methods and, if possible, make a recommendation to him on the policy he should adopt.

The urgency of the problem derived from the Librarian's desire to solve it by the start of the next academic session (viz. October 1969). The Librarian required the research team to report its findings to the Library Staff Meeting of the 18th April, 1969; this discussion forming the basis for a recommendation to University's Library Committee which was due to meet on the 30th April 1969. The Librarian would then be in a position to ask Senate to approve his decision on policy for the academic session commencing in October.

THE STRUCTURE OF THE PROBLEM

The Library in its University environment is a highly complex information system with a whole range of functions and objectives. It has a central role in the cultural, educational

SOURCE: Reprinted from the Conference Papers of the 1971 Conference of the Operational Research Society Ltd. at the University of Lancaster (Session C1: New Areas of Application), by permission of the authors and the Society.

and recreational activities of the University.

Further, very little previous Operational Research had been carried out in the library environment, although Martyn and Vickery[1] had pointed out some of the difficulties. Also the Librarian at Lancaster had in April 1968 published a paper entitled "Systems Analysis of a University Library"[2] in which the structure of the total problem was outlined. He has recently published a comprehensive review of O.R. in Libraries for "British Library and Information Science, 1966-1970"[3].

The principal interacting decision areas were considered to be the following:

1. Acquisition: the selection of serials, the selection of new monograph titles; the duplication of titles.
2. Collection Control: the determination of systems and procedures governing the use of the library's materials and services.
3. Education: the education of the user in methods of using formal information services and helping users to solve problems requiring information services.
4. Administrative Systems: administrative efficiency, user convenience, efficiency of technical processes (e.g. cataloguing, binding etc.).

The initial decision required of the research team was a choice of decision area on which to concentrate for the project outlined in this paper i.e., to determine the most important source of complaints by users. To this end a *frustration survey* was undertaken. A randomly selected sample of users were questioned about their reasons for entering the library and about the extent of their dissatisfaction. This suggested that the principal causes of frustration might be removed by changes in the Collection Control Area, particularly by changes in loan policy (including policy for both the borrowing and reference use of material) and policy on duplication of existing titles.

The decision to concentrate on "Collection Control" was also influenced by the knowledge that this decision area is more directly under the control of the Librarian than certain other areas, e.g., the acquisition of new titles, the return times for inter-library loans and so on.

The Collection Control problems of a library are bedevilled by uncertainties of many types and three examples can be cited:

Uncertainties about User Behaviour

Although it is clearly of value to a user to be able to borrow a book from the library and use it in the convenience of his own study room rather than be constrained to use it within the confines of the library building, such an issue renders the book relatively unavailable to another would-be user. However, such availability can be justified if the book is being genuinely "used" by the borrower. Unfortunately it is possible that users may borrow books to remain idle on their bookshelves rather than on those of the library.

Uncertainties about Values

The users of a library do not all have the same cultural and educational objectives and certain groups of users have conflicting objectives. For example, the professional researcher would like the book fund devoted to the acquisition of new titles, rather than the duplication of existing ones; he would further require that the collection be confined to the library (i.e. Reference Use only) or alternatively that the loan policy should allow him to borrow large numbers of titles for long periods. The undergraduate, on the other hand, is interested in a small number of titles and in a particular title for a short period. He requires heavy duplication of popular titles so that he is not thwarted in his essay writing by his own colleagues. In a similar vein one can envisage conflicting objectives between the sciences, the social sciences and the humanities.

Uncertainties about University Decisions (and Other Environmental Influences)

Decisions about University growth, both in total numbers and in terms of relative development of various academic areas, affect Collection Control problems. Similarly developments in educational technology have their influence, particularly the extent to which seminar based project oriented teaching overtakes the more traditional lecture based approaches.

It was clear to the research team that they could not produce a comprehensive solution to the problem given to them in the few months available. However, it was also clear that the real complexities could not be ignored in any short cut methods we might employ. The aim, therefore, was to produce an answer to the urgent problem of low availability and a basis for an adaptive Collection Control system such that the Library would be more responsive to the changing influences upon it.

THE ANALYSIS

The Relationship Between Demand, Loan Period, Number of Copies and Immediate Availability

Although P.M. Morse[4] has derived models relating loan policy and availability based on the mathematical theory of queues, it was considered that a simulation approach would be more realistic. A Monte Carlo simulation was constructed[5] requiring the following information for one title:

1. The number of demands to be simulated
2. The number of copies of the title
3. The maximum number of reservations permitted
4. The pattern of demand (inter-request intervals)
5. The nature of demands (reference or borrowing)
6. The pattern of return for borrowed books (return times)
7. The use made of reservation facilities by users
8. The delays involved if a book is recalled from a user by the library.

The index of performance or output used in the experiments using this simulation is a measure of "immediate availability", defined as the probability that a request (for reference use or loan) can be immediately satisfied by the book's presence on the shelf.

Background insight was obtained by producing a model of a closed-access reserve collection.

Define n as the number of copies of a given title and s as the number of requests for it in any single loan period, so that when $o \lessgtr s \leq n$ then s requests are satisfied and when $s > n$ then n requests are satisfied. If P(s) expresses the probability of s requests being made in a loan period then

$$\% \text{ Availability} = \frac{100 \left\{ \sum_{s=0}^{n} sP(s) + \sum_{s=n+1}^{\infty} nP(s) \right\}}{\sum_{s=0}^{\infty} sP(s)}$$

where
$$P(s) = \frac{e^{-r} r^s}{s!}$$

and r is the average request rate.

The Poisson assumption was found adequate for this particular collection.

The flow diagram for the simulation model for the open access collection is illustrated in Figure 1.

The Effect on Users of Changes in Official Loan Periods

Although ideally the research team would have liked to carry out experimental changes of loan period and study the consequent use of books by users, this was impossible with the time available to us. Therefore a short comparative study of University Libraries having a variety of loan policies was carried out, as follows:

> One week: Manchester
> Two weeks: Michigan, Strathclyde, Sussex
> Four weeks: Manchester, Michigan, Strathclyde
> Ten weeks: Strathclyde
> End of Term: Lancaster

The pattern which emerged consistently is that there is a very strong tendency for books to be returned or renewed at the expiry of the official loan period. Further, the proportion of books renewed at the end of a loan period varies little over the range of loan periods.

These results suggest two conclusions:

1. The Librarian has control over book return times as a result of his ability to modify official loan periods
2. The use made of a document would not seem to increase proportionately with increasing loan period: otherwise one would expect renewal probability to increase with decreasing loan period.

Measures of Performance

As indicated in the section entitled "The Structure of the Problem", above, deriving a fully satisfactory index of performance for a library system would be a complex and near impossible task. It was desirable to come as close as possible to a measure of the "genuine" use made of material under various policies. A measure of "document exposure" was suggested i.e., for books, the total time books were open and apparently in use under various schemes. However due to the urgency of the problem two

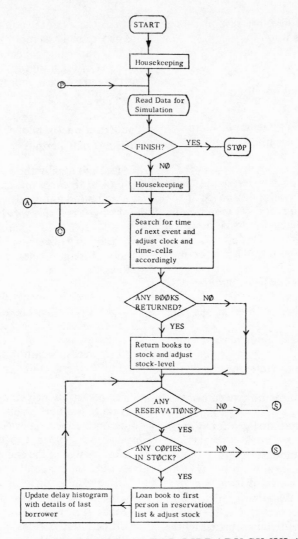

FIG. 1.   FLOW DIAGRAM FOR LIBRARY SIMULATION

rather more indirect but more readily measured indices were used:

1. Satisfaction level: in a given time period the proportion of demands on the library which could be immediately satisfied.
2. Collection bias: the proportion of the most popular 10 per cent of the library's stock off the shelves at any given point in time.

The latter index was used because, for users whose request or requirement is not title specific, the Library provides a browsing facility. The collection on the shelves in front of him will be biased towards the less popular, less used books in the subject area since the more popular ones will tend to be on loan.

Subject to constraints, the good library will have a high "satisfaction level" and a low "collection bias".

Investigation of the data collected on use of the Lancaster Library yielded the following estimates of performance:

Satisfaction Level   60 per cent
Collection Bias   45 per cent

Performance as a Consequence of Loan and Duplication Policy

Simulation experimental results together with demand distributions derived from borrowing history data were used to estimate "satisfaction level" and "collection bias" for a range of feasible alternative loan and duplication policies.

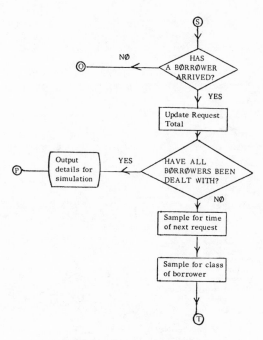

FIG. 1.   (continued)

The policies considered fall into five categories.
1. A single, but shorter, loan period
2. Selective duplication of stock
3. Loan periods determined by type of borrower
4. Loan periods determined by book popularity
5. Combined systems.

Policy 4 represents an insight appearing as a result of the study. Although obvious (after one has thought of it), we were not aware of any Library having a policy in which official loan period varied directly with estimated book popularity.

However, clearly, under the assumption that the proportion of time a book is "in-use" *whilst* on loan decreases with increasing loan period, document use will be maximised for the collection as a whole with a system based on the concept of Policy 4.

Many other factors needed to be considered other than "satisfaction level" and "collection bias" in the evaluation of policy:
a. Administrative consequences: if every book were to be considered individually to determine a loan period this would be time consuming and administratively inconvenient.
b. Capital expenditure: would the system require on-line computer control? A large scale increment in the purchase of duplicate copies would also be very expensive.

c. Consequences for Assistant Librarians: would monitoring of book popularity encroach on their research time?
d. Political consequences: if academic staff were to lose their special library privileges would this be acceptable to Senate?

The methodology used for evaluation was a weak form of cost-effectiveness analysis using a balance sheet of "pros" and "cons" in relation to each alternative policy for achieving arbitrary (but agreed) standards of service.

The System

The nature of the system implemented is illustrated in Figure 2. It requires the Librarian to state the standards of performance he requires of his library, currently in terms of Satisfaction Level (viz. 80%) and Collection Bias (viz. 15%). Also he is required to state his policy in terms of the proportion of book stock assigned to various loan (i.e. popularity) categories at the moment:

Short Loan   -   4 hourly loan
Popular Loan   -   1 week loan
Long Loan   -   end of term

Clearly these standards can be kept under continuous review.

The Collection Control system is required to meet these standards subject to a variety of

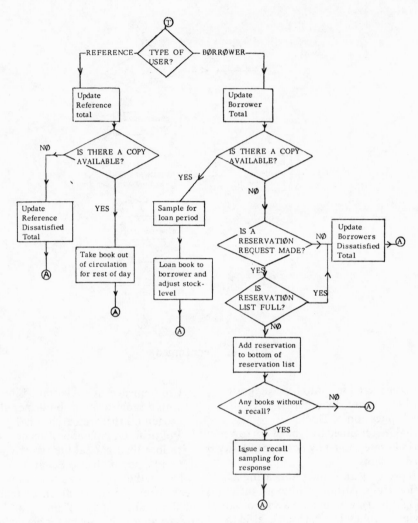

FIG. 1   (continued)

constraints (budget, administration etc.). The output can be compared with the standards and corrections made.

Allocation of books to loan categories and signals for the acquisition of duplicate copies derive from a new process of BOOK MONITOR-ING. Decisions on demand level for books are made by studying issue labels (and occasion-ally as a result of complaints or information from lecturers). If the book is LONG LOAN but its borrowing history data would suggest that standards of availability were not being met, then it would be re-allocated to POPULAR LOAN. If an unacceptably large proportion of books in a subject area or for the collection as a whole are being upgraded, this is a signal for the "acquisitions department" to selectively

duplicate.

Note: Previously duplication decisions had been left to academic departments as part of their acquisitions activity. There was no separate book fund for duplicates. Since they had no information on "availability levels" and since everyone prefers new to old, the vast majority of acquisitions were for new titles. Also Librarians are inclined to prefer new titles to further copies of existing ones.

Results

The results of implementation of the system were unexpected and dramatic. It was predicted that as a result of increased availability the satisfaction level would increase by 20 per cent and that the increase in issues per capita would be somewhat higher than this, between 20 and 30 per cent. In practice for the first year of operation total issues increased by 97 per cent which is 25-30 per cent higher than could have been predicted from expected increased "availability" and increased student numbers. It is possible that increased success in use of the Library is a positive reinforcement for further use.

COMPARISON WITH OTHER UNIVERSITY LIBRARIES

The Library at Lancaster now has heavier use per capita than any other University Library for which records are available. Sussex University library has adopted a similar policy and several University Librarians are currently examining the Lancaster system with a view to implementation in their own Libraries.

Discussion

It transpired, after the decision to propose the new system, that the study caused considerable stress and tension amongst library staff. Only the full support of the Librarian clinched the issue. Many of the library staff felt that they were being rushed. They felt that the problem had been grossly over-simplified and that insufficient attention had been paid to practical

consequences in terms of the administration of the new loan system. Now (a year or so later) the research team are, we believe, viewed with greater favour.

Although the "classical" philosophy of Operational Research was clearly not pursued in this investigation, the appearance of an "insight" on loan and duplication policy, followed by very determined implementation, has provided an excellent basis for more systematic approaches to library planning. In practical terms it has led to the formation of a Library Research Unit at the University of Lancaster, undertaking a range of research studies, projects, and consultancy investigations for Libraries.

In particular three projects are being undertaken.

1. A study of the structure of holdings of the national library system. In particular this concerns the overlap in holdings of the major libraries.

2. A study for the Council on Library Resources into the fundamental aspects of library use and especially the behavous of users in relation to library provision.

3. The development of a management game for the education of Librarians in the managerial aspects of their activities. This study is sponsored by the office for Scientific and Technical Information (OSTI).

Other work is also going on in Britain and the foundation by OSTI of the Cambridge Library Management Research Unit in 1969 should be noted.

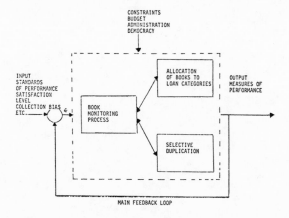

FIG. 2. THE LANCASTER LOAN AND DUPLICATION SYSTEM

REFERENCES

[1] Martyn, J. and Vickery, B. C. "The complexity of the modelling of Information Systems" *J. Docum.* 26 [3] 1970 204-220.
[2] Mackenzie, A. G. "Systems Analysis of a University Library" *Program* 2 [1] April 1968 7-14.
[3] Mackenzie, A. G. and Buckland, M. K. "Operational Research" in Whatley, H. A., ed. *British Library and Information Science, 1966-1970.* London, Library Association, 1972.
[4] Morse, P. M. *Library Effectiveness: A Systems Approach* Boston, Mass., M.I.T. Press 1968.
[5] Buckland, M. K., Hindle, A., Mackenzie, A. G., and Woodburn, I. *Systems Analysis of a University Library* Occasional Paper No. 4, University of Lancaster Library, 1970.

ABOUT THE AUTHORS

Tony Hindle: See page 28.
Michael K. Buckland: See page 28.

A National Loan Policy for Scientific Serials

D. J. Urquhart and R. M. Bunn

This brief paper should be regarded as a classic. In a few paragraphs, it sets forth a rational basis for the planning of a national interlibrary loan service for scientific serials. The most relevant available data are collected and presented. The implications of these data are then developed with forthright simplicity. In the process, the then-influential views of the British library profession are lambasted.

Urquhart and Bunn went on to implement these rationally-developed policies with the highly successful National Lending Library for Science and Technology. Some fifteen years later this remains the outstanding example of a quantitative approach to library planning, though for most of this time it aroused surprisingly little interest in North America. A fuller account of the development of the library may be found in: HOUGHTON, Bernard. Out of the Dinosaurs. The Evolution of the National Lending Library for Science and Technology. London: Bingley, 1972.

Elsewhere[1] a survey has been reported of the use of the serials in the Science Museum Library. In brief this showed that where the Science Museum Library's copy of a serial was frequently used, this serial was widely held, and that the converse was true. In fact it appears that the use of the Science Museum's copy of a periodical is a rough measure of the national loan use of library copies.

In general it seems that a small percentage of the current serial titles account for a large percentage of the use of all serials. In the Science Museum in 1956 about 350 titles accounted for 50 per cent of the total use of serials, and about 1200 titles for 80 per cent of the total use. This, despite the fact that in 1956 the Science Museum Library contained 9120 current serials, and that possibly an equal number of dead ones. In general terms it appeared that, excluding less than 2000 titles, the total national interlibrary loan use could be satisfied by one loan copy. For perhaps half the current serials in the Science Museum Library the total use of a title is less than ten times per decade. For the majority of current serials then a single copy can be used to provide a loan service without the chance of the copy not being available on demand for loan or reference being anything but microscopic.

To examine the figures of the survey further it is necessary to make some assumption about the nature of the demand. The simplest assumption to make is that the demand for any title is random with an average frequency. The use in any period can then be predicted from tables of Poisson distribution. For instance, if there are 1000 periodicals in a library which on an average are each used twice per year then in any particular year theory predicts

135 would not be used
271 would be used once each
271 would be used twice each
180 would be used three times each
90 would be used four times each
53 would be used more than four times each.

This theory thus permits an appreciable variation of an actual demand for a serial in a given period. It has not been possible as yet to test this hypothesis, but there is no obvious evidence to indicate that it is not adequate. Moreover, if the average period of loan was one-twentieth of a year and there are ten separate items (parts

SOURCE: Reprinted from the *Journal of Documentation* 15(1) March 1959, pp. 21-25, by permission of the authors and publishers. When originally published, this paper had an Appendix containing data on the use of serials in the Science Museum Library. This Appendix has not been reprinted.

and/or volumes) for each title, then if waiting lists are maintained, 1 per cent of the items requested would be on loan when required.

The loan demand for serials borrowed twice a year or less accounted for less than 8 per cent of the total demand. Thus if the Science Museum Library only lent serials used as infrequently as this or less (over three-quarters of the current titles), the availability on demand for reference purposes would be more than 99.9 per cent. These figures suggest that the traditional policy of, say, the British Museum Library of refusing to lend little-used material in case a reader should require an item when it is on loan may have no adequate statistical justification.

The problem of providing a loan service for periodicals really becomes one of catering for the rarely used periodical by ensuring that it is available somewhere in the country, and that there are sufficient copies of the more frequently used periodicals. There is general agreement that the responsibility of ensuring that the rarely used periodicals are available for loan rests with the National Lending Library. There is no general agreement, however, about the responsibility for catering for the more frequently used periodicals.

There is, for instance, an idea in the United Kingdom that these frequently used periodicals should be held regionally. This idea is derived from the regional bureau system of the National Central Library, but it has no logical basis. It is, of course, a good idea that a copy of a periodical should be held where there is any appreciable use for it without recourse to the postal service. But since in the United Kingdom it is possible for letter post to reach almost any part the next day there is no special point in arranging for copies to be located regionally. In fact because of the same mathematical reasoning that lies behind the installation in an organization of an internal telephone exchange with a limited number of external lines, there is an advantage in locating in a central collection any copies which are specifically held to meet the loan demand.

The advantages of this are illustrated in the following tables. Tables I and II have been calculated using the following assumptions to simplify the calculations.

a. Random demand with a specified average frequency.
b. All items are returned at the end of a loan period.
c. No waiting lists are maintained.

Table I shows the percentage of failures with
C. centralized collections (i.e. 2, 5, or 10 copies of the same periodical in one library);
D. decentralized collections (i.e. 1 copy in each of 2, 5, or 10 regional libraries — the average demand on each regional copy being the same).

Table II gives the number of copies required in
C. a centralized collection;
D. decentralized collections consisting of one copy in each collection. The demand on each decentralized copy being the same;
R. regionally organized collections — each region being self-sufficient, the demand on each of ten regions being the same;
to meet a specified total demand with not more than 5 per cent of failures.

Whilst the figures in Tables I and II would alter for a more realistic mathematical model of the system there is no doubt that a centralized system will be more efficient. In practice a decentralized system would be relatively more inefficient because of the difficulty of ensuring the same demand in all regions.

To reiterate, whilst there is some advantage

TABLE I
PERCENTAGE OF FAILURES

Total average demand per item per loan period	1 copy	2 copies		5 copies		10 copies	
		C	D	C	D	C	D
0.01	0.5	0.0	0.0	0.0	0.0	0.0	0.0
0.1	4.7	0.1	2.5	0.0	1.0	0.0	0.5
0.2	9.4	0.6	4.7	0.0	2.0	0.0	1.0
0.5	21.3	3.3	13.4	0.0	4.7	0.0	2.5
1.0	..	10.3	21.3	0.1	9.4	0.0	4.7
2.0	..	..	..	1.6	17.5	0.0	9.4
5.0	..	..	..	..	..	0.4	21.3

TABLE II
NUMBER OF COPIES REQUIRED TO MAINTAIN AT LEAST 95 PER CENT
AVAILABILITY ON DEMAND

Total average demand per item per loan period	D Decentralized	R Regionalized (10 regions)	C Centralized
0.1	1	10	1
0.2	2	10	2
0.5	5	10	2
1.0	10	10	3
2.0	20	20	4
5.0	49	20	7
10.0	97	30	13

in having collections to meet truly local demands there is no point in an island as small as Great Britian in attempting to cover interlibrary loan requirements for scientific periodicals regionally. This is the first principle on which a national loan service should be based.

A second principle can be derived from the fact that the use falls off with time. Thus, for instance, the survey gave the figures shown in Table III.

The actual quantities of publications of different publication dates in the Science Museum Library is not known, but the annual use of a current volume is twenty to forty times a volume fifty years old. These figures are, of course, global figures. The use of some periodicals falls off more rapidly than others. It is known that the use of material in the physical sciences falls off more rapidly than that in the biological sciences[2]. However, the table suggests that except for selected items there is little point in a special library keeping an item for more than two or three decades after publication.

For selecting the exceptions to some general rule of this sort local experience will be the best guide, but the appendix may be of value. This lists all the titles whose volumes for any of the five decades 1900-49 were borrowed ten or more times in 1956 as well as any which, whilst they do not satisfy this criterion, were used fifty or more times. For completeness the "non-loanable" titles in the Science Museum Library have been included as these titles were originally selected because they were some of the more heavily used titles. In interpreting this table it should be appreciated that the titles used are, as a rule, those given in the Science Museum Hand-list of short titles of current periodicals in the Science Library (Eighth Edition), but that the use data may relate to earlier titles of these periodicals.

TABLE III

Number of complete years since publications	Use in period	Total use in period since publication
1	34.4	34.4
2—6	27.3	61.7
7—16	18.8	80.5
17—26	11.8	92.3
27—36	3.9	96.2
37—46	1.5	97.7
47—56	1.1	98.8
57 or more	1.2	100.0

Judged by the growing volume of literature which is being presented to D.S.I.R. for the National Lending Library for Science and Technology, it appears that the concept that special libraries should dispose of their rarely used holdings is growing. It is hoped that the data in this paper and in the Appendix will facilitate this process.

The concepts in this paper apply particularly to scientific serials. For such publications the editorial policies, circulations, and arrangements for making known what is available change but slowly. For these publications it is possible to predict with reasonable accuracy the future demand for future parts. Unfortunately it is not a simple matter to apply these ideas to even the books required by scholars. It can, however, be asserted that the concept of "regional self-sufficiency" within the United Kingdom for books published in the United Kingdom after 1 January 1959 is not the best one for meeting the demand for such books with the greatest national economy. Undoubtedly it would be cheaper for each region to make a contribution towards a central collection to give "national self-sufficiency" than for each region to make purchases purely to achieve "regional self-sufficiency".

For serials in all subject fields the ideas in this paper have a direct application. The relationship between use and time since publication requires examination before some of the ideas can be applied in, say, the humanities and social sciences.

The concept of self-sufficient regions has a much better logical basis for the U.S.A. than for the United Kingdom because of the greater distances involved. Nevertheless, K.D. Metcalfe, a former Director of the Harvard University Libraries, had this to say about a national acquisition policy for the U.S.A.[3]:

> One final warning if we are to make mistakes, as we are bound to do, let us try to make them, in the case of most libraries, by not getting enough, because the law of diminishing returns will come to our aid. But, and this is a large but, let us make the mistake on the side of getting too much in the National Libraries. The total cost to the library world of this method will be less, and nationally only a drop in the bucket.

In the United Kingdom, since inevitably the size of the national "bucket" is smaller, the policy advocated by Metcalfe appears to be more essential.

REFERENCES

[1] International Scientific Information Conference 1958, *Proceedings*.
[2] Brown, C. H. *Scientific Serials* ACRL Monograph No. 16, 1956.
[3] *Acquisitions Policy of the National Medical Library*. Proceedings of a Symposium held 12th April 1956, Washington D.C., National Library of Medicine. 1957.

ABOUT THE AUTHORS

Donald J. Urquhart received his B.Sc. degree in physics and his Ph.D. in metallurgy from the University of Sheffield in Yorkshire, England and started his career in the Research Department of the English Steel Corporation.

In 1938, however, he joined the staff of the Science Museum Library in London, then directed by S. C. Bradford (see Paper IV.2). During the Second World War he worked for the Admiralty and the Ministry of Supply. In 1948, he transferred to the Information Department of the Department of Scientific and Industrial Research.

In 1956 it was decided to create a new lending library for scientific and technical literature and Urquhart was appointed to lead the Lending Library Unit which developed into the National Lending Library for Science and Technology in his native Yorkshire.

He has been a popular speaker and writer on libraries and science information, though his caustic remarks and unconventional views caused a major stir in the British library profession. Typical are his assertion that he is a professional civil servant and not a librarian and his categorization of union catalogs as "sacred cows . . . with a low milk yield".

However with the unquestionable success of the National Lending Library, the criticism of Urquhart subsided and he was elected President of the (British) Library Association.

Rosemary M. Bunn has spent most of her career in the British Civil Service. In 1956 she joined the Lending Library Unit at the Department of Scientific and Industrial Research, and thus became a member of the team which planned the National Lending Library for Science and Technology. She became a Senior Experimental Officer at the N.L.L.S.T. after its formation, and at present she is a Principal Scientific Officer. She has published a number of papers on the philosophy and development of the concept of a national lending library, as well as on other topics.

On Information Storage Models

F. F. Leimkuhler

Information Retrieval is a familiar phrase. However, the analysis of information storage problems is less common, yet is quite amenable to measurement.

In the following paper, a researcher who has specialised in this field provides a readable review which leads, through its references, into a useful selection of the work of others.

Information storage theory is not a well-defined area of research in the formal sense and one is still free to make of it what he wants. My own viewpoint is that of an industrial engineer and operations researcher who has been seeking ways to develop mathematical models for the analysis and design of library-type information storage systems. The words "storage" can evoke some bad vibrations in library circles where it is associated with the least respectable aspects of librarianship, but I choose to use the word in a broad and inclusive sense. While it may be more meaningful to define libraries as communications systems which transfer information through time and space, such transfers are accompanied by significant delays which give rise to meaningful storage problems. The study of libraries from the storage viewpoint can identify some crucial aspects of information systems which are often overlooked or ignored when the focus is on communication.

Although I have been working at storage models for several years and have advocated its practical importance to libraries, I am quite aware that it is not an easy matter to translate theory into practice. It has been my experience that action follows from need, but that better action can result if some good theory is available to help diagnose the need and to guide the remedial efforts. Our present theory is quite rudimentary from a research viewpoint and has a good way to go before it reaches the sophisticated state of, say, modern inventory theory, but the beginnings are there and there is good promise of a rich harvest.

It seems a bit ironic to me that the first important exploitations of this new study of library systems and the best guarantee of its continued support are probably going to come from outside the library proper. It is in the design of automated special purpose information systems that one has the greatest freedom to make innovations and the greatest pressure to apply a uniform economic and technical yardstick to every facet of the system. Conventional libraries are already mature technological systems in their own right. They are predicated on an earlier piece of mechanical wizardry — the printed book and a well-developed clerical work system to support its exploitation. Within these bounds most of the waste has been trimmed away in the long lean years of experience. As with a magnificent old clock, one doesn't tamper with it. If you want to keep it running, you will have to find parts made to the original specifications.

Still, I find it fruitful and hopeful to pursue the study of information storage systems in the context of conventional libraries. They offer a rich source of experimental data, and a wealth of ingenuity in an operational setting. As a "going" system, it is a good place to test the validity of one's models. Furthermore, there are plenty of indications that some radical changes in library operations are going to have to occur in the not too distant future.

SOURCE: Reprinted from *Planning Library Services. Proceedings of a Research Seminar held at the University of Lancaster, 9-11 July 1969*. (Edited by A. Graham Mackenzie and Ian M. Stuart) University of Lancaster Library, Occasional Papers No. 3 (1969), by permission of the author.

SPACE MODELS

A good first example of the nature and implications of storage theory is the book shelving model which was developed at Purdue several years ago[1,2]. The model assigns a given collection of books to a set of shelves with those lengths and heights which will minimize the shelf area required. The direct application of this model to some representative library collections has indicated that relatively efficient storage can be achieved by using only three or four different heights; and, in fact, by shelving large books on their fore edge, one can do remarkably well with only two shelf heights[3]. This result poses an interesting question to those large libraries which presently employ eight or more size classifications in their depository-type storage areas. It also calls into question the wisdom of spending extra money on variable height shelving and the practice of adjusting shelves up and down as new books are added. But these are rather minor benefits; and, perhaps, the greatest immediate importance of the model is its ability to show rigorously that one is not going to achieve dramatic reductions in space utilization through shelf arrangement alone. If all books could be stored by size on their fore edge, the best one could do is to double shelving capacity[4]. This is not by any means a long run solution to library storage problems.

Of considerable interest are two recent applications which are peripheral to the shelving problem. In one instance, the MARC catalog tapes produced by the Library of Congress were examined for the distribution of lengths of the records they contain[5]. Some 65 different record lengths were found in a random sequence. When ordered by size, they formed a bellshaped distribution. The book shelving model was applied to find the optimal record lengths to use for blocking the tape so as to produce a fixed record length tape with one, two, three, etc., different block sizes. The records would be in conventional sequence within each block size, and shorter records would cause some loss of storage space. As with books, it was found that the use of only a few block sizes could make fixed length processing relatively efficient at the expense of more storage capacity. Again, as with flipping large books on their fore edge, the model could be used in conjunction with a program for selective code compaction of longer records so as to achieve an optimal balance of processing and storage costs.

An even more esoteric application of the basic shelving model is the possibility of using it in the production of microform records. For example, in producing microfilms of conventional book material, one has to compensate for the variable sizes of book pages. What set of fixed frame sizes would achieve an optimal balance between the cost of handling variable frame sizes and the cost of reproducing blank spaces? If a single frame is used, it must accommodate the largest page size at the expense of much excess capacity for smaller pages. If only two sizes are used, what smaller size is optimal? The use of more sizes decreases lost area but increases complexity of the system. Again, as with the fore edge storage of books and the compression coding of MARC tapes, variable magnification might be used in conjunction with the selection of optimal frame sizes. This complicates the analysis considerably but allows for many more options and the possibility of a much better solution.

Another different sort of application of the book shelving model was made recently to the design of industrial warehouses, where the problem was that of determining optimal bay configurations and the assignment of variable size lots of palletized materials[6]. This might have useful implications for the design of library building and the assignment of subject groupings of varying size to different areas so as to minimize the sum of paging and space costs.

USAGE AND COST MODELS

Space models of the kind considered above have the analytic advantage of dealing with the physical measurement of inanimate objects and avoiding the more difficult problems of measuring human behavior and judgment. It is the absence of the human element which makes them most amenable to mechanical applications and which evokes the strongest suspicions of practical librarians. There are two basic ways of approaching the role of human intervention in man-machine systems. One way is to take the direct approach and concentrate on people, their perceptions and reactions to the system. This is the approach of the behavioral scientist.

A second approach is an indirect one of focusing on the physical components and attributing to them attributes which are really the net effect of some prior human action. For example, we speak of a book circulating, of it containing certain information, or of it having so much worth and relevance. This approach permits the reduction of much of the human element to measurable quantities which can be related directly to other aspects of a system. This is the approach of the economist who can infer a value measurement from the limited availability of certain resources and the desire to have more of everything rather than less.

A good example of this approach is in the work of Philip Morse and his recent book on *Library Effectiveness*[7]. Most of his models depend heavily on the notion of "randomness" in the behavior of library patrons. Tossing coins to retrieve information is an idea which seems patently absurd, if applied to some individual researcher, but is remarkably useful in measuring the collective effects of many individual choices and actions on the performance of a service system. Once we accept these measures as good approximations, we are in a position to make meaningful comparisons and recommendations for system improvement.

The analysis of depository schemes for libraries is a good example of what I call usage models. In general, despository models have argued that a considerable portion of a library's collection is so rarely used that these items could be stored elsewhere at less cost or to make room for new material. On the basis of out-of-pocket library costs alone, Lister[8] argued that several science libraries at Purdue could justify the storage of up to 60% of their holdings and achieve a small reduction in total costs. However, if some significant user delay cost is added to the charges, the advantages of depository storage are reduced drastically. The net effect of his study is to show that depositories do *not* provide an easy solution to library storage problems. Where space is limited and storage is the only answer, however, Lister's models do show how a rational, suboptimal policy can be developed.

A variation on this theme is seen in the recent study by the Center for Research Libraries[9] of the feasibility and potential benefits of a cooperative storage and lending facility for periodicals. This study is notable for its analysis of pertinent cost data from several libraries. A similar preliminary study was made in England at the University of Lancaster which showed that university libraries might utilize a national lending service for 10 to 30% of their demands depending on the user delay cost.

Perhaps a better prototype storage model of the usage variety is the one proposed by Cole[10] and refined and extended by Buckland[11]. Cole showed that a 2000 volume petroleum library could expect to satisfy the greatest number of user requests by subscribing to approximately 190 journals and holding them for about 11 years. He assumed exponential obsolescence of older volumes and a Zipf-type pattern for the marginal productivity of additional journal titles. Buckland introduced some considerable mathematical refinement to these basic relationships and was able to go beyond Cole's results and show how to include such additonal features as variable retention periods for different journals and use of interlibrary loan options. He also looked at how to meet a given level of service and minimizing a cost function that gives explicit recognition to different storage policies. An excellent review of the history of library use studies and models was made by A. K. Jain[12].

Some how the usage models, like the space models, seem to fall short of the mark in an attempt to come to grips with the critical problems of libraries. Libraries do have something in common with warehouses and bookstores but there is still a residual difference which cannot be ignored. The further development of economic models of library-type systems must focus on investment as well as operational costs. Because of their patterns of long-term storage and exponential growth, investment models may provide the better approach to the understanding of library economics. This approach would seem to be better suited to the development of system planning models and the justification of technical innovations.

RETRIEVAL MODELS

One cannot pursue information storage models very far without confronting difficult problems of information retrieval. It is interesting to observe how operations researchers and industrial engineers have tended to focus on the storage side of library systems while library scientists focus on the retrieval side. M. E. Maron has defined "The library problem" as the problem of retrieval and not of storage. He points out that the space problem is largely a problem of technique and economics — a matter of miniaturization, for which the necessary physical theory is already available, but that any use of miniaturization or mechanical storage is going to necessitate the development of a sophisticated remote access capability. The theoretical work on information retrieval which is necessary for such a development is not available now.

The separation of storage and retrieval is the critical factor in the automation of information systems and libraries. Conventional libraries must depend on direct user access to keep costs within bounds and to make card catalog systems work, i.e., we really have catalog-aided manual retrieval. Interlibrary loans, for example, are one of the most expensive kinds of services a library offers; and yet even this is cheap when compared to the cost of providing remote reference service, as for example, in the specialized information centers which the government has funded.

A thorough review of retrieval models is too large a subject to cover here and is beyond my competence to review. There appears to be a wide variety of approaches and classes of models, among which are those based on behavioristic studies of how man uses language in the transfer of information; and then there are the computer-oriented approaches which concentrate on the algebraic and physical capabilities of electronic devices.

The approach I have taken is an operational one in that it attempts to model the patterns observed in existing working systems, and to draw inferences for local optimization and evolutionary development. This is the method of operations research as opposed to basic research and is not offered as a substitute for the latter but as a complimentary approach.

It is characteristic of OR work to look for analogies from other fields and to draw heavily on the selctive experiences of past observers so as to attempt a sort of restatement of what is known about a system in the language of applied mathematics. An example is the model which appeared recently in *American Documentation*[13] where ideas were taken from the theory of military search and reconnaissance and from the earlier empirical work and wisdom of the English documentalist, S. C. Bradford. These ideas were used to formulate an analytic model that also incorporates a mathematical approach which is similar to the math used in the book shelving model, and which, by the way, is developing its own separate history within OR circles under such names as the assignment problem, the cutting stock problem, the packaging problem, and other such titles.

This approach seems promising, especially in the connection it made with Bradford's "scattering" studies, which can be related to Zipf's law and which, in turn, opens the door to some promising extensions into information theory, linguistics, and economic theory. Furthermore, the first model has called into question the proper measurement of search effectiveness and its relation to user preferences, perceptions, and behavior[14], and the relation of the latter to expert judgment of the relevance and content specification of a chunk of printed matter we call information. Thus, the models have a double payoff: they can lead to practical applications and can also open doors to new theory.

REFERENCES

[1] Leimkuhler, F. F. and Cox, J. G. "Compact Book Storage in Libraries" *Operations Research* 12(3) May-June 1964, pp. 419-427.

[2] Cox, J. G. "Optimum Storage of Library Material" Ph.D. Dissertation, Purdue University. 1964. See reviews in *Library Quarterly* 35(3), *College and Research Libraries* 26(3), and *Library Review* 20(2).

[3] Popovich, J.D. "Compact Book Storage" M.S.I.E. Thesis, Purdue University, 1966.

[4] Raffel, L. J. "Compact Book Storage Models" M.S.I.E. Thesis, Purdue University, June 1963.

[5] Stirling, K. "Cost Exchange Analysis of Variable Length versus Fixed Length MARC II Bibliographic Records" Course 244-C, School of Librarianship, University of California, Berkeley. Fall, 1968.

[6] Roberts, S. D. "Warehouse Size and Design" Ph.D. Thesis, Purdue University, 1968. (Major Professor: Ruddell Reed, Jr.)

[7] Morse, P. M. *Library Effectiveness* M.I.T. Press, 1968.

[8] Lister, W. C. "Least Cost Decision Rules for the Selection of Library Materials for Compact Storage" Ph.D. Thesis, Purdue University, 1967. (U.S. Clearinghouse Report PB 174441)

[9] Williams, G. *Library Cost Models: Owning versus Borrowing Serial Publications* Center for Research Libraries, Chicago. 1968.

[10] Cole, P. F. "A New Look at Reference Scattering" *Journal of Documentation* 18(2) June 1962, pp. 58-64.

[11] Buckland, M. K. and Woodburn, I. "Some Implications for Library Management of Scattering and Obsolescence" University of Lancaster Library Occasional Papers, No. 1. University of Lancaster Library, 1968.

[12] Jain, A. K. "A Statistical Study of Book Use" Ph.D. Thessis, Purdue University, January 1969. (U.S. Clearinghouse Report PB 176525)

[13] Leimkuhler, F. F. "A Literature Search and File Organisation Model" *American Documentation* 19(2) April 1968, pp. 131-136.

[14] Baker, N. R. "Optimal User Search Sequence and Implications for Information Systems Operation" School of Industrial Engineering and The University Libraries, Purdue University, 1968.

ABOUT THE AUTHOR

Ferdinand F. Leimkuhler, has recently been described as an elder statesman of library operations research. This status derives from his work as principal investigator for a major program of library operations research at Purdue University from 1963, and as Distinguished Lecturer of the American Society for Information Science in 1972.

He holds bachelor's degrees in chemistry and engineering and worked, in the 1950's, for the DuPont company. In 1962 he received his doctorate in engineering from Johns Hopkins University and in 1963 published a book on the trucking of radioactive materials, based on research sponsored by the U. S. Atomic Energy Commission.

Moving to the School of Industrial Engineering at Purdue University, his papers and those of his colleagues and students form a major element in the literature of library operations research. In 1968 he became visiting professor at the School of Librarianship at the University of California, Berkeley. On his return in 1969 he became Head of the School of Industrial Engineering at Purdue.

Production: Operations Research in the National Coal Board

Rolfe C. Tomlinson

The Operations Researcher will often state that many of the managerial problems in libraries are similar in form to well-studied industrial problems. The area of problem-solving which has been most conspicuously successful in the industrial context is that of "production planning". In this paper the production activities (over a number of years) of the largest British O.R. group are described. It will give the librarian an appreciation for the concept of a program of O.R. effort in a particular field of application. It will also allow him to consider similarities and differences between the problems described and production problems in libraries. Five case studies are described, ranging from stock control through to the evaluation of contract tenders. All are discussed at a non-technical level.

INTRODUCTION

Of all the aspects of a business enterprise the production process is the most tangible and the most obviously suitable for scientific study. In particular, its workings will probably be capable of being both measured and modelled. No doubt this is why so much early OR, in the NCB and elsewhere, was directed towards production problems; indeed, much of the present-day bread-winning OR lies within this field. There are two other powerful impetuses to work on the production process in the NCB. First, the finances of mining are largely dominated by production costs — that is to say, the actual production process is financially important in its own right. (This is not always the case in other industries where costs of raw materials or distribution might swamp process costs.) Second, and this point is implicit in much of what follows, there are sufficient similarities in the hundreds of production units in the NCB to make generalization a possibility. To study some aspect of production at one colliery might not in itself pay off; but if the work is easily extensible to a hundred more collieries the potential return on the work is very great indeed.

Many parts of the production process can be modelled with great precision by means of conventional applied mathematical methods, e.g. technical calculations such as are involved in the design of winding gear. Others require a statistical treatment, as in most calculations covering safety. The OR scientist's contribution is distinct from these, and for three reasons. First, he might develop models of a more complex kind of process than his colleagues the applied mathematician or the statistician — one thinks here of simulation models as an example. Second, he is more likely to be concerned with modelling not merely the physical process but also its economic consequences — he will often develop a cost model to superimpose on his physical model. Above all, however, the OR man is interested in models as tools of decision-making: he does not produce models either for himself or other specialists. Thus he will try to develop models that are comprehensible to and have the confidence of the non-specialist manager, while at the same time responding to the professional requirement that the model should help to formulate better lines of action than have

SOURCE: Reprinted from *OR Comes of Age: A Review of the Work of the Operational Research Branch of the National Coal Board 1948-1969.* by R.C. Tomlinson. London: Tavistock Publications Ltd., 1971, Chapter 4: "Production" (pp. 75-96) by permission of the National Coal Board and the author.

itherto been followed. The distinction is, of course, not clear cut. The applied mathematician and the statistician often undertake studies that are very good OR; from time to time the OR man undertakes work that the applied mathematician could not. It matters little.

The chapter distinguishes between three different aspects of the production process. In the first place, we shall be concerned with mining engineering proper, problems concerned with colliery design and control. These are dealt with in Part A. However, the best mining engineering practice is of little avail if there are no machines to work the coal or no supports for the roof. Part B is therefore concerned with what are, at first sight, engineering problems associated with equipment, etc. Then in Part C we deal with problems associated with the purchasing and stores functions, seemingly remote from the production process, but in practice very much a part of it. In each of these parts we give a brief historical review together with an indication of the work currently being undertaken. Finally, in Part D, we present five case studies to describe how work was actually carried out. Clearly, five case studies cannot be representative of twenty-one years' work, but they have been chosen both because of their importance and because of the different aspects of the work that they reveal.

(A) DESIGN AND CONTROL PROBLEMS AT COLLIERIES

Collieries have to be designed when they are sunk: decisions about where to sink the shaft, what underground roadways to drive, where to open coalfaces, and so on have to be taken at various stages before coal is won. So much is obvious. It may, however, be less obvious that collieries, or some aspects of them, are continually being redesigned throughout their life, whether this is five, twenty, or one hundred years. Partly, of course, this is because, as in all industry, technological change makes some redesign essential. More important, however, collieries have to be redesigned because, in an extractive industry, the colliery designed a year ago may, in large measure, no longer exist — coalfaces have a life measured usually in months, and even whole coal seams may become exhausted. So design is a never-ending process yielding a continual

demand for better tools.

A large range of tools is necessary to carry out colliery design. Some of these tools are tangible — the surveyor's equipment, the draughtsman's board — and some are less so — the methods for analysing borehole data, the ventilation engineer's computer program for calculating air flows — but all are necessary. The problems are diverse, e.g. what dimensions should this face have; into which part of the coal seam would we now plan to move; how should we transport the coal along this road. What kind of tools can the OR man bring to help? The tools developed have been mostly for one general purpose, namely to look at the total system that is generated by the bringing together of numerous small parts, all of which interact with one another. To put this point in more concrete terms, we are not concerned with what conveyor belt to use in order to transport a given amount of coal, but rather with the question: is this system of conveyor belts and bunkers, the design characteristics of each of which are known, a well-designed system? In large measure, the design problem in this sense is to predict, from a knowledge of the way the parts of the system will behave, how the system in total will behave. If one can make such predictions, then the problem of design can be raised from the simple question "Will the system work?" to the more difficult one "Which system will work best?" These predictions may be physical — this system will produce so much coal; or economic — the cost of this or that system will be so much. Of course, not all the important factors can be predicted in this way, judgement remains the ultimate criterion, but many bad guesses can be avoided.

If a system is to be of value, it must work — its operation must be controlled. One can regard the problems of control as distinct from the problems of design. Indeed, one is often obliged to, for example when an existing system has to cope with a new set of circumstances. However, in order to predict the way in which a complex system will behave, it is usually necessary to decide at the planning stage how the system is to be controlled. Thus if one wishes to predict the performance of a coal transport system made up of belts and bunkers, the precise way in which the flow of coal through the system is to be controlled clearly influences the performance that can be expected. The designer must, moreover, specify the checks and controls that will ensure that it is behaving according to plan. Equally, if a system is already there the type of control that is exercised essentially affects the design.

Thus the problems of design and control are opposite sides of the one coin: their solution is likely to need the same basic tools.

Historical Review of OR Work

Until the late fifties, the preoccupation of the industry was to increase its productive capacity. This meant sinking new pits and putting a lot of capital into the reconstruction of old pits. At that time, OR was not seen to have a place in the design of new pits, but a good deal of work was done at a general policy level, much of which made a considerable impact on Board policy. Thus studies were made of the circumstances in which various types of coal transport were likely to be most suitable; of the best way to drive underground roadways (driving roadways formed a major part of capital investment in new and reconstructed mines); and of methods of shaft-sinking. Most of this work was unsophisticated in terms of technique. The work on different transport systems, for example, consisted essentially of gathering and analysing sensibly a great deal of information on performance and costs of systems already installed. The work on tunnel drivage and shaft-sinking included a good deal on method improvement that would nowadays be seen as falling within the province of Method Study Branch.

It would be wrong to discount this work; it was certainly very useful and made an impact both on Board policy and on actual achievement. However, for better or for worse (and a number of influential managers think for the worse), this sort of work no longer forms a major part of OR's field of interest.

What one might call the modern age was anticipated by a number of studies that arose as the consequence of a particularly grievous mining disaster at Creswell Colliery in which not far short of one hundred men lost their lives because of an underground fire. This loss of life could have been greatly alleviated if it had been possible to warn the men much more promptly and had the conveyor belting in use at the colliery been fireproof. The inability to warn the men in sufficient time was seen to be due to deficiencies in the design of the colliery communication system. The

Branch was asked to investigate the design of such a system, and the then novel approach of computer simulation was used in the cours of this study. The performance of different telephone systems was examined by careful collection and analysis of the relevant data an their use in simulations of basically different types of telephone systems — for example, telephone systems may be hierarchical, with on central exchange fitted to several subexchanges or there may be one single central exchange that can communicate directly with any telephone in the colliery. It is not easy in retrospect to see why the communication stud was not developed and extended to a more far-reaching study of the whole problem of communication in a pit. On the production sic it did not appear as a serious problem, and the Branch were not then able to formulate their studies in such a general way.

Another important study was begun as a consequence of the decision, following the same disaster, to instal fireproof conveyor belting throughout the Board. Information or the merits of the different newly developed fireproof belts was needed very quickly in ord to determine purchasing and installation policy, and the Branch was responsible for establishing carefully designed trials to produc the necessary information as quickly and efficiently as possible.

The late fifties and early sixties saw a continuation of what one might call major ad hc policy studies. Many of the studies were now becoming more consciously economically based — what characteristics of a colliery mak it suitable for three-shift working, in what circumstances does face mechanization pay, how much should be invested in certain minin equipment, and so on? One of the most important features of these studies was that they could not provide easy generalization in the form of a direct answer to the question; instead they culminated in systematic procedures for answering the question in a specifi instance, e.g. whether colliery X should be three-shifted.

Many of these duties reflected the reduced emphasis, through pressure of events, on expanding production capacity. However, the need for systems design remained, indeed in some ways was strengthened. The sudden and largely unexpected competition from other fuels placed great pressure on mining engineers to increase productivity and reduce costs. New techniques for production and transport of the coal were introduced, all with new potential whose achievement needed fresh planning and organization — design, in fact. This was not confined to a few pits undergoing capital reconstruction, but affected almost every colliery in the country.

Review of Current OR Work

In the early sixties, the main production drive was to get all coalfaces mechanized; that is, to cut the coal from the solid and load it onto the conveyor by a machine. By 1967 this prime objective had largely been achieved, and it became clear that greater efficiency could be achieved only by getting higher production from faces that were already mechanized. On paper, it would appear that quite dramatic increases in efficiency on mechanized coalfaces should be possible; for example, the coal-winning machines spend rather less than half the available time actually producing coal, the rest of the time being lost through delays. Analysis of observational data strongly suggests that many of these delays could be avoided by better supervisory control of the operation of the coalface or by better system design of faces. Consequently, attention in the last year or two has concentrated on the management of coalfaces and their design. OR has been involved in this, with the prime objective of constructing models of coalface operations that enabled various design proposals and control procedures to be tested.

On the design side, quite simple techniques based on network analysis have been developed and their value proved in a number of applications to the design of so-called spearhead faces. (Each Area was asked to plan at least one spearhead face to produce 1,000 tons a shift — about four times the national average.) The way in which design and control interact is rather well illustrated in the use of these networks. The design aim is to ensure that production is not impeded because of other activities on the face; in network terms this means that the critical path through the network must be the movement of the machine along the face. In practice these activities are frequently delayed owing to the inherent variability in the time taken to complete operations at the coalface. A study of the network can then show what activities should be given priority to minimize production delays. Thus the design technique helps to indicate how control should be exercised in real time.

Much of the value of networks lies in the way that they force the designer to set down the logic of the process and enable him to undertake simple calculations on priorities and so on. They are of less help when the difficulties of design arise less from the scheduling of actions than from the high variation in the time that various activities can take. In these circumstances the critical path as such can have little meaning. Moreover, a change in the organization will mean a complete change in the network and its associated calculations. For these reasons simultation-type models of the coalface are being developed which enable different methods of organizing facework to be studied under conditions of uncertainty. These methods can have a wider range of application. One problem arises from the fact that work on the face is carried out in a long, narrow, dark, noisy, and dust-filled corridor where rapid movement is impossible; understandably it is very difficult to coordinate operations. Tannoy-type systems can be installed to improve coordination and a simulation study has been conducted to assess the value of such an investment resulting from the improved central control that such a system would provide.

Moving away from the coalface, we encounter next the problem of how to transport the coal from the face to the shaft bottom, from where it is wound to the surface. Simulation programs have been constructed that enable estimates of the efficiency of different transport systems to be easily made. There are two sets of programs, one set corresponding to transport systems made up of conveyor belts and bunkers, and the other corresponding to the second most common mode of transport, namely underground railway systems. The first of these sets of programs is described in a case study at the end of this chapter; the section includes an elaboration of the practical problems, a discussion of some features of the research necessary to develop suitable general programs, and some comments on the effort devoted to training the potential users of these programs.

Like the simulation model of coalface operations, these models can be used to assess the value of different types of control policy. In the case of underground railway systems, the control policy can be just as important as the design, in the sense of track layout, of the system. The main control decision is how to allocate the trains between different loading-points immediately after they have emptied their loads at the shaft. (This problem is not, of course, peculiar to mining; many transport systems give rise to essentially the same problem.) A number of different methods for making this decision have been proposed and their efficiency examined. It seems from the results obtained that a flexible allocation method — one that acknowledges the variability inherent in the system and allocates according to the present state of affairs (an inflexible system, in contrast, might be based on a pre-fixed timetable for the trains) — is much to be preferred. While this is perhaps obvious at the qualitative level, to put figures on it would be very difficult without a simulation model.

A particularly interesting application of this type was to the evaluation of remotely monitored information, which, at a cost, would allow a centrally placed controller access to complete information of relevance to the transport system, compared with the more conventional method of exercising central control via the telephone. This was, of course a study of the value to be attached to different quantities and types of information. A quantitative approach to such problems is surprisingly rare. Most of the published literature on management information systems does not attempt to put any value on the information, but is concerned rather with getting the information in the most expedient way.

We now move on to the rather more strategic aspects of colliery design. Deep mining is a risky venture, and money to be invested in a new mine is always regarded as high-risk capital. Even when the shaft and main roadways have been driven, major uncertainties exist that must be taken account of in drawing up plans for working the mine. Coal seams are faulted and even on occasions vanish unpredictably as one is working through them. The nature of the coal through the seam is not always homogeneous, and the thickness of the seam commonly varies very widely. If one proposed to work, say, five faces in a seam there is, at many collieries, a pretty fair chance that one or two of these faces will unpredictably encounter adverse geological conditions, which will greatly reduce the output from these faces. Such a circumstance can have major economic consequence because the main resources, the men and the capital equipment,

cannot be very flexibly redeployed.

The businessman faced with this sort of problem has two possible lines of action, both o which can be expensive: he can take out insurance in the form of surplus productive capacity or he can try to obtain better information.

The mining engineer can do the same. He ca develop more faces than can be worked with the resources and shaft capacity available so that if one of the faces runs into trouble the me from it can be absorbed productively on the remaining faces. Or he can spend money to improve his knowledge of the characteristics o the coal seam within which he is working. This might be done by driving extensive roadways into the seam, by drilling boreholes and so on.

The first method has been the subject of a good deal of OR study and is discussed in a case study later in this chapter. The second metho is more complicated and the issues are decidedly less clear cut. Thus if we drive road ways ahead of the requirements for current production, we may generate information abou the seam, but we may also be affecting future production techniques. For example, it may b possible to take advantage of these roadways to extract the coal between them much more cheaply than would otherwise be the case If this were so, a reduction in costs would be achieved even without the extra knowledge of the seam gained by the advance exploration. Thus the exploration can be thought of as an investment not only in knowledge but also in the possibility of cheaper methods of minin at some point in the future. The realities of the situation are a far cry from the simple economic models of pit layouts that one sees postulated; nor do existing statistical technique seem capable or providing much help. Howeve a good deal of progress has been made and in particular gaming studies, in which the colliery planner is invited to play his pit throug five years with nature as his opponent, have proved popular and effective.

Although the models developed are of immediate value to the OR staff providing a direct OR service to coalfield staff, the prime aim of practically all the present work in the field of colliery design and control is to help locall based management, planners, and work-study engineers by the provision of tools for their use. All the various models described abov are, or will be, made available in "packaged" form for use by the local staff. Many of the models are, of course, computer-based, and the way in which engineers in the coalfield have assimilated and used these novel methods, as they must be to men with no formal training in computing, has been one of the remarkable features of this work over the past year or two.

It would be wrong to conclude this general review without emphasizing that a great deal of the work described in it, certainly most of the current work, represents the results of the joint effort of OR with other staff, notably Method Study, Planning Branch, and the Computer Services. Without this collaboration progress would be impossible.

(B) EQUIPMENT AND RELATED PROBLEMS

The borderline between colliery design and equipment problems is difficult to draw. In practice the distinction is often made simple for organizational reasons; namely, the equipment problems tend to be the responsibility of different men with different loyalties and organizational pressures. Moreover, much engineering activity — in particular equipment overhaul — is administered not at colliery level but as a service from a central point used by a great many collieries. These two faces conspire to put a very different slant on the OR approach to the two types of problem.

What are these equipment problems? In the first place, what is the equipment? In the main we shall be talking about coalface machinery, the installation of which has, to a large extent, been the mainspring of the increasing productivity in coalmining. The machines that have contributed most to this increase are power loaders, which cut a strip of coal from a vertical coalface and load the coal into a conveyor, and walking roof supports, which support the roof behind the face and also serve to push the conveyor forward before being drawn forward automatically when a slice has been cut from the face.

This machinery, which can cost about a quarter of a million pounds for a single coalface, is working in appalling conditions by factory standards. It is subject not only to heavy and sudden stresses and strains, but also to the effects of use in an atmosphere filled with coaldust and water. The improvement of design

has led to great inreases in reliability, but nevertheless considerable effort has to be put into maintaining the machinery on the face and replacing failed components. In addition to maintenance at the coalface, machinery is also withdrawn either periodically or at breakdown for workshop overhaul.

The range of equipment decisions on which OR advice might be sought is wide. Questions of design, quality, and standardization — affecting the actual equipment bought — and of maintenance, overhaul, and control of plant — affecting its use — have each been studied. In the early days of the Branch most of the effort went onto the former, in trying to determine methods of comparing the overall economics of different types of equipment. In recent years, with the increasing use of expensive machinery and the corresponding recognition of the importance of keeping this machinery in operation, the Branch has become more involved in such questions as the amount of spare machinery to hold, how frequently to withdraw machines for overhaul, whether to hold a common pool of plant, and how to control machinery by ensuring that machines are withdrawn from a pit and overhauled rapidly.

The first major OR study in the maintenance field arose from the concern felt in one Area about the costs and efficiency of its central workshops (i.e. the workshops responsible for all overhaul work in the Area. For many reasons much work is carried out centrally and not at each colliery.) This first study had an important formative influence on future work in the field and will therefore be described in some detail. Two points in particular arose from it which have pervaded all subsequent work. The first is the difficulty of limiting the field of inquiry; it was found, for example, that decisions on how frequently to remove a machine for overhaul at the surface necessitated considering whether there would be a machine to replace it and this in turn led to looking at the question of how many machines to purchase. The second is that, because of the large scope of the inquiry, there were a great many people who were taking decisions that affected the outcome; the problem gradually came to be seen not just as deciding an optimum policy but as the far more difficult task of coordinating the actions of a number of people.

The problem worrying the senior management in the Area concerned was, then, that they did not know what value they were getting from their overhaul workshops. It was soon clear that not all was well. The Area had tended to build up the workshops' programme from the equipment withdrawn from collieries and needing overhaul. The workshops were stretched to capacity and, by normal criteria, operating efficiently. Unfortunately, many of the machines repaired went into a plant store and were never used. There were reasons for this; the number of faces in the Area was reducing and, in any case, new types of machinery were being installed. The simple point emerged that the overhaul programme should be built up from what was likely to be needed rather than from what was available for overhaul. But this apparently simple point created a new and still more difficult problem, namely how to estimate what would be needed. Breakdown of machines was impossible to forecast, new faces did not always start on schedule; it was clearly impossible to match the rate of repair to the rate of need, and therefore a buffer stock of overhauled machines was called for. So the problem had to be expanded still further to include the control of these buffer stocks.

But there were still many other sides to the problem. Equipment was often being sent to the workshops for overhaul when all that was required was a small repair at the colliery. The internal accounting scheme encouraged this. Equipment, in the form of complete machines, was owned by the Area and was hired to collieries. The cost for hire charges incurred at the workshops was based on averaging the total Area cost and therefore did not discriminate against a colliery which sent its machines in for overhaul unnecessarily often. How then should one fix an equitable internal accounting system?

Some senior managers in the Area had another worry. This was that the cost of the workshops per ton of coal produced in the Area was higher than that in other Areas, without any indication from available statistics that, as a result, the Area had fewer breakdowns. Others questioned the effectiveness of the existing plant registry for recording the dispostion of machines and in particular for the control of machine units (coalface machines normally consist of three or four separate units). In fact, the registry only kept records of movements of complete machines, although most of the

breakdowns involved changing a unit rather than the whole machine. The result was that no record was kept of whether or not units had been sent to the workshops. Yet another cause for concern was that overhauls of some machinery were being subjected to long delays owing to shortage of spare parts.

Because of these ramifications, it was decided that the best way to proceed would be to study a particular machine, one that was in most common use in the Area. The first attack was on spares supply, a problem met and beaten before. After a couple of months it had been established that an improved availability of spares, such as would result from the use of the stock control tables prepared by the Branch, would lead to some reduction in delays to overhauls, but that this improvement was slight compared to what would be achieved if the workshops overhaul programme could be smoothed. It was also clear that there was a need for a better record of the whereabouts of machinery, and it was agreed to appoint someone to set up such a record.

Six months after the project started the main lines of the results had emerged. An improvement to the records in the plant registry was recommended and it was suggested that the registry should be at the workshops and under the control of the workshops manager, and that deviations from the planned programme to meet expected demands for plant should be based on upper control limits on the amount of plant that was either already overhauled and waiting to be used or actually being overhauled. It was also suggested that a fixed charge should be made to the colliery each time a new machine or unit was taken from the workshops and that an incentive should be given to encourage prompt return of units.

Perhaps the main conclusion was that it was not always worth while to overhaul machinery since the cost of overhaul might outbalance the extra life given to the machine by the overhaul and it might be better to scrap the old machine and buy a new one. An estimate of additional life due to an overhaul was made, and it was easy to calculate which machines to scrap not only in absolute terms but also to make best use of the limited capacity of the workshops.

These suggestions were acted on and smoothed several paths. However, the heart of the matter, the high workshops cost in relation to other Areas, was barely touched. It as therefore decided to compare the workshops costs in the Area with those of another Area where a system of cyclic withdrawal was used whereby machines were overhauled in order of time since last overhaul. This system meant that a smooth workload was given to workshops. It was found that the running costs of overhaul and maintenance, including production losses due to breakdown, were 50 per cent higher in the Area that did not have cyclic overhaul, but that the Area practising cyclic overhaul were spending much more on new machines. When the capital charges were added to the running costs there was little difference between the two Areas. Since there was practically no difference in the observed breakdown frequencies, the results provided some reassurement to the management of the Area with the high running costs, though of course the conclusions were highly debatable in view of other differences, such as ease of coal cutting, between the Areas which would have an effect on maintenance costs.

The first study had, therefore, identified most of the problems. Fully satisfactory solutions had not been found to all of them, but at least the task was known.

The natural development from this first study seemed, at the time, to be to take one of the problems it had highlighted and to study this one problem in depth. It was tempting to choose the organizational problem, but the potential OR contribution to problems of organization was not then well recognized and an organizational study would probably have been still-born. Instead, the question of overhaul policy was examined. The work on this question is dealt with in a case study at the end of the chapter and will not be discussed further here.

While this work on overhaul policies was being done, another facet of the general problem was selected for study. Concern was being expressed at the low percentage of machinery that was actually in use at any one time. The basic question here was identified as: how many spare machines should be held to back up machines in use?

At any given time the machines constituting the pool would be in various stages of a cycle. There would be a number of machines in operation on the face, some machines being withdrawm from the face, others standing at workshops awaiting overhaul; some would be in the process of overhaul and others would

be overhauled and awaiting dispatch to collieries. The number of machines in each of these categories fluctuates in practice as machines break down, are withdrawn from collieries, are overhauled, and so on. It was decided to simulate this cycle of machine movements. The results of the simulation showed the effects of holding different numbers of spare machines, or rather spare units (machines are split into "units", it will be recalled). The more spare units held, the smaller the number of times a unit was unavailable when required. So it was possible to compare the cost of holding extra spare units with the savings that would result from fewer shortages of units (if a unit was not available one would have to be borrowed from another Area at high cost in terms of transport and loss of production pending the arrival of the replacement).

This work indicated, therefore, the number of spare units that should be held. More work was needed, however. Thus it was necessary to know when there was danger of the system getting out of control through, say, a build-up in the number of units awaiting withdrawal from the pits, or a shortage of repaired units in the "clean" pool of overhauled units available for issue. It was possible to set control levels for this so the risk of running out of machines could be reduced to an acceptable level.

While this study and its implementation were proceeding, the organization of plant pools and workshops in the Board changed. Previously each of thirty-five Areas had had its own plant pool and its own central workshops for overhauling plant. The first change to occur was a reduction in the number of Areas to eighteen and an accompanying process of rationalization of workshops so that each workshop specialized on overhaul of a certain type of equipment. Plant pools were reorganized, with the result that some of the new Areas now have their own pools while others share a pool. There are certain immediate benefits from all this. The rationalization of workshops means that it is possible to set up flow lines for overhaul and reduce the holdings of spare parts; grouping plant pools means that less spare plant needs to be held. However, there were considerable organizational difficulties.

With shared pools and rationalized workshops, adequate communication and some formalizing of rules on priorities seems essential. Recent OR work has therefore included studying the feasibility of providing workshops with a flow of information on the likely needs of Areas for overhauled machines, not solely for scheduled replacements but also for replacements owing to breakdowns. In addition it is hoped to formalize a system of priorities for overhauls that can be agreed by all concerned.

Most of the work hitherto described has been concerned with power-loading equipment, but recently attention has shifted to the overhaul policy for powered roof supports, which are the most expensive item of equipment on a coalface. These are not withdrawn from a face until the face has finished, any failures of components being repaired on the face. While normal practice has been to withdraw the supports when the face finishes, it might be worth while in some cases to transfer them directly to another face thereby achieving higher utilization of supports. Studies are being carried out of the value and feasibility of such face-to-face transfer, and this work is linked with another study which involves forecasting future demand for powered supports.

Perhaps the most important lesson from this work in the engineering field is the need to understand and take account of the large number of people that will be fundamentally affected by a decision to do things in a different way. There are separate people concerned with deciding what machines should be used on particular faces, establishing the hire charge system, running the plant pool, deciding on withdrawal policies, and running the workshops organization. In addition, while some of these people operate within an Area, others, in some plant pools and workshops, operate on a regional basis. The solutions proposed often have to be tailored to the abilities of people to implement them in terms of their position in the organization, and it is therefore important that any new system should be worked out with the managers involved. It may be difficult to reconcile the desire of the OR worker to take a wider view and develop an integrated approach with the need to retain the sympathy of the people for whom he is working. It is salutary for the OR worker to reflect continually that the manager still has to be able to fit the solution proposed into the organization as it stands or to face the difficult task of changing the organisation.

Finally, it is perhaps appropriate to reflect on the rate at which work can become obsolete. Obsolescence occurs in engineering for three main reasons. First, through changes in management; a solution accepted by one manager may be questioned by another and for good reason, and the work may have to be repeated. Second, the organization may change; the organization of plant pools and of workshops has evolved throughout the period of study. Third, the equipment being used may change; the machine studied in the first project in 1961 is by 1969 used only in special circumstances. This all means that care must be exercised in deciding the amount of effort that should be put into a study, and it should be recognized that any systems produced will need regular servicing and revision to ensure that they are kept up to date.

(C) PURCHASING AND STORES

Just as the mining engineer depends on the engineer for the development of improved equipment and the maintenance of the equipment he already possesses, so the engineer is dependent on those concerned with provisioning to get this equipment at an economic price and to ensure that both equipment and necessary spares are available when required. In one sense the division between all the functions is artificial, since design decisions at the colliery can be taken only in the light of information and assumptions about the service that the engineer and the provisioning expert can provide. For most purposes, however, it is convenient to consider the functions as separate. Those concerned with provisioning often have a different background and experience both from the engineers and from the mining engineers, and for much of the Board's history the work of provisioning has been carried out in a separate department.

Inventory control or stock control is, of course, one of the classic fields of OR application. Most of the literature on the subject is concerned with the development of systems for controlling stock levels of finished goods, often linked with production control systems, usually in manufacturing industry. Such problems are often the first to be given to an industrial OR group, and the reason for this is not hard to find. The amount of capital tied up in stock is one of the first items that strikes anyone reading a balance sheet.

On the OR side there is a body of theory that seems to correspond with reality rather more closely than most. Moreover, the results of the investigation can be embodied in simple procedures that do not require any understanding of the principles employed. One might add cynically that, provided major disasters are avoided, it is very difficult to prove or disprove whether the system is working as planned since the real savings cannot be often identified in the accounts. The NCB situation is rather different in that stock control of finished stocks, i.e. mined coal, is almost impossible in the traditional sense, and that the inventory problems are concerned with stocks of production materials, e.g. pit props, steel arches, and, in particular, spare parts for coalface and other machinery.

Purchasing and Stores in the National Coal Board is a large commercial activity by any standards. Buying, stocking, and issuing goes on at a rate of £1,000,000 per working day. When the NCB was formed, Purchasing and Stores activities were made a branch of Production Department, partly because it was felt that this was the only way to get the work done initially, and partly because it was felt that it would be wrong to inject too early into a newly established nationalized industry the full impact of centralized control. The desirability of some form of centralized control was, however, seen, and certain steps were taken, for example the introduction of a national stores vocabulary. In 1955, following the report of the Fleck Committee, a separate Purchasing and Stores Department was established to coordinate and, where appropriate, centralize the policy and decisions on all purchasing and stores matters. An early policy decision in the direction of increased central control was to establish central stores serving typically twenty or so collieries; central purchasing also began at this juncture. The record of achievement since then, as indicated by all the usual measures, such as quantities of stock held and index of purchase price, is more than impressive.

The first OR projects were started soon after the new department was set up. The folklore of OR Branch includes the belief that this work was initiated when a senior member of the Branch found himself making a cross-country train journey with a man

unknown to him. The member of the Branch sat reading a book on stock control theory and the unknown man, suitably impressed, asked what the book was about and modestly confessed to some interest in the topic; he was the Director General of the Purchasing and Stores Department of the NCB! This happy coincidence led to the first OR work.

It is interesting in retrospect to note that all the early OR effort for Purchasing and Stores Department was directed to the problem of studying stock control, although work on determining the right quality of conveyor belting to buy had previously been started for Production Department and continued under their aegis. It is clear now that inventory control is not necessarily the most profitable part of the provisioning function to study — the question of what to order (e.g. which of technically equal alternative equipment is most economic for the job, manipulating quantity discounts, etc.) is generally speaking much more important than the stock control decisions of when to order and in what quantity. There are also interactions between purchasing patterns and stock levels (e.g. the even ordering of supplies), which can reduce purchasing costs but increase stock levels. Historically, there is little doubt that stock control was chosen as a topic because it was known that a solution could be found, and examples of successful applications could be quoted as evidence.

During those early years, the foundations were laid for a stock control system that was subsequently implemented in many parts of the country. Two aspects of this early work have been influential over the years. First, an early decision was taken to develop a stock control system that minimized total costs including the costs of stock-outs as opposed to providing a given service level at least cost. This decision was taken because the alternative of fixed arbitrary service levels (95 or 99 per cent) seemed to beg the real question of deciding what the service level should actually be. And so it does. But, in the light of history, many of the difficulties in implementing our system arose because of this minimum-cost criterion. For example, such a criterion leads to a relatively poor service level for expensive spares, often contrary to the intuitive feeling of the stock controller. Above all, it presupposes that everyone thinks in terms of total cost, whereas the cost of capital seems to have an emotional significance out of proportion to its economic weighting. Second, there is the question of flexibility. The tables provided assumed certain levels of costs - ordering costs, holding costs, runout costs. If management felt that these were wrong, and they inevitably changed with time, or that the total level of stockholding was wrong, there was no convenient way of taking account of this - other than referring back to OR. Retrospectively one can see the main value of these tables was the way in which they distributed the stock amongst different items. A system enabling Purchasing and Stores staff to adjust levels to current requirements, possibly by alteration of the costs, might have been more helpful in the long run.

Nevertheless, the work was widely implemented and was of great originality. It remains the only practical work reported on the OR literature, and almost certainly the only implemented stock control system, which minimizes total cost. The system developed as a result of these early studies, some of the interesting steps in its development, and some of the lessons learned in this work, are described more fully in a later part of the chapter.

As would be expected, this work was the starting-point for a number of other studies both in the inventory control field and beyond. The question of very slow-moving engineering spares was one such topic. In fact, the great majority of engineering spares in the NCB are slow moving in the sense that demand is less than, say, ten or twelve per year; in terms of value, as much as fifty per cent of spares is held in items whose usage is less than one a year. These very slow-moving items present special problems - demand is difficult to forecast, they are usually expensive but their availability when required is often crucial to the working of the plant concerned. There is a fair risk of their being bought with the plant, never being used, and having to be scrapped. Some simple rules were developed to help in the setting of levels but, as often happens, the most valuable part of the work was in helping to establish the critical features. Once this had been done, calculations were often unnecessary.

Many other studies arose from an examination of the assumptions that had to be made in the stock control system, and in particular of the overall system of which stock control is a part. Some of these studies took the work outside the Purchasing and Stores Department. Thus it was recognized that a reduction in consumption of engineering spares could be expected to have a bigger impact than better stock control of them. This was one starting-point of the work, already reviewed, on engineering and maintenance, work which has developed far beyond its original limited aim of justifying or otherwise the current level of spares usage. But many of the questions raised remained in the purchasing and stores field. One was the value of greater or lesser centralization of stockholding - the structure, so to speak, of the system. Which, if any, items should be held only at national level? Which should be held at the coalface? Questions such as these turned out to be more important than how stocks of the item were controlled at any given level. Another was the perennial question of whether the errors in forecasts of demand can be reduced thereby reducing the stock level, part of which is held to insure against uncertainty in the forecast.

This last point, whether demand forecasting can be improved, presents an interesting example of common sense being controverted by fact. One might suppose, on common-sense grounds, that information on overhaul plans, production intentions, and machine usage could be used to produce a much more accurate demand forecast than some simple rule like "next year's demand will be twice the demand experienced in the past six months". When the data had been collected in order to test this hypothesis, it was found that they did not really help at all, since the uncertainty in the overhaul plans and so on was too great.

Another study was started at about this time into ways and means of reducing the uncertainty in delivery dates. This work led to suggestions for strengthening the cooperation between the NCB and its suppliers. Some studies were carried out which suggested that decision rules for deliveries that encompassed both the NCB and its suppliers would provide mutual benefits. For obvious reasons, this work has been difficult to implement between firms, though discussions are taking place. But it is an interesting example of the common OR experience that it is so often organizational boundaries that waste money.

All the work so far mentioned, which still continues, was and is generally reckoned a success. Work at present is largely centred on two main projects. The first is part of the Purchasing and Stores Department's much wider effort to introduce computerized stock control. This began with the coding and recording of all current stock levels and movements thereby enabling surplus and obsolete stock to be fully identified for the first time. A redeployment system for surplus and redundant stock has been added to the computer system, opening the way for the first time to the control of existing as opposed to new stock levels. The Branch is providing assistance in the formulation of a computerized stock control system by providing forecasting and setting routines. The computer system has been used to simulate the effect of different holding and run-out costs in the stock control system. Stores management can then exert direct influence over the matters that concern them, namely the level of stockholding and the service level, by using the computer to tell them, for instance, the run-out cost that will provide a required service level given a desired level of stocks. This gives the opportunity of a flexible stock control system which can more easily respond to departmental policy changes than could the system originally developed by the Branch.

The second major Branch project is perhaps more novel in direction, namely a new move into the field of purchasing, where the problems are arguably more important in terms of cash return and of commercial politics than are stock control problems. The first studies in the field of purchasing were akin to value engineering, being generally designed to explore which of several alternative buys gave best value for money. (The work on conveyor belting previously mentioned had resulted in the establishment of formal procedures for the underground testing of all new types of belting.) But few other studies of this type were successful, mainly because of the difficulty of establishing measurable evidence of the effects due to the use, for example, of different steel arches to support underground roadways. More recently our studies have turned to the problem a purchasing officer faces when he is placing a contract, in the case of the NCB usually for one year ahead, for a particular type of material that can be obtained from a number of suppliers. Many factors enter into the decisions. Quite complicated discount rules are commonly the case. Additionally, for those items for which the NCB is virtually a monopoly buyer, the long-term effect of today's decisions can have a profound effect on the commercial position in the future. In an extreme case, the NCB could bankrupt a supplier. OR methods in such a delicate field can scarcely quantify all the conditions; but if used jointly with human judgement they may be of great use. One of the case studies in the next section is concerned with this work.

(D) CASE STUDIES

This part of the chapter presents five case studies chosen to illustrate the range of work undertaken and some of the techniques employed but, most of all, to record important stages in the development of the Branch. It is, of course, tempting to select the successes, though failure is often the best instructor. By most reckonings, these cases are all successes. In each case the difference between doing what the study recommends, and some alternative policy, can be measured in millions. But the advice is not always different from what management proposed to do in any case, and the advice was not always accepted. Taken together we hope they give a not *untypical* picture of the major research studies the Branch has undertaken.

The first case study concerns the simulation of underground belt and bunker transport systems and describes some aspects of work that, at the time of writing, we certainly judge to be successful. This work has some interesting technical features, for example, some of the research undertaken to ensure applicability of a system to all of a large class of collieries, but also it involves major problems of implementation.

The second — dealing with spare face requirements — is chosen because two attempts, separated by five years in time, were made on the same problem. The first attempt was not successful and the second, although drawing on the lessons of the first, was only partially successful. Some of the reasons for this lack of success are discussed.

The third — examining the frequency of machine overhaul — is chosen for a number of reasons. It illustrates, for example, how much more important factual research can be than complicated model-building. It also leads naturally to a discussion of relationships between the engineer and the OR man.

The fourth — stock control of spares for

coalface machinery — is again chosen for a variety of reasons. It enjoys, as has already been hinted, an important place in the development of OR in the NCB: it was one of our first big successes and generated a good deal of interest in our work. But there were problems of implementation, which we now understand the reasons for, and from which we hope to learn.

Finally, we have chosen to describe work carried out on the evaluation of contract tenders. This is work in a novel field, novel not only to the NCB but probably to the OR world at large. It is also quite a good example of the potential value of OR techniques used in a purely arithmetical role and how this apparently limited use can afford considerable insight into less quantifiable features of the problem.

The Simulation of Underground Belt and Bunker Transport Systems

Technological improvements in coal production and means of transport have led to considerable increases in efficiency in British mines. However, in the design of transport systems they have created problems. When coal was produced manually, the production rate from a face was more or less predictable (although not constant) throughout a shift. Furthermore, the older methods of transport, commonly by wagons that could be moved individually, provided considerable flexibility in absorbing what variation in production rate there was. The wagons could be diverted to storing coal at times of high production and they could be rapidly disposed from face to face as required. Mechanized coalfaces, on the other hand, produce at a very variable and partly unpredictable rate. To some extent this is because they are designed to do so — the machine cuts the length of the face, and then production stops while the machine is moved forward before starting another cutting run — but also the mechanized face is more liable to unplanned stoppages, which may be due to any of a large number of causes, such as varying hardness of the coal, mechanical failure, and delays through organizational difficulty. Unfortunately, the newer methods of transport, specifically in this case conveyor belts, are rather inflexible. There can, for instance, be no question of changing the size of the conveyor belt in the short term as the production rate varies from the face. The problem can there-

fore be posed in a general way as: how much can one afford to invest in fixed transport capacity to meet a variable transport need? An example of a more specific question that someone charged with designing the transport system might have to answer is: would it pay to have a belt along such and such roadway capable of carrying the highest load that might be asked of it, or would it be better to put in a smaller belt and provide bunker storage immediately before the belt to smooth the flow of coal onto it?

An essential preliminary to answering this type of question is that one must be able to predict how well any given transport system will perform.

This is not easy to do because the variability in production rates, which obviously matters, does not take a particularly easily described form; and it is doubly difficult when there are, as there might well be, twenty or thirty roadways between the faces and the shaft, each having its own belt, when each belt may be receiving its load from more than one earlier belt in the system, and when bunker storage may be dispersed throughout the system. In the absence of any satisfactory theoretical or rule-of-thumb method for making these predictions, and it was recognized that there was none, and in view of the financial importance of the decisions involved, it was decided to develop simulation models.

One of the drawbacks to the use of simulation in problems of this type is that used only once it can be a very expensive way, and also a very time-consuming way, of getting an answer. It soon became clear that a general program, capable of simulating the performance of pretty well any belt and bunker system, was required. Moreover, the data collection involved in establishing a simulation model can be quite expensive. We therefore decided that every effort should be made to keep to a minimum the data collection necessary for using these programs. (This aim was greatly facilitated by the fact that much relevant information is available as a routine through the efforts of Method Study Branch who, usually for quite different reasons, carry out frequent studies of coalface and other operations.) Another draw back to simulation is that it does not, of itself, generate good designs; it merely predicts the performance of any given design. In order to get a good design one might have to try out a great many alternatives. A third aim of the research was therefore to provide some means of sorting out, in as simple a way as possible, what were the likely features of a good design so as to narrow down the field of possible designs that would be given the full-scale simulation treatment. It is probably sufficient to say that we were able to meet these aims both to our own satisfaction and to the satisfaction of the potential users of the programs. Three programs were developed, two of which are extremely crude and are used to give some broad indication of the designs likely to be worth assessing by the third program, which is more detailed and very much more accurate in its predictions.

A particular thread that might be worth following through to illustrate how the research was carried out is the question of what constitutes an adequate general model of production rate at a coalface for the purpose of predicting the performance of the transport system.

In the very first simulation model constructed, an extremely detailed model to generate production rates from the coalface was built in. This first model, which was constructed only as part of a proving exercise, was clearly inadequate for a number of reasons. First, it was so detailed as to lead to an excessively long runningtime for the program; second, it called for a rather more detailed specification of the coalface than could be expected without some laborious data collection; and, third, to have followed this line of development would have meant that generality could have been attained only at the expense of complicated programming which would have had to be matched with laborious data form-filling.

In the next model we therefore went as far as we dared in the opposite direction of using an extremely simple model to generate face reproduction rates. This model assumed, for instance, that once the coal-winning machine was embarked on its cutting run it kept going at a constant rate. The crudity of this model allowed much faster running of the program and called for far fewer data. Unfortunately, when we came to test the results obtained from this model against actual performances of transport systems, the results were not quite adequate, though the degree of inadequacy was remarkably small. (We were later able to explain this in terms of the real situation.)

At the expense of only a little more complication — broadly speaking the introduction of reality was obtained. It may well be, at the risk of unjustified generalization, that a useful way of going about building simulation models is to start from an exceedingly simple model and to introduce only as much complexity as is necessary to obtain an adequate representation of reality. Implicit in this statement is that one can define "adequate", which it is not always easy to do. In this context it turned out that the question could be begged because of the accuracy exhibited by the model's predictions. However, another aspect of the word "adequacy", particularly when one is constructing a general program of this type, is the need to satisfy oneself that the prediction will be accurate not only at the, in this case, dozen or so collieries where the model was thoroughly tested, but also when it comes to be applied at the remaining hundreds of pits. We satisfied ourselves on this point, although it must be conceded that not all doubts were removed, by testing many of the statistical and other assumptions in the model against themselves, so to speak. Thus we tested whether predictions of performance were significantly altered by assuming that times to cut a face were normally distributed or uniformly distributed compared with the log-normal distribution we had found to be a good fit on the faces for which data had been analysed. Similarly, tests were carried out to examine the sensitivity of the predictions to different delay patterns and so on. Again, somewhat to our surprise, these tests indicated a surprising lack of sensitivity to most of the basic assumptions. It seemed, for example, that, for most likely statistical distributions of cutting-time performance, predictions would be broadly the same; only in the extreme case in which we were bold enough to test the effect of no variability[1] were the predictions seriously different. One must refrain (with some reluctance) from drawing the obvious generalization from this result. However, it does at least appear likely that such testing of simulation models might remove doubts about their validity in other similar circumstances.

To turn now to implementation, it might be appropriate first to remark on a positive advantage of simulation as a technique: it is easily understood by the practical man, who is therefore well disposed to accept the validity of results obtained from it. This was certainly our experience in helping to implement the use of the programs. Indeed, it might almost be argued that simulation is too readily accepted by management who, in our experience, sometimes confuse the simulation with reality and forget that the simulation is merely a model. Be that as it may, the nature of simulation undoubtedly gets off to a flying start in implementation.

As one would expect in such a large organization as the NCB, with so many people to convince, the implementation strategy involved a good deal of effort. Line management, the men who will take the decisions based on the use of the programs, were given an appreciation of the programs. This took the form of a one-day exercise in general management courses in which the managers were presented with a colliery plan and asked to suggest a transport system, their proposals being evaluated overnight on the computer and the results communicated to them. The wide diversity of plans proposed by the managers indicated both the difficulty of the problem and also the arbitrariness of the methods available to them for its solution. It was gratifying for the OR people and sobering for the managers, the great majority of whom left the course convinced of the program's potential. Week-long courses for potential users of the programs were also mounted. Planning and method-study engineers came along to these courses with problems of current interest to them, and a good deal of the course was spent in practical work, filling in the data sheets and interpreting the results appropriate to the problems they had brought with them. In total, it is estimated that between three and four manyears of OR and Method Study effort went into the implementation. This includes not only the training but also the initial assistance given to the program-users back in their Areas. (It is of interest to note that the implementation effort fell not far short of the effort needed to develop the programs.) However, the implementation was outstandingly successful, and the programs have been widely used; in many cases demonstrable cash savings have been made.

Studies of Spare Face Requirements

The second problem to be discussed in more detail is the question of how many spare faces to have at a colliery. The main reason for choosing this example is that two attacks on this problem were made, separated by about five years. The first was unsuccessful in terms of implementation. The second was more successful, but cannot yet be judged a complete success. It is interesting to speculate how these levels of implementation arose.

The bones of the practical problem have been described above. One might have enough face workers at a colliery to man a half dozen faces on three shifts. Geological conditions are unpredictable. If, for unexpected geological reasons, one of these faces has to stop, production is lost and resources, including men, are idle. At the cost of investing in an extra face, or more generally extra faces, one could insure against this loss of production. The question is how many spare faces at any given colliery is it worth while to have. The extra costs incurred in having a spare face are the mining costs of developing it before it is strictly necessary, and the capital costs of equipping it (there is little point in a spare face not being fully equipped because it would take so long to move the equipment from the discarded face to the spare). To answer the question one therefore needs to estimate these costs. This is comparatively straightforward, although some rather nice points about opportunity costing are involved. What is less straightforward is to estimate the gain from having a spare face. Clearly, this depends on the degree of risk in the particular seam and on the efficiency with which the men are likely to work on a strange face if they are transferred to it. One might elaborate a good deal on this point, but let us suppose that this gain can be predicted.

In detail, both the costs and the gains will vary from colliery to colliery. If, as was the case, one wishes to develop a general method for tackling this problem that can be used at local level, an interesting question is how many of the costs can be built in, that is treated as the same for all collieries, and which should be left to be estimated by the man on the spot.

The earlier approach was to present a graph to the planners that enabled them to assess how many spare faces to have, provided they carried out all the costing themselves and provided also that they were willing and able to estimate the proportion of time for which the spare face would be used. Some notes of general guidance were also given to them which, it was hoped, would enable them to take a sensible view of the costing exercise. Very little guidance, except by precept, was given as to how the proportion of time the spare face would be used was to be estimated.

This method was practically never used. Partly this was because the OR workers chose not to push it too hard, because the gains from the right decision as opposed to what people were doing was, at that time, not too big (this was in the days when there was still much handling at the coalface and neither the cost of a spare face nor the loss in the absence of a spare face when it was needed were as big as for present-day highly capital-intensive faces). Even so, such attempts as were made to get the method used failed.

Some years later a senior official asked that a second look should be taken at the problem. Because of increased mechanization and the consequently larger cash flows involved, the problem was now more important; and moreover there was a spirited discussion among mining engineers about the whole question of spare faces. Everyone knew an OR study of the question was being made and there was a strong interest in the study. This time round the approach to the problem scarcely differed at all in terms of how the method should be presented to the planners. First, whatever costs could be built into the model — and sensitivity analysis was the guiding principle here — were built in. Second, quite specific methods were suggested for evaluating the other costs. For example, rather than a vague injunction to estimate the running costs of the equipment on the coalface, a table was provided giving estimates of these costs for different types of equipment, different lengths of face, etc. Third, a good deal of research was carried out into how the proportion of time the spare face was needed could be best estimated. In this way, one was able to say in what circumstances it would be prudent to use last year's figures as an estimate of next year's, in what circumstances it would be more prudent to use two years' records, and in what circumstances one should use different estimates for different seams within a pit. The user of the method still had to refer to a graph like the previous one. It was a simple graph which was not certain to be accurate for any specific colliery, but was judged to be accurate enough, and

certainly more likely to generate acceptance than a graph with many lines each corresponding to a different combination of colliery factors. It was possible to simplify the graph because the nature of the problem is such that the choice has to be made from among very few alternatives and the total economics is very insensitive to the choice made at the boundary between, say, one and two spare faces. This method was widely adopted, though still not universally. What lessons, if any, can be drawn?

First, why was the second approach more successful than the orginal? To begin with, one might ask whether the reasons for the difference in implementation lie within the approaches at all. It may be that the first approach "softened up" the organization so that the second approach had a much higher chance of success anyway; or it may be that the second approach gained from the wider acceptance, through other means, of OR involvement with this type of problem; or perhaps the problem was nearer to the top of management's minds the second time. Perhaps just as important a factor was the energetic way in which use of the method was pursued by members of the Branch, both by face-to-face contact with particular men at particular pits and also by participation in management training courses.

Second, why was even the second approach by no means totally successful? Again, the answer might have nothing to do with the method. For example, the problem is one on which strong opinions are held; when emotions run high, OR does not find its easiest converts. Perhaps one-third of senior management could not, at the emotional level, accept spare faces. In other cases, local management has its own method of deciding on the number of spare faces, which it is happy with and which very commonly gives the right answer, or a good answer, anyway. In such circumstances the new untried method is unlikely to usurp the proven if not quite optimal approach.

When all these things are said, one overriding question remains: is a responsible decision-maker ever going to accept a technique, however easy and however well explained, which generates his decisions for him? This question takes an extreme view of the methods described above; clearly they do not take the decisions or force them on the decision-maker, but one wonders if it looks that way to him. Certainly, in the NCB recent experience has been that what the decision-maker at this level of non-routine decision wants is tools to help him to make the decision and not decision-making tools. The simulation models described in earlier sections, with their emphasis on evaluating alternatives put up by the decision-maker in a manner he can understand, with their sense of being models to be played with in order, by experimentation, to understand the system he is taking decisions about, have been far more widely used and accepted than any optimizing techniques. Perhaps there is a moral here.

A Study of the Frequency of Overhaul

Shortly after the completion of the first OR study of engineering topics, and arising from the discussions of it, it was agreed that the frequency with which power loaders should be overhauled was a suitable subject for examination. This study appealed to the OR men since it had become clear that, while savings due to better stock control policies could be large, it ought to be possible to make even larger savings through studying the consumption of spare parts and this could only be studied by in turn studying policies on overhaul and maintenance. The topic was also one on which there were strong opinions but comparatively few facts.

The basic problem is one common to all situations in which machines are used. It should perhaps be noted, however, that there is in fact a hierarchy of problems. In the first place, one must decide whether it is worth while to have a uniform policy at all, other than the trivial policy of leaving every engineer to make up his own mind. In coalmining the conditions under which machines work are so variable from place to place, and from time to time in the same place, that no policy might be the best policy. The next question is: if a uniform policy seems desirable, what type of policy should it be? How much initiative should be left to the local engineer? Should the criterion of "age" of machine be years or tons produced or what? Having decided these matters, control parameter estimation is relevant.

The essential circularity of the arguments in the previous paragraph will not be lost to the reader. Thus one can, strictly, only decide whether to have a uniform policy by costing out its implications which in turn means determining control parameters for all feasible

policies and so on. This is a common enough situation in OR and one simply has to break into the circle somewhere. The point is not developed in general terms any further but it will be seen in what follows to have lain behind some of the difficulties experienced in this work.

What was actually done was to collect data from about thirty coalfaces on the costs, for each of the three major units of the machine in question, of underground repairs, lost tonnage, and the workshop overhaul when the unit was removed from the face. The statistical analysis of these data (in itself not a straight-forward task) showed that the average cost per ton of coal produced was less the longer the unit was on the face. This suggested that the units should be left on the face as long as possible. The main argument in favour of the then policy of withdrawing machines for overhaul after a fixed amount of work was, of course, that this would minimize the chance of units breaking down on the face and save the expensive loss of coal caused by a breakdown. The pattern of breakdowns was therefore examined in particular detail. Some of the findings might be of more general interest. For example, it was found that breakdowns to the machine as a whole were due almost entirely to breakdowns of only one of the three units. Moreover, although this unit broke down more frequently, it seemed to be just as likely to break down when it had cut a small yardage. Examination of the types of breakdown also suggested that many of the major breakdowns were the results of damage rather than wear, tending to bear out the hypothesis that breakdowns were largely independent of the age of the machine, at least within the range of ages observed.

These results suggested that the period between overhauls should be extended. There was also some statistical evidence to suggest that yardage of coal cut was a good measure of age. No machine had cut along a face more than 90,000 yards, so it was not possible to recommend that machines should run beyond this limit, but it was suggested that trials should be undertaken to see what the effect of cutting to higher yardages would be. It was also recommended that the unit that had broken down should be repaired on the face if possible; or, if not, that only it and not the complete machine should be replaced. This was already done to some extent, but there was a fear that changing units underground would lead to entry of dirt into the machine and consequent breakdown or loss of performance. A study of twenty-five such replacements showed that there was no such effect.

Though it was not possible to say definitely when a spare unit should be held underground, it was clear that it was worth while to hold some commonly used spares near the face. This was because time would otherwise be lost in bringing the spares from the surface. A list of such spares was suggested.

The results were enthusiastically received at senior levels of management. Similar studies, with broadly similar results, were carried out for other machines and there was a strong push from senior management to get the recommended policies implemented.

At lower management levels, however, the situation did not appear anything like as clear-cut, nor did the proposals seem sensible. The policy was, in fact, adopted in some Areas quite willingly, and in others it was forced on Area staff. Basically, however, there were two objections, though they became apparent only after a good deal of discussion. The main objection to the results of the study was that it had assumed that any policy of setting a target yardage for withdrawal would involve setting the same target for each face. It was argued that what should be done was to set a different yardage for each face based on the engineer's experience. How could this experience be incorporated into any agreed procedure? Second, from the engineering point of view, the policy for withdrawal was only part of a general drive to treat machinery properly rather than as inanimate blocks of metal. The whole effect on this drive needed to be considered.

This case study therefore serves to illustrate one of the main factors which the OR man has to be aware of when developing a new system — what does it look like at the receiving end? The engineer at colliery level is paid for his skill or experience; if you override this, then you lose what you pay him for. Your system must allow for this. You must also look at the pressures on him. The colliery engineer reports to the colliery manager and will be in trouble if a machine breaks down and loses production. He is less likely to be in trouble if he withdraws the machine too early; it is difficult to prove in the first place, and the cost

probably does not come back to him later.

On this issue, at any rate, the lesson has been learnt. Research is continuing, on a closer joint basis to try to develop a means of providing information that will help the engineer to give his advice. In the meantime, the work has proved of wider value than at one stage it appeared. The ideas generated are widely known and are becoming more readily accepted. The OR man can as easily claim too little as too much.

Stock Contol of Spares for Coalface Machinery

The background against which the work originated is important and is worth reiterating. In the late fifties when power-loading machines were first beginning to be used in large numbers at the coalface, they were unreliable, and repairs on the face were a common cause of production delay. Obviously, then, the supply of spares played a major role. Adequate service was essential, but overinvestment in stock was to be avoided. By the end of the decade the NCB had set up a system of about 35 large central stores, which were replenished by deliveries from manufacturers. In turn, each of these stores was responsible for topping up stocks in about 20 stores, one at each colliery served. Two questions were posed: how much stock should be held in each of these 35 central stores and 700 colliery stores? and when should an individual spare be replenished and by how much? These were the questions the OR Branch set out to answer.

After preliminary studies in which several alternative approaches were tried, a series of decisions was taken that determined the shape of the system to be designed. First, it was decided the aim of the system would be to minimize the total of the costs of holding stocks, or losing production if spares were not immediately available, and of administering the stores system. This was felt to be less arbitrary than the alternative, that of giving a particular level of service. Second, since most breakdowns could be repaired by replacing one part, and since there was no gain in considering parts jointly from the ordering and purchasing points of view, it was decided that items could be treated independently. The effect of this was that the policy which minimized the total cost for each spare individually also minimized the total cost for the whole inventory of items, and was therefore the optimum policy. Third, the cost of shortages was taken to be proportional to the number of items short, rather than the duration of the shortage, since action either had to be taken immediately (if production was disrupted) or could wait until the normal delivery was made. Fourthly, a re-order level and re-order quantity system was preferred to the cyclic review system most used at that time in the NCB. The latter has advantages from the point of view of organizing clerical labour, but these were felt to by outweighed by the facility to take actions as and when required. Thorough studies, however, predicted that the total cost for a typical group of spares would be about 16 per cent higher on cyclical review than on re-order levels; stocks would be lower, but this would be more than outweighed by increases in administrative and shortage costs. Finally, forecasting; this would remain the responsibility of the stores clerks.

A study of the pattern of demand in the lead-time showed that this followed Poisson's distribution for low demands. For high demands, a normal distribution was appropriate; however, an empirical relationship was found which enabled the variability of demand in the lead-time to be calculated from the average demand rate and the duration of the lead-time. Thus for both high and low demand rates the variability of demand in the lead-time was specified in terms of its average.

The problem of estimating shortage costs for spares was next tackled. Experience showed that very different courses of events took place when different underground machinery spares were short, so that a single shortage cost would be inaccurate if used for all items. However a pattern emerged which was used to group the spares into a small number of categories for stock control purposes. First, if production was lost when the part broke, the spare was termed priority. If not, the cost of shortage was merely the extra administrative actions needed to replenish it; these were estimated at five shillings if the shortage occured at a colliery and £2 if at a central store. If the spare was priority, then administrative costs were negligible compared with the cost of extra production lost due to the shortage. This depended upon the rate at which production was being lost (a standard figure being assumed for all coalfaces) and the time it took to get an emergency delivery. This time in turn depended

on whether the spare could be carried to the face by a miner. If so it was termed portable. The additional time to get a portable spare to the coalface from a central store rather than from a colliery store was found to be about an hour, which at the time corresponded to a loss of £20. Surprisingly, non-portable spares could be got to the coalface as quickly from central stores as from colliery stores, partly because of better handling facilities and partly because the time taken to organize transport of the spare underground was often sufficient to make some lateness in arrival of the spare irrelevant anyway. Thus there was no shortage cost at colliery stores for non-portable spares and therefore we recommended they should be completely centralized. At central stores, the shortage cost of priority non-portable spares was high. Since none were to be held at collieries a central shortage implied lost production and the cost was determined by the time needed to get an emergency delivery from a *supplier* or from a neighbouring Area; a figure of £85 was used. Finally, a central shortage of a priority portable spare was not serious, because demands would normally be to replenish colliery stocks. The cost was administrative and, like non-priority spares, equal to £2. These costs are summarized in the following table:

	Colliery stores		Area central stores	
	Priority	Non-priority	Priority	Non-priority
Portable	£20	£0.25	£2	£2
Non-portable	—	—	£85	£2

These costs have a powerful effect on the distribution of stocks. At collieries, only portable spares are held and the stockholding is composed largely of priority spares. At central stores, stocks are fairly low for all categories except priority non-portable spares; high stocks of these are held at this one point for the Area as a whole. The system thus tends to hold high stocks of important items at the point where they are most useful, to hold low stocks of unimportant items, and to avoid duplication of stockholding.

A system based on the above work was given a field trial in one of the Areas highly regarded in the Board for the quality of its stock control. The trial showed that the system would reduce stocks by one-eighth, administrative costs by a quarter, and shortages by a half. Purchasing and Stores Department recommended all Areas in the Board to use the system, which was published in 1961 as OR Branch Technical Note No. 75, and became known as TN 75.

In the years following the publication of TN 75, several Area Central Stores and colliery stores began to use the system. Very few used the system in total, though most Areas used some part of it. What were the drawbacks?

The first stumbling-block met in implementing the total system was the difficulty in getting some Areas to categorize spares as priority, portable, etc. The reasons were either that qualified engineers with experience of spares usage underground were not available or that the size of the job (up to 20,000 spares in some Areas) was daunting. Areas not categorizing used the £20 tables for all spares at collieries and the £2 tables for all spares at central stores. The effect of this was that the expected centralization of stocks, which was to have accounted for most of the stock reduction, did not materialize. Nevertheless, where this modified system was tried, it proved popular with the clerks, who rapidly proved a re-order level system was practicable, and who enjoyed having a guide to their decisions.

More serious problems were to come, however. The first stemmed from the original decision to adopt total cost as a criterion. Purchasing and Stores Department is itself controlled by the Board on total stock value; no quantitative measure of service given is demanded of it and records of the actual service given are not made as a routine. The original field trial was acceptable because it promised a stock reduction of one-eighth, with an additional free bonus of a reduction in shortages. However, as the commercial tide began to flow more strongly against coal, the Board set lower and lower permitted stock levels and by 1963-4 the stocks given by TN 75 were no longer within the budget allowed. This problem was deferred by the publication of a new set of tables based on a higher notional cost of holding stock, which naturally gave lower stock levels.

A second problem arising from the adoption of total cost as a criterion has already been mentioned earlier in the chapter, namely that expensive spares, even if quite frequently used, tended to run out more often than was felt by the stock controllers to be right.

Arbitrary revisions were made to the tables to take account of this feeling but, unless the revisions went so far as to restore stock to its former level, they seemed incapable of pleasing everyone.

In any case, however, two trends in external events have taken place in recent years that have diminished the appropriateness of TN 75. First, there has been a switch in maintenance policy. The original machines have become reliable and hence repairs on the face are less frequent. At the same time there has been an increasing tendency to hold spare machine sections at the face-end; when breakdowns occur, the section is replaced rather than the machine being stripped and the broken part being replaced by a spare. Thus there is no need for a wide range of spares at collieries. The only spares usage on the face today tends to be replacement of external parts that suffer damage. At the same time, the volume of section overhauls in central workshops has greatly increased, giving rise to a need for very good service from the central store, which is usually adjacent to the workshop. A poor service leads to large quantities of machinery held up in various states of repair, an intolerable idle investment. Since spares tend to be used as part of kits on these overhauls, the TN 75 assumption that the demands for different spares are independent is no longer strictly true.

The second external trend is a result of the Board's 1967 reorganization, which left colliery stores under local control, but placed central stores and workshops under a national authority. Subsequently, rationalization occurred. No longer was one workshop responsible for all machinery in one Area; one workshop now tends to repair one type of machine for several Areas. One purpose of this is that lower stockholding is in theory possible. However, no great reduction occurs if TN 75 tables are used. This follows from the relations between variability of demand in the lead-time and average demand in the lead-time. The value found for the original central stores no longer applies to the new rationalized stores. This is one of a large number of assumptions that need revising as time passes. Another is the rate at which production is lost; the run-out cost on a face is now very much greater. Some of these changes can be taken care of by altering parameters in the original calculations, some may need more drastic change. As so often happens, it might have been better to provide the department concerned with the means of doing the calculation, rather than to have done them for them.

The upshot of all this is that TN 75 is obsolescent. This is, incidentally, no surprise — a paper describing the system estimated its life as about five years and, on this criterion, it is already living on borrowed time. Ironically, use of it is perhaps as high now as it has ever been, but mainly because no better system is at present available. A new computerized system is now being developed, which will have the immediate advantage that stock control policies can be amended by Purchasing and Stores Department simply by writing to the computer centre. There is no longer a practical problem in changing the control levels for 20,000 items. The technical categorization into portable priority spares and so on has been abandoned and all items are now treated equally. The program will still minimize total cost, but the values fed in for the unit stockholding, ordering, and shortage costs will be under the direct control of Purchasing and Stores Department staff. This will enable them to adjust stock levels, service levels, and administrative effort directly. (In other words, the new system will, in some measure at least, be adaptive, that is its detailed operation can be changed in response to some types of change in the environment. Clearly adaptive systems are desirable, but whether the original changes in environment is an interesting speculation.) Research is now concentrating on the problem of how managers can know the effects, in both the short and the long run, of a change in control parameters. The computerized system will include a forecasting subsystem using such techniques as exponential smoothing and tracking signals, but the key problem in forecasting is how to incorporate the clerk's local knowledge, which may have been informally picked up in the Miner's Welfare Club.

Evaluation of Contract Tenders

In order to understand this study we must first define more precisely the problem of the purchasing officer. He is responsible for placing orders to ensure availability of previously determined quantities of material in accordance with previously determined specifications. We may consider him, to begin with, as having a list of quantity and quality specifications, but not having made any formal approach to possible suppliers. He will, however, have probably grouped the materials under certain broad headings (for example, tyres) each heading corresponding to a general type of material of which it is likely that a supplier of any single one item (for example, radial-ply tyres of a certain size) can supply several, if not all, of the items. In the NCB as in many large organizations, use is made of this grouping in order to obtain quantity discounts or deferred rebates. Such a grouping is also in the interest of the manufacturers since, when tendering, they will be able to take account of interactions in their own manufacturing processes among items in the group.

The purchasing officer now receives tenders from his suppliers, and he must decide, on the basis of these tenders, precisely what contracts to place with each supplier. In the NCB, contracts are mostly placed for a year. However, it would plainly be wrong to place the contracts in such a way as to achieve least cost in the immediate coming year if there were any risk that by so doing the purchasing officer was jeopardizing the future. Thus the placing of too small a contract might, in extreme cases, put the relevant supplier out of business, thus reducing competition in future years; even if the effect were not as extreme as that, the supplier might feel obliged to reduce research and development, to forgo investment in more up-to-date plant, and so on, thus increasing the chance of a higher price being asked in future years. The purchasing officer normally has a good idea of the effect that fluctuating contracts from year to year will have on a supplier. More likely than not there will be maximum and minimum cash purchases from each supplier beyond which the purchasing officer is not willing to go.

It is clear that a good deal of arithmetic has somehow to be done. Even with a simple price structure it would probably not be all that easy to decide what materials to order from whom, and the decision is made doubly difficult by the fairly complicated discount structures most suppliers seem to offer. Discounts tend to be given for total business. This means that the price of each item depends not only on the quantity of that item bought from the supplier, but also on the quantity of other items bought as well.

It is therefore difficult to work out manually

an allocation of business that satisfies all the restrictions and takes best advantage of all discounts. However, the problem can be set up as a non-linear programming problem and this has been done. The mathematical detail of this formulation will not be given, but it might be worth while to discuss exactly what features of the problem can be incorporated in the formulation.

First, the types of discount structure mentioned above can be quite easily formulated, as can the initial quantity and quality specifications.

Second, the commercial considerations also mentioned above have to be formulated in some way. One must try to develop formulations that enable the purchasing officer to simulate his commercial judgement above what the market can stand in the senses discussed above. One obvious facility of this type is to include restrictions that bind the amount ordered from a given supplier within limits. Generally, this restriction will be imposed on the total business placed with that supplier. However, in some cases it may be preferable to impose restrictions of the quantities of each item to be bought from each supplier, while in other cases one may wish to place orders in such a way that a given item is ordered from at least, say, three suppliers. The point here is that one might want to maintain a competitive situation by purchasing a particular item from several manufacturers, even though one manufacturer could supply all one's needs at a lower cost than can be obtained by spreading the purchase; alternatively, one might want to force the market in the opposite direction to encourage specialization. Restrictions to take account of these considerations can quite easily be built in.

In a complete model of the market, it would be nice to think that such features as manufacturers' delivery performance, the amount of product development he carries out, and other features that might be put under the heading of supplier's performance, could be quantified. In practice, however, we have not yet attempted

to do this and such considerations can only be taken account of by the purchasing officer using his judgement.

The computer program which has been developed to carry out this programming exercise has certainly proved useful and has led to rewarding results in the placing of contracts for which it has been used. A side gain from this system is that the purchasing officer is enabled to find out how much immediate cash he is paying in order to satisfy commercial restrictions by quite straightforward use of shadow prices and parametric programming.

Ideally, we should like to reach the stage where the purchasing officers themselves use the program without any OR assistance. There is no difficulty in principle about doing so — the purchasing officers themselves understand clearly the way to use the program and their staff could readily fill in the data sheets — but there are difficulties in detail. Some examples of these difficulties follow; they may be interesting as illustrative of the practical considerations that need to be taken into account in implementing a system of this type.

In the first place, the method is quite expensive in computer time — the basic difficulty with non-linear programs is that they can take a long time to reach even a good solution. The disadvantage of this is not only cost, but also speed of turnround — in the rush to place contracts three turnrounds a day is obviously of more value than one. In order to keep costs within reasonable bounds it is therefore desirable to make some preliminary specifications, aimed at reducing running-time without too much loss in validity of results, before putting the data to the computer. The running-time is critically dependent on the number of non-linearities a program has to consider, and therefore one of the simplifications consists of reducing this number. In practice, this could boil down to combining discount steps. Another simplification has been to combine certain types of commodity that are similar in both a physical and a price sense and to treat them as a single commodity.

NOTES

[1] It should perhaps be explained that the superimposition of production rates from several coalfaces, even if it were assumed that while producing each face produced at a constant rate, would itself give rise to a variable pattern of production because the faces would be expected to be out of phase.

This paper is based on a draft by George Mitchell, Terry Dobson, and Doug Wood.

ABOUT THE AUTHOR

Rolfe C. Tomlinson is at present Managing Director of the Operational Research Executive of the (British) National Coal Board, having previously been Director of O.R. in the same organisation. He has been concerned with Operational Research studies in this field for some years, and has written a number of papers on the subject.

The Re-Organization of Community Nursing in Westmorland

A. Hindle and G. Gregory

This very successful case study illustrates the way in which standard O. R. models developed in the industrial context can be adapted to deal with community services problems. Although many simplifying assumptions have to be made they are tested where possible and use is made of "sensitivity analysis" where data are inadequate. Sensitivity analysis is a useful precautionary measure. If a set of data is considered unreliable, one substitutes a variety of different values and recalculates the solution. If the answer still comes out more or less the same, then one's confidence is increased. If, however, the solution is substantially altered by the change in data, then one becomes more cautious, and, if possible, tries to collect better data. The models used in this study derive from "travelling salesman" situations where the concern is to minimise the expected mileage in making a number of calls.

I INTRODUCTION

In 1971 a staff-student team from the department of Operational Research at the University of Lancaster began a study to deduce the consequences, in terms of cost and nursing provided, of alternative schemes for the organisation and management of the community nursing services in rural Westmorland. The study made recommendations in two parts:
  (a) A new management structure for Westmoreland's community nurses.
  (b) A re-organisation of the nursing service bringing a closer liason with the region's general practioners.
Clearly (a) and (b) above are closely interrelated, and they were treated as such by the project team. The main O.R. interest is contained in the approach to part (b) which is described below.

Communication between general practitioners and community nurses was, prior to the study, largely on an *ad hoc* basis, depending very much on personalities. Since, in England, the parties involved are funded by different authorities it is not surprising that problems can arise, particularly in passing on full information about the conditions of patients. There are clear advantages - centralisation of records, regular communication - in having nursing teams "attached" to general practices, i.e. with doctor and nurse working as a team. (Before the study the nurse provided services to a distinct geographical district, not to a particular doctor's patients.) In addition, the concept was proposed of an integrated nursing team of variously qualified nurses which should mean more effective nursing, where nurses will do the work for which they have been trained, instead of the previous system of having a highly qualified nurse responsible for all home nursing work in a relatively small region.

All this could not be achieved without some cost. If a nursing team is attached to a general practice, they will have to travel to some of the practice's outlying patients. Furthermore effective nursing will only be achieved with planning and this takes time and therefore costs money. The benefit should be in a healthier community and in the job satisfaction of the nurses.

Probably most areas in England would claim some peculiarity which makes them different from the rest. Westmorland makes a convincing case on three counts. It is a large

SOURCE: Reprinted from *Community Nursing in Westmorland* by G. Gregory and A. Hindle, Unit for Operational Research in the Health Services, Department of Operational Research, University of Lancaster, England. (December 1972), by permission of the authors.

county (789 square miles), it has a relatively small population (approx. 72,000), yielding the lowest population density amongst English counties, and it supports a higher percentage of the population aged over 65 than the national average. Each of these factors must produce a more expensive nursing service.

The problem, in essence, is one of striking a balance between the benefits of "attachment" of nurses to doctors and the increased costs which would be incurred due to the extra travelling, since the geographical areas covered by doctor's patients overlap to a considerable degree.

II ALTERNATIVE SCHEMES

As part of the management structure, nursing teams of between two and five nurses were to be set up, each team being responsible to an area nursing manager. The problem of deciding on the community to be served by a team was a compromise between area covered by the team and the level of attachment achieved. At one extreme, if full attachment is desired, the team is attached to one or more general practices and it nurses all patients registered with the practices. Considerable overlap in the areas covered must ensue. At the other extreme the county would be divided into nursing team regions and the nurses attached to whichever practice or practices are predominant in the region. This can produce a reasonably high level of attachment, attachment being measured as the proportion of the population nursed by a team attached to the practice with which the individuals are registered. An important consideration is that once attachment has been introduced, the communication problems between nurses and general practitioners for non-attached patients are multiplied, so that even with an attachment rate as high as seventy-five per cent (a level achieved by one proposal) it is doubtful if the scheme would work because of administrative difficulties. It was decided therefore to find a scheme with a high level of attachment, accepting some overlap of team regions.

III THE TEAM REGIONS

Data were available on the numbers of

individuals in each parish (the basic geographical/administrative unit) registered with each medical practice. A map of patient density could therefore be built up for each practice and rules formulated for the allocation of parishes to practices. Most parishes have only one population centre, and they form a fine enough division to make regions which could not be improved by further sub-division. The quartiles of parish populations are 101 and 520.

As a first attempt we operated a rule whereby any parish with 50 or more people registered with a practice must be included in the region served by a team attached to that practice. If the number was between 25 and 50 the same rule was applied whenever the parish fitted in with adjacent parishes, thereby forming a cohesive nursing team region. The solution found by using these rules was robust in the sense that changes in the critical values 25 and 50 did not appreciably change the regions.

Use of these rules produced the gratifyingly high level of attachment of 97.6 per cent. This very high level is largely the result of people registering with doctors who are conveniently located. The remaining 2.4 per cent have chosen a less convenient practice or have moved into a different parish and wish to keep the services of their family doctor. It was felt that this number would be low enough so that any loss through being treated by a non-attached nursing team would be made up by "special case" consideration. Part of the job of the new "Area Manager" is to monitor such cases.

The overlap between nursing regions was approximately twenty-five per cent of the area of the county, but as most of this was rural, this figure exaggerates the time spent by nurses in overlapping regions.

IV LEVEL OF NURSING SERVICE

It is doubtful if there will ever be an entirely satisfactory measure of nursing service. The basic reason is the impossibility of assessing quantitatively (preferably costing) the benefit received by a patient from a nursing call. We have tried to overcome this by showing the effect in terms of the average number of calls possible per working day when the resources (i.e. nurses) are all given strengths. This in turn implies a demand rate for calls per person per day, and this is taken as the level of service provided. Over the last ten years in Westmorland the actual demand rate has remained stable at 0.003, or approximately one call per person per year on average. It might be more appropriate to call this the supply rate.

A further point about level of service is concerned with the differently qualified nurses in the team. If, as is intended, each nurse carries out appropriate duties, and if each team is composed of just one nurse at any level of qualification, then each nurse will cover the whole region and the total level of service will be the sum of the levels for each member of the team. The only teams wherein there is duplication in the qualifications of the nurses are those whose regions cover the more densely populated regions and it would be pointless to divide a town into sub-regions for the different nurses. Thus the assumption that each nurse covers the whole region is justifiable for all teams. What is at present unknown is the relative incidences of calls for the different levels of nursing and the average times per call for such different levels, but the model used (and described below) is sufficiently flexible to absorb these data when they become available.

V THE MODEL

The model assumes that the working day of the nurse is divided into three phases:
  (a) administration/communication
  (b) travelling
  (c) visiting
The time for administration and communication is simply a period which must be subtracted from the working day of the nurse. The amount subtracted will depend on the status of the nurse within the team.

To estimate the times for travelling and visiting, we need a model which explains the behaviour of the nurse in terms of the area and population covered and of the demand for her services.

On any day as the nurse plans her route for a given set of calls, she is faced with a "travelling salesman" problem. However it should be noted that the nurse may need to return to the nursing "centre" once or more during the day. This nursing centre may be at a Health Centre, a general practitioner's

surgery or the nurse's home. Our main task was to determine the average distance travelled when reasonably optimum daily routes were planned. The results of Beardwood, Halton and Hammersley[1] and Christofides and Eilon[2] were used as will be shown. Several assumptions were made:

(1) Every individual in the region has the same (small) probability p of requiring a visit on any day. The parameter p is the service level defined in the previous section. This is clearly an over-simplification. Many calls are made on a regular basis over a relatively short period of time. This should not affect the average travelling distance, but it does ignore the correlation of distances from day to day. Occasionally patients may need regular visits during the day (e.g. for insulin injections).

(2) The demand generated in any day is met on that day. Clearly in practice if a call is not urgent and is close to the end of her route, the nurse is likely to postpone it to the following day. The lengths of the working day will thus tend to be averaged out. Since we shall determine a criterion dependent on an *average* demand, this departure from reality in the model should not be serious.

(3) The nurse does not adjust her working rate (either in the length of visit or travelling speed) to meet the workload of the day. Again in practice the hours actually put in will be more even than our model would suggest, but in terms of averages the agreement should be good.

(4) The daily route of the nurse consists of two components:
  (a) between parishes
  (b) within parishes.
Thus she travels to the population centre of each parish where she has one or more calls to make, and then within that parish to make these calls. The assumption is justified by the fact that parishes have one village or small town which is the intersection of main roads, and the nurse would therefore almost inevitably pass through this centre. It is possible of course that she may have made calls on her way into the parish centre and thus there would be no need for "within parish" travelling. This means that our estimate would tend to be high, but since the "within" component is much less than the "between" it was considered unnecessary to make the adjustments.

Suppose now that a region consists of m parishes with populations $k_1, k_2, \ldots k_m$ in areas $a_1, a_2, \ldots a_m$. Let the distances of the parish centres from the nurse's home or base be $d_1, d_2, \ldots d_m$. The total estimated travelling distance

$$\overline{D}_T = \overline{D}_B + \overline{D}_W$$

where D_B and D_W are the between and within parish travelling distances. (Both of these are random variables because of the stochastic demand and we use $\overline{D_B}$, $\overline{D_W}$ to denote estimates of the average values of D_B and D_W.)

Using the Christofides-Eilon formula for D_B we have

$$D_B = 1.8 \frac{D_R}{C} + 1.1(a)^{\frac{1}{4}} (D_R)^{\frac{1}{2}}$$

where D_R = the sum of *radial* distances from the nursing centre to the centres of the parishes visited

A = the area of the region served by the nurse.

The critical parameter is clearly C which is meant to indicate the maximum number of calls which can be made on any trip before a return to base. If the nurse could complete all the calls for the day without a return to the nursing centre, then the first term in the expression is eliminated. However, nurses will rarely do a single complete round during the day. Unfortunately the data required to estimate C is difficult to collect and we did not attempt a detailed survey of this. Instead we determined the sensitivity of the mileage "ratios" for alternative nursing organisations to various reasonable values of C. The regions are very approximately square in shape, and we have taken $(A)^{\frac{1}{2}}$ as the length of the side of the equivalent square, where A is the area of the region. Also the scatter of parish centres within the region appears to be random. D_B is a random variable since D_R, the sum of the radial distances from the nurse's home to the centres of the parishes visited, on any particular day, is a random variable.

Thus the probability that parish i is included in the route is $1-e^{-k_iP}$. Hence the expected value of D_R is $\sum_{i=1}^{m} d_i(1-e^{-k_iP})$. Using $\sqrt{\sum_{i=1}^{m} d_i(1-e^{-k_iP})}$ for $\sqrt{D_R}$ clearly implies using a biased estimator, but nevertheless a reasonable one.

Estimation of D_W is a similar problem, except that now it is infeasible to locate all possible calls - the actual households within the parish. We use instead the formula of Beardwood, Halton and Hammersley where the distance travelled depends only on the area of the region and the number of points of call randomly scattered within it. For any parish D_W equals zero if the number of calls within the parish is either zero or one.

Thus the expected number of calls necessitating travel in parish i is

$$\sum_{j=2}^{\infty} j \frac{(k_ip)^j}{j!} e^{-k_iP} = k_iP[1-e^{-k_iP}]$$

Hence $\overline{D_W} = 0.75 \sum_{i=1}^{m} \left\{ a_i \; k_iP[1-e^{-k_iP}] \right\}^{\frac{1}{2}}$

We have once more used a biased estimator in the above. Thus the estimated total travelling distance $\overline{D_T}$ may be written as a function of p, the demand:

$$\overline{D_T}(p) = \overline{D_B}(p) + \overline{D_W}(p)$$

Computer programs have been developed for the evaluation of these functions.

VI PRESENTATION OF RESULTS

Suppose that it is agreed that a nurse is to organise her day as follows: H (hours) is the time which she spends on travelling and visiting. This is her working day apart from administrative tasks. V (hours) is the average time spent by the nurse within the home on a visit. S (miles per hour) is the average travelling speed of the nurse. Then $H = \dfrac{D_T(p)}{S} + VKp$

where $k = \sum_{i=1}^{m} k_i$, the total population within the region. Writing the relationship as

$$1 = \frac{D_T(p)}{Y} + \frac{K_p}{X}$$

where Y = HS, X = H/V, we can reduce the effects of the plan to a set of contours relating X and Y for various values of p. Thus the effect in terms of level of service, p, can be deduced for any organisation of the nurse's day. A typical set of contours is shown in figure 1.

Using this set of contours we can work through an example, as follows:

Our aim is to determine for a nursing team containing two nurses (Nurse A and Nurse B), nursing a particular region in Westmorland, the average number of visits that they can be expected to undertake per working day. The measure will be expressed as a number of visits per person (in the region) per day.

Firstly we need to calculate X and Y for each nurse where, as above, Y = HS and X = H/V.

Nurse A   H = 7 hours
           V = 20 minutes per visit
           S = 25 miles per hour
    ∴   X = 21
    and Y = 175

Nurse B   H = 8 hours
           V = 40 minutes per visit
           S = 30 miles per hour
    ∴   X = 12
    and Y = 240

Plotting these values on the graph (figure 1) we obtain values of p for the two nurses, viz.

Nurse A; p = 0.0021
Nurse B; p = 0.0018

Thus the team of nurses could provide a service level of 0.0039 visits per person per day in their particular region. Thus, if the population were 2,000 persons the team could accomplish 2,000 x 0.0039 visits per day, viz. 7.8 visits.

VII EVALUATION OF SPECIFIC PROPOSALS

Although the method described above can evaluate any specific allocation of nurses to areas within the county, three proposals were formally considered in the study and the scheme outlined in Sections II and III was one of these. Another plan was a traditional "district nursing" scheme with no overlap of nursing areas and the final plan involved "full attachment"; nurse and doctor serving identical populations. In Table I, which presents the principal results of the analysis for a part of Westmorland, these three plans are labelled "district plan", "partial attachment" and "full attachment" respectively. Some nursing mileage data after implementation of the recommended scheme are also shown in the Table.

Mileage increased by more than that forecast by the model for several reasons, among which are increased staff members, a decrease in working hours with a consequent increase in "relief" work, and a tendency for some nurses not to hand over their doctor's patients to another nurse if these patients lived outside the limits of their area. Despite these problems the nursing administration have been very satisfied with the performance of the scheme and the O.R. methodology employed has yielded valuable and gratifyingly accurate information considering the range of assumptions which had to be made.

ACKNOWLEDGEMENTS

This project was carried out under the University of Lancaster Local Authorities (Small Projects) Scheme. We would like to acknowledge the support of the University. During the study we have received help and encouragement from very many people in Westmorland - county officials, doctors and nurses. Particular mention should be made of the generous assistance of Dr. H. P. Ferrer, County Medical Officer, and Miss E. Nicholl, Superintendent Nursing Officer.

REFERENCES

[1] J. Beardwood, H. J. Halton and J. M. Hammersley (1959). The Shortest Route through many Points. *Proc. Camb. Phil. Soc.*, 55, 299.
[2] N. Christofides and S. Eilon (1969). Expected Distances in Distribution Problems. *Opl. Res. Q. 20*, No. 4, 437-443.

TABLE 1
THE PRINCIPAL RESULTS OF THE ANALYSIS OF THREE SCHEMES
FOR NURSING ORGANISATION IN NORTH WESTMORLAND

Scheme	Estimated Monthly** Mileage	Actual Mileages*
I District Plan	5174	6027
	} +8.4%	} +15%
II Partial Attachment (as implemented)	5610	6912
	} +51%	
III Full Attachment	8495	

* These are the actual monthly mileages for the region "before" and "after" implementation

** Based on   S = 20 Miles per hour
V = 20 minutes
p = 0.0030 demands per person per day

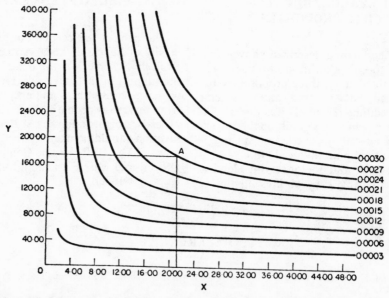

FIGURE 1.   THE EFFECT OF THE ORGANISATION OF A NURSE'S DAY ON THE LEVEL OF SERVICE SHE CAN PROVIDE.   As an example of the use of Figure 1, suppose that a nurse has 7 hr to spend on traveling and visiting. If her average time per visit is 20 min and her average travelling speed is 25 m.p.h., the resultant X and Y values are 175 and 21. The point A (175, 21) gives a p value of 0.0021 indicating that with this work pattern a service level of 2.1 calls per day per thousand people in her region could be achieved.

ABOUT THE AUTHORS

Geoff Gregory is currently Professor of Management Sciences in the Department of Management Studies of Loughborough University of Technology. He received his B.A. and M.A. from the University of Cambridge, and his M.S. and Ph.D. from Stanford. He was Tutor in O.R. at the University of Birmingham from 1958-59, and he then went to the University of Melbourne as Senior Lecturer (later Reader). From 1966-72 he was a Senior Research Fellow in the Department of Operational Research of the University of Lancaster.

Tony Hindle: See page 28.

III

THE ANALYSIS OF DECISION-MAKING

Since the aim of operations research is to assist management to determine its policy and reach decisions scientifically, it is clear that the approach implies an understanding of the decision-making process. An understanding of decision-making would seem to be a fundamental element in the rational development of the discipline and a considerable amount of research has been devoted to the problem. The level of achievement has, in some respects, been disappointing and we still know much less than we would like about the structure of choice-making at "individual", "group" and "organisational" levels. However some progress has been made and the two papers chosen for this Chapter illustrate this. They show two complementary lines of approach to the problem. In the first paper, an attempt is made to build a generalized description of the decision process, to identify the basic elements of rational choice. In the second paper the approach is normative, concentrating on the question "how ought decisions to be taken?"

Aiding the Decision-Maker — A Decision Process Model

L. P. Schrenk

The author of this paper provides a very clear description of the process of deci-sion-making. He concentrates on a single decision-maker working through the process from the definition of goals to the implementation of "action". Although intended as a descriptive model, it also has considerable value as a decision aid. Both the O.R. scientist and the manager can use it as a check-list to ensure that the decision prob-lem has been systematically tackled.

1. INTRODUCTION

Decision making is a key function performed by human operators in man-machine systems. In recent years human decision behaviour has been the subject of considerable empirical and analytical research. As a result, there is a growing body of knowledge con-cerning human as well as mathematically optimal decision processes. This paper is con-cerned with the integration and application of this knowledge to the design and operation of real-time man-machine systems. The goal is to achieve better decisions through improved structuring of the decision process and through the development and use of more effective machine aids to operator decision making.

Although the current status of relevant re-search is briefly surveyed below, the major purpose is to present a conceptual model of an idealized decision process. This model, which is derived from numerous sources and which is highly tentative, is intended to represent neither observed behaviour nor a formally optimal process. It is intended primarily as a guide to system designers and users in structuring system decision functions and as a framework for integrating know-ledge regarding operator decision behaviour. Ultimately, the model may provide a basis for task allocation, for specifying require-ments for aids to operator decision making and

for guiding further research by highlighting gaps in our knowledge.

2. OPERATOR DECISION FUNCTIONS IN ADVANCED SYSTEMS

In recent years there have been remarkable advances in machine technology, making it possible to automate many tasks which former-ly were assigned to human operators. There remain, however, certain fundamental functions which continue to require man's inclusion in complex systems. These functions, which typically involve relatively high levels of intellectual skill, include setting objectives, allocating resources, diagnosing environ-mental conditions, defining and selecting courses of action, and interpreting intricate patterns of events. Complex decision tasks of these kinds often cannot be handled by formal algorithms. In short, the prime role of man in many systems is to serve as the major decision element.

It is possible to regard virtually all aspects of human behaviour as involving decision making, in at least some limited but non-trivial way. However, this paper is concerned primarily with task situations characterized by fairly well-defined objectives, significant action alternatives, relatively high stakes, inconclusive information, and limited time for decision. Examples of such situations in-

SOURCE: Reprinted from *Ergonomics* 12 (4) July 1969, pp. 543-557, by permission of the publishers and the Ergonomics Research Society.

clude medical diagnosis and treatment, control of electrical power distribution, investment portfolio management, air traffic direction, weather forecasting, tactical command of military operations, dispatching of freight vehicles, control of manned space missions, factory production control, and many others. Increasing numbers of man-machine systems are being designed to handle these kinds of decision tasks. The proliferation of digital computers has been, of course, a prime factor in this development. Furthermore, we may expect an acceleration of the use of real-time decision systems as time-shared computer facilities become more common.

Technological innovations and more complex requirements have combined in many cases to enlarge the magnitude of the decision maker's task in man-machine systems. The scope and complexity of system activities has, in recent years, tended to increase. New capabilities for gathering, processing and displaying data have been exploited to provide greater varieties and amounts of information with higher frequency. Expanded communication capabilities have been used to provide more centralized control of widespread system operations. Often the time available for making critical decisions has diminished while the consequences of errors have grown more severe. As a result of these factors, there is an urgent requirement to evolve techniques for assisting the decision maker in complex systems.

3.   CURRENT STATUS OF DECISION RESEARCH

It is not surprising that decision making, as one of the most complex and pervasive aspects of behaviour, has received considerable study. It has been explored from many points of view — as a form of behaviour in its own right as well as in connection with many other areas of investigation. Consequently, there is an enormous and diverse literature relevant to the subject. Edwards (1954, 1961) and Becker and McClintock (1967) have provided excellent bibliographic reviews of some of this literature. Just recently, Edwards (1969) published a list of over 1300 papers concerned with behavioural decision processes. "Never again," he said.

Despite the attention they have received, I believe that it is fair to say that we are just beginning to understand human decision processes. Most of the experimental research to date has focused on highly limited and abstracted segments of decision making behaviour. Certain areas, such as man's ability to estimate simple statistical properties of event groupings (see Peterson and Beach 1967), have received much attention. Other areas, such as how people develop and use alternative hypotheses in trying to account for observed event sequences have largely been ignored. Complex decision skills need much better definition than is presently available.

One source of difficulty in attempting to assess the state-of-the-art in decision research is a surprising lack of agreement as to what constitutes a "decision". Different investigators have often meant rather different things by the term. Explicit definitions of "decision making", when they are given, generally are at variance with one another. For the present paper, decision making is defined as the selection of an alternative response to an inferred environmental situation about which complete certainty is lacking. Roby (1964) has given a somewhat similar definition.

It should be noted that psychophysical judgments regarding directly perceived events are not considered as decisions. In man-machine systems the alternative responses may be limited in number and largely pre-determined. The response alternatives may be either a set of possible conclusions regarding the environmental situation or a set of courses of action. In the latter case, one option may be to defer making a final commitment while waiting for or seeking further information.

The central problem of decision making is the resolution of inherent uncertainty, which may arise from many sources and may be concerned with a situation in the past, present or future. For example, it may reflect ambiguity as to whether some event has actually happened. It may be due to the occurrence of random events in the environment. It may be caused by unreliability in communication lines or of the information source itself. It may reflect inability to predict the outcome of some course of action. In any case, uncertainty is appropriately specified in terms of probability statements.

One view of probability is that it is the limit

approached by some long-term relative frequency. A second view is that probability is the expression of degree of belief regarding some uncertain event. Since real decision problems often involve unique events and since people can express useful opinions regarding relative event likelihoods, the subjective or "degree of belief" definition is the more useful one in dealing with operator decision processes.

Much of the research relevant to human decision making has been concerned with measuring subjective probability, with determining the identity and effects of its controlling variables, and with representing these phenomena in mathematical form. The other major parameter in behavioural decision making, value or subjectively expected utility, has received similar attention (Becker and McClintock *op. cit.*).

Research on decision processes has been done in many different contexts and, as yet, there is no adequate conceptual framework for integrating or classifying the results. Some relevant areas of study, with illustrative references, include the following: (1) statistical decision theory (Fishburn 1966); (2) game theory (Luce and Raiffa 1958); (3) concept formation (Hunt 1962); (4) problem solving (Davis 1966); (5) risk-taking aspects of personality (Slovic 1964); (6) probabilistic information systems (Edwards 1964, Briggs and Schum 1965); (7) interpersonal and group behaviour (Rim 1963); (8) signal detection (Swets *et al.* 1961); and (9) business decision making (Bierman *et al.* 1965). Of necessity, much of the above has not been considered in the present paper. Hopefully, however, the decision process concept presented later in this paper will help to provide a framework for integrating results from this diverse research, making it more usable for system design.

4. MAN AS A DECISION MAKER

What do we know about man's ability to serve as the decision-making element of a man-machine system? To begin with, he has a number of general characteristics that are relevant. For example, man can assimilate and process information only at relatively low rates and is poor at doing computations and at remembering information. Man's general capabilities

and limitations have been described many times already and do not need further elaboration here. However, there are certain properties of behaviour that are more specific to decision making. Most of these are not yet well defined but are becoming evident through the results of contemporary research.

The most common finding regarding decision behaviour is that there are significant individual differences in decision skills among people (Vernon 1957, Messick 1964). It also appears that people tend to want too much rather than too little information (Gibson and Nicol 1964, Becker and McClintock *op. cit.*) and that they may delay too long in arriving at decisions (Sidorsky and Houseman 1966, Howells and Gettys 1968). People seem unable to make full use of available information, especially when it is multi-dimensional (Rigney and Debow 1966, Kanarick *et al.* 1969). Similarly, decision makers have been found to be conservative, i.e. not to be as certain as the evidence warrants, in revising opinions on the basis of new data (Peterson and Miller 1965, Phillips *et al.* 1966). A primacy effect of giving too much weight to early information has been found (Peterson and DuCharme 1967, Dale 1968), and people appear to be unduly reluctant to change an erroneous commitment in light of new evidence (Gibson and Nicol *op. cit.*, Pitz 1969). There also is evidence that people may develop and consider too few courses of action (Kennedy and Schroder 1964, Vaughan *et al.* 1966).

Despite these limitations, people generally seem to perform surprisingly well as decision makers. They can specify probabilities with reasonable accuracy on the basis of experienced frequency (Attneave 1953, Schrenk and Kanarick 1967) and can usefully apply probability statements for decisions regarding non-frequentistic events (Beach and Wise 1968). They can understand expressed probabilities (Katter and Holmes 1965) and can judge the potential value of new information (McKendry 1965).

Most importantly, in experiments which permit an objective evaluation of human decision performance, man generally compares favourably with optimum solutions (Southard *et al.* 1964, Pitz and Downing 1967). It has been found, though, that as the decision situations becomes more complex the human decision maker shows greater divergence from mathematically optimum performance

(Kaplan and Newman 1966, Howell 1967). Nevertheless, the deviations of human from optimum performance rarely seem so large as to invalidate his potential utility as a system decision element. Despite his biases, man generally appears to give the greatest weight to the most important factors in decision problems, and to respond in appropriate ways to variations in these factors. Furthermore, people seem to show consistency in their decision-making over time (Vaughan *et al.* 1964) and seem to do certain parts of decision tasks with considerable accuracy, although sometimes with erroneous concepts of the situation (Beach 1966, Lichtenstein and Feeney 1968). These findings provide further reason to belive in the desirability of developing appropriate aids for improving decision performance.

5. IMPROVING DECISION PERFORMANCE

There are three general ways in which the performance of the human decision element in a system might be improved. The first is to select good decision makers. This approach has often been suggested but does not appear to have been seriously employed. The concept seems reasonable since people have been found to vary greatly in decision performance. However, there are some problems with this idea. For one thing, adequate criteria of "good" decision making are not available for many complex operational tasks. Usually, large numbers of identical situations cannot be obtained and in a small number of trials one cannot determine whether a desirable outcome was the lucky result of a bad decision or the expected result of a good decision. Also, a general test which might serve as a basis for selection of good decision makers has not been developed. In fact, quality of decision making may be rather task specific. A third barrier is that in real world situations other factors are usually the basis for selection. An obvious example is the selection of sonar operators on the basis of auditory acuity without consideration of their ability to evaluate and integrate multiple, probabilistic cues.

A second approach is to train people to be good decision makers. This has been attempted in various cases, but usually subsidiary to other training purposes. Training for senior military command and staff positions may be conducted through war games and exercises on paper, through simulated operations of varying degrees of realism, and through field exercises. One formal programme of instruction in decisiion making skills is a course on problem-solving techniques developed by Kepner and Tregoe (1965). The training approach to improving decision making has promise but needs further development and validation (Schroder 1965, Sidorsky and Houseman *op. cit.*, Kanarick 1969).

The third approach is to provide, through appropriate systems design, machine and procedural aids for decision makers. Human judgment would be used where required, but would be systematized and supplemented to overcome man's limitations and compensate for his biases. In the past few years there have been significant research efforts in this direction. One major area of activity has been directed toward the development of probabilistic information processing (PIP) systems. The basic concept of this kind of system is to have man define the problem and provide probability estimates and to use automatic computation to aggregate incoming information with the estimates for reaching decisions. The approach seems particularly suited to situations involving large quantities of unreliable data and short response-time requirements. Concepts for PIP systems, based on Bayesian statistics, have been explored experimentally at the University of Michigan by Edwards and his associates (Edwards 1964, Edwards *et al.* 1968), at the Ohio State University (Schum *et al.* 1966, Howell and Gettys 1968), and at the RAND Corporation (Miller *et al.* 1967). A medical forecasting application has been evaluated by Gustafson (1969). The concensus of these efforts is that better decisions are achieved by laboratory PIP systems than are obtained with unaided performance. However, validation in actual decision situations is still needed.

A number of other studies related to computer-aided decision making have been reported. Yntema and Torgerson (1961) suggested methods for having man provide a set of decision rules for computer use. This has been further explored by Pollack (1964) and Yntema and Klem (1965) with favourable results. Vaughan *et al.* (1964) developed an ingenious computer-based aid for tactical action selection.

Human judgments as to significant variables and their relative weights are presented in a readily evaluated display which also shows a recommended course of action. Schaffer (1965) studied operator monitoring of computer-derived solutions to a control problem. He found that experienced subjects improved poor solutions but degraded good ones. Shuford (1965) has reported development of an on-line decision theory system called CORTEX for computer-aided formulation and solution of problems. Another problem-solving aid concept (Gagliardi *et al.* 1965) used the computer to eliminate clearly inappropriate problem solutions in order to reduce operator workload. One other relevant programme of research, by Hanes and Gebhard (1966), has explored the usefulness and acceptability of computer aids to command decisions. They found that, under the right conditions, computer-generated advice will be accepted and can lead to improved performance.

Information display variables have been extensively studied. However, very little attention has been given to questions of how information should be encoded, organized and sequenced to facilitate operator decision processes. Studies by Herman *et al.* (1964), Ward and Jenkins (1965), and Baker and Goldstein (1966) indicate that the way in which information is encoded has important effects on decision performance. More research is needed to develop guidelines for the design of displays that will aid decision making.

To facilitate the further development of techniques for aiding real-time decision making, a better definition or model of "optimum" decision processes is required. This model should be applicable to human performance and, therefore, should not make unrealistic assumptions about levels of knowledge or information handling capabilities. Such assumptions are present in the "rational man" concepts of economic decision theory (Edwards 1954). The objective is not to specify an "ideal" decision procedure which will produce perfect choices in abstract or laboratory situations, but rather to develop a process that will yield better decisions in real situations. Such a model is consistent with ideas expressed by Back (1961), Becker and McClintock (*op. cit.*), and Raiffa (1968), and would serve several purposes. First, it should provide a framework for both classifying and integrating research findings regarding decision behaviour. Second, it should help to guide further research by highlighting gaps in our knowledge. Third, it should help to guide system designers in structuring decision tasks and in allocating decision sub-tasks to man and machine. Finally, by specifying sub-tasks in which human biases or limitations may degrade performance, guidance will be provided for the development of decision-aiding concepts.

In line with these ideas, a three-stage approach to developing decision aids is suggested. The first stage is to define in some detail the steps which compose an idealized, realistic decision process. The second stage is to specify human capabilities, limitations and tendencies for each step. The third stage is to create guidelines and methods for complementing or aiding human performance for those steps in which deficiencies are noted. This last stage may, in some cases, have to be specific to particular tasks and systems.

6. DEFINING THE DECISION PROCESS

The literature contains many statements as to what does or should constitute the process of decision making. Most of these tend to be either very general or else so highly abstracted and limited as to be essentially irrelevant to most if not all real decision problems.

The following sections present a detailed but tentative definition of an idealized-decision process. The process sequence is not intended to represent either actual decision behaviour or to fit exactly any real decision situation. Time or resource constraints might require that the process be abbreviated considerably. The model is limited in that certain important considerations are omitted. Specifically, methods for accomplishing each step are not indicated, e.g. how information should be filtered, reduced, organized and displayed. Temporal aspects of decision making are only partially indicated. In applying the model to some specific situations, the order of the steps shown could be modified or some steps might be omitted. The model shows only a single decision sequence of a series which might possibly be needed to solve a particular problem. Furthermore, although iterations within blocks of steps are to be expected, the model indicates only a few of the many possible process loops.

The decision model has been developed after considering many descriptions of decision-making processes. (The principal ones are contained in the following references: Chenzoff *et al.* 1960, Edwards 1965, Vaughan *et al.* 1964, Kepner and Tregoe *op. cit.*, Shuford *op. cit.*, Drucker 1967, Kinkade and Ranc 1967, Porter 1967, Howard 1968, and Raiffa *op. cit.*)

The model is divided into three phases. These, which are described below, are (1) problem recognition, (2) problem diagnosis, and (3) action selection.

6.1 *Problem Recognition*

The first phase of decision making is concerned with determining that a problem requiring a decision exists. Problem recognition is made up of the following steps (see Figure 1).

1. *Information input.* Typically, the first indication of a decision problem is receipt of information indicating a deviation from a desired state of affairs. Therefore, situation monitoring is an important antecedent to problem recognition. Information should be organized and presented in a manner that permits easy comprehension of situations as they develop. Although situation monitoring is not considered as part of the decision process proper, it is an important part of the design of decision systems.

2. *Objectives.* The decision maker's purpose or mission is a second factor in determining the existence of a decision problem. Objectives are often externally assigned and may contain multiple goals accompanied by explicit or implicit priorities.

3. *Perceive decision need.* The requirement for a decision is considered to arise from the existence of a discrepancy between objectives and a currently existing or forecast situation. Thus, the perceived need for a decision may result from either new information or a new objective. The problem may be either external to the system (e.g. a tactical threat) or internal (e.g. a system component failure). People may be slow in recognizing a new need for action, particularly under conditions of information overload. Performance improvements might be obtained by use of alarms and alerting displays, by simplifying information in displays to promote rapid comprehension, by showing boundary conditions that should trigger action, or by providing predictive displays that help the decision maker to anticipate problems.

4. *Assess problem urgency and importance.* When a decision problem is perceived, its priority in relation to other current problems should be determined. The time and effort appropriate to its solution should also be defined since people may devote too much energy to an interesting but low priority problem or may delay making a decision so long as to be ineffective.

6.2 *Problem Diagnosis*

The second phase in the decision process is determining the probable situation which is producing the problem. The nine steps described below comprise the diagnostic process (see Figure 2).

1. *Define possible situations.* This often requires creativity in hypothesis generation. If a Bayesian system approach is to be used, the alternatives should be mutually exclusive and include all possible alternatives. This is a difficult requirement, often involving a question of just how fine a breakdown should be used.

2. *Evaluate situation likelihoods.* In this step, *a priori* probabilities of the truth of each alternative hypothesis are assigned. If there is no basis for this evaluation it is possible to consider all alternatives as equally likely, pending additional information. There seems to be some tendency of people to ignore possible but improbable alternatives. Therefore, the display of all identified alternatives might preclude failure to consider unlikely possibilities. These sometimes have the most disastrous consequences.

3. *Is more information needed?* In many decision situations there is an option of delaying

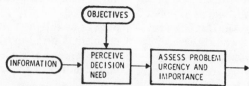

FIGURE 1.   A CONCEPTUAL MODEL OF A PROCESS FOR PROBLEM RECOGNITION.

a final decision in order to obtain more information. To make this interim decision, the decision maker should assess whether the delay and cost for additional information is warranted by the expected gain from increased decision accuracy. Research on sequential decision making suggests that people may postpone terminal decisions too long.

4. *Identify possible data sources.* If more information is desired, then the possible sources need to be specified. In many systems these sources are largely pre-determined by system designers.

5. *Judge data value versus cost.* Often there are several possible sources of information, each with its own cost in time or resources. The decision maker must choose which of these to use. Factors such as reliability, probability of useful information being provided in time and diagnostic value should be considered. One conclusion might be that the cost is excessive, so that despite the desire for more information, none should be sought.

6. *Seek more information.* Having chosen to obtain more information, the decision maker takes appropriate action to acquire it. He needs to avoid delaying action too long or seeking so much information that he overloads his ability to evaluate it properly.

7. *Re-evaluate situation likelihoods.* As new information is acquired the prior opinions regarding alternative situation likelihoods are revised. Research has indicated that people generally do not change their probability estimates to the degree warranted by the new data. New information may also suggest redefinition of situation alternatives.

8. *Do alternatives account for all data*? As a precaution against an erroneous diagnosis it may be prudent to re-assess the favoured hypothesis. People often seem to jump to conclusions too quickly. Some odd item of information might indicate a need to redefine the set of possible situations.

9. *Make diagnostic decision.* At this point a selection is made from the set of alternatives. In some cases the end product may be a limited set of weighted alternatives.

6.3 *Action Selection*

The third phase of the decision model includes the steps required to choose a course of action (see Figure 3). The process is largely based on decision theory concepts and is rather lengthy, being made up of the following

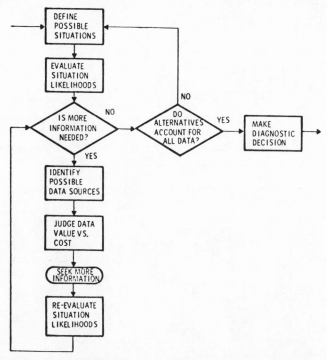

FIGURE 2.   A CONCEPTUAL MODEL OF A PROCESS FOR PROBLEM DIAGNOSIS.

seventeen steps.

1. *Define action goals.* The basic question is: given the situation, what should be done? The objectives initially specified are often too broad. Therefore, this step provides for specification of subordinate goals consistent with the major objective. Several concurrent goals may be identified. One consideration at this point should be the strategy of successive decisions. One approach, for example, is to "muddle through" or, in other words, to use small action steps, so that progress can be closely checked.

2. *Specify value and time criteria.* Goals are typically multi-dimensional in real-world situations. To assess properly the desirability of various possible actions, the relevant dimensions of goal value need to be identified. Furthermore, time factors which may place constraints on action alternatives also need to be specified.

3. *Weight decision criteria.* Once decision value criteria have been determined, their relative importance needs to be specified. Some criteria may, of course, be absolute requirements. Changes in preferences over time should also be considered. Thus, this step provides time-based, weighted criteria and boundary conditions for choosing a course of action.

4. *Specify risk philosophy.* The previous steps provide a basis for evaluating the potential outcomes of various possible actions. This step is concerned with the strategy of action selection, considering all of the possible outcomes. For example, should one choose an alternative which provides the possibility of a very desirable result along with some risk of a disastrous outcome or should one choose a more conser-

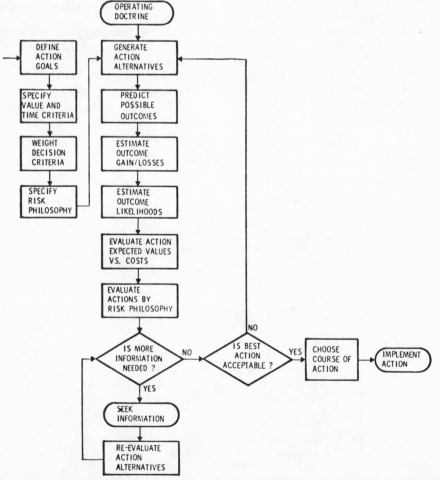

FIGURE 3. A CONCEPTUAL MODEL OF A PROCESS FOR ACTION SELECTION.

vative, safer course of action? This question, which is basic and often perplexing, has been the subject of considerable concern to decision theorists.

5. *Operating doctrine input*. The question of what action to take in response to a problem situation is often guided by operating rules or doctrine. These guidelines may specify particular actions or, at least, may limit freedom of choice.

6. *Generate action alternatives*. Although action alternatives may be dictated in advance, creativity is often required of the decision maker at this point. Since the number of possible action alternatives can be very large in some cases the definition of a reasonable set of alternatives may be a difficult task. Care must be taken not to generate too many alternatives in order to avoid overloading the decision maker. In most cases, however, people seem to consider too few rather than too many courses of action.

7. *Predict possible outcomes*. The possible outcomes of each action are next predicted. Some order of priority of consideration may be needed so as to avoid the loss of certain options due to delay. Attention to possible undesirable outcomes is important since people often seem to give this aspect insufficient attention. If the situation involves an opponent, his goals and tactics should also be considered. As possible outcomes are evaluated it may be desirable for the decision maker to simplify the decision task by dropping action alternatives which are found to be clearly undesirable.

8. *Estimate outcome gains and losses*. The next step is to determine the value of each possible outcome according to the decision criteria previously determined. At this stage certain alternatives may be dropped for failure to satisfy value or time requirements.

9. *Estimate outcome likelihoods*. At this point the probabilities of occurrence of the various possible outcomes are judged for each action which is being considered.

10. *Evaluate action expected values versus cost*. The expected value for each action is derived from the results of the previous two steps. Next, for each action, the expected value is diminished by the estimated cost of taking the action. This leaves a net expected value for each alternative course of action.

11. *Evaluate actions by risk philosophy*. The decision maker can now evaluate the alternative actions according to his previously determined decision strategy.

12. *Is more information needed?* The decision maker may, at this point, decide to defer taking action so that additional information may be gathered to improve his forecasts of action outcomes.

13. *Seek information*. As in the case of diagnosis, the decision maker may act to acquire additional information.

14. *Re-evaluate action alternatives*. As new information is obtained the estimates generated above are revised. New information may also suggest that new action alternatives be considered.

15. *Is best action acceptable?* As a final check, the course of action which seems most desirable should be reviewed to ensure that it satisfies the desired goals and value criteria and to determine if the expected gain is worth the cost of action. There should also be a check to ensure that any possible adverse consequences can be accepted or avoided. If not, then some new alternative may have to be developed.

16. *Choose course of action*. At this point the decision occurs. Usually this results in an irrevocable commitment of resources.

17. *Implement action*. This is a very important sequel to the action commitment decision in a system context. It includes defining the method of carrying out the selected action, communicating the decision to those elements which will execute it, taking precautionary action against possible adverse consequences, providing for information feedback, and monitoring the progress of action.

7. CONCLUSION

The decision process model, in its present form, may serve as a guide in structuring the decision making tasks of a man-machine system. To do this, however, requires that the nature of the expected decisions be defined and that the information needed to make the decisions be specified. The design of the decision tasks can then be determined. This includes specifying which steps should be done in advance, their allocation to man or machine, and, finally, in what ways the human operator can be aided in performing his segments of the process.

The model is, of course, tentative and needs further development, particularly to incorporate additional data on human decision processes. One approach is to study how "good" decision makers interpret and structure a decision problem and how they go about resolving it. This perhaps could be done by having experts verbalize their thinking as they solve decision problems in complex situations such as may be found in business or war games. Some provocative ideas recently described by Broadbent (1967) regarding human decision processes might be explored in this manner.

The complexity, pervasiveness and practical significance of decision making make it a particularly fascinating area of study. Experience in the world today makes evident the far-reaching consequences that may result from ill-timed or ill-conceived decisions. One of the major contributions we could make would be to find ways to achieve significantly better decisions.

AUTHOR'S NOTE

The author is indebted to his colleagues, Dr. A. F. Kanarick and Dr. A. H. Henke, for their helpful comments during the preparation of this paper.

REFERENCES

Attneave, F., 1953, Psychological probability as a function of experienced frequency. *Journal of Experimental Psychology*, 46, 81-86.

Back, K. W., 1961, Decisions under Uncertainty: rational, irrational and nonrational. *American Behavioral Scientist*, 4, 14-19.

Baker, J. D. and Goldstein, I., 1966, Batch vs. sequential displays: effects on human problem solving. *Human Factors*, 8, 225-235.

Beach, L. R., 1966 Accuracy and consistency in the combination of subjective probabilities. *IEEE Transactions. Human Factors in Electronics*, HFE7, 29-37.

Beach, L. R. and Wise, J. A., 1968, Subjective probability revisions and subsequent decisions. *Univ. Washington, Dept. Psychol. Rep.*, 68-1-25.

Bierman, H., Jr., Bonini, C. P., Fouraker, L. E., and Jaedicke, R. K., 1965, *Quantitative Analysis for Business Decisions (Revised Ed.)* (Homewood, Illinois: Richard D. Irwin, Inc.)

Briggs, G. E., and Schum, D. A., 1965, Automated Bayesian hypothesis-selection in a simulated threat-diagnosis system. In *Information Systems Sciences; Proceedings of the 2nd Congress* (Washington, D. C.: Spartan Books), 169-175.

Broadbent, D. E., 1967, Aspects of human decision making. *Advancement of Science*, 24, 53-64.

Chenzoff, A. P., Crittenden, R. L., Flores, I., Frances, A. S., Mackworth, N. H., and Tolcott, M. A., 1960, Human Decision Making as related to air surveillance systems. *USAF AFCCDD Tech. Rep.*, No. 60-25.

Dale, H. C. A., 1968, Weighing evidence: an attempt to assess the efficiency of the human operator. *Ergonomics*, 11, 215-230.

Davis, G. A., 1966, Current status of research and theory in human problem solving. *Psychological Bulletin*, 66, 36-54.

Drucker, P. F., 1967, The effective Decision. *Harvard Business Review.*, 45, 92-98.

Edwards, W., 1954, The theory of decision making. *Psychological Bulletin*, 51, 380-417.

Edwards, W., 1961, Behaviorial decision theory. *Annual Review of Psychology*, 12, 473-498.

Edwards, W., 1964, The design and evaluation of probabilistic information processing systems. *Proceedings of the 5th National Symposium on Human Factors in Electronics.*

Edwards, W., 1965, Probabilistic information processing system for diagnosis and action selection. *Information Systems Sciences; Proceedings of the 2nd Congress* (Washington, D. C.: Spartan Books), 141-155.

Edwards, W., 1969, A bibliography of research on behavioral decision processes to 1968. *Univ. of Michigan, Human Performance Center. Memo. Rep.*, No. 7.

Edwards, W., Phillips, L. D., Hays, W. L., and Goodman, B. C., 1968, Probabilistic information processing systems: design and evaluation. *IEEE Transactions. Systems Science and Cybernetics.*, SSC-4, 248-265.

Fishburn, P. C., 1966, Decision under uncertainty: an introductory exposition. *Journal of Industrial Engineering*, 17, 341-353.

Gagliardi, V. O., Hussey, R. A., Kaplan, I. T., and Matteis, R. J., 1965, Man-computer interactions in idealized tactical problem solving. *USN ONR Final Rep., Contract Nonr. 3602(00).*

Gibson, R. S., and Nicol, E. H., 1964, The modifiability of decisions made in a changing enviroment. *USAF ESD Tech. Docum. Rep.*, No. 64-657.

Gustafson, D. H., 1969, Evaluation of probabilistic information processing in medical decision making. *Organizational

Behaviour and Human Performance, 4, 20-34.

Hanes, R. M., and Gebhard, J. W., 1966, The computer's role in command decision. *Naval Institute Proceedings*, 92, 61-68.

Herman, L. M., Ornstein, G. N., and Bahrick, H. P., 1964, Operator decision performance using probabilistic displays of object location. *IEEE Transactions. Human Factors in Electronics.*, HFE-5, 13-19.

Howard, R. A., 1968, The foundations of decision analysis. *IEEE Transactions. Systems Science and Cybernetics.*, SSC-4, 211-219.

Howell, W. C., 1967, Some principles for the design of decision systems: a review of six years of research on a command control system simulation. *USAF AMRL Tech. Rep.*, No. 67-136.

Howell, W. C., and Gettys, C. F., 1968, Some principles for the design of decision systems: a review of the final phase of research on a command control system simulation. *USAF AMRL Tech. Rep.*, No. 68-158.

Hunt, E. B., 1962, *Concept Learning: An Informational Processing Problem.* (New York: Wiley).

Kanarick, A. F., 1969, The learning, retention and transfer of decision making. *Paper read at Honeywell-NTDC Technical Meetings on Learning, retention and transfer*, Orlando, Florida.

Kaplan, R. J., and Newman, J. R., 1966, Studies in probabilistic information processing. *IEEE Transactions. Human Factors in Electronics*, HFE-7, 49-63.

Katter, R. V., and Holmes, E. H., 1965, Semantics of uncertainty: some psychophysical correlates. *System Development Corp. Rep.*, No. SP-1937.

Kennedy, J. L., and Schroder, H. M., 1964, Decision making training in tactical AAW type situation. *Princeton Univ., Contract Nonr. 1858(42) Progress Rep.*, No. 2.

Kepner, C. H., and Tregoe, B. B., 1965, *The Rational Manager* (New York: McGraw-Hill).

Kinkade, R. G., and Ranc, M. P., 1967, The effect of conflicting instructions and feedback specificity on tactical decision performance. *Human Factors*, 9, 257-262.

Lichtenstein, S. and Feeney, G. J., 1968, The importance of the data-generating model in probability estimation. *Organizational Behaviour and Human Performance*, 3, 62-67.

Luce, R. D., and Raiffa, H., 1958, *Games and Decisions: Introduction and Critical Survey.* (New York: Wiley).

McKendry, J. M., 1965, Utility of information as a predictor of decision adequacy in ambiguous choice situations. *HRB-Singer Rep.*, 567-R-3.

Messick, D. M., 1964, Sequential information seeking: effects of the number of terminal acts and prior information. *USAF ESD Tech. Docum. Rep.*, No. 64-606.

Miller, L. W., Kaplan, R. J., and Edwards, W., 1967, JUDGE: A value-judgement-based tactical command system. *Organizational Behaviour and Human Performance*, 2, 329-374.

Peterson, C. R., and Beach, L. R., 1967, Man as an intuitive statistician. *Psychological Bulletin*, 68, 29-46.

Peterson, C. R., and DuCharme, W. M., 1967, A primacy effect in subjective probability revision. *Journal of Experimental Psychology*, 73, 61-65.

Peterson, C. R., and Miller, A. J., 1965, Sensitivity of subjective probability revision. *Journal of Experimental Psychology*, 70, 117-121.

Phillips, L. W., Hays, W., and Edwards, W., 1966, Conservatism in complex probabilistic inference. *IEEE Transactions. Human Factors in Electronics*, HFE-7, 7-18.

Pitz, G. F., 1969, An inertia effect (resistance to change) in the revision of opinion. *Canadian Journal of Psychology*, 23, 24-33.

Pitz, G. F., and Downing, L., 1967, Optimal behavior in a decision-making task as a function of instructions and payoffs. *Journal of Experimental Psychology*, 73, 549-555.

Pollack, I., 1964, Action selection and the Yntema-Torgerson worth function. In *Information Systems Sciences, Pro ceedings of the 1st Congress.* (New York: McGraw-Hill).

Porter, E. H., 1967, A paradigm for system analysis of command and control functions. In *USA BESRL Rep.*, S-1 (Edited by J. Uhlaner), 245-257.

Raiffa, H., 1968, *Decision Analysis: Introductory Lectures on Choices Under Uncertainty.* (Reading, Mass.: Addison-Wesley).

Rigney, J. W., and DeBow, C. H., 1966, Decision strategies in AAW: I. Analysis of air threat judgements and weapons assignments. *USN ONR Tech. Rep.*, No. 47.

Rim, Y., 1963, Risk-taking and need for achievement. *Acta Psychologica*, 21, 108-115.

Roby, T. B., 1964, Belief states, evidence and action. In *Predecisional Processes in Decision-Making: Proceedings of a Symposium, USAF AMRL-TDR-64-77* (Edited by D. P. Hunt and D. L. Zink), 27-46.

Schrenk, L. P. and Kanarick, A. F., 1967, Diagnostic decision-making in a Bayesian framework. *Proceedings of the 5th Annual Symposium on Human Factors in Electronics.*

Schroder, H. M., 1965, Factors underlying performance in a complex decision task: performance in an anti-air warfare context. *Princeton Univ., Contract Nonr. 1858(42) Rep.*, No. 9.

Schum, D., Goldstein, I., and Southard, J., 1966, Research on a simulated Bayesian information-processing system. *IEEE Transactions. Human Factors in Electronics*, HFE-7, 37-48.

Schaffer, L. H., 1965, Problem solving on a stochastic process. *Ergonomics*, 8, 181-192.

Shuford, E. H., Jr., 1965, A computer-based sysrem for aiding decision-making. In *Information Systems Sciences; Proceedings of the 2nd Congress* (Washington, D. C.: Spartan Books), 157-168.

Sidorsky, R. C., and Houseman, J. F., 1966, Research on generalized skills related to tactical decision making. *USN NTDC Tech. Rep.*, No. 1329-2.

Slovic, P., 1964, Assessment of risk-taking behavior. *Psychological Bulletin*, 61, 220-234.

Southard, J. F., Schum, D. A., and Briggs, G. E., 1964, An application of Bayes theorem as a hypothesis-selection aid in a complex information-processing system. *USAF AMRL Tech. Docum. Rep.*, No. 64-51.

Swets, J. A., Tanner, W. P., and Birdsall, T. G., 1961, Decision processes in perception. *Psychological Review.* 68, 301-340.

Vaughan, W. S., Jr., Franklin, R. D., and Johnson, R. B., 1966, Study of functional requirements of training equipment for army command tactical decision making. *USN NTDC Tech. Rep.*, No. 1341-1.

Vaughan, W. S., Jr., Virnelson, T. R., and Franklin, R. D., 1964, Information-processing tasks in tactical action selection: performance of experienced submarine officers in weighting multiple criteria for depth selection. *Human Sciences Research, Rep.* No. RR63 26 Ae.

Vernon, M. D., 1957, Cognitive inference in perceptual activity. *British Journal of Psychology*, 48, 35-47.

Ward, W. C., and Jenkins, H. M., 1965, The display of information and the judgement of contingency. *Canadian Journal of Psychology*, 19, 231-241.

Yntema, D. B., and Klem, I., 1965, Telling a computer how to evaluate multidimensional situations. *IEEE Transactions. Human Factors in Electronics*, HFE-6, 3-13.

Yntema, D. B., and Torgerson, W. S., 1961, Man-computer cooperation in decisions requiring common sense, *IRE Transactions. Human Factors in Electronics*, HFE-2, 20-26.

ABOUT THE AUTHOR

Lorenz P. Schrenk was born in Utica, New York, and took his M.A. and Ph.D. at Ohio State University. He has worked on human information processing and decision-making at the Systems Development Corporation, at Ramo-Wooldridge Data Systems Laboratories, and at Ohio State University. Currently he is manager of the Life Sciences Department of Honeywell Systems and Research Division.

Operations Research and Decision-Making

R.M. Adelson and J.M. Norman

This paper reviews the theory of logical decision. In contrast with the previous paper, the aim is not to describe decision-making but rather to prescribe how decisions ought to be made. One of the aims of operations research is to reduce this difference between "decision theory" and "decision practice".

INTRODUCTION

Since management consists largely, if not exclusively, of the making and implementation of decisions, it is axiomatic that operational research must concern itself with the decision-making process. The mental processes which most people go through in deciding on courses of action are ill understood, even by the people making them. McDonald[1] quotes a number of senior American executives as making remarks such as: "I don't think businessmen know how they make decisions, I know I don't, "I'm damned if I know" and, even, "Whenever I think I make a mistake". The one cheering fact which is apparent in McDonald's paper is that at least businessmen are aware of the distinction between a right decision and a lucky decision, and McDonald gives us one example — the case of the railroad executive who reflected with irony on the great oil field that turned up unexpectedly among the railroad's industrial sites in Los Angeles. Even so, many businessmen apparently believe that the outcome of their decisions is a certainty. For example, "I can't accept the idea that the Executive Committee could make a major mistake" and, again, "I am always sure of the results when I make an important decision" (this attitude bears on the point we discuss later of the ways in which the techniques of operational research do in fact treat the uncertainty which is inherent in all decision-making). Clearly, if operational research is to be of assistance to decision-makers it is important that its techniques rest on

a foundation of a sound Theory of Decision, since without this its results can have no more *validity* than those of the executives quoted above. This does not necessarily imply, of course, that it cannot be *successful*. Many firms whose executives are no less hunch-men than those quoted by McDonald are successful (which may simply reflect the fact that the business environment is less hostile than is generally believed). However, we claim that operational research is something different — that it is based scientifically on logic and empirical fact — that it therefore understands the reasons for its success and can build on these — that it in fact "knows itself". It behooves us, therefore, to examine these foundations now and again, to assure ourselves that they are strong enough to bear the edifice that has been erected on them. If they are not, then they must either be strengthened, or some of the superstructure taken down.

CLASSIFICATION OF DECISION PROBLEMS

Most formal attempts to construct a theory of decision start by attempting to classify problems. Ackoff[2] gives the following representation of a problem situation:

$$V = f(X_i, Y_j),$$

where V is the measure of performance or accomplishment that we seek to maximize or minimize; X_i, the aspects of the situation we can control (the "decision" variables); Y_j, the aspects of the situation over which we have

SOURCE: Reprinted from R.M. Adelson and J.M. Norman "Operational Research and Decision-Making", *Operational Research Quarterly* 20(4) 1969 pp 399-413, by permission of the authors and publishers.

no control. Johnston,[3] for example, has classified problems. His classification is: first of all according to our knowledge of the structure, whether this is complete or partial; secondly, according to our ability to predict the uncontrollable variables which are part of the problem; and, finally, according to whether the problem itself has an exact (or deterministic) structure or whether its structure is probabilistic. For each of the eight categories of decision problems thus derived Johnston is able to list some appropriate techniques to deal with this particular type of problem. Thus, for example, for problems which are deterministic, of whose structure we have complete knowledge, and in which we have complete ability to predict the uncontrollable variables, such techniques as the calculus, linear and non-linear programming can be effectively used.

It is perhaps worth noting that in fact real problems can never be classified in this way. All real life problems fall into the category in which the structure is only partially known (indeed can we ever know whether we know *all* the structure?), the uncontrollable variables are unpredictable, and the structure is probabilistic. The classification can in fact only be applied to classroom exercises, which are usually devised to fit in with it, or at best to the *models* we make of problem situations. This is not to deny, of course, that mathematical programming techniques are extremely useful even in "real" problems in sorting out the set of "efficient" strategies from those that are dominated. It even transpires, quite often, that the situation is sufficiently robust for the remaining "uncertainties" to be negligible, but where this is not so methods of taking decisions under uncertainty are needed.

DECISIONS UNDER UNCERTAINTY

The most widely known construct for decision-making under uncertainty is that of the "American School". This recognizes two factors which together determine the course of action which will be taken by a decision-maker. One factor is that of assessment of the relative "probabilities" with which various outcomes can occur. The attempts to attach probabilities to events other than spinning coins or rolling dice has necessitated the reopening of the question of the definition of "probability". The American School points out that strictly speaking *all* probabilities are conditional probabilities — conditional that is on the *information* available about the events in question and associated events. (Even the probability of 0-5 that a tossed coin falls heads is conditional on the information that the coin is "unbiased" — and how can one tell whether or not a coin is "unbiased"?), and it is not unreasonable therefore that different people should attach different probabilities to the same event (since they may have different information), i.e. probabilities are "subjective". This does not mean they are arbitrary. A reasonable man "should base the probabilities which he assigns to events in the real world on his experience with such events, and when two reasonable men are subjected to the same overwhelming experience with a certain kind of event they tend to assign to it roughly the same probability".[4] This statement is one of the cornerstones of the theory of decision-making we are discussing. It is noteworthy that no empirical evidence is given for the verification of the statement. We shall return to this later.

The second factor which is instrumental in determining decision is the decision-maker's personal valuation structure, that is the body of views he holds which enables him to give a preference for one outcome over another. It has also been necessary to include the decision-maker's valuation of "gambles" (usually referred to as "lottery tickets") in this structure.

IMPROVED DECISION-MAKING

Given these two factors, of assessment and valuation, then it can be argued that the action that the decision-maker chooses is a logical consequence of his assessment of consequences and his valuation of the outcomes in the sense that the assessment and the valuation determine the action, unless the decision-maker makes a mistake. If this is so then we should be able, in principle at least, with complete knowledge of the factors, to know the course of action which any man would choose to take in any situation. Naturally, because we can never have complete knowledge of either of these factors which are in essence, personal, we shall never be able to do this in all cases. Nevertheless, this is no pipedream, for even now, in practice, many decisions are delegated and those decision-makers who do such delegation are often happy enough with the results. However, if all decisions are determinate on the basis of probability assessment and outcome valuation, then in principle there is nothing to stop the use of computers to carry out the decision-making processes which we use now. There is a further consequence of this: if all decisions are determinate in this sense, how is it that we can speak of decisions being improved? This is important in that one of the arguments often advanced for the utilization of operational research is that it results in improved decision-making.

It is clear nevertheless that the use of the techniques of operational research *has*, in some sense, given rise to improved decision-making. For example, if a transport manager tells you that he has three depots and three hundred customers, that he has constant supplies arriving at the depots in known amounts and constant demands from the customer, and you tell him how to use the transportation method, then in some sense you have improved his decision-making. His decision-making has been improved in that, using the transportation method, his total transportation costs between the depots and the customers have now been reduced, or if not reduced, at least he now knows that his former allocation method was the correct one and he knows why. What in fact has happened? We have changed neither the assessment of outcomes nor the valuation structure; what we have changed is the process by which the transport manager has derived his preferred course of action from these factors. In a sense what we have improved are his thought processes themselves. We have shown him, in this particular situation, how to derive the consequences which he desires from his own assessment of outcomes and values. In Ackoff's format, we have made him aware of the underlying form of the function f, which relates the performance measure to the decision variables. We have shown him how to arrive at decisions which are *consistent* with his expressed valuation structure. Is this the prime role of operational research in decision making — to ensure consistency? Certainly a large amount of operational research effort is expended on this activity. We are often being told that it is important to get management to state their objectives at the outset of an operational research study. In practice, it frequently turns out that management are reluctant to state objectives, and when these are elucidated they turn out to be confused and sometimes incon-

sistent, and we now sometimes find in operational studies advice on what management's objectives "ought" to be — "maximize present worth", for example.

Churchman[5] has said that "what a man ought to do is what he would do if he had perfect knowledge", that is, perfect knowledge of the probabilities of all possible outcomes and their values to him. There is a sense in which in the ultimate this is the role of an adviser. If this knowledge could be shared by the adviser as well as, say, the managing director then there is no reason why the adviser should not choose actions on his behalf. Here, of course, we leave aside all questions of ethical and moral considerations. It might be right, for example, for a burglar to break into a particular house if this act would be in accordance with his own assessment of probabilities (of detection for example) and his own valuation structure, which are essentially personal. Given his own evaluation of risk and his peculiar valuation structure then his "right" course of action is logically determinate. Whether or not we as outsiders think it right or wrong to break into the house is irrelevant in the sense of "right" which we use in the phrase "right decision-making", where the meaning of "right" is nearer to "correct" than to "good" (in a moral sense). The point is, that it is right for him irrespective of it not being in line with what is desired by society as a whole. In the same way a managing director could value outcomes in a way with which we as observers might disagree. In what sense have we the right to tell him that he is making the wrong decision? So far as the correctness of his actions is properly based on his valuation structure is concerned we have none. All we can do is attempt to change his valuation structure itself and try to persuade him that he should value some outcomes in a different way from the way in which he values them now. But if these values are themselves decidable, then we must believe the manager has a further set of values which he must have invoked to enable him to decide on the structure of his valuation basis for the decisions he currently makes, and we find ourselves in an infinite regress. At some stage values must be undecidable. If we accept this then it becomes very difficult to speak of a man having irrational objectives. We may feel that a school-boy who will not look at the notice board to see whether or not he has passed the examination is being stupid; but if he values his state of uncertainty very much more highly than the state of knowing that he has failed then he may be acting in accordance with his own personal valuation structure. We are not in a position to criticize his decision-making in so far as it is based on what is in principle undecidable. Ultimately, the way he values outcomes is his own affair.

Can similar arguments be applied to firms? Clearly if operational research is to help firms achieve their objectives firms must have objectives. But who determines them, and how? Is it the board of directors, other levels of management or the shareholders? And is it possible that a firm or manager could have objectives which are in fact wrong? If not, by what token do we advise management that, for example, it should not choose the project which minimizes the "payback period", but should choose that which maximizes "present worth"? Or again — suppose a chemical engineer who is highly thought of in his company has for years been attempting to maximize the chemical yield from a process which he controls. We come along and tell him that he ought instead to be maximizing profit, and adjust the plant accordingly. What justification is there for this? One might argue that the engineer was making an error and not acting consistently with his "true" objectives which were to maximize profit. He believed wrongly, as the study showed, that yield and profit were so related that by maximizing the former he was at the same time maximizing the latter. But how can we say that profit is any more his "true" objective than was yield? His "true" objective might well be to increase his status and importance; to be well thought of within the firm, etc., and *yield* might be more strongly correlated with this than is profit. Indeed, there might also be ethical reasons why yield should be maximized if the raw material used is a scarce natural resource in limited total supply, which might run out in another 100 years or so. Surely for us to use it up at a faster rate than is feasible for our own requirements is a crime we are committing against our great-grandchildren?

If, however, the view is accepted that a firm's objectives are determinable in some sense, should not operational research be endeavouring to help management determine what its "true" objectives are? Should we *ever* accept management's dictum on this subject?

INFORMATION

In the past, operational research has often attempted to circumvent this problem by arguing that the function of operational research is simply to provide decision-makers with *information* on which to base decisions — it should not concern itself with the decision process itself. That is to say that operational research should concern itself only with experimental or econometric investigations into the nature of the functional relationship between the variables of the problem — thus to present management with the consequences of alternative courses of action. However, the difficulty will not be overcome so easily. In order to make the results comprehensible it is necessary to summarize them in some way into certain statistics or indexes which are presented to management. Unless we know what the valuation structure is, how do we know *which* statistics should be computed? What would be an operational research man's reaction, for instance, to a request from management that he compute the "pay-back period" for a number of different configurations of a new plant complex which is being investigated? Would he surreptitiously also compute, say, the DCF yield and report that also? And if he is then asked why he did this would he presume to tell management that this is what *should* have been asked for?

We might also point to the paradox that further information does not necessarily make one better off — if it is information which increases the probability of an undesirable event. This is implicitly recognized, for example, when a patient's relatives or doctor have to decide whether to tell him he is dying of an incurable disease. Is it better for the patient to know or not to know? Again suppose in the usual acts-states notation we have the following pay-off matrix.[6]

		State	
		1	2
Act	1	0	100
	2	1	50

If a man has the choice of either Act 1 or Act 2 or of finding out the true state at zero cost then in every theory of choice we know of he will choose to find out the true state of nature. However, if there is a time lag T between the choice of his act and the realization of the state, then if the man decides to find out the true state he may be doomed to an expectation of one unit for the whole of time T. Whereas, if he chose not to find out the true state then he could live in hope for time T of 100 units. Again, suppose an operational research man uncovers some information which would *decrease* the value of the company's shares. Is it not his duty to suppress it? One might argue that such people are living in fools' paradises, but on what grounds can we say this is wrong?

A further argument that is sometimes invoked that operational research need not concern itself with the choice of "objectives" is that it is better to proceed according to *some* plan than to travel haphazardly. The argument is that precisely *what* the plan is is less important than that there should be one, any "reasonable" objectives will do. We know of no one who has attempted to test this thesis and it can only be accepted at the present time as an act of faith. It must be remembered that it is possible to be consistently wrong, and this may give a worse result than being wrong only part of the time. The main reason, it seems to us, for proceeding in line with unchanging objectives is to impart a sense of purpose to our decision-making. It makes it possible for us later, as a result of the knowledge we have gained from the experience of operating according to the objectives which we have laid down, to exchange these objectives if necessary for what we hope is an improved set. This in itself is an instance of the use of a personal valuation structure in decision-making. Effectively we are assigning some value to acting in a consistent manner. Indeed, this procedure does make a certain amount of sense in that if one considers an individual's objectives, these are not likely to remain constant throughout his life — they are constantly evolving in the light of experience. The office boy who, on entering the firm, sets his objective as that of becoming managing director in the shortest possible time may well abandon this in the light of experience. Can a firm be said to evolve its objectives in the same way? Are a "young" firm's objectives quite different from an "old" firm's? Or a large firm's from a small firm's?[7] The suggestion that a firm's historical performance can be used to set its future objectives is in fact well known — *vide* the argument that a firm should attempt to maximize its present worth at an appropriate discount rate, this rate to be determined by an examination of its past record. This has its dangers, however, as it is an easy way of introducing an element of positive feedback. Suppose a firm has accepted this argument. It will then only accept projects which have a positive present worth at that rate i.e. which have a rate of return higher than it has so far achieved. Suppose it is successful in implementing this policy. If it re-examines its history at the end of a year, it will find that its *average* rate of return will have increased. It will therefore change its "required" rate to this new average (i.e. the historical average rate becomes the new marginal rate), and look for projects which exceed this rate. There will almost certainly be fewer of these than there were at the old rate, so it will invest less capital this year. If it is again successful, the same thing happens again until eventually it has pushed up its required rate so high that it can find no opportunities to invest at all. It therefore ceases to grow and will start to decline. Either the whole thing will go into oscillation or, if there is nothing to arrest the decline, it will continue until the firm is making no return at all.

PROCEDURE

Suppose to take a simple case, an individual feels able to assign some value (utility) to all outcomes of which he is aware in a given decision situation. How does he proceed? If he restricts himself to this set of outcomes and to a known set of alternative actions, then, in accordance with the von Neumann and Morgenstern axioms, he will act in a way which will maximize his expected utility. However, this version of the decision process takes no account of the valuation process which he must go through in deciding whether or not to look for, and consider, further alternatives and their associated outcomes. Nor does it take account of the process he must have gone through to arrive at the decision situation we have described.

Ackoff's outline of the phases of research is well known:

1. Formulating the problem;
2. Constructing the model;
3. Testing the model;
4. Deriving a solution from the model;
5. Testing and controlling the solution;
6. Implementing the solution.

In this scheme, the decision situation we have outlined is equivalent to stages 2-4 and Ackoff's list could be extended. For example, the process of deciding that there is a problem which needs to be solved should be at the top of the list.

Already we are skirting the edges of an area of difficulty. The decision situation usually described in the literature can be portrayed in the well-known two-way table which shows the values associated with each act-state of nature combination. This is a single-stage situation. Except in so far as they can be discounted to some present value, future consequences are not taken into account. Yet even the abbreviated scheme given by Ackoff exhibits the sequential characteristics of the decision-making process.

The approach using decision trees (as described by Magee[8]) or through the decision problem under uncertainty (cf. Pratt et al.[4]) overcomes this criticism to some extent. Yet the decision tree itself may be more or less infinite: the number of possible alternative sequences of:

Carry out an experiment, with some cost or reward,

Evaluate resulting information;

Carry out an experiment, with some cost or reward,

Evaluate resulting information;

etc.

may be very large indeed, and the problem of "roll-back" may be computationally infeasible. Apart from this, as we have pointed out, an individual's or firm's valuation structure itself may be liable to change over time. How can one include this in a decision tree?

PROBLEMS OF IMPLEMENTATION

We have argued that operational research must concern itself with the *whole* decision problem if it is to do a really useful job. The American School teaches that this can be done provided that probabilities can be attached to uncertain events and that a "utility function", whose expected value is to be maximized, can be obtained over the possible outcomes to the decision-maker. It is perhaps of some interest that we have not found any published case studies in which this approach has been used although the literature abounds with "examples". This may simply be a reflection of the fact that there are very few published case studies! However, discussions with management have indicated a marked reluctance to embrace these ideas, i.e. subjective probability and utility. Is this due to "stupidity" on the part of management (remember that the decision to accept a new technique is a *decision*), or is there perceived to be something basically wrong with the ideas? How good are people at determining subjective probabilities? Here, again, it is difficult to find evidence. In one of the very few papers which purport to be "real-life" case studies of the use of subjective probabilities, Harris[9] gives the prior distribution obtained by the product planning committee of a company of the "proportion of potential users who would purchase this new product". A sample of 100 customers was then taken. The results indicated that the proportion of customers purchasing was about 3 prior standard deviations from the prior mean. This speaks for itself.

In an attempt to test the validity of the statement made by Pratt et al (quoted on p. 132), one of the present authors has asked two groups of numerate people to give their subjective estimates of the probability of no rain on a certain day. In one case the results were uniformly spread about between 0.45 and 0.75, and in the other case uniformly between 0.25 and 0.75. Thus "roughly the same" has to be interpreted very loosely. Other aspects of these experiments also tended to cast doubt on the ability of even numerate people to agree on the probability of a certain event, conditional on information which is about as common to them all as one is likely to find anywhere in real life.

Empirical attempts to determine utility functions have also raised doubts as to the usefulness of the idea. As is well known, the way these utility functions are to be obtained is by asking a subject to state the sum of money which he would just be prepared to exchange for a gamble with well known probabilities between a greater and lesser sum. It is argued (see, for example, Luce and Raiffa[10]) that providing a decision-maker behaves in accordance with certain plausible axioms, he must have a utility function. That utility functions for individuals *exist* is not in question, as Swalm,[11] in a most interesting piece of empirical work, has shown, and since firms presumable obey the same desiderata, firms must have utility functions as well. But how are these to be determined? By asking management? Swalm has obtained amazing differences between executives within a particular firm. These might be due in part to the well-known fact that "objectives" of different parts of an organization might be in conflict. This is perhaps a problem for the organizational theorist. It might help to explain the differences (although they appear to be too large for this) but it doesn't help us to resolve them.

The American School, it seems to us, has begged these questions (and several others) completely. Indeed, Raiffa and others base their case on the need for consistency, as Swalm points out, and we have commented elsewhere on this. It is certainly easy to demonstrate that mortals are often inconsistent. A famous example was concocted by Allais.[12] In this, subjects are asked to state a preference for either (A) a large sum (e.g. £1,000,000) with certainty, and (B), a gamble in which the prizes are:

0 with probability 0.01

£1,000,000 with probability 0.89

£5,000,000 with probability 0.10

They are then asked to state their preference between two gambles (C) and (D), where (C) offers

0 with probability 0.89

£1,000,000 with probability 0.11

and (D) offers

0 with probability 0.90

£5,000,000 with probability 0.10.

It has been observed many times, with many groups of people with different backgrounds and different levels of training, that a majority plump for A and D. These choices are inconsistent with the axioms of Utility Theory. This fact has been used by its detractors to fley the theory, and by its protagonists to point out how necessary it is, since without it people are inconsistent, etc. This seems to us to be very unsatisfactory. How can we make a "rational" choice between these alternatives? To be more specific, and bringing the problem a little nearer home, the writer would have a great deal of difficulty in choosing between say £10,000 with certainty and say £50,000 with probability 0.9, zero otherwise — not because he is *indifferent*

between them but because he cannot solve the decision problem posed. What he would do with the money if he got it is very relevant. The larger figure might open up opportunities which would not exist under the smaller figure. In other words, a very complex decision-tree stems from this decision — the so-called simple choices which one is asked to make to determine a utility function are in reality not simple at all but are possibly as difficult as the so-called involved ones which are supposed to be solved with the aid of decision theory. If forced to make a choice in this situation, he would certainly do so, but would be conscious of the fact that perhaps he had made a mistake, and if faced again with the *same* problem (let alone a related one) might plump for the opposite choice next time (on the grounds that one of them must be right), were he not conscious of the fact that his interrogator might think him unstable. Indeed, if faced with this problem he might almost feel inclined to call in operational research consultants.

One of the most hopeful developments can be found in the work of Borch,[13] who has presented a very simple model of a dynamic investment problem. It is shown that a particular decision should be taken according to a certain utility function, whose form is derivable from the model. In order to do this, however, it is necessary to know something about the statistical nature of the opportunities which arise, Borsch makes some particularly simple assumptions, but we would suspect that it is lack of detailed *empirical* work in this area which is responsible for the current unsatisfactory state of decision theory.

A less happy resolution of the utility problem is to prescribe a function of particular mathematical form, for which the quadratic is very popular. The portfolio approach usually attributed to Markowitz[14] is based on this, and one hears reports from time to time that this has been successfully "sold" to portfolio managers — despite the fact that Pratt[15] has shown that a quadratic (indeed any polynomial) is in a sense "irrational".

DECISION AND CHOICE

One of the most telling criticisms of studies of this kind is that the answers given may be, as pointed out above, coloured by what the individual believes the interrogator wants to say to him or will think of his answers. They may be very different from what the individual would do in a real-life situation. Is it possible for us to determine this by observing the actions he takes in the kind of circumstances with which we are concerned? The difficulty here is that all we can observe is the man's choice behaviour. We can observe the actions he takes but not know why he takes them. Discussing the feasibility of ascertaining values by direct response, Churchman writes: "Possibly experimental economics can accept the proposal that values could be directly ascertained by pointing out that it is not interested in the internal 'pleasure feeling' aspect of the response but rather in the external *choice* made by the subject; hence the experimenter does not have to pose questions about internal feelings; he can directly observe what the subject really does." Here Churchman is making a distinction between decision and choice. We can observe choice but we can only infer decision. Dunlop puts this another way: "There can be choice without decision, but there cannot be decision without choice." At what stage in the process does a man *take* a decision? We often speak of a man deciding to do something and then changing his mind. Howard[17] defines a decision as "an irrevocable allocation of resource"; further, he writes, "a decision is not a mental commitment to follow a course of action". Howard claims that this definition serves to identify the true decision-makers in an organization. This does not seem to be the case. Those who decide on, for example, a stock control policy within an organization are not, in general, the same people as those who decide how much to produce from day to day, or how long the machines which produce the goods should be kept running in each production run. It is true that those who actually make the specific production decisions do determine the actions which take place, yet there is a distinction between the commitment to an action and the carrying out of that action. This is the distinction that we make when, speaking in terms of levels of authority within a firm, we speak of policy decisions, on the one hand, and executive or administrative decisions, on the other, where the observable difference between the two lies in the level in the hierarchy of the firm at which these decisions are taken.

COMPUTATION

Even when we know, or think we know, with some assurance, the manager's valuation structure in so far as it involves a particular problem, as indeed we might do with the kind of manager who still does not know about the transportation method, we can come up against severe computational difficulties when we try to compute the solution to the problem. An examination of the operational research literature in the last two or three years reveals many instances in which operational research scientists, seemingly unable to derive an analytic solution to a well-structured model, have used stimulation. This gives rise to the unhappy feeling that perhaps we are trying to get at the basis of decision-making in terms of valuation and assessment and at the same time are unable to derive the solutions to problems in which these factors are either known or can be taken as known. As an aside we may note that there is a computational limit to the size of problem that can ever be solved (shown by Bremerman[18] on the assumption that information is stored as some form of energy). There is good ground here for giving encouragement to the heuristic approach and justifying it by experimentation on models.

A SUGGESTED PROCEDURE FOR JUSTIFYING COMPUTATIONALLY DIFFICULT DECISIONS

How is it possible to justify actions which we take? This is a question that the sort of man who claims experience alone is the basis for his decision-making is unable to answer. Yet most of us will reason that some courses of action, in particular, are better than others. It is for this kind of reason that we feel justified in recommending, for example, decision rules based on queueing theory models or simulations. The justification we can give, however, is not that the actions we recommend will necessarily work out better in practice than others. In risky situations we have to distinguish between good decisions and good outcomes and make allowance for the element of good fortune which enters into all non-deterministic decision-making. Even in deterministic situations we may have to justify our choice of action by reference to a model simply because experimentation in the situation we are modelling is either too expensive or too time consuming. The archetypical operational research approach is to derive a model in which some sense fits the problem and from the model to derive a solution (compare Ackoff's six stages).

$$\text{Problem} \xrightarrow{\text{I}} \text{model} \xrightarrow{\text{II}} \text{solution.}$$

The arrow we have labelled I represents a kind of reduction. It is true but trite to remark that it is impossible in a model to completely represent the structure of the problem with which we have to deal. What we try to do is to portray in the model the relevant elements of the problem structure (this is what Stafford Beer[19] refers to as a homomorphism). Stage II is not a reduction in the same sense but a step is certainly involved here. We draw attention to this because frequently a model is confused with its solution. Thus we frequently find references in the literature to linear programming as a model, though it would be more appropriate to think of linear programming as a technique of stage II; as a way of deriving a solution from a model and not itself a model. Dantzig[20] points out that Stigler's least-cost-diet problem could not be solved until the advent of linear programming. In our scheme we would say that Stigler had derived a model that performed stage I but was unable to perform stage II.

It frequently happens that a model is so complicated that its solution is thought to be impossible or at least impracticable. In many cases what is then done is to change the model and effectively to retrace stage I. Under our scheme we show this as follows:

$$\text{Problem} \xrightarrow{\text{I}} \text{model}$$
$$\downarrow$$
$$\text{revised model} \xrightarrow{\text{II}} \text{solution}$$

What is happening in this event is that the original model is being discarded. All we have to show for a justification of the stage I reduction is an intuitive feeling of reasonableness. It does not seem possible to us to justify by any rational means the appropriateness of a model. All we can do is to point to the various homomorphic relationships and assert that these are the ones that matter. What has happened if we change the model on account of the difficulty involved in solution is that we have discarded all these intuitive ideas of reasonableness for purely pragmatic considerations. What seems to us a better procedure is to reduce the model itself in some well-defined fashion:

$$\text{problem} \xrightarrow{\text{I}} \text{model} \xrightarrow{\text{IA}} \text{reduced model} \xrightarrow{\text{II}} \text{solution.}$$

We still have merely our intuitive notions of appropriateness for the reduction of stage I, but these are all we have to go on anyway and it is precisely these notions that are discarded in the previous procedure. What we have gained in this procedure is a justification for the reduction of the model at stage IA. Admittedly the procedure does involve us in additional reduction. Our justification for IA needs evidence which is based on the same kind of reduction applied to other models in which we do know the solution to the complete model and can compare the cost of the reduced model with the cost of the solution to the complete model. An example may make this more clear. We can easily conceive of a sequential problem which seems to cry out for a dynamic programming model and yet for one reason or another, for example, because of the high dimensionality of the state description, the model is impossible to solve. In this situation it might be possible to reduce the model by some tested technique, for example, by using expected values instead of random variables whenever these occur. Suppose then that under this technique we are able to derive an optimal solution to the reduced model: we are justified in stating that this solution is an approximate solution to the complete model and hence to the original problem? What justification there is lies in the results of previous computational experiments which have been carried out using this approximation technique and so far these have all proved successful.

Our purpose in this paper, however, is more than merely to make a plea for further experimentation in heuristic problem solving. Research which extends the field of application of the techniques of operational research is important, but just as important are investigations into the theory which underlies them. At the beginning of this paper we spoke of a general lack of understanding of the nature of decision-making and our main theme has been to discuss the reasons for this and to try to point to ways in which it might be overcome. Perhaps the major route would be a more thorough examination of the philosophical and statistical questions which underlie our subject.

REFERENCES

[1] J. McDonald (1955) "How Businessmen Make Decisions" *Fortune.*

[2] R.L. Ackoff (1962) *Scientific Method: Optimizing Applied Research Decisions.* John Wiley, New York.

[3] J. Johnston (1963) "Decision Theory: New help in Solving Business Problems". *Progress.*

[4] J.W. Pratt, H. Raiffa, and R. Schlaifer (1965) *Introduction to Statistical Decision Theory.* McGraw-Hill, New York.

[5] C.W. Churchman (1961) *Prediction and Optimal Decision.* Prentice-Hall, New Jersey.

[6] This example is taken from D.J. White *Decision Theory,* Allen and Unwin, London.

[7] Steindl has suggested that large firms use their economic scale advantage to "buy" security, i.e. large firms do not go to the wall relatively as frequently as small ones. Cf. J. Steindl (1965) *Random Processes and the Growth of Firms* Griffin, London.

[8] J.F. Magee (1964) "Decision Trees for Decision-Making" *Hvd. Bus. Rev.* 42(126).

[9] L. Harris (1967) "New Product Marketing: A Case Study in Decision-Making under Uncertainty" *Appl. Statistics* 16(39).

[10] R. D. Luce and H. Raiffa (1957) *Games and Decisions* John Wiley, New York.

[11] R. O. Swalm (1966) "Utility Theory - Insights into Risk Taking" *Hvd. Bus. Rev.* 44 (123).

[12] M. Allais (1953) "Le comportement de l'homme rationnel devant le risque: Critique des postulats et axiomes de l'ecole Americaine" *Econometrica* 21 (503).

[13] K. Borch (1966) "A Utility Function derived from a Survival Game". *Mgmt. Sci.* 12B (287).

[14] H. M. Markowitz (1959) *Portfolio Selections: Efficient Diversification of Investments.* John Wiley, New York.

[15] J. W. Pratt (1964) "Risk Aversion in the small and in the large" *Econometrica* 32 (122).

[16] W. Dunlop (1951) "The Representation of Choice". *Terminological Rev. Q. Bull.* No. 3. (Quoted in Footnote 6.)

[17] R. A. Howard (1966) "Decision Analysis: Applied Decision Theory". Paper presented at the IFORS Conference, Boston, 1966.

[18] A. Bremerman (1962) "Optimization through evaluation and recombination" Paper presented at the Conference on Self-Organising Systems, California, 1962.

[19] S. Beer (1966) *Decision and Control.* John Wiley, London.

[20] G. B. Dantzig (1963) *Linear Programming and Extensions,* Princeton.

ABOUT THE AUTHORS

Ron Adelson took his B.A. and M.A. at the University of Cambridge and a Diploma in Operational Research at the University of London. Between 1959 and 1965 he worked as Operational Research Officer for the British Iron and Steel Research Association (BISRA) and for the Distillers Co. Ltd. In 1965 he was awarded the Bronze Medal of the Operational Research Scoeity, and in the same year he became a Lecturer at Imperial College, London, In 1967 he took up his present appointment as a Senior Lecturer in the Department of Operational Research of the University of Lancaster. His principal research interests lie in the field of industrial and institutional investment.

John Norman holds a B.A. degree in Philosophy, Politics and Economics from Oxford University, where he was a scholar in Mathematics at Wadham College, an M.Sc. in Operational Research from the University of Birmingham and a Ph.D. from the University of Manchester. In 1966-7 he held a Foundation for Management Education Fellowship jointly at the Massachusetts Institute of Technology and with Arthur D. Little Inc. Dr. Norman's industrial career included work in the fields of computer programming, systems analysis, transportation, inventory control and production scheduling. He has also worked on problems of capital investment in electrical distribution systems and in efficient resource utilisation in hospitals. More recently his work has involved the construction of cost-based models for university planning and budgeting, and the design of a computer based production control system. His principal research interests are in Dynamic Programming and Decision Theory.

IV

PROBLEMS OF DATE AND MEASUREMENT

The collection of data and the measurement of parameters are essential parts of an operations research study. In the first place, data are needed to validate the theoretical model and to ensure that it is capable of predicting the observed results. Secondly, before the model can be used in any operational situation it is necessary to define the characteristics of that situation in suitable terms. These requirements mean that, not only must the operations researcher determine exactly what data are required, but he must also devise suitable methods of collecting and organising these data with reasonable attention to accuracy, reliability and cost.

In many cases, the limitations imposed on the type of data which can be collected will determine some of the characteristics of the model. These limitations can have a variety of causes, some of which may well be outside the control of the researcher, and he must therefore take them into account when he is designing the model.

The collection and organization of data may well be the most time-consuming part of an O.R. study, particularly in libraries which are in existence to provide a service and must interface with human customers. Thus much of the data about a library's operations may be concerned with the behaviour of the users and the researcher may have to use methods of data collection which are not necessarily very accurate or reliable, such as questionnaires and interview techniques.

The seven papers in this Chapter illustrate some of the methods used to collect data about libraries and some of the statistical methods used to organise these data. Emphasis has been placed on the development of Bradford's Law of Scattering, showing how successive researchers have advanced the understanding of this law, and how it can provide basic data for a variety of studies in the field of librarianship and information science. The law is a good example of how the development of a probability distribution in librarianship and information science can bring together seemingly diverse data in a coherent and meaningful form. The final two papers illustrate some of the problems in designing useful measuring instruments in the library context. The reader should also consult Ford's review of "library user surveys" in Chapter VI of this *Reader*.

Measuring a Library's Capability for Providing Documents

Richard H. Orr, Vern M. Pings, Irwin H. Pizer,
Edwin E. Olson, and Carol C. Spencer.

The paper which we have chosen to open this chapter shows how a research team, having devised a measure of performance for libraries, used that measure as a basis for a series of comparisons of a number of libraries. They developed a methodology (the "Document Delivery Test") which can be used in any library situation to give a reasonably consistent measure of the effectiveness of that library. The methodology has been tested in a number of situations.

In this example, the problem of measuring the behavior of the users was overcome by the use of records of their past behavior in the form of citations. The problems associated with this method are discussed.

INTRODUCTION

In the scheme of classifying library services adopted for this project, perhaps the most basic service a library performs is that of making available to its users the documents they need.[1] Developing a method of assessing, quantitatively, a library's capability for providing this service, which we call "document delivery," therefore had a high priority; and this developmental task was one of the first undertaken. This article presents a general method of measuring such capabilities that can be adapted for different types of libraries and for different kinds of users. It also describes two specific applications of the method that have been developed into operational tests of capability, ready for general use. The first of these tests is designed to measure the capability of a medical school library for meeting the document needs of users engaged in biomedical research. The second test is designed to measure, analogously, the capability of "reservoir" libraries for filling loan requests from libraries serving biomedical populations.

Weaknesses of Existing Methods

We will not attempt to review and evaluate all the different ways that have been employed to assess library collections. Two recent books on library "surveys" cover the more commonly used methods and at least touch upon their weaknesses[2,3]. Here we will comment briefly on those methods that attempt to provide quantitative data bearing directly upon the adequacy of library collections and have some claim to be called "objective."

If a library had a complete record of all the documents its users tried to obtain from it without success, one might think that these data, together with data on its "successes" in meeting requests, would provide a good measure of its adequacy. However, even if it were possible to maintain such a record — and this is obviously impossible in open-stack libraries, and most unlikely in any library with a catalog freely accessible to users — the record of "failures" would be biased. Users learn the strengths and weaknesses of a library's collection; and if there are alternative sources for the documents it does not own, they often turn to these sources without making their needs known to the library's staff. A library that is able to fill all but a small percentage of the needs its users make known, therefore, can be either a library that actually does have almost everything its users need or one that is being bypassed, except

SOURCE: Reprinted from the *Bulletin of the Medical Library Association*, 56 (3) July 1968 pp. 241-267, by permission of the publishers. An Appendix to this paper was lodged with the National Library of Medicine and has not been reprinted.

for the particular needs it can fill.

Recognition of the error of judging adequacy by unfilled requests alone has led librarians to search for other means of assessment. Most of these employ "standard" or "*ad hoc*" lists of serial and book titles, against which holdings are checked to learn what proportion of the titles is owned by the library being assessed. The lists are variously based upon the subjective judgement of some recognized authority, collective judgements of groups of librarians or of users, data on borrowing or in-library use of titles, coverage of indexing/abstracting services, exhaustive or selective bibliographies for selected subjects, or frequency of citation in segments of literature defined by subject classification. In commenting on "list-checking" as a general method, Williams states that, unless a very large number of titles is covered, any such lists "must be regarded as samples . . . one assumes that there is a correlation between the percentage of listed books held by the library and the percentage of other desirable works that are in its collection"[4].

Checklists based on citation frequency, or based on utilization data, have an important potential advantage. If such lists adequately represent the document usage of the specific populations served by the libraries to be assessed, then the *relative* desirability of titles can be weighted according to the likelihood of their being requested, based on the frequency with which they have been cited, or used, in the past. Provided this condition is met, either of these two bases would, in theory, be appropriate for constructing lists that could be employed to estimate what proportion of its users' collective document needs can be filled by a library's collection. But the techniques previously used to insure that the resulting lists adequately represent users' needs leave much to be desired. Why this is true will be discussed later in connection with the development of the present method. However, even if this essential condition were met, the kinds of numerical measures derived from list-checking in the past — principally the proportion of listed titles owned by a given library — have two critical weaknesses. First, the measures do not consider the library being assessed as part of a larger system — they reflect only its self-sufficiency. Second, they do not take into account a variable vitally important to a user — the time required to obtain the document

he wants.

Given enough time, a library can fill a user's request for almost any published document that is known to exist — provided, of course, that he is interested in the document's content, rather than its form, and will be satisfied by a facsimile copy of the original. From the user's point of view, therefore, the real criterion for assessing a library's document delivery performance is not *whether* the library can supply the document he wants, but *how long* it takes. Data on the length of time required to fill user's requests by borrowing from other libraries are reported by some libraries, most commonly in annual reports; and we know that a number of large libraries with closed stacks have assessed their performance in terms of the time required to deliver documents into the hands of requesters, though there appear to be relatively few published reports of such studies[5],[6]. Although it seems probable that others have attempted to measure the time required for users to obtain documents from open stacks, we found only one published report containing data on this type[6]. Apparently no one has tried to measure "delivery speed" for *all* requests, regardless of whether the requests are met from the library's own collection or by borrowing from other libraries; and this is the kind of a measure of a library's capability we wanted to develop.

A General Method for Measuring Document Delivery Capability

Our approach to measuring a library's capability for providing the documents its users need is basically very simple — take a representative sample of the documents they need and test the library to see how long would ordinarily be required for them to obtain these documents. Translating this basic idea into an operational test suitable for a particular library, or for a particular type of library, requires answers to two key questions: First, how can appropriate document samples be established? Second, how can the test be administered to achieve an acceptable balance between realism and practicality? The proper answers to these questions will vary depending on the nature of a library's users, on the purposes for which the test data are intended, and on what is "practical" in a given case.

In the course of developing tests designed specifically for academic biomedical libraries and for reservoir libraries serving the bio-medical community, it became apparent that the basic idea, and the general method that evolved from it, were applicable to any library. The method can be illustrated best by des-cribing how these tests were developed. We will give the rationale underlying each of the more important development decisions in the hope that these details will be useful to those who may want to develop similar tests, appropriate for other types of libraries, or for other kinds of users. In addition, although the two tests that resulted from these decisions can be used with-out knowing the rationale and assumptions on which they are based, we feel that knowledge of the "why's" is essential for understanding the tests' advantages and disadvantages and for using them most effectively.

A TEST FOR ACADEMIC BIOMEDICAL LIBRARIES

Deciding on Test Samples

As a first step in answering the question, "How can document samples appropriate for testing academic biomedical libraries be estab-lished?" it was necessary to define, opera-tionally, the appropriate "universe" of documents from which to draw test samples. For the reasons already discussed, the universe of all the documents that had been borrowed from the library to be tested was not appropriate, nor was the universe of all the documents its users had tried to obtain from it, even if the latter universe could be operationally defined. If one assumes that the staff and students of a medical school should be able to turn to its library for any published document they need for their work, then the document universe to be sampled might, ideally, be defined as all the published documents this user population had read or consulted during the recent past, *regardless of where or how they actually obtained these documents* — from the medical school library, from other libraries, from colleagues, by purchase, etc. In principle, all such documents could have been obtained through the library, even if they were not in its collection. But this definition does not specify the operations by which all documents in this universe can be identified. Although there is a variety of direct techniques for determining,

with greater or lesser accuracy, what documents a given user population reads or consults (for example, reading diaries and questionnaires), establishing appropriate test samples by any of these techniques would be a formidable task in itself.[7] However, a simple and practical *indirect* technique suggests itself for the segment of the user population that publishes papers — sample the universe of documents they cite in their publications, since one can reasonably assume they have read most, if not all, of these documents. But it should be recognized that any samples established in this way cannot be considered truly representative of the document universe one would ideally like to sample; that is, all published documents read or consulted by all members of the population.

Since authors customarily cite "primary sources" whenever possible, certain types of commonly used documents — such as review articles, textbooks, handbooks, and other types of "derivative" literature — will probably be underrepresented as compared to their actual use in any sample drawn from the documents authors cite; and abstracting/indexing tools are unlikely to be represented at all. Nor is the frequency with which a given primary-source document is cited necessarily proportioned to how many people have read it, since authors do not cite a completely random selection of all the primary-source documents they read, but rather select those most directly pertinent to their work and, more often than not, those they consider most "valuable." If one decides to use samples of cited documents, he must consider how this compromise with the postu-lated "ideal" sampling plan will affect the utility of the test. The decision will mean that a library's capability for delivering the kind of primary-source literature that is read by many, but cited by few, will be inadequately tested; to the extent that this kind of literature is actually less directly pertinent to the user population's work and is also less valuable to them, this consequence will not be a serious disadvantage. This decision will also mean that test results will not accurately reflect a library's capability for supplying the "derivative" literature its user population reads; how serious this consequence is will be examined later.

Assuming for the moment that sampling cited documents is an acceptable compromise, at least as far as *authors'* reading is concerned, what about the "nonauthor" segment of the medical school population? Professional staff who are actively engaged in either basic or clinical research can be assumed to be authors, almost by definition. Other professionals are less likely to write papers, although some publish didactic or review-type papers; and students are unlikely to be authors, unless they are graduate students. Unfortunately, for the nonauthor segment of a medical school population, there seems to be no simple and practical indirect technique for establishing samples of what they read. For the nonauthors among the professional staff, sampling their reprint files and the documents they cite in lectures are possibilities; but the practical difficulties are imposing. For establishing samples of students' reading, reserve book records and lists of assigned readings are unacceptable since they are biased by the library's holdings.

In view of the practical problems of sampling nonauthors' reading, it was necessary to examine closely the possible disadvantages of employing test samples drawn solely from literature cited by the author segment of the population. From the foregoing analysis, we concluded that there were two major theoretical disadvantages to employing samples of cited literature — the derivative literature read by the user population will be under-represented; and where the document needs of the author and non-author segments of the population differ, non-author needs will be under-represented. We saw no way to determine, a priori, how much these theoretical disadvantages would actually affect the utility of test results. After trying to estimate the probability of developing a practical test based on other techniques for establishing test samples, and concluding that the probability was low, we asked ourselves whether a test that measured *only* a library's capability for supplying primary-source documents important to researchers would be useful. It seemed to us that, *if its limitations were clearly understood*, such a test could be useful for managing academic medical libraries, particularly since no comparable methodologic tool exists. The scales were tipped further toward proceeding to develop a test employing samples of cited literature when another consideration was added — the fact that, at least with respect to the *variety* of documents it can provide, researchers' needs pose the most severe demands on a library's capability. For the medical school population as

a whole, therefore, such a test would be unlikely to overestimate this aspect of document delivery capability — underestimation was much more probable.

Once we decided to accept this compromise with ideal sampling, the last major decision regarding the test sample hinged on a philosophical question — should the capability of a school's library be assessed solely on the basis of how well it can supply documents used by the authors in its *own* user population? What if most of the school's current authors happen to be heavily concentrated in a few departments or happen to be provincial in their reading habits? If the library's collection is "tailored" to accommodate the reading patterns of the school's present staff very well, but these patterns happen to be substantially different from those of medical schools in general, should such a collection be considered "good" — particularly in view of the high rate of turnover among medical school staff and the rapidity with which research interests may change? We begged the question by deciding to conduct trials of the test with two different kinds of samples — samples drawn from "local citation pools," i.e., pools representing the literature cited by the authors in a library's own user population, and samples from a "national citation pool" representing the literature cited by U. S. biomedical researchers as a whole.

Deciding on Test Procedures

The second key question, "How can the test be administered to achieve an acceptable balance between realism and practicality?", required a similar analysis of alternatives. Academic biomedical libraries typically have open stacks; and when a user wants a specific document from the collection, he usually gets it from the shelves himself. The most realistic way to administer the test, therefore, would be to recruit a group of real users and assign a few of the items in the test sample to each user; the recruits would then go to the library, individually, and try to obtain copies of the test items. They would record how long it actually took to obtain each of the items, including those that had to be borrowed on interlibrary loan. For many reasons, including the fact that the number of items in a test sample might well be large, it was obvious that administering the test in this "ideal" way would be definitely impractical for academic medical libraries — therefore, some compromise with complete realism was necessary. The most attractive alternative was to simulate what would happen if real users were to try to obtain the items in a test sample. Since we were interested in testing the capability of a library, not the capability of its users, we could simplify matters by assuming that the users to be simulated were reasonably knowledgeable, and that, if an item were properly shelved, they could find it without wasted effort and with only minimal help from library staff. The simulation, however, should not assume any special knowledge of the particular library being tested, other than what could be learned from its public catalog and from other "location" tools normally available to users.

We decided to conduct trials with the medical librarians on the project staff administering the test by simulating knowledgeable users. The decision to have librarians simulate users, rather than employing real users, meant that care would be required to insure that test results would not be affected by any "professional courtesies" a library's staff might extend to those administering the test, nor by the staff's awareness that a test was underway.

Selecting a Time Scale

Our original plan was to have a librarian search the library for each item in the test sample and record how long was required to find it. However, this plan had one major difficulty — if the sample consisted of hundreds of items, searching the collection for each item separately and recording the exact time required to obtain it would obviously require several days, even if all the items happened to be "on shelf" and, therefore, quickly obtainable. But was such precise data necessary to assess the time required to obtain documents in terms that have *practical* meaning for users? Our experience suggested that users do not perceive "delay time," or "delivery speed," on a linear scale — that is, a ten-minute delay is not necessarily twice as "bad" as a five-minute delay, nor is it necessarily three times as "good" as a half-hour delay. The length of delay that will materially affect a document's value to a user varies widely — on some occasions, a delay of a few minutes can make a difference, on others a delay of a week or more is unimportant. When ordered by relative urgency, the ways in which users commonly express how soon they need a

particular document seem to fall into a relatively few, broad categories that can be typified as "within a few minutes," "within an hour or so," "sometime today," "within a week," etc. The nature of this progression, and the fact that sensory perceptions are typically measured on logarithmic, rather than linear scales, suggested that a similar scale might be appropriate for users' perception of delay time.

To explore this idea, we constructed a simple logarithmic scale with the unit value equal to the smallest time interval that might reasonably be expected to make any real difference to users, except in extraordinary cases. This smallest interval was assumed to be ten minutes. On the resulting "user-time" scale, values of 1, 2, 3, and 4 correspond, respectively, to intervals of 10^1, 10^2, 10^3, and 10^4 minutes. When these intervals are converted to convenient units of ordinary time and rounded off, they become ten minutes, two hours, a day, and a week, which agree closely with the categories of users' expressions described earlier. This agreement encouraged us to believe that, for the purposes of the test we were trying to develop, great precision in measuring the time required to obtain test documents was not essential. We therefore decided that, in administering the test, it would suffice if the "searchers" merely determined which of the five categories of delivery speed each test item fell into — not more than ten minutes; more than ten minutes, but not more than two hours; more than two hours, but not more than twenty-four hours; more than twenty-four hours, but not more than one week; and more than one week.

The decision to categorize delivery speed, rather than attempting to treat it as a continuous variable, was critical to success in developing a practical, reliable document delivery test that takes into account users' primary criterion for judging the effectiveness of document delivery service — speed. The searchers had to collect only enough information about the current status of a test item to place it somewhere within one of the relatively broad categories of delay time. This meant not only a great saving in the time required to administer a test, but also, and more importantly, one could have greater confidence that test findings with regard to delivery speed would correspond to what real users would find, and that test results would be reproducible from one searcher to another.

Generating Citation Pools and Drawing Test

Samples

When the key questions about sampling and test administration had been answered, preparation of the test samples began. For each of four medical schools, a local citation pool was generated by sampling the documents cited in the recent publication of its staff. Three of these schools maintained institutional bibliographies or files of staff publications; and a sample of 1963, 1964, and 1965 publications in these bibliographies were used as "source articles" for generating their respective citation pools. At the fourth school, the library collected staff publications for the same three years to serve as source articles for its citation pool. Each of the resulting pools consisted of at least 4,000 citations. Test samples were drawn from these pools by random procedures.

To generate an analogous citation pool for U. S. Biomedical researchers as a whole, we needed a similarly unbiased list of source articles — unbiased in the sense that it was not influenced by any library's holdings or by the coverage of abstracting/indexing services. The *NIH Research Grants Index* includes a list of all researchers who are principal or coprincipal investigators on NIH grants, and all publications resulting from these grants are also listed. These researchers comprise a major fraction of all U. S. scientists engaged in biomedical research, and the great majority of scientists listed are in academic institutions[8]. The volumes for fiscal 1963, 1964, and 1965 were sampled to obtain source articles by generating a single national citation pool. Test samples were drawn from this pool in much the same manner as was done for the local citation pools. Details on how the local and national citation pools were generated, and on how test samples were drawn from these pools, are given in the Appendix to this paper, which has been deposited with the National Library of Medicine.[9]

Characteristics of Test Samples

To obtain an idea of the kinds of documents represented in the citation pools, and therefore of the "characteristics" of test samples, we analyzed some 600 items drawn at random from the national citation pool. Roughly four-fifths of all the items were from English-language publications, and about 90 percent were from serial titles. Twenty serial titles accounted for

almost a third of all the items; but the remaining two-thirds were scattered in 223 other serial titles and in over 50 different nonserial titles. Of the serial items, 93 percent were in titles covered by *Index Medicus* and, therefore, represent "core" biomedical literature. Publication dates of items ranged from 1866 to 1965. Table I summarized the distribution by age; only twenty items carried 1964 or 1965 dates. More detailed analyses of the age of items and of their "scatter" among different titles can be found in the Appendix, which also includes a discussion of how the characteristics of these items compare with those of documents circulated by, or used in, academic biomedical libraries. The local citation pools have not been similarly analyzed; but by inspection, they appear to be much the same as the national citation pool.

Exploratory Trials and Test Standardization

Exploratory trials of the test were conducted at the libraries of Wayne State University College of Medicine and of Upstate Medical Center, State University of New York. The principal aims of these trials were: (1) to discover any unforeseen difficulties in administering the test, (2) to develop standardized procedures to insure that two different searchers would get the same results when they independently administered the same test sample in the same library, and (3) to determine how large test samples should be to give acceptably consistent test results when *different* samples from the same pool were administered in the same library.

The first trials were made with small test samples consisting of only fifty items each, which the searchers (V. P. and I. P.) administered first in their own libraries and later in each other's libraries. We soon found that much of the searchers' time was being spent in correcting and completing the citations of test items. Some of the documents cited did not meet our criteria for "published," or publicly available, documents — documents that *any* library can purchase or borrow from government or private sources through regular channels and that are listed in at least one of the standard bibliographic tools. Test results, when the same sample was administered in the same library varied materially from one "searcher" to the other because they sometimes made different decisions about the identity of a document cited incorrectly or ambiguously. This was undesirable, not only because the reproducibility of test results was reduced, but also because the test was supposed to measure document delivery capability *alone*; and in our scheme for classifying library services, document delivery presupposes that the user has an unambiguous bibliographic description of the document wanted. It therefore proved necessary to develop rather extensive "cleaning" routines to insure that, before a test sample was used, all the citations referred unambiguously and correctly to published documents. To avoid any bias that might result from discarding legitimate citations because they could not be readily cleaned or verified, we required that a reasonably exhaustive search be done before rejecting a citation; the final rejection rate was 1 percent. To reduce further the possibility of ambiguity, it also proved desirable to edit the citation until they included only the minimal essentials of bigliographic information. The instructions for cleaning and editing test-item citations are given in the Appendix.

TABLE 1
AGE DISTRIBUTION OF ITEMS IN NATIONAL CITATION POOL

Publication Date of Item	Percent of All Items (600)
1956-1965	73
1946-1955	16
1936-1945	6
1926-1935	2
1916-1925	1
1866-1915	2

Median Date 1959
Modal Date 1961

In addition to the problems caused by poor citations, the exploratory trials showed that the routines for searching and for recording test data had to be carefully standardized if different searchers were to obtain the same results. After considerable experimentation, explicit and detailed instructions for test administration and a standardized form for recording test data were developed. Repeated trials demonstrated that, when these instructions were followed and the standard forms were used, there was rarely any difference among test results obtained independently by different searchers.

TABLE 2
TEST-ITEM "AVAILABILITY STATES"

1. Not in collection
2. In collection but stored off immediate premises
3. On open shelf in expected location
4. Checked out on reserve loan
5. Checked out on faculty loan
6. Checked out on student loan
7. Checked out on I-L loan
8. Checked out on other type of loan
9. In bindery
10. In process
11. In storage on immediate premises
12. In special location (e.g. closed stack)
13. Among documents to be reshelved
14. Recorded by library as "missing"
15. Other known states (e.g., set aside for photocopying)
16. Found on shelf at time of second search
17. Unable to determine state even after second search
18. Other outcome of second search

The citation for each item in a test sample is typed at the top of one of the standard forms, which are designed to facilitate hand tabulation or machine processing of test data. The materials for a test consist of a set of these forms — one for each item in the test sample — and a cover sheet for recording certain general information about the test and the library tested. The searcher records the "availability state" of a given test item on its form by simply marking one of the eighteen mutually exclusive alternatives shown in Table 2; most of these availability states are familiar to librarians. The form also specifies what additional information about an item is required, if any. When the searcher cannot establish the state of a test item on his first attempt, he makes a second search later, shortly *after* reshelving has been done; and the test item is then categorized as being in one of three "second-search" states (States 16, 17, and 18). Copies of the instructions for test administration and of the standard recording form are included in the Appendix.

Data obtained by administering six small test samples of fifty items each at two libraries suggested that a sample of 300 items should be large enough to give results of acceptable reliability — that is, results obtained with different test samples from the same pool would agree closely enough to be useful for at least some purposes. These trials also indicated that a test with a sample of this size could probably be administered in less than half a day, which seemed acceptable from the standpoint of practicality.

Other exploratory trials suggested that non-librarians could be trained to administer tests consistently. However, this possibility was not pursued further; and in all the trials that will be reported later, medical librarians on the project staff administered the tests. An exploratory trial was also carried out to assess the feasibility of self-administration — that is, test administration by staff of the library being tested. In this trial, a test sample with 155 items was mailed to a group of hospital and academic libraries, and the libraries' own staffs carried out the test with only the standard written instructions as a guide. Fourteen of these libraries completed the test and returned test data to us for analysis; none reported any particular difficulty in carrying out the test. It was not possible to have independent searchers check the test data obtained by self-administration; but in each case, the results were about what one would expect from knowledge of the library's resources.

Full-scale Trials

After test procedures had been standardized, trials at Wayne and Upstate were extended to include tests of each library with a sample of 300 items drawn from its local citation pool and with two different samples of 300 items (Samples NA and NB) from the national citation pool. To date, five other medical school libraries have been tested with Sample NA, and two of these libraries have also been tested with a sample of 300 items from their respective citation pools. These five libraries were not selected as representative of academic biomedical libraries in general; their selection was dictated by practical considerations. Two were selected primarily because they were known to have files of faculty publications for the years 1963, 1964, and 1965. This was an important consideration because, without such a starting point, the time and effort required to generate a local citation pool is truly formidable. The remaining three libraries were selected primarily because they were geographically accessible to project staff and were sufficiently heterogeneous to provide some variety. Since none of the five libraries was either very small or very large, and we wanted to get an idea of how extremes in size might affect results, we also ran tests with Sample NA at a "small" and a "large" nonacademic library.

Primary Test Data

The primary data obtained by searching a library for the items in a test sample consist of the numbers of items found in each of the eighteen availability states. Table 3 summarizes the primary data for the seven academic libraries that were tested with Sample NA and shows the corresponding data for the "small" and "large" nonacademic libraries with the same sample. The latter data are included only to suggest how extremes of size might affect the results of tests of *academic* libraries, and no inferences as to the capabilities of these two libraries for serving the needs of their particular user populations should be drawn from these data. Insofar as hospital libraries are intended primarily to serve practitioners, Sample NA, which reflects the needs of researchers, is obviously inappropriate for testing the "small" nonacademic library; and since the "large" nonacademic library has a collection that is specialized for its principal function, which is to serve as a "reservoir" upon which other libraries can draw, Sample NA is inappropriate for testing its capability also. Although it may be reasonable to assume that test data for an academic library with only 9,000 volumes would resemble those for the "small" nonacademic library, a similar assumption about the test data for the "large" nonacademic library is more questionable.

Although the primary test data can be useful for certain purposes without further processing, a single figure-of-merit summarizing a library's document delivery capability is highly desirable for other purposes; for example, for comparing libraries or for relating test results to some standard value. Before any summary measure with the desired properties can be calculated, however, the primary data must be "weighted" to reflect delivery speed.

Coding Primary Data for Delivery Speed

The user-time scale discussed earlier is used to translate the primary test data into numbers indicating how long it would take a user to obtain the test items from the given library. The delivery speed for each item in the test sample is coded either as 1 (less than ten minutes); 2 (more than ten minutes, but not more than two hours); 3 (more than two hours, but not more than twenty-four); 4 (more than twenty-four hours, but not more

TABLE 3
SUMMARY OF PRIMARY DATA FROM TESTS WITH SAMPLE NA (290 ITEMS)*

Distribution of Test Items	Library Tested								
	Academic							Nonacademic	
	A	B	C	D	E	F	G	"Small"	"Large"
Not in Collection	11%	12%	16%	17%	27%	28%	42%	52%	13%
On Shelf	85%	76%	80%	74%	67%	66%	56%	46%	81%
On Loan	2%	6%	4%	2%	4%	3%	1%	1%	3%
In Other States	1%	6%	0%	6%	2%	2%	1%	0%	3%

Since values are rounded to the nearest whole number, columns may not total exactly 100 percent. Of the availability states shown in Table 2, States 4, 5, 6, 7, and 8 are subsumed in this table under "On Loan"; and States 2, and 9 through 8, are subsumed under "In Other States." Libraries A through G are medical school libraries. The "small" nonacademic library is the library of Harper Hospital (Detroit) with approximately 9,000 volumes, and the "large" library is that of the College of Physicians of Philadelphia, with roughly 250,000 volumes; for the reasons discussed in the text, test values for these two libraries should not be interpreted as measures of their capabilities for providing the documents needed by their primary users.
* Sample NA, as drawn, consisted of 300 test items; however, in the course of using this sample, a few test-item citations proved to be ambiguous, and a few more inadvertently omitted from tests in one or more libraries. The percentages shown here are based on the 290 test items with unambiguous citations that were searched in all nine libraries.

than seven days); or 5 (more than seven days). The "speed code" assigned to a particular item is based on how the searcher categorized its availability state at the time of the test, plus certain supplementary information obtained by the searcher, if knowledge of its availability state is not sufficient, in itself, to establish the proper speed code. For some of the availability states, the speed code assigned is the same in all cases. For example, any item the searcher finds on the open shelves in the expected location at the time of the first search, and without questioning library staff, is always coded as Speed 1, since it seems reasonable to assume that a knowledgeable user, given an adequate bibliographic description of the document, could obtain the item himself in ten minutes or less in almost any academic biomedical library. A speed code of 2 is always assigned to an item found in a "special location" to which access is controlled by library staff, or if it is found among documents awaiting reshelving. However, for test items in some of the other states, the speed code varies with circumstances and depends upon supplementary information. For example, when a test item proves to be out on loan, information regarding the library's loan periods is used in determining the proper speed code for that item. All the rules for speed coding have been standardized, and the process has been reduced to a strictly clerical operation that

can be performed manually or, if desired, programmed for a computer. A complete set of these rules is included in the Appendix; and with the exception of the rule for speed coding items not owned by the library, they will not be discussed further here.

Estimating Delivery Speed for Test Items not Owned

Items not owned by the library tested posed a special problem. It was obviously impractical to ask the library to initiate a purchase order or an interlibrary loan request for each of these items and wait to see how long it took to obtain them. However, we decided that the time required for interlibrary borrowing could be estimated closely enough for the purposes of the test and that we could safely assume borrowing would be a faster way to obtain most of the test items than purchase. Our original method for estimating interlibrary borrowing time was to ask the library to provide two dates for each of the last fifty documents borrowed from any source, either as an original or a photocopy: the date on which the document was requested by the user, and the date when the loan was ready for him to pick up. The intervals between "user-request" and "user-ready" dates were then calculated, and the median interval for the fifty transactions was taken as the "most likely" estimate of how long would probably be required to borrow any test item. For all libraries, the median interval was materially less than the mean interval, since the latter is greatly influenced by a few very long intervals. All test items not owned by the given library, and also those found to be "lost" or "missing", were then speed coded on the basis of this median interval. The precision of this estimate is actually critical only when the median interval is close to seven days; then a difference of a day one way or the other can mean the difference between coding the speed as 4 or 5.

After this method had been used for several trials, the question arose as to whether it might bias the test results materially under one or both of the following conditions: (1) when the tested library's commonly used sources of interlibrary loans are local libraries from which loans are obtained very rapidly, and these local transactions have not been included in its regular records of interlibrary loans; or (2) when the library's local environment is rich in resources, and its users are accustomed to going to these resources directly instead of asking the library to borrow for them. The former condition might hold for a medical library that is part of a university library system in which there is much unrecorded "intrasystem" borrowing. Under the second condition, the median time for interlibrary borrowing calculated from the library's records might not be a fair estimate of how long would be required to obtain test items, since the documents it had been borrowing might be relatively "exotic" ones, for which it is difficult to find rapid loan sources.

To assess the theoretical possibility that, under these two conditions, this method of estimating interlibrary borrowing time might materially bias test results, an alternative method was tried with eight of the nine libraries tested with Sample NA. In this alternative method, an attempt is made to estimate the probable borrowing time for each test item individually, rather than using a single estimate for all test items. Details of both the original and the alternative method are given in the Appendix, together with an analysis of differences in test results with the two methods. These differences proved to be relatively small in all cases.

Experience with the alternative method indicated that it entails considerably more effort than the original method — both for the library being tested and for anyone processing the test data. In addition, it seemed to be more subject to possible error. The major difficulty encountered with the original method was that relatively few libraries record the type of data needed — the dates when the user requested the document and when the document was ready for him. If records of the time required for borrowing are maintained, the dates recorded are usually those when the *library* initiated a request and when it received the loan materials. Since users' requests are commonly batched for processing, and incoming loan materials are "processed" before they are ready for the user, there is usually a material difference between the interval calculated from library records and the interval we need. In most libraries, it is impossible to establish the user-request and user-ready dates in retrospect; and we have to work with the dates on interlibrary loan request forms and add such rough estimates of processing time as the library can give. This problem with the original method is compounded in the alternative method. As a result, we have considerably less confidence that estimates of interlibrary borrowing time by the alternative method reflect typical performance and allow for the borrowing library's processing time. This consideration, plus the fact that the alternative method puts significantly greater demands on the libraries tested, led us to conclude that any benefits it has over the original method are questionable and that even if the benefits are real, the cost in terms of test practicality outweighs the benefits. We, therefore, decided to continue using the original method.

Calculating a Capability Index

After the availability state for each item in a test sample has been translated into a number representing delivery speed, the next step is to convert this mass of numbers into a single figure-of-merit. One can summarize the results by averaging the delivery speeds for all test items to obtain a "mean speed" — which will vary from 1, if all test items are found "on shelf," to 5, if the library owns none of the test items and borrowing them would require more than a week. The mean speed, however, does not meet our criteria for a summary measure — that it be intuitively meaningful and readily interpreted. Therefore, we change the mean speed into a "Capability Index" (CI) by a single arithmetical transformation.[10] The CI assumes a value of 100 when all test items are found "on shelf," and a value of 0 if none of the test items would be obtainable in a week or less.

TABLE 4
FACTORS INFLUENCING TEST RESULTS

EXTRALIBRARY FACTORS	LIBRARY FACTORS
1. Searcher Error	1. Capability
2. Sampling Error	a. Intrinsic Capability (own resources)
	b. System Capability ("coupling" with other resources)
	2. Activity of Collection
	a. Short-term Activity (in-library use)
	b. Long-term Activity (loans)

Factors Influencing Test Results

Table 4 outlines the factors that can affect test results. Since it is undesirable, methodologically, for "extralibrary" factors to influence test results, these two factors can be thought of as sources of error. "Searcher error" represents inconsistency in test results from one searcher to another, all other factors being constant. "Sampling error" is the variation in test results that occurs when tests are conducted with different samples from the same pool, even if all other factors are unchanged. "Capability" is a theoretical construct representing a library's ability to deliver documents *if its collection were not being used*. It has two components. The first consists of the library's "intrinsic capability," which is determined not only by the nature and size of its collection, but also by how well the collection is arranged and stored for accessibility and how well the "order" of the collection is maintained. Usually none of these determinants of intrinsic capability changes very rapidly; therefore, for a given library, this component of capability would not be expected to cause material differences in the results of tests performed a few days or weeks apart. The second component, "system capability," relates to the help a library can get from other libraries in local, regional, and national systems; it

is governed by how closely a library is "coupled" with the collective resources of these systems. Although one can think of a few things that could change this coupling rapidly — for example, installation of TWX — most of the factors determining this component of capability also change relatively slowly. "Activity of collection" represents service loads at the time of the test. It likewise has two components that can influence test results. At the time of a test, some of the test items owned by the library may not be immediately available, either because they happen to be in use within the library (short-term activity), or because they are out on loan (long-term activity). All of the factors shown in this table must also be considered when interpreting the results of testing *different* libraries — for example, if one library happens to be very busy at the time of the test, whereas a second is not, this can cause their test results to be different even if the two libraries actually have the same capability.

Controlling for Variables

For interpreting test results, and for assessing the relative influence of different factors (variables) on the test results, it seemed desirable to develop a convenient means of "controlling" the CI so that one could see what it would be if one or more of the four library variables were held constant. If one wants to compare test results for different libraries, or the results for a given library tested at different times, the value of having "options" for calculating the CI with different variables controlled is especially clear. We therefore worked out the following options for calculating CI:

Option 1 — all factors uncontrolled. The CI is calculated on the basis of the availability states in which test items were actually found at the time of the test.

Option 2 — short-term activity controlled. The CI is calculated as if all test items that were in use within the library at the time of the test had been "on shelf" instead and, therefore, immediately available.

Option 3 — long-term activity controlled. The CI is calculated as if all test items on loan at the time of the test had been "on shelf."

Option 4 — both short-term and long-term activity controlled. The CI is calculated as if all test items in use within the library *and* on loan had been "on shelf."

Option 5 — system capability controlled. The CI is calculated as if all test items not owned (and all items missing or lost) would require more than one week to obtain.

Option 6 — all of the above factors controlled.

Details on how the CI is calculated by these six options are given in the Appendix. Scoring a test — that is, calculating the CI — using these options is relatively simple and can be done manually. For convenience and speed in scoring multiple tests, however, a computer program was written.

In Table 5, the primary test data shown in Table 3 have been converted into CI's, and the values for "percent not in collection" in Table 3 have been subtracted from 100 percent to give the "percent of test documents owned" in the last column here. In all cases, the "percent of test document owned" is numerically very close to the CI by Option 6; these two figures would be identical except that some test items owned by a library may not be immediately available even when the activity of the collection is controlled — that is, test items found in availability states 2, 9, 10, 11, 12, 14, and 17 (Table 2). In Table 3, the libraries were ordered on the basis of the proportion of test items owned. One can see that, when ranked on the basis of their CI's by any of the

options, the order is much the same. The range of CI values among the libraries varies materially with different scoring options. When none of a library's major loan sources are nearby, the CI's by Options 5 and 6 are the same as by Options 1 and 4, respectively; and the difference between the CI's by Options 5 and 1, or between Options 4 and 6, provides a rough measure of how much of a library's borrowing is from nearby sources. The CI's by Option 4 are shown in bold face because they constitute the best basis for any general comparisons of the relative capability of different libraries; it seems neither logical nor fair to put heavily used libraries at a relative disadvantage, and both short-term and long-term activity are controlled by this option. For a given library, the difference between the CI's by Options 1 and 4 gives an indication of how heavy the service load was at the time of the test.

Reproducibility of Test Results

For comparing the results of two tests of a given library performed at different times to determine whether its capability has changed, or for comparing the test results of different libraries, one needs to know how reproducible or "reliable," the test results are — that is, how much of any *apparent* difference could have

TABLE 5
SUMMARY OF TEST RESULTS WITH SAMPLE NA (290 ITEMS)

Library Tested	Capability Index						Percent of Test Documents Owned
	Option 1	Option 2	Option 3	Option 4	Option 5	Option 6	
Academic							
A	86	86	88	88	86	88	89%
B	81	82	86	87	81	87	88%
C	81	81	84	84	81	84	84%
D	83	84	85	85	78	81	83%
E	76	76	79	79	69	72	73%
F	75	75	77	77	67	70	71%
G	67	67	68	68	57	57	58%
Nonacademic							
"Small Library"	60	60	61	61	47	48	48%
"Large Library"	83	83	85	86	83	86	87%

All values are based on a total of 290 test documents and are rounded to two significant figures. The scheme employed here for designating the libraries tested is the same as in Table 3.

been caused by the "extralibrary" factors, or sources of error, that are shown in Table 4, rather than by any real difference in capability.

As mentioned earlier, exploratory trials — in which different searchers, working independently, tested the same library with the same sample at the same time — indicated that the CI should not vary at all when the searchers are adequately trained in the standardized test procedures finally adopted. Although it is unrealistic to assume that anyone, no matter how well trained, can always achieve error-free performance on a task that requires hundreds of small decisions, we feel it is reasonable to expect that, after relatively short training in administering the test, careful searchers will make few errors. For a given library, the CI by Option 4 should rarely vary more than one point from one searcher to another if they are both using the same test sample and if the library's capability has not changed between tests. Variation in test results caused by "searcher error" can, therefore, be considered insignificant, provided searchers are properly trained.

The other source of error in test results cannot be reduced to insignificance in any test that is practical for wide use. "Sampling error" — that is, the variation in test results to be expected when a library is tested with different samples drawn from the same citation pool — can be reduced only by increasing the number of items in the test sample, which increases the time and effort required to administer a test. In the full-scale trials using a sample of 300 test items, searchers could complete a test in about three to four hours, which seems very acceptable for a practical test. Statistical studies of test data from all the full-scale trials with Sample NA show that, if one were to test a library repeatedly with different samples of 300 test items drawn from the same citation pool, the CI by Option 4 should not vary more than ± 5 points in 95 of 100 such tests, provided the library's capability did not change between tests. These studies also indicate that, under similar conditions, if the CI's of two libraries differ by six points or more, one can conclude that, in 95 out of 100 cases, they have different capabilities. A difference of six points or more is equally significant when a given library is tested at different times to assess changes in its capability. The statistical studies are described in the Appendix, which also reports the

results of actually retesting two libraries with different samples drawn from the national citation pool.

When sampling error is considered, a conservative interpretation of the CI's shown in Table 5 (Option 4) is that there is no evidence of any real difference in the capability of Libraries A, B, C, and D. However, one can be reasonably confident that Libraries E and F have less capability, as measured by this test, than Libraries A, B, C, and D — and also that the capability of Library G is significantly different from that of any of the others. Thus, the seven academic libraries that participated in these trials seem to fall into three classes as far as their document delivery capability is concerned.

Using a larger sample would give the test more "power" to detect small differences in capability, but the point of diminishing returns is reached rapidly. Increasing the size of the sample to 600 items, and thereby doubling the time required to perform a test, would decrease the "uncertainty" in CI's relatively little — to ± 4 points, rather than ± 5. We believe that a sample of 300 items represents an acceptable compromise between precision and practicality and that test "reliability" with such samples will probably be adequate for most purposes.

TABLE 6
COMPARISON OF CI'S BASED ON TESTS WITH SAMPLES FROM NATIONAL CITATION POOL (SAMPLE NA) AND FROM LOCAL CITATION POOLS

Library Tested	Sample From National Pool	Sample From Library's Local Pool
A	88	90
B	87	93
C	84	87
D	85	90

All CI's are calculated by Option 4 and rounded to two significant figures. All samples included approximately 300 test items.

Test Results with Samples from Local Citation Pools

As stated earlier, we initially decided to develop the test with samples drawn from local citation pools, as well as with samples drawn from the national citation pool. Table 6 compares the results of tests of four libraries using samples from their respective local citation pools with test results based on Sample NA from the national citizen pool. One can see that, for all four, the CI based on samples from local citation pools is somewhat higher than the CI based on samples from the national pool. However, the difference is greater than four points for only two of the libraries, and only in the case of Library B is it large enough for one to be highly confident that the difference is not attributable to sampling error. The mean CI for all four tests with locally derived samples proves to be significantly higher than the mean for tests with Sample NA — 90 as compared to 86. Statistical tests of significance are given in the Appendix. This overall difference may be interpreted as evidence that, to some extent, the collections of this group of libraries are "tailored" to the special interests of their respective faculties — that is, their collections are *relatively* more adequate for their local user populations than for biomedical researchers in general. An alternative explanation is that local user populations' reading habits have been influenced by the collections of their libraries — that they tend to read, and cite, what is readily available rather than what is *potentially* available.

The general practicability of tests based on samples drawn from local citation pools is questionable. Relatively few medical schools seem to maintain complete bibliographics of all staff publications; and to compile such a bibliography as a starting point for generating a local citation pool is, in itself, no small undertaking. Even when a suitable bibliography already exists, carrying out all the procedures required to prepare a test sample is relatively costly in terms of man-hours of work, much of which can be done only by professional librarians with a good knowledge of biomedical literature and bibliographic tools. Although some libraries may want to undertake the work required to prepare test materials specific to their own user population, tests based on samples from a national citation pool have more potential for general utility. Once prepared, a sample from such a pool can be used to test a large number of libraries, and the cost of preparation is spread over many uses. In weighing the relative advantages and disadvantages of tests based on the two types of samples, in addition to the matter of practicality, there is also the "philosophical" question touched upon earlier in presenting the rationale of establishing test samples. These considerations led us to decide that, for a test intended for wide use, samples from a national citation pool are definitely preferable.

Effect on Test-item Age

Drawing test samples from any pool representing cited documents means that relatively few of the test items will have been published very recently; and if "ready-made" bibliographies, such as the NIH *Research Grants Index*, are used as a starting point to generate the citation pool, then the literature of the previous few years will always be materially under-represented relative to its frequency of use at the time the test samples are used. When samples for the trials of this test were prepared in the latter part of 1966, we used the three most recent issues of the *NIH Research Grants Index* (RGI) then available to generate the national citation pool; nevertheless, the test samples contained no documents published in 1966, and few from 1964 or 1965 (see "Characteristics of Test Samples," above). The resulting citation pool actually represented the literature biomedical researchers were actively using during a period some two to four years before the samples were prepared. This fact explains why, when Sample NA from this pool was employed in the full-scale trials, which were conducted during 1966 and 1967, an average of only about 3 percent of all test items proved to be on loan at the time of the tests (see Table 3). If the sample had represented the literature that biomedical researchers were actively using at the time the tests were performed, a materially higher percentage of the test items undoubtedly would have been found to be on loan, and in other availability states that reflect use — for example, States 13 and 16 (Table 2).

The question therefore arises as to how relative "obsolescence" of test samples may affect the utility of test data. The answer depends upon what the data are to be used for. If one is interested in assessing the effect of varying service loads on the document delivery service a library can provide, or the effect of binding policies on capability, obsolescence will be highly undesirable. However, if test data are to be used for comparing the capabilities of different libraries, or for determining changes in the capability of a given library over a period of time, then a moderate degree of obsolescence is acceptable; for such uses, the variation caused by service loads will be controlled anyway, since CI's will be calculated by Option 4. In general, for most applications in which it is desirable to control for service loads (activity of collection), moderate obsolescence will not materially reduce the utility of test results; but it has some disadvantages. An example is where there has been a *recent* and sharp increase in the number of serials a library receives, and one wants to determine how this change affects its capability. Unless the file of these newly acquired serials extends back three years or more, the library's CI based on samples drawn from citation pools will show little or no change attributable to its new acquisitions. The effect of an expanded serial acquisition program will not be reflected in a library's CI for several years unless back files are acquired, and the same consideration holds for a cut-back in acquisitions. We have devised a way to "correct" a sample for the moderate obsolescence inherent in the use of any citation pool; however, the technique is not applicable to any nonserial test items in the samples. This technique, which is described in the Appendix, may be useful for special applications. Another example of a disadvantage caused by moderate obsolescence is that a library's speed in acquiring new nonserial titles is not reflected in the test results.

Should the citation pool employed for samples be *grossly* outdated, a significant number of recently founded journals will not be represented in test samples; and if some of these journals are heavily used by biomedical researchers, tests with these samples may overestimate the capability of libraries that have not acquired the more important new journals. It should be possible, however, to avoid gross obsolescence if one uses the most recent bibliographies available for the given user population as a starting point for generating the citation pool.

Preparing a Test Sample for a National Survey

After the full-scale trials indicated the test was practical and had acceptable reliability, we prepared a test sample suitable for use in a national survey of academic medical libraries. For this purpose, the original national citation pool was "updated" as described in the Appendix, and that sample was drawn from this updated pool. At the time this article was being written, this test sample was being used in a national survey conducted by the University City Science Center under a contract from the National Library of Medicine. If this method of assessing the document delivery capability of academic medical libraries proves a useful tool to those responsible for managing such libraries, and follow-up tests are desirable, new test samples can be drawn periodically from the same pool after it has been updated by the technique employed for the present test sample. Since, with this technique for updating the national citation pool, only about one-third of all the citations in the pool will be changed each year, the comparability of test results from year to year should be insured, and the effort required to prepare new samples will be relatively small.

Limitations of the Test

In describing the major decisions made in the course of developing this test, we have attempted to point out the implications of each decision as they relate to possible theoretical limitations or "weaknesses" of the test. We have also emphasized that the *practical* importance of these theoretical limitations usually depends on how, and for what purpose, test results are to be used. Some of the limitations are inherent in the procedures for test administration and scoring; others relate to test samples. Here we will review and summarize what seem to be some of the more important considerations regarding these two types of limitations.

Test administration assumes that a property trained searcher, proceeding according to standardized instructions, can simulate a real user sufficiently well that the searcher's findings with regard to availability of test items will *approximate* what the user would find if he visited the library and tried to obtain these items himself. If, in a particular library, this assumption is not valid for some reason, then the test results for that library will not be a valid measure of its document delivery capability. In typical medical school libraries, where the catalog and main stacks are freely accessible to users, it is difficult to conceive of circumstances that would invalidate this assumption. However, if the test is used in any other type of library, the validity of this assumption must be examined carefully. For example, in libraries where users do not usually serve themselves and where most of the stacks are not open, the searcher could not

158 ORR, PINGS, PIZER, OLSON AND SPENCER

simulate users by going to the shelves himself. For a realistic simulation, each item would have to be requested from the library staff. If a test sample of 300 items were to be administered in this way, within a few hours, it would put a heavy load on library staff; and their performance under the test conditions would be atypical. To test libraries of this type, other procedures for test administration will need to be devised.

Test scoring is based on the assumption that a test item can, with *reasonable* accuracy, be assigned to one of five categories of delivery speed on the basis of the availability state recorded by the searcher, plus a limited amount of supplementary information about the library being tested. For most medical school libraries, this assumption should be valid. But in a very large academic library, and in libraries where users *typically* find it difficult to determine document locations, it may not be valid to assume that a user can obtain any test item that is "on shelf" in ten minutes or less. Such a violation of the assumption will assume importance only under certain conditions — for example, when different libraries are being compared, and the assumption is seriously violated in some of the libraries, but not in others.

Another theoretical limitation of test scoring relates to the scheme used to code, or weight, the five different categories of delivery speed. Although the present scheme has some logical merit, it may not accurately reflect the relative values that users actually place on the different categories of delivery speed — perhaps being able to obtain a document within ten minutes is actually ten times "better" than having to wait more than a week, rather than being only five times better, as the present weighting scheme implies. Aside from the difficulty of determining, in any objective manner, how users value delivery speed, there is another reason why this theoretical limitation seems largely "academic." The CI is relatively insensitive to changes in the weighting scheme. If the tests summarized in Table 5 were scored by assigning a weight of 10 to all items not available in less than a week, rather than a weight of 5, the CI's would be practically the same as those shown.

The relatively "coarse" categorization of delivery speed employed in the present scoring procedure represents another theoretical limitation — for example, an item requiring two days to obtain is scored the same as an item

requiring three or four days, and a delivery time of two weeks falls into the same speed category as one of a month or more. The assumption is that, for most users and most needs, the differences in speed *within* a category are not as important as the differences *among* categories. Again, we believe that, for most academic medical libraries, this assumption is reasonably valid. However, for other types of libraries it may not be; and in any library where this assumption is questionable, the utility of the CI will be reduced to the degree that the present delivery-speed categories do not accommodate all the distinctions that make a practical difference to its users.

The principal limitations imposed by the present test samples are those inherent in the use of any citation pool as the source for test samples. Employing samples drawn from cited literature means that certain types of document needs — particularly those for "derivative," or secondary-source documents — and the needs of nonresearch segments of academic user populations are under-represented. Because researchers' needs for primary-source documents pose one of the most severe demands on a library's capability, we do not consider this limitation a critical weakness for a test of the document delivery capability of academic biomedical libraries. However, one must always keep this important limitation in mind when interpreting test results and avoid overgeneralization. If a library has a high CI, it does not necessarily follow that it has a high capability for meeting all the document needs of all of its users; one can think of grossly unbalanced acquisition policies that might result in a low capability for meeting some types of document needs in the face of a high CI.

An additional limitation imposed by using citation pools is that the age distribution of items in such pools cannot be typical of document use patterns at the time a test is performed. This weakness is accentuated when the citation pool is generated from ready-made bibliographies like those employed in establishing the test samples for the present trials. Where test results are to be used primarily for comparing the capability of different libraries, moderate obsolescence of test samples is now a critical disadvantage. But if the purpose is to study how service loads or binding policies can affect a library's performance, then this limitation assumes real importance.

Prospects for Improving the Test

Perhaps the most important of these limitations is that imposed by under-representation of some document needs in the test samples. Although, for a specific library, it is undoubtedly technically possible to establish a sample truly representative of all the published documents its entire user population reads or consults in the course of its work, the task would seem to require an investment of effort and time that relatively few academic libraries can make. While we cannot rule out the possibility that a practical technique might be developed to establish an ideal test sample, completely representative of document needs and appropriate for testing any academic medical library, we are not optimistic about the prospects.

After experience with the test in its present form, if librarians find it is a valuable tool, but its practical utility is materially affected by the coarseness of the present delivery-speed categories, then finer and more numerous categories can be defined. However, such an improvement probably cannot be realized without accepting either a higher incidence of categorization error, or an increase in the complexity of test administration and in the time required to administer a test. The former will decrease test reliability, and the latter will decrease practicality. In contrast, if it is felt that the present scheme for numerically weighting the delivery-speed categories can be modified to reflect users' values more accurately, this modification can be made easily and without adverse effects.

Advantages of the Test

Earlier, under "Weaknesses of Existing Methods," we touched upon some of the shortcomings of methods that have been used in the past to obtain quantitative assessments of a library's capability for supplying the documents its users need. One could evaluate the merits of the present test as compared to these existing methods. However, in discussing the test's limitations, the standard was an ideal measure, rather than existing measures; and in discussing its advantages, the same standard will be used. As compared with the test's limitations, we believe that its advantages are more apparent; therefore, they will be reviewed and summarized more briefly.

In the enumeration of major advantages that follows, the first four advantages are related to the general method of measuring document delivery capability, of which the present test is a specific example, and the remainder are related to the CI as a means of expressing test results. First, unlike the requests that users make of a library, the test items are not biased by what users know about the inadequacies of the library's collection, nor by their perceptions of the time and effort required for interlibrary borrowing. Second, because test samples are selected by random procedures, the reliability of any quantitative data the test provides is statistically determinant — knowing the confidence one can have in the accuracy of data is very important when considering their practical implications and making decisions based on them. Third, the test is outstandingly practical. It does not interfere with a library's normal routine and can be carried out in a few hours. Fourth, where strict comparability of test results for different libraries is not important, tests can be administered by a library's own staff. Fifth, test results can be expressed as a single figure-of-merit that reflects delivery speed — the user's primary criterion for the specific service being assessed. Sixth, this figure-of-merit, the CI, measures a library's capability for this service relative to that of a perfect library that has everything needed, always immediately available. The CI is, therefore, readily understood by users and fiscal authorities, as well as by librarians, and can be used to set goals that are intuitively meaningful to all concerned. Seventh, the CI is convenient and appropriate for comparing the capabilities of different libraries and for evaluating changes in the capability of a given library over a period of time. Last, this index accommodates the reality that today libraries are, functionally, components of larger systems and can provide the highest level of service for *any* given cost only by achieving an optimal balance in their dependence upon self-owned versus shared resources.

Interpreting Test Results

The importance of considering chance variation when interpreting test results have been stressed earlier. Here it seems desirable to discuss two other general considerations that should always be kept in mind when thinking about what test results may "mean."

Measuring capability by means of this test is not equivalent to *evaluating* the service tested.

The figures given by a test do not, in themselves, indicate whether a library is "good," "adequate," or "poor" — answering this question entails a value judgement. Whoever interprets test results must decide what the test results for a given library should be evaluated against — whether to compare them with typical, or "average," values for similar libraries, with the test values for a particular library considered to be a model, or with values representing goals set for future achievement. The trials conducted in developing this test involved a group of libraries that cannot be considered representative of U. S. medical school libraries in general; and the test results reported here, therefore, are of little use for indicating what typical values may be, or for suggesting what values may represent desirable and feasible goals.

"Capability" is a theoretical construct, representing how a library would perform if it were operating under the artificial conditions assumed for test purposes. A library's CI is, therefore, analogous to the power rating for an engine — it approaches being a measure of everyday performance to the extent that the assumed conditions approximate reality. In actual operations, a library's theoretical capability can, of course, never be fully realized. The CI calculated by Option 1 is closer to being a measure of actual performance than when the various factors affecting service are controlled in scoring. However, it reflects only the operating conditions at the time of the test; and unless service loads and other conditions happen to be reasonably typical at that time, it can be misleading. In addition, because of the obsolescence of the present test samples, it cannot reflect the full effect of service loads and technical processing activities on a library's performance.

Potential Uses of the Test

Some of the potential uses of the test and of test data have been suggested or implied earlier; however, it may be helpful to summarize the major uses previously touched upon and to mention a few additional possibilities.

When the test data from the national survey of medical school libraries become available, they can be used by appropriate bodies to establish national standards and goals for document delivery service, if this is considered desirable. These data will also make it possible for individual libraries to see how they compare with other libraries and to set their own goals for improvement. If periodic tests are carried out in such a way that test data are comparable from year to year, progress toward national and individual goals can be judged. In addition, the test samples developed for the national survey and for the developmental trials may be used by individual libraries for self-administered tests to obtain data useful for planning and management. These test samples may also be suitable for some research purposes.

If the present test samples are not suitable for some particular purpose, samples specifically designed for the purpose can be established and used within the present test framework. For example, a library can establish a test sample drawn from publications cited by its own users and compare the test results based on this sample with those based on a sample from the national citation pool; and samples appropriate for testing libraries serving dental or other health science schools can be established.

In a later article, we plan to report on a method that represents another potential use of test data. This method enables a library manager to employ test data in a systematic evaluation of the relative "cost effectiveness" of alternative ways to improve his library's document delivery capability.

A TEST FOR RESERVOIR LIBRARIES

Early in the course of developing a document delivery test for academic biomedical libraries, it became apparent that the same general method could be applied to measure a library's capability for supplying the documents needed by other libraries, as contrasted to the documents needed by its individual users — that is, its specific capability for serving as a source of interlibrary loans, which may be called its "reservoir capability." Existing means for assessing reservoir capability are even less satisfactory than those for measuring capability for serving individual users ("regular capability"). The proportion of interlibrary loan requests a library actually fills is perhaps even less satisfactory as a measure of reservoir capability than the analogous figure is as a measure of regular capability. Many factors other than a reservoir library's capability affect this proportion — for example, whether most of the borrowing libraries have a list of their holdings, and whether it is considered a loan source of "last resort." Since a document delivery test of reservoir capability (a "reservoir DDT") could be a useful tool in regional and national planning, when the feasibility of such a test became apparent, our original contract with the National Library of Medicine was modified to include the development of a reservoir DDT analogous to the test described in the first section of this article, which will be referred to hereafter as the "regular DDT." This application of the general method for measuring document delivery capability can be described more briefly because the development steps and the resulting test procedures are generally similar to those for the regular DDT.

In developing a test appropriate for reservoir libraries, the same two key questions had to be answered — "How can appropriate document samples be established?" and "How can the test be administered to achieve an acceptable balance between realism and practicality?"

Deciding on Reservoir DDT Samples

Within a given geographical region, all the loan requests initiated by libraries serving biomedical user populations are the potential load upon any system that may be established to handle biomedical loan requests on a regional basis. The library (or libraries) accepting formal or informal responsibility for acting as the regional reservoir will be required to handle some portion of this load. The size and nature of this portion will undoubtedly vary from one region to another, depending upon existing practices, and upon the philosophy of regional service that is adopted.

Ideally, before deciding how to establish test samples appropriate for a reservoir DDT, one would like to know exactly how a regional reservoir's responsibilities are defined; however, in the present stage of development of most regional systems, these responsibilities have not yet been clearly set forth in operational terms. Lacking this knowledge, one might make the simplifying assumption that a reservoir library could be called upon to handle *any* interlibrary loan request generated by the region's biomedical population. Under this assumption, test samples would ideally be drawn at ran-

dom from the universe of all such requests. But realizing this ideal poses many practical difficulties. It would be necessary to establish a different test sample for each region where a reservoir DDT was to be administered by randomly drawing test items from a pool representative of the region's interlibrary loan requests. To generate such a regional pool would require the cooperation of scores of libraries in providing lists of all the requests they initiated during some period that was long enough to insure it was "typical." Although an effort of this magnitude may be justifiable to obtain test data for planning and managing a particular regional system, our aim was to develop a *generally* useful test; and generating such pools for a number of different regions would require considerably more time and resources than were available.

We therefore decided to explore other ways to establish test samples. One possibility was to use a sample consisting of items that the development trials for the regular DDT had shown were not owned by one or more of the libraries tested — these items obviously represent potential requests on some reservoir library. However, the libraries tested in these trials were principally medical school libraries; and although a sample made up of such items might be representative of loan requests from academic libraries, the bulk of requests actually made on major de facto reservoir libraries are from hospital and industrial libraries. This technique for establishing a test sample was therefore challengeable on theoretical grounds. Its big advantage was that such a test sample could be established quickly. We decided to employ a sample established in this way for developmental trials of the reservoir DDT and later, while these trials were proceeding, to establish another test sample that would be more appropriate for use in a national survey of major de facto reservoir libraries.

Instead of focusing on regional systems, if one looks at regional reservoir libraries as components in the national system for handling interlibrary loan requests, their function can be viewed as "filtering" the requests from their respective areas that would otherwise go directly to NLM. To the degree that these regional filters are effective, the average time required for mail transit of requests and loan materials will be shortened, the quantitative load on NLM will be reduced, and its resources will be conserved for filling those requests that cannot be handled regionally. This formulation of a reservoir library's function suggests another way of establishing a sample appropriate for testing the capability of a de facto reservoir library. In principle, one could identify all the requests that are currently going to NLM from its region *without* being first checked against its holdings; and the reservoir library could be tested with a sample of such requests, which would not be biased by its holdings. Although this may constitute an ideal sampling plan, the procedure would definitely be impractical. However, the nature of current requests on NLM indicates that, in the informal system that presently exists, much of the total national demand for interlibrary loans is not being filtered through de facto reservoir libraries; and one can argue that a sample of the requests NLM currently receives will be a reasonable approximation of what would be obtained by the "ideal" sampling plan. We therefore decided to prepare a sample drawn from current requests on NLM for later use in the national survey.

Deciding on Reservoir DDT Procedures

Once the question of test samples had been resolved, the second key question remained — "How to administer the test to achieve an acceptable balance between realism and practicality?". This question proved considerably more difficult than the corresponding question for the regular DDT; and as a result, the compromise between realism and practicality that had to be accepted is less satisfactory. In the regular DDT, a searcher could simulate an individual user reasonably well, but by analogy, the "users" in the reservoir test are other libraries transmitting their requests from a distance. Actual service conditions could be realistically simulated only by sending several hundred test items to the library as "interlibrary loan requests"; and this way of administering the test seemed out of the question. Also, in the regular DDT, we measure a library's capability for providing documents on a selfservice basis and can therefore assume that variations in service load will not materially affect document delivery time — at least up to the point where the stack area becomes so crowded that users get in each other's way. In contrast, the capability of a reservoir library to deliver documents depends not only upon its collection's

adequacy, physical accessibility, organization, and control, but also upon the availability of staff to process requests as soon as they arrive. Since staff is always limited, a reservoir library's processing speed is sensitive to changes in its service load.

An additional difficulty in devising a reservoir test is that the criteria for assessing capability are more complex than for the regular DDT. At present, most de facto reservoirs do not routinely forward to another loan source all requests they cannot fill themselves; therefore, one cannot postulate, as in the regular DDT, that the essential criterion for assessing perfomance is not whether a library can supply a document, but only how long it takes. Any test measure of a reservoir library's capability must reflect the proportion of test items it can supply, as well as the time required to supply them.

From the borrowing library's viewpoint, the overall time required to obtain an interlibrary loan is the sum of three intervals — the time required for its request to reach the reservoir library, the time required for the reservoir to process the request and prepare the loan (original or facsimile copy) for delivery, and the time required for the loan to arrive from the reservoir library. If the analytic scheme depicted in Table 4 is applied to a reservoir library, one can see that only the second interval is determined by the "intrinsic capability" of the reservoir library; the first and third intervals are determined by its "system capability." In the regular DDT, we could use data from a library's records of its interlibrary borrowing to assess its system capability; however, it was obvious that, for the reservoir DDT, analogous data could not be obtained from routine library records. We therefore decided that, if the reservoir DDT was to be completed on a single visit of a few hours, as the regular DDT is, we would have to limit our aim to assessing only one component of capability — the library's intrinsic capability. But even with this limited aim, the questions of what to measure, and how, were not simple; and answering them required a careful analysis of the interlibrary loan transaction.

The loan operations that depend entirely upon a reservoir library's intrinsic capability are those that are under its immediate and *direct* control. They begin with receipt of a request and usually end when the material to be loaned (an original document or a facsimile) is ready to be delivered to the borrowing library, either by a common carrier (e.g., the U.S. mail) or by an agent of the borrower. Relatively few de facto reservoirs currently have their own messenger or delivery service; therefore, delivery to the borrowing library is not included among the operations that typically depend entirely on intrinsic capability. In all cases, however, the total time that elapses between when a request arrives at the reservoir library, and when the loan is *ready* for delivery, may be considered to be under its direct control. This interval, which we call the library's "total processing time," can be divided into two segments — "request-processing time," which ends when the library's staff has the requested document physically in hand, and "loan-processing time," which starts when the requested document is in hand, and ends when the original or a facsimile copy is ready for delivery.

From this analysis, it follows that a complete assessment of a reservoir library's intrinsic capability requires information about its typical total processing time, as well as about how large a proportion of potential requests it can be expected to fill. A test analogous to the regular DDT, in which someone searches the reservoir library's collection for each of a sample of test items representing potential loan requests, will provide the latter information; but how can total processing time be assessed in the course of administering such a test? In this case, the searcher will actually be simulating a member of the library staff who is trying to locate documents that have been requested; and if one assumes that the staff can always begin to process a request as soon as it is received, then at least a rough estimate of the library's request-processing time can be made from a knowledge of the availability state of test items at the time of the search. This estimate will, of course, not include the time-consuming process of correcting citations, since test items will have verified citations. To use the resulting estimate as a crude measure of the *total* processing time requires a second assumption — that, on the average, request-processing time bears a reasonably constant relation to total processing time. This second assumption may or may not hold in real operations, but the first is clearly unrealistic. However, since we could think of no other way to measure total processing time that preserved one of the best features of a DDT —

its practicality — we decided to accept the sacrifice of realism entailed by these assumptions. We felt that, despite the theoretical weaknesses of its claim to prima facie validity, a reservoir DDT administered in the same way as the regular DDT could provide useful data. The time estimate that can be derived from test data should be a reasonable approximation of the *shortest possible* time in which the tested library could process real requests for documents like those represented in the test sample; and the test data should provide a good idea of the adequacy of its collections for providing such documents.

In accepting this compromise, we were also influenced by the fact that we had already decided to develop another method, unrelated to the DDT, for measuring, directly, a reservoir library's "typical" total processing time and also its system capability. The data provided by this independent method would supplement DDT data and compensate for their deficiencies. This method has now been developed and will be reported in a later article in this series.

Trials of the Reservoir DDT

A sample consisting of 244 documents that were not owned by at least one of five libraries tested with a regular DDT was prepared for trials of the reservoir DDT. The sampling method is described in the Appendix, which also includes an analysis of the characteristics of this sample (Sample R). Sample R was used for tests of four de facto reservoir libraries — the libraries of Wayne State College of Medicine, of the Upstate Medical Center of the State University of New York (SUNY), of the New York Academy of Medicine, and of the College of Physicians of Philadelphia. These libraries range widely in size and in the number of interlibrary loan requests handled. We also tested the National Library of Medicine and two "library complexes" with the same sample. At the time of the test, one of these complexes — the Library of Upstate Medical Center and the other SUNY libraries in Syracuse and Buffalo — was actually operating as a functional unit in responding to interlibrary loan requests. The second library complex — the Library of Wayne State College of Medicine, the other libraries of Wayne State University, and eight Detroit hospital libraries — is potentially capable of operating as a functional unit.

Procedures for administering the reservoir DDT and recording test data were the same as those developed for the regular DDT, with one modification. In testing library complexes, if a test item was not owned by the first library searched, or if it was not immediately available at this library, its availability at other libraries in the complex was ascertained by telephone or teletypewriter. If more than one of the libraries owned the item, its availability state in the library where it could be obtained most quickly was recorded.

Coding Reservoir Test Data for Delivery Speed

In Table 7, the primary data from trials of the reservoir DDT employing Sample R have been categorized by grouping the more commonly observed availability states on the basis of the *least* time that would probably be required for the reservoir library's staff to put their hands on a copy of the test item. This categorization seems to be about as fine as one can make with reasonable certainty from inferences based on the searcher's record of the availability state of test items. In this table, the category numbers represent the speed codes assigned in translating the primary data into numerical form for test scoring. Detailed rules for assigning speed codes for the reservoir test are given in the Appendix.

These four delivery-speed categories seem to constitute a natural, if rough, way to characterize the speed with which a reservoir library can handle a request. However, the time scale implied does not have the theoretically desirable properties of the one used for the regular DDT, since the intervals are neither equal nor logarithmic. If Category 4 is considered to cover a time interval extending to infinity, one can rationalize assigning a speed of 4 to test items that are, in fact, functionally unavailable from the reservoir library when it does not routinely arrange with other libraries to fill any request it cannot meet. This artificiality is introduced into scoring so that reservoir test results can be summarized by a Capability Index analogous to that for the regular DDT.

The same speed-coding rules can be used for reservoir library complexes in which a request to any component of the complex is filled by whichever component can do it most quickly, given two assumptions: first, that the components employ some electronic means for intercommunicating; and second, that the sum of the processing times for the component receiving the request and for the one filling the request is not so much greater than the processing time for a single component that the time scale underlying the speed coding

TABLE 7
SUMMARY OF PRIMARY DATA FROM RESERVOIR DDT WITH SAMPLE R (244 ITEMS) CATEGORIZED BY AVAILABILITY

Availability Category	Percentage of Test Items						
	Wayne	Upstate	College of Physicians	New York Academy	NLM	"Wayne* Complex"	"Upstate* Complex"
1 — Available within a few hours ..	66	72	73	78	84	82	81
2 — Available within a day, but requiring more than a few hours	0	1	1	>1	3	3	1
3 — Available within a few weeks, but requiring more than day	3	1	3	5	0	>1	1
4 — Functionally unavailable	31	26	24	17	14	14	16

NOTE: *For reasons discussed in the text, the values should not be interpreted as definitive measures of the capabilities of these libraries for filling the kinds of interlibrary loan requests typically directed to reservoir libraries.*

Since values are rounded to the nearest whole number, columns may not total exactly 100 percent. Category 1 includes items on shelf at time of first search; Category 2 includes items stored off premises but retrievable within a day, plus items in use at time of first search but back on shelf at time of second search; Category 3 includes items checked out on loan; and Category 4 includes items not owned, plus items library had declared "missing" or could not locate at time of either search.

* "Wayne Complex" consists of the Wayne State College of Medicine Library, the other libraries of Wayne State University, and eight Detroit hospital libraries; "Upstate Complex" consists of the Library of the Upstate Medical Center, State University of New York (SUNY), and the other SUNY libraries in Syracuse and Buffalo.

rules is seriously violated.

Calculating the CI for Reservoir Tests

There are only four possible speeds in the reservoir DDT, rather than five as in the regular DDT; therefore, the formula for calculating the CI for the regular DDT was modified so that the range of 0 to 100 points would be maintained.[11] In this test, the factors influencing the CI are the same as those outlined in Table 4; and scoring options analogous to those for the regular DDT serve to control for the number of test items in short-term use at the time of the test (Option 2), for the number on loan (Option 3), or for both simultaneously (Option 4). Since a reservoir library's system capability does not influence the CI in this test, there are no Options 5 and 6. Details on the scoring options are given in the Appendix.

In Table 8, the values in the columns headed "Total Sample R" are based on the primary test data shown in Table 7. When calculated by Option 4, a reservoir library's CI is very close, numerically, to the percentage of test items owned; where there is a difference between these two values, it represents test items that were owned but functionally unavailable ("missing" or "can't locate") at the time of the test. Values for the CI by Option 4 are printed in bold face because, for the reasons discussed in connection with the regu-

lar DDT, these values are the most appropriate ones for general comparisons among libraries.

Implications of Reservoir DDT Trials

In reporting data from trials of the reservoir DDT, we have identified the libraries by name, in contrast to the practice followed in reporting trials of the regular DDT. These libraries constitute a much more heterogeneous group than the academic libraries tested in the trials of the regular DDT; and we feel that, to consider the methodologic implications of the trials, one should know something about the nature of the libraries tested. Because some of these libraries are unique, they could hardly be described and remain anonymous. Since they have been identified, we feel it necessary to emphasize that, unlike the test data from the trials of the regular DDT, data from the reservoir DDT trials are based on a test sample that, for the reasons discussed earlier, does not have a good claim to be considered "appropriate." Sample R is adequate for methodologic purposes — such as determining reproducibility, obtaining an idea of the range of the CI, etc. — but one should not consider the values shown in Tables 7 and 8 as definitive measures of either the absolute or the relative capabilities of these libraries for filling the kinds of inter-

TABLE 8
SUMMARY OF RESULTS OF RESERVOIR DDT WITH SAMPLE R

Library Tested	Total Volumes (X 10³)	Total Sample R (244 Items)			"Biomedical" Items in Sample R* (213 Items)		
		Percent Owned	CI		Percent Owned	CI	
			Option 2	Option 4		Option 2	Option 4
Wayne	68	69%	67	**69**	76%	71	**76**
Upstate	75	74%	73	**74**	82%	81	**82**
College of Physicians	228	76%	74	**76**	84%	82	**84**
New York Academy	358	83%	80	**83**	88%	85	**88**
National Library of Medicine	1300	86%	86	**86**	92%	92	**92**
"Wayne Complex"	984	86%	85	**86**	89%	89	**89**
"Upstate Complex"	615	84%	83	**84**	91%	90	**91**

NOTE: *For reasons discussed in the test, the values should not be interpreted as definitive measures of the capabilities of these libraries for filling the kinds of interlibrary loan requests typically directed to reservoir libraries.*
* Any document published in a serial covered by *Index Medicus*, listed in "Biomedical Serials 1950-1960," or included in the *NLM Catalog* was considered "biomedical."

library loan requests that are typically directed to de facto reservoir libraries.

Although all test items in Sample R represent documents actually used in the course of biomedical research, some of these documents fall outside the usual subject classification of biomedical literature. The right side of Table 8 indicates how the test values change when they are calculated on the basis of only those test items classified as biomedical by the stated criteria. From the methodologic viewpoint, it is interesting that, although the CI based on biomedical test items alone is materially higher in all cases, the ranking of libraries on this basis is much the same as that based on the CI for the total sample. One could interpret the size of any difference between these two CI's as an indication of how closely the scope of the library's collection of biomedical literature — the larger the difference, the more strictly "biomedical" the collection. The present data suggest that the libraries tested may differ in this respect, and the differences are in the direction that might be expected; however, the chance variation attributable to sampling error must be considered.

With this test sample, the CI for both library complexes is high, even when only "biomedical" test items are counted in scoring. This finding is not surprising in view of the total document resources commanded by these complexes (see "Total Volumes," Table 8). From the present data, one might conclude that a reservoir library complex that includes at least one "good" university library has about as much capability for providing interlibrary loans as the largest medical library. However, for the reasons that have been discussed, basing such a conclusion on test data with Sample R is unwarranted. The capability of reservoir complexes deserves further investigation with a more definitive sample, such as the one described later. If complexes also score very high with a more definitive sample, there is still the question of the formidable organizational problems involved in creating a complex that actually responds as a functional unit. These problems can block the realization of a complex's theoretical capability unless they are solved.

Reliability and Practicality of the Reservoir DDT

Statistical studies reported in the Appendix

indicate that the CI for the reservoir DDT is at least as reproducible, or reliable, as for the regular DDT. With a test sample of 300 items, the CI (Option 4) for a reservoir library can be expected to vary no more than ± 5 points in 95 of 100 repeated tests with different samples from the same document universe. For the values shown in Table 8, which were based on a test sample of only 244 items, the corresponding limits are ± 6.

The reservoir DDT is also equally practical to administer. Although administering a test at one of the very large reservoir libraries will require longer than administering a regular DDT at a typical medical school library, it can be done in roughly half a day in most cases. Individuals trained to administer the regular DDT can also administer the reservoir DDT, since the searching and recording procedures are the same. Because the trials entailed relatively few tests, we did not develop a computer program to score the reservoir test; however, like the regular DDT, the scoring procedure can be automated.

Preparing a Reservoir Test Sample for a National Survey

The rationale for assessing the capabilities of major de facto reservoir libraries as "filters" in the national medical library system has been discussed earlier. A sample suitable for such an assessment has been established by selecting some 300 test items from all the interlibrary loan requests NLM received during fiscal 1967, using random procedures described in the Appendix. When the citations for these test items appeared questionable, they were verified and corrected as necessary. From NLM's records, we established that 97 percent of the items in this sample (Sample NLM-1) is in its collection. At the time this article was being written, Sample NLM-1 was being used for testing major de facto reservoir libraries as part of the national survey mentioned earlier in connection with the regular DDT.

There is the possibility that Sample NLM-1 may be too "difficult" to give results that accurately reflect capability for meeting the kinds of requests that regional reservoirs will be called upon to handle. This question could be answered by testing some libraries with both Sample NLM-1 and a new sample randomly selected from the total interlibrary loan traffic among the nation's medical libraries. However, establishing such a sample will require a substantial effort and considerable time. A less definitive assessment of this possibility might be carried out with a sample established by selecting items from the total traffic within a smaller geographic area.

Limitations and Advantages of the Reservoir Test

Most of the general considerations concerning the limitations and advantages of the regular DDT apply equally well to the reservoir DDT. However, this test has certain additional limitations, which will be summarized here. As has been discussed, in this test "users" can be simulated less realistically and completely than in the regular DDT; and only the intrinsic component of a reservoir's capability can be assessed. Since the scheme for weighting test data for delivery speed entails an artificiality not entailed in scoring the regular DDT, and the time scale for delivery speed has less desirable properties, the CI for the reservoir test cannot be considered as satisfactory a figure-of-merit to summarize test results. The latter weakness, however, pertains only to the CI and not to the primary test data. These data can be used to assess a reservoir's collection and its "housekeeping" controls, without attempting to summarize them in a single figure-of-merit.

Perhaps the most important advantage of the reservoir DDT is that this test makes it possible to assess the adequacy of collections in terms of the demand that will be made on libraries assuming formal responsibilities for regional service in the evolving national medical library system — the "potential demand," in contrast with the "expressed demand" that de facto reservoirs currently feel. The latter is markedly influenced by many factors that will change when regional services are formalized and integrated into a true national system.

Potential Uses of the Reservoir Test

The potential uses of the reservoir DDT can be summarized very briefly. The data obtained in the national survey from testing major de facto reservoir libraries with Sample NLM-1 will be useful for predicting how the load on NLM will change as current plans for regionalizing interlibrary loans are implemented. The national survey data should also be useful for planning regional services, in that they will indicate the adequacy of a reservoir library's present collection for meeting its future responsibilities. In conjunction with data supplied by the method we have developed for measuring typical processing time and for assessing system capability, the primary test data from the national survey will give a comprehensive picture of a reservoir's intrinsic and system capabilities.

For purposes where strict comparability of test results among different libraries is not required, the reservoir DDT can be self-administered using Sample NLM-1 or Sample R.* For example, the reservoir DDT employing Sample NLM-1 should be an excellent tool to explore the potential of reservoir library complexes for meeting regional needs. Libraries in the process of assuming regional responsibilities may want to test themselves with samples drawn from the interlibrary loan traffic in their particular region. However, once a library's regional loan services are fully operational, the potential demand for loans should become expressed demand quite rapidly; and at that time, such tests will be unnecessary, since its *actual* performance in meeting this demand is the ultimate measure of the adequacy of its collection.

CONCLUSION

We belive that the general method for measuring document delivery capability presented here is basically sound and should be applicable to many types of libraries. The weaknesses of any specific application of the method — that is, any operational test designed for a particular type of library — stem from compromises regarding preparation of test samples and test administration that are dictated by practical considerations. In applications where acceptable compromises can be achieved, the method has unique advantages over the subjective and objective methods currently employed to assess a library's capability for providing the documents its users need. The tests for academic and reservoir biomedical libraries developed in this project appear to meet this requirement. But, in the last analysis, whether the necessary compromises are acceptable must be judged by those who use the test results as aids in making decisions.

Neither of these tests assesses all aspects of a library's capability for supplying all the documents needed by all segments of the pertinent user population — individuals in the case of the test for academic libraries, and other libraries in the case of the test for reservoir libraries — and both can be improved by further refinement. Nevertheless, we are convinced that the tests can be useful in their present form. Actual experience in using them will be the best guide for efforts to increase their utility and minimize their disadvantages.

Like many powerful tools, these tests require an appreciation of their limitations as well as their advantages. If these limitations are clearly understood, we believe that the tests will prove to be valuable tools for planning and managing library services.

ACKNOWLEDGEMENTS

In addition to the libraries of Wayne State University College of Medicine and of the Upstate Medical Center of the State University of New York, the following libraries participated in the full-scale trials of one or both of the document delivery tests: the medical school libraries of Albany Medical College, the State University of New York at Buffalo, the University of Louisville, and the University of Pennsylvania; the libraries of Harper Hospital (Detroit), the College of Physicians of Philadelphia, and the New York Academy of Medicine; and the National Library of Medicine. Without the help generously provided by the staffs of these libraries, and the active cooperation of numerous other libraries in the exploratory trials, this work would have been impossible.

Many individuals on the professional staffs of the Medical Library of Wayne State University, the Upstate Medical Center Library of the State University of New York, and the Institute for Advancement of Medical Communication assisted in this effort. Of these, the following made material contributions: at Wayne, G. S. Cruzat, M.L.S.; at Upstate, Carol A. Salverson, M.L.S.; and at the Institute, Sol Rabin, Ph.D., George Shaffia, M.L.S., Reginald W. Smith, M.S.L.S., and two Research Fellows supported by USPHS Grant HE 5414, Paul L. Garwig, M.S., and Joseph E. Lovett, Jr., B.S. On statistical questions, David S. Salsburg, Ph.D., Assistant Professor of Statistics, University of Pennsylvania, and Bernard Warner, Ph.D., Senior Research Staff Member, Management Science Center, University of Pennsylvania, provided valuable counsel.

NOTES

Author's Notes

[1] This work was supported in part by U.S. Public Health Service Contract PH 43-66-540 from the National Library of Medicine.

[2] A later paper (*Bulletin of the Medical Library Association*, 60 (3) July 1972, pp. 382-422) gives the results of a project in which the test was administered at 92 libraries, discusses weaknesses that were disclosed, and illustrates how the test data can be used in a mathematical model to predict the effects of alternative actions to improve capability.

Editor's Note

In 1968 standardized Document Delivery Tests based on the above article were employed in the U.S. to assess the capability of 92 medical school libraries for meeting the document needs of biomedical researchers and the capability of 15 major resource libraries for filling interlibrary loan requests from biomedical libraries. The report on the survey is of considerable interest not only for the results obtained but also for the methodological problems involved. For details see Orr, R. H. and A. P. Schless. Document delivery capabilities of major biomedical libraries in 1968: results of a national survey employing standardized tests. *Bulletin of the Medical Library Association* 60 (3) 1972, 382-422.

Footnotes

[1] This classification scheme is described in Part I of the present series of papers, to which this paper belongs. Part I covers the project's overall objectives and its conceptual framework, and appears in the *Bulletin of the Medical Library Association* 56 (3) July 1968, pp. 235-240.

[2] Line, M. B. Library Surveys. Hampden, Connecticut, Shoestring Press, 1967. 146 p.

[3] Tauber, M. F. and Stephens, I. R. Library Surveys. New York, Columbia University Press, 1967. 286 p.

[4] Williams, E. E. Surveying Library Collections. In: Tauber, M. F. and Stephens, I. R. *op. cit.*, p. 23-45. (See especially p. 32).

[5] Voerhoeff, J. The Delft circulation system. *Libri* 16: 1-9, 1966.

[6] Meier, R. L. Information input overload: features of growth in communications-oriented institutions. *Libri* 13: 1-44, 1963.

[7] Line (*op. cit.*, p. 42-44) and Parker and Paisley (Parker, E. B. and Paisley, W. J., Research for psychologists at the interface of the scientist and his information system. *Amer. Psychol.* 21: 1061-1071, Nov. 1966.), recently reviewed these techniques and discussed some of their advantages and disadvantages.

[8] Orr, R. H., Abdian, G., and Leeds, A.A. Generation of information: published output of U. S. biomedical research. *Fed. Proc.* 23: 1297-1309, Nov. - Dec. 1964.

[9] The Appendix also includes other materials, which are described in later sections of this paper.

[10] Capability Index = $\dfrac{5 - \text{Mean Speed}}{4}$ x 100.

[11] Capability Index for reservoir DDT = $\dfrac{4 - \text{Mean Speed}}{3}$ x 100.

ABOUT THE AUTHORS

Richard H. Orr was born in Kansas and educated at the University of Chicago (A.A. and B.S.) and the University of Southern California (M.D.). He was employed at the Southern Pacific Hospital, San Francisco from 1950-53, and from 1953-55 he was a Research Fellow at the University of California Medical Center. From 1955-57 he was Medical Director of Grune and Stratton Inc. (medical publishers) and since 1958 he has been Director of the Institute for the Advancement of Medical Communication. In 1971 he came to England as Senior Visiting Research Scientist at Aslib, and during 1972-73 he was an Honorary Research Fellow in the University of London. He is well-known for his outstanding contributions to medical librarianship and library management and has been on the editorial boards of numerous journals in the library field.

Vern M. Pings took his M.A.L.S. and Ph. D. at the University of Wisconsin and soon afterwards became Librarian of Ohio Northern University, Ada, Ohio. In 1960 he moved to the School of Librarianship of the University of Denver and then from 1961-71 he was Medical Librarian at Wayne State University School of Medicine. During this time he held a number of visiting lectureships, etc., and was an active member of more than one research team. In 1971 he became Acting Director of the University Libraries of Wayne State University, and in January 1972 he became Director. He has published numerous articles and books on medical librarianship and on other topics.

Irwin H. Pizer was born in 1934 in Wellington, New Zealand. He took his M.S. at Columbia University School of Library Service and during 1960-61 was an Intern at the National Library of Medicine. From 1964 to 1969 he was Librarian and Professor of Medical History at the State University of New York Upstate Medical Center and from 1969-71 he was Associate Director of Libraries at the State University of New York at Buffalo. During the years 1966-70 he was also Director of the SUNY Biomedical Communication Network. Since 1971 he has been University Librarian and Professor of Library Administration at the University of Chicago Medical Center, Chicago.

Edwin E. Olson teaches at the School of Library and Information Services, University of Maryland, College Park. Professor Olson has a B.A. degree from St. Olaf College, Northfield, Minnesota and M.A. and Ph.D. degrees from the American University, Washington, D.C. He has had considerable experience of studying library systems including work with the Institute for the Advancement of Medical Communication and as a consultant to Westat Research.

Carol C. Spencer holds degrees in Chemistry and information science and is Director of Regional Services, Mid-Eastern Regional Medical Library Program, College of Physicians Library, Philadelphia.

Sources of Information on Specific Subjects

S. C. Bradford

A classic contribution to library science, Bradford's paper, published nearly forty years ago, can be identified as one of the first systematic attempts to analyze bibliographic data. It is the starting-point from which "Bradford's Law of Scattering" has since been developed.

It is interesting to note the structure of the paper: the first paragraph outlines the problem and the observations which have led to its isolation, in the second paragraph alternative hypotheses are put forward to explain these observations, and there then follows an explanation of the methods of measurement used and a detailed analysis of the data. The results of this data analysis are used to support the postulation of a "law of (the) distribution of papers on a given subject in scientific periodicals."

Those who are concerned with progress in science and invention are aware of the need for the provision of an efficient service for abstracting and indexing scientific and technical literature. It is, therefore, somewhat disquieting to find on inquiry that, although the 300 abstracting and indexing journals notice 750,000 articles each year, which is the same as the total number of papers published in their fields; owing to duplication of effort, only 250,000 different articles are dealt with and 500,000 are missed. This is the more difficult to understand when the skill and money spent on these services are realized. It seemed worth while to inquire whether the cause of this failure might not lie in the manner in which the literature of a subject is distributed among the periodials that contain it, and an investigation was consequently undertaken by Mr. E. Lancaster Jones in the Science Library. The results fully confirm this view.

It might be supposed that the bulk of the papers on a special subject would be published in a few journals specially devoted to that subject, or to the major subject of which it forms a part, together with certain border-line journals and some of the more general periodicals. An alternative hypothesis to be investigated is that, to a considerable extent, the references are scattered throughout all periodicals with a frequency approximately related inversely to the scope. On this hypothesis, the aggregate of periodicals can be divided into

TABLE
APPLIED GEOPHYSICS, 1928-1931, INCL.

A.	B.	C.	D.	E.
1	93	1	93	0
1	86	2	179	0.301
1	56	3	235	0.477
1	48	4	283	0.602
1	46	5	329	0.699
1	35	6	364	0.778
1	28	7	392	0.845
1	20	8	412	0.903
1	17	9	429	0.954
4	16	13	493	1.114
1	15	14	508	1.146
5	14	19	578	1.279
1	12	20	590	1.301
2	11	22	612	1.342
5	10	27	662	1.431
3	9	30	689	1.477
8	8	38	753	1.580
7	7	45	802	1.653
11	6	56	868	1.748
12	5	68	928	1.833
17	4	85	996	1.929
23	3	108	1,065	2.033
49	2	157	1,163	2.196
169	1	326	1,332	2.513

SOURCE: Bradford, S. C. "Sources of Information on Specific Subjects." *Engineering* 137(3550) 26 Jan 1934, pp. 85-86.

LUBRICATION, 1931 - June, 1933
(FEW 1933 REFS.).

A	B	C	D	E
1	22	1	22	0
1	18	2	40	0.301
1	15	3	55	0.477
2	13	5	81	0.699
2	10	7	101	0.845
1	9	8	110	0.903
3	8	11	134	1.041
3	7	14	155	1.146
1	6	15	161	1.176
7	5	22	196	1.342
2	4	24	204	1.380
13	3	37	243	1.568
25	2	62	293	1.792
102	1	164	395	2.215

Column A gives the number of journals producing a corresponding given number of references.

Column B gives the corresponding number of references during the period surveyed.

Column C gives the running sum of the numbers of Column A.

Column D gives the running sum of the numbers of Column B multiplied by A.

Column E gives the common logarithms of Column C numbers.

classes according to relevance of scope to the subject concerned, but the more remote classes will, in the aggregate, produce as many references as the more related classes. The whole range of periodicals thus acts as a family of successive generations of diminishing kinship, each generation being greater in number than the preceding, and each constituent of a generation producing inversely according to its degree of remoteness.

The investigation covered, in the first place, the references quoted, in the course of four and two and a half years, respectively, by the current bibliographies of Applied Geophysics and Lubrication, which are prepared in the library. The source of each reference being given, it was possible to arrange the sources in order of productivity, the results being set down in columns A and B of the table, in the previous column.

A glance at these figures shows that in each case there are a few very productive sources, a larger number of sources which give moderate production, and a still larger number of constantly diminishing productivity. In each case by far the largest number of sources give only a single reference during the whole period of the survey. No definite boundaries between the various classes are indicated, but the sources can be graded roughly according to the following basis:

a. Those producing more than 4 references a year.
b. Those producing more than 1 and not more than 4 a year.
c. Those producing 1 or less a year.

In the case of applied geophysics (see columns C and D):

In class a there are 9 sources producing altogether 429 references,
In class b there are 59 sources producing altogether 499 references,
In class c there are 258 sources producing altogether 404 references.

In lubrication, assuming that practically all the references relate to the two years 1931 and 1932 only,

in class a there are 8 sources producing 110 references
in class b there are 29 sources producing 133 references
in class c there are 127 sources producing 152 references

The groups thus produce about the same proportion of references in each case, and the number of constituents increases from group to group, by a multiplier which, though by no means constant, approximates fairly closely to the number 5, especially for the two larger groups. This suggests that the running total number of references given in column D might be proportional to the logarithm of the corresponding number of sources in column C, *i.e.*, to the corresponding number in column E. And, in fact, if curves are plotted, as in Fig. 1, page 86, with E as abscissae and D as ordinates for both cases, the later portion of each curve is remarkably close to a straight line. We can thus say that the aggregate of references in a given subject, apart from those produced by the first group of large producers, is proportional to the logarithm of the number of sources concerned, when these are arranged in order of productivity.

In the diagram, Fig. 2, let P be the point at which the straight line part of the curve commences. Draw $P_1 X_1$ and $P_1 Y_1$ perpendicular to the axes of X and Y respectively. On O Y mark off $Y_1 Y_2$ and $Y_2 Y_3$ each equal O Y_1. Draw $Y_2 P_2$ and $Y_3 P_3$ parallel to $Y_1 P_1$, cutting the curve in P_2 and P_3, and draw $P_2 X_2$ and $P_3 X_3$ both parallel to $P_1 X_1$. Let the distance O X_1 be r units and the equal distances $X_1 X_2$ and $X_2 X_3$ be s units in length. Then, if α, β and γ are the natural numbers corresponding respectively to the logarithmic abscissae O X_1 O X_2 and

O X_3, we have

$$\log \boldsymbol{\alpha} = r, \text{ or } a = 10^r$$
$$\log \boldsymbol{\beta} = r + s, \text{ or } \boldsymbol{\beta} = 10^{r\,+\,s} = 10^r \times 10^s$$
$$\log \boldsymbol{\gamma} = r + 2s, \text{ or } \boldsymbol{\gamma} = 10^{r+\,2s} = 10^r \times (10^s)^2$$

Putting $10^s = n$, we see that the natural numbers $\boldsymbol{\alpha}, \boldsymbol{\beta}$ and $\boldsymbol{\gamma}$ are related to each other as $1 : n : n^2$

The journals in the group represented by O X_1 form a nucleus of those more particularly related to the subject in question. Therefore, the law of distribution of papers on a given subject in scientific periodicals may thus be stated: if scientific journals are arranged in order of decreasing productivity of articles on a given subject, they may be divided into a nucleus of periodicals more particularly devoted to the subject and several groups or zones containing the same number of articles as the nucleus, when the numbers of periodicals in the nucleus and succeeding zones will be as $1 : n : n^2 \ldots$

The question now arises, what limit can be assigned either to the aggregate of sources, or the aggregate of references produced, in any given subject? We know that the former number cannot exceed the total number of current scientific periodicals, say 15,000. But all the data known hitherto relate only to known sources actually discovered in preparing bibliographies. How can we determine whether a mass of sources is in fact absolutely sterile in each subject, and how determine this number? One approach to this hidden factor is suggested by the scope of the sources actually found. On examination, we can establish the fact that the a and b groups above are periodicals of scope obviously and *a priori* relevant to the subjects investigated. They are journals which would almost inevitably suggest themselves as being concerned with these subjects, among others. On the other hand, the c groups are very mixed, including some sources which, by their scope, we might expect to find more productive; but including also journals of very general scope in which we should hardly expect to find references. We are surprised, on the one hand, by the lack of productivity of the former, and, on the other hand, by the productivity of the latter. We can only draw the general conclusion that a large number of references are produced by sources which, *a priori*, are "unlikely."

Again, if we examine the annual aggregate of sources of references, we find that each successive year brings forth a new crop of sources of references, and that many sources produce a reference one year, but fail in later years. In fact, in the applied geophysics case, each of the four years produced about 40 sources which gave a reference that year and none in the other three years. Also, if we take the successive periods 1929, 1929-30, 1929-31, and 1929-32, *i.e.*, one, two, three and four-year periods, it is found that the number of references arising from sources which produce not more than one reference per annum is, in the four periods, 86, 184, 320, 404 respectively. As each year produces about 350 references, it may be deduced that, in any given period of years, the c group will produce approximately 25 per cent to 30 per cent of the total quantity of references. These will arise from sources which fluctuate over a wide range, and may in the aggregate involve a thousand or more periodicals.

It is conceivable that there could be specified in each of the two test cases a list of a thousand sources that would include all the producers yet found and all which might be found in a ten years' survey. But there is no means of ascertaining the limit necessary in any given case, and no guarantee that in the bibliographical work a considerable number of articles have not been ignored. In the lubrication case, it is significant that a small sample of journals, selected at random from a general list as being possible sources of references, yielded in a ten-year survey 4 "producers" out of 14. These 4 produced only 15 references in the ten years, none producing an average of 1 a year, so that all would come in group c. Out of these 4, only one actually occurs in the list of producers in the bibliography 1931-33, and this one is not in fact the greatest producer in the ten-year period tested. These 14 periodicals examined represented a sample, very small naturally, of the aggregate of regular journals dealing with general science, physical and chemical sciences and engineering and industry. This class would exclude periodicals of the annual or semi-annual type, and those dealing with natural history, medicine and other subjects unlikely to produce references to lubrication. It might thus represent a sample of 14 from an aggregate of say, 3,000 possible periodicals of the former type. As, out of the 14, 4 were found to be productive, we get, as a very rough approximation, a figure of

$$\frac{2}{7} \times 3,000 = 850 \text{ (say)}$$

for the number of productive sources in a ten-year period.

Two further tests were made, each based on an examination of the relevant classes in the subject catalogue of the Science Library during a five-year period in which about 500 periodicals, on all branches of science and technology, have been indexed. The tests showed that the lubrication references came from 14 sources, and the applied geophysical references from 19 sources. Assuming that the periodicals indexed by the library represent about $\frac{1}{30}\left(=\frac{500}{15,000}\right)$ of the total number of similar periodicals in existence during the five-year period, we get

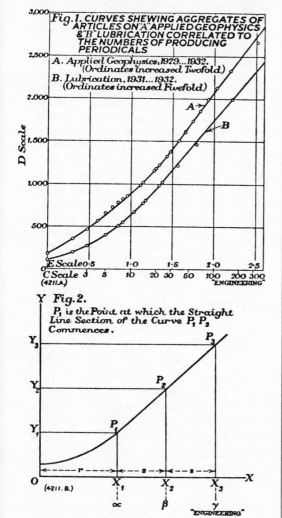

Fig. 1. CURVES SHEWING AGGREGATES OF ARTICLES ON "A" APPLIED GEOPHYSICS & "B" LUBRICATION CORRELATED TO THE NUMBERS OF PRODUCING PERIODICALS

A. Applied Geophysics, 1929...1932.
   (Ordinates increased Twofold)
B. Lubrication, 1931...1932.
   (Ordinates increased Fivefold)

Y Fig. 2.
P_1 is the Point at which the Straight Line Section of the Curve $P_1 P_3$ Commences.

the figures 14 X 30 = 420, and 19 X 30 = 570 for the numbers of actual sources of references on lubrication and applied geophysics res-

pectively, in a five-year period. These figures are both considerably less than the figure 850 obtained above for lubrication periodicals, which is to be attributed mainly to the difference in the period of the survey, as will be seen.

Other considerations tend to confirm the hypothesis that the number of sources must increase almost linearly with the period of the survey. The numbers of known geophysical sources contributing not more than one reference a year to the bibliography were as follows: —

> 86 in the year 1929
> 155 in the 2-year period 1929-1930.
> 230 in the 3-year period 1929-1931.
> 258 in the 4-year period 1929-1932.

and these form the major portion of the known sources, which were respectively 145, 218, 281 and 326. The increments each successive year are 73, 63 and 45, the last figure being probably smaller than it should be, because the survey of the literature of 1932 is still incomplete.

It is reasonable to assume that the known geophysical sources would increase over the whole ten-year period, though the increment might tend to diminish each year, say be 10 per cent.

Thus the number of known sources in a period of n years might be

$$S_n = a + (b + br + br^2 + \ldots \text{ to } n \text{ terms})$$
$$= a + \frac{b(r^n - 1)}{r - 1}$$

where, for the geophysics bibliography,

$$\left.\begin{array}{l} a = 60 \\ b = 85 \\ r = \dfrac{9}{10} \end{array}\right\} \text{ approx.}$$

giving

$$S_n = 60 + 850 (1 - 0.9^n)$$

or in the limit $S_\infty = 910$.

Again, putting $n = 5$ and 10, successively, we have, for applied geophysics,

$$S_5 = 410$$
$$S_{10} = 615$$

These are the "bibliographical" or "known" sources.

For lubrication, we know that a two-year survey produced 164 bibliographical sources compared with the 218 of applied geophysics, say 25 per cent less. We can therefore assume, for lubrication

$$S_5 = 310$$
$$S_{10} = 460$$

Comparing S_5 here with the value $S_5' = 420$ estimated for the actual sources, we get a figure

$$S'_{10} = 460 \times \frac{420}{310} = 620$$

for the actual or total sources in lubrication, on a ten-year basis. Considering the approximate character of the analysis, this figure is sufficiently comparable with the 850 obtained above.

It seems safe to say, therefore, that the number of journals which contain articles on the subjects in question is of the order of a thousand. But the periodicals themselves could not be specified without scrutinising a much larger number of periodicals during a long period. And even when the actual producers during a period of years had been ascertained, new sources would certainly appear during a further period. It follows that the only way to glean all the articles on these subjects would be to scrutinise continually several thousands of journals, the bulk of which would yield only occasional references or none at all. And because this work is altogether impracticable, a large portion of the total number of references on a given subject is regularly missed by the abstracting journals.

For the same reasons special libraries cannot gather together the complete literature of their subject, except by relinquishing altogether their specific character and becoming practically general libraries of science. In practice one-third of the contents of special libraries is usually related definitely to their scope, the remaining two-thirds comprising literature on border-line and less related subjects. These publications are duplicated in many other libraries, and their representation in any one is altogether inadequate.

In methods of abstracting and indexing, a radical change is needed. Periodical literature must be abstracted by source, and not by subject, as hitherto. All the important articles in each periodical should be catalogued, those coming within the scope of a particular bureau should also be indexed, the titles of the remainder being forwarded to the bureaux specially concerned, or to a clearing house. A standard classification must be adopted, so that references to the same subject would be brought together by the classification, irrespective of source or abstracting bureau, when, without increase of labour, a complete index to scientific literature would be achieved.

ABOUT THE AUTHOR

S. C. Bradford was one of the founders of modern bibliometrics - his "Documentation," published in 1947, is cited in a host of papers which have been published since his death in 1948. He held the degree of D.Sc. (from the University of London) and was a Fellow of the Library Association. He worked at the Science Museum in South Kensington from 1899 until 1938, when he retired. From 1925-38 he was Chief Librarian of the Science Library. He was co-founder (with Professor A.F.C. Pollard) of the British Society for International Bibliography, and in 1927 he helped to found the British National Section of the International Federation for Documentation. (amalgamated with the Association of Special Libraries and Information Bureaux in 1948). He published a number of papers on bibliometrics, as well as papers on physical chemistry and a book on his favorite recreation activity entitled "The Romance of Roses."

Bradford's Law and the Bibliography of Science

B. C. Brookes

Bradford's hypotheses on the laws underlying the distribution of papers in scientific periodicals have been taken up by other researchers and a mathematical relationship, known as Bradford's Law of Scattering, has been established. The author is able to demonstrate both the theoretical and practical implications of this Law, and to show that it is more than just the "statistical curiosity" which some authors have taken it to be. The Law provides the means to test the completeness of a bibliography, allows the bibliographer to estimate the number of items in the complete bibliography, provides the librarian with data with the help of which he can determine the most effective way to spend his limited serials budget, and may also be of use in estimating the coverage of the literature in an hierarchical library system.

In 1948 Bradford[1] formulated an empirical law of scientific periodical literature in the following terms:

"If scientific journals are arranged in order of decreasing productivity of articles on a given subject, they may be divided into a nucleus of periodicals more particularly devoted to the subject and several groups or zones containing the same numbers of articles as the nucleus, when the numbers of periodicals in the nucleus and succeeding zones will be as $1 : n : n^2 : \ldots$"

Bradford also drew a graph to illustrate the law (Fig. 1). Along the x axis he ranked the periodicals $1, 2, 3 \ldots n \ldots$ in decreasing order of productivity of papers relevant to the given subject on a logarithmic scale; along the y axis he marked cumulative totals of papers, $R(n)$. When $R(n)$ is plotted against $\log n$, the resulting graph begins with a rising curve AC which at some critical point C runs into a straight line CB. Bradford's formulation of this law is quite clear, but he did not express it in the form of a mathematical equation. As a result of this omission it has taken twenty years for the significance of this law to be recognized.

During these twenty years the law has been regarded only as a statistical curiosity. Its validity has been tested from time to time with varying degrees of apparent success, chiefly because the law has not always been interpreted as Bradford formulated it. There has also been a search for the underlying formula, particularly for series with terms such as $(n + a_n)$ which might yield sums of the form required, and more elaborate formulations

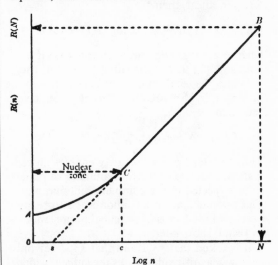

FIG. 1. BRADFORD'S DIAGRAM OF THE "LAW" OF SCATTER" SHOWING THE INITIAL CURVE *AC*, THE "NUCLEAR ZONE" AND THE LINEARITY *CB*.

SOURCE: Brookes, B. C. "Bradford's Law and the Bibliography of Science," *Nature* 224, 6 Dec 1969 pp 953-955.

have been published from time to time. It has only recently been noticed[2] that the law has to be expressed in two parts:

$$R(n) + \alpha n^\beta \quad (1 \leq n \leq c) \quad (1a)$$
$$+ \kappa \log n/s \quad (c \leq n \leq N) \quad (1b)$$

These two equations refer separately to the rising curve and to the linearity, and satisfy Bradford's verbal formulation and his graph precisely.

The constants are not all independent. The value of α is the number of relevant papers published in the most productive periodical; it clearly increases with the timespan of the bibliography. It is found that $\beta < 1$ always: its value is constant only if the bibliography is restricted to some relatively short time-span, say two to five years. For bibliographies with longer time-spans such as those recently analysed by Goffman and Warren[3] on mast cells and schistosomiasis, which both ranged over a century, it is found that β takes a series of successively decreasing values — of 0.85, 0.73 and 0.40 for mast cells and of 0.91 and 0.86 for schistosomiasis.

The constant κ is the slope of the linearity. All bibliographies are finite and the final increment, from the least productive periodical, cannot be less than 1. If N is the rank of this last periodical, then

$$r(N) = R(N) - R(N-1) = -k \log (1-1/N) \approx k/N = 1$$

when N is large enough, as in this case it is. And so $k=N$, that is the slope of the linearity indicates the total number of periodicals in the bibliography. So equation (1b) can now be rewritten

$$R(N) = N \log N/s, \quad (c \leq n \leq N) \quad (1c)$$

Thus the slope of the linearity enables an estimate to be made of the total number of papers to be expected in the complete bibliography. This estimate has been found to be surprisingly exact and the fact is of practical importance — as I shall show later.

It is found that $s \leq 1$ and that $s = 1$ for only narrow scientific subjects: as the subject widens, so does s. In fact, s could become an objective measure of subject breadth, for it can be shown that if r wholly independent bibliographies of equal size, each with $s = 1$, are added together to become a composite bibliography then the composite value of s is r.

The value of c, which is related to s, has not yet been found to be less than 3, and that when $s = 1$. So the value of c increases also as the breadth of the subject increases. As the curve is found to run smoothly into the linearity, certain analytical conditions have to be satisfied: they are that

$$1/\beta = \log_e c/s = R(c)/N$$

For strict conformity with Bradford's law, certain conditions have to be imposed on the bibliography. They are (1) the subject of the bibliography must be well defined; (2) the bibliography must be complete, that is, all relevant papers and periodicals must be listed; (3) the bibliography must be of limited time-span so that all contributing periodicals have the same opportunity of contributing papers.

Nevertheless, it is found that the form of the graph is surprisingly stable even when these conditions are not fully satisfied. The more one analyses sets of bibliographic data in this way, the more one is surprised by the stability of the Bradford law and of the characteristic form of the bibliograph.

MECHANISM UNDERLYING THE LAW

The underlying mechanism of this empirical law is not fully understood. The generation of a Bradford distribution is a stochastic process which is at present being explored by computer simulation techniques. There seem to be two mechanisms which compete in part. The linearity arises if successive choices are made initially from a small number of possible items, but only if each item selected becomes a "success" which strengthens the probability of that same item being selected again. As the total number of selections grows, so does the number of items from which selection is made. Gradually a few of the items emerge as the most "popular" choices but, as they do, a restrictive factor comes into play, though it bears only on a limited number of the most popular selections. These most popular selections remain, however, the most popular selections but with their freedom of growth restricted in part. Without such restriction the resulting graphs are always wholly linear (on semi-log paper) and of the form

$$R(n) = k \log n/s$$

where $s \leq \frac{1}{2}$, that is, they are Zipf distributions.

To obtain the required Bradford-Zipf combination it is therefore necessary to impose on the c most popular choices a restriction of the required intensity and proportional to some as yet unknown function of (c-n) which, for $n < c$, will fade away to zero as n approaches and finally reaches c.

In bibliographical terms the Bradford law implies that when the first papers on a new subject are written they are submitted to a small selection of appropriate periodicals and are accepted. The periodicals initially selected attract more and more papers as the subject develops but, at the same time, other periodicals begin to publish their first papers on the subject. If the subject continues to grow, however, there eventually emerges a Bradford "nucleus" of periodicals which are the most productive of papers on the subject. As this occurs, the pressure of the thrusting new subject on the space of these periodicals increases until restrictions are imposed by limitations of space and by editorial decisions to maintain a balance of scientific interest among all the papers published. Assuming that the initial growth of literature in any new subject follows an exponential law in time, conformity with the Zipf law would require a uniform increase with time of the numbers of papers published on the new subject by each contributing periodical, but this kind of growth does not continue; one relief is the establishment of new specialist periodicals. The initial rising curve of the Bradford nucleus to the Zipf linearity is the indication of the kind of restrictive pressure which leads to a Bradford deficiency from the Zipf expectation of ($\alpha + N \log s$) papers from the nucleus of periodicals.

If this hypothesis, which combines the free play for all of the "success-breeding-success" mechanism together with restraints on the most popular few is valid, then it should apply to other phenomena subject to similar conditions. Conversely, if these conditions are not fully satisfied, then Bradford-Zipf distributions should not be obtained. So let me specify again the requirements for exact conformity with the law in more general terms.

The Bradford-Zipf distribution can be expected to arise when selection is made of items, characterized by some common element, which are all equally open to selection for an equal period and subject to the "success-breeds-success" mechanism, but when the selection of a most popular group is also, but to a weaker extent, subject to restriction. It is thus a general law of concentration over an unrestricted range of items on which is superimposed a weaker law of dispersion over a restricted range of the most frequently selected items.

The Bradford law remains empirical until it is better understood. But if it can be demonstrated to be widely applicable, reliable and useful in practical operations there is no need to wait until the underlying theory is completely established. In the chaotic field of scientific documentation there is plenty of work for it to do in helping to design information systems, in rationalizing library services and in making more economic and fruitful use of the 29,000 scientific periodicals estimated to be in current production.

BIBLIOGRAPHIC APPLICATIONS OF BRADFORD'S LAW

The collection of a complete bibliography by human search is still an exhausting task even with the bibliographic aids now available. There is unfortunately no indication to the searcher when his task has been completed. All that he knows is that as he approaches the end of his task, his search becomes increasingly unrewarding until finally he stops. The advent of computerized bibliographic search systems such as MEDLARS has therefore brought a flood of new bibliographic data. The advantage of the computer is that it completes any search it makes on the literature within the system and maintains a constant standard of "relevance" throughout.

Fig. 2 shows the actual and estimated "complete" bibliograph of a MEDLARS print-out on muscle fibres. It is typical of good bibliography, though even this shows, towards the end, a slight fall-off from the Bradford idea in $R(N)$, though N is correctly estimated. The bibliograph of a good but "selected" (and therefore incomplete) bibliography on computer science is shown in Fig. 3 to indicate its larger deviation from the Bradford ideal.

All such bibliographs of periodical literature so far examined have either corroborated Bradford's law or else the discrepancies have been plausibly accounted for.

The number of abstract serials and other aids to bibliographic searching now exceeds

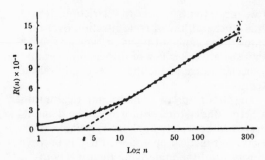

FIG. 2. BIBLIOGRAPH OF MEDLARS PRINT-OUT ON MUSCLE FIBERS: $N = 313$, $E = 313$, $R(N) = 1,402$, $R(E) = 1,346$; $s = 3.6$, $c = 18$.

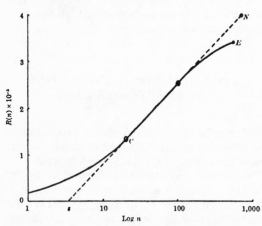

FIG. 3. BIBLIOGRAPH OF A GOOD BUT "SELECTIVE" (AND THEREFORE INCOMPLETE) BIBLIOGRAPHY ON COMPUTER SCIENCE: $N = 750$, $E = 522$; $R(N) = 4,050$, $R(E) = 3,436$; $s = 3.4$, $c = 18$.

1,000 and so they too should be candidates for Bradford analyses. Statistical data on the use of bibliographic aids are, however, scarce. The only published data known to me are those of Wood and Bower[4] of the National Lending Library which refer to abstracting serials used in the social sciences. The bibliograph (Fig. 4) conforms closely with the law — a fact of practical importance though it would be reassuring to have corroborating evidence from other sources.

Data on citations are readily available but their bibliographs conform only in part to the Bradford-Zipf distribution. Some citation data yield Zipf distributions only. For example, data on citations in *Plasma Physics* — published by East and Weyman[5] — yield

two successive Zipf distributions with $s_1 = 1/2.08$ and $s_2 = 1.00$ respectively (Fig. 5). In this case, therefore, there is no Bradford restriction. But this is not surprising because there is no restriction on the number of citations that may be made. Data on citations given by papers in *Physics of Fluids* to papers in other periodicals, also given be East and Weyman[5], seem to conform with the Bradford-Zipf law (Fig. 6), but the estimated end-point is 248

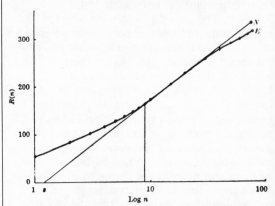

FIG. 4. BIBLIOGRAPH OF THE USE OF ABSTRACTING SERIALS IN THE SOCIAL SCIENCES (WOOD AND BOWER): $N = 75$, $E = 77$; $s = 1.21$, $c = 9$.

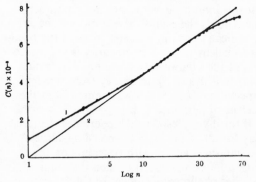

FIG. 5. BIBLIOGRAPH OF CITATION DATA IN *PLASMA PHYSICS* (EAST AND WEYMAN): TWO ZIPF DISTRIBUTIONS, $s = 1/2.08$, $s = 1.00$.

while the actual end-point is 372 citations. The explanation is that citations are not bibliographically homogeneous: citations to other papers by papers in *Physics of Fluids* are not all to other papers which would be classified as "physics of fluids": they may refer to mathematics, electronics, and so on. So citations do not conform with the Bradford-

Zipf conformity of the distribution of the citing papers.

If the publishers of books of a bibliographically well defined subject, for example mathematics, are ranked 1, 2, 3 . . . *n* . . ., and *R(n)* is the cumulative sum of books published within a given period, then *R(n)* conforms with the Bradford law. The required conditions are fully met.

The issues of books by a library seem to satisfy the Bradford conditions but, until a computerized issue system can do the count automatically, such data cannot be checked without an inordinate amount of clerical work.

PRACTICAL APPLICATIONS OF THE LAW

In the management of special libraries the bibliograph offers a check on the completeness of any allegedly complete bibliography — a check that has hitherto been missing. For any specified subject it is necessary to analyse the productivity of only at most the *c* + 5 most productive periodicals in order to estimate the complete bibliography. Thus much time and effort can be saved in trying to estimate the magnitude of the bibliographical area and the cost to the library of attempting to cover the

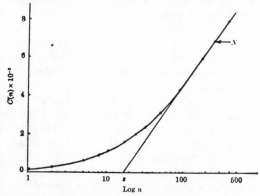

FIG. 6. BIBLIOGRAPH OF CITATIONS IN *PHYSICS OF FLUIDS* (EAST AND WEYMAN): THE END-POINT DOES NOT CONFORM; *N* = 248, *E* = 372.

whole or any specified fraction of the complete bibliography. Thus, if *f* is the specified fraction, this fraction of the complete bibliography is covered most economically if the Bradford ranked series is cut at *n* where

$$N \log n/s = f\, N \log N/s, \ (c \le n \le N)$$

that is where $n/s = (N/s)^f$.

Thus, for $N = 2,000$, $s = 5.0$, $N/s = 400$. And so to cover half the output of papers from the 2,000 contributing periodicals it is necessary to take only the $s(N/s)^{1/2}$ or 100 most productive of the 2,000 periodicals. The same technique can be applied to bibliographic aids. It should be noted that the technique is valid only if $n \ge c$, but a special library would normally take at least the "nuclear" periodicals in its subject.

If the total expenditure on periodical provision is limited to the fraction *f* of the sum needed to cover the subject completely, the buying of periodicals may be supplemented by the buying of photocopies of the relatively few relevant papers published in the peripheral periodicals. For $n \ge c$, the number of papers expected in the periodical of rank *n* is N/n; the cost of such papers is therefore approximately An/N each, where *A* is the average cost of annual periodical subscriptions. As soon as $An/N > P$, the average cost of photocopies, it pays to switch from periodicals to photocopies. We then have

$$An + PN (\log N/s - \log n/s) = f\, A\, N$$

an equation for *n* which can best be solved graphically by reference to the bibliograph.

It is known that scientific periodicals "age", that is interest in and references to back issues decline broadly in conformity with the negative exponential law

$$R(t) = R(0)\, e^{-t/a}$$

where $R(t)$ is the sum of the references to issues of age *t* or more, and where *a* is a constant characteristic of each scientific subject. It is therefore possible to organize the periodicals in a special library so that ageing issues are discarded as they reach any prescribed minimum level of utility. If it is worth while just retaining (for a few seconds only) new issues of the *n*th of the *N* periodicals, the fraction of the total utility thus discarded is $n/(N \log N/s)$ so that equal increments of utility would be discarded from the remaining collection if the process were continued with the discarding, one by one, of the periodicals ranked $n - 1$, $n - 2, \ldots$ down to $n - c$.

The law could also be applied to the planning of special library systems; the model considered here consists of a national, a regional and a local library. The local special library is assumed to be interested in a scientific subject whose complete periodical bibliography consists of N periodicals with the characteristic constant s. Of these N periodicals, the national library takes all, the regional library takes n_1 and the local library takes n_2, where $c \leq n_2 \leq n_1 \leq N$. Most of the periodicals taken by the regional and national libraries will be in the outer Bradford zones of the subject and therefore contain papers of interest to other special libraries as well.

If it is assumed that the use made of periodicals is proportional to the numbers of relevant papers they contain, then $R(n)$ is proportional to usage. Thus a scientist interested in the subject and seeking specific papers will find $f_2 = R(n_2)/R(N)$ of the papers he needs in his local library, $f_1 = [R(n_1) - R(n_2)]/R(N)$ of his residual needs in the regional library, and the remaining fraction, $[R(N) - R(n_1)]/R(N)$, in the national library. Substituting $R(n) = N \log n/s$ we obtain

$$n_2/s = (N/s)^{f_2} \text{ and } n_1/s = (N/s)^{f_1 + f_2}$$

It has been shown[6] that f_1 and f_2 can be related to the "viability ratios" of the libraries. If the local library does not attain, for any given potential user, a certain minimum viability, he will by-pass it in favour of the library next in the hierarchy. This factor depends on the user's estimates of the "costs" to him of using the various libraries and varies from one potential user to another. These viability ratios are likely to be lognormal variates. A library operating at the median value of the ratio is attracting half its potential users, and analysis shows that the viability ratio of a local library in relation to a regional library varies inversely as the "distance", measured in terms of user cost, of the local from the regional library. Thus the local libraries more remote from the regional library can operate viably with a smaller stock than those that are nearer.

For all such problems of viability and rationalization of library systems the Bradford-Zipf distribution is of great value. Subject bibliographies can be resolved or composed without difficulty, for example, but its principal advantage is that it has an optimization principle automatically built into it. The Bradford cut-off is the optimum cut-off for all purposes.

THEORETICAL PROBLEMS

The Bradford-Zipf distribution is empirically found to be very stable. But it would be reassuring to have a theoretical explanation of its stability. Ordered distributions such as Bradford and Zipf have so far attracted little theoretical attention.

Though the Bradford-Zipf distribution, which is first organized by arranging all the contributing "sources" in order of productivity, is not a conventional statistical distribution, such a distribution can be derived from it by inverting the distribution to express the numbers of periodicals, $p(r)$, expected to produce r papers. The probability density function of this distribution is

$$p(r) = \frac{1}{1 - \gamma^r} \frac{1}{1 - \gamma^{r+1}} \quad r = 1, 2, 3 \ldots N/c$$

where $\gamma = e^{-1/N}$ so that $\gamma < 1$. This expression reduces to $p(r) = N/r(r + 1)$ when r/N is small enough, but it has to be modified to allow for the Bradford restriction when $r > N/c$.

The behaviour of the Bradford-Zipf distribution for $n < c$ also requires theoretical analysis. It is not clear why the exponent β, if not constant throughout, seems to take a series of distinct discrete values.

In conclusion, when remaining doubts about the applicability of the Bradford-Zipf to bibliographic work, and the reliability of the estimates derived from its application, have been more thoroughly tested, it seems to offer the only means discernible at present of reducing the present quantitative untidiness of scientific documentation, information systems and library services to a more orderly state of affairs capable of being rationally and economically planned and organized.

NOTES

[1] Bradford, S. C., *Documentation* (Crosby Lockwood, London, 1948).
[2] Brookes, B. C., *J. Doc.*, 25, 58 (1969).
[3] Goffman, W., and Warren, K. S., *Nature*, 221, 1205 (1969).
[4] Wood, D. N., and Bower, C. A., *J. Doc.*, 25, 108 (1969).

[5] East, H., and Weyman, A., *Aslib Proc.*, 21, 160 (1969).
[6] Brookes, B. C., *J. Lib.* (in the press).

ABOUT THE AUTHOR

B. C. Brookes read mathematics and physics at Oxford and took his first degree in 1932. He has taught at University College London since 1949 when he was appointed Lecturer in the Presentation of Technical Information. In 1966 he was appointed Reader in Information Studies and now teaches in the Library School. He has written numerous articles on various aspects of librarianship and information science.

Empirical Hyperbolic Distributions (Bradford-Zipf-Mandelbrot) for Bibliometric Description and Prediction

Robert A. Fairthorne

A review of past work on the characteristics of a particular type of statistical distribution (the hyperbolic distribution) and its application in a variety of fields. Bradford's Law of Scattering is shown to be a particular application of this general distribution in the field of "bibliometrics," and the various interpretations of the Law are dealt with chronologically. This paper gives a glimpse of the variety of activities which have been studied and the powerfulness of brief formulae to describe the complex structure of many different things.

Since 1960, and especially during the past three years, many papers have appeared about particular manifestations and applications of a certain class of empirical laws to a field that may be labelled conveniently "Bibliometrics". This term, resuscitated by Alan Pritchard (see page 348), denotes, in my paraphrase, quantitative treatment of the properties of recorded discourse and behaviour appertaining to it.

In this field the law cited is usually that named after Bradford[4,5] or Zipf[59,60] according to whether the interest is in vocabulary or periodical literature or physical access, in the rate of diminishing returns, or in the cumulative yield from a given input. The behaviour is hyperbolic; that is, the product of fixed powers of the variables is constant. This type of behaviour has been observed for a century or so in fields ranging from meteorology to economics, and has given rise to many particular explanations appropriate to the particular fields. Thus it has received many names according to its exponents, in both senses of that word.

A recent note by Buckland and Hindle[10] and subsequent correspondence[20,52,11,8] have outlined the application of the Zipf-Bradford (rectangular hyperbolic, or harmonic) relation to aspects of library management and aligned it with some cognate studies in other fields.

This paper, and its bibliography, supplement Buckland and Hindle. It aims to help present and future workers to build on what has been done already. To this end I, as have others, interpret earlier work as particular applications of a certain type of statistical distribution. Inevitably this attempt at unification is largely a précis of Benoit Mandelbrot's researches.[2,42,43,44,45,46,47]

This approach, besides thwarting wasted effort, has the advantage that it makes available statistical tools that are neutral towards rival explanations of this type of behaviour. Actually, as Fairthorne[17] pointed out in 1958, it is non-conformity, rather than conformity with it, that needs explanation. It is difficult to defeat in situations where the objects or actions of interest are built from a finite repertoire of elements — alphabet, vocabulary, authors, journals, arm and leg movements, species, phonemes — whose co-occurrences are at most weakly correlated and whose quantitative properties are additive. More generally, as pointed out by Mandelbrot[46,47] it is characteristic of any phenomena that are self-similar in that their parts differ from the whole only in scale.

So far as possible I outline mathematical matters plainly and briefly enough to lie within the tolerance of a generally educated reader,

SOURCE: Fairthorne, R. A. "Empirical Hyperbolic Distributions (Bradford-Zipf-Mandelbrot) for Bibliometric Description and Prediction," *J. Docum.* 25 (4) Dec 1969 pp 319-343.

while giving enough clues and references for the mathematically skilled to follow up.

The bibliography necessarily and properly overlaps that of Buckland and Hindle, and should be taken as supplementing theirs. With few exceptions I have read all the works that I cite.

EMPIRICAL LAWS

The same social phenomena may have many different causes, acting severally or in concert. Together with the uniqueness of social events, which makes them unrepeatable in detail, this strongly hampers the isolation of social causes. Day to day struggles with these uncomfortable facts make economists, engineers, administrators, librarians, and other servants of social demands, very wary of general principles claimed to be the mainspring of widely ranging phenomena. The wariness varies directly with the generality of the principle. Even in physics some general principles such as the conservation of energy, Hamilton's principle, and Lagrangean equations apply to so many possibilities as to be useless unless these are strictly isolated and controlled within a laboratory or conceptual model. Permissible general principles are those of logic and mathematics, provided that these can be shown to correspond with reality not only before deduction, calculation, and symbol manipulation, but also after.

On the other hand, though causal insensitivity hampers explanation, it correspondingly helps prediction. Provided that the unknown causes are not augmented or replaced by different ones, the general pattern of events is likely to be repeated. Given enough carefully collected and presented data, both the pattern and its persistence can be estimated usefully in numerical terms. This can be very useful, pending explanation. For instance, gravitation is far from being explained, though there is precise and comprehensive enough knowledge of gravitational behaviour to construct stationary satellites and, in due course, live in them. But for wider tracts of useful activity even rougher knowledge will suffice. Often all that is needed is reasonable assurance that water will flow into the sink and not on to the ceiling.

In social situations even this kind of assurance is weakened by the awkward fact that the situations are created by people. All measurements are necessarily retrospective, so social prophecies based upon them are liable to be either self-defeating or self-fulfilling just because they have been made. Indeed, "quality control" consists of making and then defeating prophecies of future unfavourable behaviour. I use the word "prediction" in this sense of detecting changes soon enough to correct or allow for them. I do not use it in the sense of successful prophecy, guaranteed in advance of its success.

The indispensable basis of this kind of prediction is careful and extensive observation. This demands not only skill, patience, and endurance, but also inspiration about what may prove relevant. One cannot observe everything. Then the data must be described rationally and conveniently. Description also needs inspiration, because the manner of description is, consciously or unconsciously, a partial explanation.

Not so long ago the presentation of empirical data had an ambiguous status. Many of its devotees compensated for lack of insight and experimental skills with exotically graduated graph paper, "curve fitting" with typographically elegant expressions inappropriate to the subject matter, arbitrary parameters equinumerous with the data and, as even now, the darker activities euphemistically named "adjustment of experimental data". Widespread use and understanding of statistical disciplines has done much to remove the black magic from empirical description. One can discuss and compare similar patterns of behaviour in widely removed fields without assuming that they have the same proximate cause. For instance, the pattern of events known as the Poisson distribution is exhibited both by the number of soldiers kicked to death by horses within a given period, and also by the number of loans in certain libraries within a given period. This does not prove that library borrowers have the motives of homicidal horses. Nor, of course, does it disprove it. The deductions are no more than that at any given time most books were not being borrowed and most soldiers were not being kicked to death, that neither the borrowers nor the horses were working in concert between themselves, and that individual drives to borrow or kill were manifested so often on the average. Because rare events, occurring independently of each other at constant average rates, are common in many otherwise unrelated activities, the Poisson distribution can be used in them for prediction, in the sense defined above.

From this antiseptic viewpoint I will discuss a certain class of empirical descriptive "laws" that long have been known to fit certain phenomena of psychology, meteorology, linguistics, signalling errors, economics and, presumably, any other phenomena with the necessary formal properties. Amongst these are certain types of bibliographic behaviour, as was noted some time ago without much effect. In the past two or three years this has been rediscovered and applied with fair vigour. This resurgence of interest comes because of the growing demands on library and cognate services. Far more people are now working at, and paying for, library and documentary work than earlier. Moreover, workers are now quite as numerate as they are literate, sometimes more so. Only a few years ago writing on such topics in the mathematical frame of mind resembled shouting into a hollow tree. Also we can now delegate heavy computation to automatic machines. Above all, this increased interest has been made possible by those who have collected and presented essential data about who and how many and in what way and when and where and by what name. One can get by without being a skilled mathematician or without having access to a computer or even without an audience. One cannot get anywhere without reliable observers.

Empirical description can take many forms. Hitherto the one most often used in our field is a relation between quantity and yield. For instance Bradford's law relates the number of periodicals, arranged in order of decreasing productivity, to the number of technical articles of specified type contained between them. Direct descriptions of such relations may not be available, or may be too cumbersome, but sometimes we can still describe how they are generated in terms of difference, differential, or integral equations. These cannot always be resolved, even numerically, but detailed solutions are rarely needed. For instance, the equations governing vibrating systems and their more complicated descendants, control systems, are usually far too complex for other than particular numerical solutions at best. But usually what matters is not the exact shape of the vibrations, but under what conditions they will grow, die away, or

remain stable. Powerful ways for studying the stability of interconnected systems have been developed during this century.

Goffman and Newill[25,26,27,29,30] have applied these to their "epidemic" model of the spread of scientific ideas, as manifested by publication. Communication of ideas by recorded discourse is assumed to be governed by processes formally equivalent to communication of disease by microorganisms and of signals by machines. Information Retrieval then corresponds to processes that enhance the spread of infection by favouring the contacts of infectives with susceptibles. Goffman and Newill use control system theory to study the growth, decay, and stability of such processes. Analysis of Selye's bibliography of mast cell research, 1877-1963, and Warren and Newill's of schistosomiasis, 1852-1962 gives grounds for wider application of this model of the growth and dispersion of recorded discourse.

SOME EXAMPLES OF HYPERBOLIC DISTRIBUTIONS

At present the Goffman-Newill theory seems to be the only bibliographical model that involves time explicitly, treating the situation as a process. The others give synoptic views of consolidated data. Almost all of them, whatever their starting-point, end with some kind of hyperbolic distribution in which the product of fixed powers of the variables is constant. In its simplest discrete manifestation an input increasing geometrically produces a yield increasing arithmetically. This is the empirical relation between stimulus and response observed by Weber (1846) and between periodicals scanned and articles retrieved observed by Bradford[4] (1934). Different manifestations of the hyperbolic distribution for both discrete and continuous variables are found in many fields and named variously after Fechner, Zipf, Pareto, Bradford, Willis, Berger-Mandelbrot, and others. But these are names associated with particular explanations for particular manifestations of this type of behaviour, not names for the type of behaviour itself.

These manifestations can be regarded as samples from one or other of a family of statistical distributions first studied in detail by Paul Lévy[39] (1925). This has properties as appropriate to some types of behaviour as the Normal Gaussian distribution has to others. I give some examples, in chronological order. All these bear on the bibliometric application.

Coin-tossing

From the beginning of the eighteenth century there have been extensive studies of problems arising from the situation where two men, traditionally named Peter and Paul, toss pennies. Peter pays Paul one penny if the result is "heads", Paul pays Peter one penny if the result is "tails". One problem is to find the probability that, on the $2n + 1$ throw, one of the players has for the first time to draw upon his capital. That is, that up to this time his losses have never exceeded his gains. For an unbiased penny this probability is

$$p(n) = C(2n, n)/2^{2n}(n + 1) \qquad (1)$$

where $C(2n, n)$ is the number of selections of n items from a collection of $2n$ distinct items.

For large enough n this expression tends to

$$p(n) = (2\sqrt{\pi})/n^{-3/2} \qquad (2)$$

From this point it can be shown that the probability of the interval between successive points of financial equilibrium exceeding $2n$ throws varies inversely with the square root of n. That is, it is a hyperbolic distribution.

This result and discussion of the problem will be found in many textbooks. Feller's[22] treatment is thorough whilst, as usual, Whitworth's[56] classic deals with it elegantly in terms of elementary algebra, under the heading of "Questions of priority".

Little more than changes of nomenclature suffice to apply this result to taxonomic trees, random walks, intermittent errors in signalling and, as the first exact equation suggests, to the relation between ideally chosen and assigned descriptors and the size of the collection labelled with them.

Weber-Fechner psycho-physical laws

In 1846 Weber found experimentally that the just noticeable increase of a stimulus is pro-

portional to the initial magnitude of the stimulus. This implies that the stimulus must increase in geometrical progression to produce an arithmetical increase in the response.

Fechner (1860) developed this as support for his philosophical views on the mind-body relation. He assumed that the Weber rule would hold for subdivisions finer than the just noticeable. In the limit this leads to

$$R = k \log (S/s) \qquad (3)$$

where R is the number of just noticeable increments of response or sensation above its value at the threshold, S is the magnitude of the stimulus, s its threshold value.

Modestly, but confusingly, Fechner called this the Weber Law. Formally it is the same as the Bradford distribution.

Pareto distribution

The economist Pareto[48] showed in 1897 that the distribution of wealth in various communities could be represented quite well by taking the proportion of $P(u)$ of incomes equal to or exceeding a given value u as in inversely proportional to some power of u, the exponent being greater than zero and not exceeding unity: to wit

$$P(u) = ku^{-\theta} \quad (1 \leq u, 0 < \theta \leq 1) \qquad (4)$$
$$= 1 \quad (0 \leq u < 1)$$

Because it is a more general distribution, and applies to a very wide range of phenomena outside economics, including the coin-tossing problem of equilibrium, it is often called the "Paretian distribution".

Willis taxonomic distribution

Willis[57] observed in 1922 that for some biological families the number of genera $g(s)$ having exactly s species could be given by the relation,

$$g(s) = k \, s^{(1+\theta)} \, (0 < \theta \leq 1) \qquad (5)$$

Alternatively, taking s as a continuous variable, the number of genera $G(s)$ having at least s species is

$$G(s) = K \, s^{-\theta} \qquad (6)$$

k, and *K* being appropriate constants.

Usually θ is around one-half, as in the coin-tossing problem. This is no coincidence. Taxonomic trees can be regarded as generated by successive dichotomies, just as the trees proper to random walks and to coin tossing are generated by successive dichotomies, right-left, or gain-loss, and also as the trees appropriate to sentences are generated by segmentation into words by spaces.

Yule[58] (1924) modelled the Willis distribution by assuming species and genera to multiply at random, but at constant rates whose ratio is θ.

Benoit Mandelbrot[44] treated this distribution from many points of view in 1955. Fundamentally he took it as a sample drawn from a population conforming to a more general distribution that has many properties desirable in taxonomy and linguistics, amongst others. It is stable, in the sense that parts of it are distributed in the same way. Thus splitting or lumping together of genera or species result in populations that follow the same law, and the relation between families and genera is the same as between genera and species. Later Mandelbrot was to develop this property of stability or self-similarity and apply it to many phenomena, including variations in market prices[46] and intermittent error bursts in communication systems.[2,47] *Mutatis mutandis*, his studies are strongly relevant to bibliometrics.

Lotka's distribution of literary productivity

In a study of literary output by scientists Lotka[40] (1926) found that the number of authors who had published *n* papers in a given field was roughly $1/n^2$ the number of authors who had published one paper only.

This relation implies that, if it holds good for all authors in a given field, their number would be finite and less than $\pi^2/6$, approximately 1.65, of the number of single-article authors, even if the total output were infinite. This is unlikely. The relation underestimates the number of more prolific authors but applies fairly well for the less prolific.

Bradford's law of literary yield

In 1934 Bradford[4,5] published a study of the dispersion of articles on specific topics. He found that if periodicals were ranked into three groups, each yielding the same number of articles on a specified topic, the numbers of periodicals in each group increased geometrically. That is, for successive yields of *n* articles, one had to search successively *a, ab,* and ab^2 periodicals if the latter were ranked in order of decreasing yield. Proper choice of origin and scales can reduce this to the Weber-Fechner relation, (3) above.

The relation can be expressed in many ways, and in continuous as well as discrete variables. For instance, in continuous variables,

$$F(x) = k \; log \; (1 + cx) \qquad (7)$$

where $F(x)$ is the total yield from the more productive fraction *x* of the periodicals, and *k, c*, are constants.

$$f(x) = A/(1 + cx) \qquad (8)$$

where $f(x)$ is the yield from a periodical of rank *x*. That is, *x* is the proportion of periodicals that have yields not less than $f(x)$. *A, c* are constants.

$$P(u) = (C/u) - D \qquad (9)$$

where $P(u)$ is the proportion of periodicals having a yield not less than *u*. That is, the expression gives the rank in terms of yield per periodical.

All these are obviously equivalent. The constants are functions of the median, which is the smallest fraction of the periodicals that can produce half the total number of required articles.

Equivalent expressions can be formed for discrete variables, but these are more of a typographical strain than are the continuous expressions. The constants for discrete expressions involve the median and the number of periodicals each having the smallest yield, usually one article per periodical, or the number of periodicals each having the largest yield.

Kendall[35] published this form of the Bradford distribution, and related it to Zipf, in 1960. Though this was known before it does not seem to have achieved publication. The Bradford distribution is treated in more detail below. It is outlined here to relate it to the others in this section.

Zipf and Least Effort

Zipf[59,60] (1935, 1949) greatly developed
and extended the scope of an empirical relation, noted by Estoup[14] in 1916, between
the rank of a word in order of frequency, and
the frequency of its appearance in a long
enough text. A "word" is here any string of
letters bounded by spaces and used in the text.
It therefore comprises more than dictionary
entries. The rank of a word, r, is the number of words, including itself, that have at
least the same frequency, f(r), of occurrence.
Zipf's relation is

$$f(r) = k/r \ (k \text{ approximately } 1/10) \qquad (10)$$

He explained this, and other manifestations
in many fields, as the consequence of a
general principle of Least Effort. In particular
applications the practical value of this
principle depends on how well one can enu-
merate actions and their consequences,
and estimate the effort they demand. Fortunately in some important and well defined
situations relations of this kind can be predicted without calling in the aid of Least
Effort, except in the very weak form of excluding
any significant amount of obviously irrational behaviour. Therefore occurrence of
the Zipf type of relation can be made use of
without denying or endorsing the principle.
Benoit Mandelbrot[42,43] (1953, 1954),
using considerations based on information
theory, obtained a more general and better
fitting form. He took the "effort" or "cost" of
words as the delay resulting from their
transmission as a sequence of letter patterns
or phonemes, separated by spaces or pauses.
Assuming that the aim of language is to
allow transmission of the largest variety
of signals (i.e. "information" in the specialized
sense of that word in information theory)
as is possible with the least delay, he used
the techniques for matching codes to
message usage. Thus he obtained the relation
between word frequency f(r) and rank of
word, r as;

$$f(r) = k \ (r + c)^{-\theta} \qquad (11)$$

The constant c improves the fit for common
words, which have low r, or if the relation (11)
is interpreted as a Bradford distribution,
for the most productive periodicals. The ex-

ponent improves fit for large r; that is,
for the rarer words or less productive periodicals. For most natural languages θ is rather
larger than unity, and for languages with
constrained vocabularies and rules of use it
is less than unity. A perfectly applied indexing
language would tend to have a horizontal
curve, with θ zero, because every term
would be used on the average equally often.
Parker-Rhodes and Joyce[49] (1956) obtained the derivative of the Zipf relation. This
gives the number of words n(u) in a given
vocabulary that occur in a long enough
text with relative frequency u. Their relation
is the same as Lotka's, above, for the number
of authors of given productivity; to wit

$$n(u) = ku^{-2} \qquad (12)$$

They derived this by assuming, amongst
other things, that words in the vocabulary are
stored and scanned in order of decreasing
frequency, that that duration of scansion is
proportional to the number of words scanned,
and that the language concerned evolved
so as to give maximum variety ("information")
for a given duration of scansion. They then
used maximum likelihood methods to
obtain (12).
This entails maximizing the sum of products
u log u taken over the entire vocabulary.
Mandelbrot's derivation also requires
maximization of this sum of products, although
his hypotheses make no assumptions about
the manner of storing and scanning. In fact the
sum of products u log u over all elements
of choice in a system must arise whenever one
tries to estimate the optimal use of a repertory of entities to build up compounds, provided that the "cost" of a compound is the
sum of the costs of its components. This sum
is often called the "entropy", "negentropy",
or "(selective) information", but is not
necessarily associated with quantities that
deserve these names.
In a series of papers, 1953 through 1958,
Fairthorne[15,16,17,18] expounded and applied
this Least Cost principle to various problems
in documentation and retrieval from coding,
through the power required by different
alphabets, to the marshalling of books on
shelves.
In 1969, Booth,[3] independently developing
the last application in detail, inverted the
Parker-Rhodes and Joyce argument. Discus-

sing the layout of books in libraries he derived the optimal least-frequent most-distant arrangements by assuming a Zipf distribution of book usage, instead of deriving the Zipf relation from an assumed storage and access procedure. His use of Zipf in this application was, of course, supported by empirical evidence on library borrowing. Booth then suggests the possibility of some equivalent mechanism for average minimum access time in human cognitive processes, very similar to that assumed by Parker-Rhodes and Joyce to derive the Zipf relation.

Buckland and Hindel[10,11] (1969) review applications of Zipf to many aspects of library management. This paper and its bibliography supplements theirs, but does not supplant it.

Distribution of initial digits

For a long time people dealing with numerical tabulations have noticed that if the numbers are expressed without zeros on the left, the initial digits occur with roughly logarithmic frequencies. About one third of the initial digits will be "1"s, rather under one half will be either "1"s or "2"s, and so on. It is not difficult to show that for large enough tables, without arbitrary constraints, the relative frequency $P(d)$ of numbers commencing with any of the digits "1" through "d" is

$$P(d) = log_{10} (d + 1) \qquad (13)$$

Obviously this will not hold in a tabulation displaying, say, the populations of towns having at least 4,000 inhabitants. Apart from such drastically truncated samples the relation holds very widely. Goudsmit and Furry[31] (1944) and Furry and Hurwitz[23] (1945) showed analytically why it is so stable.

The general form is

$$P(d) = log (d + 1)/log R \qquad (14)$$

where R is the radix of the representation.

If d is taken as a continuous variable, this expression gives the rate of yield of entries per initial digit as

$$p(d) = 1/(d + 1) . ln R \qquad (15)$$

The symbol "d" is not only the name of a numeral, it also represents its rank in order of decreasing frequency. So the distribution of initial digits follows the simple Bradford and Zipf laws.

Although the expression of numbers by "significant digits" alone necessarily suppresses the absolute magnitude of the number so represented, many people who should know better have taken (14) as a law of distribution of magnitudes in the physical universe; e.g. Benford[1] (1938). It has been remarked[17] that, if so, the law must be awkward to enforce, because the distribution alters if the observer chooses to write down the magnitude in, say, duodecimal instead of decimal notation. If he wrote it down in binary notation, all entries would commence with a "1".

It is not a property of the external world, but of how we talk about it. So also is the Zipf-Mandelbrot relation a property of how we are compelled to talk within a framework of words and spaces, not a property of what is talked about. The Bradford relation is probably a property of how editors talk about subjects in terms of authors within a framework of distinct periodicals. Certainly it is not a property of whatever authors write about.

These "laws" are laws in the legal or arbitrary sense, not laws of nature. As with any social arrangement we can change them if we have the inclination to do so, and the power to persuade others to conform. This option is not available with the laws of nature. Things fall to earth, not away from it, whatever the consensus of opinion.

Some linguists, e.g. Herdan[33] who disapprove of Mandelbrot's explanation of the Zipf relation, also of Zipf's, treat this legal and social aspect of the relation as a weakness. In the context of linguistics, this is a curious objection. Language itself is the supreme social artifact.

How we talk about things, or go about things, is to some extent a matter of convention. There are many ways of doing them without violating natural laws. But there is a hard core of combinatorial necessity. For instance, however we choose our guests at a cocktail party or other such gathering of six people, at least three of them will either be previously known to each other or previously mutual strangers. However we choose our means, these means are necessarily finite and discrete and, like the guests (who are finite and mathematically discrete), must conform to combinatorial laws.

The following example shows how this can lead to a hyperbolic distribution directly without any behavioural hypothesis.

The length of rugged coastlines Equi-populated regions

The British physicist L. F. Richardson (1881-1953) devoted the last twenty years of his life studying empirically possible proximate causes of war. Amongst these are population densities and boundaries in common. In a posthumous paper[50] (1961) intended as an appendix to his final work[51], itself published posthumously, he studied empirically, experimentally, and mathematically various ways of measuring these factors.

He divided the world into sixty regions of equal population. This is the two-dimensional version of Bradford's approach to literary productivity but, unlike the division of a sequence into quantiles, can be done in many ways. Richardson's regions were determined by the requirements of being simply connected (i.e. not ring-shaped or similarly awkward) and as broad as they were long, so far as this was consistent with common boundaries and leaving existing political boundaries intact.

He found the relation between population (1910 statistics) p, in millions, of a region in terms of its rank r to be

$$p = 1/(0.127\, r + 0.06)^3 \qquad (16)$$

excluding the population of China. Lack of statistics about this country much hampered his work.

Richardson compares this with the laws of Pareto and Zipf. The latter, he comments, "offers theoretical, but rather vague, explanation."

To arrive at this geographical subdivision he had to solve massive mathematical and empirical problems. Amongst these was the estimation of the length of a boundary. Usually one measures the length of an irregular outline by approximating to it with a polygon; for instance, by stepping along it with a pair of dividers of constant opening. Sometimes this leads, conceptually or practically, to a unique limit; whatever the opening of the dividers, the measurement tends to be the same limit as the opening is decreased. Curves that considerably conform to such treatment

are said to be rectifiable. Not all mathematical curves are rectifiable and, in the physical world, most curves are not. Fortunately one is rarely interested in lengths along the arc, usually we are concerned only with the distance between points that lie on the curve.

Richardson found empirically that the relation between the length $L(u)$ of an outline or curve, and the length u of the side of an approximating polygon or divider opening was (omitting terms that vanish with u)

$$L(u) = ku^{-\theta} \qquad (17)$$

For a rectifiable curve θ is zero, and the length is determinate. For most coast lines it is a small positive number. The west coast of Britain, which is very irregular, has an exponent of 0.25.

Mandelbrot[47] (1967) shows that if θ be written $D - 1$, then D corresponds to a dimension , even though it may be fractional. One of the characteristics of dimension is that a parallelepiped of dimension D can be dissected into N parallelepipeds similar to it in the ration $N^{1/D}$. For example, you can dissect a rectangle into N similar rectangles whose sides have the ratio $N^{1/2}$ to the side of the original rectangle.

The relation between the ratio of similarity r, the dimension D, and N, the number of similar parts is

$$D = -\log N/\log r \qquad (18)$$

Mandelbrot suggests that fractional dimensionality is in some way a measure of self-similarity between the parts of a system and the whole. Such self-similarity leads to hyperbolic distributions.

CHARACTERISTICS OF HYPERBOLIC DISTRIBUTIONS

These examples come from many disjunct activities, and they could be extended indefinitely. For instance, the distribution of prime numbers is approximately a Bradford distribution, because all numbers are unique products of primes. Whatever their origin, all involve hyperbolic distributions which, in terms of a continuous random variable u, are of the form (4); to wit

$$P(u) = ku^{-\theta} \quad (1 \leq u < \infty, 0 < \theta \leq 1)$$
$$= 1 \quad (0 \leq u < 1) \qquad (4 \ bis)$$

where $P(u)$ is the probability of the variable exceeding the value u.

The many rather bewildering variations from this form come from expressing it in terms of rank or in terms of probability density, the latter increasing θ by unity. Also, if one expresses the relations in terms of discrete variables, as one should, they look very different. In this survey I have shifted from discrete to continuous variables without giving the rather massive formal justification required, but this does not mean that one can change from discrete to continuous variables without risk of losing essential features.

Essentially the hyperbolic distributions arise from properties of discrete collections, or the attempts to quantize non-discrete phenomena. So for investigation into causes or for theoretical mathematical development, one must treat the problem to begin with in its exact discrete form. For application of the results, the continuous form is much more convenient as a rule, and can be adjusted to fit a given range with reasonable accuracy.

Another source of variation is presentation of these relations in terms of logarithms, so that they become — if one is lucky enough to know the correct origin and scale — straight lines when plotted on logarithmically scaled paper. If the exponent is exactly unity, its cumulative expression, e.g. (3) and (7), plots as a straight line on semi-logarithmic paper. So it will if the exponent is not exactly unity, deviating noticeably from a straight line only for large enough values. Some of the various "drops" reported (e.g. Groos[32] [1967]) in Bradford plots may be in part due to the exponent not being exactly unity.

The limits of validity of the relation are part of the relation. If they are varied in each application, they must be regarded as additional parameters. Some years ago I remarked, as have others, that a straight line law connecting any empirical data always can be achieved with the aid of suitably scaled logarithmic paper and a robust conscience. Even more can be achieved if you give yourself the option of declaring the limits of the straight line portion only after you have plotted the data.

In many applications the scale and limits are determined, not by the phenomena themselves, but by the sensitivity, resolution, and range of the methods of observation or presentation. For instance, in the Pareto distribution of incomes, no income can be less than the least monetary unit. The same situation is self-similar, so a segment of it can be scaled into the form (4), whatever the instruments of observation and mode of reporting. In this it is unique (Mandelbrot[46] [1965]). The uniform, equiprobable, distribution is the special case when the exponent is zero. This is obviously self-similar.

Self-similarity characterizes the Bradford distribution, because if we subdivide any of the original zones into sub zones, they will follow the same law, though with a different parameter. Again, any part of a taxonomic tree is on the average similar to any other part, differing mostly in scale and degree of refinement. Trees of the same kind can represent also the building of words from letters, number-words from numerals; phrases from words and spaces, levels of physical access or administrative access into libraries, encyclopaedias, or computer stores; all numbers from prime numbers; random walks and coin-tossing; and so on indefinitely. It is not surprising that the hyperbolic distribution is so widespread in documentary and managerial contexts, where activities are of similar pattern at different levels of design and by necessity.

These hyperbolic distributions belong to a class studied in detail by Paul Lévy[39] (1925). The most useful ones have the property that the sum of two such distributions is itself a similar distribution. That is, it is stable in the statistical sense. A better known stable distribution is the Normal or Gaussian distribution, which is also the only stable distribution to have finite moments. The hyperbolic distributions have infinite moments, of course, but these are rather sensitive to sample size.

Distributions with infinite moments are quite respectable. For instance the Cauchy distribution, which is generated by the intercept of a randomly rotating line with a fixed straight line, is a straightforward example. But such distributions do not yield gracefully to the usual powerful methods based on the moments of a distribution. Instead of these one must use the median, quantiles, and their higher equivalents. Indeed, these arise naturally in phenomena giving rise to hyperbolic distributions. Bradford, for instance, divided the range of periodicals into three zones of equal yields.

Looking at them from another point of view, it may be helpful to point out that the Normal Gaussian distribution can be generated from binomial distributions with integer exponents, the hyperbolic from binomial distributions with fractional exponents. For example, the exact expressions for financial equilibrium in coin tossing, (1) above, are the coefficients in the expansion of a bionomial square root. This observation gives a clue for modelling discrete processes of indefinite length.

A modern and more accessible treatment of Lévy distributions is given by Gnedenko and Kolmogoroff[24](1954). Mandelbrot[45] and Fama[21] (1963), applying them to the variation of speculative prices, discuss in some depth the stability of these distributions which, quite reasonably in this context, are what Mandelbrot calls "Stable Paretian Laws".

Up to this point I have surveyed the hyperbolic laws as a whole, with bibliometric applications as particular cases. This unifies the formal aspects of this type of behaviour, and collects tools for dealing with it, without invoking any hypothesis about the proximate causes of such behaviour.

I will now outline the rather isolated and amnesic progress of such studies within the field of bibliometrics.

THE BRADFORD DISTRIBUTION

Bradford[4] published in 1934 a paper showing the dispersion amongst scientific periodicals of articles about applied geophysics and about lubrication. The paper was reprinted with minor alterations in 1948.[5] In both of these largely unrelated topics he grouped the source periodicals into three zones, in order of decreasing yield, each zone yielding the same number of required articles. Bradford found the number of periodicals in each zone to increase geometrically. He used this finding to estimate the number of periodicals that contained articles on a specified subject and concluded that, unless many pertinent articles were to be lost, periodical literature must be abstracted by source and not by subject.

Though in public and, rather ambiguously, in private Bradford tended to belittle this finding, he did make use of it. His private conversations gave me the impression that he was sure it was important, but equally sure that he had not enough evidence or explanation to sustain it in public debate.

Vickery[53] (1948) cleaned up and extended the mathematical side of Bradford's communication. In particular he showed that if the relation held generally, it must hold for any subdivision into groups of equal yield, not just for high, medium, and low yielding quantiles.

A dozen years passed before the Bradford distribution again became the main topic of a published paper. In 1960 Kendall[35] showed that it applied to the bibliography of operational research, and studied it from a statistician's point of view. He showed that it was structurally similar to the Zipf relation, and took the important step of regarding any particular manifestation of the relation as a sample of a more general statistical distribution.

There seems little doubt of Kendall's priority of publishing an explicit statistical study of the Bradford distribution and its equivalence to Zipf's.

Though Kendall was the first to publish, the Bradford-Zipf equivalence was fairly widespread amongst those few already working in the field. This is indicated by Fairthorne[18] (1958) referring to the importance of "deviations from some Bradford-Zipf-Mandelbrot relation" in the distributions of words and of notions over items indexed by them. Up to 1960 the interest and paid time of the few mathematically inclined workers in documentation was directed mainly on index languages and their coding to deal with unpublished reports and to patent specifications. They were not unacquainted with conventional periodicals and, in those early days, some had even read books with hard covers, but immediate problems lay with unpublished items and their retrieval.

Cole[12] (1962), making use of the papers of Bradford, Vickery, and Kendall, plotted the proportion of total yield $F(x)$ against the logarithm, $ln(x)$, of the most productive fraction of sources that yielded it. He drew his data from the fields of engineering, biology, chemistry, and physics. For all these subjects he got a fairly straight line. For petroleum literature he proposed an empirical formula which can be written, as Leimkuhler was to point out, as

$$F(x) = 1 + 0.185 \ln x \qquad (19)$$

Leimkuhler[37] (1967) examined existing studies and examples of Bradford's distribution and derived various formulations for discrete and for continuous variables. As Vickery had found, a fundamental parameter is the ratio b_m between the numbers of source periodicals in successive zones, when the periodicals are grouped into m zones of equal yield, with the periodicals in decreasing order of yield. The relation between these ratios for different numbers of zones, $m, n,$ is:

$$b_n^n = b_m^m = b_2^2 \qquad (20)$$

This perhaps may be seen more readily if one considers subdivision into mn zones. The ratio b_{mn} should be the same whether you first divide into m zones, and then subdivide each into n or divide into n zones, and then subdivide each into m. The relation (20) between the rations is the only one that permits this.

Any particular collection is a sample of the actual population of productive periodicals. Assuming that this sample is the most productive part of the actual population, Leimkuhler studied the effect of collection size on Bradford parameters.

Brookes[7,8] (1968, 1969) reviews the literature from Bradford onwards, and formulates the distribution directly from the consideration that, by hypothesis, the number of pertinent articles yielded by the nth ranking periodical exceeds that of the $(n + 1)$th by $b\ln[n/(n - 1)]$, where b is the ratio between successive equi-yielding zones of periodicals. For the most refined subdivision, this difference of yield must be one article.

The distribution is thus determined by b_2, which is found immediately from the median value, and by the number of periodicals with minimum yield, usually one article per periodical. The last determines the greatest number of zones into which a particular collection can be subdivided.

Brookes aims to derive simple techniques for using the Bradford distribution as a working tool of operational research or quality control.

Leith[38] (1969) showed that his personal collections of references in radiation- and cell-biology follow Bradford distributions. He draws the same conclusion for personal reading that Bradford did for special libraries. That is, by reading only the "core" periodicals of your speciality you will miss about 40% of articles relevant to it. Qualitatively this review supports his view.

Goffman and Warren[28] (1969) used their studies of mast cell and of schistosomiasis literature, discussed above, also to investigate the Bradford distribution. They found that in both subjects the ratio of periodicals to authors was almost the same, around 0.27, and the average output of authors over five year periods did not vary over the entire eighty years covered by the bibliographies. Moreover, these ratios of articles per author — 1.1 for mast cell literature and 1.5 for schistosomiasis — were roughly equal to the minimal Bradford ratio b corresponding to the most refined subdivision of the periodicals.

These findings of Goffman and Warren hint, to me, that the Bradford distribution of periodical articles arises from an author-editor balance, rather than subject-periodical. Short of publishing one massive periodical containing all articles by all authors, there are two policies for partitioning their output. One is to publish periodicals such that each makes use of as many authors as possible, subject to the constraints of practical publishing; e.g. *Nature, Science, Readers Digest*. The other policy, also subject to economic constraints, is to publish the output of a group of authors that is changed no more than the attrition of authors demands. To these editorial policies correspond author policies. Both policies are largely unconcerted, and the situation tends to be stable. Because authors commonly write within a special field these days, the situation can be interpreted in terms of subject matter, but it is plausible that the editor-author interaction is basic.

This is speculation, but there is no doubt that after many years the observations of Bradford have at last helped to forge a tool useful in management of and research into bibliographic matters. Many will be glad that his name is used to label this tool.

VOCABULARIES, CODING, ACCESS

Zipf[59,60] had proposed a general Least

Effort principle that was not, perhaps, stated with a precision commensurate with its claimed far reaching consequences. Nevertheless, principles of this kind exist in many activities, but arise out of the nature of the activity rather than as manifestations of a universal principle. For instance, in communication engineering messages must be coded as patterns of physical events so as to allow the greatest variety of patterns to choose from. At the same time they must use as little power, cause as little delay, and be masked as little as possible by extraneous physical events, generically called "noise". In 1958 many previous applications of these considerations were united in Shannon's "Information Theory", a name later changed by him to "Communication Theory" in the interests of semantic hygiene.

An essential tool in this theory is a measure of average variety of complication of signals. This takes the form of a sum of products, — $p \log p$, summed over the values of p for each element of the repertory of signal patterns, and is therefore less than unity. Hence the minus sign, which is put in to make the sum positive.

This measure is called, in this context, the "(selective) information", a name that ever since has been a lure for loose thinkers.

It has the same form as the measure of thermodynamic entropy and, in certain very circumscribed situations, can be identified with it. For our purposes it is a measure of the average variety, complication, or freedom of choice, allowed by a given repertory of patterns used with stated frequencies. Why and for what they are used does not come into it. This quantity is used a great deal in combinatorial and statistical theory, and crops up over and over again in applications, from Bradford's distribution to problems in sorting and marshalling and access to files. Information Theory has therefore supplied a useful label for an existing concept. Whether it has supplied more than a label is subject to dispute that does not concern us here.

Shannon's theory appeared in the summer and fall of 1948, too late for discussion at the Royal Society Conference on Scientific Information held earlier that year. Nevertheless some people, including some at Aslib, recognized at once its relevance to various documentary problems, especially to coding for what Mooers was to call (the next year) Infor-

mation Retrieval.

The most thorough study of information theoretic methods appropriate to this problem was not directly aimed at it, but at the more general problem of the coding of messages into words and spaces in natural languages. From 1952 onwards Benoit Mandelbrot attacked this problem. In a symposium paper[42] (1953) he gives, in English and mathematics, a comprehensive and very condensed account of motivation and development. Many ideas of this paper deserve and still await exploitation. Brillouin[6] summarizes the method used in his chapter on coding problems. A less technical summary, in French, was published by Mandelbrot[43] in 1954. Here he is concerned mainly with the application of his techniques to natural languages, but the relevance to indexing and similar languages is obvious. More obvious, in fact, than their relevance to linguistics in general. About this there is some debate because Mandelbrot bases his stand on the views of de Saussure, which are not accepted unanimously by linguists. Fortunately this debate does not affect the validity or invalidity of his methods when applied to other activities.

Concurrently, from 1952 through 1958, a sequence of papers by Fairthorne[15,16,17,18] reprinted later in 1961[19], attempted to explain, mainly in non-technical English the scope and limitations of information theoretic methods in documentation, and stated results concerning vocabularies and their coding, sorting and marshalling, access to files, keyboards, and bookshelves, amongst others.

The basis of such methods are the combinatorial properties of compounds built up by repetition and combination from a fixed repertory of elements. This may be an alphabet of letters and spaces; a set of numerals; a vocabulary of words or phrases with spaces or pauses; fixed teams of authors; periodical title lists; pigeon holes; prime numbers; phonemes; standardized actions in clerical or manipulative activities; and so on. With each of the elements is associated a positive number, its "cost", which may be its financial cost, its mass, length, distance, or duration, or any other measure of significant inconvenience, from duration of a word to rotation of a typewheel or length of a bookshelf. If the total cost of any compound be the sum of the costs of its elements, and the restrictions on permissible combinations not too arbitrary, the costs of all compounds can be represented analytically or computed. Otherwise, and always as a check, one relies on observation. Zipf, for instance, investigated the cost as being the length of words (number of letters) occuring naturally in various environments. Mandelbrot took his cost as being the duration of words and spaces.

Consider an alphabet of n letters, each of the same length or duration, or requiring the same effort or money to print or write. Suppose, at first, that all combinations of letters are permitted, and that we will ignore the space as a character. That is, words will be considered as isolated occurrences. (In fact spaces and hierarchies of spaces are a most important type of character in segmented sequences.) Clearly there are n one-letter words, n^2 two-letter words . . . n^r r-letter words, and so on. Their costs are $1, 2, \ldots, r, \ldots$ units respectively. Thus we have the familiar geometrico-arithmetical correspondence between the number of words with their costs that we have observed so often between sources and their yields.

If here we assume that the less costly words are used more often, in isolation, than more costly words and that equally costly words are used equally often, we arrive immediately at the Zipf-Bradford hyperbolic distribution with exponent unity, sometimes called the "harmonic" distribution.

In most applications by no means all compounds are permitted, there must be special elements with the properties of spaces, and the elements will have different costs. Nevertheless, if one considers the costs averaged in various plausible ways, the result is qualitatively the same. Instead of n being a whole number, and instead of the hyperbolic exponent being unity, both may be fractional.

To determine the values is a technical task. Traditionally information theorists take an unnecessary detour through difference equations. Actually the direct attack is by way of generating functions and their resolution into partial fractions. Fairthorne[18] (1958) developed a very general type, in the form of analytical continued fractions, for a unified treatment of storage and retrieval languages.

The important property of "vocabularies" generated in this way is that they are insensitive to quite extreme restrictions on rules of use, as noted above when discussing the Initial Digit distribution. Therefore any assumption

about fairly rational use of the repertory leads to hyperbolic distributions, whatever the precise linking of cost to frequency of use. Deviations will occur only when the calculated costs cease to be the dominant costs, or inconveniences, because of changed circumstances. These are most likely to affect first the very cheap or very expensive compounds.

Mandelbrot's major contribution has been to bring together and organize a set of phenomena and of appropriate mathematical tools hitherto scattered around. For instance, in his discussion[44] of the language of taxonomy he uses the techniques and concepts of statistical thermodynamics, but based on the Levy hyperbolic, instead of the Normal Gaussian, distribution. Since then he has continued to develop, sharpen, and apply these tools.

Nevertheless in 1969 one read in a documentation journal the suggestion that the Bradford-Zipf relation was perhaps the symptom of some law or "information flow", the last two words undefined. The unwillingness, of inability, of information retrieval specialists to retrieve information about information retrieval is notorious. It is also extremely expensive.

As mentioned above, Parker-Rhodes and Joyce arrived at the Zipf distribution of exponent unity by using information theoretic or statistical methods (the distinction is here mainly terminological) but rather differently from Mandelbrot, who obtained a more general result. Many others at that time I know to have been working on similar problems on similar lines. Few if any achieved publication other than as internal memoranda.

Up to the late 1950s the most pressing problems concerned indexing vocabularies and their coding into forms congenial to various devices. All these ingredients were regarded as commercial commodities. Thus, though the growth of indexing vocabularies with the size of the collection came in for much attention, especially after 1950, studies of it were mainly *ad hoc* and confined to one's own system. Nevertheless the approximately straight line relation on log-log paper, and the importance of its slope, were fairly well known. Those with the appropriate background recognized the equivalence of Zipf and Bradford laws. But data were scanty, pressures then as now were on development rather than on research, and there was no audience for publication.

Although it is impossible to give individual credit for unpublished and inaccessible contributions I can, and should, credit the Documentation Committee of the Advisory Group on Aeronautical Research and Development of NATO for their encouraging pioneer work and discussion about mathematization and mechanization of documentary tasks in the early 1950s. As well as encouraging research, it had the more difficult task of discouraging mystique and misunderstanding about both mathematics and machines. Thus it laid a fairly sound foundation for the machines when they were ready for documentary tasks. Unfortunately that was late enough for the foundations to have been forgotten.

Wall[54],[34] (1957, 1964) reports that in 1956 T. E. Boyle of DuPont Engineering Department suggested, in private correspondence, use of Zipf's findings to predict the number of "keywords" or the like in what are now called "co-ordinate indexes". In 1959 Costello and Wall[13] gave an empirical formula relating the number t of indexing terms, of the undisciplined Uniterm kind, and the number of documents n indexed by them.

$$t = 4170 \ log_{10} \ (n + 730) - 11620 \qquad (21)$$

Wall favours a log-normal distribution, rather than a hyperbolic, of the use of indexing terms; that is, the logarithm of the documents per term is dispersed about its mean value according to the normal Gaussian distribution. He seems to have chosen this distribution because the results plotted as a straight line on available "probabilty" paper. So they would have on ordinary logarithmic paper. Numerically and graphically there is little difference, because segments of the tail of a Gaussian distribution are not readily distinguishable from segments of a hyperbolic distribution. Unfortunately there is not, so far as I know, any small-sample test of goodness of fit for logarithmic plots.

Houston and Wall[34] (1964) fitted the log-normal distribution to nine indexing vocabularies. Wall[55] elaborated on this work in another paper published the same year. In this he displayed generalized hyperbolic as well as log-normal distributions for various relations in index term use. Also he

gave procedures for predicting term use as a function of index size. These are entirely empirical and extremely elaborate, using many arbitrary parameters. The last did not, as an unkind critic commented, outnumber the data, but there was enough to make some theoretical justification and practical interpretation most desirable. However Wall did cite and use extensive data from the more monstrous indexes, vocabularies, and subject heading lists of the time. It is worth noting that he in some cases obtained a Zipf-Bradford relation between the rank of a term and its frequency of assignment.

Zunde and Slamecka[62] (1967) use an information theoretic approach, but seem unacquainted with the work of Mandelbrot and others. Their criterion of index efficiency was matching if input and output "entropy"; i.e. of variety or complication. This certainly is a measure of the efficiency of signalling. Also it is a measure of the convenience of natural language, in the sense of permissible variety. Natural language has no "efficiency" in the engineering sense. The least-cost principle applies only to short-term inconvenience, dealt with more or less instinctively.

Index languages, like other deliberately constructed languages, do have efficiencies with respect to the end for which they were constructed. As is well known, efficiency here by no means implies convenience. If an indexing language were perfectly efficient, every item would be used equally often and every item would be assigned the same number of index terms. Plotted as a cumulative distribution, the perfect indexing system would give a horizontal line along the rank axis, a vertical line, and a line parallel to the axis. Normally index term distributions approximate to this as a S-shaped curve, which become straighter and closer to the simple Bradford line as the index language becomes more convenient (i.e. closer to natural language) and less efficient in the sense of terms needed to index an item.

Zunde and Slamecka do obtain these S-shaped curves, but take goodness of fit with simple Zipf as the criterion of virtue. The more general Mandelbrot relation, had they known of it, would certainly have fitted the plotted curves for overall slope and for common and rare terms. They also accept a log-normal distribution of term usage, and use it to calculate source "entropy" for collections of various sizes. Probably they get much the same numerical results as they would from any plausible arbitrary distribution, but the log-normal hypothesis certainly does not simplify their calculations.

Zunde and Dexter[61] (1969), investigating the joint use of indexing terms by groups of indexers, arrive at a hyperbolic distribution between a function of the number of distinct terms used by a number of indexers, and the number of indexers. They cite Lotka, Zipf, and Bradford, but not Mandelbrot and the others who have published on information theoretic methods in this field. Internal evidence suggests that they are going to repeat this earlier work unwittingly.

In this they will not be alone. A paper of Krautwurst,[36] citing Zipf and Zunde and Slamecka (1967) purports to apply information theory to analysis of an indexing vocabulary. Apart from listing some of the elementary expressions of information theory, this paper does no more than to put new labels on old curves. One hopes that the resurgence of interest in the information theoretic approach does not also mean that it will become fashonable.

CONCLUSIONS

This survey has shown the hyperbolic distributions to be the inevitable result of combinatorial necessity and a tendency to short-term rational behaviour whenever a group of people have to use a repertory of given elements to form compounds, and when one aspect of the "cost" or inconvenience of these elements is dominant.

Usually the elements and their use arise from the way people choose to observe, arrange, or talk about things, not from the nature of the things themselves. Therefore designers and administrators can cheat these laws by changing the elements, their costs, and the rules for using them. The laws themselves give the limits of improvement and a yardstick for quality control. Disobedience of the laws is more significant than obedience, because it indicates that conditions have changed.

This survey itself supports Bradford's conclusion from his law; that to know about your speciality you must go outside it. You must be neither too local nor too contemporary. The past is a profitable prelude.

ACKNOWLEDGEMENTS

Mr. Alan Pritchard was not only the involuntary donor of the term "Bibliometrics," but also the voluntary donor of a most helpful bibliography. Mrs. Elizabeth Mack of Aslib, and Messrs. Wright and Seymour of the Royal Aircraft Establishment, Farnborough, went well beyond the call of duty in helping me to read what authors had actually written.

REFERENCES

[1] Benford, F. Proceedings of the American Philosophical Society, vol. 78, 1938, p. 551.

[2] Berger, J. M. and Mandelbrot, Benoit. A new model of error clustering on telephone circuits, IBM Journal of Research and Development, vol. 7, 1963, p. 224-36.

[3] Booth, A. D. On the geometry of libraries. Journal of Documentation, vol. 25, no. 1, 1969, p. 28-42.

[4] Bradford, S. C. Sources of information on specific subjects. Engineering, 1934, Jan. 26.

[5] Bradford, S. C. Documentation, Crosby Lockwood, 1948.

[6] Brillouin, L. Science and information theory. Academic Press, 1956.

[7] Brookes, B. C. The derivation and application of the Bradford-Zipf distribution. Journal of Documentation, vol. 24, no. 4, 1968, p. 247-65.

[8] Brookes, B. C. The complete Bradford-Zipf "bibliograph". Journal of Documentation, vol. 25, no. 1, 1969, p. 58-60.

[9] Brookes, B. C. Library Zipf (letter). Journal of Documentation, vol. 25, no. 2, 1969, p. 155.

[10] Buckland, M. K. and Hindle, A. Library Zipf. Journal of Documentation, vol. 25, no. 1, 1969, p. 54-7.

[11] Buckland, M. K. and Hindle, A. Library Zipf (letter). Journal of Documentation, vol. 25, no. 2, 1969, p. 154.

[12] Cole, P. F. A new look at reference scattering. Journal of Documentation, vol. 18, no. 2, 1962, p. 58-64.

[13] Costello, J. C. and Wall, E. Recent improvements in techniques for storing and retrieving information. In Studies in co-ordinate indexing, vol. 5. Documentation Inc., 1959.

[14] Estoup, J. B. Gammes stenographiques. 4th edition. 1916.

[15] Fairthorne, R. A. Automata and information. Journal of Documentation, vol. 8, no. 3, 1952, p. 164-72.

[16] Fairthorne, R. A. Information theory and clerical systems. Journal of Documentation, vol. 9, no. 2, 1953, 101-16.

[17] Fairthorne, R. A. Some clerical operations and languages. In Proceedings of the Third London symposium on information theory, 1955. Butterworth, 1956.

[18] Fairthorne, R. A. Algebraic representation of storage and retrieval languages. *In*: Proceedings of the International Conference on scientific information, Washington, D. C. 1958. Area 6. National Acedemy of Sciences, 1959.

[19] Fairthorne, R. A. *Towards information retrieval*. Butterworth, 1961 (reprinted, Archon Books, 1968).

[20] Fairthorne, R. A. Library Zipf (letter) *Journal of Documentation*, vol. 25, no. 2, 1969, p. 152.

[21] Fama, E. F. Mandelbrot and the stable Paretian hypothesis. *Journal of Business*, vol. 36, 1963, p. 420-9.

[22] Feller, W. *An introduction to the theory of probability and its applications*. Vol. 1, second edition. Wiley, 1957.

[23] Furry, W. H. *and* Hurwitz, H. Distribution of numbers and distribution of significant digits. *Nature*, vol. 155, 1945, p. 52-3.

[24] Gnedenko, B. V. *and* Kolmogoroff, A. N. (*trans*. K. L. Chung). *Limit distributions of sums of independent variables*. Addison-Wesley, 1954.

[25] Goffman, W. An epidemic process in an open population. *Nature*, vol. 205, 1965, p. 831-2.

[26] Goffman, W. Stability of epidemic processes. *Nature*, vol. 210, 1966, p. 786-7.

[27] Goffman, W. A mathematical approach to the spread of scientific ideas. *Nature*, vol. 212, 1966, p. 449-542.

[28] Goffman, W. *and* Warren, K. S. Dispersion of papers among journals, based on a mathematical analysis of two diverse medical literatures. *Nature*, vol. 221, 1969, p. 1205-7.

[29] Goffman, W. *and* Newill, V. A. Generalization of epidemic theory; an application to the transmission of ideas. *Nature*, vol. 204, 1964, p. 225-8.

[30] Goffman, W. *and* Newill, V. A. Communication and epidemic processes. *Proceedings of the Royal Society*, Series A, vol. 298, 1967, p. 316-34.

[31] Goudsmit, S. A. *and* Furry, W. H. Significant figures of numbers in statistical tables. *Nature*, vol. 154, 1944, p. 800-1.

[32] Groos, O. V. Bradford's law and Keenan-Atherton data. *American Documentation*, vol. 18, 1967, p. 48.

[33] Herdan, G. *The advanced theory of language as choice and chance*. Springer, 1966.

[34] Houston, N. *and* Wall, E. The distribution of term usage in manipulative indexes. *American Documentation*, vol. 15, 1964, p. 105-14.

[35] Kendall, M. G. The bibliography of operational research. *Operational Research Quarterly*, vol. 2, 1960, p. 31-6.

[36] Krautwurst, J. Die Beurteilung eines Thesaurus mit informationstheoretischen Hilfsmitteln. *Nachrichtung fur Dokumentation*, vol. 20, 1969, p. 68-72.

[37] Leimkuhler, F. F. The Bradford distribution. *Journal of Documentation*, vol. 23, no. 3, 1967, p. 197-207.

[38] Leith, J. D., jr. Biomedical literature: an analysis of journal articles collected by a radiation- and cell-biologist. *American Documentation*, vol. 20, 1969, p. 143-8.

[39] Lévy, P. *Calcul des probabilités*. Part 2, chap. 6. Gauthier-Villars, 1925.

[40] Lotka, A. J. The frequency distribution of scientific productivity. *Journal of the Washington Academy of Sciences*, vol. 16, 1926, p. 317-23.

[41] Lynn, K. C. A quantitative comparison of conventional information compression techniques in dental literature. *American Documentation*, vol. 20, 1969, p. 149-51.

[42] Mandelbrot, Benoit. An information theory of the statistical structure of language. *Proceedings of the symposium on applications of communication theory, London, Sept. 1952*. Butterworth, 1953, p. 486-500.

[43] Mandelbrot, Benoit. Structure formelle des textes et communication. *Word*, vol. 10, 1954, p. 1-27.

[44] Mandelbrot, Benoit. On the language of taxonomy: an outline of a "thermostatistical" theory of systems of categories with Willis (natural) structure. *Information Theory*; papers read at a symposium on information theory, London, Sept. 1955. Butterworth, 1956, p. 135-45.

[45] Mandelbrot, Benoit. The variation of certain speculative prices. *Journal of Business*, vol. 36, 1963, p. 394-419.

[46] Mandelbrot, Benoit. Self-similar error clusters in communication systems and the concept of conditional stationarity. *IEEE Transactions on Communication Technology*, vol. 13, 1965, p. 71-90.

[47] Mandelbrot, Benoit. How long is the coast of Britain? Statistical self-similarity and fractional dimension. *Science*, vol. 156, 1967, p. 636-8.

[48] Pareto, V. *Cours d' économie politique*. Vol. 2. Section 3. Lausanne, 1897.

[49] Parker-Rhodes, A. F. *and* Joyce, T. A theory of word-frequency distribution. *Nature*, vol. 178, 1956, p. 1308.

[50] Richardson, L. F. The problem of contiguity. *In*: General systems: yearbook of the Society for General Systems Research, vol. 6, 1961, p. 139-88.

[51] Richardson, L. F. *Statistics of deadly quarrels* (ed. by Qunicy Wright and C. C. Lienau), Boxwood Press, Pittsburgh, 1960.

[52] Smith, D. A. Library Zipf (letter). *Journal of Documentation*, vol. 25, no. 2, 1969, p. 153-4.

[53] Vickery, B. C. Bradford's law of scattering. *Journal of Documentation*, vol. 4, 1948, p. 198-203.

[54] Wall, E. Use of concept co-ordination in the DuPont Engineering Department. *In*: Conference on multiple-access searching for information retrieval. Proceedings, 1957. AD - 147491, U. S. Defense Documentation Center.

[55] Wall, E. Further implications of the distribution of index term usage. *In*: Parameters of information science; proceedings of the American Documentation Institute annual meeting, 1964, vol. 1, p. 457-66. American Documentation Institute, 1964.

[56] Whitworth, W. A. *Choice and chance*. Chap. 5, 5th edition, 1901 (reprinted, Stechert, 1942).

[57] Willis, J. C. *Age and area; a study in geographical distribution and origin of species*. Cambridge University Press, 1922.

[58] Yule, G. Udny. A mathematical theory of evolution based on the conclusions of Dr. J. C. Willis. *Philosophical Transactions of the Royal Society*, Series B. vol. 213, 1924.

[59] Zipf, G. K. *Psycho-biology of language*. Houghton Mifflin, 1935.

[60] Zipf, G. K. *Human behaviour and the principle of least effort*. Addison Wesley, 1949.

[61] Zunde, P. *and* Dexter, M. E. Indexing consistency and quality. *American Documentation*, vol. 20, 1969, p. 259-67.

62 Zunde, P. *and* Slamecka, V. Distribution of indexing terms tor maximum efficiency of information transmission. *American Documentation*, vol. 18, 1967, p. 104-8.

ABOUT THE AUTHOR

Robert A. Fairthorne was born in 1904 at Farnborough, Hampshire, England and has spent most of his working life in various departments of the Royal Aircraft Establishment. He has been a Visiting Research Professor at both Western Reserve University, Ohio, and at the State University of New York at Albany. He has published numerous articles on information science and librarianship as well as on mathematical, technical and computational matters.

The Ambiguity of Bradford's Law

Elizabeth A. Wilkinson

We have seen in the previous paper that a number of researchers have studied Bradford's Law and that its formulation would appear to have been well-established. However, careful analysis shows that none of these studies have produced mathematically-equivalent results and that Bradford himself put forward two different interpretations. Wilkinson is able to demonstrate that the graphical formulation of the Law appears to describe the situation found in practice more accurately.

INTRODUCTION

Bradford's law of scatter describes a quantitative relation between journals and the papers they publish. We are far from knowing how and why such a relationship exists, but fortunately it it not necessary to wait for complete understanding before making use of such empirical laws.

As Fairthorne[1] has pointed out " . . . gravitation is far from being explained, though there is precise and comprehensive enough knowledge of gravitational behaviour to construct stationary satellites and, in due course, live in them. But for wider tracts of useful activity even rougher knowledge will suffice. Often all that is needed is reasonable assurance that water will flow into the sink and not on to the ceiling."

Despite the limitations of our understanding of such laws, then, Bradford promises useful application in the design of more rational and economic information systems. Further, such an empirical law may be seen as a particular manifestation of a more fundamental law; we may hope to progress from sink filling to satellite construction.

It is therefore encouraging from both points of view to note that the literature on Bradford's law is now growing, even if applications have hardly begun. Since the law was formulated in 1948,[2] there have been contributions from Vickery,[3] Barrett,[4] Leimkuhler,[5] Brookes,[6] Fairthorne,[1] Goffman and Warren,[7] and Naranan.[8] Yet the most remarkable feature that emerges from a study of these papers is that no two ot these contributions interpret the law in mathematically identical terms. It is ironic that after reading the literature on Bradford's law the first question that arises is: what *is* Bradford's law?

Hopefully, one turns back to Bradford's *Documentation*. But here again ambiguity is found. Bradford formulated his law in two ways: firstly by means of a graph and secondly in words. But these two formulations can be shown not to be mathematically equivalent — a fact which only Vickery[3] appears to have noticed. As Bradford himself offers two different formulations, the next questions that arise are: which of these two formulations better expresses Bradford's intentions, which of them better fits the empirical data, which should be called Bradford's law of scatter?

THE DISPARITY BETWEEN THE VERBAL AND GRAPHICAL FORMULATIONS

Consider a set of journals contributing papers on a particular topic, ranked 1, 2, . . . , n in order of decreasing productivity, with $R(n)$ the cumulative total of papers published by the first n journals.

Bradford's verbal formulation of the law as it appears on page 116 of *Documentation* reads:

"If scientific journals are arranged in order of decreasing productivity of articles on a given subject, they may be divided into a nucleus of periodicals more particularly devoted to the

SOURCE: Wilkinson, E. A. "The Ambiguity of Bradford's Law," *J. Docum.* 28 (2) June 1972 pp. 122-130.

subject, and several groups or zones containing the same number of articles as the nucleus, when the number of periodicals in the

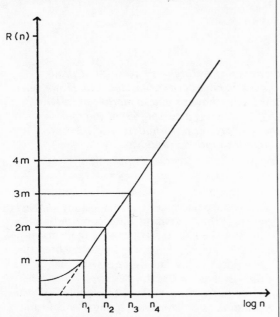

FIG. 1. THE GRAPHICAL FORMULATION OF BRADFORD'S LAW

nucleus and succeeding zones will be as $1 : a : a^2 : \ldots$ "

Bradford formulated the law graphically as shown in Fig. 1 (page 115 of *Documentation*). He plotted $R(n)$ against $\log n$ as defined above and noticed that the resulting graph was a rising curve which ran into a straight line after some critical point.

Vickery has pointed out the disparity between these two formulations. He showed that if n_m journals contribute a cumulative m papers, where n_m is larger than the nucleus, the verbal formulation is equivalent to the expression

$$n_m : n_{2m} - n_m : n_{3m} - n_{2m} : \ldots :: 1 : a_m : a_m^2 : \ldots ,$$

while the graphical formulation is equivalent to the expression

$$n_m : n_{2m} : n_{3m} : \ldots :: 1 : b_m : b_m^2 : \ldots$$

The disparity between the two formulations becomes much clearer on examining the mathematical equation relating $R(n)$ and n in each case. The equation for the verbal formula-

tion may be established as follows:

$$n_m : n_{2m} - n_m : n_{3m} - n_{2m} : \ldots :: 1 : a_m : a_m^2 : \ldots ,$$

for all m larger than the contribution from the nucleus.

i.e $n_{rm} = n_m \, (a_m^r - 1)/(a_m - 1)$

and $n_R = n_m \, (a_m^{R/m} - 1)/(a_m - 1)$
        $n_R \, (a_m - 1)/n_m + 1 = a_m^{R/m}$
        $R(n) = m \log [n(a_m - 1)/n_m + 1]/\log a_m$

i.e $R(n) = j \log (n/t + 1)$ for $n \geq n_m$,
          where j and t are constants.

Leimkuhler has expressed the same relation in terms of the proportion of total productivity (papers), $F(x)$, contained in the fraction x of journals. Leimkuhler's expression can be derived as follows:

$F(n) = R(n)/R(N)$, where N is the total number of journals

i.e. $F(n) = j \log (n/t + 1)/j \log (N/t + 1)$

And since $x = n/N$, we have Leimkuhler's equation

$$F(x) = \log (1 + \beta x)/\log (1 + \beta), \text{ with } \beta = N/t$$

Brookes, on the other hand, has developed the graphical formulation of the law and has shown that it may be expressed by the equation

$$R(n) = k \log n/s \text{ for } n \geq n_m,$$

where k and s are constants

In summary then, the distribution of papers on a particular topic among contributing journals is expressed by

$R(n) = j \log (n/t + 1)$ for the verbal formulation, and
$R(n) = k \log n/s$ for the graphical formulation

Further, as will be shown in the appendix, the constants of these equations are not equal; i.e. $j \neq k$ and $t \neq s$. The verbal and graphical formulations are not, therefore, mathematically equivalent, nor do they converge for large n.

WHICH OF THE FORMULATIONS EXPRESSES BRADFORD'S INTENTIONS?

Bradford first developed a theory of the distribution of articles among journals by considering the range of journals as "a family of successive generations of diminishing kinship". This theory is expressed by the verbal formulation. In attempting to substantiate his theory, Bradford plotted empirical data and observed the straight line form of the graph.

As Vickery has pointed out, he mistakenly assumes this to be a restatement of the verbal formulation.

The verbal formulation, then, expressed Bradford's *theory*, the graphical formulation expressed his *observations*.

WHICH FORMULATION BETTER FITS THE EMPIRICAL DATA?

Subsequent interpretations of the law of scatter have been based on one or other of Bradford's formulations. Brookes[6] developed the graphical formulation and has published empirical data which closely follow the log linear form of the distribution. The "nucleus" of journals can be calculated with relative ease and Brookes established a simple method of estimating the total number of contributing journals and papers on a particular topic. The method works particularly well with data from computerized retrieval systems. In contrast, Leimkuhler[5] developed a model based on Bradford's verbal formulation, and on testing his model against empirical data found again a "relatively close agreement between the observed and theoretical distributions". Apart from Leimkuhler's observations, there has been little published evidence corroborating the verbal formulation, possibly because of the difficulty in this case of establishing the nucleus and hence the starting point of the geometric progresion.

It is evident that any testing of the formulations that has so far been published, has been performed on different sets of data. A comparative test between the two formulations against the same data will show more clearly which formulation gives the better fit.

A COMPARATIVE TEST OF THE TWO FORMULATIONS

A method for testing the two formulations which obviates precise calculation of the nucleus has been developed, and is fully described in the appendix. The method may be summa-

rized as follows:

Assume that the journals contributing papers on a particular topic are ranked $1, 2, \ldots, n$ in the usual way. If p journals contribute a cumulative S papers (where S is larger than the contribution from the nucleus) and q journals contribute $2S$ papers, then the total numbers of papers and journals are given by the following formulae:

(i) — in the case of the verbal formulation,

total number of journals =

$$S/\log_e a - p/(a-1)$$

where $a = (q-p)/p$

total number of papers =

$$S \log [\{S(a-1)/p\}\log_e a]/\log a$$

(ii) — in the case of the graphical formulation,

total number of journals = $S/\log_e \beta$

where $\beta = q/p$

total number of papers =

$$S \log [\{S\beta/p\}\log_e \beta]/\log \beta$$

Table 1 shows the estimates of the total number of papers and journals for four different subjects according to the two formulations. The values of p, q, and S are taken from the observed data and the estimates are calculated using the formulae above. The percentage error of each estimate compared with the observed value is indicated.

The data for Agricultural Economics and Rural Sociology have been collected by H. Buntrock.[9] The muscle fibre data is the response to a MEDLARS search.[10] The data for schistosomiasis[11] comprises Selye's bibliography, 1877-1963, and the data for mast cells[12] comprises Warren and Newill's bibliography, 1852-1962.

It is not the purpose of this paper to discuss the absolute accuracy of the estimates according to each formulation. However, it is worth pointing out that Bradford's law relates a complex set of papers on a topic to the journals which publish them; that is, all the papers which are relevant must be included in the data and the criteria for recognizing a relevant paper should be consistent. The accuracy of the estimates would be affected by the extent to which the empirical data fall short of this completeness. In the event of serious disagreement between estimated and observed values, we must reject the data, the empirical law or both.

TABLE 1
COMPARISON OF RESULTS FOR TOTAL NUMBER OF JOURNALS

	p	q	S	Observed total	Graphical formulation Estimated total	% error	Verbal formulation Estimated total	% error
Agricultural economics	40	191	3,454	2,116	2,210	4.4	2,586	22.1
Muscle fibre	25	176	604	313	310	-1.0	331	5.8
Schistosomiasis	20	126	3,023	1,738	1,643	-5.5	1,807	4.0
Mast cells	20	85	768	587	531	-9.5	642	9.5

COMPARISON OF RESULTS FOR TOTAL NUMBER OF PAPERS

	p	q	S	Observed total	Graphical formulation Estimated total	% error	Verbal formulation Estimated total	% error
Agricultural economics	40	191	3,454	12,205	12,320	1.0	13,510	10.5
Muscle fibre	25	176	604	1,346	1,383	2.7	1,415	5.1
Schistosomiasis	20	126	3,023	9,914	10,270	3.6	10,810	9.0
Mast cells	20	85	768	2,378	2,502	5.2	2,797	17.6

Nevertheless, the purpose of the present discussion is to establish which formulation more closely refelcts the practical situation, shown by existing published data regardless of possible incompleteness. For the four sets of data considered, the estimates according to the graphical formulation are closer to the observed values in six of the eight cases.

CONCLUSION

It is unfortunate that while Bradford's findings stimulated a more scientific approach to information studies, the ambiguity of his conclusions has led to a certain amount of confusion and uncertainty. There is little to be gained from trying to establish which of the formulations Bradford would have adopted had he realized the disparity. In theory Bradford predicted the verbal formulation; in practice he observed the graphical formulation.

From the results above it would seem that the graphical formulation more closely describes the practical situation, or at least describes it equally well. There would be certain advantages, also, in applying Bradford's law as manifested by the graphical formulation. There is a simple mathematical equation; a minimum of observed data is necessary to estimate the total numbers of journals and papers; the nucleus is identifiable.

However, the most important point to be made is that in its present form Bradford's law *is* ambiguous and that existing work has been based on two different formulations. The search for a "fundamental law" may be based on one or other or neither formulation, but from a theoretical point of view, it is important to appreciate that the two are different. From the practical point of view, the application of Bradford's law will not be encouraged until the predictions of that law are consistent. In terms of Fairthorne's analogy, we must first agree that water does flow into the sink, before expecting people to make use of the fact.

The author acknowledges a grant for research from the Office for Scientific and Technical Information.

REFERENCES

[1] Fairthorne, R. A. Empirical hyperbolic distributions (Bradford-Zipf-Mandelbrot) for bibliometric description and prediction. *Journal of Documentation*, vol. 25, December 1969, p. 319-43.

[2] Bradford, S. C. *Documentation*, Crosby Lockwood, 1948.

[3] Vickery, B. C. Bradford's law of scattering. *Journal of Documentation*, vol. 4, 1948, p. 198-203.

[4] Barrett, A. J. Linking research and design. *Aslib Proceedings*, vol. 14, p. 438-53.

[5] Leimkuhler, F. F. The Bradford distribution. *Journal of Documentation*, vol. 23, no. 3, September 1967, p. 197-207.

[6] Brookes, B. C. Bradford's law and the bibliography of science. *Nature*, vol. 224, 1969, p. 953-6.

[7] Goffman, W., *and* Warren, K. S. Dispersion of papers among journals, based on a mathematical analysis of two

diverse medical literatures. *Nature*, vol. 221, 1969, p. 1205-7.

[8] Naranan, S. Bradford's law of bibliography of science: an interpretation. *Nature*, vol. 227, 1970, p. 631-2.

[9] Based on an unpublished compliation by H. Buntrock from Survey of the world agricultural services. Prepared on behalf of AGRIS panel of experts by H. Buntrock. Rome, FAO, 1970.

[10] Unpublished compilation by B. C. Brookes from a MEDLARS print-out (private communication).

[11] Warren, K. S., *and* Newill, V. A. Schistosomiasis, a bibliography of the world's literature from 1852-1962. Western Reserve University Press, Cleveland, 1967.

[12] Selye, H. The mast cells. London, Butterworth, 1968.

APPENDIX

The appendix describes a method of estimating the total numbers of papers and journals on a particular topic for both formulations of Bradford's law, given that p ranked journals contribute S papers, and q ranked journals contribute $2S$ papers.

(i) Verbal Formulation

We have established that the equation relating the rank of a journal, n, and the cumulative number of papers contributed by the first n journals, $R(n)$, is as follows:

$$R(n) = j \log (n/t + 1)$$

for $n \geq n_m$ and some constants j and t.

Now, $R(n) = S$ when $n = p$ and
$R(n) = 2S$ when $n = q$

i.e.
$$S = j \log (p/t + 1)$$
$$2S = j \log (q/t + 1)$$

$$\therefore \quad p^2/t^2 + 2p/t + 1 = q/t + 1$$

$$t = p^2/(q - 2p) \quad (1)$$

and
$$j = S/\log [(q - p)/p] \quad (2)$$

Let N be the total number of journals in the collection. The last journal must contribute not less than one integral paper.

i.e.
$$R(N) - R(N - 1) = 1$$

$$\therefore \quad -j \log [(N - 1 + t)/(N + t)] = 1$$

$$-j \log [1 - 1/(N + t)] = 1$$

But for large N and taking logarithms to base e,

$$\log [1 - 1/(N + t)] \approx -1/(N + t)$$

$$\therefore \quad j/(N + t) = 1$$

and
$$N = j - t$$

Thus from (1) and (2)

Thus, the total number of journals in the collection is given by $S/\log_e a - p/(a-1)$, where $a = (q - p)/p$, and the total number of papers in the collection is given by

$$(S/\log_e a) \log_e [\{S(a - 1(/p\} \log_e a].$$

(ii) Graphical Formulation

Brookes has shown that the equation relating $R(n)$ and n is as follows:

$$R(n) = k \log n/s \text{ for } n \geq n_m \text{ and some}$$
$$\text{constants } k \text{ and } s.$$

$R(n) = S$ when $n = p$, and $R(n) = 2S$ when $n = q$

i.e.
$$S = k \log p/s$$

$$2S = k \log q/s$$

$$\therefore \quad s = p^2/q \quad (3)$$

and
$$k = S/\log (q/p) \quad (4)$$

Let N be the total number of journals in the collection. The last journal must contribute not less than one integral paper.

i.e.
$$R(N) - R(N - 1) = 1$$

$$\therefore \quad -k \log [(N - 1)/N] = 1$$

$$-k \log (1 - 1/N) = 1$$

But for large N and taking logarithms to base e,

$$\log (1 - 1/N) \approx -1/N$$

$$\therefore \quad k/N = 1$$

and
$$N = k.$$

Thus, from (3) and (4),

$$N = S/\log (q/p)$$

and $R(N) = [S/\log(q/p)] \log [(Sq/p^2) \log (q/p)]$

Thus the total number of journals in the collection is given by $S/\log_e \beta$ where $\beta = q/p$, and the total number of papers in the collection is given by $S \log_e[(S\beta/p) \log_e]/\log \beta$.

Note that from a comparison of equations (1), (2), and (3), (4) that the constants of the equations of the two formulations are not equal.

ABOUT THE AUTHOR

Elizabeth A. Wilkinson graduated in Mathematics and Information Studies from University College London, England in 1969. She was an Assistant Information Officer at the University of Manchester Regional Computer Centre during 1969-70, and in 1971 she returned to University College London to carry out a project on the development of a stochastic model of literature distribution. She has since taken up an appointment as Lecturer in the Department of Library and Information Studies at Loughborough University.

The Application of Psychometric Techniques to Determine the Attitudes of Individuals Toward Information Seeking

Victor Rosenberg

The most difficult problems of data collection and measurement are usually encountered when it becomes necessary to consider the attitudes and motivations of the users of the library or information service. This study is concerned with these problems and is a good example of how a carefully-designed questionnaire can be used to elicit information about the way in which individuals attempt to satisfy their information requirements. The results may well be of paramount importance for information system design.

ABSTRACT

A structured questionnaire was administered to professional personnel in industrial and government organizations, asking the subjects to rank eight information gathering methods according to their preference in given hypothetical situations. The subjects were then asked to rate the methods on a seven point scale according to (a) ease of use and (b) amount of information expected. The subjects were divided into two groups determined by their time spent in research or research related activities. The groups were designated "research" and "nonresearch".

A statistical analysis of the data from 94 subjects (52 in research, 44 in nonresearch) showed that no statistically significant differences were present in either the rankings or ratings between research and nonresearch personnel. A high significant correlation was found, however, between the preference ranking and the ease of use rating within both groups, whereas no significant correlation was found between the preference ranking and the amount of information ratings.

The results of the study infer that the ease of use of an information gathering method is more important than the amount of information expected for information gathering methods in industrial and governmental environments, regardless of the research orientation of the users.

INTRODUCTION

Many recent studies have attempted to investigate the behavioral aspects of the information gathering process. Generally, these studies have developed an insight into the ways by which scientists obtain information, and have developed the methodology for such studies. A number of studies have also sought to determine the actual information needs of scientists. Generally neglected, however, are attempts to discover (a) why individuals prefer certain methods, (b) what attributes of information gathering methods are important, and (c) if the study of the information seeking process should be restricted to research scientists. The purpose of this study is to investigate such questions, in an attempt to make the interpretation of results from information-user studies more meaningful.

Most efforts in the actual development of information retrieval systems have been based, either explicitly or implicitly, on the assump-

SOURCE: Reprinted from *Studies in the Man-System Interface in Libraries Report No. 2. The Application of Psychometric Techniques to Determine the Attitudes of Individuals Toward Information Seeking.* By Victor Rosenberg. Bethlehem, Pennsylvania. Center for the Information Sciences, Lehigh University. July 1966. In this reprinting, some of the preliminary matter and appendixes II and III (which contain the data collected) have been omitted.

tion that the greatest need for improved availability of information exists among research scientists. Although differences exist in the types of information required by different professions, it is not at all clear that the basic principles underlying the development of retrieval systems should be different for different environments.

METHOD

To obtain the data for the investigation, a structured questionnaire was administered to a selected group of subjects. The questionnaire was designed to minimize the inconvenience of the subjects while extracting the necessary information.

The questionnaire first asked the subject to indicate whether he spent more than fifty percent of his time in research or research related activities. This question separated the subjects into two groups: (a) "research" and (b) "nonresearch". All data were analyzed between the two groups.

Part I of the questionnaire presented the subject with three hypothetical situations which required information and which would be likely to be part of his general experience. The situations presented concerned research for a proposal, research for a journal article, and research on work being done in a particular field. The purpose of a given hypothetical situation was to establish a frame of reference within which the subject was asked to rank eight information gathering methods. The same eight methods were presented in each of the hypothetical situations, but in each case rearranged in a different, random order, minimizing the possibility of subsequent questions being influenced by previous ones (i.e., order effects).

The information gathering methods were selected from a group of methods which appeared in an earlier study (Rosenberg, 1965).[1] From a list of twenty-three items, the most popular, on the basis of choice by the subjects of that study, were selected and modified. The methods were thus representative of generally used information seeking techniques.

Part IIA of the questionnaire, listing the same eight methods as in Part I, asked the subject to rate each method by the criterion of ease of use. The subject rated the method on a seven point scale ranging from "extremely simple" to "extremely difficult".

Similarly in Part IIB, the subject was asked to rate the methods by the criterion of amount of information expected, rating the methods from "very little" to "very much" information expected. As in Part I, the order of presentation was randomized. Part II was prepared in four sets, each set listing the methods in a different random order, to minimize any possibility of order effects. A sample questionnaire appears as Appendix I.

SELECTION OF SUBJECTS

The population from which the sample was taken was professional personnel employed by scientific organizations. The sample was more specifically defined as persons holding at least a bachelors degree, employed in organizations with interests in scientific research.

An attempt was made to secure employee directories from which to draw a random sample. The cooperating organizations indicated, however, that the release of such directories was against corporate policy, so that an alternative sampling procedure was used. Six organizations cooperated in the project, and in each case a quantity of questionnaires was sent to a cooperating individual, who was instructed to distribute the questionnaire to professionals in his organization representing as many departments as possible. The questionnaires were returned by mail.

The cooperating organizations were : International Business Machines Corporation, Research Division, San Jose, California; International Business Machines Corporation, Thomas J. Watson Research Center, Yorktown Heights, New York; Merck and Company, West Point, Pennsylvania; Arthur D. Little, Inc., Cambridge, Massachusetts; Air Products and Chemicals, Inc., Allentown, Pennsylvania; and the United States Naval Air Turbine Test Station, Trenton, New Jersey. The choice of cooperating organizations was dictated only by the effort to obtain approximately equal numbers of subjects for both the research and non-research categories. Within the limited objectives of the study, the sample was sufficiently diverse to eliminate any obvious bias.

RESULTS

The entire distribution of the questionnaire to the six cooperating organizations totalled 175. One hundred and six questionnaires were completed and returned. Eleven percent (12) of the returned questionnaires were rejected because certain parts of the questionnaire were incorrectly or incompletely filled out. Table 1 shows the distribution statistics for the questionnaire. Since no due date was given to the subjects, some of the questionnaires were returned after the completion of the analysis and therefore were not included in the sample.

TABLE 1.
DISTRIBUTION DATA

Total questionnaires	No. returned correct	No. returned reject
175	94	12

The subjects were divided into the "research" and "nonresearch" categories on the basis of question number one. The resulting set of usable questionnaires contained 52 (55 percent) in the research category and 44 (45 percent) in the nonresearch category.

The data resulting from Part I of the study consisted of sets of ranked items for each of the three hypothetical situations, listed in the data as questions (Table 2). Thus for each group of subjects there were three sets of ranks and the degree of consistency in the ranking was measured within each group, for each question separately and averaged for the set of all three taken together. The data for Part I is tabulated in Appendix II.

TABLE 2.
HYPOTHETICAL SITUATIONS
LISTED AS QUESTIONS

No. 1 You are working on a design for a procedure or experiment and wish to know if similar work has been done or is currently being done by someone else.

No. 2 You are preparing a proposal for a new project either to the management of your organization or to an outside agency. You wish to substantiate the proposal with a thorough bibliography. The proposal involves approximately $60,000.

No. 3 You wish to gather information in order to write an article in your area of specialization for a trade or research journal.

To measure the consistency of ranking among subjects, the Kendall coefficient of concordance, W, was used. The test ascertains the overall agreement among k sets of rankings (i.e. the association among them). If there were perfect agreement among the subjects in their ranking, each method would have the same rank for each subject. The Kendall coefficient of concordance is an approximate index of the divergence of the actual agreement shown in the data from the maximum possible (perfect) agreement.[2]

Computing W for each question in a given group,

$$W = \frac{s}{1/12 \ k^2 \ (N^3 - N)}$$

where

s = sum of squares of the observed deviations from the mean of the totals R_j,

thus,

$$s = \Sigma \ (R_j - \frac{R_j}{N})^2$$

k = number of sets of rankings, i.e. the the number of subjects

N = number of items ranked

and the denominator, $1/12 \ k^2 \ (N^3 - N)$ is the maximum possible sum of squared deviations.

For the data shown in Appendix II, the resulting coefficients of concordance are shown in Table 3.

TABLE 3.
KENDALL W FOR PART I

Group	k	Question			
		no. 1	no. 2	no. 3	Average
Research	52	0.452	0.511	0.539	0.501
Nonresearch	44	0.326	0.352	0.469	0.382

The statistic, W, is linearly related to the X^2 (Chi-square) by the formula:

$$X^2 = k(N-1)W$$

The X^2 statistic is used to test the statistical significance of W. In the resulting chi-square table (Table 4) all entries are significant at the 0.05 level.

TABLE 4.
X^2 FOR PART I

Group	k	Question no. 1	Question no. 2	Question no. 3	d.f.
Research	52	164.528	186.004	196.196	7
Nonresearch	44	100.408	108.416	144.452	7

The correlation between the rankings of the two groups was measured by applying the Spearman rank correlation coefficient: r_s to the ranks of the totals of each method for each question and for the totals over the three questions. Kendall[3] claims that the best estimate of the ranking of N items is the ranking of the sums of the various rankings, provided W is significant. The ranks of the various sums (Table 5) are used to find r_s .

TABLE 5.
RANKS OF TOTALS

Methods	Q_1 R	Q_1 NR	Q_2 R	Q_2 NR	Q_3 R	Q_3 NR	totals R	totals NR
1	1	4	2	3	1	1	1	1.5
2	2	2	1	1	2	2	2	1.5
3	8	8	8	8	8	8	8	8
4	6	6	4.5	6	5	6	5	6
5	5	5	3	4.5	4	4	4	5
6	3	1	4.5	2	3	3	3	3
7	7	7	7	7	7	7	7	7
8	4	3	6	4.5	6	5	6	4

Note: R = research, NR = nonresearch

The methods are listed by numbers which are interpreted in Table 6. The fractional rankings represent ties which are averaged for the computation.

The statistic, r_s, is calculated by the formula:

$$r_s = 1 - \frac{6 \sum_{i=1}^{n} d_i^2}{N^3 - N}$$

where

d_i = the deviation between two ranks

and

N = number of items ranked.

For the data shown the r_s in each case is significant at the 0.05 level.

TABLE 6.
NUMBERING OF METHODS

The numbering of information gathering methods in the text corresponds to the following listing:

Methods

No. 1 Search your personal library.
No. 2 Search material in the same building where you work, excluding your personal library.
No. 3 Visit a knowledgeable person — 20 miles away or more.
No. 4 Use a library that is not within your organization.
No. 5 Consult a reference librarian.
No. 6 Visit a knowledgeable person nearby (within your organization).
No. 7 Write a letter requesting information from a knowledgeable person — 20 miles away or more.
No. 8 Telephone a knowledgeable person who may be of help.

TABLE 7.
R_S BETWEEN GROUPS

	Question no. 1	Question no. 2	Question no. 3	totals
r_s =	0.833	0.786	0.976	0.923

The statistic r_s is a one tailed test showing that a significant relationship exists in the data. It is a nonparametric test having an efficiency of 91 percent when compared to the Pearson r.[4]

The data in Part II of the questionnaire were ratings given to each method on the criteria (a) ease of use and (b) amount of information. The data for Part II are tabulated in Appendix III and the methods are referred to by numbers as listed in Table 6.

For the data of the "ease of use" ratings the null hypothesis was that no difference existed in the mean ratings given the methods by the two groups (i.e. H_0 : $\mu R = \mu NR$ for all methods). The null hypothesis was tested using standard t tests corrected by Sheffe's method, which is the most conservative of the generally used procedures for correcting critical values when a number of t tests are used.[5] The results of the t tests for the "ease of use" ratings are shown in Table 8. The t tests were calculated by the computational formulae:[6]

$$t^2 = \frac{(n_a - n_b - 2)(n_b \sum X_a - n_a \sum X_b)^2}{(n_a - n_b)(n_b L_a - n_a L_b)}$$

TABLE 8.
T TESTS FOR EASE
OF USE RATINGS.

	Methods							
	No. 1	No. 2	No. 3	No. 4	No. 5	No. 6	No. 7	No. 8
t =	.780	.434	.752	.419	.362	.375	.507	.792

where:

$$L_a = n_a \sum X_a^2 - (\sum X_a)^2$$

$$L_b = n_b \sum X_b^2 - (\sum X_b)^2$$

and

n_a = sample size for group 1
n_b = sample size for group 2

and X_a & X_b are the scores.
None of the results of the t test are significant at the 0.05 level.

A similar analysis was performed on the data from Part IIB, the "amount of information" ratings. The results of the t test for these data (Table 9) again show no significant difference at the 0.05 level.

TABLE 9.
T TESTS FOR AMOUNT
OF INFORMATION RATINGS

	Methods							
	No. 1	No. 2	No. 3	No. 4	No. 5	No. 6	No. 7	No. 8
t =	.718	.989	.754	1.007	.587	.548	.398	.596

The results from Parts I and II were then compared by finding correlation coefficients between the sets of ranks and the sets of ratings for each group. To find the correlation coefficients a ranking was derived from the average ratings of the methods in each case and compared to the ranks given by the subjects (Table 10). The Spearman rank correlation was used for this test (Table 11). The correlation of the ranks derived from the ease of use ratings to the subject rankings were significant for both research and nonresearch groups, while the correlation of the ranks derived from the amount of information ratings to the subject ranking were not significant for either group. Significance was determined at the 0.05 level in all cases.

TABLE 11.
SPEARMAN RANK
CORRELATION COEFFICIENTS

Derived Rankings from	Subject Rankings	
	Research	Nonresearch
Ease of Use	0.868	0.887
Amount of Information	-0.166	-0.113

INTERPRETATION OF RESULTS

The initial test determining the degree of agreement among the subjects in the ranking of the methods showed that the subjects applied essentially the same standard in ranking the eight methods.[7] The ranking of the totals for each group can be taken as the best estimate of the ranking based on the given data. The

TABLE 10.
DERIVED RANKINGS

	Research							
Method	No. 1	No. 2	No. 3	No. 4	No. 5	No. 6	No. 7	No. 8
Subject Ranking	1	2	8	5	4	3	7	6
Derived Ease of Use Ranking	1	2	8	6	5	4	7	3
Derived Amount of Information Ranking	3	7	6	8	4	5	1	2

	Nonresearch							
Method	No. 1	No. 2	No. 3	No. 4	No. 5	No. 6	No. 7	No. 8
Subject Ranking	1.5	1.5	8	6	5	3	7	4
Derived Ease of Use Ranking	1	3	8	7	5	4	6	2
Derived Amount of Information Ranking	1	7	5	6	3	8	2	4

significance of the statistic, W, is not inte-
preted to mean that the estimated rankings are
correct by an external criterion, but rather
that they are the best estimate for the given data.
The fact that W was significant in all cases
was considered important because the subsequent analysis was based on the reliability
of the rankings of the totals.

The comparison of the estimated rankings
for the two groups using the Spearman test
showed that there was no significant difference
between the two groups in the rankings. The
null hypothesis was, H_0 : The ranks are identical. The net result of the first two tests was
that the two groups used essentially the same
criterion within the groups for ranking the
items and that, on the basis of the test, there
was essentially no difference between the
two groups in the resulting rankings.

For the data in Part II, t tests were applied
to test for significant differences in the mean
ratings on a given method between the two
groups. The null hypothesis for comparison of
the two means on a given rating of a method was
$H_0 : \mu_r = \mu_{nr}$. Since no difference was
found to be significant on the basis of the data,
it was inferred that no meaningful differences
existed between the average ratings of the
group (i.e. for each method, both groups gave
the same average rating). This shows that,
given a set of methods, both groups gave
essentially the same response in each case
when asked to rate the methods according to
ease of use and amount of information expected.

To test the correlation between the results
of Part I and the results of Part II, the ratings of
Part II were converted to ranks by ranking the
mean ratings. Since the rankings of Part I
were on an ordinal scale, the inferences about
the correlation of the data was kept at the
ordinal level. Thus the inferences say nothing
about the relative magnitude of the ratings,
but only about their rank.[8] The results of
this analysis showed a marked correlation
between the ease of use ratings and the subject rankings for both research and nonresearch, and a marked lack of correlation
between the amount of information ratings
and the subject rankings.

The statistic used to test the correlation, r_s ,
ranges from +1 to -1. A value for r_s of +1
corresponds to perfect agreement, and a value
of -1 corresponds to "perfect" inverse
agreement (i.e. the highest subject ranked

item has the lowest derived rank, etc.). Thus
values close to +1 reflect a high degree of
agreement between the two variables, whereas
a value close to zero represents randomness
or lack of agreement. On the basis of this
statistic, it is clear that the subjects preference
ranking was far more closely related to his
evaluation of the method's ease of use than to
his evaluation of amount of information expected. Alternatively, a subject's preference
for a method of getting information is more
likely to correspond to his estimation of the
method's ease of use than his estimation of
amount of information expected. This inference holds for both research and nonresearch
personnel.

The actual methods listed in the questionnaire and the hypothetical situations which
served as a framework for the rankings and in
some sense for the rating also, played a
relatively minor part in the study. No attempt
was made to make inferences about the
methods themselves except that one was
ranked or rated above another. Thus the hypothetical situations and methods themselves
served only to gather data about the relationships between the two groups of subjects and between the ratings and the rankings
The interest in the relationships between
the sets of data exclusively served as a justification for the use of the structured questionnaire. No attempt was made to discover (a)
what a subject felt he would actually do, or
(b) what a subject actually does in the given
situations. Such observations have been reported in what are generally known as
information user studies, some of which are
listed in the bibliography.

A significant limitation of the procedure
used in the investigation was that there was
no way of validating the questionnaire to
test its sensitivity to the variables to be
measured. General procedure requires the
test to be administered to samples where
differences in the tested variable are known to
exist to determine the sensitivity of the test
to the variable in question. Since the experimental hypothesis was that no differences
existed between the two groups tested, no
population could be found where differences were known to exist. The consistency
of the data and the significance of the tests,
however, imply that the testing procedure was
valid. The similarity of the results to the results of studies observing actual behavior

also provides support for the validity of the experimental procedure.

DISCUSSION

Although much research has been done to study the information gathering behavior of professional personnel, very little has been done to establish the reasons for the observed behavior. The relative priority of the most frequently used channels has been established by almost all studies, and in almost every case, the analysis has shown that one of the most significant factors in determining the priority is the availability of the source. The implication is that the information gathering behavior of users is dictated primarily by the facilities available and changes to reflect a change in the availability of facilities. The importance of availability of information is consistent with the results of the present study and implies that the primary attribute of any information gathering method is its ease of use.[9]

Although the methods listed in the study were only secondarily important, the overall preference listing of the methods shows an interesting correlation to a study where actual performance was measured. In a study investigating the utilization of information sources in research and development proposal preparation (Allen, 1964), information sources were divided into three categories: (a) literature search; (b) consulting with laboratory specialists; and (c) consulting with outside sources. The data from the study show, among other things that the mean times spent in each activity were: (a) 28.4 man hours; (b) 17.2 man hours; and (c) 11.6 man hours, respectively. If one divides the information gathering methods of the present study in a similar manner (Table 12), there seems to be a one to one relationship between the preference rankings given and the results of Allen's study, if preference can be equated with time spent.[10]

The comparison of the two studies shows that there is substantial agreement between the results of the present study giving the subject's opinion of preference and Allen's study showing actual performance. Such agreement combined with the general inference of user studies concerning the importance of availability can be considered a substantiation of the validity of the present study.

It may also be inferred from the agreement between the two studies that asking the subject for opinions concerning information gathering

TABLE 12.
COMPARISON OF TWO STUDIES

Method	Overall Average Rank	Allen's Category	Average Man-Hours
Search your personal library.	1	Literature Search	28.4
Search the material in the same building where you work, excluding your personal library.	2		
Visit a knowledgeable person nearby (within your organization)	3	Consulting with Lab. Specialists	17.2
Consult a reference librarian.	4		
Write a letter requesting information from a knowledgeable person — 20 miles away or more.	7	Consulting Outside Specialists	11.6
Visit a knowledgeable person — 20 miles away or more.	8		

Note: Two of the methods were not decidable (Nos. 4 and 8).

behavior yields data as meaningful as the data from observation studies, provided the sample is sufficiently large. Since observation studies are more complex and difficult to control, the use of structured questionnaires requesting opinions could greatly simplify and thereby expand the scope of studies investigating information gathering behavior.

The scope of the study was limited to professional personnel in government and industrial organizations. The inferences of the study are assumed to hold only for this population. Hanson (1964), in a study of information seeking behavior found that industrial and government personnel differed from those in academic institutions in a number of ways. He found the organizational differences more pronounced than the differences across disciplines.

. . . we find that the differences in needs and demands for information associated with the kind of employment are on the whole greater than those associated with discipline. That is to say, although there are differences between scientists and engineers as such, and between for instance physicists and chemists, these are less marked than the differences between people, irrespective of discipline, working in industry and those working in, say, academic institutions. Comparing these last two we find that people working in industry wanted information more quickly than the academics; . . . In most respects people working in Government establishments behaved in much the same way (as those in industry).[11]

Hanson's study seems to substantiate the result that fewer significant differences exist between professional disciplines within industry and government organizations than between types of institutions and that the professionals are primarily concerned with the ease of obtaining information.

CONCLUSIONS

From the results of the experiment, it is reasonable to conclude that: (a) research and nonresearch professional personnel in industry or government do not differ to any appreciable extent in their evaluation of information

gathering methods; and (b) the preference for a given method reflects the estimated ease of use of the method rather than the amount of information expected. These conclusions in conjunction with the results of observation studies imply further that the basic parameter for the design of any industrial information system should be the system's ease of use, rather than the amount of information provided, and that if an organization desires to have a high quality of information used, it must make ease of access of primary importance.

Since the optimization of all variables has not yet become a practical reality, the design of an actual system usually permits the optimization of some parameters only at the expense of others. If all other variables such as cost, environment, etc., are held constant, a system can be designed to provide a maximum amount of information at the expense of effort, or it can be designed to minimize effort at the expense of information yield. Cast in the terms of information retrieval, one can maximize either recall or precision. In industrial environments, the design criteria should lean toward the minimization of effort (i.e. precision).

A secondary conclusion, supported by the correlation of the results with observation studies, is that user surveys can be accomplished by the use of a well designed structured questionnaire technique, without resorting to direct observation, if the sample is large enough. The questionnaire technique is far more efficient and less expensive than observation surveys.

On the basis of the present study, it appears that further research using similar techniques could accurately identify the relationship of information system characteristics to the system environment. Such further research might, for example, examine the relationships between academic and industrial environments. A further examination of the factors involved in the concept "ease of use", (e.g. time, distance, or intellectual effort), should also prove useful in providing a more detailed description of the information gathering process and system environments.

REFERENCES

[1] Rosenberg, V. *The Attitudes of Scientists Toward Information Seeking Activities*, Lehigh University, Bethlehem, Pa., 1965. (Unpub.)

[2] Siegel, S. *Nonparametric Statistics for the Behavioral Sciences.* McGraw-Hill, New York, 1956, pp. 229-239.
[3] Siegel, p. 238.
[4] Siegel, pp. 202-213.
[5] Winer, B. J. *Statistical Principles in Experimental Design.* McGraw-Hill, New York, 1962, pp. 85-89.
[6] Winer, p. 31.
[7] Siegel, p. 238.
[8] Hays, W. L. *Statistics for Psychologists.* Holt, Rinehart and Winston, New York, 1963, pp. 68-76.
[9] Bureau of Applied Social Research. *Review of Studies in the Flow of Information Among Scientists.* Columbia University, 1960.
[10] Allen, Thomas J. *The Utilization of Information Sources During R & D Proposal Preparation,* Rept. no. 97-64, Alfred P. Sloan School of Management, Massachusetts Institute of Technology, Cambridge, Mass., October, 1964.
[11] Hanson, C. W. "Research on Users' Needs: Where is it Getting Us?" *Aslib Proceedings,* vol. 16, no. 2, February 1964, p. 69.

BIBLIOGRAPHY

Allen, T. J. *Problem Solving Strategies in Parallel Research and Development Projects,* Alfred P. Sloan School of Management, Massachusetts Institute of Technology, Cambridge, Mass., June 1965.

_____ *Sources of Ideas and Their Effectiveness in Parallel R & D Projects,* Alfred P. Sloan School of Management, Massachusetts Institute of Technology, Cambridge, Mass., July 1965.

_____ *The Utilization of Information Sources During R & D Proposal Preparation,* Report No. 97-64, Alfred P. Sloan School of Management, Massachusetts Institute of Technology, Cambridge, Mass., October, 1964.

Allen, T. J. and Andrien, M. P. Jr. *Time Allocation Among Three Technical Information Channels by R & D Engineers,* Alfred P. Sloan School of Management, Massachusetts Institute of Technology, Cambridge, Mass., August 1965.

Bailey, C. A. and Davis, R. A. *Bibliography of Use Studies.* Drexel Institute of Technology, Philadelphia, Pa., 1964.

Bureau of Applied Social Research. *Review of Studies in the Flow of Information Among Scientists.* Columbia University, 1960.

Carlson, W. M. "Scientists Requirements." in A. Kent and O. E. Taulbee (ed.). *Electronic Information Handling.* Spartan Books, Washington, D.C., 1965.

Fishenden, R. M. "Methods by Which Research Workers Find Information," in the *International Conference on Scientific Information Proceedings,* National Academy of Sciences — National Research Council, Washington, D.C., 1959, vol. 1, pp. 153-169.

Glass, B. and Norwood, S. H. "How Scientists Actually Learn of Work Important to Them," in the *International Conference on Scientific Information Proceedings,* National Academy of Sciences — National Research Council, Washington, D.C. 1959, vol. 1, pp. 185-187.

Guilford, J. P. Psychometric Methods. McGraw-Hill, New York, 1954.

Halbert, M. H. and Ackoff, R. L. "An Operations Research Study of the Dissemination of Scientific Information," in the *International Conference on Scientific Information Proceedings,* National Academy of Sciences — National Research Council, Washington, D.C. 1959, vol. 1, pp. 87-120.

Hanson, C. W. "Research on Users' Needs: Where is it Getting Us?" *Aslib Proceedings,* vol. 16, 100.2, February 1964.

Hays, W. L. *Statistics for Psychologists.* Holt, Rinehart and Winston, New York, 1963.

Horner, S. "Information Gathering Habits of Workers in Pure and Applied Science," *Industrial and Engineering Chemistry,* 46 (January 1954), pp. 228-236.

Menzel, H. "Planned and Unplanned Scientific Communication," in the *International Conference on Scientific Information Proceedings,* National Academy of Sciences — National Research Council, Washington, D.C. 1959, vol. 1, pp. 199-244.

Rosenberg, V. *The Attitudes of Scientists Toward Information Seeking Activities,* Lehigh University, Bethlehem, Pennsylvania, 1965. (Unpub.)

Siegel, S. *Nonparametric Statistics for the Behavioral Sciences.* McGraw-Hill, New York, 1956.

Winer, B. J. *Statistical Principles in Experimental Design.* McGraw-Hill, New York, 1962.

Wuest, F. J. *Studies in the Methodology of Measuring Information Requirements and Use Patterns,* Report No. 1, Lehigh University, Bethlehem, Pa., May 1965.

APPENDIX I
THE QUESTIONNAIRE

Questionnaire

This is a questionnaire which seeks to determine your evaluation of various methods of gathering information. There are three hypothetical problems which you might encounter in your work. Below each hypothetical problem are various methods for gathering the information necessary for the solution of the problem. You are asked, in Part I, to rank all the items as to their usefulness in the given situation and then, in Part II, to evaluate each item as to the amount of information it will provide and as to the method's ease of use. These are relative judgements and are made by checking the appropriate number on the seven point scale.

If you would be interested in a summary of the results of the questionnaire, place your name and address below.

Thank you for your cooperation.

V. Rosenberg
Center for the
Information Sciences
Lehigh University
Bethlehem, Pennsylvania 18015

_____

_____

Question No. 1

Do you spend more than 50% of your time in what you consider research or research related activities?

_____ Yes

_____ No

Hypothetical Situation No. 1

You are working on a design for a procedure or experiment and wish to know if similar work has been done or is currently being done by someone else.

Please rank the methods listed below according to your preference for getting the required information. No. 1 for most useful, etc.

_____ Search your personal library.

_____ Search your material in the same building where you work, excluding your personal library.

_____ Visit a knowledgeable person - 20 miles away or more.

_____ Use a library that is not within your organization.

_____ Consult a reference librarian.

_____ Visit a knowledgeable person nearby (within your organization).

_____ Write a letter requesting information from a knowledgeable person - 20 miles away or more.

_____ Telephone a knowledgeable person who may be of help.

Hypothetical Situation No. 2

You are preparing a proposal for a new project either to the management of your organization or to an outside agency. You wish to substantiate the proposal with a thorough bibliography. The proposal involves approximately $60,000.

Please rank these "methods" according to their usefulness in this situation.

_____ Telephone a knowledgeable person who may be of help.

_____ Consult a reference librarian.

_____ Use a library that is not within your organization.

_____ Search material in the same building where you work, excluding your personal library.

_____ Visit a knowledgeable person nearby (within your organization).

_____ Search your personal library.

_____ Visit a knowledgeable person - 20 miles away or more.

_____ Write a letter requesting information from a knowledgeable person - 20 miles away or more.

Hypothetical Situation No. 3

You wish to gather information in order to write an article in your area of specialization for a trade or research journal.

Again please rank the "methods" listed below.

_____ Visit a knowledgeable person nearby (within your organization).

_____ Visit a knowledgeable person - 20 miles away or more.

_____ Search material in the same building where you work, excluding your personal library

_____ Search your personal library.

_____ Telephone a knowledgeable person who may be of help.

_____ Write a letter requesting information from a knowledgeable person - 20 miles away or more.

_____ Consult a reference librarian.

_____ Use a library that is not within your organization.

Part IIA

Please rate each of the information gathering methods, as listed below, according to the criteria indicated by circling the appropriate number on the seven point scale.

Please give these ratings without referring back to Part I.

1. Visit a knowledgeable person - 20 miles away or more.

EASE OF USE

extremely simple | 1 | 2 | 3 | 4 | 5 | 6 | 7 | extremely difficult

2. Search your personal library.

EASE OF USE

extremely simple | 1 | 2 | 3 | 4 | 5 | 6 | 7 | extremely difficult

3. Use a library that is not within your organization.

EASE OF USE

extremely simple | 1 | 2 | 3 | 4 | 5 | 6 | 7 | extremely difficult

4. Visit a knowledgeable person nearby (within your organization).

EASE OF USE

extremely simple | 1 | 2 | 3 | 4 | 5 | 6 | 7 | extremely difficult

5. Consult a reference librarian.

EASE OF USE

extremely simple | 1 | 2 | 3 | 4 | 5 | 6 | 7 | extremely difficult

Part IIA (Cont'd.)

6. Search material in the building where you work, excluding your personal library.

EASE OF USE

extremely simple | 1 | 2 | 3 | 4 | 5 | 6 | 7 | extremely difficult

7. Write a letter requesting information from a knowledgeable person - 20 miles away or more.

EASE OF USE

extremely simple | 1 | 2 | 3 | 4 | 5 | 6 | 7 | extremely difficult

8. Telephone a knowledgeable person who may be of help.

EASE OF USE

extremely simple | 1 | 2 | 3 | 4 | 5 | 6 | 7 | extremely difficult

Part IIB

Please rate each of the information gathering methods, as listed below, according to the criteria indicated by circling the appropriate number on the seven point scale.

Please give these ratings without referring back to Part I.

1. Visit a knowledgeable person nearby (within your organization).

	AMOUNT OF INFORMATION EXPECTED	
very little	1 2 3 4 5 6 7	very much

2. Write a letter requesting information from a knowledgeable person - 20 miles away or more.

	AMOUNT OF INFORMATION EXPECTED	
very little	1 2 3 4 5 6 7	very much

3. Use a library that is not within your organization.

	AMOUNT OF INFORMATION EXPECTED	
very little	1 2 3 4 5 6 7	very much

4. Consult a reference librarian.

	AMOUNT OF INFORMATION EXPECTED	
very little	1 2 3 4 5 6 7	very much

5. Telephone a knowledgeable person who may be of help.

	AMOUNT OF INFORMATION EXPECTED	
very little	1 2 3 4 5 6 7	very much

Part IIB (Cont'd.)

6. Search your personal library.

	AMOUNT OF INFORMATION EXPECTED	
very little	1 2 3 4 5 6 7	very much

7. Search material in the building where you work, excluding your personal library.

	AMOUNT OF INFORMATION EXPECTED	
very little	1 2 3 4 5 6 7	very much

8. Visit a knowledgeable person - 20 miles away or more.

	AMOUNT OF INFORMATION EXPECTED	
very little	1 2 3 4 5 6 7	very much

ABOUT THE AUTHOR

Victor Rosenberg is an Assistant Professor at the School of Librarianship of the University of California at Berkeley. A graduate of Lehigh University, Pennsylvania, he gained his Ph.D. from the University of Chicago. He is Chairman of the Education Committee of the American Society for Information Science, and is a member of the Board of Directors of the University of California Art Museum Council. He has published a number of papers on the use of statistical methods in the evaluation of information systems.

Measuring Readers' Failure at the Shelf

John A. Urquhart and J. L. Schofield

Since its inception in 1969, the University of Cambridge Library Management Research Unit has been responsible for the development of methods of data collection in British libraries. The "Failure Survey" described in this paper is designed to provide data on the availability of books in the library and the frequency with which users of the library fail to find the books for which they are looking. Checks are made to ensure that the users are in fact cooperating with the survey to a reasonable extent, and consideration is given to the possible effects of non-cooperation on the results of the survey.

The paper illustrates the difficulties of collecting data on the way in which users interact with the library.

INTRODUCTION

Nowadays we recognize the need to quantify the problems of librarianship so that management can plan their policies on a rational basis. There is a particular need to develop measurement techniques which can be used to describe library processes, and provide management with up-to-date information. Such techniques must operate within three constraints:

they must be inexpensive to operate;
they must not interfere with existing services;
they must provide reproducible results.

One of the main tasks of our research has been to develop these techniques in several areas of library management. The technique described here is concerned with measuring reader's failure at the shelf and we intend to show in this and later papers how it can be used to provide librarians with answers to some of their more pressing questions, such as:

(i) Which particular books are in such heavy demand that they are often unavailable?
(ii) How successful are readers at finding the books they are looking for?

(iii) What are the reasons for their failure?
(iv) What steps can be taken to reduce their chances of failure?

Surveys in America and this country have shown that in some libraries up to 50% of readers' requests are for books that are not on the shelves when required, so that the questions outlined above are quite important — particularly difficult to answer in an open access library.

TECHNIQUES OF SURVEY

To tackle this problem of non-availability we have developed simple and direct survey techniques which require little clerical work and staff time. So far we have installed the survey at four university libraries, at Cambridge, Sussex, Glasgow, and Bradford. Our original survey was at Cambridge University Library and the method of survey used in that library and the results obtained will be considered in this paper. The method of survey in the other three libraries was an adaptation of the original method. This adaptation and the results obtained will be considered in a later paper.

SOURCE: Reprinted from the *Journal of Documentation* 27 (4) Dec. 1971 pp. 273-286, by permission of the authors, the publishers, and the Office for Scientific and Technical Information.

In the Cambridge method readers were asked to record their own failure to find a book on the shelf in the open access areas by placing a pink slip in the place of the book they were looking for. These pink slips were hung in bundles every six feet or so along the shelves, and all the reader had to do was to pull off one of these slips, write down the class mark (call number) of the book he was looking for — or author and title if he did not remember the number — and pop the slip back on the shelf where the book should have been. Later on in the survey we also asked him to record his status — whether MA, BA, 3rd-year graduate or 1st- or 2nd-year undergraduate. Those with MA status are graduate staff over twenty-five or members of the Faculty, and can borrow books for a whole term.[1] Those with BA status are research students under twenty-five and 3rd-year undergraduates are the only undergraduates who have borrowing rights. Both BAs and 3rd-year undergraduates can borrow books for a fortnight.[2]

Every book consulted was reshelved by members of the staff. During the survey a co-loured slip inside a returned book indicated whether it had been at the binders or the labellers or borrowed by an MA, BA, or 3rd-year undergraduate; books used within the library contained no slips. When a book which had caused failure was finally reshelved the reshelver took out the corresponding pink slip and matched it with the coloured book slip, if there was one, and placed it in a collection box. The pink slip could then be filed by class mark for each type of failure.

At the end of the period of survey, which was also the end of the term, all books should have been returned, so any pink slips left on the shelves were checked to see why they were there — whether because the slip was in the wrong place, or was incorrectly filled in, or because the book was still missing, or because the slip had not been pulled out when the book had been returned.

The survey was carried out for two separate periods from 3 November to 31 December 1969, and from 2 January to 31 March 1970.

During the second survey we distinguished between 3rd-year and BA borrowers with different coloured slips in the reshelved books; we also collected additional statistics which enabled us to find out more about user behaviour.

EFFECTIVENESS OF SURVEY

Before we started our survey doubts were expressed to us as to whether readers would co-operate. We did our best to catch the readers' attention, putting notices in the lifts and on the tables, and instructions on the end of every other shelf and on the slips themselves. But probably our best advertisement was our bundles of pink slips, hooked on to the shelves all over the library with opened-out paper clips.

We checked the degree of co-operation by interviewing the readers as they left the shelf areas. We asked them three questions:

(i) Are you aware of the survey taking place?
(ii) Have you failed to find any of the specific books you were looking for?
(iii) If you have failed have you filled in a failure slip for each failure?

Over 1,000 readers were interviewed during the two surveys and 67% said they had fully co-operated. This percentage did not vary significantly over the period of investigation.

RESULTS OF THE SURVEYS

During the first survey, which lasted for nine weeks, 3,347 failure slips were recovered; 2,875 of these were returned by the reshelvers and 472 slips were found left on the shelves. During the second survey, lasting thirteen weeks, 6,220 slips were found; 5,317 of these were returned by the reshelvers and 903 slips were found left on the shelves. The causes of failure are listed in Table 1.

As can be seen from the Table, the two terms' figures are remarkably consistent. In both periods the three main causes of failure, MA borrowing, internal use, and other borrowing, each accounted for about 30% of the total failure, and even the less important causes of failure show little percentage change.

When we come to examine individual classes of books we find the same degree of failure from one term to the next. See Table 2(a). The class marks do not correspond with UDC or DDC.

TABLE I.

Causes of failure	No. of slips		% of total failures	
	Autumn 1969	Spring 1970	Autumn 1969	Spring 1970
A borrowing	934	1,675	27.9	26.9
A borrowing		407		6.5
	966		28.9	
rd-year borrowing		1,279		20.6
nternal use*	954	1,896	28.5	30.5
e-labelling and re-binding	21	60	0.6	1.0
issing books	90	124	2.7	2.0
verdue books	19	38	0.6	0.6
naccounted for	116	355	3.5	5.7
ncorrect copying of class marks	141	176	4.2	2.8
ooking in the wrong place	44	104	1.3	1.7
nknown (book found with slip on shelf)	62	106	1.9	1.7
	3,347	6,220		

* Books consulted within the library, but not borrowed.

TABLE 2(a).

Class Mark		No. of failures		%		Spring 1970 Failures/1,000 volumes of stock
		Autumn 1969	Spring 1970	Autumn 1969	Spring 1970	
*a	0-99	103	169	3.6	3.2	} 28.1
b	100-199	219	498	7.6	9.4	43.4
c	200-299	575	1,251	20.0	23.5	43.4
d	300-399	210	373	7.3	7.0	9.4
e	400-499	170	232	5.9	4.4	5.3
f	500-599	407	874	14.2	16.4	21.8
g	600-699	284	350	9.9	6.6	11.2
h	700-799	470	813	16.4	15.3	16.4
i	800-849	7	6	0.2	0.1	0.9
j	900-999	8	14	0.3	0.3	15.0
	P1-P339		253			6.9
	P340-P448		37			0.6
	P460-P898	422	373	14.6	13.8	8.3
	Books from other areas of library		74			0.6
		2,875	5,317			

Classes 0-999 and books from other areas of the library are monographs.
Classes with prefix P are periodicals.

*a Theology
  b Philosophy
  c Education, Social Sciences, and Law
  d Medicine and Science
  e Fine Arts, Useful Arts, Biography, Archaeology, Anthropology, and Local History

f History
g History and Geography
h Literature
i Literary subjects
j General

It is interesting to compare the number of failures with the estimated number of volumes of stock for that particular subject area. It can be seen that failure is higher in certain areas of the library. This is borne out by Table 2(b) which shows that during the Spring term, of the nine floor areas of the library with open access, only three — ground, fourth, and fifth floors of the library's North wing — accounted for over two-thirds of the failure. These floors contain economics, political and social sciences; history; and geography, English, and foreign literature respectively.

TABLE 2(b).

Class mark by floor			Total no. of failures
* a NW Ground	Monographs	1-238	1,759
b NW 1		240-364	447
c NW 2		365-449	190
d NW 3		450-536 / RA-RH	364
e NW 4		537-689	984
f NW 5		690-799 / 900-999	859
SW 3	Periodicals	P1-339	253
SW 4		P340-P448	37
SW 5		P460-P898	373
Other areas			51
			5,317

*a Theology, Philosophy, & Social Sciences
 b Education, Law, Medicine and Science
 c Science, Fine Arts, and Useful Arts
 d Biography, Anthropology, Archaelogy, and Local History
 e History
 f Geography, Literature, and General.

The percentage failure in terms of the book stock does not seem very high, but it should be remembered that in a very large library there are many books which are very rarely consulted. More revealing is a comparison of the term's borrowings with the number of failures (Table 3a).

If we take into account the fact that only two-thirds of the failures were recorded then the true ratio of failure to borrowing would be higher by 50%. So, for example, in the Spring term the ratios would be as follows:

TABLE 3(a).
RATIO OF FAILURE TO BORROWING

		Borrowed	Caused failure
Autumn term	MA	9,200	934
Spring term		13,243	1,675
Autumn term	Other	7,200	966
Spring Term		12,104	1,686

TABLE 3(b).
RATIO OF FAILURE TO BORROWING IN SPRING

Borrower	Borrowed	Caused failure	Apparent ratio	Real ratio
MA	13,243	1,675	1 in 8	1 in 5
BA	4,781	407	1 in 12	1 in 8
3rd-year	7,323	1,279	1 in 6	1 in 4

PATTERN OF FAILURE

Many of the books borrowed or used internally caused more than one failure. This pattern of failure is recorded in Table 4. As would be expected, in the Spring term, with its longer period of survey, more individual titles failed and the average number of failures per title also increased.

The table shows that books failing twice or more in the Autumn term accounted for 46% of the failures and books failing twice or more in the Spring accounted for 60% of the failures. In both cases about 500 books accounted for

TABLE 4.

No. of titles which caused:	1 fail	2 fails	3 fails	4 fails	More than 4 fails	Total no. of titles failing	Total no. of failures
Autumn	1,549	336	73	40	46	2,044	2,875
Spring	2,102	510	203	122	150	3,087	5,317

just under half the failures. To put it in more dramatic terms, 500 books out of 500,000 in open access accounted for half the readers' recorded failure. They were not necessarily the same 500 books each term, but it is worth noting that if the 500 books causing half the failure in the Autumn had been duplicated, the failure in the Spring might have been less. For example, if the 413 monographs failing two or more times in the Autumn had been duplicated, or an extra copy kept in reserve in time for the Spring term, 575 failures in the second term could have been eliminated. And if extra sets of the forty periodical titles failing three or more times in the Autumn had been available for the Spring term, 299 failures, or about 45% of all periodical failure could have been eliminated in the second term.

As we have shown previously a minority of readers did not co-operate in the survey. We consider, however, that the results received from

FURTHER RESULTS FROM THE SPRING TERM

Status of Reader Failing. In the Spring term we asked readers to record their status on the failure slips, so we were able to find out how much different groups of users were failing and what type of use was causing their failure. These inter-relationships are set in in Table 5.

It can be seen that far more undergraduates failed than other types of users.

In Table 6 we compare only MAs, BAs, and 3rd-year students. The figures in brackets refer to the number of failures we would expect on a pro rata basis if cause of failure and status of borrower were *not* related.

It can be seen that each group of borrowers caused relatively more failure to members

TABLE 5.

		Failure by:						
	MA	Non-Resident MA	BA	3rd-year	1st/2nd year	Other	Unknown	Total
Borrowed by								
MA	301	43	199	536	437	44	123	1,683
BA	50	2	63	140	119	7	31	412
3rd-year	105	13	120	606	304	13	122	1,283
Internal	222	29	181	590	656	31	200	1,909
Labelling	7	2	5	18	10	0	2	44
Binding	4	0	3	4	4	0	1	16
Totals	689	89	571	1,894	1,530	95	479	5,347*

* This figure is taken from the day by day tally of failure slips returned.

the majority of readers give, by and large, a representative picture of the situation. The relative significance of the causes of failure should not be affected. On the other hand, since one of the reasons for readers not putting slips on the shelves was because a slip was there already, our figures might tend to underestimate the proportion of multiple failures.

of its own group than to members of other groups.

Table 7 shows the relative contribution of the causes of failure to each group of borrowers.

As the table shows, MA borrowing caused nearly half of the MA failure, but only a third of the BA and undergraduates' failure. Internal use accounted for a third of the failure for each group except 1st/2nd-year, where it accounted

TABLE 6.

| | Failure by: | | | |
	All MAs	BA	3rd-year	Total
Borrowed by:				
MA	344	199	536	1,079
	(255)	(189)	(635)	
BA	52	63	140	255
	(60)	(45)	(150)	
3rd-year	118	120	606	844
	(199)	(148)	(497)	
Total	514	382	1,282	2,178

With these figures the myth of markedly different reading habits for different groups of user is finally exploded. MAs may read different ent books from undergraduates, but not in the area where it hurts most — where books are failing. These figures should be of significance in any discussion on undergraduate libraries.

Failure rates. During a fortnight in March we made a total count of all books returned on three floors in the library and compared these numbers with the number of failures they

TABLE 7.

| | | Failure by: | | | | | |
	MA	Non-Resident MA	BA	3rd-year	1st/2nd-year	Other	Unknown
Causes of failures in %'s:							
MA borrowing	43.7	48.9	34.9	28.3	28.6	46.3	25.4
BA borrowing	7.3	2.3	11.0	7.4	7.8	7.4	6.4
3rd-year borrowing	15.3	14.8	21.0	32.1	19.9	13.7	25.0
Internal Use	32.3	32.9	31.7	31.2	42.9	32.6	41.0
Labelling	1.4	1.1	1.4	1.0	0.8	—	2.2
Binding							
All causes of failure	100.0	100.0	100.0	100.0	100.0	100.0	100.0

TABLE 8.

| | | % Failure by: | | | | | |
	Total	All MAs	BA	3rd-year	1st/2nd year	Other	Total
Borrowed by:							
All MAs	1,560	22.0	12.8	34.4	28.0	2.8	100.0
BA	381	13.7	16.5	36.8	31.2	1.8	100.0
3rd-year	1,161	10.3	10.3	52.2	26.2	1.0	100.0

for nearly half.

On the other hand, because of the larger total number of failures by undergraduates, every group of borrower caused more failure to this group than to any other group. Thus every time a book borrowed by an MA caused failure it did so in the ratio two MAs to one BA to six undergraduates; a book borrowed by a BA caused failure in the ration of one MA to one BA to five undergraduates; a book borrowed by a 3rd-year undergraduate caused failure in the ratio of one MA to one BA to eight undergraduates; and a book used internally caused failure in the ratio of one MA to one BA to six undergraduates.

had caused. This enabled us to calculate the success and failures rates for different sections of the library. The failure rate was taken to be the estimated number of failures divided by the estimated demand — demand was taken to be equal to the use plus estimated failure. The estimated failure figures were found from the observed failure figures by multiplying by a factor of 20/13, since the participation rate was 65%.

As would be expected the failure rates were greatest on the North wing floors, where the number of failures was greatest.

Another interesting result was the ratio of internal to external book use. In the periodicals

TABLE 9.
RESULTS OF THE SURVEY

	South Wing 5		North Wing 5		North Wing G	
	1st week over 8 days	2nd week over 7 days	1st week over 8 days	2nd week over 7 days	1st week over 8 days	2nd week over 7 days
Internally used books returned	755	654	766	523	796	745
Externally borrowed books returned	144	145	514	561	341	447
Estimated number of failures	69	68	265	360	115	131
Estimated demand	968	867	1,545	1,444	1,252	1,323
Failure rate	7%	8%	17%	25%	9%	10%
Hence success rate	93%	92%	83%	75%	91%	90%

on the fifth floor South wing it was five to one, but for the monographs in the North wing it was less — two to one on the ground floor and just about one to one on the fifth floor.

Waiting time for a book. Newly completed failure slips on the fifth and ground floors North wing were dated each day from 6 February until 19 February. Returned slips with such dates were then examined to determine the waiting time from the recording of failure to the return of the book. The results are set out in Table 10. The most surprising result is the high waiting time for internally used books. One week after failure over half the books had not returned to the shelves and after three weeks over a fifth. Since these figures apply to waiting time *after* failure, the real period during which books causing failure are retained for internal use must be even greater. Assuming demand for a particular book to be random, then the estimated period of retention is twice the waiting time after failure, i.e. twenty-three days. It should be pointed out that this estimate probably does not apply to internally used books which do not cause failure, but popular books are certainly kept off the shelves for longer than the official three-day reservation period.

Books borrowed by BAs and by 3rd-year undergraduates show similar patterns of waiting, the waiting time being ten and eight days respectively. If we ignore books which could have caused waiting for more than a fortnight — books borrowed by BAs and 3rd-year undergraduates should be returned within a fortnight — the average waiting time is five and a half days in both cases. Books borrowed by MAs cause an average waiting time of a month. It is difficult to be precise

TABLE 10.
WAITING TIME FOR BOOKS
THAT HAVE CAUSED FAILURE.

Day	Category of Borrower			
	Internal	BA	3rd-year	MA
Same	6	6	10	3
+ 1	23	1	11	2
+ 2	13	8	18	4
+ 3	12	6	18	2
+ 4	10	1	14	10
+ 5	8	1	10	8
+ 6	15	2	13	5
+ 7	11	2	7	3
+ 8	5	0	6	3
+ 9	8	1	7	2
+ 10	7	2	10	3
+ 11	5	2	5	1
+ 12	5	4	5	3
+ 13	9	3	11	5
+ 14	3	1	2	3
+ 15-19	8	1	6	9
+ 20-24	5	1	7	11
+ 25-29	9	0	9	13
+ 30-34	5	2	2	16
+ 35-39	8	3	0	25
+ 40-44	6	0	1	32
+ 45-49	4	0	0	30
+ 50-54	1	1	0	23
+ 55-59				
Total	186	48	172	216
Mean time	11.4 days	10.3 days	8.3 days	30.1 days

about the actual effect of MA borrowing since this seems to be different at different periods of the term. There is a steady level of borrowing by MAs throughout the term but half the books are returned within the last fortnight, so we assume that many users failing near the beginning of the term are having to wait at least two months. Of the 216 books borrowed by MAs during this period and causing failure, 126 were still out after a month, and sixty-three of those were returned six weeks later at the end of the term.

Pattern of demand. Comparison of dates on the individual failure slips enabled us to deduce whether demand for particular titles was random or concentrated. Our conclusion is that there was no particular concentration of demand for popular books, but there may have been a slow decline over a period of weeks. This kind of result may seem at variance with the experience of other libraries, but it should be noted that in many cases the University Library here is not the primary source of books for undergraduates.

Relationship between failure and recall. The number of recalls for the Spring term was twelve for books borrowed by BAs and 3rd-year undergraduates and seventy-nine for books borrowed by MAs. Since the number of failures for books borrowed by BAs and 3rd-years taken together was about the same as for books borrowed by MAs, it is reasonable to suppose that users who considered recalling a book were far less likely to make a recall if the book was due back within a week or so.

The estimated number of failures for books borrowed by MAs was 2,577, compared with seventy-nine recalls, so only about one in thirty-three of those readers failing due to MA borrowing made a recall.

COMPARISON OF THE TWO SURVEYS

The total number of failures due to borrowing in the Spring term, 5,317, was nearly double those of the Autumn, 2,875, although the period of survey was only one and a half times longer. Any increase in demand should show a proportionally greater increase in failure. For example, figures for BA and 3rd-year borrowing, and failure due to this borrowing, show a 14% increase in demand rate and a 23.5% increase in failure rate. We would expect the number of failures to be approximately proportional to the demand squared, so the percentage increase in failure should be twice the percentage increase in the demand.

The same subject areas of the library stock

were in great demand in both periods of the survey, and demand for various types of books seemed consistent, even down to the individual title. In a study of periodicals failing both in the Autumn term and the Spring term, we found that 164 titles failed in the Autumn, 202 in the Spring, and of these eighty-six titles failed in both terms. In the Autumn term the forty most heavily used titles caused three-fifths of the failure, and they accounted for nearly half the failure in the Spring. Only six of these forty did not reappear in the failure records for the Spring term.

A recent study of books failing in the Economics class shows a similar picture. If failures due to MA borrowing are ignored, 42% of the books failing three times in the second period also failed in the first period, 67% of those books failing four times, and 70% of those books failing more than four times.

It is reasonable to conclude that the more a book fails in one term the more likely it is to fail subsequently.

USING THE RESULTS OF THE SURVEYS

We hope we have demonstrated the wealth of information which can be derived from a carefully thought out survey based on reader failure at the shelves. Not only have we developed a method which can pinpoint individual books in heavy demand, but, more important, we have shown that a good deal of user behaviour in libraries need not be the subject of inspired guesses but can be measured in quantitative terms. As a result of the surveys we now know that as far as the Cambridge University Library is concerned:

(i) nearly all the reader failure at the shelf is caused by other readers using the books rather than by incorrect use of the library by the reader;

(ii) MA borrowing, other borrowing, and internal use of books each make an equal contribution to that failure;

(iii) most of the failure occurs on only three floors — ground, fourth, and fifth floors of the North Wing containing economics, political and social sciences; history; and geography, English and foreign literature respectively;

(iv) about half the failure in periodicals has been caused hitherto by the same forty titles;

(v) while each group of borrowers causes relatively more failure to its own group than to other groups, there is a considerable overlap in the use of popular books by different groups of borrower;

(vi) someone who is looking for a book in use has to wait on average at least a month if it has been borrowed by a BA, at least eight days if borrowed by an undergraduate, but over eleven days if used internally;

(vii) there is no evidence that there is a sudden rush for particular books, although demand for a particular title may fall over a period of time.

Knowing the cause of failure we are now in a position to recommend what steps can be taken to reduce that failure. As far as the Cambridge University Library is concerned we have suggested certain simple adjustments to library procedure which should cause a significant drop in failure. These are:

(i) changing the system of internal reservation so that books can be renewed for the succeeding day only and complete reshelving of all books on the tables once a week. This should considerably cut the waiting time for internally used books;

(ii) making the method of recall more attractive so that more than the present figure of 1 in 33 of the readers failing due to MA borrowing decide to recall;

(iii) operating more restricted loan periods for books from heavily used sections;

(iv) preparing a list of popular periodical and monograph titles. This list could be of help to librarians when they come to select new titles.

Should any of these recommendations be adopted it would be possible to measure their effect by reintroducing the Failure Survey at some future date.

We have also compared failures of titles in a particular subject area with the holdings of those titles and their use in the corresponding departmental library. From this comparison we were able to recommend which titles should have extra copies.

COST OF SURVEY

One of the main considerations in any survey is its cost. Apart from the initial installation and the analysis of the results the actual filing

time in our surveys only took about one hour per day, while interviews averaged an hour and a half a week. Some extra time was also spent in putting borrowing slips in the books and reshelving, say another hundred hours. Thus, over the whole period of investigation an average of two and a half hours per day of staff time was needed to service half a million books in open access.

Our total cost estimate for the Cambridge survey for two terms was as follows:

Materials	£15
Installation time	£20
Running time (250 hrs at 40p per hour	£100
Analysis time (70 hrs at £1 per hour)	£70
	£205

or about 2p a completed failure slip.

SUMMARY

In this paper we have tried to stress the simplicity and usefulness of the "Failure Survey" method. It is simple because:

(i) the readers do most of the essential recording — it is to their ultimate benefit;

(ii) the technique concentrates on the small percentage of books in a library which are in great demand.

It is useful because:

(a) it pinpoints the particular books and journals which are in such heavy demand that they are often unavailable;

(b) it shows the failure rate of readers to find known books on the shelves;

(c) it indicates the causes of such failure;

(d) it provides a sound data base from which can be drawn further conclusions about reader behaviour and the effectiveness of the library services.

In later papers we will show what further management information can be found from the application of Failure Surveys to the problems of university libraries.

NOTES

[1] A "term" is taken here to mean three months and corresponds to the Cambridge word "quarter".

[2] The Cambridge university library is primarily a research library, though it is heavily used by undergraduates. Primary provision for them is made in the libraries of the faculties, departments and colleges.

ABOUT THE AUTHORS

John A. Urquhart read mathematics and statistics at the University of Leeds, England. From 1966-69 he was employed as a Scientific Officer at the Marine Laboratory, Aberdeen and was involved in a number of studies for the fisheries industry. He was an Assistant in Research at the University of Cambridge Library Management Research Unit from 1969-72. He is currently at the University of Newcastle-upon-Tyne Libraries.

J. L. Schofield is the Assistant Director of Research of the Library Management Research Unit of the University of Cambridge, England. Before taking up his present appointment he was engaged on management studies in industry and for the Ministry of Defence. His publications have included many contributions to the literature of library management.

V

THE EVALUATION OF POLICY

The assessment of whether or not a particular library service, or any aspect of that service, is "good" or "bad" can no longer be left solely to individual subjective judgement and opinion. If a decision is to be taken to follow one course of action in preference to another, it should be taken, as far as is possible, on the basis of objective information about the relative effects of the two policies in question. This means that a serious attempt has to be made to measure all the relevant parameters of the system under consideration, including the expected costs of implementation, the expected increase in effectiveness which will occur should the new system replace the old, and the expected benefits (of all kinds, both positive and negative) which the new system will produce. In the social services, of which libraries are one, the measurement and evaluation of costs and benefits is extremely complex, primarily because one has to deal with human clients in a situation in which one's own objectives are by no means clear. The idiosyncrasies of human behaviour, and the needs of human individuals may have to be considered in an environment which is not tuned to the maximization of any particular measure of its performance.

Two related techniques, known as "cost-benefit analysis" and "cost-effectiveness analysis" have been developed in an attempt to derive a methodology for solving overall policy questions of this kind. In this Chapter, these techniques are described and examples of their use in practical situations are given. Wilson, in the first paper, presents a simple and straightforward account of the principles of cost-benefit analysis, and Chambers and Hindle consider the applicability of such techniques to public policy planning. Jestes, Hitch and McKean, and Flowerdew present case-studies depicting the successful use of these techniques in three different areas, and the Chapter is concluded by Simon's paper on the role of economic analysis in non-profit-making organisations, taking libraries as a typical example.

The Technique of Cost Benefit Analysis

Alan G. Wilson

The paper which introduces this chapter has been chosen because it provides a straight-forward introduction to the techniques, methods and aims of cost benefit analysis. Wilson describes, by means of simple examples, the factors which would be considered in a cost benefit analysis, and introduces the related problems of measurement and value. The examples are taken from local government, but their lessons are equally applicable to libraries. In all cases, the problem is to decide the best method of investment in a particular situation, given a set of objectives and a set of constraints.

I INTRODUCTION

Suppose we want to apply cost benefit analysis to some investment project to be carried out by some agency. First, this investment usually has to be compared with something, either with alternative investments, or with doing nothing at all. How does cost benefit analysis then differ from other techniques? Of prime importance is the fact that it tries to examine all consequences of the investment project. This means looking at all agencies which either incur costs because of the investment, or receive benefits, whether these are financial or not. It also means looking at all the consequences *in time* of the project. Let us consider each of these in turn:

What does it mean to consider all agencies or persons affected? A simple example of this may be a private decision of a company to build a new factory which involves a smoky chimney. The firm may take this decision on the basis of its private costs and benefits, and implement the project if its private rate of return is high enough. What cost benefit analysis does in addition is to take account of the effect of the chimney smoke on nearby housewives' washing lines, and the general inconvenience to nearby residences. This sort of cost is sometimes called a social cost. Thus, in using cost benefit analysis we shall usually try to consider costs and benefits which are *external* to the private accounts of the agency, in addition to the usual ones.

It is often considered that this is one of the most important duties of government agencies, as opposed to private ones. In other words, activities which generate large social costs and benefits, as a proportion of the total, are more likely to be government activities. Yet another way of putting this, would be to say that governments undertake activities which would be difficult in the private market because the bulk of the costs and benefits are social in the sense that they are not recoverable by market operations. An extreme example of this might be the provision of coastal lighthouses: the beneficiaries are nearby ships, but the costs could not be recovered from them by a private company. This view of governmental activity, is an extreme one and we may often have other reasons for developing different types of government activity, whether central or local. However, the point illustrates the importance of cost analysis for the public sector; when investment decisions are to be taken in the public sector, social costs and benefits should be taken into account as well as the private cost of the government agency concerned. It can also be used as an efficiency test for public authorities, which do not have the usual commercial tests open to them.

The second major result of considering all the effects of an investment project, is that we should look ahead in time to cover the whole life of the project, and not just its first year, or

SOURCE: Reprinted from *Cost Benefit Analysis in Local Government* (London: Institute of Municipal Treasurers and Accountants, 1969) pp. 17-22, by permission of the author and publishers.

its first operating year, as is often the case in practice. This implies that *discounting* techniques must be developed, and a suitable rate of interest chosen. It can easily be seen why this is necessary. The investment decision is being taken at a particular point in time. Suppose a rate of interest has been chosen at 6 per cent. Suppose this means that £100 held now is worth £106 in a year's time, if 6 per cent interest has been added. This means that if a project produces benefits of £106 in one year's time, then this should be discounted by the 6 per cent interest rate to a *present value* of £100. Generally, where possible, we shall work with present values of cost or benefit time streams which have been discounted at some rate of interest. More later about the rate of interest, which is obviously crucial to the whole procedure.

Some Illustrative Examples

Three examples considered at this stage are intended to illustrate the dangers of public authorities (or private bodies for that matter) taking decisions which are not in the community's interest because they are not using cost benefit techniques in their investment appraisal.

The first example is concerned with a municipal transport undertaking. The hypothetical situation is as follows: the transport undertaking is run on a break even basis, and attempts to keep its operating costs as low as possible. This means in particular that it tries to minimise "dead mileage" — that distance covered by the buses between depots and pick up points, where no revenue is collected. The planning department of the authority then proposes in its development plan to resite the main depot of the transport undertaking so that its operating costs would increase. The transport department (or a private company if the buses are privately run) might then oppose the whole scheme on these grounds. Its break-even policy may be in jeopardy, and an increase in fares may lose it its passengers, and so on. The cost benefit technique we have been examining would get over this problem by considering all the effects of moving the main transport depot: it would look at the increased operating costs of the transport department, but it would also examine the increased benefits to traders and the public, and to the council,

which result from the planning department's scheme. If this technique is not adopted, and the objections of the transport department carry the day, then in a situation where the benefits in one department far outweigh the increased costs in another, there is a danger of the community losing substantial benefits. It may have been more sensible to subsidise the transport department for their loss, out of the benefits of the new scheme if it is thought desirable to maintain the break even policy.

The second example concerns a development problem. A local authority is carrying out major redevelopment. It has a large cleared site in the town centre and it is going to lease sites to private developers. The planning authority of that council has the alternatives of expanding the central area shopping centre, or encouraging out of town or suburban shopping centres. Some of the out of town centres may even be outside the boundaries of the authority in the county. What should the council do? A cost benefit analysis would attempt to set out all the costs and benefits, including social costs and benefits, and compare the two alternative plans. Two key differences may emerge. If the expanded centre plan is adopted, then land values will rise in the centre, and the city council will benefit from increased income. In the decentralised plan, however, land values at the centre will fall. The next key difference concerns traffic congestion. The expanded centre plan will reduce it. Only the benefits of higher land values would show in the city's accounts, and if the city were to act selfishly, it is clear that a bad decision could be made. A cost benefit approach, however, would suggest that the expanded centre plan should only be undertaken if its benefits to the city exceeded the social costs imposed by the plan. This is an oversimplied version of something which could happen, but it does illustrate the potential value of cost benefit analysis.

We can conclude our examples with an example of a dispute between local authorities: Town X and nearby town Y are each expanding their shopping centres. Assume they are each motivated by the potential gains to their own town. Then X will expand to try to capture some of the custom of Y, as well as its own residents, and vice versa. There is obviously a danger of wasteful use of resources if decisions are taken on this basis. Cost benefit analysis could almost certainly suggest a cheaper solution which achieves the same benefits, and thus increases the *net* benefit for each town over the selfish solution.

II   WHAT TO INCLUDE

First, care must be taken in defining the project proper. This consists of enumerating the costs and benefits which are incurred by the agency which is carrying out the project. For example, in considering a motorway project, the effects of the projects on feeder roads must be considered. If one of the benefits is the reduced accident level of the motorway, then the possibly increased accident level of unimproved feeder roads must be considered also. When the project is being defined, some estimate must also be made of its lifetime. This is sometimes difficult to guess, especially in the case of projects which may be overtaken by technological change.

The second major class of costs and benefits are the external ones: those which accrue to bodies external to the promoting body. The costs and benefits which should be included from this sector, are those which involve technological change, or change in productive capacity, in some sense, such as the change in operating costs of a private individual's car, but that we should not include changes which are purely financial and do not involve the use of real resources. An example of the second type of benefit would be the increase in land values which might take place in the neighbourhood of a transport improvement. The usual reason for not including such benefits is that it involves double counting. In the example given, the increased land values result from improved accessibility, and the benefits have already been counted on behalf of the people who actually travel.

It is appropriate at this stage to mention the technique of drawing up social accounts to describe investment projects. These have the form of ordinary accounts, and will begin with an orthodox account framework within which, say, a council may examine a project, but which also contains a number of social accounts, each documenting the costs and benefits under appropriate heads. These accounts then, show explicitly the *incidence* of the costs and benefits. It can be impor-

tant to show the entries even when they cannot be measured, since it is a presentation which emphasises differences between alternatives so that the argument can be concentrated on these differences. If a complete set of accounts is drawn up in the first place, then it will be certain that a decision to exclude certain costs will not have been made without due consideration.

III   HOW TO MEASURE OR VALUE

This question raises issues which may well be the crux of a whole cost benefit problem, and the answers may also decide whether the cost benefit technique is possible or not. If a private profit maximising firm manufactures a product and sells it, the cost benefit analysis of an investment decision may be straightforward. The firm incurs capital and running costs in producing the goods; it sells the goods at some market price, and the income from sales forms the benefit system. It has also paid market prices for its factors of production. The possible difficulties here are associated with imperfections in the market, so that market prices may not reflect the "true" value of the costs and benefits, or with accounting for the incidence of taxes, and the extent to which they should be included. This is mentioned, simply to illustrate that a social cost benefit calculation will be very much harder. Consider the last example: the development of two adjacent shopping centres. The variables which appear here include the length of time it takes customers to get to the shopping centre, and the range of choice available to them when they get there. The question we are asking now is a two stage one: how to put values on variables and, when we have decided this, how to actually carry out the measurement.

Let us consider one example of the measurement and evaluation of a "difficult" social variable. In the cost benefit analysis of alternative transport plans for a city, a large proportion of the benefits may consist of traveling time saved by workers making the journey to work in peak hours, after the investment in the new transport network has been made. How do we value such time saving, and how do we actually measure it? First, the aim must be to reduce all costs and benefits to money values. So in this case, we want the value that people actually put on time saved. One of the obvious difficulties is going to be that this is likely to be a different figure for different people. The millionaire commuting to his office may value his time much more highly than a lowly paid manual worker, and so may be prepared to pay more for faster travel. In the first instance, however, we may have to content ourselves with getting averages for categories of people. The clue to measurement has actually been given: there is a trade off between traveling time and money. In the case of working time saved, the answer may be to adopt the wage or salary rate as a measure of the value of time. In the case of non-working time, it is more difficult, but we can observe people to find out what their trade-off is between time and money. For example, a survey may be carried out which obtains the time and cost of the journeys to work of a set of people, and the time and cost of the best alternative in each case. It may then be possible to devise a method of statistical analysis which extracts the amount people seem to be prepared to pay to travel more quickly. There are complications of course, such as the element of choice associated with comfort and convenience, but value of non-working time can be extracted in this way.

Let us summarise the possible answers to this question of how to value and measure costs and benefits: —

In many cases money valuations exist through the market price mechanism.

Some adjustment may be necessary if the market is very imperfect, or to take account of taxation effects. (One example of a market imperfection, for example, is the relative pricing of road and rail travel: rail users more or less pay the costs of their journey. Road users pay less than their costs, since they do not pay the social costs of the congestion they cause, especially in cities. However, it does not necessarily follow that "true" market prices should be used in a cost benefit calculation if, as in the road case, it may not be politically feasible ever to charge them. In the road-rail case that may lead to heavy investment in railways, but under-used railway stock and congested roads remain.)

In the case of more difficult variables, values can be imputed by observation, as in the valuation of time, cited earlier. The difficulties are acute in many cases and ingenious methods have been devised, especially for benefit measurement. A further set of valuation assumptions has to be made in relation to the incidence of costs and benefits. So far, for example, we have implicitly tended to assume the constant marginal utility of money. This is, that £1 is worth £1 to any man, whether he is rich or poor. In some cost benefit calculations, it may be thought desirable to assume that £1 is worth less to a rich man than to a poor man. In such evaluations, a redistribution of income may be implied, and this may be one of the goals of the government which is carrying out the calculation.

It should perhaps be emphasised, in this context, that cost benefit analysis is politically neutral. It is a tool which may tell you the best investment alternative given a set of goals or aims by the agency applying the analysis.

IV   WHAT INTEREST RATE TO USE?

The third main question concerns the choice of interest rate, which was mentioned earlier. There are at least three possible choices:
(i) The social time preference rate.
(ii) The rate of interest at which the government lends and borrows: this is, roughly, the risk free rate of interest.
(iii) The opportunity cost rate of interest.
The problem would not be so severe if these rates were roughly the same, but there is evidence that they can differ markedly in different circumstances. However, their use depends on the investment criteria which we adopt anyway, and this will be discussed shortly.

The social time preference rate is a positive rate of interest which expresses the value human beings place on having assets here and now rather than at some time in the future. It may be argued, for example, that such a rate exists because of the inevitability of death: we might not be here to enjoy it in the future! From assumptions of this kind, using the kind of life tables used by insurance companies, a social time preference rate can be calculated but it seems to come out very low, of the order of 1 or 2 per cent.

The second rate of interest, the rate of interest on long term Government securities, is much higher than 1 or 2 per cent at the present time.

The third possible rate of interest is the opportunity cost rate of interest, which has obvious attractions if an opportunity cost can be calculated for the project undergoing a cost benefit analysis. This is the rate of return on the project which could be undertaken if the project being evaluated were not carried out, and so freed the capital for this alternative opportunity. Once again, we shall return to this when discussing investment criteria.

V   RELEVANT CONSTRAINTS

The final question asks what constraints are to be associated with the project being evaluated. Let us list the types of constraints which might apply, and be used in the cost benefit calculation. There are:

(i) Physical constraints: first, the production function which relates input and output, and which enters directly into the clculations. There may also be external physical constraints: if there is a question to be answered on the optimum timing of a project for example, there may be external constraints on the time of implementation.

(ii) There may be legal constraints. This may be the case for example in the evaluation of a development plan, where some alternatives may be excluded by the legal constraints on land use.

(iii) There may be administrative constraints on what can be administratively coped with. The difficulty of implementing road pricing may be an illustration of this, though the report of the Smeed Committee suggested that the constraint was not serious.

(iv) There may be constraints which the evaluating agency may wish to apply on income distributional effects. A scheme may involve some people becoming much better off (i.e. having higher incomes) at the expense of others who become worse off. Economic theorists may argue that a scheme is worth carrying out if the beneficiaries gain enough to be able to compensate the losers, and yet still benefit themselves. But such compensation is rarely feasible in practice, and so some constraints may apply against impermissible income redistribution effects.

(v) Finally, there remains the problem of budgetary constraints.

VI   INVESTMENT CRITERIA

We should finally look at investment criteria

more formally. First, then, let us list the possible criteria assuming that there are no constraints, and that all projects are independent. The investment rule would then be to carry out projects if:

(i) The present value of benefits exceeds the present value of costs, hence the ratio of the present value of benefits to the present value of costs exceeds unity.

(ii) Where a constant annuity with the same present value as the benefits exceeds a constant annuity with the same present value as the costs.

(iii) Where the internal rate of return of the project exceeds the chosen discount rate.

The only term not defined so far is the "internal rate of return." This is that rate of interest used to discount benefits and costs which produces equal present values for benefits and costs. It is, roughly, the social rate of return on a project.

Under the assumptions we have made, each of these criteria is equivalent to the others. In other words, they could be used to rank a list of projects in order of rate of return, and the ranking would be the same in each case.

It is worth noting also at this stage the importance of including social costs and benefits. When these are included, projects become worthwhile according to our criteria which would not be worthwhile (that is have an excess of benefits over costs) in a conventional accounting framework. This is true of the Victoria Line in London for example. We have gone some way, in other words, to formulating precisely the effects which pressure groups are often trying to impress on politicians to influence government decisions. The great virtue of cost benefit analysis is that these external social views can now be analysed quantitatively, in many cases, in the context of all other related effects. This is the importance of the social accounting framework referred to earlier.

The investment criteria we have used have been stated under rather restrictive assumptions, and so an indication should be given of how two of the more important of these can be relaxed.

The first important restriction was on projects being independent. There are circumstances where it is possible to evaluate interdependent projects without too much extra work, but care must be taken. Suppose, for example, we have projects A and B, and the output of A affects the output of B and vice versa. These projects can now be evaluated by considering the three projects: A on its own, B on its own, and thirdly, A and B together.

The second restriction was the assumption that there was no budgetary constraint: that projects should be carried out provided the present value of benefits exceeded the present value of costs. This will not be possible in the case where there is a budget constraint, and available capital has run out before all projects satisfying the proposed criteria can be carried out. Perhaps the obvious way to deal with a constraint is to rank all projects being considered, say according to benefit/cost ratio, and to carry out those at the top of the list progressing downwards until all funds are used up. It should be noticed that in this case, the choice of discount rate chosen may affect the *order* in which the projects are ranked. At least one author has suggested using a rate of interest which is rather low, and near to the social time preference rate and then cutting off with a benefit/cost ratio which is greater than 1 to take account of budget constraints. This could have a different effect from using a higher rate, and perhaps even increasing the rate until all the projects which exceed it come within the budget. There may be cases of budget constraint where it is more effective to use an opportunity cost argument, especially where there are very high opportunity costs.

ABOUT THE AUTHOR

Alan G. Wilson read Mathematics at Corpus Christi College, Cambridge, England and from 1961-64 was a Scientific Officer at the National Institute for Research in Nuclear Science. From 1964-66 he was a Research Officer at the Institute of Economics and Statistics of the University of Oxford, and he then became a Mathematical Advisor to the Ministry of Transport. From 1968-70 he was Assistant Director of the Centre for Environmental Studies. Since then he has been Professor of Urban and Regional Geography at the University of Leeds. He has published over 50 papers in a variety of academic journals.

Problems in Planning for Service

M. L. Chambers and A. Hindle

This paper reviews the application of operations research to public policy planning and discusses "cost-benefit" and "cost-effectiveness" analysis. In particular, it pinpoints the limitations of O.R. at the strategic level but nevertheless indicates its relevance and importance. It discusses the "political" use of O.R. and the extent to which it can be misused to justify decisions which have already been taken. The theory of sub-optimisation is briefly outlined and the pros and cons of this approach discussed. The importance of measuring non-monetary outputs is stressed throughout the paper.

INTRODUCTION

This paper considers the role of Operational Research in social planning. Since this is a relatively new field of application it is important that the rationale of the Operational Research approach is critically reviewed. By examining some of the previous work in this field we therefore aim to highlight the major difficulties encountered.

We shall define planning as anticipatory decision making. It is an inherently difficult activity in that it usually involves a complex set of interacting decisions and is concerned with future activities in a dynamic environment. Wrong decisions will usually prove costly because of the fact that plans ordinarily involve the provision of expensive facilities having long lives and inflexible uses. Alternatively, but equally critically, the plans may concern sweeping reforms which will be difficult to reverse.

The special difficulties of applying the Operational Research approach to social planning derive from the nature and organisation of community services. These difficulties are of two types. Firstly, models of the planned process may be difficult to construct, especially if the success achieved by the plan depends significantly on community behaviour. Secondly, measures of effectiveness are usually very difficult to devise, not only because of the usual problems of combining objectives measured on different scales but also because

of the problem of identifying the relevant value system.

The layout of the paper is as follows. In the next section we describe the social planning process and highlight the source and nature of social objectives. Following this, we discuss the nature of previous contributions of Operational Research in this field of application prior to a detailed treatment of the technical problems involved in plan assessment. These problems of plan assessment are considered in three sections — the first examining the difficulties of model building, the second the forms of measure of effectiveness and the third the detailed evaluation of costs and benefits. We conclude with a general discussion in which we present our views on the potential role of Operational Research in social planning.

SOCIAL PLANNING

The objectives associated with the activity of all complex organisations derives from the functioning of political processes. This property has particular relevance to social planning in a democratic society. The political processes allow for the explicit conflict of individual values such that the influence and dominance of certain values can emerge. In industrial organisations the political structure is relatively autocratic so that the majority of individuals have little opportunity to influence policy decisions. In relation to the community ser-

SOURCE: Reprinted from "Problems in Planning for Service", paper presented to the "second annual conference" of the Department of Operational Research of the University of Lancaster, England, April 1967, by permission of the authors.

vices, however, attempts are made to ensure that each individual has some "say" in the values associated with the performance of these services. In an autocratic system it is usually possible to identify one individual or a small group of individuals as a reference group for the formulation of objectives. In democratic organisations, however, the recipients of the service provided are indirectly responsible for its provision and, although a delegated authority can often be identified, it is not immediately clear whether this authority or the total community should be considered the relevant source of objectives.

In many respects the process of planning in the social field is functionally similar to planning in other complex organisations. Several attempts have been made to develop a detailed model of the planning process (see e.g. Jessop, 1966). However we rest content here with a general description of its salient features. If broadly defined planning is not clearly distinct from other forms of decision taking involving, as it does, the selection of one course of action from several alternatives. It is, however, characterised by the extent to which the course of action is specified in detail and the scale and originality of the outcome. Thus it can be contrasted with management strategy on the one hand and management control on the other, although it is closely linked with both.

Management can be considered to initiate planning activity as a response to a discrepancy between objectives and performance. Tentative ideas about the source of the discrepancy and possible solutions will be entertained at a strategic level. This may be followed by a planning brief representing an input to the planning function proper. The initial activity of planning consists of studying the problem highlighted in the planning brief in order to search for alternative interpretations and solutions. This may lead to a detailed assessment of alternative plans and a decision being taken on which plan to implement. The selection of this plan together with arrangements for its implementation concludes the planning process. There follows, however, a closely related control activity during which the implementation and performance of the selected plan are monitored and modifications made if the level of success falls below expectations.

The larger number of interacting decisions involved in planning has important implications on the process of plan selection. There may be many simultaneous planning activities taking place such that tentative plans are often based on assumptions about the outcome of other planning decisions. Integration is required in order to ensure a coherent overall plan in line with the objectives and resources of the organisation. Also the dynamic nature of the environment affects the type of plan likely to be selected. If, as is often the case, the environment is changing rapidly there are obvious advantages in incorporating flexibility and short life into the facilities provided. This flexibility is often more easily achieved by modifying human response to the process, rather than the hardware. For example, the use of differential taxes on vehicles according to their size in order to encourage the use of small cars has been suggested as an alternative to the provision of increased parking facilities.

The outcome of any planning process is a plan. Several attempts have been made to specify the components of a complete plan. Harris and Ackoff (1966) suggest that a plan should have the following five parts.

(a) A statement of the aims and objectives of the planned process and a specification of the degree to which each should be attained at specified points in time. For example, that a new hospital should be built handling a certain number of new out-patients per week as from a certain date.

(b) A specification of the courses of action by which these aims and objectives are to be obtained. By the provision, for example, of an out-patient department having certain facilities and procedures.

(c) A specification of the resources required in order to obtain the objectives by the courses of action prescribed together with a statement on the methods by which the resources are to be generated so as to be available when and where required. For example, the provision of capital investment, the training of staff, etc.

(d) A specification of the organisation of the system that is to implement the plan. The allocation of responsibility, in our example, for the design and building of the new hospital.

(e) A specification of the system for controlling the implementation and performance of the plan. For example, to determine the actual performance of the out-patient department in relation to the specified objectives.

In general, Operational Research in planning has been concerned with the assessment of plans detailed with respect to the first three parts of the above specification. In the next section we begin to consider the more general aspects of this activity.

THE ROLE OF
OPERATIONAL RESEARCH

Prior to a consideration of the role of Operational Research in social planning, it will prove helpful to outline the rationale of the Operational Research approach in general. The values held by management in relation to the performance of the system under their control determine the specific objectives which they wish to achieve. A statement of these objectives will normally be obtained from management during the formulation phase of an Operational Research study. During the assessment phase, the initial problem is to model the consequences of alternative courses of action available to management. The outputs of the models must be relevant to the objectives. These outputs are again given values by the management in order to develop a decision function. Providing the initial formulation of objectives is compatible with the value set obtained at the decision stage the output derived from an analysis of the decision function may be expected to be acceptable to management. If, on the other hand, the initial objectives are seen to be incomplete in light of the response of management to the Operational Research activity a more complete model is required. Thus the Operational Research activity adapts to the value system of the management.

Thus the role of Operational Research in social planning is primarily concerned with modelling the performance of plans aimed at providing a community service and with developing meaningful measures of effectiveness for these services. A detailed discussion of this activity is postponed to the following three sections. However, we discuss below certain less technical contributions concerned with the setting of objectives and the implementations of plans. In addition, we described the experience which has been reported on the operation of large scale planning systems.

The Operational Research literature is filled with a yearning for involvement in objective formulation activity. However, from our discussion of the rationale of the Operational Research approach it is clear that ultimate objectives must be set by the management. We mentioned earlier that it is not absolutely clear in social planning whether the source of objectives should be delegated authority or the wider community. Clearly from a short term viewpoint implementation can only follow from a consideration of the values of the specific decision maker. However for longer term studies this approach may be less reasonable. These difficulties are further accentuated by the lack of hierarchical structure in the management of community services. In particular the relative position of local and national authorities is likely to prove a significant source of conflicting pressures. Also many of the organisations providing services are typified by anarchy. Decisions in hospitals, for example, derive from the deliberations of large committees of equals. It should be emphasised that these comments refer to the formulation of overall objectives. Hitch (1953) makes the valuable but often neglected point that as far as individual plans are concerned the objectives should be set to serve the overall objectives of the total plan. The only professional contribution which the Operational Research scientist can make to the formulation of objectives derives from this principle.

Relatively little attention has been given to the implementation aspects of planning in Operational Research studies. Some contributions have, however, been made to the efficiency of implementation of particular projects, by, for example, the use of PERT and other critical path techniques. There has been, nevertheless, a marked inability to incorporate considerations of plan activation and implementation in the process of plan assessment itself. Gross (1966) in a detailed discussion of implementation problems states that " . . . before national planning is seriously undertaken the task of getting action seems relatively simple — particularly to the proponents of planning. Afterwards the national planners themselves find shocking gaps between plans and performance." He further maintains that some types of resistance to implementation can be predicted and hence should be included in the assessment of the plans.

Experience of using the type of planning

system described in the previous section for United States defence planning has been reported by Hitch (1963). Prior to the introduction of the system described, military planning and financial budgeting had been undertaken by separate departments and since budgets looked only one year ahead, medium and long term plans were always financially infeasible even if the weapon systems were properly integrated. The system described by Hitch rectifies this and also contains provisions for modifying the overall plans in the light of revised assessments of the enemy threat, break through or breakdown of weapon system development, alterations to the estimated costs of development or deployment, and so on. Although similar considerations of the integration of physical and budgeting aspects of plans must be present in fields other than defence, very little information on the methods used has been reported. It would be interesting to compare the different systems in use and their relative success.

MODELLING THE PLANNED PROCESS

In order to select amongst the alternative plans under consideration, it is necessary to predict the performance of each planned process. The costs of implementing each plan can then be compared with its expected benefits and the best plan identified. In this paper we are, of course, mainly concerned with the use of explicitly formulated scientific models for predicting performance. We should, however, be unwise not to recognise that science has at present a limited capability to construct explicit models and should not, therefore, underestimate the human capability to construct implicit ones. The implicit model, for example, possessed by a car driver of the car's responsiveness to its controls and interaction with its environment would seem, judging from the success of performance, to be superior to any explicit model that scientists could currently produce. Of course, in many situations the predictive power of scientific models has proved far superior to models derived in other ways, but in relation to some phenomena science is still making a somewhat hesitant start. This is particularly true of the explanation and prediction of human behaviour. Simon (1957) in his book "Models of Man"

illustrates clearly the present limitations of scientific endeavour in this area. Very often in fields such as health and education, the relevant aspects of system performance depend significantly on human behaviour and these deficiencies in basic scientific knowledge therefore prove a stumbling block in social planning.

Most models developed for real-life planning are partly explicit and partly implicit because of the size of the problems and the difficulties discussed above. This infeasibility of constructing total models, together with the related difficulty of devising overall measures of effectiveness, led Hitch to argue strenuously in favor of sub-optimisation in the well known Hitch-Ackoff controversy on national planning. (Ackoff 1957, 1958; Hitch 1957). Hitch's viewpoint has sometimes been misconstrued as a case against the use of low level criteria whereas his real point is that sub-optimisation is the only possible approach in dealing with large scale systems.

For the purposes of subsequent discussion, it is convenient to subdivide the types of models relevant to planning into the following three categories:

(a) Models for forecasting the changes which will occur in the environment if no plan is implemented.

(b) Models for predicting the performance of plans in a hypothetically fixed environment.

(c) Models for describing the way in which the environment will respond to the planned process or be affected by it.

In social planning, these often correspond to models of demand for community services, the capability of the planned process to meet a given demand and the way the process will affect the demand. In order to clarify the nature of these three types of model, it may be helpful to discuss a problem of planning in the police field outlined by Sargeaunt (1966). The first part of this problem is to predict the increase in number of crimes committed if no significant changes are made in police activity. The second part of the modelling process requires an estimate to be made of the way in which plans to increase manpower, improve forensic methods and introduce superior equipment will increase crime prevention and detection. At the final stage it is necessary to model the effect of the measures designed to increase crime prevention and detection on criminal activity.

Before discussing these model types in more detail it is important to note that outputs required from models for community services vary a great deal in general nature and are in some cases difficult to quantify. In this context Kendall (1965) remarks, "I have been concerned to ascertain whether it could be possible to measure the productivity of a hospital. One knows that some hospitals are better than others; one can compare them in all sorts of respects. The question is whether any of this material could be formalised and brought to a number or a series of numbers which would enable you to rank them in some kind of order. The answer is 'No'." That Kendall was being unduly pessimistic has yet to be demonstrated in practice.

Models for forecasting changes in the environment are usually very unsophisticated. Simple assumptions are frequently made about the form of the model and then its parameters are estimated from historical data. For example, in hospital planning forecasts of morbidity rates are usually obtained from straight-line extrapolations of past statistics. Forecasts of this type are notoriously unreliable, not least because of the possibility of radical technological developments. Thus predictions of the requirement for tuberculosis sanatoria derived in this way following the last war resulted in the building of many now useless buildings in remote country areas. An alternative to basing forecasts on past data is to rely more on relevant expert opinion. This approach has been used in a very detailed way in planning urban renewal. Surveys have been undertaken, for example, in which qualified building inspectors estimate the useful lives of existing properties. A case in which these two forecasting approaches were combined is illustrated by the government white paper, "The Long-Term Demand for Scientific Manpower". In this, estimates of demand are obtained by making assumptions about the permanence of critical ratios such as work force to population, manufacturing industry to other industry, students to teachers, etc. and then projecting trends in population growth, industrial development, and teacher supply twenty years into the future. The forecasts derived were then doctored to allow expert opinion to modify the outcome.

Beer (1962) pinpoints the precarious nature of these forecasts by noting that if, as is possible, the level of technological sophistication in the iron and steel industry was raised to that already existing in the oil, chemical and electronics industries the increased demand produced would of itself, be greater than the total increase projected. As a result of the unreliability of these forecasts, Beer concludes that it is better not to attempt detailed forecasting of an uncertain future but that it is preferable to design processes which are adaptable — "Away, then, with attempts to forecast the state of affairs in 1970 — which is known only to God." Ackoff (1966) takes a very similar line in considering that planning should be concerned with making provision for the inevitable.

Modelling the performance of a planned process in a given environment has proved easiest where significant phenomena are physical. Thus, although details of work in the military field are not fully published it seems that appreciable successes have been achieved in modelling weapon system performance. Similar success has been gained in modelling transport systems and in relation to water resource projects. However the difficulty of modelling increases when the output depends more significantly on human behaviour. This difficulty should also have proved frustrating in those marketing problems where performance depends on consumer response. An example in social planning is the prediction of criminal behaviour in response to police activity — here Sargeaunt (1966) notes that no worthwhile models of criminal response have yet been developed. Work in the hospital field provides interesting examples of situations which system performance is concerned with, physical and economic phenomena on the one hand through to physiological and psychological factors on the other. At the physical end of this spectrum are the innumerable models of out-patient waiting time produced since 1950. Economic models have been developed by Feldstein (1966) and Barr (1966). In these, patient throughput, expressed in terms of standardised treated cases, is considered as a function of resource inputs such as medical and nursing staff levels. At the physiological level, Howland (1960) suggests an adaptive control model in which a hospital is regarded as a system for controlling and regulating parameters like body temperature, heart rate and blood pressure. Thus, performance is considered as a function of the homeostatic balance of patients. Finally, Revans (1961) develops a model based on psychological theory whereby performance, considered in terms of morale, is related to the degree and nature of communication between people in the hospital. He, in turn, relates morale to certain superficial indices of the effectiveness of treatment of patients such as length of stay and crude mortality rates. The relative abundance of physical models as compared with those concerned with patient health and welfare suggests that the difficulties of modelling these latter factors have forced work to concentrate on less relevant aspects.

Our final group of models is concerned with the way in which a plan and the environment interact and in particular with the nature of the public response to the plan. Models of this type tend to be little more than assumptions. For example, in studies examining flood control schemes it is usually supposed that farmers will use all land freed from the danger of flooding in some optimal way. Again, in road projects, very simple and apparently arbitrary assumptions are usually made about the amount of traffic which will be diverted from existing slower roads. Rarely is any market research undertaken to gauge the likely community response to social plans. This is surprising when considered in relation to the cost of many social plans and when contrasted with the attention given to market research in the commercial field. The response of people to a plan depends largely on the existence of unsatisfied needs. These needs are translated by complex processes into specific demands for service. In particular, the demand is likely to be a function of the type of service provided. For example, in relation to the demand for medical care, a specific request for service depends on an individual's assessment of his state of health and his knowledge of the type of services available. Attempts to provide services to meet popular expectations are very likely to stimulate almost insatiable demands as the iceberg of unsatisfied need is revealed. This is demonstrated particularly clearly in the health field by extensive studies carried out by Logan into the need for medical care. He (1964) states that in the average general practice for every ten known diabetics, there are a further ten undetected and one hundred latent cases. Another source of complex interaction between plans for service and the nature of community demands derives from the effectiveness of the service. The timing of the eventual defeat, for example, in the game against nature played by a health service will depend on the effectiveness of medical treatment at each stage in the battle.

The existence of complex interations between needs, demands, the supply of services and the effectiveness of services led Beer (1962) to suggest a model for the planning of technical education based on Ross Ashby's homeostat. Beer suggests that the models used in social planning often consider demand and supply separately with little or no interaction between the two. He points out however that in the case of technical education the interaction between the supply of education and the demand for technologists is not only intense but present in most subsystems of the total system. The model he suggests comprises a polystable system responsive to the needs for technical education. Although the model is outlined it is unfortunately not constructed in detail.

MEASURES OF EFFECTIVENESS

Once the stage has been reached at which we have models predicting some of the relevant outputs of rival plans, we require to determine which plan is the best. Since it is unlikely that any one plan will be best in all respects, an attempt is usually made to develop a criterion of overall effectiveness. The need for such a measure has, however, been questioned on the grounds that, since the decision maker is the only valid source of the values to be associated with each output, it would seem less devious to allow him to choose directly between the plans. Whilst this may be true in situations involving a strictly limited number of alternative plans and outputs, it will ordinarily be difficult to present the relevant information in a form comprehensible to the decision maker when the number of plans and outputs is large. Thus, in these cases at least, a measure of effectiveness is probably essential and even in the simpler cases the decision maker may well prefer to have the output information summarised as a single number.

Accepting, therefore, the desirability of a

measure of effectiveness we must consider the difficulties and feasibility of constructing one. As mentioned in the previous section, some of the outputs of social systems have proved difficult to quantify and some quantification would seem a necessary preliminary requirement to the development of a measure. Further, it may well prove difficult to determine the true values held by the decision maker in relation to the various outputs, especially if he must provide precise numerical statements himself. We noted earlier that doubts about whether these problems can be overcome contributed to Hitch's belief in the necessity for sub-optimisation in national planning. However, whilst treating low level problems will often allow consideration to be focussed on a single input and a small number of outputs, this only removes the essential difficulty to the next higher level. Further, the varied and non-economic nature of many outputs in the social field sometimes frustrates even this approach. A good example is reported by Ackoff (1962) when he describes a problem concerning the planning of a dental service. He takes the objective to be to maximise dental health for the maximum number of people at minimal cost. Unfortunately no one, including dentists, has managed to define dental health and therefore it proved impossible to specify a single output as its measure. The inputs and outputs which thus had to be used to characterise the service were,

(a) The various types of dental ailment to be treated.
(b) The number of people treated for each type of ailment.
(c) The cost of the service to those who are treated.

The problem was to determine what services should be offered and what charges should be made. In order to do this it is necessary to determine, for example, whether it is better to clean the teeth of one thousand patients or to repair cavities in three hundred and clean teeth in five hundred, assuming equivalent costs. Likewise, the relative value of providing dentures to senior citizens or offering orthodontia to junior citizens has to be assessed. Although Ackoff states that he managed to devise ingenious methods for comparing plans, he indicates that it proved impossible to combine the numerous outputs into a single measure.

In the remainder of this section we discuss three major points stemming from the above discussion. These are,

(a) The various types of effectiveness measures which have been proposed for use in social planning.
(b) The decision algorithms used in relation to these measures.
(c) The approaches relevant in the case of sub-optimisation.

Throughout this discussion we shall assume that evaluation of costs and benefits is possible but we will return to the detailed difficulties involved in the next section.

The simplest measure of effectiveness used in social planning is the difference between the total value of all benefits and the total value of all costs. Both costs and benefits are usually discounted to allow for social time preference although the precise choice of interest rate is as problematical as in other fields. If the benefits and costs are given the values which would obtain in a fully competitive economy, this measure is in line with the social welfare function suggested by Pigou (1920). This measure has been extensively used especially in the United States of America and has in fact been given legal sanction in the Congress Flood Control Act of 1936. Conceptually it is an attempt to stimulate the market economy in the social field where it is not possible for the market economy to work. The essential feature of this Pigovian measure is that every pound is given equal weight to whomsoever it accrues. Foster (1966) emphasises this disregard for income distributional considerations, stating "if one alternative (plan) will confer great benefits on a maharajah, whilst another benefits large numbers of peasants, the logic of the Pigovian approach is that one selects whichever has the high present value irrespective of income distribution effects."

Several measures have been suggested which do include income distribution considerations so that, for example, the poor may be favoured more than the wealthy. One approach is to give different weights to the costs and benefits according to the section of the community to whom they accrue. An alternative method is to maximise the ordinary Pigovian function subject to constraints on the income distribution effects. Foster (1966) also queries whether the Pigovian measure, even with allowances for distribution of income effects, is adequate in that it seems only remotely relevant to the real aims of political decision making.

One theory of political decision making is that decisions are made to maximise votes because of the desire to stay in power. (Downs 1957). A measure of effectiveness that has been suggested which is based on this notion regards the benefits of a project as the votes likely to be gained and the costs as the votes likely to be lost, each vote being given equal weight. This measure may obviously itself be criticised and several alternatives have, in fact, been suggested, though not to our knowledge applied. All measures of effectiveness of this type described above may have relevance to certain individual decision makers in particular circumstances. One general criticism is, however, that they are formulated and, in practice, seem to be used without any consideration of whether they reflect the value system of the specific decision maker. Therefore it seems unlikely that a good match will be obtained. The measures are based either on idealogical value systems or on the values of a hypothetical decision maker.

In relation to the question of decision algorithms, it will be convenient to concentrate attention on the simplest measure of effectiveness discussed above, namely the present value of all benefits less that of all costs. Although the choice of this measure is not critical to the arguments below, we naturally assume that all plans will be evaluated on the same basis. That this may not be the case in practice, especially if the evaluation is undertaken by different bodies, is illustrated by Eddison (1966). He remarks, "it was a jest of fate for the Government to sanction the building of the Victoria line — using evidence of . . . cost-benefit analysis — at almost the same moment that British Railways announced the closure of many of their existing lines — using rigid calculations that the lines did not individually take enough revenue in tickets to cover their operating costs. Some evidence has since been adduced to suggest that cost-benefit analysis applied to some, at least, of the railway lines would have shown them to provide more in terms of social welfare than will the Victoria line."

Prest and Turvey (1965) in a general survey of cost-benefit analysis present a very succinct discussion of decision algorithms and below we draw substantially from this.

Where there is no interaction between plans, where the dates of implementation are given and where no constraints are operative, the choice of a plan to maximise the simple Pigovian measure of effectiveness can be expressed in any of the following four ways,

(a) Select all plans for which present value of benefits exceeds the present value of costs.

(b) Select all plans where the ratio of present value of benefits to present value of costs exceeds unity.

(c) Select all plans where the constant annuity with the same present value as benefits exceeds the constant annuity (of the same duration) with the same present value of costs.

(d) Select all plans where the internal rate of return exceeds the chosen discount rate.

In this rather idealised case, therefore, the identification of plans meriting implementation follows from direct calculation.

When the simplifying assumptions made above are removed, the selection of plans can become more difficult. Thus where the costs and benefits of two projects A and B are interdependent in the sense that the execution of one affects the costs and benefits accruing in the other, they must be treated as constituting three mutually exclusive schemes, namely, A alone, B alone, and A and B together. For instance, if the plans concern communications between two towns, it is necessary to consider as three distinct schemes; road improvement, rail improvements and a combination of the two. The mutually exclusive nature of the plans now considered must, of course, be allowed for in formulating the decision rules. Mutual exclusivity can also arise for technological reasons. Thus a road intersection can be built as a cross road, a roundabout or a flyover. Similarly a large or small dam, but not both, can be put in one place. Where there is freedom of choice of implementation date of a plan, this should be chosen to maximise the present value of benefits less costs at the time of making the decision. This can, of course, be computationally troublesome. It is, however, the presence of physical, distributional, or budgetary constraints which usually lead to the greatest computational difficulties particularly when several constraints are involved. It will be apparent that the derivation of optimal plans, in situations where constraints are combined with mutual exclusivity and optimal timing considerations, may involve some very difficult problems in mathematical programming. We shall not discuss the computational algorithms that have been proposed but relevant discussions are to be found in the work of Marglin (1962, 1963) and Dryden (1964).

In practice, cost- benefit studies usually concentrate almost exclusively on economic costs and benefits and, further, only consider those factors which can be predicted from explicitly formulated models. Thus the measures of effectiveness are deficient in that they ignore those costs and benefits that can be derived only from the decision maker's implicit understanding of the process. They do, however, include relevant costs and benefits that would be omitted from a more strictly financial accounting statement. The incompleteness of the measures, nevertheless, means that it is no longer allowable to compute optimal plans by directly applying the decision algorithms described above, since the omitted costs and benefits may well modify the choice which should be made. This point may be clearly illustrated by reference to two examples outlined by Litchfield (1962). The first concerns the preservation of an historic building, known as the Old Mint, in San Francisco. A conventional financial analysis showed that the taxpayer would benefit to the extent of $2.2 million by its demolition. A wider consideration of costs and benefits, however, suggested that there was a net economic advantage in retaining it. In this example, therefore, although the architectural value of the Old Mint was not included in the measure, its inclusion would have only strengthened the case for retention. In the second example, however, which concerns the provision of a three acre park in San Francisco, both straight financial and cost benefit calculations gave an economic disadvantage in building the park but the inclusion of other incommensurable factors presumably reversed the balance since the park was, in fact, built.

The final topic to be covered in this section concerns the approaches relevant in sub-optimisation. In order to simplify this discussion we shall suppose that all benefits have been reduced to a single measure and similarly all costs. Similar considerations apply to the choice of these separate measures as to the choice of an overall measure of effectiveness. However, in sub-optimisation, even if the cost measure and the benefit measure could be combined into an overall measure, it would not be permissible to select amongst the alternative plans by maximising the overall measure since the size of the chosen plan would bear only an accidental relation to the requirements of higher level criteria. Instead, the approach which has to be adopted is to determine the admissible set of plans, this set being defined such that any plan contained in it is not dominated in respect of both cost and benefit by any other plan. This admissible set of plans may be generated by maximising benefits with a variable restriction on cost or alternatively, by minimising cost with a similar restriction on the benefits required. Just as optimisation is valid in the case of high level criteria only if all costs and benefits are included, so the above approach breaks down if some relevant factors are omitted from the measures. The selection of one plan from the set of "good" plans so generated has to be made by either a formal or informal consideration of higher level criteria. These ideas can, of course, be extended to more than one measure of input and more than one measure of output (see e.g., Hitch 1953). This approach can also be applied at the highest level if the measures of costs and benefits cannot be combined though, as noted earlier, the presentation of data on the admissible set will prove virtually impossible if the number of different measures involved exceeds three or four. Hitch (1953) states the underlying philosophy of the sub-optimisation approach as being, "it is far more important to demonstrate that some course of action. . . are better than proposed courses . . . , than to spend one's life seeking the optimum optimorum."

EVALUATING COSTS AND BENEFITS

In the previous section we assumed that it is normally possible to place values on all relevant costs and benefits. Here we discuss the problems of evaluation in detail. The nature of the values required will clearly depend on the measure of effectiveness to be used; they may be expressed in monetary units if the criterion is Pigovian or, for example, in the votes won and lost if Down's criterion is used. It should be noted that the feasibility of obtaining meaningful values for some types of factor, by any means, has been questioned by some writers. Thus Hitch (1953), in considering how best a family should spend its income, doubts whether it is possible to obtain the utility associated by the family with various goods and services. He states, "we could not write down the family's general utility function because the family could not tell us what it was, and we could not conceivably derive it from any other source." Two methods which have been suggested for assessing values are firstly to derive them by observing market behaviour and secondly, or alternatively, to estimate them by simulating the decision environment. We discuss the difficulties and relevance of each of these approaches below.

Since, in the social field, the market-price mechanism, if it operates at all, does not operate freely it is impossible to obtain market values directly. If, therefore, it is the market values that we seek they must be imputed in some way. In some cases this may be relatively simple; thus, for example, the water provided to irrigate previously unproductive land may be taken as the market value of the crop produced less the costs incurred in its production. In other cases, it is much more difficult to develop a reasonable argument to support imputed market values. A case in point concerns the loss of recreational fishing waters which has been variously assessed as equal to the market value of the fish caught or the wages the anglers could have earned by working instead of fishing.

Several specific problems of evaluation have received a great deal of attention in the literature and, by way of illustration, we consider the value to be placed on time saved by improvements in transport systems. All evaluation procedures suggested make the doubtful assumption that one minute saved on each of sixty occasions has the same total worth as a single saving of sixty minutes. They also usually distinguish between working time saved and leisure time saved, valuing the former at the recepient's normal wage rate and latter by noting that leisure time can be substituted for one of the following.

(a) Wages earned by workers.
(b) Transport expenditure, by those who travel in their own time and are able to choose between faster more expensive modes of travel and slower, cheaper ones (see Moses and Williamson 1963).
(c) Housing and transport expenditure, by people who can choose between a more expensive house near to their work and a less expensive house further away (see Mohring 1961).

We feel that the deficiencies of each of these methods will be self-evident. The fact that time saving is often assessed at up to fifty per cent of the total benefits accruing from a transport project, however, emphasises the desirability of a more accurate method of evaluation.

Apart from the difficulties of finding satisfactory methods for imputing market values, there are a whole range of other practical drawbacks encountered in estimating them. For example, the market values of some factors may be expected to rise over the project life, even relative to the general level of prices, but it will inevitably be difficult to predict the precise nature of the increase. Again, a plan may be large enough to itself affect market prices but the extent of this influence will usually be difficult to gauge. Also the market behaviour observed in the private sector will rarely be fully competitive so that an imputed value may not be based on true market values. A particular case of a divergence between market prices and social costs and benefits derives from taxes on expenditure. Correcting for these shortcomings, whilst necessary, obviously allows scope for subjective bias.

Despite the enormity of the difficulties in the way of imputing market values we feel that, as with measures of effectiveness, a more fundamental question that has to be asked, is whether market values are likely to adequately represent a particular decision maker's viewpoint. Whilst they may do so, it seems unlikely to take an extreme case, that a decrease in prostitution resulting from a social plan would be costed against the plan by many decision makers, let alone at its market price.

The alternative to utilising market values is to obtain values by studying choices made by the decision making group. Although the principle of this approach is applicable to the study of real life decision, the specific techniques developed are more appropriate to the nalysis of verbally expressed preferences. There is little evidence of these techniques having been used in social planning although some applications in other fields have been reported. The approach is typified by the method of Churchman and Ackoff (1954) in which subjects first rank the alternative factors and then place provisional relative values on them. These initial values are subsequently tested by presenting the subject with choices between groups of the factors and the values are reined if they are at variance with the choices made. The critical difficulty of all such approaches is the uncertain reliance that can be placed on verbal statements of preference or choices made in unrealistic situations.

DISCUSSION AND CONCLUSIONS

It remains for us to summarise and discuss the points that we have raised, and to give our views on the future role of Operational Research in social planning.

One major consideration that we have frequently noted concerns the choice of the value system to be used in setting objectives. We have expressed a preference for regarding the appropriate delegated authority as the valid source of objectives, except in studies without specific implementation in mind, when the viewpoint of the community at large may be more appropriate. However this may be, it seems to us that one completely inadmissible source of objectives is the Operational Research investigator himself. This is not to say that the Operational Research scientist may not play a very useful role in helping the decision making groups to clarify their objectives, but for the Operational Research man to actually impose his own value system seems to us to remove the study from the realms of science to that of politics. Failure to observe this principle in the past is indicated by the following quotations given by Bryk (1966) from a House of Representatives Report;

"The almost obsessional dedication to costs effectiveness raises the specter of a decision maker who knows the price of everything and the value of nothing,"
"Knowledge of an esoteric mathematical ability does not inherently accord one wisdom and judgment."

Whilst therefore recognising the advisory role of Operational Research, we should emphasise that we strongly deprecate the use of Operational Research to justify decisions that have already been made. That this use must on occasions be suspected may be illustrated by again quoting from the above House of Representatives' Report, which states that the value of a project is often increased by "pumping it up with cost-effectiveness."

On the technical side, the major difficulties we have identified are those concerned with modelling, especially when the performance of a plan depends significantly on human behaviour, and those concerned with measuring effectiveness, which appears to be especially difficult in social systems because of the non-monetary nature of the outputs. We have noted that our present inability to model large systems completely and to devise overall measures of effectiveness has resulted in a strong move being made towards sub-optimisation in social planning. Our viewpoint here is briefly as follows.

We consider that progress in modelling will only come from detailed studies of particular facets of total planning problems. We feel, however, that whilst this work is being undertaken, great care must be taken to ensure against undue emphasis being given to objective predictions derived from partial models as compared with the subjective ones obtained from relevant experts. That there is a real danger here will be evident to anyone familiar with the delightful oversimplifications often evident in the papers used in maing high level decisions in Government Ministries.

Whilst therefore accepting the need for much low level work to be undertaken in order to develop models, we are not at all convinced that the suboptimisation approach avoids the real difficulties of measuring effectiveness in several of the community services. This essential difficulty of measuring effectiveness seems to us to stem from the problem of properly measuring outputs like level of health, the extent of law and order and the standard of education, and these problems are present whether we consider, for instance, the health service as a whole, a particular hospital or an individual general practice. If Operational Research is to make any contribution to the central issues involved in social planning, these problems of measuring non-monetary outputs must be solved. This is essential even if the outputs are not combined with the monetary inputs to yield an actual measure of effectiveness.

REFERENCES

ACKOFF, R.L. (1957). Operations Research and National Planning. J. Operations Res. Soc. Amer. Vol. 5. 457-468.

ACKOFF, R.L. (1958). On Hitch's Dissent on Operations Research and National Planning. J. Operations Res. Soc. Amer. Vol 6. 121-124.

ACKOFF, R.L. (1962). Some unsolved problems in problem solving. Operational Res. Quart. Vol. 13. No. 1. 1-11.

ACKOFF, R.L. (1966). Adaptive National Planning. Paper to Conference 'Science in Planning,' Department of Operational Research, University of Lancaster.

BARR, A. (1966). Unpublished Correspondence

BEER, S. (1962). An Operational Research Project in Technical Education. Operational Res. Quart. Vol. 13. No. 2. 179-199.

BRYK, O. (1966). All is not well. The C.E. Newsletter of the Operations Res. Soc. Amer. Vol. 1. No. 6. 1-5.

DOWNS, A. (1957). Economic theory of democracy. London, Harper.

DRYDEN, M.M. (1964). Capital Budgeting: Treatment of Uncertainty and Investment Criteria. Scottish J. of Polit. Econ. Vol. XI.

EDDISON, R.T. (1966). Social Effects of Policies and their Measurement: Introduction and Commentary. In 'Operational Research and the Social Sciences,' Ed. J.R. Lawrence. Tavistock Publications, London. 295-304.

FELDSTEIN M. (1966). Economic Analysis for Health Service Efficiency. Ph. D. Oxford University.

FOSTER, C.D. and BEESLEY, M.E. (1963). Estimating the social benefit of constructing an underground railway in London. J. Royal Statist. Soc. A. 126. 46-78.

FOSTER, C.D. (1966). Social Welfare Functions in Cost-Benefit Analysis. In 'Operational Research and the Social Sciences,' Ed. J.R. Lawrence. Tavistock Publications, London. 305-318.

GROSS, B.M. (1966). Activating National Plans. In 'Operational Research and the Social Sciences,' Ed. J.R. Lawrence. Tavistock Publications, London, 449-482.

HARRIS, B. and ACKOFF, R.L. (1966). Strategies for Operations Research in Urban Metropolitan Planning. Paper to Int. Fed. Operational Res. Soc. Conference, Boston.

HITCH, C. (1958).Sub-optimisation in Operations problems. J. Operations Res. Soc. Amer. Vol.1. No. 3. 87-99.

HITCH, C. (1953). An appreciation of systems analysis. J. Operations Res. Soc. Amer. Vol. 3. No. 4. 466-481.

HITCH, C. (1957). Operations Research and National Planning — A dissent. J. Operations Res. Soc. Amer. Vol. 5. 718-723.

HITCH, C. (1963). Plans, Programs, and Budgets in the Department of Defense. Operations Research. Vol. 11. No. 1. 1-17.

HOWLAND, D. (1960). The development of a methodology for the evaluation of patient care. Engineering Experiment Statio Ohio State University.

JESSOP, W.N. (1966). A model for City Planning. Paper to Int. Fed. Operational Res. Soc. Conference, Boston.

KENDALL, M.G. (1965). Discussion point. Response to paper 'Statistics and intellectual integrity' by S. Paul Chambers. J. Royal Statist. Soc. Vol. 128. Pt. 1. 15.

LICHFIELD, N. (1962). Cost-benefit analysis in urban redevelopment. RR. 20. Real Estate Research Program. Inst. Business and Economic Research. University of California, Berkeley.

LOGAN, R.F.L. (1964). Studies in the Spectrum of Medical Care. In 'Problems and Progress in Medical Care.' The Nuffield Provincial Hospital Trust, Oxford University Press. 3-54.

MARGLIN, S.A. (1962). Cost-benefit Analysis. In 'Design of Water Resource Systems: New Techniques for Relating Econom ic Objectives, Engineering Analysis, and Governmental Planning,' A. Maass et al. London. Macmillan.

MARGLIN, S.A. (1963). Approaches to dynamic investment planning. Amsterdam, North Holland.

MAHRING, H. (1961). Land values and the measurement of highway benefits. J. of Polit. Econ. Vol. LXIX.

MOSES, L.N. and WILLIAMSON, H.F. (1963). Value of time, choice of mode, and the subsidy issue in urban transportation. J. of Polit. Econ. Vol. LXXI.

PIGOU, A.C. (1920). Economics of Welfare. London. Macmillan.

PREST, A.R. and TURVEY, R. (1965). Cost-benefit analysis: A survey. The Economic Journal. No. 300. Vol. LXXV. 683-73.

REVANS, R.W. (1961) Standards for Morale: Cause and effect in hospitals. The Nuffield Provincial Hospital Trust.

SARGEAUNT, H.A. (1966). Planning for the allocation of resources in the Police Force. Paper to Conference 'Science in Planning,' Department of Operational Research, University of Lancaster.

SIMON, H.A. (1957.). Models of Man. New York. Wiley.

WESTCHURCHMAN, C. and ACKOFF, R.L. (1954). An approximate measure of value. J. Operations Res. Soc. Amer. Vo No. 2. 172-187.

ABOUT THE AUTHORS:

Mike Chambers holds a degree in Statistics from London University. He started his career at t Air Ministry working on the cost-effectiveness of different defence systems. Then he lectured Bradford University, where he was responsible for designing an industrially oriented degr course in statistics, operational research and computing, and also consulted for several firms production problems. Since being at Lancaster University he has worked on both industrial pr blems in the production, marketing, distribution and corporate planning areas, and on gover mental problems, particularly those concerned with police operations.

His main research interests are in applications to the problems of planning, especially in the public sector.

Tony Hindle: See page 28.

An Example of Systems Analysis: Locating a Book in a Reference Room

Edward C. Jestes

In this paper, a simple example of the application of cost-benefit analysis to a problem in the field of librarianship is described. The fact that the application of these techniques is not necessarily difficult, even in complex situations, is emphasized. The author, a professional librarian, has used a simple, but effective approach and the paper describes the study lucidly and with attention to detail.

Systems analysis is defined in Edythe Moore's[1] excellent introduction to the concept as "organized common sense." This paper presents an example of systems analysis.

The analysis could be considered to be hypothetical in part because so many estimates and assumptions were made. However, because the system which was studied and the modified system which is proposed are so simple, more detailed collection of data is not warranted and would only add to the total cost of the analysis.

The analysis was done in a large university library (about 25,000 students and 3,000,000 books). The writer was not on the library staff, and the staff was unaware of the study. The analysis is of a patron entering a reference room with the title of a book in mind, perhaps obtained from the main card catalog. He is aware that card catalogs reveal call numbers by which books are located, but beyond that he has never attempted to locate a book in this particular reference room. It is apparent that this is only a subsystem of a system of entering a reference room to determine a fact without a particular book in mind, which in itself is another subsystem of locating facts and ideas in the entire library.

REQUIREMENTS OF AN IDEAL SYSTEM

From the entrance to the Reference Room there should be a direct line of sight to the main locating system, the card catalog or the librarian. The catalog should be convenient to use, that is, it should not require stooping and it should have enough working space to accommodate at least four people simultaneously (or some other number determined by a study).

The information on the card should enable the user to locate the book in the room directly or by referring to a chart or floor plan.

The distance between the card catalog and the book should be the shortest, yet it should be the most convenient possible. When the user finds the book, there should be lighted space available to use it, that is, a podium or table.

TABLE 1.
PRESENT TERMINOLOGY

PENCILED TERMS* ON CARDS	CORRESPONDING TERMS ON FLOOR PLAN
Biographies	Biography
Desk	None
Dictionaries	Same
Directories	Same
General Reference Desk	General Reference Service
Indexed Books	Same
Periodical Indexes	Same
Periodical and Newspaper Reference	Same
Reading Room	None
Telephone Directories	Same
U.S. & British Trade	Trade and Bibliography

* Various abbreviations of these terms occur on the cards.

The Present System

Entering the Room. The door on the entrance to the reference-study room is labeled

SOURCE: Reprinted from *Special Libraries* 59 (9) November 1968 pp. 722-728, by permission of the author and publishers.

"Reference Room. General Reference Service." Many of the catalog cards for reference books in the main card catalog are stamped or typed "Reference and Bibliography." This difference in terminology is a minor annoyance. In the large room the sounds of chairs, rustling paper and sharp reports of books being dropped (?) echo through the otherwise hushed atmosphere.

To the left are rows of tables and chairs; to the front and about 20 yards across the room a sign, "Thesis Bibliography," can be seen. To the immediate right is a long table with a sloping top and with the label "Periodical Indexes." Further to the right and about 25 feet away is a fairly large sign on the end of a table, "Periodical and Newspaper Reference," above which is a smaller sign — difficult to read because of the glare from its acetate cover — "Reference Room Catalog."

The desk and reference librarian are to the right and are almost hidden from view by the intervening table and books. On approaching the desk a second card catalog, about 25 feet away, can be seen.

The Card Catalog. All of the drawers of the card catalog are below waist level and the user must back away from it and bend over to read the labels. The top of the catalog is clear, and about three persons can use it for placing drawers and writing call numbers. However, three persons will block all others from use of the catalog.

There are six different divisions of the catalog: 1) A-Z, the largest number of drawers and presumably the author-title catalog, 2) Trade and National Bibliography, 3) Unbound Serials, 4) Shelf List, 5) Abbreviations, and 6) Subject Analysis.

A floor plan of the room is on the top of the card catalog, but the glare from its acetate cover is annoying. Instructions on the plan are:

"To find a book, look in the reference and bibliography card catalog" (which is labeled "Reference Room Catalog").

"Most of the books are shelved by call number order, Cases 1-81."

"If the book is shelved in a special location, the location is written in pencil below the call number."

"The chart of the room shows the location of each section."

The relationships between the penciled instructions and sections on the floor plan are listed in Table 1.

To summarize the bottlenecks, the card catalog is not obvious on entering the room and it is inconvenient to use; the special penciled instructions on the cards do not (in about 50% of the cases) match the terms on the floor plan; the plan is too general; and the distance to many of the books is too great. (The room is about 62 feet wide and about 240 feet long.)

Analysis of the Present System

It is assumed that the patron knows the title of a reference book. An analysis is made of the sequence of steps, and the time and cost of the patron in locating the book. Emphasis is on the use of the card catalog because even if he asks for the book at the reference desk, there is a good chance he will be directed to the card catalog.

The steps and decisions the patron must take can be graphically displayed in a flowchart. The symbols (Figure 1) are defined as used in this paper (generally following IBM Flowchart Template, Form X20-8020).

COST AND TIME ESTIMATES

Cost Per Minute of User's Time. It is assumed that out of every 100 catalog users 35 are undergraduates, 35 are graduates, 5 are faculty and 25 are various members of the library staff (who need to locate a book but who are not maintaining the catalog). Their time is assumed to be worth the following amounts:

Undergraduates	$2/hr. or $0.033/min.
Graduates	$4/hr. or $0.067/min.
Faculty	$10/hr. or $0.167/min.
Library Staff	$4/hr. or $0.067/min.

Time and Cost Estimates at the Catalog. The mean time that it takes to find the call number and to look at the floor plan is estimated to be 1.5 minutes (this is based on a very small sample and needs statistical checking as do all the other time and cost estimates in this analysis).

The cost of the 1.5 minutes at the catalog is calculated by multiplying: (No. of Users) $\times$ (1.5 min.) $\times$ ($/min.) with the following results:

Undergraduate (actually user-$ units)	35 X 1.5 X 0.033 = $1.73

Graduate	35 X 1.5 X 0.067 = $3.51
Faculty	5 X 1.5 X 0.167 = $1.27
Library Staff	25 X 1.5 X 0.067 = $2.51
Totals	100 users $9.02

This is $0.09/user for 1.5 minutes (as a weighted average).

To the Desk or Walk to Book? It is estimated that about 10% (1,500) of the books in the reference room are behind the desk and must be asked for. Because many of these books are those that are highly used, it is estimated that about 25% of the catalog users are directed to the desk and about 75% walk to the book located in the room.

SYMBOL	DEFINITION
▭	A major processing function.
◇	A decision required (usually involves a yes or no answer).
▭	Terminal. The beginning or end of a program.
⬡	A predefined group of processes not shown in detail.
←	The direction of procedures.
O	On-page connector (see another part of the flowchart).

FIGURE 1.   FLOWCHART SYMBOLS

Time and Cost Estimates of Asking for Book at Desk. The mean waiting time of a user is estimated to be one minute (with a range of 0.5-2 minutes), of which it takes 0.5 minutes for the librarian to get the book and hand it to the user. The cost is calculated by multiplying: (No. of waiters) X (1 minute) X ($/minute) with the following results:

Undergraduates	9 X 1 X 0.033 = $0.297
Graduates	9 X 1 X 0.067 = $0.603
Faculty	1 X 1 X 0.167 = $0.167
Library Staff	6 X 1 X 0.067 = $0.402
Totals	25 $1.469

FIGURE 2.   SYSTEM SCHEMATIC: The Major Processes in Finding the Book

The cost of the reference librarian to hand **the book to 25 users is (25) X (0.5 minutes) X ($.067) = $0.837.** The total cost to hand a book to 25 users then is:

$$\begin{array}{r} \$1.469 \\ +\$0.837 \\ \hline \$2.306 \end{array}$$

or $0.09/user (as a weighted average)

Time and cost Estimates of Walking to the Book. It takes one minute to walk to the farthest corner of the 240 foot long reference room from the card catalog. This is just walking time and does not include time for scanning for call numbers. It is estimated that the mean time spent walking and scanning is 3.5 minutes with a range of 0.5 minutes to 6 minutes.

The cost of walking-scanning is calculated by multiplying: (No. of walkers) X (3.5 minutes) X ($/minute) with the following results:

Undergraduates	26 X 3.5 X 0.033 = $ 3.00
Graduates	26 X 3.5 X 0.067 = $ 6.09
Faculty	4 X 3.5 X 0.167 = $ 2.34
Library Staff	19 X 3.5 X 0.067 = $ 4.45
Totals	75 $15.88

or $0.21/user (as a weighted average)

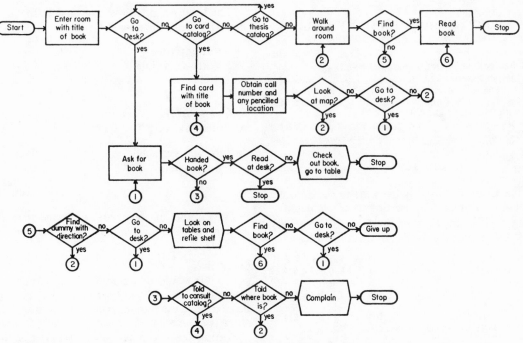

FIGURE 3.   FLOWCHART OF STEPS REQUIRED TO FIND A BOOK IN THE REFERENCE ROOM

Total Weighted Average Costs per User to Get a Book.

To get book at desk:	Catalog use	$0.09
	Desk Service	+$0.09
		———
		$0.18/user

To walk and scan:	Catalog use	$0.09
	Walk-Scan	+$0.21
		———
		$0.30/user

ALTERNATIVE SYSTEMS

Several alternative systems might be:
1. A more detailed floor plan and decision-locator chart.
2. More information on the card (that is, case number).
3. Additional librarians to direct users.
4. Rearrange room; bring books closer together.
5. Arrange all books in one call number sequence.

More Detailed Floor Plan and Locator Chart. The flowchart for this system would be identical with that for the existing system. The new locator chart is shown in Figure 4; the cost of the new chart and floor plan is in Table 2.

The floor plan of the reference room would be as it is, except the terminology would be made consistent with the penciled locations on the cards and the beginning and end call numbers for each section would be indicated as well as a few intermediate call numbers for large sections. Alternate case numbers would also be shown.

Maintenance of Floor Plan and Chart. The Locator Chart would probably not need any alterations for 2 to 5 years. The Floor Plan would have to be slightly altered only when, an addition or deletion of a book was at the beginning or end of a section. This would be accomplished by pasting the new call number over the old. It is estimated that this is required each three months and if done by the librarian or library assistant, it would take about 0.5 hour at a rate of $4.00/hour for a yearly cost of about $8.00 plus ink, paper and paste. This amounts to about $0.67 month and is considered negligible.

Estimated Time and Cost of Using the New Chart and Floor Plan. The new chart and plan will add an estimated 0.5 minutes to the time for use of the card catalog, that is, raise

TABLE 2.
COST OF PRODUCING NEW FLOOR PLAN AND CHART

Librarian's time to rough draft and plan: Two 8-hour days at $4.00/hr.	$ 64.00
Changing and correcting penciled location in card catalog: Three 8-hour days at $2.00/hr.	$ 48.00
Draftsman: One-and-a-half 8-hour days at $3.00/hr.	$ 36.00
Material	$ 4.00
Total	$152.00

the mean card catalog use time to two minutes. The cost of catalog use time is recalculated by multiplying (No. of users) X (2 minutes) X ($/minute) with the following results:

Undergraduates	35 X 2 X 0.033 =	$ 2.31
Graduates	35 X 2 X 0.067 =	$ 4.69
Faculty	5 X 2 X 0.167 =	$ 1.67
Library Staff	25 X 2 X 0.067 =	$ 2.35
Totals	100	$11.02

or $0.11/user (weighted average)

The walking-scanning time will be reduced from an estimated mean of 3.5 minutes to an estimated mean of 1 minute (with a range of 0.5 minutes to 3 minutes) for 75 of the 100 users. The cost is calculated by multiplying: (No. of users) X (1 minute) X ($/minute) with the following results:

Undergraduates	26 X 1 X 0.003 =	$0.858
Graduates	26 X 1 X 0.067 =	$1.742
Faculty	4 X 1 X 0.167 =	$0.668
Library Staff	19 X 1 X 0.067 =	$1.183
Totals	75	$4.451

or $0.06/user (weighted average)

The total weighted average cost to locate a book by using the new chart and floor plan is:

Catalog time	$0.11/user
Walk-scan time	+$0.06/user
	$0.17/user

Savings of the Chart-Plan System. The new system would save $0.13/user:

Present system	$0.30/user
New system	$0.17/user
	$0.13/user

The number of users required to use the new system before the initial cost is paid off is $\frac{\$152.00}{\$0.13/user}$ = 1,169 users. At a rate of 75 users per day it would take about 16 days to pay off the initial costs. If one operating year (24 days/month for 9 months) is 216 days and if there is an estimated 75 walk-scanners in one operating year. At a savings of $0.13/user this would amount to $2,106.00. For the first year the initial cost reduces this by $152.00 to $1,954.

It is assumed in these saving figures that each user has to look up a title each time and that there are no repeat uses of the same book which would short-circuit the system.

Case Number on Catalog Cards. This system would require an estimated two week's work by a clerk at $400/month, and, in addition, either a new floor plan or greatly altering the present plan. With the same amount of savings as with the Plan-Chart system, it would take about twice a long to pay off and the maintenance costs would be greater (every card

STEP I. Obtain *Call Number* and any Location *Penciled* below Call Number.

STEP II. Penciled Location	What To Do
None	In Call Number order in study area. See map.
Biographies	To your left in corner of room.
Desk	Give title and Call Number to librarian.
Dictionaries	Behind you, against far wall.
Directories	On far side of Reference Desk.
General Reference Desk	Give Call Number to librarian.
Indexed Books	In Call Number order in study area. See plan.
Periodial Indexes	To your right.
Periodical and News- paper Reference	Behind this sign.
Telephone Directories	Behind you, across room.
Trade & National Bibliography (Loan Hall)	Go to the Loan Hall.
U.S. & British Trade	Behind you, across room.

FIGURE 4. NEW LOCATOR CHART

would have to have a penciled case number).
Additional Librarians on Duty at the Card Catalog. This sytem would cost at least $7,500/year per librarian, and this cost would be a continuing cost.
Arrange Books in Call Number Sequence. This system would cost an estimated $1,200 (3 assistants working for one month at $400/ month). It would also place some of the most used books at the far end of the room and would, therefore, greatly increase the walking time.

RECOMMENDATIONS

It is recommended that the proposed Chart-Floor Plan system be installed. If data are desired, it is recommended that a librarian spend one week timing and counting users at the catalog and following them to the book. This would cost about $125 of salary time with negli-ble equipment cost if the librarian has a watch with a second hand. If the new system were then installed, a one-week follow-up study could be done for an additional $125 of salary time.

CONCLUSIONS

The system for locating a reference book in a large university library was basically sound. The application of systems analysis found a few inconsistencies which tend to annoy patrons and which increase the number of unnecessary directional questions for the reference librarian. By quantifying and placing a dollar value on the time of both librarians and patrons the cost of installing the modified system can be justified.

REFERENCE

[1] Moore, Edythe. "Systems Analysis: An Overview" *Special* Libraries, v. 58: no. 2, p. 87-90 (Feb. 1967).

ABOUT THE AUTHOR

Edward C. Jestes is a geologist turned librarian. Born in Nairobi, Kenya he received A.B., M.A. and Ph.D. degrees in geology from the University of California at Los Angeles. He performed military service in Japan and Korea and at various times taught geology at UCLA, the University of Hawaii and Washington State University. However in 1965-66 he went to the University of California at Berkeley for an MLS and took up a post of reference and map librarianship at the Davis Campus of the University of California.

An Illustrative Application of Economic Analysis

Charles J. Hitch and Roland N. McKean

Perhaps the most comprehensive attempt (to date) to apply operations research and cost-effectiveness analysis to the evaluation and control of public policy has been in the military and defense arena. In this case study, the authors present a simplified application of the cost-effectiveness method to a decision concerning the composition of an intercontinental military air transport fleet. They consider the nature of the problem, including the wider issues involved and the extent to which it can be sub-optimised. The objective or mission is defined and alternative means of achieving this objective are deduced and described. A cost-effectiveness criterion is derived and the best alternative plan identified.

To exemplify the potentialities and limitations of systematic quantitative analysis, we shall apply some of these techniques to a choice faced by a military service. This application reflects the "way of looking at military problems" that has been stressed, that is, the systematic consideration of alternative policies and the gains and costs of each. The example therefore embraces the various elements discussed above — a manageable "sub-problem" of choice, a mission or objective, alternative means of achieving that objective, costs entailed by each means, models to trace out the relationships among these elements, and a criterion for choosing the preferred means. In this chapter we simply present the analysis. In subsequent chapters, we shall refer to it in order to elucidate general points about the selection of criteria, uncertainty, the treatment of time streams, and the use of analysis in planning research and development.

THE PROBLEM

In order to exhibit both the merits and the pitfalls of quantitative analysis, we have turned to a real problem of military choice. It is a problem of procurement or force composition —

that of choosing in 195x an intercontinental military air transport fleet for the decade 1958-1967. Because we wish to focus attention on method rather than on the substance of this particular analysis, the alternative policies — in this case, alternative transport fleets — are hypothetical. The assumed characterizations, such as payloads and ranges, of the aircraft considered here do not correspond to those of existing transports. The planes cannot be labeled "turboprops" or "turbojets"; they are simply hypothetical aircraft whose function is to help illustrate the possibilities of systematic analysis. The context, however, is sufficiently realistic and detailed to bring out many of the complexities, and the calculations have been carried out fully in order to make the illustration complete.

Deciding on the best intercontinental air transport fleet appears to be a manageable sub-optimization. Certain higher-level questions — for instance, should the United States have an intercontinental airlift capability? — are put aside. Attention is confined to the lower level question: If the United States is to have such a capability during the period 1958-1967, what is the most efficient fleet for the mission? This decision appears to have no marked repercussions on broader defense policies or on international negotiations, so we

SOURCE: Reprinted by permission of the publishers from *The Economics of Defense in the Nuclear Age* by Charles J. Hitch and Roland N. McKean, Cambridge, Mass.: Harvard University Press, Copyright 1960 by the Rand Corporation.

can safely "factor out" the problem for more or less separate examination. (If the choice affected the design of equipment to be transported, this effect would have to be taken into account, but the alternative aircraft do not in fact seem to have differential implications for the design of tanks, guns, gear, and so on.)

THE MISSION OR OBJECTIVE

The assumed mission comprises two tasks, routine worldwide resupply of our military bases at *all* times and deployment in the event of a peripheral war. (Air transport needs in an all-out war are not considered, for they appear to be less than the requirements for tactical deployment in limited conflicts.) These tasks, while specified in considerable detail, are intended to be representative airlift missions. Both are stated in terms of cargo and passenger tonnages to be delivered via 20 "channels" (see Tables 3 and 4 in the appendix at the end of this chapter). A channel is specified by an origin and one or two overseas destinations. For most of the channels, several round-trip *routes* are available for delivering the required tonnage. Thus Travis Air Force Base, California, to Tokyo, Japan, is Channel 17, and five routes can be used:[1]

Route 1: Travis-Tokyo-Travis
Route 2: Travis-Midway-Tokyo-Midway-Travis
Route 3: Travis-Hickam-Midway-Tokyo-
    Midway-Hickam-Travis
Route 4: Travis-Hickam-Wake-Tokyo-Midway-
    Hickam-Travis
Route 5: Travis-Hickam-Johnston-Wake-Tokyo-
    Midway-Hickam-Travis

To allow for changes in routine air resupply needs and in the availability of various aircraft, the 10-year period studied was divided into Period I, four years, 1958-1961 inclusive, and Period II, six years, 1962-1967 inclusive. The magnitude of the deployment task is assumed to remain unchanged throughout the 10 years. The magnitude of the routine resupply mission is assumed to increase from about two and one-half times 1954 levels in Period I to about five times 1954 levels in Period II. This assumption of rapid growth in traffic seems justified by trends observed in the past 10 years.

The representative deployment task consists

of the movement to Bangdhad, a hypothetical city in the Far East, of one infantry division (combat echelon) from Travis Air Force Base, California, one fighter-bomber wing from Travis, and two fighter-bomber wings from Tokyo. In addition, one week's supply of fuel and ammunition for the fighter-bomber wings is to be brought in from Manila. This airlift is to be accomplished in 10 days.

THE ALTERNATIVE MEANS

The aircraft considered for the transport fleet were limited, for present purposes, to four: the C-97[2] (the currently used piston-engined aircraft), the HC-400 (HC standing for "Hypothetical Cargo" aircraft), the HC-500, and the HC-600. The last three aircraft are turbine-engined aircraft, and the higher the "HC-number", the larger the size of the aircraft.[3] Perhaps the best way to summarize the physical characteristics of these aircraft is to show their respective "payload-range" curves, which picture the combinations of cargo and range that are feasible in each aircraft (see Figure 1). These curves play a major role in the calculation of results.

Some of these aircraft are supposed to be on hand, while others are presumed to be procurable within specified production limits. Table 1 gives initial inventories and the possibilities of procurement in each of the two periods. Notice that for each of the turbine-engined aircraft, the number available increases over time, with HC-400 production ahead of HC-500 production, and the latter ahead of HC-600 production.

Since the problem pertains to a series of points in time, simplified here to two time periods, the alternatives are not just fleets, but fleet *sequences*. That is, what we seek is not actually an optimum fleet but rather the best Period I-Period II sequence of fleets. Note that what is best in Period I depends in part upon the aircraft available and most useful in Period II, and what is best in Period II depends upon the aircraft procured in Period I — a real-life complexity that cannot be shrugged off by the analyst.

Since (in this chapter) we treat these aircraft as candidates for procurement, we assume that they have already been "developed," at least as far as the prototype stage.

TABLE 1.
AIRCRAFT AVAILABLE (ILLUSTRATIVE ANALYSIS)

Aircraft type	Initial inventory	Maximum number procurable	
		Period I 1958-1961	Period II 1962-1968
C-97 (and equivalent)	400	0	200*
HC-400	100	400	700
HC-500	0	50	100
HC-600	0	0	125

* By 1962 the introduction of new tanker aircraft into the Air Force will presumably bring about the retirement of KC-97 tankers. If desired, these could then be modified at a nominal cost for use as C-97 transport aircraft.

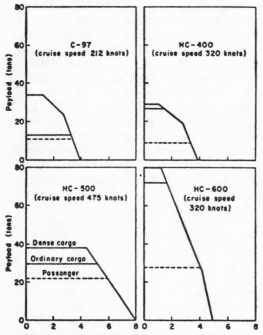

FIGURE 1. PAYLOAD-RANGE CURVES OF THE ALTERNATIVE AIRCRAFT.

THE COSTS

The costs that we wish to measure are the additional system costs attributable to each fleet sequence. Our first step is to identify just what it is that we are costing. We focus attention upon the wartime deployment and wartime resupply missions that each fleet must be capable of carrying out, because they appear to constitute the largest job the transport fleet will have to do. The fleet is occupied during peacetime, however, with peacetime resupply. Since large parts of the costs appropriate to the comparisons being made are operating costs, we must consider this peacetime resupply activity. If transport aircraft could be mothballed in a highly ready state (and if it were economic to prepare for war in this fashion), then the only operating costs in our comparisons would be those incurred during the conduct of the war. And since the wartime task we have postulated is short-lived, these costs would be negligible compared to the large initial costs of procuring the fleet. Quick response from a mothballed fleet, however, is difficult to obtain. Crews and maintenance personnel need practice, and the complicated aircraft of today must be operated to remain operable. In short, *practice* of the whole fleet appears to be requisite to readiness. A further important reason for operating the fleet in peacetime is that once it has been procured, it may as well be used if the benefits thereby derived exceed the operating costs. The man with a family of five who has bought a station wagon for vacations and Sunday outings will not ordinarily be averse to using it to drive to work. And if he is a careful car buyer, he will consider the operating costs of this commuting in making his selection.

We assume, therefore, that six hours daily flying for each aircraft in the fleet is necessary to a capability of immediately achieving ten hours daily flying whenever the occasion warrants. Hence, in determining fleet costs over the ten-year period, we include the operating costs of the ten years of six-hours-a-day "practice" flying. We presuppose that whatever useful work is accomplished in the course of this "practice" flying is the same for all fleets considered, so we do not bother to give any credit for this incidental (but not unimportant) accomplishment. We shall also ignore the relatively small wartime additions to the total of operating costs.

Let us turn now to the main cost components: procurement costs, installation and training costs, attrition, and annual operating costs. Here we shall simply outline the nature of these components. (For the calculations, the cost relationships had to be somewhat simplified in order to be put into "linear" equations.)

The *procurement cost* of an aircraft includes both the cost of the airframe and an initial outlay for spare parts (a by no means neglible addition). While one might argue that the latter is really an operating cost, the Air Force *does* buy spares when it buys aircraft. Procurement costs would be quite simple to calculate were it not for certain "set-up" costs and "learning" phenomena in aircraft production. Before mass production can begin, a large investment must be put into tooling (jigs, dies, fixtures, and so on) which can be used for no other aircraft. Moreover, this investment is the same whether 50 or 500 aircraft are produced.[4] And as production gets under way, the efficiency of the whole operation improves through learning. These two effects (of set-up costs and of learning) together bring about a decline in procurement cost per aircraft as the number of aircraft produced increases.

Installations and training costs, like procurement costs, are initial, rather than annually recurring, costs. The purchase of one particular vehicle for the fleet requires an outlay for buildings, kitchens, ground handling equipment, and so on, and for the training of crews and maintenance personnel. One of the difficult questions that must be decided is whether the resulting equipment and proficiency depreciates faster or slower than the aircraft for which it was purchased. Another is the extent to which this equipment and proficiency is of use with other types of aircraft. Must these accoutrements be retired along with their aircraft? No pat answers to these questions are possible.

Attrition costs result from peacetime "practice" flying operations. They differ, for present purposes, from other annual operating costs in that they must be paid for by the purchase of replacement aircraft, the cost of which, as indicated above, depends on the total number procured. Our troubles with attrition costs would end here if we were not concerned with the design of a whole fleet and with the numbers of aircraft each manufac-

turer can provide by certain points in time. The case of piston-engined aircraft is particularly troublesome. If, in the fleet sequence being costed, retirement of these aircraft is being carried out at a rapid rate, then attrition should be costless: an attrited aircraft constitutes a retirement. If retirement is not called for, then the attrited aircraft — no longer being produced — must be replaced by newer aircraft having an equivalent capacity. But this kind of replacement alters the composition of the fleet — the very thing we are trying to cost. For the newer aircraft that are still in production, an attrited aircraft is replaced by a new one, except when rapid retirement takes place. Whenever the number called for by a fleet sequence presses hard against the manufacturer's limits, we must make sure that the phasing-in is not so fast as to leave no production capacity for attrition replacements.

Annual operating cost is the most easily dealt with of the four cost components discussed. It is almost directly proportional to the level of the peacetime "practice" flying-hour program and includes such items as wages (both crew and ground support personnel), fuel and maintenance.

In order to measure the extra costs attributable to each fleet sequence, we should avoid including sunk costs, that is, expenditures already made and therefore irretrievable. Thus, we must not include in our costs the procurement expenditures for the aircraft already in the fleet. If these older aircraft cannot be sold or put to alternative uses, in effect and for present purposes, they are free. This point, which will be discussed more fully in Chapter 11, applies equally to the 100 HC-400's and to the 400 C-97's in the initial inventory.

THE CRITERION

As in most problems, there are some considerations that we cannot successfully include in a single definitive test of preferredness. Several considerations of this sort will be pointed out in interpreting the results. The principal criterion, however, will be minimum cost over the years 1958-1967 of maintaining the specified airlift capability. That is, the system that can achieve the objective at lowest cost will be regarded as the best system (unless this test is overruled by the "outside" considerations). In applying this criterion, we have not discounted the streams of cost or gain (see Chapter 11 for a discussion of discounting). In this comparison of air transport fleets, discounting the future at plausible rates seems unlikely to affect the results; in fact, discounting the costs at as high a rate as 25 per cent leaves the ranking of the fleets unchanged.

THE MODELS AND THE PROCEDURE

The models comprise the relationships that enable us to estimate the cost and effectiveness of alternative fleets. Details of the models and computations are shown in the appendix at the end of this chapter. Here we shall indicate only briefly the general nature of the procedure.

The technique for finding the least-cost fleet is the one described in the discussion in another part of this book[5] — that is, seeking points of tangency between exchange curves and output-isoquants. In other words, the models show how the transport aircraft can be traded for each other while holding total cost constant, and how they can be substituted for each other while keeping the quantity of output constant.[6] The ratio of two aircrafts' marginal costs (that is, the costs of buying and operating an additional

plane) shows how they can be traded for each other while holding total cost constant. The ratio of the aircrafts' productivities (tons of cargo that can be delivered per flying hour) over each channel shows how they can be substituted while keeping the quantity of output constant. Finally, knowing the effects of trading one aircraft for another, we exchange them (on paper) until we determine the least-cost combination that will do the job.

The models also show the costs of certain fleets other than the least-cost one. The reason for this is that we may legitimately be interested in certain other fleets, in which case we should know their economic implications.

RESULTS AND CONCLUSIONS

The results are presented in Table 2. The fleet that entailed the lowest cost, which we shall call the "basic least-cost" fleet, employs all three of the new aircraft in Period II (when the HC-600 becomes available), the C-97's being retired at the end of Period I. Least-cost fleets were also calculated with certain planes excluded. We did this for two reasons: (1) to determine the sensitivity of the costs to the presence of those planes, and (2) to identify the best fleet in case some special consideration eliminated one of the transports. It turns out that costs are not

TABLE 2.
COST AND COMPOSITION OF ALTERNATIVE FLEETS, PERIODS I AND II*

	Basic least-cost		Least-cost excluding HC-600		Least-cost excluding HC-500		Least-cost excluding HC-500, HC-600		Least procurement	
Composition (numbers of aircraft)	I	II	I	II	I	II	I	II	I	II
C-97	103	0	0	0	309	0	0	0	400	472
HC-400	151	151	229	229	161	161	399	486	103	103
HC-500	50	53	50	78	—	—	—	—	8	8
HC-600	—	53	—	—	—	113	—	—	—	0
Cost** (millions of 1956 dollars)	$3,986		$4,039		$4,295		$4,587		$5,129	

* A dash (—) indicates that the model is not available in that particular period. A zero (0) indicates that it is inefficient to use that aircraft even though it is available.

** These cost figures are the amounts as estimated by the mathematical models (see the appendix) *plus* adjustments for those elements of cost that could not be allowed for in linear relationships.

sensitive to the presence of the HC-600, for its elimination raises the expected cost negligibly. The results are more sensitive to the employment of the HC-500, for its elimination increases the cost of carrying out the mission by about 300 million dollars. Eliminating both of these aircraft raises the expected cost by about 600 million dollars.

The most striking result, however, is the marked inefficiency that would result from adopting a "least-procurement" policy — that is, a policy of buying no more new aircraft than would be necessary to carry out the task. The operating costs of the C-97 are sufficient to make this a very expensive policy. costing over a billion dollars more than the least-costs fleet. In this instance, as in many others, it is not economic to "make do" with old equipment. Economizing does *not* mean minimizing cash outlays in the current time period.

The array of results in Table 2 also brings out some interesting interrelationships between the decisions for each of the two periods. For example, if the HC-600 is excluded, it becomes efficient to use more HC-400's in Period II. This fact in turn makes it economical to procure more HC-400's in Period I. As a consequence, the exclusion of the HC-600, instead of thrusting more work on all three of the remaining aircraft, leads to the elimination of the C-97 even in Period I!. That is, in these altered circumstances, it is economical to replace the C-97 immediately. The same thing happens if both the HC-500 and the HC-600 are excluded. On the other hand, if the HC-500 is excluded, it is economical to lean very heavily on the C-97 in Period I (the HC-600 being available only in Period II), and procure a comparatively large number of HC-600's (113) in Period II. The impact of these interrelationships on the composition of efficient fleets is by no means intuitively obvious.

In interpreting the results, we must recognize that there are relevant considerations outside our principal criterion. For instance, manning requirements may be an important aspect of the different fleets in addition to their effectiveness and cost (as reflected in our measures). If the military were free to adjust pay (and other policies) so as to get the personnel desired, dollar costs would fully reflect the advantages and disadvantages of various fleets with respect to manpower requirements. But since manpower ceilings

and legislation on pay structure have to be considered, the Services may be unable to obtain the desired personnel at the indicated costs. In other words, heavy manpower requirements may pose some difficulties that are not reflected in costs. Another outside consideration is the effect of each fleet on base saturation. After preliminary investigations, it was assumed here that the various airbases could handle the traffic and refueling in all cases. Yet, clearly, different fleets do impose different burdens on these bases, and even if the accomplishment of the mission is not impaired in any way, the differential burdens and strains may properly bear on a final decision.

Still another consideration outside the main criterion is uncertainty. There is great strategic uncertainty. Is this mission a representative one? Is the composition of the least-cost fleet sensitive to changes in the mission? There are also uncertainties about many other matters such as technological developments, cost figures, and performance in particular instances. These tables show "best estimates" or estimates of the outcome that can be expected on the average, and other outcomes are clearly possible. In the face of these uncertainties, we may prefer, not the least-cost fleet to carry out the designated mission, but a modified version that offers insurance against very unfavorable outcomes. As a consequence, before interpreting the above results, one should make some additional calculations — to see how well the interesting fleets would perform in certain other contingencies, or to determine the least-cost fleet for altered versions of the mission.

Nonetheless, it is fairly clear, in this illustrative analysis, that an economical fleet will employ a large number of newly procured aircraft. It will employ not only the HC-400 but also at least one of the two larger transports (the HC-500 and HC-600). We cannot here compare the impacts of various fleets on such things as base saturation and manning requirements; but consideration of these factors is virtually certain to favor still further the larger turbine-engined transports, the HC-500 and the HC-600.

We wish to stress that this analysis pertains to a *relatively* low-level and uncomplicated choice. It is defined in such a way that we do not worry about spillover effects on

other missions or about enemy reactions.
Yet even in this analysis, there are many difficulties in selecting a criterion, spelling out
the objective, measuring aircraft productivities,
estimating costs, and interpreting the results. The following appendix, on the models
and computations, emphasizes further the
subtlety of some of these problems. For
example, it makes a difference what cargo
"mix" is to be moved in this mission. Also,
aggregating the possible trips and routes
into a manageable number of channels raises
some nice questions. It is important, therefore, to be careful in preparing and appraising
relatively simple analyses such as this one.
In more complicated choices, it is all the
more important to be clear on the methodological issues. In the following chapters
we turn to a more thorough examination of
several of these issues.

APPENDIX ON THE MODELS AND THE COMPUTATIONS[7]

As indicated in the text, the aim of the analysis is to find the least costly fleet sequence
from among all those with the required capability. How is this to be done? Once the input
data — to be described below — have been
gathered, it is a straightforward matter to
construct a Period I fleet and a Period II fleet,
each possessing at least the required capability. For comparisons to be of much use,
however, these fleet sequences must have in
common two further characteristics that make
their construction more difficult.

First, aircraft production availabilities must
not be exceeded.[8] In the case of the C-97,
which is no longer being produced, the beginning inventory must not be exceeded until
the retired KC-97's become available for
conversion to transports in Period II.

Second, none of the fleets entering the
comparisons should have *more* than the required capability. This stipulation causes
more difficulty than might at first appear.
While it is easy to make sure that a fleet has
enough capability, it is another matter to
ask that it have no more than enough, for
reshufflings of the assignments of aircraft and
jobs can sometimes result in unused capacity. We must be sure, in other words, that
each aircraft is contributing the most it can to

fleet accomplishments. Fleets that possess
this characteristic of having the required
capability but no excess capability, we shall
refer to as *efficient*[9] fleets.

Before going on to the question of how to
construct these efficient fleets, it will be useful
to discuss the choice of fleet sequences to
compare. Even with as few as four aircraft, the
number of interesting and relevant fleets —
not to mention Period I-Period II combinations
of fleets — is large, so large in fact that it
becomes difficult to know what comparisons
to carry out. Even if production availabilities
permitted, little would be learned from a
comparison between, say, a "pure" fleet of
HC-500's and a "pure" fleet of HC-600's. The
HC-500 might be an economic aircraft to
procure as a complement to, say, the HC-600,
but poor as a general purpose aircraft. The
HC-400 *might* be an economic procurement
only as a stopgap measure prior to HC-600
production. The HC-600 might be a good
Period II procurement if the HC-500 is bought
in Period I, but a poor procurement if the
more nearly similar[10] HC-400 serves as
the stopgap.

Obviously the method of choosing the comparisons to be made should be systematic.
The method described below achieves this end
and at the same time ensures that the fleets
chosen are *efficient* ones. The procedure
consists, first of all, in using mathematical
means to find the fleet sequence that costs the
least among all those that meet requirements
without exceeding available production.
The next step is to determine the best fleet in
case one of the transports is ruled out by
special considerations. This fleet is determined by arbitrarily barring one of the aircraft
in the first least-cost sequence, and solving for
the least-cost fleet among those remaining.
In the next step a different transport may be
eliminated, and the former one restored, or
both may be barred. The process continues in this fashion to form new fleet sequences — each of which, it will be noted, is
the least costly in its class. The direction
the procedure takes in each case is dictated
partly by the analyst's interests, and partly by
the outcome of the preceding calculations.

There are several reasons for our being interested in these other fleets. For one thing,
our measure of the "equal capability" of the
fleets being considered ignores such matters
as runway requirements, cargo handling

characteristics, and vulnerability. Moreover, this "equal capability" refers to only one war situation out of the many that might occur. To experienced eyes one of our fleet sequences — as capable as the others according to our crude measure — may appear to be superior in some respect, say, in vulnerability or versatility. One of the purposes of our comparisons is to show the economic implications of these other fleets that might be favored. Our procedure helps us chart a pertinent segment of the spectrum of efficient fleets.

AIRCRAFT PRODUCTIVITIES

We shall express the productivity of a given aircraft on a given channel in terms of the number of tons of a specified cargo that can be delivered per flying hour.[11] Since several routes are usually available for each channel, we must first determine an aircraft's productivity on each route. The productivity of an aircraft on a channel will then be its productivity over its most productive route.

For the calculations, we need to know the performance of the various transports and the nature of the job to be done. As for the job, the data in Table 3 form the basis of our requirements for each of 20 channels. Channel numbers 57-61 give the tonnage requirements for the tactical deployment, and Channels 01-47 give those for routine resupply in Period I. Period II requirements are twice those of Period I for Channels 01-47, and the same as those of Period I for Channels 57-61. Table 4 gives a sample description in terms of round-trip distances and "critical legs" of representative channels.

As for the performance of the transports, their payload-range curves have already been given in Figure 1. Note that they pertain to three types of payload — passengers, ordinary cargo, and dense cargo (such as petroleum, oil, lubricants, and ammunition). When passengers are to be carried, Table 3 states this explicitly. We shall suppose that the only airlift of dense cargo takes place on the Clark to Bangdhad resupply run, Channel 61. When dense cargo is carried, the full weight-allowable cabin load of an aircraft can be used. However, when passengers or ordinary freight is to be airlifted, the cubic capacity of an aircraft may limit the payload. As a

result, separate payload-range curves for determining allowable passenger loads are given, as well as the cubic capacity of each aircraft for cargo purposes. We assume throughout that our ordinary cargo has a uniform density of 12 pounds per cubic foot. With this information we can modify the top part of each payload-range curve to ensure that cubic capacities are not exceeded. Thus we have for each aircraft three payload-range curves — for passengers, for ordinary cargo, and for dense cargo.

TABLE 3.
TEN-DAY CARGO AND PASSENGER REQUIREMENTS BY CHANNEL (INCLUDING ROUTINE RESUPPLY, WARTIME DEPLOYMENT, AND WARTIME RESUPPLY)

Channel*	Passenger tons**	Cargo tons
01	—	—
03	—	—
05	50	80
07	25	51
09	25	82
11	31	72
13	45	88
15	—	—
17	557	531
19	—	—
21	—	—
23	111	185
25	27	26
27	44	95
29	10	36
31	112	203
33	74	342
35	45	88
37	—	—
39	—	—
41	26	127
43	538	1,156
45	74	179
47	117	499
57	200	1,000
59	1,600	4,000
61	—	20,000

* Channels 01-47 are for routine resupply. The requirements for Channels 57-61 are for the tactical deployment in the event of peripheral war.

** Nine passengers to a ton. The tonnages listed (for both passengers and cargo) are hypothetical. They have been made up for the purpose of illustrating the method of analysis.

The points in our route network where fuel is pre-positioned play a part in the determination of the critical legs in each route. We have assumed that sufficient petroleum, oil and lubricants are available for transport purposes at all points except Bangdhad. Thus, for every route except those including a Clark-Bangdhad leg, the payloads will be determined on the basis of the customary payload-range curves and the critical legs. On routes involving Clark-Bangdhad flights, however, we must use payload-radius curves[12] *as well as* payload-range curves.[13] Whereas usually the critical leg of a route is simply the longest leg, it may or may not be the leg that limits payload on routes involving radius work.

The payload of a given aircraft on a given route is found by reading from the appropriate payload-range curve the number of tons corresponding to the length of the critical leg on this route. This means, of course, that over some of the shorter, noncritical legs of a

route, an aircraft may be less than fully loaded. Transloading would be the only way to use this capacity, however, and this is probably more expensive than unused aircraft capacity.

The round-trip flight of an aircraft on a given route is determined in two steps. We first divide the round-trip route distance by the aircraft's cruise speed. Since the resulting time estimate does not allow for delays in descents and ascents and in ground handling during intermediate fueling stops, we add 15 minutes for each landing and 15 minutes for each take-off. This sum we regard as our estimate of flight time.

The productivity of a given aricraft on a given route is now determined by dividing the appropriate round-trip flight time. For example, let us find the passenger productivity of the HC-600 on Route 2 of Channel 17. (We shall

TABLE 4.
PARTIAL DETAIL OF MATS ROUTE STRUCTURE ASSUMED FOR ANALYSIS

Channel*	Route*	Critical leg** (N. mi.)	Round-trip distance (N. mi.)	Route description***
05	1	1280	2180	Nouasseur§ — Tripoli-R (i.e., Return)
07	1	3290	6060	Nouasseur§ — Dhahran-R
07	2	2210	6060	Nouasseur-Tripoli§ — Dhahran-R
07	3	1330	6240	Nouasseur-Tripoli-Cairo§ — Dhahran-R
09	1	2320	4360	Dover§ — Lages-R
09	2	1630	4920	Dover-Stephenville§ — Lages-R
11	1	1050	1300	Dover — Bermuda-R
13	1	3180	4860	Dover§ — Keflavik-R
13	2	2250	4940	Dover-Stephenville§ — Keflavik-R
17	1	4650	8860	Travis§ — Tokyo-R
17	2	3220	10120	Travis§ — Midway-Tokyo-R
17	3	2460	11040	Travis-Hickam-Midway§ — Tokyo-R
17	4	2410	11420	Travis-Hickam§ — Wake-Tokyo-Midway-Hickam-Travis
17	5	2150	11520	Travis§ — Hickam-Johnston-Wake-Tokyo-Midway-Hickam-Travis
19	1	4670	8620	Travis§ — Eniwetok-R
19	2	2700	8980	Travis-Hickam§ — Eniwetok-R
19	3	2150	9040	Travis§ — Hickam-Johnston-Eniwetok
23	1	2150	4280	
25	1	1480	2940	
27	1	1550		
29	1	1550		
31	1			

* Channel and route numbers are not the same as MATS designations.
** Includes distance to nearest alternate.
*** Symbols are as follows: § denotes critical leg. R denotes return.

make the calculation precise so that the result will correspond with that shown in Table 5.) From Table 4 we see that the critical leg on this route is 3,200 miles. Entering Figure 1 at 3,200 miles and reading the passenger curve, we find that the HC-600 has a payload of about 28 tons — 27.8 tons, if we could read the figure accurately enough. The round-trip distance on Route 2 is 10,120 miles; dividing this figure by the cruise speed of the HC-600 (320 knots), we have 31.68 hours as the time for the round trip. Adding 15 minutes for each of the 4 landings and 4 take-offs in the round-trip, we get 33.68 flying hours as our estimate of total flight time. Passenger productivity then is payload over flight time: 27.8/33.68, or 0.824 tons per flying hour.[14]

The productivity of each aircraft on each channel is shown in Table 5. Cargo and passenger productivities are given separately. Since the dense cargo appears only on Channel 61 — all of this requirement is dense cargo — it was not necessary to have a third tabulation. All of these productivities refer to "overload" or "emergency" operating conditions.

In one respect, the importance of which is difficult to judge, the measures of productivity we have been discussing are unrealistic. Notice that we always assume an aircraft to be doing one or the other — but not a mixture — of two jobs: passenger transportation and cargo transportation. Now, if it were true that when an aircraft was loaded to capacity with one of these commodities, no capacity remained for the other commodity, then only the most critical could object. Mixed loading, in this case, could always be simulated in our calculations by unmixed loading: three aircraft each with a third cargo and two-thirds passengers would for present purposes be equivalent to one aircraft of cargo and two of passengers. As aircraft engineers will be quick to point out, however, fuselage shapes spoil this nice equivalence. When an aircraft carries passengers over short or intermediate ranges, its capacity is limited by space rather than by weight. Even so, in some aircraft there remain oddshaped spaces unsuitable for passengers but perfectly good for cargo. The belly compartment of a C-97 is an example. The reverse also holds. For structural reasons, one transport has a large bubble across the upper fuselage. Cargo can be carried in this space, but difficulty of access makes it unattractive for cargo purposes. Thus, when the aircraft is loaded with cargo to its easy-access cube capacity, there still remains space for a good many passengers.

COST COEFFICIENTS

TABLE 5.
AIRCRAFT PRODUCTIVITIES BY CHANNEL (TONS PER FLYING HOUR)

Channel	Cargo				Passengers			
	C-97	HC-400	HC-500	HC-600	C-97	HC-400	HC-500	HC-600
1	1.337	3.478	5.321	9.130	.957	1.202	3.946	3.550
5	.494	1.207	2.161	3.169	.365	.471	1.603	1.390
7	.700	1.481	2.922	4.123	.500	.642	2.167	1.895
9	2.115	5.365	7.968	14.083	1.513	1.854	5.909	5.475
11	.593	1.271	2.649	3.540	.451	.580	1.964	1.712
13	.274	.559	1.513	1.544	.217	.279	1.122	.824
17	.340	.728	0	0	.243	.312	0	0
19	.712	1.583	2.971	4.417	.509	.653	2.203	1.928
23	1.015	2.598	4.139	7.000	.726	.922	3.069	2.722
25	1.000	2.536	4.088	6.912	.717	.910	3.032	2.687
27	.324	.811	1.292	2.211	.231	.291	.958	.860
29	1.146	2.896	4.627	7.863	.819	1.035	3.432	3.057
31	.662	1.355	2.772	3.721	.473	.608	2.056	1.796
33	1.055	2.360	4.288	6.633	.755	.956	3.180	2.824
35	.790	1.844	3.275	5.025	.565	.722	2.429	2.132
41	.372	.756	1.591	2.149	.266	.335	1.180	1.045
43	.219	.467	.959	1.303	.164	.210	.711	.622
45	1.208	3.094	4.642	8.123	.864	1.069	3.442	3.158
47	.494	.968	2.015	2.594	.353	.448	1.494	1.324
57	.182	.358	.840	.959	.138	.176	.623	.520
59	1.604	2.135	5.579	5.720	.780	.988	3.279	2.919
61								

The complexities of the cost relationships have been described. In this section we shall outline the simplifications and approximations that make our problem a mathematically tractable one. Of course, as soon as the cost relationships are simplified for use in the minimization problem, the resulting fleets only approximate the true least-cost fleets whose name they bear, but the approximation is close enough to justify the trouble connected with the minimization procedure.

The unknows of our problem are the numbers of aircraft (of each type) procured and the numbers (of each type) operated[15] in each period. So long as cost inputs to our problem can be used as coefficients of numbers of aircraft procured or numbers of aircraft operated, no difficulties arise, for this type of treatment yields the simple linear expressions so convenient in computing. One of the costs that can be dealt with in this manner is operating cost. Unfortunately, not all the components of cost can be represented in this convenient fashion, as is clear in the earlier discussion. The following measures were therefore taken. The total procurement cost curves, like that portrayed in Figure 2, were approximated by straight lines with positive intercepts, as in the dotted line in the same figure. These curves are drawn, that is, just as though the costs of tooling and learning were covered by a sutstantial initial investment, after which the *marginal* cost (the cost of an additional vehicle) remained exactly the same. Notice that the approximation is good except in the very low ranges. If it is found that this low range is critical, the approximation should be changed and the computation repeated. Obviously, foresight helps in making a good approximation at this stage.

Of the aircraft presently under consideration, only the HC-600 has a markedly curved procurement-cost function; the straight-line approximation for this aircraft resulted in a positive intercept of $50 million. Since 100 HC-400's have already been produced, the marginal procurement cost can be assumed to be constant. No HC-500's have yet been procured, but we assume that the initial tooling and learning outlay (an analytical fiction) has already been made. Both the cost of the first 100 HC-400's and the initial outlay for HC-500 production are therefore *sunk* and we do not even need to determine them; all we

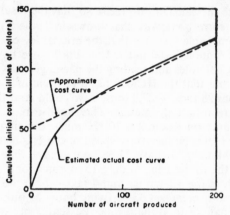

FIGURE 2.   CUMULATIVE PROCUREMENT COSTS

need here are the (constant) marginal procurement costs for these two aircraft. With these simplifications, the only mathematically troublesome aspect of procurement cost that remains is the positive intercept on the HC-600 curve. Our procedure will be to forget this intercept for the moment, proceed as if it were zero, and when we have achieved a tentative solution, check to see whether the $50 million initial outlay would affect the answer.

We shall assume that the useful life of any one of the new aircraft is ten years. It will be supposed that the C-97's are usuable throughout both periods, whatever their age at the beginning of our study. Since we are only attempting to determine costs over a ten-year period, a credit will be given for the undepreciated portion of any one of the new aircraft procured midway in our period.

In our treatment of attrition, foresight again comes into play. We start the analysis with a hunch that the C-97's will be retired in favor of the newer aircraft, and charge nothing for attrition of the former. (Had this assumption turned out to be wrong, charges for attrition would then have been introduced.) Attrition of the newer vehicles is covered by further procurement at marginal procurement cost — the amount being added in with operating cost.

Installations costs we simply add in as a part of the initial cost of an aircraft. This treatment assumes that installations depreciate at the same rate as the aircraft itself, that they are specialized for use with particular aircraft, and that they cannot be inherited. Not much can be said in defense of this procedure except that it simplifies computation, and that the re-

TABLE 6.
COST COEFFICIENTS — COSTS PER ADDITIONAL AIRPLANE
(MILLIONS OF 1956 dollars)

	C-97	HC-400	HC-500	HC-600*
Period I:				
Operating Cost Coefficient	3.69	3.13	8.13	7.12
Initial Cost Coefficient	0	1.20	3.00	2.68
Total**	3.69	4.33	11.13	9.80
Period II:				
Operating Cost Coefficient	5.54	4.70	12.20	10.68
Initial Cost Coefficient	0	1.80	4.50	4.02
Total**	5.54	6.50	16.70	14.70
Grand Total**	9.23	10.83	27.83	24.50
Initial Outlay for Production	0	0	0	50

* For purposes of comparison, the HC-600 coefficients are given in Period I even though the aircraft is not available in this period.

** The reasons for summing these coefficients, and the conditions under which they can properly be summed, are explained in the section on "Optimizing Procedure."

sulting error is probably small.

The cost numbers used explicitly in the mathematical model are costs-per-additional-aircraft and will be called *cost coefficients*. They are based on the assumptions just described. Because separate fleets are to be designed for Period I and Period II, which are four and six years long respectively, separate cost coefficients must be given for each. We will need two sets of coefficients in each period: initial cost coefficients (based on procurement and installations costs) and operating cost coefficients (based on operating and attrition costs). The complete set of coefficients, along with the initial production outlays, are presented in Tabel 6.

AGGREGATION OF CHANNELS

The use of an electronic computer to find the least-cost fleet sequence with the desired characteristics is perfectly feasible. Standard computing procedures exist which can be adapted to the present problem with very little alteration. Close examination of the inputs to the problem, however, indicated that moderate channel aggregation would bring the solution within reach of hand computation. This procedure, despite the more burdensome arithmetic task involved, has the advantage of allowing the analyst to see the "insides" of the problem more clearly. Those parameters and relationships on which the solution depends critically are more clearly brought to

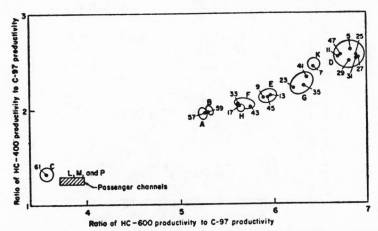

FIGURE 3. COMPARATIVE RATES OF SUBSTITUTION
FOR THE VARIOUS CHANNELS

light.[16] (For these reasons hand computation of preliminary simplified models is especially helpful.)

Our object is to aggregate the 40 channels into a smaller number of groups without losing too much detail. From the standpoint of a given pair of aircraft, one channel differs from another only to the extent that the substitutability of the two aircraft on one channel is different from their substitutability on another channel. Their substitutability on a particular channel depends upon the ration of their productivites (defined above as tonnages carried per flying hour). Therefore, the ration of productivities for two aircraft will be called their subsitution ratio. Channels with almost the same ratio can be treated as a single channel, and their requirements can be added together.

Channels that are similar for one pair of aircraft, however, may be quite different for another pair. One way to investigate this question is to plot one set of such substitution ratios against another, as in Figure 3, where the ratio of HC-600 productivity to C-97 productivity is measured on the horizontal axis and the ratio of HC-400 productivity to C-97 productivity is measured on the vertical axis.

In this first graph the points to fall into quite obvious clusters, with one or two exceptions. Circles[17] have been drawn around the points aggregated, and the new aggregate "channels" are denoted by captial letters. In Figure 4, where the HC-500:C-97 rate of substitution is plotted against the HC-400:C-97 rate of substitution, we see the same aggregation. While there is nothing *necessary*

about the particular aggregation chosen, it does appear to be a reasonable one. This is true even of Channel H, which appears to be an unlikely choice, when only Figure 3 is studied, but which is an obvious choice in Figure 4. Distinct clustering of points is neither necessary nor sufficient for aggregation. What is important is that the points aggregated be fairly close together on both graphs. All of our circles have diameters sufficiently small to avoid introducing much distortion into the problem. From this point on, therefore, we shall deal in terms of the aggregate channels A, B, C, D, E, F, G, H, K, L. M and P.

OPTIMIZING PROCEDURE

The derivation of a least-cost fleet is accomplished by trading aircraft X for Y as long as the ratio of Y's productivity to X's is in excess of the ratio of Y's marginal cost to X's marginal cost. By means of such trading, we keep finding combinations of aircraft that carry out the mission at a lower total cost.

Marginal costs[18] are somewhat complicated, in part because the procurement decisions of one period will affect the marginal costs in the other. The marginal cost of procuring an aircraft for the Period I fleet is Period I operating cost plus the Period I share of depreciation *if this vehicle is continued as a member of the Period II fleet.* In this case, the Period II marginal cost is Period II operating cost plus the Period II

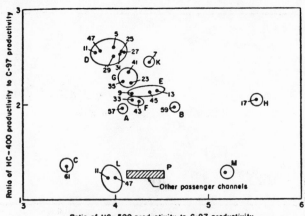

FIGURE 4.   COMPARATIVE RATES OF
SUBSITUTION: ANOTHER SET

share of depreciation. If, alternatively, some retirement of this aircraft type takes place in Period II — that is to say, if the number of this type in the Period II fleet is less than in the Period I fleet — then the marginal cost in Period I is Period I operating cost plus the *whole* ten-year depreciation of the aircraft. The Period II marginal cost in this case is only the Period II operating cost. For the piston-engined aircraft in the beginning inventory, procurement costs are sunk, so that the marginal costs in Period I and Period II are equal to the respective operating costs in those periods. The same applies to the newer aircraft, to whose procurement the Air Force is already committed, just so long as the number of aircraft in the fleet does not exceed commitments. As soon as more than the committed number enter the fleet, then *all* of the aircraft of this type must compete on the basis of procurement plus operating costs. In any case where production availabilities of new aircraft or beginning inventories of out-of-production aircraft are exceeded, the appropriate marginal cost figures must be increased enough to ensure that these constraints are met, just as though fictitious rental charges designed to equate demand and supply were being exacted. Notice that while a separate contest among aircraft goes on for the work on each individual channel, the local outcome depends on the global outcome because marginal costs are related to the totals of each aircraft type that appear in the fleet.

One outcome is possible which, while it appears troublesome at first sight, serves to point up some of the interesting time-phasing aspects of our problem. Suppose one of the new aircraft is a good competitor in Period I but a poor competitor in Period II, still newer types having become available in quantity. If we start by carrying out our cost-productivity comparisons on the assumption that marginal costs in the two periods include the respective shares of depreciation, then it may happen that the solution will show that the number of a certain aircraft type in the Period II fleet is smaller than the number of the same type in the Period I fleet. This is an inconsistent result, since the aircraft retired will in fact have contributed a full ten years of depreciation to total cost. But if we attempt to correct this situation by putting the full ten years of depreciation for this aircraft into Period I mar-

ginal cost, and none into Period II marginal cost, the result may turn out to be that the Period I fleet of this aircraft type is *smaller* than the Period II fleet — a *still* inconsistent result since the aircraft procured at the beginning of Period II will have contributed six years of depreciation to total fleet costs. The answer to this anomaly is that a sufficient portion of Period II depreciation must be shifted from Period II marginal cost to Period I marginal cost to bring about equality of the Period I and Period II fleets of this aircraft type. This aircraft is intermediate in its economic worth between a Period I stopgap vehicle and a full-fledged Period II competitor.

To make the calculations, we need to know the number of each aircraft type that would be required to carry out each of the 39 (unaggregated) channel jobs *alone*. This number can be computed as follows:

$$\text{Number of Aircraft Required} = \frac{\text{10-day Requirement}}{\left(\begin{matrix}\text{Tons per} \\ \text{flying hour}\end{matrix}\right) \times 10 \left(\begin{matrix}\text{Flying hours per} \\ \text{aircraft per day}^{19}\end{matrix}\right)}$$

When these aircraft requirement figures have been derived — one for each aircraft on each channel — they are aggregated by the channel groups defined in the last section. Since the traffic requirements change from Period I to Period II, it is necessary, of course, to determine these aircraft requirements separately for both periods. Notice the very important fact that *aircraft* requirements, not *traffic* requirements, are the numbers aggregated. The results of this computation are given in Table 7.

Another item needed before the minimization problem can be attacked consists of the lists of productivity ratios. We can derive these ratios from the aircraft-requirement figures of Table 7, arriving at the *weighted* average for each aggregate channel of the productivity ratios of the channels aggregated. Thus, for example, on Channel C in Period I:

$$\frac{\text{C-97 Productivity}}{\text{HC-500 Productivity}} = \frac{\begin{matrix}\text{Number of HC-500's that would be needed} \\ \text{to do the whole Channel C job in Period I}\end{matrix}}{\begin{matrix}\text{Number of C-97's that would be needed} \\ \text{to do the whole Channel C job in Period I}\end{matrix}}$$

$$= \frac{35.85}{124.69} = 0.288$$

This ratio means that the C-97 is 28.8 per cent as productive as the HC-500 on Channel C. In Table 8, these ratios are given for each aggregate channel and each pair of air-

TABLE 7.
NUMBER OF AIRCRAFT OF EACH TYPE REQUIRED TO CARRY OUT EACH CHANNEL JOB ALONE

| | Aircraft type | | | | | | | |
| | Period I | | | | Period II | | | |
Channel	C-97	HC-400	HC-500	HC-600	C-97	HC-400	HC-500	HC-600
A	20.2	10.3	5.0	3.9	20.2	10.3	5.0	3.9
B	219.9	111.7	47.6	41.7	219.8	111.7	47.6	41.7
C	124.7	93.7	35.8	35.0	124.7	93.7	35.8	35.0
D	9.2	3.6	2.3	1.3	18.3	7.2	4.7	2.7
E	10.8	5.1	2.5	1.8	21.7	10.2	5.0	3.6
F	36.2	17.8	8.5	6.3	72.5	35.6	17.0	12.6
G	5.0	2.2	1.2	.8	10.1	4.5	2.4	1.6
H	19.4	9.5	3.5	3.4	38.8	19.0	7.0	6.9
K	1.0	.4	.2	.2	2.1	.8	.5	.3
L	1.6	1.3	.4	.4	3.1	2.5	.8	.9
M	25.7	20.0	5.0	6.8	51.3	39.9	9.9	13.5
P	156.6	123.0	35.0	41.4	191.7	150.7	43.0	50.4

craft.[20] There is much redundancy in the table, but this makes it all the easier to compute, and separate lists for each pair of aircraft are worth the trouble.

The various tables that have been presented are all that we need to solve for a series of least-cost fleets. We shall not attempt to reproduce the computational process here,[21] but will describe the optimum assignment of aircraft to channels that resulted from the Fleet I computation. With the aid of the cost and productivity information presented earlier, the reader will then be able to check for himself whether the conditions for an optimum hold and whether the fleet we claim to be less costly than any of the others with the required capability is *in fact* less costly. As in many other mathematical problems, obtaining the solution is rather difficult, but recognizing the solution is quite easy.

The aircraft assignment of Fleet I is shown in Table 9. We know that this fleet is the least costly because it is possible to find a set of prices (that is, costs) which, for the assignment portrayed, satisfies the least-cost condition:[22] Namely, a given aircraft is in the fleet only if, on any channel where it operates, the ratio of its productivity to the productivity of any other aircraft on that channel is *at least as great* as the ratio of its marginal cost to the other aircraft's marginal cost. The set of prices consists of:

$ 3.69 million for the C-97 in Period I
5.34 million for the HC-400 in Period I

TABLE 8.
PRODUCTIVITY RATIOS

	Channel	C-97	HC-400	HC-500
	A	51		
	B	51		
	C	75		
	D	39		
	E	47		
HC-400	F	49		
	G	44		
	H	49		
	K	41		
	L	81		
	M	78		
	P	79		
	A	25	48	
	B	22	43	
	C	29	38	
	D	25	65	
	E	23	49	
HC-500	F	23	48	
	G	24	55	
	H	18	37	
	K	23	56	
	L	25	31	
	M	19	25	
	P	22	28	
	A	19	37	78
	B	19	37	88
	C	28	37	98
	D	15	37	58
	E	17	36	73
HC-600	F	17	35	74
	G	16	36	66
	H	18	36	98
	K	16	38	68
	L	27	34	109
	M	26	34	136
	P	26	34	118

An example of how the Table is to be read:

An HC-400 is 38% as productive as an HC-500 on Channel C.

TABLE 9.
AIRCRAFT CHANNEL ASSIGNMENT — FLEET 1

Channel	Period I				Period II			
	C-97	HC-400	HC-500	HC-600	C-97	HC-400	HC-500	HC-600
A		10.3						3.9
B		111.7				111.7		
C	103.4		6.1			31.4		23.2
D		3.6				7.2		
E		5.1						3.6
F		17.8						12.6
G		2.2						1.6
H			3.5					6.9
K		0.4						
L			0.4					0.9
M			5.0				9.9	
P			35.0				43.0	
Total	103.4	151.2	50.0	—	0	151.2	53.0	52.7

12.80 million for the HC-500 in Period I
5.54 million for the C-97 in Period II
5.49 million for the HC-400 in Period II
16.70 million for the HC-500 in Period II
14.70 million for the HC-600 in Period II

We see that the C-97 price in Period I and the HC-500 and HC-600 prices in Period II are the same as the corresponding cost coefficients in Table 6. This is as it should be, for in each of these cases no production limit or inventory limit has been reached, and in the cases of the latter two aircraft no retirement takes place in Period II. In Period I the HC-500 price is somewhat higher than the corresponding cost coefficient in Table 6 because the Period I production limit of 50 aircraft is reached before the requirements have been satisfied on those channels where the HC-500 excels. In this case the fictitious rental charge referred to earlier has equated demand and supply for this aircraft.

The most interesting pricing phenomenon in this fleet concerns the HC-400. The Period I price is higher and the Period II price lower than in Table 6. Part, but not all, of the Period II share of depreciation is being charged to Period I. The reader may recall that this phenomenon is compatible only with equal numbers of HC-400's in the Period I fleet and the Period II fleet.

With these prices, the reader can check whether price and productivity ratios are consistent with the assignment presented. Perhaps the most instructive step would be to attempt to find a less costly fleet by a small change. For understanding the mechanics of the model, of course, new prices should accompany these charges, and the conditions for the solution checked.

NOTES

Author's Note
This chapter was written by C. B. McGuire, who participated in a study of military air transport systems carried out for the U.S. Air Force in the Logistics Department of RAND's Economics Division. D. M. Fort and A. S. Manne helped in the development of the model. The *methods* used in this illustrative analysis are similar to those of the original study.

Editor's Note
In reprinting this chapter as a paper, the figures and tables have been renumbered.

Footnotes
[1] Still other routes can be devised, of course, but the ones listed cover most of the interesting possibilities.
[2] We can regard other piston-engined aircraft as being included in this category, as they can be translated into "C-97 equivalents."
[3] This statement is correct, whether size is taken to mean maximum "weight allowable cabin load," "space allowable

cabin load," or "takeoff weight."

    [4] This statement exaggerates the picture only slightly.

    [5] Interested readers should consult *The Economics of Defense in the Nuclear Age.* by Charles J. Hitch and Roland N. McKean, Cambridge, Mass.: Harvard University Press, 1967. pp 114-118.

    [6] In the language of economics, the models trace out the "marginal rates of substitution" in incurring costs and in producing transport services. These are the trade-offs referred to in Chapter 7. of Hitch and McKean, *op. cit.*

    [7] We shall try to present enough information to indicate clearly the manner in which the calculations were made and to enable the reader to go over especially important computations.

    [8] By "production availability" is meant the number of aircraft that can be produced in a *single* facility. A second facility would lift this limitation, of course, but since the costs of additional tooling and learning make these extra aircraft substantially more expensive, this alternative has, for simplicity, been ignored.

    [9] See Chapter 7 where this concept of efficiency is discussed in a more general context. (Hitch and McKean, *op. cit.*)

    [10] Similar in the sense that the HC-400 performs relatively better on those same channels where the HC-600 performs relatively better.

    [11] Tons delivered per *hour*, rather than per *flying hour* is a better definition of productivity, but since the same daily flying capability is assumed for all of our aircraft, the two definitions are equally satisfactory here.

    [12] A payload-radius curve shows maximum payload for any given radius, the radius being the distance to which the aircraft carries the payload when it must return without refueling at destination.

    [13] Of course, where the Clark-Bangdhad leg comprises the whole channel, as in Channel 61, only the radius curves need be used.

    [14] Carried out to the nearest thousandth to correspond with figures in Table 5.

    [15] These two sets of numbers need not be the same since an aircraft may be procured at the beginning of Period I as a stopgap measure and then be retired at the beginning of Period II (i.e. not operated in Period II).

    [16] These remarks should not be construed as a *general* argument for hand computation as opposed to electronic computation, for with special measures, the latter can, of course, also answer some of the subtler questions mentioned. Too often, the virtues of hand computations in this respect are forgotten.

    [17] Some of the passenger channels are not plotted separately because they fell so close together. They all lie in the shaded rectangle.

    [18] To repeat an earlier definition, "marginal cost" is the extra cost of buying and using an additional airplane.

    [19] The number of flying hours obtainable per aircraft per day is assumed to be the same for all aircraft types, ten hours.

    [20] The mathematically inclined reader will notice that these productivity ratios need not be precisely the same for Period I and Period II on aggregate channels composed of both deployment and routine resupply work, such as P. Since the difference is small, however, we use the ratios from Period I throughout.

    [21] The solution can be obtained by the use of a somewhat extended version of the method of Lagrange multipliers (H.W. Kuhn and A.W. Tucker, "Non-Linear Programming," in *Proceedings of the Second Berkeley Symposium on Mathematical Statistics and Probability*, Berkeley, University of California, 1951)

    [22] Moreover, this is still the least-cost fleet after we take into account the $50 million initial outlay for HC-600 production (a quantity that could not be allowed for in this linear model).

ABOUT THE AUTHORS

Charles J. Hitch gained his B.A. with highest distinction from the University of Arizona in 1931, and was a Rhodes Scholar at the University of Oxford in 1934. During the years 1935-48 he was fellow, praelector and tutor at Queen's College, Oxford, and from 1948-61 he was Chief of the Economics Division of the RAND Corporation. From 1961-65 he was Assistant Secretary of Defense (Comptroller) and since 1967 he has been President of the University of California at Berkeley. He is a past-President of the Operations Research Society of America.

Roland N. McKean took his A. B., A. M., and Ph.D. at the University of Chicago. From 1951-64 he was a research economist at the RAND Corporation, and from 1964-67 he was Professor of Economics at the University of California, Los Angeles. Since 1968 he has been Professor of Economics at the University of Virginia. He has published a number of books and papers on his principal professional interest, public finance.

Cost-Benefit Analysis in Evaluating Alternative Planning Policies for Greater London

A. D. J. Flowerdew

A particular approach to the evaluation of "inputs" and "outputs" in social planning is known as "cost-benefit" analysis. This methodology is discussed in the papers by Wilson and by Chambers and Hindle. In this paper, Flowerdew describes a practical case study in which a cost-benefit approach is used. It concerns a particular set of planning alternatives for the urban development of London, England. Very many transportation planning problems have been subject to similar methods of analysis.

"Andy Cobham: Do I have to know about economics before I'm permitted to build my cities?"

Arnold Wesker. *Their Very Own and Golden City*

1. INTRODUCTION

The Greater London Council was set up in 1963 as part of a major re-organisation of local government in London. It covers an area of 620 square miles, with a population of nearly 8 million, and is more than five times the size of the former London County Council with more than double the population. At the same time 32 new London Boroughs were established, with populations of about a quarter of a million each, covering the whole area apart from the square mile of the City of London. Local authority functions and powers are split between the G.L.C. and the London Boroughs. In particular, the planning function is divided, with the G.L.C. carrying out a strategic role and the Boroughs being responsible for detailed planning in their areas.

The major task of G.L.C. planning is the preparation and maintenance of the Greater London Development Plan, due to be submitted to the Minister of Housing and Local Government sometime around the date of presentation of this paper. This Plan will consist of a series of policy statements on subjects like population, housing, employment, transportation, open space and shopping. These policy statements will be supplemented by maps, and by research material presented simultaneously, product of a research group about 50 strong, possibly the largest planning research team in the world.

Research in planning, as in other fields, has several aims. It has to specify the data which must be collected for analysis, it must carry out the analysis of data to define more precisely the planning problems to be solved; it must forecast the likely effects of alternative planning policies, including the "do-nothing" alternative, and it must evaluate these effects, so as to guide decision-makers on which policies should be adopted. It is with the last of these activities that I am concerned here.

2. STRATEGY

The use of the word strategy is intended to imply that the policies for each major subject should be consistent with each other. It would be foolish, for instance, to adopt a policy of encouraging economic growth while at the same time lowering housing densities, maintaining the Green Belt and

SOURCE: Reprinted from *Cost-Benefit Analysis* (Papers presented at a Symposium held in The Hague in July, 1969, under the aegis of the NATO Scientific Affairs Committee.) Edited by M.G. Kendall, London: English Universities Press, 1971, pp. 109-120, by permission of the author and publishers.

discouraging commuting. There would then be no labour to produce the economic growth. This seems obvious, but there is an understandable tendency, for planners, politicians and private citizens alike, to suggest that through their ingenuity in devising plans, the interests of every section of the community can simultaneously be advanced. If policies are considered separately, the self-deception can be maintained, but when they are taken together, in the light of the constraints placed by availability of capital, labour and land, it is clear that planning is a question of compromise, or of allocating scarce resources, not of panaceas. Three examples for illustration: much housing in Inner London is crowded or unfit; housing considerations suggest re-housing at lower densities, and taking more land, but the same areas are often desperately short of parks and play areas. Traffic management schemes (usually re-routing traffic round one-way systems) have succeeded in maintaining Central London traffic overall journey speeds, despite a large growth in the volume of traffic;[1] but the use of formerly quiet residential streets by fast and heavy traffic has increased environmental costs. Satisfying housing demand efficiently implies more investment in public housing and low price accommodation in poor areas, and in owner-occupied property in the better-off places, yet this policy is likely to increase social problems associated with one-class communities, the effects of which are realised in extreme form in parts of the United States. These examples could be multiplied.

The major strategic issue for London is that of centralization versus decentralization. In over-simplied terms, is it better to encourage the centralization of activity in London, or to shed as much as possible of the activity to new or expanded towns, counter-magnets, or new cities in other parts of the country. For some time now, both central and local government have been pursuing a policy of decentralization influenced by the Barlow Report (1940,[2] the Abercrombie plan and the views of most of the planning profession. Whether for this or for other reasons, the population of the G.L.C. area has been falling slowly since the early 1950's, and is expected to fall quite dramatically in the next decade.

Now that decentralization policies are beginning to bite, should public authorities continue to encourage them or should they hold back and remove some of the existing constraints and incentives? (The constraints and incentives include: Office Development Permits, Industrial Development Certificates, regional subsidies such as capital allowances, SET rebates, etc. — central government; land use zoning and plot ratio restrictions and new and expanded towns schemes — local authority.) It is almost impossible to quantify how far the projected population decrease is caused by planning measures, and how far it is a natural process: moreover to get a complete picture it would be necessary to consider how much is invested by Government in London relative to the rest of the country. So to obtain the basis for a judgement it is necessary to examine in detail the likely costs and benefits of the alternative strategies.

The main costs and benefits to be considered are:

(i) productivity. Output per man in manufacturing industry is higher, job for job, in Greater London than in the rest of the country — in particular the rest of S.E. Region. Not much can be deduced from these figures (which date from 1958; 1963 Census of Productivity data are not available at the time of writing). But on a detailed analysis the most plausible hypothesis seems to be that the productivity differences reflect external economies of scale. In so far as these result from specialisation, close geographical ties between firms and their customers, suppliers and competitors or the volume and range of services available, one might expect such a productivity difference to exist also in the service sector where direct productivity measurement is not possible. If the productivity differences are real, one could expect losses in output from decentralizing economic activity. The problem of measuring this loss with any degree of precision remains.

(ii) housing and infrastructure. Costs here depend very much on the pace of decentralization. It seems unlikely that many areas of London would have vacant property, beyond the usual float of vacancies required by the market. What is most likely is that decentralization would reduce the need for new building and bring down occupancy rates. There is an obvious benefit here, which may be partly offset by the construction of a greater number of new dwellings. Much of the social infrastructure however is likely to cost more on decentralization — at least that which is associated with urban uses, and with the possible exception of roads (see below). If open space provision is also regarded as infrastructure, on the grounds that it is a community need, decentralization would bring benefits. Measurement of these factors is clearly quite complicated: perhaps a rough guide could be obtained by comparing new or expanded town costs to the extra costs of renovating or re-building an equivalent number of houses in the conurbation, including land costs where new land has to be taken for modern density standards, and with some allowance for increasing open space provision.

(iii) congestion and travel. Congestion costs in London are well known to be heavy, both on road and rail, and journeys to work are often formidably long. Such factors can be costed, but there are some quite difficult problems to consider. Since expensive and extensive transport investments are on the way, against what system should one measure congestion costs? And what assumptions are to be made about future pricing policy and other controls, on road and rail, parking and taxes? In principle one should no doubt compare optimum pricing and investment policies for the centralization and decentralization cases (if the implied assumption of rational behaviour on the authorities' part is sustainable) but such a study would need to be of an order of magnitude more sophisticated than the £1 million, 5 year London Transportation Study. This study, advanced for its time, nevertheless failed to take into account the price demand relationship, failed to produce a social rate of return calculation for the G.L.C.'s proposed roads programme as such and failed to produce a meaningful comparison of the relative merits of investment in road and rail improvements.

While one can look for short cuts on some of these points, a clear indication of the right strategy must wait for the next batch of information and research. Crude numerical studies carried out at the G.L.C. suggested that the answer was not obvious. In this situation a compromise strategy for London seems right at the present time — not to resist the trend for people and firms to move out, but to be more selective in operating the incentives for them to do so.

This section has dealt with strategy at some length, in the hope of dispelling the rather widespread belief that the solution to London's problems is obvious, and planning should therefore be concerned with means of getting there, rather than with considering what the overall objective should be.

3. POLICIES/PROJECTS

More was achieved (and far more research effort was used) in carrying out cost benefit studies into particular policies or projects. Four case studies will be described here. Two were in fact carried out in support of policy research, two intended to help in development projects, but in effect all four can be regarded as case-studies. The case studies are disguised in this account to avoid identification, and simplified to avoid the paper becoming too long: I hope nevertheless to put over some of the flavour of the work. They deal respectively with Central London redevelopment, a suburban town centre proposal, residential density, and a proposed new civic centre.

3.1 Central London Redevelopment

Central London — broadly the area surrounded by the mainline termini — contains within it many areas which do not resemble or function as effective parts of the centre of a large conurbation. Commercial inertia, coupled with the additional friction on changing land use which planning policies impose, have left areas which attract the attention of architects, planners, and entrepreneurs as potential sites for ambitious redevelopment. This study concerned one such district: the Committee was to be advised on the most suitable land use zonings for the district, part of a Comprehensive Development Area. For various reasons a number of unconventional possibilities were eliminated and the alternatives were boiled down to three:

A. retention of commercial and some office uses
B. replacement of these by residential and
C. a mixture of A and B.

Capital costs of acquisition and clearance and resulting land values had been estimated in the normal way, showing a very large loss of Scheme B over Scheme A, which was not much reduced by the compromise proposal. But this was unlikely to satisfy the Committee as clinching the matter, especially since it had requested particular attention to be paid to the problem of traffic congestion. It was suggested that Scheme A should be debited with the cost of road works to cater for the traffic generated by commercial uses, but in the dense mesh of Central London a road scheme could hardly be judged within the limited area of this one district. Anyway there were other factors to consider. There was thought to be a case for increasing the residential population of the centre to cut down on commuting problems. A cost-benefit study was called for.

The major factors to be incorporated in the study, apart from those in the financial appraisal, were taken to be the effects on road congestion of removing the traffic generated by commercial land-uses; the change in commuting expected by increasing household potential in the centre; and environmental changes. In assessing these factors, two complicated problems of principle arose. The first is that one needs to make assumptions that alternative locations for residents in Scheme A and for firms in B (unless assumed to go out of business): the second that we are recommending land-use zonings, not actual buildings, so that costings, traffic generations, etc., can only be taken as average values. Because of this second problem we baulked at assessing the environmental changes: it seemed wrong to suppose that new commercial development would ipso facto be better or worse than new housing. The first problem was treated by assuming that the change from commerce to residential would not be compensated by an equivalent change in the reverse direction elsewhere in Central London, and that if housing is not provided here it would have to be increased at the fringe of the conurbation.

3.2 Congestion Costs

If one form of development is likely to generate more traffic than another on an already overcrowded network of roads, this traffic will impose extra external costs on the environment. These external costs will arise because the traffic generated by the development will tend to reduce the speed and hence the journey times of the traffic already on the network. The consequent reduction in speed cannot of course be precisely calculated, but estimates of the average reduction in speed have been produced by the Road Research

Laboratory in the work for the Smeed Report on Road Pricing (1964).[3] The formula used in that report relates the marginal social cost of congestion for an additional vehicle mile of traffic on the network to current vehicle speeds, the desired speeds of vehicles and to the social costs of additional time spent in travelling, which is composed of evaluation of an individual's time together with that portion of operating costs which varies with operating time. The desired speed which is assumed corresponds to the speed at which traffic would flow along the network in the absence of other vehicles. The equation takes the form

$$M = b (d-v)/v^2,$$

where M is the marginal social cost of an additional vehicle mile, b is a constant derived from the mix of traffic on the roads, the marginal operating costs, and time values, d is the desired speed and v the actual speed on the network.

To apply this formula to traffic generations it was necessary to derive an estimate of the most likely number of additional generations by type of vehicle, time of day and distance travelled. Since we were dealing with Central London redevelopment it seemed reasonable to suppose that all trips were radiating out from the centre. This was a useful assumption since it meant we did not have to take into account the direction of travel. There is a reasonably good relationship between distance from the centre of London and vehicles' average speeds. We assumed that desired speeds would also be likely to increase as distance from Central London increased since the density of the road network itself becomes less, the obstructions fewer, and one would not expect free flow in Central London in any case to reach the levels that it does on suburban roads. The formula can now be applied to produce a marginal social cost derived from the number of additional traffic generations which can in turn be related to the amount of floor space provided. Figure 1 overleaf illustrates the process.

Estimating the social cost of congestion on public transport posed rather different problems. We were fairly easily able to calculate the expected effect on the length of journey to work. Clearly providing more homes in the central area and fewer jobs is likely to reduce the average length of travel, and our best estimate was that this was approximately two train

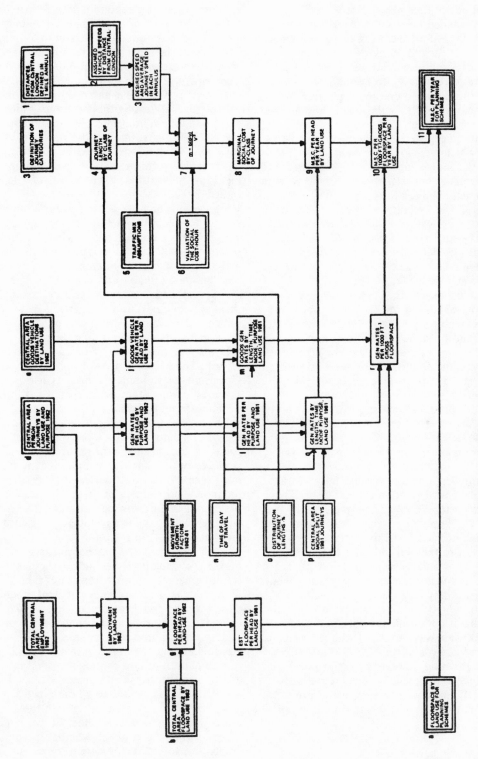

FIGURE 1. THE CALCULATION OF MARGINAL SOCIAL COSTS OF VEHICULAR CONGESTION FOR PLANNING ALTERNATIVES

loads of commuters per day. It is less easy, without detailed knowledge of British Rail and London Transport operating costs, and what the policy is for providing extra services once congestion in overcrowding terms has reached a certain level, to evaluate the social cost involved, even if one could get a reasonably good measure of the social cost of discomfort from overcrowding.

At this stage, therefore we examined the figures which we had already obtained. Inclusion of the congestion costs effects had reduced the differential between Scheme B and Scheme A by something like a third, indicating that road congestion was certainly a significant factor in location policy but it did not seem in this case to be sufficiently large to outweigh the financial losses involved. It was our judgment that the public congestion cost was not likely to be greater than that on the roads. We therefore concluded that Scheme B — and the same applied to Scheme C — were not really improvements on Scheme A. It is however worth noting that the same calculations, applied to particular sites in the area, did not necessarily show the same results. There were instances where a particular proposed commercial development, while showing a purely financial profit, produced a social loss when congestion costs were taken into account. This indicates that it may be of some value to go through these calculations in considering whether or not to adopt such schemes.

The implications for land use policy as a whole in Central London are less clear. The analysis briefly described above can really not be taken to apply to anything other than marginal alterations in the existing land use pattern. In so far as it indicates that road congestion is not an argument for reducing the amount of land allocated to employment generating uses, it may be taken as one justification for continuing this kind of activity and possibly expanding it within the central area, a policy which in some ways conflicts with the objectives, for example of the Location of Offices Bureau. It would however be rash to make any such sweeping conclusions on the basis of a purely marginal study, which in itself has not covered by any means all the important factors.

4. TOWN CENTRES

Most of London's shopping centres are located at junctions of main roads and along stretches of busy arterial routes in and out of London. In the inner areas the buildings themselves are often fifty and more years old. The growth of traffic since the war, in particular the growth of car based shopping, had led to great interest by the local authorities in preparing renewal schemes. At the same time private developers, finding that the scope for office building was limited by controls, have tended to turn to shopping redevelopments as the next best likely source of a high return on capital.

As a result there are getting on for a hundred shemes for redevelopment of shopping centres within Greater London alone. Many of these schemes include both development of roads and shops, and the more ambitious ones often incorporate a public transport interchange and a number of new civic buildings. Many of them are envisaged as a partnership between public and private development, public development being responsible for roads, very often some housing and civic buildings as well. The Ministry of Housing and Local Government will prepare a priority list of schemes to which they are prepared to allocate resources from a central pool.

The criteria for priorites in these town centre redevelopment schemes — and there must be priorities for the total expenditure involved would come to thousands of millions of pounds – must take into account two factors. Firstly, the individual viability of these schemes interpreted not in a narrow commercial sense — will the shops pay the developers? — but in a social sense — do the total benefits for this scheme provide an adequate social return on the costs involved? Secondly, whether the resulting balance of provision is desirable, for it may be that two redevelopment schemes close together could each in isolation provide an adequate return, but the combination of them results in an over provision of shopping. Hence planning must take into account the overall pattern of new centres provided in addition to the merits and demerits of each individual case. The study to be described here in outline was concerned solely with the evaluation of individual schemes. It was undertaken in order to establish whether it would be possible to institute a system for evaluating each town centre proposal, in the same way that the Ministry of Transport assesses road proposals, and allocates money on the basis of the results. The centre studied in the pilot was typical of many redevelopment schemes. The existing centre lay at the intersection of two major roads, and it was proposed to redevelop within a ring road so that most of the new shopping development would be in a pedestrian precinct.

It proved possible to establish a rate of return for this particular scheme although a number of difficulties were encountered, some of which really need to be overcome before it could be claimed that the method is really sound. One of the most difficult of these was in evaluating the benefits from improved shopping facilities. The only data available were on increased rents paid by shopkeepers to the developers which had to be forecast, of course, to produce a commercial rate of return. This return does not however take into account any additional benefits for the shopkeepers which may be created nor benefits to the shoppers themselves. The only benefits credited to the shoppers themselves were savings in accident costs, because vehicle/pedestrian conflict in the centre would be virtually eliminated. In fact no non-financial costs and benefits were assessed, except for traffic. The analysis of traffic was based on an assignment technique, developed especially to deal with small networks. Incidentally, this showed the ring road to be a rather poor solution to the traffic problem, since the road was of too low capacity to handle the peak flows of vehicles, and traffic distances were increased on this network against the previous one. (The scheme was later revised with a much more satisfactory road network.)

A rate of return was however calculated, and it was about 5%. Taking into account unquantified factors, which on the whole seemed to be against the scheme, with the exception of consumer surplus for shoppers, it was concluded that the scheme was perhaps a doubtful starter. A more detailed description of the study is given in Saalmans (1967).[4]

5. DENSITY

Among the most pressing redevelopment problems are the large areas in Inner London of mainly 19th century housing where a high building density and high occupancy rates combine to produce severe overcrowding. Some few of these areas — Earl's Court, Hampstead, etc. — have been largely taken over by groups of single people or childless families for whom high density living can be attractive, and who can afford rents which will maintain the property in good condition. But much is in really bad condition and at or approaching slum level. Redevelopment is clearly desirable, and in at least some cases money should not be lacking — two of the richest London Boroughs, Westminster and Kensington and Chelsea contain large chunks of such property in Paddington and North Kensington — but the problem of overspill or what to do with the surplus population if redevelopment is confined to approved residential densities, is tricky.

In any case, if density standards are to be taken seriously, a critical examination is necessary. We decided to take as a case study a small area, currently inhabited at 250 persons per acre, and compare the effects of redevelopment at densities equivalent to 250, 140 and 75 persons per acre, assuming the overspill population could be housed on the fringe of the conurbation. Again this was a marginal study; it was recognised that if low densities turned out preferable for large areas of Inner London, further comparisons would have to be made with housing beyond the Green Belt.

The most easily quantified factors, land and construction costs, journeys to work and congestion costs, turned out to be fairly evenly balanced, the extra costs involved in high density construction being nearly equal to the cost of acquiring more land on the fringes. Two more intangible factors appear capable of a decisive influence on the study.

The first is the cost of compelling some proportion of people to move from where they live, involving some disruption of communities, family ties, and so on. Measures of these costs are not yet established: it is possible that some limits could be set by considering what extra rents unwilling movers would have to pay to move back, or unwilling stayers would need to pay to move out. Social surveys could establish what proportion would accept a move. From these data a crude measure could be obtained. The social cost involved depends on how it is decided who would stay; if matters can be arranged so that those who are least resistant to moving do so, the cost can be minimized.

The second intangible factor relates to the benefits obtained from housing of various types. High densities do not necessarily mean high flats of course, but the higher the density the less easy it is to match the provision of dwelling types to the preferred choices of the families. So benefits from reducing densities can be expected by enabling people to occupy more preferred types of housing.

Two approaches are possible here. One is to infer relative preferences from rent levels in the private housing market. The main objection to this procedure is that private and public housing markets in London cater on the whole for very different classes of people, not so much with regard to income level, as to family structure and geographic mobility. The second approach is via a survey in which people are asked, first to rank their choice of housing types, and second to estimate the differential rent which would induce them to shift to a less preferred type, or allow them to go to a more preferred type. There are obvious difficulties in this approach, but it is hoped that it can be tried.

6. CIVIC CENTRE

When the London Boroughs were set up many of them were amalgamations of existing authorities: consequently their municipal and civic facilities are spread over a number of locations. There is an argument for centralizing these, and we carried out a study on one such proposal. Three alternative sites for the new centre were to be compared, and it was also proposed to incorporate some new facilities.

The list of costs and benefits considered were as follows:
- (i)   Construction, demolition and clearance.
- (ii)   Land costs and replacement of public open space.
- (iii) Effect of concentration on costs and services.
- (iv)   Journey to work costs.
- (v)   Accessibility of residents to exisiting facilities.
- (vi)   Benefits from new facilities.
- (vii) Running and maintenance costs.
- (viii) Imponderables (aesthetic: civic pride).

The first two items in the above list were obtained: there was some uncertainty with

regard to one site, located in the middle of a proposed large open space, there being some support for the view that use of the open space would be enhanced by the civic centre. On balance it seemed best however to include the replacement cost of open space, because of the counter argument that breaking up a continuous green area could have a greater social cost than using the whole of a small area. (By analogy taking 10 acres out of Hampstead Heath could not necessarily be compensated for by an equivalent acreage not adjoining the Heath.)

Sketchy studies were carried out on (iii), (iv) and (v), enough to indicate the rough orders of magnitude and demonstrate that they were relatively small. Taking a generous view the capitalized value of benefits would be around quarter of a million pounds, compared with construction costs of several millions.

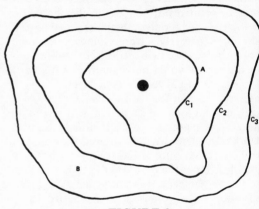

FIGURE 2

Benefits from new facilities were estimated by a Hotelling type analysis, using data from an existing recreation centre (Swiss Cottage) and an existing Central Library. The method used analyses the costs paid to use such facilities, including travel costs and time valuation, and produces an implied demand curve. It is illustrated in Figure 2.

The central blob represents some attraction such as a swimming pool, fishing pond, library, etc. The squiggly lines are equi-cost contours dividing up the map into regions where the cost of travel to the blob is the same. Thus it costs c_1 to travel from point A and between c_2 and c_3 to travel from point B. The population inside c_1 is p_1, and the number visiting the blob from this region is n_1; similarly the population between c_1 and c_2 is p_2, and so on, Normally one would have:

$$\frac{n_1}{p_1} \geq \frac{n_2}{p_2} \geq \frac{n_3}{p_3}$$

It is assumed that the population is homogeneous within each ring with regard to their desire to vist the blob (an assumption that would not be satisfied if they had chosen where to live because of proximity to it). But if this is so, then of the people living inside C_1, at least a proportion N_2/p_2 must be receiving some surplus benefit, since this proportion of people travel from outside the ring. If we assume a linear demand curve then their benefit will be

$$p_1 \left\{ \frac{n_3}{p_3} \left(\frac{c_2 + c_3 - c_1}{2} \right) + \left(\frac{n_2}{p_2} - \frac{n_3}{p_3} \right) \left(\frac{c_2 - c_1}{2} \right) \right\}$$

Similarly we can calculate a surplus for those inside C_2. Even without assuming a linear demand curve, we can estimate upper and lower bounds for the total surplus. Details need not be described here.

There are considerable problems in applying this method to real data, not least the existence of competing facilities in the neighborhood (to account fully for these one needs to use a gravity model formulation). But the figures produced — about £85,000 per year for the recreation centre and £25,000 for the library — seemed plausible. The method of course does not take into account health and education benefits except in so far as these are appreciated and valued by consumers.

The last two items were not estimated. The short fall between capitalized benefits and costs was around £5 million and it seemed unlikely that they could possibly make up the difference. Item (vii) is likely to increase the cost side, especially for new facilities.

Analysis of the separate elements of the proposal showed that the Recreation Centre was the best bet, though in no case were benefits more than 80% of the costs.

ACKNOWLEDGEMENTS

The work described in this note is to be credited to members of the Cost Benefit Studies Section rather than to me. The people concerned are Carol Barnett, Robin Carruthers, Richard Carter, Donald Hoodless, Frank Little, Peter Saalmans, Bob Stannard, and Ray Thomas. To each of them grateful thanks, and also to Donald Cross and Ian Carruthers, Head and Deputy Head of Survey and Research Group and to many other colleagues too numerous to mention.

AUTHOR'S NOTE

This paper is based on work carried out by the Cost Benefit Studies Section, Survey and Research Group, Planning Department, Greater London Council, which I was in charge of from February 1966 to December 1968. It does not necessarily reflect the policy of the Greater London Council in any way.

REFERENCES

[1] Thomson however puts this down to better driving and better cars. See Thomson, J. M. "The Value of Traffic Management" *J. Transport Economics and Policy* 2 (1, 2 and 3) 1968.
[2] *Royal Commission on the Distribution of the Industrial Population* (Barlow Report) Cmd., 6153, H.M.S.O., 1940.
[3] *Road Policy, the Economic and Technical Possibilities* (Smeed Report) H.M.S.O., 1964.
[4] Saalmans, P. D. "Evaluation of Town Centre Redevelopment Schemes" *Proceedings of the P. T. R. C. Seminar on Urban Renewal Cost Benefit* 25-31, 1967.

ABOUT THE AUTHOR

A. D. J. Flowerdew read mathematics and moral science at Kings College Cambridge and from 1957-61 did activity sampling and stock control for the National Coal Board. From 1961-66 he worked for Richard Thomas and Baldwins, and from 1966-68 he was in charge of the Cost-Benefit

Studies Section of the Greater London Council Planning Department. In 1968 he became Deputy Director of Research and Head of the O. R. group for the Royal Commission on the Third London Airport. Since 1971 he has been a Senior Lecturer in the Department of Economics at the London School of Economics and Political Science. He is currently a consultant on a number of projects, including one on the value of secondary information systems for the Office for Scientific and Technical Information (OSTI).

Some Principles of Practical Welfare Economics

Julian L. Simon

In this paper, Simon examines the possible applications of economic techniques to the problems of non-profit-making organisations (which include nearly all libraries). The most important characteristic of these organisations is that, unlike commercial organisations which normally expect a tangible return for their services or products, they are forced to allocate scarce resources without any payment in return. The author proposes a systematic method for solving the resource allocation problem in welfare organisations and concludes that, provided the analyst is willing to make sufficient assumptions, it should be possible to bring economic techniques to bear on welfare problems, and to expect reasonable and useful results from such analyses.

Non-profit organizations must often allocate scarce resources without return payment of any kind. It is this non-exchange characteristic that really defines the hard-core problems in welfare economics. Such non-exchange transfers form a large part of total resource transfers in our society. These are some examples:

1) Decisions of non-profit institutions about how to distribute their resources among several kinds of output. Should a hospital allocate marginal dollars to new ambulances or new surgical equipment? Should a nation spend more for infantry and less for missiles?

2) Decisions of non-profit institutions about whether a given output is worth the cost. Should a hospital ask the community for money to buy new surgical equipment? Should a nation spend more or less for defense? Should a state hire more highway police to reduce the number of accidents?

3) Decisions about intra-institutional transfers in profit and non-profit organisations. This is the transfer-price problem which appears within organizations like the Soviet Union and General Motors. Though the latter operates for profit, and sells its product through a public market, transfers within the firm do not take through a market and there is *quid pro quo* in common money.

4) Decisions of communities about the regulation of private-enterprise actions that have a public cost. Should a town require factories to render their sewage harmless? L. W. Kapp has discussed specific examples.[4]

5) Taxation and other community decisions that affect income distribution. How much more welfare is provided by a dollar tax reduction for a poor family compared to a dollar reduction for a rich family? Such issues must be considered, in addition to the macroeconomic and growth problems that usually come into the argument.

These decisions will be made with or without assistance from economists. The appropriate question is whether economic analysis and investigation can *improve* the quality of decisions even a little compared to the ordinary common-sense reasoning that now underlies the decisions.

From one point of view, economics need make no special provisions for non-exchange transfers by non-profit institutions. If the institutions would specify objective revenue and cost functions, the calculi of business economics could be adopted bodily.[9] But the specification of these functions is often the most important part of the job, and if economists do not do it prior to offering the standard business-economics solutions, the specification job just will not get done rationally. There is not profit-and-loss pressure to force trial-and-error learning upon non-profit decision-makers, as there

SOURCE: Reprinted from *Management Science* 13 (10) June 1967, pp. B621-B630, by permission of the author and publishers.

is in firms in an enterprise economy.

Economic analysis of non-profit situations can also work in the other direction, by making explicit the assumptions that are implicit in non-profit policy decisions. For example, the value that a hospital or community places upon a given probability of saving a human life may be deduced from decisions to purchase or not to purchase hospital equipment and services. And elsewhere I show that a marginal dollar of wages that might be lost to a cigarette worker if cigarette advertising were banned is associated with the increase of 100 hours of human life[7].

Ferreting out implicit assumptions can also help rationalize subsequent decisions. If a hospital discovers that its decisions about surgical equipment, ambulances, and other expenditures all approximate a value of $50,000 for the life of a thirty-year-old adult, this then provides a yardstick to be used in future decisions. Future decisions can then benefit by some consistent rationality and the equivalence of marginal utility, even if all the decisions are too high or too low.

The common responses of economists to the kinds of problems under discussion are either to avoid them like the plague, or try to handle them with a variety of more-or-less satisfactory dodges, among which are:

1) Reversion of all non-profit institutions to private enterprise. To the problem of university library decisions about which books to buy and store, some economists will advocate selling the library to an entrepeneur who will then price the library services appropriately and who will discontinue all un-profitable activities. Unfortunately this is not a caricature.

2) Refer to free markets for valuations. The Soviet Union sets certain resource prices in accordance with free-market prices. And General Motors sets some prices for transfer or resources among divisions by what the resources can be bought (or sold) for outside the firm.

3) Restrict the problem to economic or easily-measurable quantities. A benefit/cost study of a proposed recreation lake, for example, may reckon only the economic revenues to the region and ignore the recreational benefits. And on the cost side, only the dollar costs and not the displacement-agony costs will be reckoned. Or, defense analysts may maximize the bang for a buck, but they ignore the value of human security and the cost of human life that may be attendant on the various alternatives.

The following pages try to set forth some practical advice for the practical use of economics in non-exchange welfare situations, and in other cases in which the relevant quantities are not measurable in dollars. The main objective is to inject into theoretical welfare economics a little of the vitality and excitement that always accompanies factual data. On this, Mishan[5] says:

> [The fact that] few welfare propositions can be predicted which are not in the same breath qualified out of existence . . . is to a large extent, a consequence flowing from our ignorance of the world we live in. . . . What the subject badly needs is a strong infusion of empiricism . . . to bring it down to earth feet first.

PROCEDURE IN SOLVING AN EXEMPLARY WELFARE PROBLEM

The remainder of the paper sets forth some sequential principles of how to make non-market allocation problems sensibly determinate. Each how-to-do-it principle is really a label for a key decision plus some guidance for making the decision. These how-to-do-it principles are mostly in the context of a research-library problem, though I shall also allude to other concrete problems. The problem is to determine how many and which books a major university research library should move from the conventional housing in the stacks of the research library into much cheaper housing in storage libraries. The problem is not formulated precisely at this stage of the paper because, as we shall see, the process of problem formulation is much of our subject matter and represents muh of the practical work of welfare economics.

Storage-library housing is much cheaper — perhaps 10¢ per book per year as compared to 25¢ per book per year in the regular stacks. The economies stem from the utilization of less-valuable non-central land locations, and compact storage in a consecutive-number system that segregates books only by size. The major welfare cost of transferring a book to a storage library is that scholars cannot browse in storage libraries, which may interfere with research or prevent serendipitous discoveries.[10] The problem is not cosmic but it is not trivial either; it involves a major part of the annual budgets for large libraries. The problem can also be generalized to decisions about *which* books the library should purchase.

The library problem is a good example for these reasons:

a) The problem is relatively uncomplicated compared to many decisions made by nations, cities, national charitable organizations, etc. The lack of complexity stems partly from the non-earthshaking importance of the problem and partly from the relatively small number of people and dollars involved.

b) The decisions are on-going and repetitive, rather than one-time situations. This makes it possible to develop information from past decisions for use on future decisions.

c) Facts are available. And the facts are familiar to the reader. It may even be a problem which involves the reader emotionally, though scholars in the humanities tend to be more passionate about the problem than do economists.

Step 1. Setting Forth the Problem

As with all other decision problems, the trick is to set up the non-exchange problem in such a way that it demands appropriate answers.

In at least some classes of books used for scholarly research — economics books, for example — it is possible to rank-order books by their expected use in any period of time, with various statistical devices. The rank-order of the value of books as rated by well-known economists has a high correlation with the rank-order of frequency of use.[11] This means that we can assume that books can be rank-ordered by *value* with statistical routines.

The problem, then, is how far down the rank-order should be the cut-off point, above which books are kept in expensive conventional stacks and below which they are sent to storage. In other words, the problem is to find the point at which the utility of the marginal book equals the marginal utility in the appropriate comparison system, a procedure which obviates the need for the concept of consumer surplus. Formally, we might write that we want to maximize

(1) $U = f(S, M, ???)$

(2) $? = ?$

where U is some appropriate measure of utility (discussed later), S is the number of books in university storage libraries, and M is the number of books in conventional library housing. The question marks within parentheses in Equation (1) indicate that we have not yet specified whether other variables will be included in the discussion or what they will be. The question marks in Equation (2) indicate that we have not yet stated any constraints for the maximization.

Step 2. Establish the Correct Locus of Decision

The solution differs depending on whether we assume: (a) that the library's budget is fixed and the decision is whether to spend money to store books or on other library services; or (b) that the expenditures for books compete with other at-large university expenses rather than competing only with other library-service expenditures. In other words, we must decide whether the locus of decision is the library administration or the university administration. In formal terms, we have not decided whether to maximize

(3) $U = f[S, M, N]$

or

(4) $U = f[S, M, N, P]$

where N is other library services, and P is other university-wide services. i.e., we have not decided whether it is the total cost of $S + M + N$, or of $S + M + N + P$, that will be considered fixed. This decision should be based on the institutional facts of what is already fixed and what is not fixed. If there were reason to believe that the university administration had a fixed, long-term plan for the over-all library budget, then the appropriate locus for decision would be the library administration. Otherwise, the university administration would be the appropriate locus. In the actual situation to which this article refers, the university administration seemed to be the appropriate locus, i.e., the relevant equation is (4).

There is often considerable conflict over the appropriate locus for decision. Perhaps Congress orders the Air Force to increase its supply of Weapon A. The Air Force asks for an increase in its appropriation in order to do so. Congress replied that the Air Force should take funds away from other expenditures. And the argument rages.

286   JULIAN L. SIMON

The higher the administrative level at which the budget is considered fixed, the better will be the allocation of funds, assuming rationality. For example, the local director of the Internal Revenue Service office will not mail out a routine blank form; he insists that you come to his office to get it because,he says, he does not have sufficient staff to handle the mailing. That is another way of saying that within his fixed budget, other services with even better payout ratios are below the cut-off point, by his reckoning. But if the local budget is considered to be flexible, and the constraint is at the state or national level, it is much more likely that the local office will assume the burden of the 5¢ stamp and addressing the envelope, saving the taxpayer dollars of time to go and get the form. And if we consider that the total government budget is not fixed with respect to any items with demonstrable social benefit, the form would surely be mailed out.

Similarly, if total library budgets were flexible with respect to all items, libraries would employ more reference librarians to handle bibliographic questions telephoned in by faculty members and others; librarians can handle many such questions more quickly, at a lower rate of pay, and without personal transportation costs.

On the other hand, the higher the administrative level at which the budget is considered not fixed with respect to a possible expenditure, the less efficient and more costly is the decision-making process. Fortunately the President and the Secretary of the Treasury have too much sense to worry about the unavoidable misallocation of resources represented by my spending $2 worth of time that a 5¢ stamp could handle. It is a misunderstanding of this point that makes possible those Congressional investigations of the 6000 oyster forks aboard a Navy destroyer. Such flaws must appear no matter how good a routine is, if the routine is to have any generality.

As a practical matter it is efficient to handle decisions in bundles, by fixing budgets at lower levels, as long as the marginal decision is not far out of line compared to the marginal decisions in other budgets at the same level, or unless a very large bundle of decisions are involved — as, for example, the bundle of decisions about the individual books in the library — which total a large sum relative to the size of the budget. In such cases, it pays to move the locus of the decisions up one or more administrative levels.

Sometimes the analyst must make it clear to decision-makers that increasing expenditures for one resource *must* force a decrease for *something* else. Economists accept this fact as they accept breathing. But non-economists work on other sets of assumptions. There are many eminent scholars who refuse to surrender the view that "the library should have everything." And to them "everything" is not a figure of speech. It is often necessary for the analyst or decision-maker to conduct educational programs as part of his research into welfare allocations.

Step 3. Make the Necessary Assumptions

Arrow [1] caused consternation for a while by demonstrating the indeterminacy of welfare situations under some sets of assumptions. But if you make enough assumptions, you can assure yourself of a determinate solution.[12] One of the assumptions will usually be tantamount to a cardinal scale of utility, which often seems justifiable in the specific set of circumstances.

In the library problem we assume:
a) All dollar-costs of handling and storing books are known.
b) Only the patronage of the faculty counts.
c) One faculty-member's work is as important as another's. This avoids problems of inter-personal valuations (which are implicitly made by the administration, however). Non-equal valuations could easily be incorporated into the solution.

Step 4. Identify the Alternatives Competing for the Resources

This step is intertwined with Step 2, choosing the locus of decision. In the library case, expenditures for recreational facilities, grounds, scholarships, etc. The basis for this assumption for one particular university is the attitude epitomized by a chancellor's statement.[13] This means that the relevant choice is between the marginal amounts of books, and the marginal expenditures for other university projects relevant to scholarly productivity.

Step 5. Disaggregate the Value Comparisons as Far as Possible

Decisions should be made for the smallest units that can be controlled separately by the administrator. Instead of debating whether the national budget should contain another billion for defense at the expense of a billion for education, one should ask whether the million required for the marginal school is a better expenditure than a million for the marginal helicopter. But if military decisions must be made for the unit of a helicopter *group,* then the comparison should be between a group of helicopters and an equally-costly package of education expenditures.

In the library case, the analytic comparison should not be between a half million dollars more for book storage, versus a half million for the marginal university project — perhaps a new laboratory. Rather, we must find ways of comparing the value of keeping a marginal book (its marginality is determined by its rank-order of expected value) against other marginal university projects that would cost $2.50 (the cost of keeping the book for another ten years).

Disaggregation helps the comparer make good comparisons by reducing complexity. A man can sensibly decide whether a given book is worth a given cost to a university (under well-defined conditions discussed later). He way also be able to decide sensibly that a small group of books each with a given expected value is worth the expenditure for each of them, though this decision will seem harder than the decision for just one book. But it is enormously more difficult to look at a list or pile of 50,000 heterogeneous books *en masse* and make a sensible decision as to whether they are worth the cost of keeping them.

The disadvantage of disaggregation is the increased decision-making time required. The trick is to develop *routines* by which disaggregated comparisons can be made with little extra labor. In this case we can automatically rank-order the disaggregated units so that only a few comparisons need be made at the margin by an expert. This is quite feasible, whereas it is too expensive to have an expert consider each book, volume by volume, to see if it should be stored.

Step 6. Set Up a Framework for Individual Value Comparisons

This step is usually big trouble, and demands a high order of common sense and close understanding of the realities of the over-all situation.

There are at least two reasonable ways to proceed in the library problem. First, one could make individual value comparisons and then combine them. Second, one could analyze the library decisions that have been made in the past to determine the implicit marginal values. Once they have been made explicit, those marginal values can then be examined for soundness and used as explicit standards to routinize future decisions. We shall consider the latter procedure first.

A. Identification of marginal book-purchase decisions to determine the mean value rendered by marginal books. Several methods are possible:

1) Search out those books that were bought perhaps five years before, and that had least use (value) in the five years. Then apply the prediction apparatus to them as of their purchase dates, and the *predicted* value might well approximate the expected value of marginal purchases. The prediction would be something less than .02 uses per year (really!).

2) A second method is to ask acquisitions librarians to identify those purchases that were marginal decisions and determine the actual use (value) after a period of time. The mean value of the books would be the operational marginal value (use). We would expect it to equal the .02 uses/year estimate above.

3) Libraries occasionally purchase entire collections. The mean use per dollar of cost of one or more collections would provide another yardstick.

Once established, the actual use-value of marginal purchases might seem too high or too low, comparing the cost of the books against the value of the same amounts spent for other university projects, which might lead the administration to change its procedures.[14]

We cannot immediately adopt the above estimate as the cut-off value for book storage, because the cost of purchasing and then housing a book is greater than the cost of simply housing a book already owned. The marginal use-value must therefore be adjusted downwards for *keeping* books. If, for example, the discounted-present-value of the cost of purchasing plus housing is twice as great as the present value of housing costs alone, the marginal (expected) use for storage should be half the use required for purchase.

B. Value comparisons from polls of book

users. This method is difficult conceptually. It might also be sufficiently difficult in practice so that it could be used only as a "mental experiment" — that is, by inserting administrative estimates of the quantities instead of actually surveying to determine the quantities.

This is a voting method. But the issues on which the voter casts his ballot must be stated in a more sophisticated fashion than for political voting. Methods of combining the votes constitute another difficulty.

We could begin by segregating groups of low-value books in each academic field by expected value (use). One bundle contains books with .01 expected uses per year, other bundles with .02, .03, .05, .10, .20, etc., expected uses per year. Then tell a representative faculty member in the field that the extra cost of retaining each of the books in conventional stacks is $.15 per year ($.25 for conventional minus $.10 for storage facitities) and that retention of the book competes with the expenditure of the same funds on other university-provided aids to his research, such as laboratory equipment or funds to pay research assistants. Then ask the faculty member to proceed down the ordered groups of books until he reaches the group for which he is indifferent between retaining the books and spending the funds on other aids to his scholarly work.

To obtain a proper valuation the comparison must be between books and other scholarly aid to the *particular* faculty member. If the comparison were stated as between books in his field and aids to some *other* scholar, or between books and faculty expenditures at large, then the comparison would appear to be between books whose absence have a cost to the individual faculty member but not to others outside his department, and other services whose absence would be a cost falling mostly or entirely on other people. In other words, it makes a difference in one's evaluation whose ox is being gored.

This procedure provides a cut-off standard for each field, and the library could proceed immediately upon that basis. No aggregation of individual valuations is necessary.

A complication exists in fields where no other aids to scholarship compete with books for funds. In the humanities a researcher may not even need research assistance, and certainly not laboratories, equipment, and the like. It might then be reasonable to offer a choice between the university spending money to house books in his field against an expenditure for at-large university services such as a faculty club. The individual faculty member might then be instructed to choose between given groups of books and the value of the university service to *him.* The total value of the university service would then be estimated as the *aggregate* value of scholars in *all* the fields.

Faculty members might also be instructed to act as if they were choosing for the university as a whole, rather than for the value to their own work. But it seems to me that judgments made from such a "universalistic" point of view would necessarily be less accurate than "particularistic" judgments, just as commissars cannot estimate what mixes of goods will provide most gratifications to groups of consumers.

A variant of this general approach is to find the indifference-value of an average *use* of a book, rather than of the book itself. The procedure would be to ask a professor, when he is returning a book that he has withdrawn, how large a sum the university would have to spend on other services to equal the value he had obtained from his use of the book in hand. The mean value of uses would then be calculated, and all books whose predicted use exceeds the criterion would be retained. For example, if the mean value of a use of economics volume is calculated to be $3, then each book whose expected use is above .05 uses per year would be retained. ($3 value of a use ÷ $.15 cost of housing conventionally rather than in storage.

CONCLUSIONS

Economic techniques can help institutions make welfare judgments about non-exchange transfers, if the analyst is willing to make sufficient assumptions. The usefulness of the analysis depends on the realism of the assumptions and the coordination of the model to reality, especially in the process of determining values by comparison with other alternatives. The series of decision steps outlined above may help carry out such analyses.

NOTES

Author's Note

This paper is an outgrowth of a research project at the University of Chicago Library under a grant from the Council on Library Resources.

Footnotes

[1] Arrow, Kenneth J., *Social Choice and Individual Values,* Wiley, New York, 1951.

[2] Fussler, Herman H. and Simon, Julian L., *Patterns of Use of Books in Large Research Libraries,* University of Chicago Library, 1961.

[3] Hicks, J.R., "Annual Survey of Economic Theory: the Theory of Monopoly", *Econometrica,* Vol. III (1935). Reprinted in G. J. Stigler and K.E. Boulding, *Readings in Price Theory,* Irwin, Homewood, Ill., 1952.

[4] Kapp, K. William, *The Social Costs of Private Enterprise,* Harvard U. Press, 1950.

[5] Mishan, E.J. "Survey of Welfare Economics 1939-59", *Economic Journal,* June 1960.

[6] Simon, Julian L. "The Economics of Book Storage in Large University Libraries", Ph.D. Thesis, University of Chicago, 1961.

[7] Simon, Julian L. "Cigarette Advertising and the Nation's Welfare", *Illinois Business Review,* May 1964.

[8] Williamson, Oliver T., "Peak-Load Pricing and Optimal Capacity under Indivisibility Restraints", *American Economic Review,* Sept. 1966.

[9] In 1950 J.R. Hicks wrote of his 1935 survey of monopoly theory: "The great weakness of this article . . . is its failure to perceive that the significance of monopoly theory lies in the direction of welfare economics" (Hicks, J.R. *op. cit.,* p. 383).

[10] Other costs, such as the cost of actually transferring a book to storage, and messenger costs, are considered in detail in Simon, J.L. (1961) *op. cit.* Nor shall we consider here the possible gains from re-educating scholars to use shelf-list catalogs.

[11] Both of these propositions are investigated empirically and discussed in length in Fussler, H.H. and Simon, J.L. *op. cit.*

[12] Williamson comments that Turvey " . . . was able to get so far with the fishery problem . . . precisely because he was willing to make simplifying assumptions and thereby provide a fundamental welfare motivation . . . " (Williamson, O.T. *op. cit.,* p. 811)

[13] Chancellor Kimpton once wrote that the essence of the University of Chicago was: "a passionate dedication to pure research and scholarship," and that the school is "research-oriented and faculty-oriented."

[14] We have skipped over the issue of measuring value, and of considering the use of books as an index of value. These issues are explored conceptually and empirically in Simon, J.L. (1961) *op. cit.*

ABOUT THE AUTHOR

Julian L. Simon received his B.A. in experimental psychology from Harvard and an M.B.A. and Ph.D. in Business Economics from the University of Chicago. From 1959-61 he was Associate Director of the Library Use Study at the University of Chicago (reported as "Patterns in the Use of Books in Large Research Libraries" (University of Chicago Press, 1969). In 1963 he became Assistant Professor of Advertising at the University of Illinois (Urbana), and from 1966-69 he was Assistant and Associate Professor of Marketing at the same university. Since 1969 he has been Professor of Economics and of Marketing at the University of Illinois, although in 1970-71 he was the First Lipson Professor of International Marketing in the Department of Demography of the Hebrew University, Jerusalem.

VI

THE USER

The librarian, in his role as manager of a library service, is concerned to satisfy the needs of the users of his library. He needs to concern himself with the behaviour of library users (both actual and potential) in an attempt to provide the kind of service which is best suited to their needs. Operations researchers, and workers in related fields, have, in the past, been accused of ignoring the human element in the systems which they have studied. However, as the papers in this Chapter show, they are now well aware of this pitfall, and much work is being undertaken in the area.

Although behavioural variables are difficult to handle, it is essential that the attempt is made and that, as far as possible, assumptions about user behaviour are tested scientifically. Ford presents an overview of previous research in the field and Elton and Rosenhead illustrate that, in some circumstances, human behaviour can be modelled. Revans presents a case study in which both "hard" and "soft" data are combined in an analysis of a hospital problem, and finally Ackoff raises some fundamental questions about "methodology" when dealing with problems having a significant sociological content.

Research in User Behaviour in University Libraries

M. G. Ford

There have been many studies concerned with the user and his interaction with the library. However, as has been emphasised in many of the preceding sections of this Reader, this, the human aspect of the library service, is one of the most difficult areas to study. Nevertheless it remains one of the most important. In this paper, Ford summarises the major user studies of the past and, in doing so, considers separately three areas of interest to librarians: Factors which affect demand for library services, the interaction between the library and its users, and the way in which use is made of library materials.

INTRODUCTION

The task of the librarian is to achieve his library's objectives. A simplistic statement, perhaps, but it is rare that a library's objectives are defined in any terms other than the broadest — for example, "to meet the needs of its users". In fact, the definition of objectives in any service organization is likely to be an iterative process, but the explicit commitment to users' needs (however mystical this concept may be) requires the librarian to examine users' behaviour as a first step to determining policy. Since a complete state-of-the-art in user behaviour would fill a substantial book, this survey is restricted to drawing together some threads of research of potential application in university libraries. Methodological problems are not discussed here, since these are adequately reviewed elsewhere.[39,56,62]

One of the problems in this field is the lack of any systematic use of terminology. One model of information communication was developed by Saul and Mary Herner in order to help them organize a review of research in information needs and uses.[39] Their model has six components:

sources or originators	methods or activities
recipients	messages
channels or media	information

Thus:

(SOURCE) (METHOD) (MESSAGES)
The source / writes or speaks / ideas, research results, etc. / which are transmitted by /
(CHANNEL) (RECIPIENT)
journal, meeting, etc, etc. / to the recipient, who
(METHOD)
reads or hears / the message and is thus informed. At this point the message is converted into INFORMATION. A conceptual model of this kind is necessary if a research study is to achieve its objectives. The general objectives of any study of user behaviour can be summarized as:

1. the explanation of observed phenomena
2. the prediction of behaviour
3. the control of behaviour by manipulation of conditions.

In order to achieve these objectives it is necessary to carry out certain activities, i.e.:

1. the description of user behaviour
2. the definition of concepts
3. the theorization of causal and quantitative relationships between information use and related factors.[62]

Now although these activities can be (and indeed have been) pursued independently, they are only fruitful when related to each other. It is deceptively easy to describe information use,

SOURCE: Reprinted from the *Journal of Documentation* 29 (1) March 1973 pp. 85-106, by permission of the author and publishers.

and many researchers have taken the easy
road. It requires an effort of will to ponder on
the work that has gone before, to synthesize a
body of theory, and having theorized, to
formulate a hypothesis, to test it, and to refine
the theory in the light of new findings. An
increasing number of researchers of information
needs and uses are adopting the more scientific approach, but the greater proportion
of published research findings on user behaviour in university libraries fails to match the
ideal pattern. It is unfortunate that in the past
library researchers have often not carried
out their own objectives, even when they
have defined them. The classic study of loan
records at Leeds University[77] is an example
of this. The stated object of the survey was,

> ' . . . to ascertain and measure the demand made by the
> three main types of readers . . . '

It was considered that the measurement of
use would satisfy this objective, and in the
end only recorded loans were analysed. No
attempt was made to relate recorded use to
acutal demand. A later survey at Leeds[98]
commences by stating that the previous survey
of borrowing use showed what demands
were made upon the library's stock — the
author is using the terms synonymously. This
would not be confusing but for the fact that
the author later uses "demand" in its proper
sense when discussing availability.

There are several possible ways of organizing a survey of research; it seems fruitful
to consider them in relation to the three main
problem areas of interest to all libraries:

1. the factors affecting demand for library
   services
2. the interaction between libraries and users
3. the utilization of library materials.

These three areas are all bound together
of course; for example, the interaction between
a library and its users in itself affects the
level of demand; but meaningful limits can
be placed on each of the areas of concern
for the purposes of hypothesizing and data
gathering. Thus the level of demand can
be related to the state of the user on entry to
the library: the library-user interaction can
be studied in terms of success and failure
at various stages in the library; and the utilization of library materials can be studied in
terms of the effects of such use on the users.

A useful critical bibliography of library use
studies is that by DeWeese.[28]

FACTORS AFFECTING THE DEMAND FOR LIBRARY SERVICES

The factors affecting demand are apparently innumerable, but it is possible to group
them in five categories:

1. the information sources or channels available
2. the uses to which the information is put
3. the individual user
4. the systems of which the user forms a part
5. the consequences of use.[78]

The last of these closes the loop, in that
successful use of libraries can generate further demands.

Information Channels. Channels are the
means by which ideas, opinions, facts, and
interpretations are communicated. These
channels may be formal — books, journals,
research reports, slides, audio tapes,
gramophone records, films — or informal —
after-dinner discussions, casual meetings with
colleagues, correspondence. The line between formal and informal channels is
difficult to draw; a reasonable approximation
might be that formal channels are susceptible of use by a number of people, not
necessarily at the same time, while informal
channels operate on an individual interpersonal basis. Channels may also be classed as
primary and secondary: the primary channel
carries the actual message, while the secondary
channel leads one to the primary channel.
Review articles, abstracting journals, and
indexes are all secondary channels.

Some of the channels — books, journals,
indexes, etc. — are of course the prime concern of librarians. The librarian is an expert
at manipulating the channels under his care
to derive the maximum benefit to the users
of the library. It is possible to regard the
library as a rather complex market place for
information channels, with the librarian as
its manager. The level of need of the individual user determines the channel which
the librarian recommends him to use. Thus
the general inquirer may be directed to an
encyclopaedia, the specialist to an erudite
monograph. To assist in this task of direction,

the librarian creates secondary channels peculiar to his own library — catalogues, lists of recent acquisitions, subject bibliographies, and guides to resources. Other secondary channels — abstracting journals, indexes, etc. — are purchased ready-made by the library; and decisions must be made on which to buy and which to create in the library.

There are two principal factors which determine the use of particular channels. The first of these is *accessibility*. The perceived cost of using an information channel weighs heavily with the user; and in at least one study was shown to be the strongest single predictor of use.[3] O'Gara took distance as a measure of accessibility, and found that that probability of interpersonal communication decreased as the square of the distance between the persons' normal place of work.[74] At a lower level of analysis, the library can be treated as a single channel; and Frohmann found that the distance measure was applicable to library use.[32] Indications of a similar relationship were found at Durham[83] and Edinburgh Universities some years ago. Within the library itself Harris found evidence to reinforce the hypothesis that improved exposure leads to increased use of materials and services.[37] Supermarkets have, of course, been working on this principle for many years; and the law of retail gravitation has already been suggested as a basis for the location of new public libraries.[85]

It may be argued that in universities there is a need for library materials transcending such mundane factors as distance to be travelled to obtain information; but there is an increasing body of evidence to suggest that there is a large amount of latent demand which can be stimulated by improving the accessibility or availability of material.

A second factor affecting use of a given channel is *quality*. It has been demonstrated that the quality of information channel governs the acceptability of the information received. The natural conclusion to be drawn is that the best channels should be made the most accessible also. We are talking here, though, of quality as perceived by the user. If a decision based on information received from a given channel turns out to be successful, the decision maker will tend to value that channel more highly. This

is the point where the channel and the user are beginning to interact, and some work in this field has been reported by Streufert.[93] The interesting thing is that continuing failure does not seem to depress the value placed on a channel; but this effect may be a function of the field of Streufert's research — apparently in military decision making almost any information is better than none at all. Some interesting case studies of undergraduates' information-seeking behaviour have been described by Taylor.[95]

Uses of Information. In simple terms, information has only one use — i.e. the assistance of problem solving. Different types of problem may require different types of information. The requirements of library users can be tentatively classified as:

1. *Personal*
   Conditions of work — heating, lighting, draughts, sound-proofing, ease of entry/exit — turnstiles, porters etc. Amenities — location of lavatories, smoking rooms, food, drink.

2. *Technical*
   Discipline — rules of library use, fines, sanctions.
   Operations — signposting methods of borrowing/returning books accessibility of library personnel

3. *Task*
   The nature of the work in hand.

Although personal information requirements are extremely variable, conditions of work and amenities in a given library are fixed for significant periods of time. Thus it is important to cater for as many variations as possible right from the outset.[31,91,92] Consideration of the habits of university library users should lead to the elimination of hog-bristle carpets (tough on the feet) and to the introduction of beds (Gifford and Sommer[34] have adequately demonstrated the arguments in favor of this latter move).

The technical aspects of library use are under the control of the library; this is a major area of interaction. The book stock, the catalogues, the library staff, are all information channels, use of each being dependent on accessibility, ease of use and perceived relevance. Harris's work on accessibility has already been referred to;[37] and a more recent study[110] describes the effects of minor changes in a small college library in which too many items were being borrowed 'illegally' because the issue desk was not permanently manned — the situation was alleviated by placing 'proper receptacles' for book cards at convenient points within the library.

The effects of signposting in libraries have not been explored in depth; Carey describes the use of a range of devices, including permanent visual information, tape recorders, and induction loops which are intended to make library use a continuous learning process.[23] Intuitively, this approach seems better than the lecture-tour syndrome, and more likely to reduce 'noise'.

The general question of 'noise' in the communication theory sense, has not been examined in libraries, although Willmer has outlined an approach to measure the effectiveness of a library in these terms.[106] The amount of noise generated by filing rules in catalogues is considerable — apparently enough to drown the signal completely in many cases, since surveys of reader failure invariably show that users are frequently unable to find items in the catalogue, although library staff are able to trace the same items using only the data supplied by the user.[21, 29, 99, 100]

Other technical aspects of library use, and the effects of their complexities need not be described at this stage. It is important to stress however, that much of librarians' time is devoted to communicating information about information channels housed within the library; and since the librarian has more control over this factor than over any other, it is worth investigating the effectiveness of the secondary channels traditionally created by librarians, such as catalogues,[35, 67] classification schemes and shelf arrangements.[16, 58] It is significant that surveys of information gathering often place library catalogues and librarians low down on the list of useful secondary channels.

So far we have discussed the use of information which affects the user's ability to get what he wants; the most important of his information requirements are those related to the task in hand. Allen found evidence to suggest that the channel selected was task-specific; and different channels vary in their usefulness at different stages of a research project.[4, 105] It is difficult to trace any useful findings on the utilization of information — the what-where-

when-how-and-why of book use. It is easy to discover how many books are borrowed by a user; but the amount of use made of these books is largely unknown, although some recent studies (as yet unpublished) undertaken in a number of British universities suggest that the amount of use is extremely low in relation to the retention time. It is conceivable that alternative methods of supplying information are more effective than books. A better understanding of how and when books and other channels are used could lead to improvements in a library's service.

The individual user. At different times a wide variety of characteristics have been postulated as having effects on user behaviour. Some of these are more easily listed than investigated; and it is not always easy to draw the line between the individual and his environment. Work on perception and cognition is relevant here; in the abstract, quality, utility, relevance, and accessibility can be measured only as perceived by the individual user in relation to a particular task. For many users, however, accessibility and quality can be treated as fixed, and as "% properties" of information channels; thus in a university, the position of the library is fixed relative to the individual's normal place of work.

One important factor in learning is the variation in comprehension between individuals; and factors influencing comprehension have been studied by Kottenstette.[48] In this study, materials of differing degrees of difficulty were read by students in hardcopy and microform, and reading rates and comprehension were measured. It was found that there was no difference in the comprehension achieved between the two forms of presentation; but easy material took longer to read in microform than in hardcopy. This suggests that microform catalogues may not be desirable, despite their cost advantages in an automated world.

Maizell examined relationships between creativity and information gathering patterns amongst chemists.[68] In general the more creative chemists made more use of a wider variety of channels than did their less creative brethren; a significant finding was that the most creative chemists tended to rely on their own efforts rather than rely on information services, and they preferred to search for specific data themselves rather than use library reference services. It may be of course, that both creativity and information gathering habits are dependent on another, unidentified variable.

Factors such as experience, seniority, educational level, professional activity, and orientation are all potentially related to information-seeking behaviour.[86] There are possible links between personality and subject of study. Krulee and Nadler[50] found that science students placed higher values on independence and learning for its own sake than engineering students, who were more concerned with personal success and vocational training; as always, it is difficult to disentangle cause and effect. Differences have been observed for a long time in use made of different channels by workers in different disciplines, but these findings are not always helpful. Bernal observed differences between pure and applied scientists;[11] scientists seem to make more use of formal channels.[2, 70] This difference has not yet been explained, although Wolek has suggested that engineers, being concerned with making things that work, cease to make use of formal channels when their design is more or less frozen, and minor systems modifications arise out of interpersonal communications with close colleagues.[107] Alternative suggestions are that engineers cannot read, or that formal channels provide the wrong service. This is a case where a mere survey of use offers no guidance as to the true explanation and relevant solution.

Systems and organizations. Each user is a member of a number of systems each of which may influence his information-gathering behaviour in some way. For example, there are the effects of national frontiers on communications; the foreign language barrier is well documented[42] but there may well be other effects independent of language, explicable only in terms of xenophobia or of "national character." On this last point, it is necessary to point out that most of the research on information transfer has been done in the USA, and it is not known whether all the findings can be generalized to include the UK. In one international study it was found that UK physicists relied more on formal channels of communication, while US physicists used informal channels more.[90] If cultural factors are operating, then general pronouncements based on findings of research done in the USA must be declared 'not proven'.

The status of an individual within his own organization is a key factor in information transfer. Although informal communication networks are widespread, they tend to operate at a senior level; junior members of a system tend to rely heavily on formal channels.[109] Thus in a university, junior lecturers are more likely to use library facilities than professors, who are usually well endowed with review copies, preprints, articles to referee, and so forth. Moreover, it is these non-users who sit on library committees and finance committees before which libraries have to compete with departments for funds. Perhaps the libraries' universal complaint of lack of funds is justified. Line found that older researchers were more likely to be satisfied with their local libraries;[60] this may be an expression of this seniority factor.

Allen[2] has revealed the apparent importance of "technological gatekeepers" in research laboratories — individuals who act as filters of information for their research teams. A similar pattern emerges in sociological studies of opinion formation in communities.[53] It would be interesting to know whether any similar effects can be observed among students, or whether in fact it is the teachers who effectively fill this role. The studies of catalogue use done by Cambridge LMRU do confirm that teachers are the major source of references to items sought by students. Although teaching needs generate the greatest proportion of demand in universities, we know very little about the nature of this demand other than its variability. The provision of a 'short-loan' collection[18, 90] is an attempt to meet the extreme demands but we need to know more about teaching methods before an efficient pattern of stock provision can be achieved.

Every university library user is a member of a subject group, each with its own long-established pattern of communications behaviour.[5, 11, 15, 60, 90] Some of these subjects are traditionally more library-oriented than others. There are differences within subject groups, however. In one study it was found that teachers of psychology who had graduated from 'good' universities planned their undergraduate courses quite differently from those who had 'not so good' universities behind them.[5] The 'good' teachers showed much more awareness of the latest research and made use of review journals and 'Advances'-type publications; by implication they knew more about library resources. Other studies touch on the differences between subject groups in the way in which books are used. Line found that the 'harder' social scientists — geographers, statisticians, psychologists — were more likely to use books in a consecutive mode, while the 'softer' workers — anthropologists, sociologists — were more likely to use several books in conjunction.[60] This suggests that libraries serving the 'harder' disciplines could make do with smaller bookstocks (backed up with a good interlibrary loan service) than libraries serving the 'softer' subjects.

All users are members of a particular social system, and their position in society affects their opportunities, but the influence of social class on library use is a neglected factor in universities; Luckham's work on public libraries[66] is relevant here. Evidence from the USA shows that science and technology students tend to come from working-class and lower middle-class backgrounds, while upper- and middle-class students tend to go for the humanities and social sciences.[50] There are indications that this situation is paralleled in the UK.[1] This pattern suggests a strong correlation with exposure to literature in the home — it may be that by the time a student gets to university it is too late to alter his information-seeking behaviour. The influence of gender on library use has been examined,[55, 59] but this effect could be an expression of subject and/or social class — distribution of female students is notably different from that of males in respect of both these factors.[103] Enough perhaps has been said to show the effects on information use of systems to which users belong. One all-pervasive effect of the cultural system is the premium placed on productivity and priority, and the effects of these twin factors on libraries need no further elaboration.

INTERACTION BETWEEN LIBRARIES AND USERS

A library"s primary objective must be to maximize the successful use of the services which it provides; and since successful use breeds more intensive use[17] it is desirable to discover in what ways the library is succeeding or failing to meet its users' needs. Although there have been many surveys of library use, very few of these give any more information than "how many did what". This kind of survey is rarely of use outside the institution in which it is done; sometimes not even there. Much of the

data collected is no more than informative; where inferences are drawn, it is seldom possible to determine whether particular local conditions are affecting the results. The lack of an adequate theoretical framework places severe restrictions on the interpretation of diverse results. Why for example do freshmen borrow more books than seniors at one college,[9] while at another, the reverse is true?[52] More intriguingly, why at Newcastle University did the use of the catalogue apparently increase by 300% between February 1968 and November 1969?[73] What are we to make of the fact that the age of books used by a social science research worker is related to the number of books he owns?[60]

Measures of effectiveness. In order to determine a library's effectiveness, it is necessary to define a suitable measure. Traditionally, librarians have counted issues (which are one measure of satisfied demand) but these data are rather meaningless unless they are related to a measure of total demands during the same period. 'Satisfaction level' (defined as the proportion of demands immediately satisfied during a given time period) was at one time suggested as the most useful single measure of library effectiveness.[19] There is little data available on satisfaction levels, although a comparatively high figure of 88% was reported from Birmingham in 1964,[102] and an earlier survey at Leeds[98] hinted a much lower figure. Orr, has proposed and used a Document Delivery Test[75] which yields an unobtrusive measure of a library's effectiveness very similar to satisfaction level. There are difficulties attached to the measurement of satisfaction level, and since it is extremely likely that demand is affected by satisfaction level, a single measure of this kind may not be particularly useful. A number of partial approaches to the measurement of satisfaction level have been made,[19, 21, 99, 100] and surveys such as these can yield useful data on the reasons for failure, and these in turn may suggest remedial programmes. Thus at Lancaster a failure survey led to a change in loan policies,[19] The results of the shelf failure survey at Cambridge[99] suggest that the reshelving procedure for books used within the library requires investigation; and examination of results from a number of sources leads to the conclusion that in general, libraries are inadequately oriented to the user, or users need better instruction in the use of libraries, or university teaching staff need instruction in the accurate citation of references, or any combination of these.

An alternative measure of effectiveness is document exposure, suggested by Hamburg.[36] This is the amount of actual eyeball-to-page contact during the time the book is on loan. The measure seems of more practical use than that of item-use-day proposed some years ago by Meier,[71] and is closely related to the measure of 'reader-book-contact-hours' suggested by Richard Morley.[111] This brings into the measure the amount of in-library use — always a difficult item to measure,[19, 33, 83, 100] but of extreme importance. In terms of actual reading time, it seems likely that the amount of use of books in libraries is perhaps twice that made when they are officially borrowed.

Catalogues. Although the catalogue is the most reliable guide to a library's stock, there are strong indications that users prefer going straight to the shelves, even when the author and title of a book are known.[59, 83] This strong user preference has not been reflected on a large scale in the organization of any library (apart from the National Lending Library, which has few personal users). Perhaps it is too early to say that a self-organizing shelf-location system, based on title, is the optimal scheme, but it is a hypothesis worth testing. Certainly it seems likely that users remember titles more readily than authors, [7, 63, 94] and that 'known-item' searches are more common than subject searches; [63] we do not yet know enough about users' lack of enthusiasm for catalogues, nor about the degree of subject browsing (although Fussler & Simon[33] found it low), nor about the degree of substitutability of individual titles. The whole topic of browsing has been treated discursively in a recent book.[43] Although there is a *prima facie* case for some kind of subject arrangement on the shelves of a university library, it may well be that close classification is sub-optimal; Bryant & Line[16] report the recent application at Bath University of 'broad' shelf classification combined with close classification recorded in the catalogue, although the idea is not new.

Use of catalogues has been studied in a number of contexts, but again mostly in a quantitative fashion.[63, 69, 73] One factor which has emerged is that students who have used large public libraries are more ready to use catalogues than are other students.[59] This

effect is difficult to pin down; familiarity with large public libraries does make users more at ease in university libraries, but some US findings are that size of public library previously used does not affect ability to use the university library competently.[51] Admittedly competence is not the same as familiarity, but one would have thought the two were related; the test of library competence used is in fact suspect.[32]

Instruction in Library Use. Library staff come very low down in the priorities of users when the choice of information channels is made. It has been suggested that this represents the triumph of experience over hope.[57] The low demand for channels like librarians and catalogues, when compared with the books on the shelves, is a perennial concern of librarians. Knowing the imperfections inherent in reliance on the shelves, they are anxious to instruct the users in the advantages of the other methods available. The major difficulties occur because of the lack of properly stated objectives in most libraries.

The consensus is that libraries are a good thing; but opinions as to their value in given situations vary widely. Some teachers believe that their lectures provide all the information that students need; some librarians say that conditions would be unbearable if all students did try to use the library. Apart from these two groups, there is a substantial body of opinion to the effect that,

1. libraries are a good thing
2. the average man does not know how to use them
3. libraries will be more effective if people are given guidance in using them.

The teacher's role in promoting the use of the library cannot be neglected. After all 'It is now and always will be the classroom and its ideals and methods which, by and large, determine the extent of activity at our loan desk'.[104] This view is confirmed by the experimental work at Monteith College.[46] If the teacher believes that the library plays an important part in providing materials for his subject, then his students will also believe and will use the library. Where the teacher believes the library to be unimportant, it seems that the successful students are those who use the library least.[40] There are two questions that arise here:

should all teachers encourage their students to use libraries? and should training in library use be given by teachers? This is not the place to enter into the value of libraries to society, but we can say that in a university the necessity of library training follows naturally if we assume any one of the following:

1. the library's functions include acquiring instructional materials, making them available, and interpreting them to the users;
2. students (and other users) are unfamiliar with the functions and uses of the library;
3. students need to acquire skills in bibliographic method appropriate to their subject of study;
4. librarians and teachers are concerned that students should acquire these skills;
5. students require guidance and instruction;
6. undergraduate courses are geared to student needs.

If it is accepted that library training is necessary, our second question requires an answer: should training in library use be given by teachers? The debate — teacher or librarian? has probably been going on for as long as the activity itself, and the arguments have been well-rehearsed by Bonn.[12] It does seem that for library instruction to be successful, it must be integrated with the official curriculum. There is a wide variety of possibilities, given this basic premise, and several experiments in this field have been reviewed recently,[38] and it is a popular area for conferences.[54, 88, 101] Taylor has described the plan for the ultimate in the library-college concept at Hampshire College[96] where the goal is the orientation of the library to the user. Steps along this road are to include a programme of continuous user instruction at points (such as catalogues, indexes, etc.), within the library where problems are likely to arise, and the employment of students as reference assistants. Another application of point-of-use-self-instruction (this time in the UK) has been described by Carey.[23]

The methods of reader instruction have not changed much in the last century: lectures, guide books, and on-the-spot assistance were all in use by 1892.[12] Teaching machines and computer-assisted instruction have made little impact as yet, although there have been some applications of both in recent years.[6]

The lecture, commonly given to freshman students at the beginning of their first session,

must surely be a waste of time. The library, with its vague connection with academic work, can hold little attraction for a student struggling to adjust to university life. The tours which are often associated with such lectures similarly rely on the students' overtaxed memories for their impact. All too often the librarian slips into jargon, or relapses into an uninspired restatement of rules and regulations. At a later stage in the student's career, however, lectures may have some value.

Modern versions of the lecture (tape/slides, films, video tapes[25, 108]) can be more effective as they can be made available on a more continuous and individual basis. This is, of course, true also of teaching machines. One interesting fact that has emerged is that no one means of instruction seems to have any advantage over any other in terms of effectiveness in imparting knowledge. A series of lectures is as good as a teaching machine or a film.[6, 51]

Printed guides are almost universal in university libraries; librarians are always eager to produce these, but the results too often resemble textbooks of librarianship. Thus for example:

"The symbol "Q" in the middle of a class-mark to indicate geographical sub-division of a subject . . . represents the figures "09" and is so filed. Other letters occurring in class'marks are filed in normal alphabetical sequence."

It may be of course that users take this in their stride and remember it — if they happen to read it. We do find the occasional student who gets " . . . the greatest feeling of satisfaction when I can go straight to an item because of a technical filing rule I know! One of my favourites is the Umlaut rule — filed as if it were an "ae" instead of an "a" . . . "[13] The interesting thing is that the author uses this quote to illustrate the appreciation of some students who had taken a course in bibliography and library instruction at his college. It does not seem to have occurred to either of them that by changing the Umlaut rule more users might be able to find items directly without needing to know such technical details. After all, a and ä are treated as the same letter in the standard German dictionaries for filing purposes!

The operational side of library use can best be taught on the spot in the library. Carey's approach, already referred to, using an integrated system of colour coding, tape recordings and inductance loops for directing users round the library and giving instruction in catalogue use and other techniques has a lot of attractive features.[23] The subject approach is the side that needs the active co-operation of the teaching staff: various ways of doing this have been tried,[97] but the best solution is probably a programme of seminars structured on real problems.[14] The use of "subject specialists" and more recently, experiments using information officers at Durham,[83] Bath, [61] and elsewhere,[26,27,44] are further attempts to increase the users' awareness of library materials.

Taylor reports on the behaviour of undergraduate students in information-seeking situations;[95] in his experiment the students reported on the methods they adopted to discover the answers to specific questions. In similar situations, a generalized search strategy was described by Carlson.[24] These observations were made on reference librarians, whose search strategy is possibly more formal than non-librarians, but even they use inconsistent techniques which could be improved by training. The significance of this research is that human search behaviour can be generalized sufficiently to cover a wide variety of information-seeking situations, and this should prove of use in the design of educational programmes. The concepts and methods of instruction for library users have been covered adequately in the literature in recent years, and the bibliographies in Bonn,[12] Tidmarsh,[97] and Mirwis[72] should be consulted for further information.

The effectiveness of library instruction is less well documented, perhaps because of the difficulty of evaluating any educational programme. The learning process has not been studied in great detail in the UK, but in the USA where library orientation tests are widespread in application, there have been several studies of their apparent effectiveness. The most important of the publshed tests seem to be the *Peabody Library Information Test*[89] and *A Library Orientation Test for College Freshmen*.[30] These tests have been reviewed by Buros.[22]

The Feagley test[30] was designed to discover areas in which college freshmen needed courses of library instruction. It covers nine areas of knowledge:

1. definition of terms
2. interpretation of the information on a catalogue card
3. choice of subject-headings in a card catalogue
4. arrangement of headings in a card catalogue
5. literature reference books
6. sources of biographical information
7. choice of indexes
8. interpretation of information in periodical indexes
9. abbreviations.

The American liberal arts emphasis is very pronounced.

A lot of effort has been expended in determining the relationship between performance in library orientation tests and other factors. The commonest result is that sholastic aptitude is linked with the ability to use library resources;[84] in one study in which Feagley's test was used,[45] it was administered to fourth-year students in a teachers' college, and a positive correlation ($r = 0.41$) was established between academic grade and score on the test. Perkins administered the Feagley test to a large number of students in several teachers' colleges.[82] He also used the Peabody test. He did not relate the scores achieved to any significant factors, but analysed in detail the incorrect responses to the questions. In a short preliminary section of his book he reviews the findings of some other workers who correlated Grade Point Average with performance in the test. One particularly interesting study attempted to determine the correlation between performance in two different tests of library competence. The low correlation achieved ($r = 0.385$) suggests that

"One or both of the tests is a poor test or that one or both of the tests do not measure what it (they) purport to measure."

Other studies have shown that performance in library tests is not related to the level of library service available to the student before coming to the college;[51] and that all methods of instruction appear to be equally effective in improving students' performance in library tests. The most systematic study to date is the work of Knapp[46] in which a variety of psychometric tests were used; while Grade Point Average did not correlate with library competence (apparently contradicting the findings of Joyce) library performance did correlate with the Terman Concept Mastery test.

At the end of all this, we are left with a feeling

of uncertainty as to what library orientation tests actually test. The contradictory findings which emerge lead us to question the validity of these tests — they really test common sense and general knowledge — and Perkins' conclusions (quoted above) would seem to be justified. Adequate tests of library competence will have to be devised before it will be possible to measure the interaction between libraries and their users, and to discover the mechanisms of the learning process. The increasing use of audio-visual aids is arousing interest in the evaluation of teaching methods and some work on this has been done at the University of Surrey.[25]

THE UTILIZATION OF
LIBRARY MATERIALS

Although several surveys of book borrowing based on the analysis of loan records have been reported, there have been few startling discoveries. The most significant result is that Arts students borrow more than Technologists: is this due to a fundamental difference in the library needs of the two groups, or an expression of the lower, non-book oriented, social origins of technologists, compounded by a long tradition of librarians trained in the humanities? It is also significant that students confine their borrowing almost exclusively to course materials.[47,52,83] Teachers and researchers seem to have wider interests, if the classification numbers of books are any guide: indications are that as much as half of a university lecturer's borrowings may be in subject-fields other than his specialism.

One of the interactions between the library and the user which has a bearing on utilization is the influence of the loan period on book retention time; it seems that borrowers (in general) retain books until they are due for return.[18,20] A number of studies of scientists' reading habits (reviewed by Barber[8]) have shown a very low allocation of time to reading, so that in many cases the amount of use made of books must be very small relative to the length of time the books are on loan. We know nothing about the *quality* of use of course. Another neglected area is the in-library use of books — neglected probably because of the difficulties of recording data. Fussler & Simon[33] reported that a book was likely to be

used three to nine times in the library for each time it was borrowed; and a similar range of values was obtained at Lancaster[19] and Durham.[83]

The continued support of libraries implies a belief in their value; it is however difficult to measure the value of a library or its contribution to a measurable output of its users. It has been shown that a scientist's performance correlates with the level of his communication with colleagues.[81] Paisley & Parker showed that an individual's productivity of research correlates strongly with the amount and diversity of his information inputs,[79] confirming the earlier work of Maizell.[68] Various US studies have correlated academic achievement with various aspects of library use. Thus Kramer & Kramer showed that drop-out rates were higher for non-library users than for users;[49] but their conclusion that the lack of library use *caused* the drop-outs is open to question. It has been shown that use of a library has a significant influence on pupil achievement in some aspects of social studies learning.[10] This study was conducted in elementary schools in the USA on a sample of ten-year-olds, and it is possible that instruction in library use is most effective at this stage. Otherwise, there are no adequate demonstrations of definite influences of libraries on anything else. In one recent study, non-users of the library were found to differ significantly from the users only in the fact that they were non-users.[65]

According to George Orwell " . . . survival . . . is itself an index of majority opinion"[76] and libraries are therefore good things to have. The desirability of encouraging people to use them depends on the philosophy of education currently supported by the social and political system.

CONCLUSIONS

From the foregoing we can draw a number of conclusions. There is a general lack of theory, and an equal lack of adequate definition of concepts. An example of this lies in the various actions taken to encourage and improve the use made of libraries. Here the definition of objectives of such activities are at best hazy, and in consequence the actions taken are frequently inadequate; the failure is compounded by the lack of suitable means of testing the effects of activities such as reader instruction.

A further consequence of the inadequate theory is that the results of surveys of information seeking behaviour cannot always be satisfactorily interpreted. When we find that engineers read less than scientists, it is possible to postulate a number of explanations; such as,

1. engineers cannot read
2. engineers don't need to read
3. engineers use more informal channels
4. libraries provide the wrong kind of service.

The adoption of a more scientific approach — testing hypotheses formulated on a base of well-developed theory should lead to a more satisfactory state of affairs.

Although many studies of information-seeking behaviour have been done, there remain some severe gaps in our knowledge. One of the most important of these relates to the utilization of library materials — we know practically nothing about the what-why-how-when-and-where of book use. Another gap in the record is the lack of longitudinal studies. There are many cross-sections of user behaviour, and of chan-

nel usage, but few researchers have followed up earlier work. A notable exception is the work of Lubans;[64,65] the survey reported by Line & Tidmarsh[59] attempts to measure the effects of changes introduced after an earlier study[55] but the two surveys were done on entirely different populations, and the results are inconclusive. Consecutive surveys done by PEBUL[83] on the same population used identical questionnaires of the 'instant diary' type, but as these were anonymous it is difficult to draw any firm conclusions. The lack of longitudinal studies of library users leads to an incomplete knowledge of the interaction between libraries and their users, and possible effects on the demand for library services arising therefrom. Other factors affecting the demand for library services which are imperfectly understood include the influence of social class on people's attitudes to libraries; this may prove to be an important determinant of engineers' reading habits. Perhaps the most important finding of this review of research in user behaviour is that it has yet to be demonstrated that the use of libraries has any definite influence on anything else.

ACKNOWLEDGEMENT

This survey is based on a report prepared for a research project funded by the Council on Library Resources, Inc. currently in progress at the University of Lancaster, England.

REFERENCES

[1] ABBOTT, J. *Student life in a class society.* Oxford Pergamon. 1971. ISBN 0080156541.

[2] ALLEN, T.J. *Managing the flow of technical information.* Ph.D. thesis. Cambridge, Mass., Alfred P. Sloan School of Management, Massachusetts Institute of Technology, 1966.

[3] ALLEN, T.J. & GERSTBERGER, P.G. *Criteria for selection of an information source.* (Working Paper 284-67) Cambridge, Mass., Alfred P. Sloan School of Management, Massachusetts Institute of Technology, 1967.

[4] ALLEN, T.J. & others. *Time allocation among three technical information channels by R and D engineers.* (Working paper 184-66.) Cambridge, Mass., Alfred P. Sloan School of Management, Massachusetts Institute of Technology, 1966.

[5] AMERICAN PSYCHOLOGICAL ASSOCIATION. *The use of scientific information in the undergraduate teaching of psychology.* (Project on scientific information exchange in psychology, report 17.) Washington, D.C., American Psychological Association, 1967. (PB-174 652).

[6] AXEEN, M.E. *Teaching the use of the library to undergraduates: an experimental comparison of computer-based instruction and the conventional lecture method.* Ph.D. thesis. Urbana, Ill., University of Illinois, 1967. (Co-ordinated Science Laboratory, report R-361.)

[7] AYRES, F. H. & others. Author versus title. *Journal of Documentation,* vol. 24, 1968, pp. 266-272.

[8] BARBER, A.S. A critical review of the surveys of scientists' use of libraries. *In* SAUNDERS, W.L. *ed. The provision and use of library and documentation services.* Oxford, Pergamon. 1966, pp. 145-179.

[9] BARKEY, P. Patterns of student use of a college library. *College & Research Libraries,* vol. 26, 1965, pp. 115-118.

[10] BECKER, D.E. *Social studies achievement of pupils in schools with libraries and schools without libraries.* Ed.D. thesis. Philadelphia, University of Pennsylvania, 1970.

[11] BERNAL, J.D. Preliminary analysis of pilot questionnaire on use of scientific literature. *In. Report of the Royal Society Scientific Information Conference,* London, Royal Society, 1948, pp. 101-102, 589-637.

[12] BONN, G.S. *Training laymen in the use of the library.* (The state of the library art, vol. 2;1). New Brunswick, N.J. Rut-

gers University Graduate School of Library Science, 1960.

[13] BOONE, M.D. An experiment in library instruction: the initial step in the identification of library users' needs at a liberal arts college. *In. Use, mis-use and non-use of academic libraries*. New York, New York Library Association College & University Libraries, 1970, pp. 31-41.

[14] BRISTOW, T. Instruction or induction: the human approach to student involvement in library materials. *In Seminar on human aspects of library instruction, 9th December, 1969 . . . Proceedings*. Cardiff, Standing Conference of National and University Libraries, (1970), pp. 3-23.

[15] BRITTAIN, J.M. *Information and its users: a review with special reference to the social sciences*. Bath, Bath University Press, 1970. ISBN 090084308X.

[16] BRYANT, P. & LINE, M. Cataloguing and classification at Bath University Library: on the track of white elephants and golden retrievers. *Library Association Record*, vol. 73, 1971, pp. 225-227.

[17] BUCKALND, M.K. An operations research study of a variable loan and duplication policy at the University of Lancaster. *Library Quarterly*, vol. 42, 1972, pp. 97-106.

[18] BUCKLAND, M.K. & HINDLE, A. Loan policies, duplication and availability. *In* MACKENZIE, A.G. & STUART, I.M eds. *Planning Library Services: procedures of a research seminar*. (University of Lancaster Library Occasional Papers, 3). Lancaster, University of Lancaster Library, 1969. ISBN 0901699012.

[19] BUCKLAND, M.K. & others. *Systems analysis of a university library: final report on a research project*.(University of Lancaster Library Occasional Papers, 4). Lancaster, University of Lancaster Library, 1970. ISBN 0901699020.

[20] BURKHALTER, B.R. & RACE, P.A. An analysis of renewals, overdues, and other factors influencing the optimal charge-out period. *In* BURKHALTER, B.R. *ed. Case studies in systems analysis in a university library*. Metuchen, N.J., Scarecrow Press, 1968, pp. 11-33.

[21] BURNETT, A.D. Reader failure: a pilot survey. *Research in Librarianship*, vol. 1, 1966, pp. 142-157.

[22] BUROS, O.K. *Readings: tests and reviews*. Highfield Park, N.J. Gryphon Press, 1968.

[23] CAREY, R.J.P. Making libraries easy to use: a systems approach. *Library Association Record*, vol. 73, 1971, pp. 132-135.

[24] CARLSON, G. *Search strategy by reference librarians*. Sherman Oaks, Calif., Hughes Dynamics, 1964. (PB-166 192)

[25] CHESSHYRE, H.A. & HILLS, P.J. Evaluation of student response to a library instruction trials programme using audio-visual aids. *In* LINCOLN, C.M. *ed. Educating the library user: Proceedings of the fourth triennial meeting of IATUL . . .* 1970. Loughborough, University of Technology Library, 1970, pp. K1-11. ISBN 0950141100.

[26] CORNEY, E. The information service in practice: an experiment at The City University. *Journal of Librarianship*, vol. 1, 1969. pp. 225-235.

[27] DE HART, F. E. *The application of special library services and techniques to the college library*. Ph. D. thesis. New Brunswick, N.J. Rutgers University Graduate School of Library Science, 1964.

[28] DE WEESE, L.C. A bibliography of library use studies. *In* JAIN, A.K. *A statistical study of book use*. Ph.D. thesis. Lafayette, Ind. Purdue University, 1967. (PB-176 525)

[29] DUREY, P. A survey of student library-use at the University of Keele, 1967. *Research in Librarianship*, vol. 2, 1968. pp. 3-8.

[30] FEAGLEY, E.M. & others. *A library orientation test for college freshmen*. New York, Columbia University Teacher's College, 1955.

[31] FISHMAN, D. & WALITT, R. Seating and area preferences in a college reserve room. *College & Research Libraries*, vol. 33, 1972, pp. 284-297.

[32] FROHMANN, A. *Determinants of library use in an industrial firm*. (Term paper.) Cambridge, Mass., Alfred P. Sloan School of Management, Massachusetts Institute of Technology.

[33] FUSSLER, H.H. & SIMON, J.L. *Patterns in the use of books in large research libraries*. Chicago, Ill., University of Chicag Library, 1961.

[34] GIFFORD, R. & SOMMER, R. The desk or the bed? *Personnel & Guidance Journal*, vol. 46, 1968, pp. 876-878.

[35] GROSE, M.W. & LINE, M.B. On the construction and care of white elephants. *Library Association Record*, vol. 70, 1968, pp. 2-5.

[36] HAMBURG, M. & others. Library objectives and performance measures and their use in decision making. *Library Quarterly, vol. 42, 1972, pp. 107-128.*

[37] HARRIS, I. W. *The influence of accessibility on academic library use*. Ph.D. thesis. New Brunswick, N. J., Rutgers University, 1966.

[38] HENNING, P. A. & STILLMAN, M. E. eds. Integrating library instruction in the college curriculum. *Drexel Library Quarterly*, vol. 7, nos. 3 & 4, 1971.

[39] HERNER, S. & HERNER, M. Information needs and uses. *Annual Review of Information Science & Technology*, vol. 2, 1967, pp. 1-34.

[40] HOSTROP, R.W. *The relationship of academic success and selected other factors to student use of library materials at College of the Desert*. Ed.D. thesis. Los Angeles, Calif., University of California, 1967.

[41] HUMPHREYS, K. W. Survey of borrowing from the main library, University of Birmingham. *Libri*, vol. 14, 1964, pp. 126-135.

[42] HUTCHINS, W. J. & others. University research and the language barrier. *Journal of Librarianship*, vol. 3, 1971, pp. 1-25.

[43] Hyman, R.J. *Access to library collections: an inquiry into the validity of the direct shelf approach, with special reference to browsing*. Metuchen, N.J. Scarecrow Press, 1972. ISBN 0810804344.

[44] JANDA, K. & RADER, G. SDI: a progress report from North Western University. *American Behavioral Scientist*, vol. 10, 1967, pp. 24-29.

[45] JOYCE, W.D. A study of academic achievement and performance on a test of library understanding. *Journal of Educational Research*, vol. 54, 1961, pp. 198-199.

[46] KNAPP, P.B. *The Monteith College Library experiment*. New York, Scarecrow Press, 1966.

[47]KNAPP, P.B. The reading of college students. *Library Quarterly,* vol. 38, pp. 301-308.

[48]KOTTENSTETTE, J.P. Student reading characterisitics: comparing skill-levels demonstrated on hard copy and microform presentations. *In* NORTH, J.B. *ed. Proceedings of the ASIS vol. 6.* Westport, Conn., Greenwood Publishing Corp. 1969, pp. 345-351.

[49]KRAMER, L.A. & KRAMER, M.B. The college library and the drop-out. *College & Research Libraries,* vol. 29, 1968, pp. 310-312.

[50]KRULEE, G.K. & NADLER, E.B. Studies of education for science and engineering: student values and curriculum choice. *I.R.E. Transactions in Engineering Management,* vol. EM-7, 1960, pp. 146-158.

[51]LADNER, M.M. *The relationship between available pre-college library service and ability to use the library.* M.A. thesis. Atlanta, Ga., Emory University, 1966.

[52]LANE, G. Assessing the undergraduates' use of the university library. *College & Research Libraries,* vol. 27, 1966, pp. 277-282.

[53]LAZARSFELD, P.F. & others. *The People's choice.* 3rd edition. New York, Columbia University Press, 1968.

[54]LINCOLN, C.M. *ed.* Educating the library user: Proceedings of the Fourth triennial meeting of IATUL, Loughborough, April 1st-3rd, 1970. Loughborough University of Technology Library, 1970. ISBN 095014100.

[55]LINE, M.B. Student attitudes to the university library. *Journal of Documentation,* vol. 19, 1963, pp. 100-117.

[56]LINE, M.B. *Library surveys.* London, Bingley, 1967.

[57]LINE, M.B. The information uses and needs of social scientists: an overview of INFROSS. *Aslib Proceedings,* vol. 23, 1971, pp. 412-434.

[58]LINE, M.B. & BRYANT, P. How golden is your retriever? *Library Association Record,* vol. 71, 1969, pp. 135-138.

[59]LINE, M.B. & TIDMARSH, M. Student attitudes to the university library: a second survey. *Journal of Documentation,* vol. 22, 1966, pp. 123-135.

[60]LINE, M.B. & others. *Information requirements of researchers in the social sciences.* (Investigation into information requirements of the social sciences, research report, 1.) Bath University Library, 1971. (OSTI report 5096).

[61]LINE, M.B. & others. *Experimental information officer in the social sciences, 1969-1971: Final report.* Bath University Library, 1972. (OSTI report 5118).

[62]LIPETZ, B.A. Information needs and uses. *Annual Review of Information Science & Technology,* vol. 5, 1970, pp. 3-32.

[63]LIPETZ, B.A. *User requirements in identifying desired works in a large library: Final report.* New Haven, Conn., Yale University Library, 1970. (ERIC report ED-042 479).

[64]LUBANS, J. Student use of a technological university library. *IATUL Proceedings,* vol. 4, 1969, pp. 7-13.

[65]LUBANS, J. On non-use of an academic library: a report of findings. *In Use, mis-use and non-use of academic libraries,* New York Library Association College & University Libraries Section, 1970, pp. 47-70.

[66]LUCKHAM, B. *The Library in society.* London, Library Association, 1971. ISBN 0853653445

[67]McGREGOR, J.W. In defense of the dictionary catalog. *Library Resources & Technical Services,* vol. 15, 1971, pp. 28-33.

[68]MAIZELL, R.G. Information gathering patterns and creativity. *American Documentation,* vol. 11, 1960, pp. 9-17.

[69]MALTBY, A. & SWEENEY, R. The U.K. catalogue use survey. *Journal of Librarianship, vol. 4, 1972, pp. 188-204.*

[70]MARQUIS, D.G. & ALLEN, T.J. Communication patterns in applied technology. *American Psychologist,* vol. 21, 1966, pp. 1052-1060.

[71]MEIER, R.L. Efficiency criteria for the operation of large libraries. *Library Quarterly,* vol. 31, 1961, pp. 215-234.

[72]MIRWIS, A. Academic library instruction — a bibliography, 1960-1970. *Drexel Library Quarterly,* vol. 7, 1971. pp. 327-335.

[73] MORRIS, W. E. M. *Catalogue computerisation project:* Final Report to OSTI, 1967-1971. Pt. 2: Catalogue Use Survey. Newcastle, University of Newcastle Computing Laboratory & Library, (1972) (OSTI report 5110)

[74]O'GARA, P.W. *Physical location as a determinant of communication possibility among R and D engineers. S.M. thesis. Cambridge, Mass., Alfred P. Sloan School of Management, Massachusetts Institute of Technology, 1968.*

[75]ORR, R.M. & others. Development of methodologic tools for planning and managing library services: II. Measuring a library's capability for providing documents. *Bulletin of the Medical Library Association,* vol. 56, 1968, pp. 241-267.

[76]ORWELL, G. Lear, Tolstoy and the fool. *Reprinted in Shooting an elephant and other essays.* London, Secker & Warburg, 1950.

[77]PAGE, B.S. & TUCKER, P.E. The Nuffield pilot survey of library use in the University of Leeds. *Journal of Documentation,* vol. 15, 1959, p. 1-11.

[78]PAISLEY, W.J. Information needs and uses. *Annual Review of Information Science & Technology,* vol. 3, 1968, pp. 1-30.

[79]PAISLEY, W.J. & PARKER, E.B. *Scientific information exchange at an interdisciplinary behavioral science convention.* Stanford, Calif., Stanford Institute for Communication Research, 1967. (PB-174 837)

[80] PEACOCK, P. G. The short loan collection in a university library. *Journal of Librarianship,* vol. 4, 1972, pp. 130-136.

[81]PELZ, D.C. & ANDREWS, F.M. *Scientists in organizations: productive climates for research and development.* New York, Wiley, 1966.

[82]PERKINS, R. *The prospective teacher's knowledge of library fundamentals.* New York, Scarecrow Press, 1965.

[83]*Project for evaluating the benefits from university libraries: Final report.* Durham, University of Durham Computer Unit, 1969. (OSTI report 5056).

[84]RILEY, L.E. *A study of the performance on a library orientation test in relation to the academic achievement and scholastic aptitude of a selected group of freshmen college students at Tuskegee Institute.* M.S. in L.S. thesis. Atlanta, Ga., Atlanta University School of Library Service. 1962.

[85]ROBERTS, R.G. Reilly's Law: the law of retail gravitation. *Library Association Record,* vol. 68, 1966, pp. 390-391.

[86]ROSENBLOOM, R.S. & WOLEK, F.W. *Technology, information and organization: information transfer in industrial R & D.* Boston, Mass., Harvard Graduate School of Business Administration, 1967.

[87] SAUNDERS, W.L. & others. Survey of borrowing from the University of Sheffield Library during one academic year. *In* SAUNDERS, W.L. *ed. The provision and use of library and documentation services.* Oxford, Pergamon, 1966, pp. 115-143.

[88] *Seminar on human aspects of library instruction, 9th December 1969 . . . Proceedings.* Cardiff, Standing Conference of National & University Libraries, (1970).

[89] SHORES, L. & MOORE, J.T. *Peabody Library information test.* Minneapolis, Educational Test Bureau, 1940.

[90] SLATER, M. & KEENAN, S. *Results of a questionnaire on current awareness methods used by physicists prior to publication of "Current Papers in Physics".* New York, American Institute of Physics, 1967. (PB-178 368).

[91] SOMMER, R. The ecology of privacy. *Library Quarterly,* vol. 36, 1966, pp. 234-248.

[92] SOMMER, R. Reading areas in college libraries. *Library Quarterly,* vol. 38, 1968, pp. 249-260.

[93] STREUFERT, S. & CASTORE, C. H. *An implication for the information search concept: effects of increasing success and failure on perceived information quality.* Lafayette, Ind., Purdue University, 1968. (AD-668 529).

[94] TAGLIACOZZO, R. & others. Access and recognition: from users' data to catalogue entries. *Journal of Documentation,* vol. 26, 1970, pp. 230-249.

[95] TAYLOR, R. S. *Question-negotiation and information-seeking in libraries.* (Studies in the man-system interface in libraries, 3.) Bethlehem, Pa., Lehigh University Center for the Information Sciences, 1967. (AD-659 168).

[96] TAYLOR, R. S. *The making of a library: the academic library in transition.* (Hampshire College working papers, 2). New York, Becker & Hayes, 1972. ISBN 047184831X

[97] TIDMARSH, M. N. Instruction in the use of academic libraries. *In* SAUNDERS, W. L., *ed. University and research library studies.* Oxford, Pergamon, 1968. ISBN 0080127266.

[98] TUCKER, P.E. The sources of books for undergraduates. *Journal of Documnetation.* Vol. 17, 1961, pp. 77-95.

[99] URQUHART, J. A. & SCHOFIELD, J. L. Measuring readers' failure at the shelf. *Journal of Documentation,* vol. 27, 1971, pp. 273-286.

[100] URQUHART, J. A. & SCHOFIELD, J. L. Measuring readers' failure at the shelf in three university libraries. *Journal of Documentation,* vol. 28, 1972. pp. 233-241.

[101] *Use, mis-use and non-use of academic libraries.* New York, New York Library Association College & University Libraries Section, 1970.

[102] VICKERY, B. C. & others. Report by Birminghan University Library on surveys carried out in 1964 on the use of the library by undergraduates, graduates students and staff. *In* UNIVERSITY GRANTS COMMITTEE, *Report of the Committee on Libraries.* London, H.M.S.O., 1967, pp. 213-228.

[103] WESTERGAARD, J. & LITTLE, A. Educational opportunities and social selection in England & Wales: trends and policy inplications. *In Social objectives in educational planning.* Paris, O.E.C.D., 1967, pp. 215-232.

[104] WATKINS, D. R. Some notes on "orienting the library to the user". *In Use, mis-use and non-use of academic libraries,* New York, New York Library Association College & University Libraries Section, 1970, pp. 43-45.

[105] WHITE, M. D. *Communications behaviour of academic economists.* Ph.D. thesis. Urbana, University of Illinois, 1971.

[106] WILLMER, M.A.P. Noise in the library. *Library Association Record.* Vol. 71, 1969, pp. 303-304.

[107] WOLEK, F. W. The engineer: his work and needs for information. *In* NORTH, J. B. *ed. Proceedings of the ASIS annual meeting, vol. 6.* Westport, Conn., Greenwood Publishing Corp., 1969. pp. 471-476.

[108] WYATT, R.W. P. The production of video-tapes for library instruction - an account of experience at Brunel University. *In* LINCOLN, C.M. *ed. Educating the library user: Proceedings of the Fourth triennial meeting of IATUL . . . 1970.* Loughborough University of Technology, 1970. pp. 21-25. ISBN 0950141100.

[109] ZALTMAN, G. *Scientific recognition and communication behaviour in high energy physics.* New York, American Institute of Physics. (PB-179 890).

[110] ZELKIND, I. & SPRUG, J. Increased control through decreased controls: a motivational approach. *College & Research Libraries,* vol. 32, 1971, pp. 222-226.

[111] Private communication.

ABOUT THE AUTHOR

Geoffrey Ford read geology at the University of Leicester and took a Post-Graduate Diploma in librarianship at the University of Sheffield. From 1965 to 1967 he worked in the Science Library of the University of Durham, and from 1968-69 was a member of a team working on a project for evaluating benefits from university libraries. In 1969 he became a systems analyst at the University of Bristol, and investigated the feasibility of cooperative automation between five university libraries in the South-West of England. Since 1972 he has been Assistant Director (Research) of the University of Lancaster Library Research Unit where he has been involved in two research projects; one (funded by the Council on Library Resources) was designed to investigate user behaviour in university libraries, while the second project is based on the use of management games in education for librarianship.

Micro-Simulation of Markets

Martin C. J. Elton and Jonathan Rosenhead

Unfortunately this paper may prove hard-going for any other than professional operations researchers. However, it is very common for librarians, managers and researchers to recognize and state the need for improved models of human behavior and response. In this paper, the authors illustrate how this need can be met and how behavioral models can be realised in practice.

1. INTRODUCTION

There is a growing realization that the considerable variety of marketing tools which are at least partly under the control of a firm's marketing manager do not operate independently. For example, a strenuous advertising campaign will have little effect if the product is not widely available for purchase. In similar but more intricate ways, the effects on consumer behaviour and on sales of product characteristics, price and price promotions, package size, outlets, shelf-facings, point-of-sale displays, sales force activities and media advertising are all interrelated.

The realization of the complexity of the system which is a market has coincided with an increasing belief that formal modelling is likely to lead to improved managerial decision-taking. This has given rise to a dilemma for operational researchers. In any market the number of variables, most of them probabilistic, many of them human and imperfectly understood, which are involved is very considerable. A tractable mathematical model of one segment of the market (say, the effect of price on purchase decision) cannot be validated in the real world because of all the unexplained factors. A mathematical model of the *total* market system is not tractable by analytic methods.

It is this dilemma which has led to the current interest in *simulation* models of the total market. The sectors of the market system can each be represented fairly simple; the complexity enters in the interaction of the different sectors; and simulation can produce predictions of market behaviour which would not be feasible analytically.

1.1 Micro-simulation

In defining what micro-simulation is, we have to make two distinctions; between simulation and analysis, and between micro-models and macro-models.

Simulation is a method of making deductions from a mathematical model of a system.[100] Instead of using mathematical manipulation to draw general conclusions about the behaviour of the system, simulation uses the model as a working analogy of the real system. This working analogy can be used to produce repeated realizations of the behaviour through time of the system as modelled. Thus one does not arrive at explicit equations expressing the behaviour of systems of this general type; rather one achieves a number of potential histories of the system, from which the effects of possible modifications to the system can be predicted.

A *micro-model* is one in which the elements are disaggregated, and relate to purposive entities within the system rather than to aggregated concepts or statistics. Thus a macro-model might represent the way in which national spending on consumer durables is related to gross national product, the level of unemployment, etc. A micro-model might represent an individual's purchase decision in terms of his income, job security, etc. To obtain aggregate results from a micro-simulation it is necessary to repeat the simulation for a

SOURCE: Reprinted from the *Operational Research Quarterly* 22 (2) June 1971 pp. 117-144, by permission of the authors and publishers.

sample of decision-makers representative of the whole population.

1.2 Micro-simulation of Markets

The nature of micro-simulation is brought out more clearly by examples than by definitions. The micro-simulation models of market situations which have been constructed are of widely differing complexity. At one extreme Day[50] has simulated the selections made by members of a taste-test panel confronted with a choice between two ice-cream samples with different levels of chocolateness. He made only two assumptions — that consumer preference was normally distributed across the available range of chocolate content, and that the probability of choosing one or other sample could be expressed by a simple formula representing the consumer's ability to discriminate between the taste of ice-cream which has his preferred chocolate content and the tastes to the two alternatives offered. At the other extreme Amstutz[8] has constructed a generalized model of consumer purchase which incorporates factors such as the consumer's demographic characteristics, income and perceived need; brand availability and price, and the consumer's attitudes towards and awareness of different brands; the consumer's response to advertising, word-of-mouth information, experience with the product and the passage of time; the retailer's promotional effort, related to his expected profit; the salesman's effort and the probability that he will change jobs, related to his sales rate, length of service, salary and commission; and so on.

Micro-simulation is particularly appropriate for representing a system in which there are many similar decision-makers, each making repeated decisions of the same type: sufficient data can then more often be found to validate the behavioural hypotheses within the model. Consumer non-durable markets are systems which have this characteristic.

Our definition of micro-simulation inevitably leaves some marginal cases which fall between micro and macro. In particular there are simulation models, such as those using Forrester's[11] *Industrial Dynamics*, where the elements are not individual consumers but commercial enterprises. In other simulation models, individual decision-taking is explicitly represented, but the decision-maker is not a consumer. We have included such intermediate models in our study only when they have contributions of value to make to the practice of micro-simulation.

1.3 General Considerations

A number of articles have been written which describe the nature and advantages of micro-simulation models of markets in a simple and vivid way, easily accessible to non-experts. Orcutt[4] does this elegantly at the level of the national economy. Starr[2] stresses the advantages of the computer as the test market of the future, and gives an example of the sort of marketing situation which mathematical analysis cannot handle but which simulation can. There is also a useful article of this type by Bauer and Buzzell.[1]

It should be stated that, at the time of writing, the development and use of micro-simulation models of markets is still a subject of controversy. Some practitioners (for example, Davis[97]) state that our knowledge is too imperfect for the construction of comprehensive marketing models. Others give the difficulties of validating simulation models as their objection. Still others simply believe that the old ways are best, and that aggregated analytic models with suitable sophistications are adequate to the needs of the situation.

As indicated by our earlier remarks, we cannot accept this last proposition. The other objections are ones we would agree with, up to a point. But, given the potential value of the simulation approach, they seem to us to be arguments for increased activity in the area rather than reasons to abandon it entirely.

Our purpose in writing this paper is to give an integrated presentation of the application of the micro-simulation approach to the study of markets. In particular we wish to emphasize the methodological considerations which we believe should govern the use of the approach; the technical problems which are only rarely specified in the literature; and the need to be eclectic in the selection of model formulations. Much of the discussion is also relevant to the simulation of social systems other than markets. We have backed our presentation wherever possible with references to published work which while not exhaustive are nevertheless copious. Where we have failed to do so, we would plead in mitigation that out study is concerned with an area which is both diffuse and rapidly growing; and also that relevant and important research for commercial organisations does not always result in publications. It is our hope that this paper may provide at least a first guide to the territory, and that the inclusion of a considerable bibliography will be of assistance to those who intend to branch out on their own.

1.4 Plan of the Paper

Section 2 deals with problems of methodology — When is simulation called for? What is the appropriate level of detail? How can the model be formulated, validated and used? Section 3 is concerned with the technical problems of building and using micro-simulation models, such as the choice of basic units and of time intervals, data requirements, the testing of the model and the design of simulation experiments. In Section 4 is presented a wide range of sources for particular model formulations, while Section 5 describes published case studies. Section 6 contains information on related fields of study, and on the costs of micro-simulation, as well as some concluding thoughts.

We have adopted an indexing system for the references which permits movement in either direction between the index and the text. As an aid to those with particular interests the references are grouped into general categories in the bibliography. Those works which span several categories have been allocated to the categories to which they seem to make the most significant contribution.

2. METHODOLOGICAL

The methodological problems connected with the use of microsimulations are formidable. They may be summarized as:
When is simulation the indicated tool?
What is an appropriate level of disaggregation?
How is the model to be constructed?
How is the model to be treated?
How is the model to be used?

2.1 When to use Simulation

The circumstances which make simulation at the micro-level a productive approach are dealt with extensively in the review articles

referred to in Subsection 1.3, and (at a rather more technical level) by Orcutt.[5] In brief, simulation is a means of making deductions from a mathematical model or hypothesis. As such it is (as shown in Figure 1) an alternative to mathematical analysis. When the mathematics is tractable, analysis is normally the most efficient means of making deductions from the model to compare with observations from the real world. However, the mathematics is often intractable, particularly when the model involves a large number of interacting variables, many of them probabil-

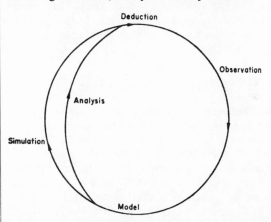

Figure 1.   THE PLACE OF SIMULATION IN MODEL FORMULATION AND TESTING.

istic, and when the model is dynamic — that is, the state of the modelled system at any time depends on its states at earlier points in time. These factors all apply to micro-models of markets.

Models of the market need to be micro-models if we are to understand and hence explain (rather than just describe) market behaviour. This can be illustrated by analogy with psephology — the study of elections and their results. In its simpler manifestations, election results are described in terms of the percentage "swing" in votes from one party to another. But these swings are aggregates which disguise many, perhaps contrary, tendencies. Those who vote for one party at an election may at the previous election have voted for a third party or abstained. Or they may have only come on to the electoral roll in the interim, while others will have departed. To understand the electoral process we must descend to a level of detail below the aggregate.

Similar arguments apply to models of

markets. Orcutt *et al.*[6] make the general point that an advantage of micro-simulation is that hypotheses are made about entities to which a manager or social scientist can intuitively relate. That is, the model represents the actions of a human decision maker, rather than the behaviour of some aggregated concept. Frijda,[20] in a stimulating article on problems of methodology, makes the similar point that model formulation in these areas must rely on analysing the researcher's introspection.

Orcutt[21,22] emphasizes that to test the hypotheses and to estimate the parameters which any model of a social system must incorporate requires large amounts of data. Only by considering micro-components can we provide this.

2.2   The Level of Disaggregation

The errors which can result from inappropriate aggregation have been ingeniously explored by Orcutt *et al.*[23] and by Stasch.[25] The former constructed and ran a simple micro-analytic model of the economic behaviour of a number of homogeneous spending units. Conventional least-squares estimation of the model parameters was applied to the simulation output at three different levels of aggregation. Appreciable increases in bias, in standard error of estimates and in the difficulty of detecting mis-specified model formulations occurred at each level of aggregation.

A similar technique was used by Stasch to investigate how aggregation affects discrimination between different hypotheses. He constructed a model of the adoption of an innovation, in terms of interpersonal contacts between members of his simulated population. Twenty-one hypothetical models (including the actual generator) were then simulated, and their outputs compared with the original "observed" simulation data at three levels of aggregation. The most aggregated data were quite unable to discriminate between the hypothetical models. As increasingly disaggregative measures were used more of the erroneous hypotheses could be rejected.

Both these examples deal with the effect of data aggregation, not with the effect of using a macro-model to fit a micro-reality. This problem is less accessible to quantitative exploration.

2.3   Model Construction, Testing and Use

The problems of model formulation, testing and use cannot be treated separately. There is a need for restraint in model formulation which springs from the very power and bluntness of the simulation instrument. Simulation removes the restriction that models need be analytically tractable, and so makes possible the development of models of a scale and complexity limited only by cost and by computer size. There is a danger of constructing models because they are possible without regard to how they can be validated. This problem is discussed by Frijda[20] and Rosenhead.[24]

Models should be constructed initially in the simplest form which appears capable of explaining the phenomena of interest. Formulations of particular relationships within the model can be based on historical information, generally accepted theories (where they exist — see Section 4), or on the educated intuitions of management and researcher. (Churchman[96] emphasizes that the "facts" of science exist only because the scientist has been bold enough to make assumptions.) The model construction should permit each formulation to be "unplugged" — that is, replaced by another formulation or modified without requiring any but minor revision of the rest of the model. Orcutt[4] and Orcutt *et al.*[6] emphasize this need for modular modelling.

Starting from the initial version of the model it is possible to investigate how sensitive its outputs are to the precision with which the values of particular model parameters are estimated, or to the replacement of one particular formulation by another. These procedures can offer great savings in research effort and in the cost of data collection. To test all the individual hypotheses which go to make up a simulation model would involve designing and carrying out numerous experiments either in a laboratory environment or in the real world. To obtain precise estimates of all the model parameters can necessitate massive data collection. At any stage in the model construction it is important that resources should be employed so as to reduce the residual variation by as much as possible. In this way the model can develop most speedily to the point where it has value to management — a major tactical consideration in maintaining support for a project which must necessarily continue for several years.

One of the best illustrations of evolutionary modelling is given by Urban and Karash,[56] who describe a marketing simulation based on a number of different classes of consumer, rather than on individual consumers. They illustrate how a succession of increasingly complex models can be developed and used.

Among the advantages claimed by Urban and Karash are an increased managerial understanding and acceptance; an orderly development of data base and data analysis capability; the reduction of project risk by the availability of opportunities for review; learning by model builders about the level of detail for the model and about managers; and the availability of short-term benefits.

Amstutz[94] has advocated a characteristically distinctive approach to model formulation and testing: to base model-building entirely on the *managers'* perceptions of the market, though incorporating the results of interaction between the managers and the scientists. Model sectors are tested by comparing their predictions with real-world observations. When these are not in accord, the managers are invited to reformulate the situation in co-operation with the model-building team. The submodel is only changed in accordance with managers' reformulations, which has implications at the testing stage. This approach is elaborated by Little.[65]

A simulation marketing model can make contributions of value to management before its predictive ability has been demonstrated. For example, Claycamp and Amstutz[10] draw an analogy with war games — by playing with the model the manager will be able to obtain "experience" useful in his day-to-day decision-making. That is, the simulation can be used as a management training device. At a later stage the output of an unvalidated model can yet be indicative to management of the qualitative effects of possible marketing strategies. Ackoff[93] suggests the use of a model as a standard against which to compare operating data; deviations from prediction may lead to management action (management by exception) or revision of the model.

At what point then can one regard the model as validated? As indicated in Section 3, there are no accepted statistical goodness-of-fit tests for the outputs of models of this type. Testing is therefore a subjective procedure — a

model is "valid" when management accepts it as such for its purposes. (See, for example, Sisson.[7]) This methodology of model development implies that even when the model has been accepted there will be some untested hypotheses, some subjectively or inadequately estimated parameters in the model. Therefore there must be continuing improvements to the model even after it has been adopted by management. There is no sharp distinction between the development and testing phase of model construction and its use. The former shades into the latter.

The use to which a marketing model is put is of course very much a matter for individual managements. Its principal value is to permit evaluation of the joint effects of the diverse actions which make up a marketing policy. This may be done on an *ad hoc* basis, examining the implications of particular proposed policies, or, more purposefully, searching for improved policies. If the second alternative is adopted, the space of feasible policies may be explored systematically using techniques of experimental design or of experimental optimization.

3. TECHNICAL PROBLEMS OF MICROSIMULATION

Conway[30] has written an excellent paper drawing attention to the neglected tactical problems which occur in running any simulation — problems of how to set up the starting conditions for a run, and of how to handle the variability in simulation output. If microsimulation models have especial problems, they result from the high level of detail involved — the large quantity of survey data required, the large number of decision takers who may be simulated and the lengthy chains of simple decisions that may be considered for each individual. In this Section we discuss some of the problems of technique that arise is consequence. It is not possible to be exhaustive in the space available, but, in being illustrative, we attempt to single out the problems that arise most frequently.

3.1 Model Construction

First we must define some terms; we use the terminology of Orcutt:

Component, decision unit — the basic
building block, generally an individual or
a family;

Operating characteristics — the behavioural relations used to generate output
from a decision unit or to update its
status variables;

Status variables — the variables which are
updated as the simulation proceeds, and
used to describe the components;[101] a
particular value is an output from an
operating characteristic at one stage, an
input to an operating characteristic at
the next.

By way of example, a rule for brand-selection
would be an operating characteristic. The
attitudes which influence the choice would be
status variables. These attitudes would be updated in the light of experience with the
product, according to rules which would
themselves be operating characteristics.

Once he has decided to construct a micro-
simulation the following fundamental questions
face the model builder whatever the situation studied:

 (i) What are the decision units to be?
 (ii) How are these to be characterized?
 (iii) What are the boundaries of the model?
 Can the model be uncoupled? (See
 Sub-section 3.1.3 below.)
 (iv) How long is the time interval between
 successive simulations of an individual's
 behaviour?
 (v) How many decision units are to be used?
 (vi) What input data are to be used both to
 start the series of simulation runs, and
 for comparison with output so as to serve
 as a basis for testing and control?

3.1.1. *The decision units.* In marketing simulations the decision units will probably be
individual purchasers, although it may sometimes be necessary to model the behaviour
of other members of the family who consume.
If the behaviour of the whole market is to
be considered other decision-making units
to be included are retailers and competing
organizations.

Not all models are based on individuals.
Some use the family as an entity; others,
in industrial markets, are based on individual
firms.

3.1.2. *Characterization of the decision units.*
Some of the variables used to differentiate
decision-makers will be demographic —

age, income etc. The particular demographic
variables employed must depend on the natur
of the market. Of more general interest are
the status variables, which are updated
during the simulation. In a particular case the
characterization chosen will be affected by
the type of data that can be made available.
However, status variables are frequently
attitudinal. In such cases much of the detail
of the model, in the present state of our
knowledge, is incapable of direct testing. An
example of this is Lavington's[53] model, in
which purchasing probabilities are computed
in terms of "stimulus elements" in the brain.
There is a divergence of opinion as to the
validity of such approaches. One argument
advanced is that if the model works well, that
is a sufficient justification. A counter-view
is that if too much detail is included (particularly if it is inherently untestable), irrelevant
variables will clutter-up the model without
their irrelevance ever being discovered.

Another point to be resolved is whether or
not there is to be a one-to-one correspondence between the computer's sample of
desicion-making units and some units in the
real world. If there is, the model can be considered to predict the behaviour of the real
panel and is capable of being checked
against this; alternatively it is possible to
generate a sample of individuals with
attributes which are proportional to their
incidence in the population at large. (Balderston and Hoggatt[46] generate preference
orderings over possible suppliers in this
way for their customers.) Of course if interaction between different attributes of the
individual are important, then data must have
been collected from one particular sample
in order to obtain the necessary joint distribution functions.

3.1.3. *Boundaries of the model.* This is
one of the first considerations of any marketing
model, whatever its type. It is governed by
the use to which the model is to be put.

Orcutt *et al.*[6] point out that it is sometimes necessary to divide a model into parts
because of computer restrictions. This is the
case in their comprehensive economic
model; rather than match up individual
purchasers and retailers for each purchase
he introduces a common interface, the market, which both affect and by which both
are affected. A customer is not matched
with a particular supplier; instead he con-

siders purchase in terms of the endogenously determined market price. If he purchases, this changes the observed level of demand at that price and so influences supplier behaviour in subsequent periods.

3.1.4. *Length of the time intervals.* Orcutt[4] draws attention to the requirement of block-recursiveness. In a micro-simulation individual decision units are considered sequentially. Each unit is taken through a period of simulated time, during which period the status variables of the other units are assumed to be fixed. So although decision units interact, unit i's behaviour only affects j's in later periods. (The situation is illustrated in Figure 2.) This is clearly only an approximation to reality, and the approximation becomes less valid as the time

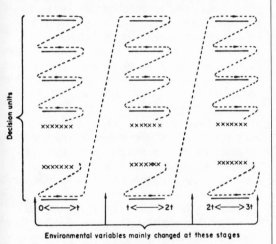

Environmental variables mainly changed at these stages

Path of computer model - → -

FIGURE 2. SEQUENTIAL PROCESSING OF A MICRO-SIMULATION

intervals grow longer. The length of the time-interval t (in Figure 2) must be a compromise — if it is too long the approximation to reality is insufficiently close, but if it is too short the computer-time required may increase unacceptably.

3.1.5. *Number of decision units.* This is primarily a statistical matter, the larger the number, the smaller the sampling variance. Ideally the number should be increased until the value of the marginal gain in accuracy is balanced by the cost of including the marginal unit. This, however, is as hard to evaluate in practice as it is easy to recommend in theory.[102]

One of the authors has experience of a model in which there are two classes of consumers, the behaviour of one of which is considerably more variable than that of the other. To improve precision relatively more of the former are included in the model, and the results are weighed accordingly.

3.1.6. *Input data.* Time series information for a set of the decision units is essential for model validation and parameter estimation. In a few consumer markets it is considered virtually impossible to collect reasonable panel data and this raises formidable problems.

It is advisable to collect data which can be used to monitor the values of the status variables. Although these are of little interest in their own right, they can serve as a useful check that the model is "under control".

In addition to data for initializing the model and for input during simulation runs, it is also necessary to provide data to establish the operating characteristics. It is unlikely that the organization's routine data collection will be of adequate scope, so it may be necessary to arrange for the collection of supplementary information. As the model progresses a need will develop for historical data on the market as a whole — advertising schedules of competing brands, price and distribution levels, as well as information on the attitudes and behaviour of consumers — with which to compare the output of the model. At an early stage steps should be taken to collect these data on a continuing basis, to provide a history of adequate length.

The parameters of the model's operating characteristics may be estimated externally or internally. If externally, the parameters are estimated at the level of the decision units so as to give the best fit to the data; this requires highly disaggregated data, preferably in the form of time series. If internally, the parameter values are chosen in such a way that the model itself gives the best fit to the data; this can be done, for example, by a search over the parameter space using the maximum-likelihood method. The distinction is not rigid — some parameters may be estimated one way, some another.

Although internal estimation may require less data, it does require more computer time, since each point in the function space requires a simulation run. Methodologically external estimation is preferable since it serves to test the model at the same time, and since it makes fuller use of the information in the disaggregate data.

3.2. Running the Model

3.2.1. *Model efficiency.* Since micro-simulation models require so much computer running time it is particularly important that the simulation procedures should be efficient. Consideration must therefore be given to variance reduction techniques and the elimination of transient effects.

Meier *et al.*[14] (Chapters 7 to 9) present a useful, non-technical discussion of these issues; the chapters are readily understandable and selective, rather than advanced and comprehensive. More technical are the works of Tocher[19] and of Hammersley and Handscomb.[12] The latter has a section on variance reduction techniques which will be of value to the mathematically inclined, while the former covers a wider range of subject matter.

A choice confronting all who construct computer simulation models is that of programming language — many are available with differing characteristics. Teichroew and Lubin[26] give a comparative survey of six of them. The particular details have inevitably been outdated by subsequent developments but the general principles stated for choice between languages remain valid. It certainly remains true that there is no one simulation language which is best for a wide variety of problems. Tocher[27] discusses the distinguishing characteristics of simulation languages — data structures, language syntax and facilities — but does not give a detailed comparison of the available languages.

3.2.2. *Use of results from field experiments.* The results of field experiments even if conducted independently of the research in hand, can make valuable contributions to model validation in two ways. First, it is necessary that the model should reproduce the results. It is particularly valuable if in some of the experimental results the control variables lie in hitherto unexplored territory. The goodness-of-fit of the model and experimental results at these points should be comparable to the fit at those experimental observations at which the control variables have more customary values.

Secondly, provided data collection has not only been at an aggregate level there may be some highly relevant additional data to use. The researcher is well advised to collect information at the level of the individual in marketing experiments even if he does not have a micro-model in mind. By doing so he may check for latent effects — such as attitude changes — that will have perceptible aggregate effects during the time span of the experiment.

Thus micro-simulation models and field experiments are complementary: the latter provide data and, maybe, operating characteristics for the former, whereas the former provide a base for the generalization of the results of the latter.

3.2.3. *Testing the models.* How a model is tested depends to some extent on the philosophy underlying its construction. No generally accepted statistical goodness-of-fit tests exist for simulation models, partly because of philosophical differences and partly because of the complexity of simulation output. The position is reviewed by Naylor and Finger,[39] in one of the few articles to advocate the use of statistical test procedures in the validation of simulations. Schrank and Holt[43] have commented that for a complex model which necessarily contains residual errors its truth or falsity is less relevant than its degree of usefulness. This approach would preclude the application of standard statistical tests.

Generally the problem is that of comparing time series, the one from the real world, the other from the simulation model. This applies whether one is testing one of the sub-models or the model *in toto*. The letters of Radosevich,[41,42] Naylor[36,37] and Clarkson[28] in *Management Science* well illustrate different standpoints as to the testing of simulation models; they draw attention to the fact that different test procedures are needed for testing the fit between model output and real data, and for validating behavioural postulates.

The most commonly advocated test (for example, Amstutz,[8] Clarkson,[48] Feldman[86]) for comparing the time series is the Turing[92] test. In this test someone well-acquainted with the real world situation compares sets of real and simulated series; if he cannot distinguish between them the model passes the test.

Other methods compare the number of

turning points and other mathematical properties of the observed and simulated series. (See, for example, Cyert.[49]) Fishman and Kiviat[31] and Naylor et al.[40] describe the more mathematically advanced technique of *spectral analysis*. The latter paper lists the advantages of spectral analysis, two of which are that it deals directly with the autocorrelation present in a time series (this presents considerable difficulty to other techniques), and that it makes relatively simple the construction of confidence bands and the testing of alternative hypotheses.

These methods can only test the models in situations in which the controllable and uncontrollable variables (for example, one's own and competitors' advertising) take on values that they have had in the past, so that series of observations from the real world do exist. When the variables move outside such ranges one's confidence in the model's predictions will depend on the level of disaggregation at which it has been tested — the more disaggregated the better. For example, if the model has reproduced total sales satisfactorily it could still be that predictions of sales to different sectors of the market are producing balancing errors; if the sectors respond differently to changes in advertising, errors are likely to emerge when simulating an advertising situation that has not been observed before. The moral, drawn earlier, is that micro-simulations and planned experiments are not alternative approaches, but are complementary to each other.

3.2.4. *The problem of experimental design.* The ultimate purpose of microsimulation models is to enable the manager to make better decisions by appreciating more fully the implications of the alternative courses open to him. This is done by running the simulation model under different conditions: simulation runs are series of experiments in the simulated world. The highly detailed simulations considered in this paper are costly of computer time, and in consequence the efficient design of experiments is of great importance.

The subject has recently been receiving the increased attention it deserves. A useful survey of the state of the art is that of Naylor[16] (a collection of papers which also covers several of the other technical problems treated in this chapter). The review paper of Naylor et al.[38] discusses both the principles of experimental design for simulation models and

the main problems that arise; it has a particularly useful bibliography. Although the example they use is of a macro-simulation the principles are equally valid for micro-simulation. The paper distinguishes two reasons for experimentation — finding a response variable optimum, and relating response variables to controllable variables — which require different techniques. The first is normal in marketing, where a typical problem might be to decide the advertising expenditures in different media, or to set the price of the product so as to maximize sales. The second, however, applies to economic simulation models, where one must first discover which variables exert the greatest influence on the response. The next step is to explore how the response varies as a function of these variables; only then does one attempt to develop *explanatory* models to describe *why* the response works. (This is therefore, a reversal of the procedure used in marketing models.)

In either case, whether the experimentation is aimed at discovering an optimum, or at the exploration of the relation between the controllable variables and the response, a useful intermediate stage may be the application of screening devices. These are means of identifying variables which have the greatest effect on the responses of interest. Hunter[33] provides a valuable paper based upon Box's pioneering work. Hunter and Naylor[34] cover much the same ground, as well as treating response surface techniques — that is, techniques for finding settings of the control variables which maximize the response. An illuminating example of the use of these techniques is given by Bonini.[47]

In cases where it is appropriate to compare alternative marketing decisions rather than to seek an optimal one, it is necessary first to find whether there are genuine differences between the responses to the alternatives; and then, if possible, rank or quantify such differences. Naylor et al.[40] provide a useful introduction to the statistical considerations involved. Spectral analysis also has a role in the examination of alternative marketing decisions. Just as (see the preceeding subsection) it can be used to compare a simulated with a real world time series, so it can also be used to investigate differences between two simulated times series, each the result of possible alternative management decisions.

Other sources of techniques in experimental

design are Cochran and Cox[29] and Jacoby and Harrison.[35] Unlike the former which is a standard work on experimental design in general, the latter is devoted to experimenting with simulation models; it contains many valuable suggestions, but will not be accessible to the non-specialist reader.

4. OPERATING CHARACTERISTICS

The central model formulations in marketing micro-simulations are those concerning the behaviour of consumers. The formulations (or operating characteristics) must be descriptive rather than normative, since we are interested not in the behaviour of a theoretical "rational" man, but in the observable behaviour of real people.

The individual decisions for which operating characteristics are required fall into two main categories — those concerned with the response to marketing pressures, and those concerned with the workings of the social system on which the market operates. Operating characteristics of the second type will tend to be specific to particular marketing applications, while those of the first type are likely to be of more general application.

An objection is sometimes raised that individuals frequently do not arrive at decisions in the formalized manner specified by computable operating characteristics. This is clearly true. Some of the misunderstandings about the status of operating characteristic formulations would be avoided if reports of simulation models followed Frijda's[20] advice to distinguish clearly between what is essential theory, and what is mere mechanism for programming convenience — for example, the generation of random numbers, or the setting of counters to control the program operations.

4.1. General Sources

Amstutz[8] gives a comprehensive set of formulations of marketing decisions and their effects, incorporating everything from the consumer's decision to talk about a brand, to the distributor's decision to fire a salesman. It is unclear which formulations have been tested and which are interesting hypotheses. The book may most usefully serve as a quarry of possible sub-models from which researchers can excavate those which seem most appropriate.

Berelson and Steiner[76] also provide a mine of information about scientific findings on human behaviour. Many of the results are suggestive of possible formal models relevant to market behaviour. However, the findings are often phrased in qualitative rather than quantitative terms, and the absence of consistent references to the sources of the reported findings produces added difficulties.

Montgomery and Urban's[66] survey of management science in marketing is an invaluable compendium of mathematical models of different parts of the marketing process. There are sections on advertising decisions, pricing decisions, distribution decisions, personal selling decisions and new product decisions. There is also a section on models of over-all market response, in which an attempt is made to compare the stochastic (that is, analytic) and the simulation approaches. The authors urge the assembly of a model bank, from which practitioners could draw according to their needs.

Nicosia[67] provides not so much a set of operating characteristics for market processes, as a set of conceptual schemes within which models can be built. He summarizes the contribution of Parsons, the schools of Katona and Lazarsfeld, and stimulus-response theory; and proposes a comprehensive scheme which is intended to avoid some of the inadequacies he finds in these theories. This work contains a wide-ranging bibliography. Katona[63] analyses from a psychologist's viewpoint the effect of such factors as the level of income, and changes in it, on the consumer's decision to spend or save; he emphasizes the habitual nature of such decisions.

A work of particular value is that of Engel et al.[61] The authors develop a conceptual model of consumer motivation and behaviour which is both comprehensive and lucid; and the model is supported by a thorough exploration and evaluation of empirical evidence from both marketing and behavioural science. Research results are presented on such facets of behaviour as the number of alternative brands considered by the consumer, and the effect on readership and awareness of advertisement size, position and repetition.

4.2 Aspects of Behaviour

An aspect of consumer behaviour which has received extensive attention from a school of researchers at Harvard is its dependence on perceived risk. The consumer's perceived risk has a number of components — uncertainty about buying goals, uncertainty as to which brand or product best satisfies the goal, and uncertainty about the possible adverse consequences if the product fails to satisfy. Cox[60] has brought together a collection of papers which discuss, at the theoretical and the empirical level, the way in which perceived risk affects brand or product choice, and how consumers acquire and handle information to make the perceived risk acceptable.

Foote[71] has edited a collection of papers treating decision-making within family units. Major purchase and other financial decisions are analysed in terms of interactions between different members of the family.

Orcutt et al.[17] describe a pioneering demographic simulation in which the births, deaths, marriages and divorces of a population of twelve thousand are represented. Major individual economic decisions, for example house purchase, are associated with these events, and the demographic simulation was to have been the starting point for a simulation of the United States economy. This has not materialized to date.

The same authors have republished the central portion of this work as a shorter article.[6] Included are a model of a market with the function of distributing demand among a number of sellers, and a model of the operations of a bank.

An important element in many markets is the diffusion by word of mouth of a product's reputation. Rogers,[83] in a classic volume, reviews work on the spread of innovations carried out in a variety of research traditions. He gives his own analysis of the process of personal innovation, from awareness through trial to adoption, and discusses the individual and environmental circumstances which affect the process. Coleman et al.[85] present a sociological study of the way in which adoption of a new product spreads (among doctors) from identifiable opinion leaders. Abelson and Bernstein[44] and McPhee et al[87] each in the context of voting, model the process of discussion among simulated individuals of matters of mutual interest. Hagerstrand,[51] dealing with the

spread of new farming methods, produces a good fit to reality with a simple model in which the probability of adoption is based principally on the proximity of a neighbor who has made the advance. Festinger[79] presents a general psychological theory relating the information sources chosen by an individual to his need to reduce any inconsistencies (or dissonance) among his knowledge, opinions or beliefs about himself or his environment. Arndt[68] describes empirical tests of the theories of Cox and of Festinger; the book also demonstrates that cut-and-dried operating characteristics are rarely available.

There are a variety of other works which examine parts of the market system theoretically or empirically. Rosenhead[24] develops formulations for attitude change under product experience and advertising, for decision taking based on several factors, and for elements of the G.P.-specialist-patient system which provides the market for ethical pharmaceuticals. Axelrod[69] describes an experiment which compared the effectiveness of various attitudinal measures as predictors of purchasing behaviour. Coleman[84] gives an analytic development of the way in which variability of response probability within a population affects the observable change of behaviour, for example in brand-switching. Peckham[74] gives empirical data on the percentage of supermarket shoppers who will substitute a different brand or package-size if their choice is not available. Simmons[75] used the same technique for a similar problem from the standpoint of the United Kingdom rather than the United States. McConnell[73] describes some effects of a gaming simulation of the United States beer market, which suggest that price perceptions of a brand vary in a surprising fashion as the price of a competing brand is changed. Emery[70] has reported a similar result.

Any selection of operating characteristics concerning explicit marketing variables is inevitably subjective. Further examples of models of particular marketing phenomena could easily be gathered from the marketing literature. Empirical data are much more inaccessible, though many relevant studies must exist as the private property of individual firms. But in the last resort the operating characteristics incorporated in a model will be, in part, special to the particular market; and therefore there is no substitute for the collection and study of data from the actual market which is to be modelled.

5. CASE STUDIES

It is only in recent years that micro-analytic simulations have become computationally feasible. The consequent shortage of case studies is aggravated by the commercial secrecy which surrounds the implementation of marketing science. Such integrated models as are reported are often only partially described; or the description is fairly complete, but no output is described; or the output is described, but no comparison is made with real-world data.

5.1. Complete Case Studies of Consumer Behaviour

Published studies mainly relate to industrial markets or to manufacturer/trader markets. The only overall model that we have found in the literature in which the decision units are individuals is the Claycamp and Amstutz[10] study of ethical pharmaceuticals. The interactions of patients, with individual histories of treatments and complaints, and of doctors, with memories of drugs' past effectiveness and with attitudes partly determined by controllable marketing variables, are simulated. These interactions determine present treatments and prescriptions which themselves will influence future recovery of patients, attitudes of doctors and so on. Information on the model's financial and computer requirements (not included in the published report) will be found in our concluding chapter.

Urban and Karash[56] have given a detailed description of their "Sprinter" family of models, which evolve in complexity from a simple brand loyalty model to include factors such as awareness, forgetting, price-effect, samples, point-of-sale displays, shelf-facings, number of sales representatives' calls and word-of-mouth advertising.

Herniter et al.[52] describe in some detail a marketing micro-simulation package to simulate up to 500 consumers, 50 time periods, 10 brands and 10 stores. The interaction of brand choice and store choice is one of the features of this model. A fairly full account is given of experiments carried out with the

model. However, little information is given of the source of the sub-model formulations; many of the parameters are estimated by obtaining a best fit to the observed market shares of all brands, using a steepest-ascent search procedure.

A most useful contribution is that of Balderston and Hoggatt[45, 46] who have developed a simulation model of the lumber trade on the West coast of the United States. The flow of both material and information between producers, wholesalers and retailers is simulated. Decisions on choice of trading partners are determined by preference orderings built up endogenously. New firms enter the market if average profits are greater than an entry threshold. A valuable feature of the study lies in the clear way in which a real model is used to illustrate important methodological concepts.

In Lloyd-Jacobs'[54] simulation study of a mining industry the basic elements are several hundred mines, and the decision units are the mine managements. The author emphasizes that sensitivity analysis should be used to guide the allocation of research effort to different parts of the model. He also advocates the simulation approach as a means of integrating management's fragmentary knowledge of the system it manages.

5.2 Other Case Studies

In view of the shortage of published case histories it is reasonable to refer here to a number of papers which either deal with segments of a market model or describe a total model of the decisions of an individual who is not a consumer.

Cyert[49] describes a simulation of a department store's ordering and pricing, based on a study of the buyers' behaviour over a period of time. Operating rules are derived which enable very satisfactory predictions to be made.

Clarkson[48] gives another thorough account of the simulation of the behaviour of one decison-maker — the trust investment officer of a bank. The model simulates his decisions in choosing investment strategies for particular accounts by scanning through stored information on the economy, and on particular industries and companies, and applying certain decision-rules. The model produced investment portfolios which were closer to the investment officers' actual behaviour than the predictions of more straightforward models.

Bonini[47] describes fully a simulation of the information and decision systems within a firm, in a marketing context. The intention behind the work is to explore the consequences of a set of postulates, rather than to establish a valid general representation of organizational behaviour. The model incorporates the planning process, the control system and the actual operations in the environment. Several hundred variables are produced as output, including the levels of price, stocks, costs, sales and profits. A full description is given of the experimental design used to explore the implications of the model.

Both Rosenhead[24] and Warner[57] present detailed flow diagrams of particular markets. The former, like Claycamp and Amstutz,[10] deals with the prescribing of drugs, and the latter models a grocery market. Both models have reached the programming stage, but neither has been fitted to data yet. Weiss[3] provides a less detailed formulation for a micro-simulation model in a paper setting out the strengths of simulation approaches to marketing problems.

Case studies have, in the future, a most important role to serve. They will increase management confidence in the approach and show how the models may be used.[103] They will provide the management scientist with estimates of the necessary investment in manpower and computer time. They will illustrate the sorts of difficulties that can arise and how they may be overcome. They will bring evidence to bear on methodological arguments. They will reduce the need for papers such as this.

6.   CONCLUSION

There are a number of different fields which are relevant, important or vital to the successful simulation of markets. Many of these fields are not home territory to operational researchers — indeed it would be surprising to find an individual from any profession or discipline who was expert or knowledgeable in all these fields.

It follows that this is an area in which the legend that operational research is carried out by interdesciplinary teams can most usefully be revived. Ideally a team might consist of a psychologist, a sociologist, a statistician, a marketing man and an expert computer programmer; it may also be useful that one of the first four should have experience of writing simulation programs.

Unfortunately ideals are rarely achieved. In the absence of the desired specialist, non-specialists may wish to acquire at least a general knowledge of the relevant disciplines. We give here some sources which can provide an introduction to these fields.

6.1.   Related Fields

There is now over ten years' entensive experience in the design and running of (mainly industrial) computer simulations. The theoretical aspects of simulation are treated by Tocher.[19] His approach to simulation puts great emphasis on its role as a sampling experiment for the derivation of complex sampling distributions, but he gives a thorough grounding in simulation procedures, from the generation of random numbers onwards. Chorafas[9] provides examples of the simulation of a wide variety of systems — industrial, commercial and military. Shubik[18] gives a bibliography of simulation and allied fields containing over 300 items covering the period up to 1960; very few of them are directly concerned with marketing. Naylor's[15] very useful bibliography contains over 400 items covering the period up to 1968. I.B.M.'s[13] bibliography on simulation might be useful if it were legible. None of the bibliographies are annotated.

Mathematical sociology is a comparatively new and rapidly growing field. Holland and Steuer[80] provide a bibliography with brief notes about each of more than 450 items. Few of them would contribute directly to the sort of study we have described, but the directions which this subject is taking could well be suggestive to model builders.

Psychology is more immediately relevant to the study of individual decision-making. Edwards and Tversky[78] have edited a collection of papers on decision-making which analyse the notions of utility and subjective probability. Models of both riskless and risky choice are considered, and the extensive experimental probing of the way in which individuals make choices is surveyed. In the same series of publications Jahoda and Warren[81] have edited a collection of papers on attitudes. Something called as "attitude" is a frequent component of marketing models, and this book is a valuable corrective to the sometimes uninhibited use of the concept. Of particular relevance are the sections on attitude change, and on the relation between attitudes and behaviour.

Luce et al.[82] provide a survey of mathematical psychology, including mathematical models of social interaction, stochastic learning theory and stimulus sampling theory. A more extensive presentation of mathematical learning theory is given by Bush and Mosteller.[77] Computer simulation of personality is treated in Tomkins and Messick.[90] These reports of attempts to simulate such human processes as problem-solving, the development of perception and language, neurotic processes and cognition provide stimulating examples of the possible range of simulation models.

The collection of validating data for a model presents both practical and methodological problems. A particular problem is that of devising measures of people's preferences. A detailed study of psychological scaling methods is provided by Torgerson.[91] Handyside[72] gives a briefer handbook on attitude scaling, which many non-experts will find a most helpful introduction. An introduction to content analysis, a group of techniques for the quantitative description of the content of verbal or written communications is given by North et al.[88] Content analysis has been under-used in studies of the consumer decision process; however, there is a discussion of its application to the analysis of advertising material in Stone et al.[89]

Lastly there is the very extensive literature on markets and marketing. In a field growing so fast no comprehensive list of references can be given. Nevertheless, Langhoff,[64] Buzzell,[59] Alderson and Shapiro,[58] and Frank et al.[62] provide collections of marketing science papers of wide interest. The integrated account of marketing science formulations presented by Montgomery and Urban[66] is a valuable contribution.

6.2   Scale of Effort

A corollary of the paucity of case studies is that there is very little published information about the costs, in time, money and other resources, of developing a micro-simulation model of a market. However, through the co-operation of their authors we have been able to collect cost information for several of the case studies reported in this paper.

The Balderston and Hoggatt lumber-trade model (see Balderston and Hoggatt[45]) took 3 years of elapsed time and 8 man-years of effort to develop. Computer time cost nearly $30,000, and total costs amounted to $100,000; the follow-up study of Preston and Collins[55] cost an additional $10,000. It is clear that much of the cost goes on development. Hoggatt[98] (private communication) writes that "I would estimate that the original model could be programmed from scratch in six weeks for a total cost of $1000". However, because of rapidly changing computer technology — time-sharing, more powerful languages — historical costs are not likely to be an accurate guide to the costs of future projects.

Urban and Karash[56] in their paper give estimated costs for the development of the three stages of their evolutionary model building, from mod I (the simplest) through to mod III (the most complex). We reproduce this below.

	Mod I	Mod II	Mod III
Data collection cost ($000's)	0-10	25-50	50-75
Model analysis cost ($000's)	0-5	10-15	15-25
Model acquisition cost ratios	1	3	5
Computer run times per iteration	1 sec	10 sec	20 sec
(Sds 940 computer and 36 period iteration)			

Urban[99] (private communication) states that the development time was 3 years (with 3 to 5 men), and that the computer time should be costed at about $600 per hour of central processor time.

Amstutz[95] in a private communication states that the development costs of micro-analytic behavioural simulations have ranged from $100,000 (for "a relatively simple model structure with a limited number of measures in a narrowly focused environment") to a cumulative maximum of $3 million (in a case where "management has, over a period of approximately ten years, developed a reasonably comprehensive model of their entire environment"). The cost of data acquisition on an on-going basis ranges similarly from $2000 per month up to $20,000 per month, depending on whether the data cover just sales and distribution, or deal also with consumer predispositions and response. A full-scale simulation run of the drug model (see Claycamp and Amstutz[10]) involves 1 to 2 hr of computer time on a machine of size comparable to an IBM 360/65. However "it is possible to generate meaningful output from a portion of that model answering a particular strategic marketing question by expending a few seconds of time".

It can be seen from these examples that there is a wide range of expense options when developing a micro-simulation. As remarked by Urban and Karash,[56] the evolutionary approach to model building offers the possibility of graduated involvement by management, matching their investment to their confidence in the model and also to the short-term benefits it can provide. However, it would seem to us unrealistic at this time to expect a reasonably comprehensive model to reach a stage at which its output would have predictive power in under two to three years, with an involvement over that period of a two-to-three strong team.

6.3 Future Developments

The art of micro-simulation is as yet comparatively underdeveloped. The need for more work can be seen in many areas. One simple need is for the publication of more case studies of the work currently proceeding.

An area which needs particular attention is that of the testing and validation of simulation models. The present position ("it works if management says it works") is less than satisfactory, and there is a need for more objective test procedures. More experience is needed in the development of modular simulations — where particular formulations can be unplugged and others substituted with a minimum of fuss.

Lastly there is a need from management for a revised attitude to work of this kind. Management, and management scientists, still tend to think of research in terms of individual projects. What is required, if comprehensive models of markets are to be developed successfully, is the support of programmatic research. That is, research should be viewed as a series of interlinked projects building up understanding of the whole market process. This understanding can most usefully be integrated in the context of a comprehensive micro-analytic simulation model of the market.

6.4. *Coda* (by S. Messick, quoted in Tomkins and Messick[90])

A computer so solid and stern
Can simulate man to a turn
Though it lacks flesh and bones
And erogenous zones
It can teach — but, oh, can man learn?

REFERENCES

To provide potential users with additional information on its nature and subject matter, we have classified each work referred to in this paper into one of a number of categories. No such categorization can be unambiguous and ours is no exception. Some of our allocations between categories are unavoidably subjective. A particularly difficult boundary is that between what we have called "general" and "sectional" works. By "general" we mean that the work either surveys a whole field or presents an integrated view of some major aspect. By "sectional" we mean that the work is of narrower scope.

The different subject-matter divisions may need some explanation. Our Terminology is:

Introductory works (for managers or specialists): works which, in a short compass, offer their respective audiences an understanding of the broad nature of the subject.

Simulation: the theory and practice of simulation, at the macro- or micro-level.

Case studies: reports on the construction and operation of micro-simulations of purchasing or other individual decisions, and detailed descriptions of particular models.

Studies of markets: theoretical or empirical studies of the market situation, including the nature of purchasing behaviour.

Behavioural science: theoretical or empirical studies in behavioural science, excluding works explicitly on purchasing behaviour.

Following each publication in the list we have recorded the section(s) of our paper in which it is referred to.

Introductory works for managers   Section
[1] R. A. Bauer and R. D. Buzzell (1964) Mating behavioural science and simulation. Hvd. Bus. Rev. 42, No. 5.   1.3
[2] M. K. Starr (1965) Computers: The marketing laboratory. In *Models, Measurement and Marketing*   1.3, 5.2
(Ed. P. Langhoff). Prentice-Hall, Englewood Cliffs.
[3] D. L. Weiss (1964) Simulation for decision-making in marketing. *J. Marketing* 28, No. 3.   5.2

Introductory works for specialists   Section
[4] G. H. Orcutt (1960) Simulation of economic systems. Am. econ. R. 50, No. 5.   1.3, 2.3, 3.14
[5] G. H. Orcutt (1963) Views on simulation and models of social systems. In *Symposium on Simulation*   2.1
Models: Methodology and Applications to the Behavioural Sciences. (Ed. A. C. Hoggatt and F. E.
Balderston). South Western, Cincinnati.
[6] G. H. Orcutt, M. Greenberger, J. Korbel and A. M. Rivlin (1962) A stochastic micro-analytic   2.1, 2.3, 3.1.3, 4.2
model of a socio-economic system. In *Quantitative Techniques in Marketing Analysis* (Ed. R. E.
Frank, A. A. Kuehn and W. F. Massy). Irwin, Homewood.
[7] R. L. Sisson (1969) Simulation: Uses. In *Progress in Operations Research*, Volume III   2.3
(Ed. J. S. Aronofsky). Wiley, New York.

Simulation: General   Section
[8] A. E. Amstutz (1967) *Computer Simulation of Competitive* Market Response.   1.2, 3.2.3, 4.1
M. I. T. Press, Cambridge.
[9] D. N. Chorafas (1965) *Systems and Simulation*. Academic Press, New York.   6.1
[10] H. J. Claycamp and A. E. Amstutz (1968) Simulation techniques in analysis of marketing   2.3, 5.1, 5.2, 6.2
strategy. In *Applications of the Sciences in Marketing Management* (Ed. F. M. Bass, C. W. King and
E. A. Pessemier). Wiley, New York.
[11] J. Forrester (1961) *Industrial Dynamics*. Wiley, New York.   1.2
[12] J. M. Hammersley and D. C. Handscomb (1964) *Monte Carlo Methods*. Methuen, London.   3.2.1
[13] *Bibliography on Simulation*. I. B. M. White Plains (1966).   6.1
[14] R. C. Meier, W. T. Newell and H. L. Pazer (1969) *Simulation in Business and Economics*.   3.2.1
Prentice-Hall, Englewood Cliffs.
[15] T. H. Naylor (1969) Simulation and gaming. *Computer Rev.* 10, No. 1.   6.1
[16] T. H. Naylor (Ed.) (1969) *The Design of Computer Simulation Experiments*. Duke   3.2.4
University Press, Durham.
[17] G. H. Orcutt, M. Greenberger, J. Korbel and A. M. Rivlin (1961) *Micro-analysis of*   4.2
Socio-economic Systems. Harper & Row, New York.
[18] M. Shubik (1960) Bibliography on simulation, gaming, artificial intelligence and allied   6.1
topics. *J. Am. statist. Ass.* 55, 292.
[19] K. D. Tocher (1963) *The Art of Simulation*. English Universities Press, London.   3.2.1., 6.1

Simulation: Model construction   Sections
[20] N. H. Frijda (1967) Problems of computer simulation. Behav. Sci. 12, 59.   2.1, 2.3.4
[21] G. H. Orcutt (1968) Data needs for computer simulation of large scale social systems. In   2.1
Computer Methods in the Analysis of Large-scale Social Systems. (Ed. J. M. Beshers). M.I.T.
Press, Cambridge.
[22] G. H. Orcutt (1968) Research strategy in modelling economic systems. In *The Future of*   2.1
Statistics (Ed. D. G. Watts). Academic Press, New York.
[23] G. H. Orcutt, H. W. Watts and J. B. Edwards (1968) Data aggregation and information   2.2
loss. Am. econ. Rev. 58, No. 4.
[24] J. V. Rosenhead (1968) Experimental simulation of a social system. *Opl. Res. Q.* 19, No. 3.   2.3, 4.2, 5.2
[25] S. F. Stasch, Disaggregative Measures in Validating Simulations of Social Science   2.2
Phenomena. Presented at TIMS ORSA Joint Meeting, San Francisco, May 1968.
[26] D. Teichroew and J. F. Lubin (1966) Computer simulation - Discussion of the   3.2.1
technique and comparison of languages. *Comm.* ACM9, No. 10.
[27] K. D. Tocher (1969) Simulation: Languages. In *Progress in Operations Research*,   3.2.1
Vol. III (Ed. J. Aronofsky). Wiley, New York.

Simulation: Running and testing   Section
[28] G. P. E. Clarkson (1968) Letter to the Editor. *Mgmt. Sci.* 14, No. 10.   3.2.3
[29] W. G. Cochran and G. M. Cox (1957) *Experimental Designs*. Wiley, New York.   3.2.4
[30] R. W. Conway (1963) Some tactical problems in digital simulation. *Mgmt. Sci.* 10, No. 1.   3
[31] G. S. Fishman and P. J. Kiviat (1967) The analysis of simulation-generated time series.   3.2.3
Mgmt. Sci. 13, No. 7.
[32] R. H. Hayes (1969) The value of sample information. In *The Design of Computer*   3.1.5
Simulation Experiments (Ed. T. H. Naylor) Duke University Press, Durham.

[33] J. S. Hunter, Experimental Designs in Simulation Analysis. Princeton   3.2.4
University (mineographed).

[34] J. S. Hunter and T. H. Naylor (1970) Experimental designs for computer   3.2.4
simulation experimants. *Mgmt. Sci.* 16,7.

[35] J. A. Jacoby and S. Harrison (1962) Multivariable-experimentation and simulation   3.2.4
models. *Naval Res. Logist. Q.* No. 2.

[36] T. H. Naylor (1968) Letter to the Editor. *Mgmt. Sci.* 14, No. 6.   3.2.3

[37] T. H. Naylor (1968) Letter to the Editor. *Mgmt. Sci.* No. 10.   3.2.3

[38] T. H. Naylor, D. S. Burdick and W. E. Sasser (1967) Computer simulation experiments   3.2.4
with economic systems: The problem of experimental design. *J. Am. statist. Ass.* 62, 1315.

[39] T. H. Naylor and J. M. Finger (1967) Verification of computer simulation   3.2.3
models. *Mgmt. Sci.* 14, No. 2.

[40] T. H. Naylor, K. Wertz and T. H. Wonnacott (1969) Spectral analysis of data generated   3.2.3, 3.2.4
by simulation experiments with econometric models. *Econometrica* 37, No. 2.

[41] R. Radosevich (1968) Letter to the Editor. *Mgmt. Sci.* 14, No. 6.   3.2.3

[42] R. Radosevich (1968) Letter to the Editor. *Mgmt. Sci.* 14, No. 10.   3.2.3

[43] W. E. Schrank and C. C. Holt (1967) Critique of "Verification of computer   3.2.3
simulation models", *Mgmt. Sci.* 14, No. 2.

Case Studies
Section

[44] R. P. Abelson and A. Bernstein (1963) A computer simulation model of   4.2
community referendum controversies. *Publ. Opin. Q.* 27, No. 1.

[45] F. E. Balderston and A. C. Hoggatt (1962) *Simulation of Market Processes.*   5.1, 6.2
Institute of Business and Economic Research, University of California, Berkeley.

[46] F. E. Balderston and A. C. Hoggatt (1963) *Simulation* models: analytic variety   3.1.2, 5.1
and the problem of model reduction. In *Symposium on Simulation Models: Methodology
and Applications to the Behavioural Sciences* (ed. A. C. Hoggatt and R. E. Balderston).
South-Western, Cincinnati.

[47] C. P. Bonini (1963) Simulation of Information and Decision Systems in the   3.2.4, 5.2
Firm. Prentice Hall, Englewood Cliffs.

[48] G. P. E. Clarkson (1962) Portfolio Selection: A Simulation of Trust Investment.   3.2.3, 5.2
Prentice-Hall, Englewood Cliffs.

[49] R. M. Cyert (1966) A description and evaluation of some firm simulations. In   3.2.3, 5.2
Proceedings of the I.B.M. Scientific Computing Symposium on Simulation Models
and Gaming. I. B. M., White Plains.

[50] R. L. Day (1965) Simulation of consumer preference. *J. Advert. Res.* 5, 6.

[51] T. Hagerstrand (1965) A Monte-Carlo approach to diffusion. *Arch. europ. Sociol.* 6, 43.   4.2

[52] J. Herniter, V. Cook and B. Norek (1969) Microsimulation Evaluation of   5.1
Advertising Budget Strategies. Working Paper, Marketing Science Institute, Cambridge, Mass.

[53] M. R. Lavington (1970) A practical microsimulation model for consumer   3.1.2
marketing. *Opl. Res. Q.* 21, No. 1.

[54] D. Lloyd-Jacobs (1969) The use of simulations for market forecasting. *Long*   5.1
Range Planning 2, No. 1.

[55] L. E. Preston and N. R. Collins (1966) *Studies in a Simulated Market.*   6.2
Research Program in Marketing, Graduate School of Business Administration,
University of California, Berkeley.

[56] G. L. Urban and R. Karash (1969) Evolutionary Modeling in the Analysis of   2.3, 5.1, 6.2
New Products. Working Paper 424-69, Sloan School of Management M. I. T., Cambridge.

[57] B. T. Warner (1966) A model for total marketing. In *Computer in Advertising.* The   5.2
Institute of Practitioners in Advertising, London.

Studies of markets: General
Sections

[58] W. Alderson and S. J. Shapiro (Eds) (1963) Marketing and the Computer.   6.1
Prentice-Hall, Englewood Cliffs.

[59] R. D. Buzzell (1964) *Mathematical Models and Marketing Management.* Harvard   6.1
University, Cambridge.

[60] D. F. Cox (Ed.) (1967) *Risk Trading and Information Handling in Consumer Behaviour.*   4.2
Harvard University, Cambridge.

[61] J. F. Engel, D. T. Kollat and R. D. Blackwell (1969) *Consumer Behaviour.* Holt,   4.1
Rinehart & Winston, New York.

[62] R. E. Frank, A. A. Kuehn and W. F. Massy (1962) *Quantitative Techniques in*   6.1
Marketing Analysis. Irwin, Homewood.

[63] G. Katona (1951) *Psychological Analysis of Economic Behaviour.* McGraw-Hill, New York   4.1

[64] P. Langhoff (Ed.) (1965) *Models, Measurement and Marketing.* Prentice-   6.1
Hall, Englewood Cliffs.

[65] J. D. C. Little (1970) Models and managers: The concept of a decision calculus.   2.3
Mgmt. Sci. 16, No. 8.

[66] D. B. Montgomery and G. L. Urban (1969) *Management* Science in Marketing   4.1, 6.1
Prentice-Hall, Englewood Cliffs.
[67] F. M. Nicosia (1966) Consumer Decision Processes - Marketing and Advertising   4.1
Implications. Prentice-Hall, Englewood Cliffs.

Studies of markets: Sectional   Sections

[68] J. Arndt (1968) *Insights into Consumer Behaviour*. Allyn & Bacon, Boston.   4.2
[69] J. N. Axelrod (1968) Attitude measures that predict purchase. *J. Advert. Res.* 8, No. 1.   4.2
[70] F. E. Emery (1963) *Some Psychological Aspects of Prices*. Document No. 669, Tavistock   4.2
Institute of Human Relations, London.
[71] N. N. Foote (Ed.) (1961) *Household Decision-making*. New York University, New York.   4.2
[72] J. D. Handyside (1960) A general introduction to attitude scaling techniques. In *Attitude*   6.1
Scaling. The Market Research Society, London.
[73] J. D. McConnell (1968) The development of brand loyalty - An experimental study. *J. Marketing*   4.2
Res. 5, No. 1.
[74] J. O. Peckham (1963) The consumer speaks. *J. Marketing* 27, No. 4.   4.2
[75] M. Simmons (1968) Point of sale advertising. *J. Market Res. Soc.* 10, No. 2.   4.2

Behavioural science: General   Sections

[76] B. Berelson and G. A. Steiner (1964) *Human Behaviour. An inventory of Scientific*   4.1
Findings. Harcourt, Brace & World, New York.
[77] R. R. Bush and F. Mosteller (1955) *Stochastic Models for Learning*. Wiley, New York.   6.1
[78] W. Edwards and A. Tversky (1967) *Decision Making*. Penguin, Harmondsworth.   6.1
[79] L. Festinger (1957) *A Theory of Cognitive Dissonance*. Harper & Row, New York.   4.2
[80] J. Holland and M. D. Steuer (1969) *Mathematical Sociology - A selective annotated*   6.1
bibliography. L. S. E. Weidenfeld and Nicolson, London.
[81] M. Jahoda and N. Warren (1966) *Attitudes*. Penquin, Harmondsworth.   6.1
[82] R. D. Luce, R. R. Bush and E. Galanter (Eds.) (1963-1965) *Handbook of Mathematical*   6.1
Psychology, Volumes 1-3, Wiley, New York.
[83] E. M. Rogers (1962) *Diffusion of Innovations*. Free Press of Glencoe, New York.   4.2

Behavioural science: Sectional   Sections

[84] J. S. Coleman (1964) Models of Change and Response Uncertainty. Prentice-Hall,   4.2
Englewood, Cliffs.
[85] J. S. Coleman, E. Katz and H. Menzel (1966) Medical Innovation: A Diffusion Study.   4.2
Bobbs-Merrill, Indianapolis.
[86] J. Feldman (1962) Computer simulation of cognitive processes. In *Computer Applications*   3.2.3
in the Behavioural Sciences (Ed. H. Borko). Prentice-Hall, Englewood Cliffs.
[87] W. N. McPhee, J. Ferguson and R. B. Smith (1963) A theory of informal social influence.   4.2
In *Formal Theories of Mass Behaviour* (Ed. W. N. McPhee). Free Press of Glencoe, New York.
[88] R. C. North, O. R. Holsti, M. G. Zaninovich and D. A. Zinnes (1963) *Content Analysis -*   6.1
A Handbook with Applications for the Study of International Crises. North-Western
University Press, Evanston.
[89] P. J. Stone, D. C. Dunphy and A. Bernstein (1965) Content analysis at simulmatics.   6.1
Am. behav. Scient. 8, No. 9.
[90] S. S. Tomkins and S. Messick (Eds.) (1963) *Computer Simulation of Personality*.   6.1, 6.4
Wiley, New York.
[91] W. S. Torgerson (1958) *Theory and Methods of Scaling*. Wiley, New York.   6.1
[92] A. M. Turing (1956) Can a machine think? In *The World of Mathematics* (Ed. J. R. Newman)   3.2.3
Simon & Schuster, New York.

Miscellaneous   Sections

[93] R. L. Ackoff (1967) Management misinformation systems. *Mgmt Sci.* 14, No. 4.   2.3
[94] A. E. Amstutz (1969) Talk to Marketing Study Group of the Operational Research   2.3
Society. London, January 1969.
[95] A. E. Amstutz (1970) Private communication.   6.2
[96] C. W. Churchman (1965) Reliability of models in the social sciences. In *Models,*   2.3
Measurement and Marketing (Ed. P. Langhoff). Prentice-Hall, Englewood Cliffs.
[97] J. Davis (1968) How O. R. is uncovering marketing ignorance. *Financial Times*, 11 January.   1.3
[98] A. C. Hoggatt, Private communication (1970).   6.2
[99] G. L. Urban, Private communication (1970).   6.2

Notes

[100] In this paper we shall not regard simulation as incorporating gaming.

[101] A status variable must be capable of being changed during the simulation. So marital status could be a status variable but sex, probably, not.

[102] A related problem arises at a later stage of the simulation process. When operating the model, what is the optimal duration for simulation runs? Hayes[32] adopts a Bayesian approach to a restricted version of this problem - that of deciding run lengths when choosing between specified alternative courses of action or hypotheses.

[103] Starr[2] gives a concocted case study which presents the fundamentals of the simulation solution of marketing problems to the non-technical manager in very clear fashion.

ABOUT THE AUTHORS

Martin C. J. Elton is currently in charge of an interdisciplinary group which is undertaking research into the effectiveness and impact of telecommunications systems. He is also a consultant to the Institute for Operational Research and the Tavistock Institute of Human Relations. He took his M. A. in Mathematics at Kings College, Cambridge and his Ph.D. in Operational Research at the University of Lancaster. Whilst on the staff of the Institute for Operational Research he undertook a study on the scope for operations research in libraries and information services.

Jonathan Rosenhead is a Lecturer in Operational Research at the London School of Economics. Born in 1938, he studied mathematics and statistics at Cambridge and at University College London, before spending five years in industry and consultancy in Britain, and a year at the University of Pennsylvania. He has published articles on topics in statistics and operational research, in particular on the simulation of social systems, and on flexibility in planning. Current interests include the study of the social role and impact of the management sciences.

Hospital Attitudes and Communications

R. W. Revans

This paper describes an interesting case study in relation to hospital communication problems. It illustrates that "hard" and "soft" characteristics of a system can be comprehended together, can be considered side by side in an O. R. project. The measurable aspects of resource availablity and utilization are combined with survey data on social attitudes to produce an "organic" model of the hospital. This shows that attention to communication problems can improve morale in the hospital and further lead to improved hospital efficiency measured in cost terms.

THE RANKING OF HOSPITAL CHARACTERISTICS

Consider Table 1

TABLE 1
RANK ORDERS OF FIFTEEN
ACUTE GENERAL HOSPITALS

Hospital	Rank order of five parameters				
	P	K	Q	M	S
A	1	5	2	1	1
B	2	1	9	2	3
C	7	6	1	5	6
D	4	3	12	8	2
E	3	2	6	6	14
F	6	4	7	7	7
G	8	12	3	4	9
H	5	10	5	14	13
I	14	11	10	3	10
J	13	15	4	12	4
K	11	9	13	9	8
L	9	13	8	11	11
M	12	7	15	13	5
N	15	8	11	10	12
O	10	14	14	15	15

P = Sisters' opinions of senior staff
K = Sisters' attitudes towards student nurses
Q = Stability of qualified nursing staff on wards
M = Mean length of patient stay, general medical
S = Mean length of patient stay, general surgical
Coefficient of concordance,
W = 0.51; significant at 0.1 per cent

The Mean Length of Patient Stay

Table 1 ranks fifteen acute general hospitals by five observables. The meaning of two of these, M and S, are already well understood; they are the rank orders of the rapidity with which general medical and general surgical cases are discharged. It is necessary to ensure that as far as possible like is being compared with like. The hospital with the shortest average length of patient stay is ranked first; and the hospital with the longest average length of patient stay fifteenth. These general averages vary from 9 days to 16. In Tables 2 and 3 two other examples are given to suggest that, although the figures of Table 1 are drawn from those two wide ranges of diagnostic classes known as general medical and general surgical cases, there is also, within any given general hospital, a significant tendancy for all specific diagnostic classes to remain a length of time determined by that particular hospital. There is a significant concordance between the mean lengths of patient stay of all diagnostic classes in the same hospital. Hospitals where appendicectomies or hernia repairs are discharged sooner than average tend also to discharge their cardiacs and diabetics sooner than average, and vice versa. This fuller result is not, of course, suggested in *Table 1*, although there is some positive correlation between M and S as there shown.[1]

SOURCE: Reprinted from *Hospital Attitudes and Communications*, edited by J. R. Lawrence, Tavistock Publications, 1966, pp. 601-617, by permission of the author and publishers.

TABLE 2
RANK ORDERS OF AVERAGE LENGTH OF PATIENT STAY
FOR TWELVE LARGE GENERAL HOSPITALS

Hospital	i	ii	iii	iv	v	vi	vii	viii	ix	x	xi	xii	xiii	xiv	xv	xvi	xvii
a	1	1	2	3	1	2	1	5	1	2	4	1	3½	1	2	3	10
b	4	2½	1	2	2	10	3	1	4	5	5	2	5	7	1	5	1
c	5	8	3	10	3	8	2	2	8	4	3	3	11	9	8	2	7½
d	3	2½	5½	8	10	3	6	10	10	6	2	7	2	10	5	11	2
e	7	6	8½	1	5	5	10	6	2	9	6	12	9	3	6	8	6
f	8	7	4	12	11	6	5	9	11	1	1	4	8	8	3	1	12
g	2	5	5½	7	4	9	9	7	5	7	8	10	12	4	9½	9	3½
h	6	4	7	5	6	4	12	11	7	10	11	5	10	2	7	6	5
i	10	10	8½	4	9	7	8	4	3	8	9	8	3½	6	11	4	7½
j	9	12	10	6	7	11	4	3	9	12	7	11	1	5	4	7	3½
k	11	9	11½	11	12	1	7	12	12	3	12	6	6	11	12	12	11
l	12	11	11½	9	8	12	11	8	6	11	10	9	7	12	9½	10	9

Identification of symbols used for each of seventeen diagnostic classes

i   Allergic, endocrine, metabolic, and nutritional diseases
ii Diseases of central nervous system
iii Diseases of arteries and veins, and other diseases
    of circulatory system
iv Pneumonia
v   Other diseases of respiratory system
vi Diseases of respiratory system
vii Appendicitis
viii Hernia of abdominal cavity

ix Other diseases of digestive system
x   Diseases of urinary system
xi Diseases of bones and organs of movement
xii Diseases of skin
xiii Benign neoplasms
xiv Diseases of heart
xv Malignant neoplasms
xvi Diseases of genital organs; male
xvii Diseases of genital organs; female

The coefficient of concordance of the entries in this table is 0.32 and is very highly significant

TABLE 3
RANK ORDERS OF PATIENT STAY
FOR FIVE COMMON DIAGNOSES
AT FIVE HOSPITALS

Hospital	i	ii	iii	iv	v
I	1	1	2	1	1
II	2	2	3	3	2
III	3	3	1	2	3
IV	5	4	4	5	4
V	4	5	5	4	5

Identification of symbols used for each of five diagnostic classes

i appendicectomy   iv cholecystectomy
ii hernia repair   v respiratory complaints
iii partial gastrectomy

The coefficent of concordance of the entries in this table is 0.85 and is very highly significant.

N.B. In this table, rank order is ascending. Hospitals that
keep their patients longest rank 5, those which discharge them most rapidly rank 1.

The Stability of Hospital Staffs

The variate Q of *Table 1* is the rank order of ability of the hospital staff to retain its qualified ward staff, namely, its sisters and staff nurses. [This ability is expressed by the ratio of the average number of ward sisters and staff nurses (calculated monthly over two whole years) actually on the payroll of the hospital to the average number allowed by the hospital establishment over the same period.] A hospital that is continually short of qualified staff should not only deplore the emaciated service that it must offer to its patients but should also ask itself why the vacancies arise. The results of *Table 1* might have been expressed in other indices of staff stability, such as the mean length of service of individuals in particular grades; it has, however, proved extremely laborious to collect accurate information of individual periods of service in this way. Nevertheless, in the group of hospitals for which *Table 3* is drawn the records of several thousand employees were individually investigated, and it was shown that the hospital with a high wastage rate of one class of nursing staff also tended to have a high wastage rate of other classes. The results of this study are set out in *Table 4*; it can be readily appreciated that, on one hand, Cols. Q, M, and S of *Table 1* and, on the other, *Tables 3* and *4*, taken together, are saying the same thing.[2]

In preparing *Table 1* it was not possible to repeat this detailed analysis, and the index Q shown in *Table 1* was accepted as a simpler measure.

TABLE 4
RANK ORDERS OF MEAN LENGTH OF STAY OF DIFFERENT HOSPITAL STAFF FOR THE FIVE HOSPITALS OF TABLE 3

Hospital	i	ii	iii	iv	v	vi
I	1	2	2	1	1½	1
II	4	1	1	2	4½	2
III	2	3	3	4	1½	3
IV	5	5	4	5	3	4
V	3	4	5	3	4½	5

Identification of symbols used for each of six classes of hospital staff.

i Matrons and deputy matrons
ii Sisters
iii Staff nurses
iv Assistant nurses
v Domestics
vi Student nurses

The coefficient of concordance of the entries in this table is 0.59 and is significant at about 0.1 per cent.

N.B. In this table, rank order is descending. Hospitals ranking 1 keep their staff longest, those ranking 5 lose them soonest.

The Measurement of Supervisory Attitudes

The indices P and K are more complex than Q, M, and S; there may be some who even doubt their validity. P is, however, a rough-and-ready estimate of the extent to which the ward sisters in these fifteen hospitals have confidence in their seniors and in the hospital organization; it has been determined through a system of standardized, confidential, and non-collusive interviews. K, which has been determined in the same interview, is an estimate of the extent to which the sisters see it as their responsibility to help in the integration of student nurses placed in their charge. Since this is a paper on the sociology of hospitals, it is necessary to explain how P and K have been measured, and hence what, it is believed, they signify.

The relations between ward sisters and their superiors

The ward sister is a person of great importance, since it is her business to see that the senior organization of the hospital supplies her ward with what the patients need for their recovery; it is also her business, therefore, to report to the senior organization the needs of the patients *as she perceives them.* The most casual observation of the ward sister's difficulties shows that she is continually thrust into situations of tension for three principal reasons. First, she works under a system of authority which, even when understandable, she may find irksome and frustrating; second, she works in a culture of intensive specialization, in which at times any member of another service, medical, paramedical, or lay, may, in an access of insecurity or status awareness, become unco-operative or even hostile; third, she is enveloped by emergency and change, both of which demand that authority and functional specialism shall engage to the fullest extent in effective two-way communication with those who rely upon their help. Since her means of contact are frequently obstructed, there are days on which the life of the ward sister is one crisis succeeded by another. Consider, for example, the sister who has been nettled by the off-hand rejection of a comment which she has made to a doctor about the condition of a patient; the doctor, himself puzzled by the case, may have made it clear to the sister that he regards her opinion as of no importance or even, indeed, as a confusing interruption of his own thoughts. A minute later the sister may relieve her feelings with a comment about that doctor or, indeed, about all the doctors in that particular hospital. She is effectively saying, "The medical staff here tend to treat suggestions from the nurses with less consideration than they deserve."

In the same way a sister may have reason to feel that she is not getting from the matron the support that her problems deserve. A ward sister, in a moment of tension, may pass some such remark as this: "The matron and her administrative staff are no longer as closely in touch with ward problems as they should be." Sometimes the sisters are aware of the positive part they play in helping to improve the hospital organization; they may make observations such as: "The sisters in this hospital are confident that any solutions to their problems reached at their formal meetings will always be put into effect." If this is not so they may briefly remark, "Formal meetings of sisters with the senior staff at this hospital seem little more than somebody laying down the law." At other times the situations of tension in which the sister finds herself are more directly connected with the physical organization of the hospital; a conflict has arisen with the diet kitchen, the dispensary, or the X-ray department, and the sister feels she is getting less co-operation than she should reasonably expect. She may then observe, "Ancillary departments such as the pharmacy, kitchen, or maintenance seem [to the sister] to be organized for their own benefit rather than for that of the wards." We have collected many such comments upon important matters of hospital organization and culture that seem clearly and vigorously to express the perceptions of the sisters who pass them. Several sets of such remarks have been assembled, and sisters in about forty different hospitals have been invited to say to what extent they themselves agree or disagree with these comments. Consider, for example, the item, "The medical staff here tend to treat suggestions from the nurses with less consideration than they deserve." Sisters are invited to suggest, in conditions of complete confidence and anonymity, and also in which it is impossible for any one sister to know the responses of any other, to what extent they agree or disagree with this remark. A five-point scale of response is permitted, namely, strongly agree, agree, uncertain (or don't know), disagree, and strongly disagree. If twenty sisters in a particular hospital strongly agreed with this remark, whereas only five disagreed with it, and in some other hospital only five agreed and twenty strongly disagreed, one would be able to conclude that there were significant differences between the opinions held of the medical staff by the sisters in the two different hospitals. The variate P now under discussion measures the extent to which the sisters feel themselves in easy and fruitful contact with their superiors.[3]

The variate P turns out to be normally distributed. It is also possible to show, by analysing the variance of P, that there are highly significant differences in the average values of P between hospitals; averages taken over all the sisters in different hospitals differ from each other to a much greater extent than do the estimates of P made by individual sisters within particular hospitals. Although the response of any particular sister to any particular statement must be subjective, there is so great a unanimity between the independent responses of all the sisters in the same hospital to the same set of statements that we are obliged to recognize an objective hospital

effect. We can therefore assert with confidence not only that the concept P is meaningful but also that we can form a numerical estimate of it for any given hospital.

The relations between ward sisters and their subordinates

Consider such statements as these:

"Sisters can devote time to instructing the student nurse only at the expense of what may be more important demands."
"Even during their preliminary training, student nurses are given glamourized ideas of their future work."
"The sister who wishes to get on in her profession must seek frequent changes of hospital."
"Student nurses should be taught not to speak to the doctor unless spoken to first."
"Even in a ward with two or more consultants, the sister should always deal with them herself."

These statements, made by ward sisters, throw light upon the attitudes they hold towards the training of student nurses and their integration into their ward teams. An analysis of the daily activity of large numbers of sisters reveals that few of them give more than 1 per cent of their time to their first-year student nurses. It is not surprising, perhaps, to discover that one of the major fears of the student nurse is that she will be expected to perform for a patient some service in which she has not been adequately instructed. Ward activity studies also show that some sisters spend as much as 50 per cent of their time on clerical and related duties; nor would it be unfair to add that some sisters appear to justify their withdrawal from the stresses of the ward by engaging in elaborate clerical exercises. Other sisters, whether deliberately or not, diminish learning opportunities of the student nurses by forbidding them to ask questions of the doctors; others insist upon themselves transacting all ward affairs directly with the doctors, and hence upon giving no supervisory responsibility to their juniors. Finally, in some hospitals sisters are a highly transient class and student nurses are perfectly well aware that they have no deep attachment to the hospital nor to the training that should be given upon its wards.

This batch of statements may therefore be scored to give some indication of the extent to which the ward sisters are concerned about their student nurses, who provide the bulk of the bed-side care; it may be scored, as was the batch of statements indicative of P, to form another variate, here called K. This variate is also normally distributed, and an analysis of its variance shows that there are highly significant differences between hospitals. As with P, therefore, we are entitled to calculate the mean value for K for each hospital, and hence to arrange our sample of fifteen in rank order. The conclusions of a professional sociologist (herself not much older than the majority of the student nurses among whom she worked) enable us to observe K through the eyes of the girls themselves:

"There was little evidence of the existence of bad personal relations except in individual isolated cases, between the new student nurses and the other members of the nursing staff. What did emerge from the various comments made by the student nurses was that they felt there was a general lack of meaningful relations with other people in the hospital. Many complained of the break-up of the preliminary school set, saying that it was impossible to meet the other student nurses that they knew. Some felt that the ward sisters did not spend sufficient time instructing them in the wards. They mentioned that the ward sister did not always welcome them to the ward, did not always say "Good morning" and was not always particularly approachable. They did not always know who to go to if they were in difficulties or wanted information."[4]

Another constraint, called H, upon the student is the commitment of the nursing staff to the observance of hierarchical precedence; unfavourable measures of H suggest hospitals with extensive rules intended to discipline the student nurses. Attitude surveys show not only that the girls often regard such rules and the manner of their enforcement with amused contempt but also that they conspire together in order to break them.

The Concordance of Hospital Characteristics

We may now return to *Table 1*. The coefficient of concordance is 0.51. This means that hospitals that rank high in any one of the five variates (P, K, Q, M, S) rank high in the other four; or that hospitals with a low rank in any of these variates have a low rank in the four others. The most casual examination of the table shows, of course, that there are some hospitals that rank high in one variate and low in one or more of the others. One must expect some departures from any general law in real-life situations, even although there is a significant association between high

ranking in one variate and high ranking in others. In spite of its obvious exceptions, therefore, we must accept *Table 1* as evidence that the hospital perceived by the sisters, and so by others, to possess a good communication system has not only a stable professional staff but also enables its patients to recover more rapidly. This is perhaps not a surprising conclusion, since the main task of a hospital is to communicate to its patients that optimum succession of biological and mental stimuli that is the sinew of patient recovery. If this communication system becomes opaque, disjointed, uncertain, overloaded, attenuated, or simply ranshackle it must necessarily delay or distort whatever it is that makes for such stimuli; the metabolism of the hospital system slows down, there is an eruption of administrative chilblains, and the recovery of the patient becomes retarded. In simple English, if a message about a special diet is held up because the ward sister is on bad terms with the dietician the patient on the special diet is bound to suffer; if the junior nurse who observes what she believes to be an important change in the patient's condition is forbidden by hospital tradition to report this to the doctor unless he specifically asks her about it she is not only not helping that patient but is also probably accumulating a frustration which will itself contribute at some later date to a decision not to continue with her training. For those whose interest in the clinical affairs of the ward demands more than the arid statistical arguments of this essay, there is abundant evidence in the recent books by Elizabeth Barnes[5] and by Anne McGhee.[6]

INTER-GROUP COMMUNICATION

The Senior Staff and the Atmosphere of the Ward

We might argue here that P and K are like two meteorological indices, measuring those qualities of the atmosphere of the ward which, according to Anne McGhee, are so much determined by the attitudes of the sisters. What is important to the administrator is that, as *Table 1* suggests, this ward atmosphere seems to be determined not only by the sister herself but also by that sister's relationships to the senior staff of the hospital;

in determining these relationships the hospital itself makes a contribution no less important than that of the individual sister. That this is so is shown not only by the significant concordance of *Table 1* but also by the significant results found in the analysis of the variance of *P*, within and between the hospitals.

Professional Groups and Communication Problems

Elizabeth Barnes reaches similar conclusions. Her final paragraphs are on the importance of communications within the hospital and, in particular, on the importance of improving communications between the various professional groups of which the hospital is composed.

Status Groups and Communication Problems

Professional expertise is not the only major cause of division within the hospital community. Whatever the need for supervisory effectiveness to be based upon overt authority, the integration of the nursing staff into a cohesive corps is often bedevilled by considerations of rank and status. Consider the responses to this statement, also made by a ward sister: "The tradition that nursing staff of similar status should keep together at meal-times is essential to the efficiency of the hospital." About one-half only of several hundred sisters interviewed disagree with this statement; 39 per cent agree with it, and 11 per cent are not sure how to interpret it. There are many other remarks that enable an estimate to be made of the extent (measured by a variate *H*) to which any hospital is committed to such hierarchical beliefs, and statistical treatment of the results shows some hospitals to be significantly more committed than others. One finds that in hierarchically inclined hospitals the student nurses tend to place great stress upon the importance of their own "set" or that group of them who enter the hospital training school together at any given time. As any one set (to the extent that it survives) moves upward through the hospital, steadily gaining in seniority, so it may become the shield and refuge of its members; in moments of difficulty each will seek consolation from the others, and the student nurse who finds she needs help, advice, or instruction will often seek it at the next coffee-break from a fellow set-member on another ward rather than on the instant from her own sister or immediate senior. In a few hospitals one finds emphasis in still other directions upon the horizontal (namely, within given status classes) rather than upon the vertical (namely, within given wards or service departments); not only do all, say, second-year student nurses of the April set tend to form a front against all other sets, but resident staff may have little in common with the non-resident, and the full-timers may see themselves positively threatened by the part-timers. The problem for the hospital administration (using that expression in its widest sense) is again one of communication. What, one may ask, is it that endows the organism in the first place with its tendency to hierarchical division? Or, indeed, is the whole idea that it is *possible* to form a team on the ward a misconception that can serve only to distract attention from more fruitful subjects of contemplation?

The Downward Transmission of Attitudes to the Wards

It is easy to show that the perception that the sister has of those in authority above her, whether one of co-operation or of hostility, is substantially transmitted to those in turn responsible to her. The correlation between the *P* and *K* scores of several hundred individual sisters is of the order of +0.55; the correlation between the hospital averages of *P* and *K* for nineteen hospitals in a particular sample was +0.72. Both of these results are highly significant. But correlation coefficients alone, although interesting, do not identify causes. It is, however, reasonable to suggest that the attitudes of the senior staff towards the sisters, namely, the attitudes that in turn determine *P*, are of the first importance. The doctor who is not concerned to use the sister's opinion of the patient is not likely to stimulate that sister in teaching her student nurses the value of observation; the sister who has learned to regard her formal meetings with the matron as a frustrating waste of time is unlikely to encourage frank discussion among her own ward staff with a view to contributing fruitful ideas of benefit to the hospital as a whole; the ward sister who is at loggerheads with the specialist departments of the hospital (who may also be at loggerheads among themselves) is unlikely to teach her student nurses much that is useful about the contributions that these specialist departments have to offer the patients. It is more economical to conclude, as Occam's Razor would have us do, that the community of ward sisters who feel themselves unable to help their student nurses is getting little support from those above, rather than that a whole hospital full of unco-operative individual sisters has come together at random. This is not to say that the particular handful of senior staff are, as persons, outstandingly thoughtless, negligent, or insensitive. The fact, however, remains that the key relationship in the social structure of the hospital is that between the ward sisters, with the patients on their hands, and the whole array of central services, from the doctors, the matron, and the secretary to the physiotherapists, the engineer, and the barber. And if, as may apparently so readily happen, this relationship in particular deteriorates, the hospital will have a high rate of staff turnover and a slow rate of patient recovery.

HOSPITAL MODELS AND COMMUNICATION NEEDS

The results presented in *Table 1* and briefly discussed in the following paragraphs have been obtained from research into a miscellany of hospital problems; some of these have touched on highly practical issues, such as the location of hospital stores or the improvement of hospital transport systems; other inquiries on the sickness rates of the student nurses and, in particular, the significant changes in these rates as the same individual girls move from one hospital to another in the course of their training; still other inquiries on the success or failure of hospital cadet schemes, the efficacy of hospital costing schemes, and the structure of hospital committee systems. It would be convenient if, as a result of this miscellaneous programme, we would begin to develop what the operational research worker describes as a "model" of the hospital as an organism. In practice, this organism is so complicated as to defy, with our present limited knowledge of systems analysis and symbolic notation, any simple representation. Of this, however, we can be quite sure: a hospital treats a patient at five distinct stages: (a) an admission stage, which must embrace preliminary correspondence with the general practitioner, with another hospital or some other antecedent source, and with the patient's relatives; (b) a diagnostic stage, during which the complaint from which the patient is suffering is either discovered or confirmed, and some decision made as to the treatment the patient shall receive; (c) a treatment stage, which may consist in a single and decisive act, like a surgical operation, or some slower cycle of therapy during which the patient is likely to remain in the same ward; (d) a control stage, during which the progress of the patient after treatment is observed, so that it may be determined whether the operation or the therapy is doing what, at the diagnostic stage, it was expected to do; (e) a discharge stage, during which the patient is being prepared to leave the hospital in a condition, it is to be hoped, more satisfactory than that in which he was admitted. Such a model is capable of considerable elaboration, and it is possible to locate in it the roles and interactions of the main physical services of the hospital, such as the pathological laboratory and the medical records section. In trying to build such models one becomes impressed with the importance of rapid communications between one department and another, and, at the patient level, between persons on the same ward. Exercises of this type, therefore, make all the more impressive some of the results stated by Elizabeth Barnes. She describes how the majority of the members enlisting in the seminars set up in the participating general hospitals to discuss their pscho-sociological problems were able to perceive for the first time the importance of communication between different groups. One striking finding of the studies described in her work was that most professional hospital staffs had previously been completely unaware of the necessity for improving methods of communication between themselves.

THE DEVELOPMENT OF SOCIAL SENSITIVITY

As in the interesting essays in self-analysis reported by Elizabeth Barnes, we found that the medical staffs were in general indifferent to the attempts being made to discover how to improve hospital communications.

Little is known about the possibility of making members of institutions or of professional communities more critically aware of the impact that they make upon each other. Some interesting experiments have been reported from the University of California in Los Angeles by Tannenbaum, Wechsler, and Massarik;[7] to some extent the work of Johnson Abercrombie, aimed at sharpening self-perception, belongs to the same field of exploration. The researches of Rensis Likert at the University of Michigan on managerial and supervisory authority support the main ideas of this present essay.[8] The seminars reported by Elizabeth Barnes, although in a detailed sense unplanned, are among the most promising excursions beyond the sombre horizons of our administrative ignorance. The work of D. H. Clark of Fulbourn Hospital, Cambridgeshire, on administrative therapy, is also full of relevant suggestion.[9] Joan Woodward, as in so many other directions, also has something of interest to say upon the social forces at work to help or hinder the quest for enlightenment.[10] The Engineering Experiment Station of the Ohio State University is at present engaged upon a comprehensive and highly original study of social stratification on the hospital ward and its relation to clinical performance; the care with which its experiments are designed offers lessons to all students of institutions as social organisms.[11] The work of Gillian MacGuire on the possible influence that certain hospitals have upon the process and difficulties of their student nurses is also original and important.

ATTITUDE SURVEYS AND HOSPITAL PROBLEMS

From Manchester we have made an attempt to examine, among others, the two hospitals at the bottom of *Table 1* and *Tables 3* and *4*; representative attitude surveys have been conducted, with members of the university meeting in free interviews a total of over 600 persons. These voluntary and confidential interviews, each of which lasted between ten minutes and three-quarters of an hour, were patterned on a stratified sample of all staff at the hospitals. The interviewers merely explained to those who appeared that they were generally interested in the way each particular hospital functioned; they did not solicit opinions upon any particular aspects of hospital life. The programmes of interviewing were spread over about two months in each hospital, and from time to time brief reports were made back to the staff of the main findings and of any actions which the management committees were able to take upon them. It was, however, perfectly clear, after the results of the many hundreds of interviews had been classified, that each hospital had deep and organic problems on which little effective progress was to be expected from mere administrative decisions alone.

One result is of interest, because it tests the reliability of the attitude survey as a research instrument. Three hospitals with markedly different problems were chosen for survey: the first, A, has recently had to close wards because it cannot get nurses to remain in its service, the second, B, was in much the same condition three years ago, but then achieved a change of matron, who worked steadily to improve relations with her nurses; the third, C, in an old building too small for the load it is carrying, but has no serious staff problems. The points raised by the staff at the interviews could be broadly classified under two headings: primarily to do with interpersonal relations (training, promotion, communications, discipline, recruitment, social and recreational functions) and those to do with working conditions (hours, pay, food living quarters, transport, buildings, uniform, supplies, equipment, procedures). *Table 5* shows the responses from the staff interviewed, drawn at the three hospitals from all ranks, consultants to cleaners; not all comments are critical. But even when favourable comment is offset against the unfavourable, *Table 5* still shows that hospital A has an abnormally high comment rate about interpersonal relationships and hospital C an abnormally low one; at hospital B, where great efforts had recently been made to improve these relationships, the comment rate was about the average of A and C. On physical conditions, on the other hand, hospital C had a high comment rate and hospital B a low one; the rate at hospital A was about the average of B and C. Numerically, these results are highly significant, and the content of the comments is hence of interest to those who are trying to understand the problems of these particular hospitals.

TABLE 5
NUMBERS OF STAFF INTERVIEWED AND NUMBERS OF COMMENTS PASSED UPON INTERPERSONAL RELATION- SHIPS AND UPON WORKING CONDITIONS, FOR THREE COM- PARABLE GENERAL HOSPITALS

Hospital	No. of Staff interviewed	Number of comments	
		Interpersonal relations	Working conditions
A	188	856	461
B	129	478	234
C	120	346	440

PARTICIPATION AS A LEARNING PROCESS

A number of problems deeply seated in the hospital organisms have been identified from the attitude surveys, and means must be contrived whereby all who are affected by them must devote time to their analysis and solution. Typical problems uncovered are these: the arrangements for moving patients between the wards and the operating theatres; the preparation of the off-duty rota; the demands of the clerical work created, whether usefully or not, by ward routines and practices. Each of these problems affects many people at different levels within the hospital, from the consultants to the porters. One or two such problems should be carefully studied by an operational research group that includes not only a sociologist but also an administrator and that, as is suggested below, can draw upon the support and advice of the medical and nursing professions; this group should then attempt to initiate a course on administrative therapy by placing its findings for interpretation, analysis, and action in front of a committee representing all the interested factions or professional groups within the hospital; administrative therapy can be a true learning process, in which those who participate get valuable information about their own behaviour.[12] It should be the first concern of the leader of the operational research group to ensure that all members of the representative committee perceive what the structures of the problems are; if necessary, he should en-

sure that each of them can clearly state the objections or difficulties of any other faction hostile either to the changes which his own faction would advocate or to the position his own faction is striving to defend. The leader of the operational research group would need to have learned so much about the problems of the hospital as to be able to suggest what the effect would be of taking any action advocated by any particular faction, or of failing to take such action should other factions disagree with it. The operational research group might need to meet the interprofessional or interfaction committee as many as twenty times; the group leader should be free to tell the committee members if, and why, in his view, they are making no useful progress, or even if they are expressing *ex parte* views that can only bring damage to the hospital as a whole. It therefore follows that the leader of the group must not be a paid member of the staff of that particular hospital. Experiments of this type are in progress, but they have already struck one major difficulty. This does not lie within what might be called the operational research exercise itself; it lies in the lack of contact between the management committee and its own hospital problems. While the writer, who has had many years of experience in local government, believes that the judgment of the good amateur or lay committee is, in the final analysis, always sounder than that of the professional experts, he is very conscious of the difficulties of making lay committees face up to the professional conflicts within their own authority. No doubt conferences and other educational activities such as are promoted by the Association of Hospital Management Committees all have their place, but something radical also seems to be called for.[13]

The Participation of the Professions

Communication systems cannot be improved by the disinterested ministrations of mere experts; these systems begin and end with the attitudes that a few important members of the staff have towards their work and towards each other. One can renovate a hospital lighting system by employing competent electricians to overhaul it; one can deal with confusion in the hospital accountancy system by installing a reliable computer. But whether or not one can in fact do much to improve the communication system of a hospital is a debatable question. Deeply seated human attitudes are involved; the success of any learning process, by the participation of the senior staff of the hospital in the solution of hospital problems, depends, to a large extent, upon those who are called upon to catalyse this participation. It may be that there are some in the hospital service ready to turn to outsiders for help in their present difficulties, but the writer sees little evidence that, when it comes to the point of changing traditional attitudes or established practices, the service as a whole, will listen to those who are, after all, not professionally qualified. It is of no use for the outsider to deplore this fact; the professional palisades justifiably thrown up by the doctor and the nurse in defence against the charlatan and the imposter are not readily lowered to admit the sociologist, the operational research worker, or even the non-medical statistician. There is, of course, every reason why both doctors and nurses should themselves make excellent research workers in this field, since the concept of an organic system is a biological one, although, in the sense now being used, at a level of complexity and abstraction higher than that derived, say, from dissecting a dogfish. The practical difficulty to be overcome is to enable the hospital service to call upon operational research groups in whom the medical and nursing professions would have confidence. Such groups must be drawn partly from institutions, such as universities, interested in social research, partly from within these professions themselves, since the essential problem of communication, involving perception, social awareness, professional status, functional specialism, and so forth, lie behind the palisades themselves. The lay outsider can suggest method, design, and experiment; he can collect evidence, carry out complex statistical analysis, point out the significance of results and so forth. To convince the medical or nursing staff he must work closely with professionally qualified colleagues drawn from the ranks of doctors and nurses themselves.

Lessons from the Emergence and Development of Work Study

Over the past decade the hospital service has become increasingly interested in work study. A large number of hospitals have had both nurses and junior administrators trained in its techniques. What seems to be needed now is that a number of young doctors, future hospital secretaries, and nurses of the rank of deputy matron should be trained in methods of social investigation and, indeed, of operational research. This would demand that they should participate in existing research projects in the social sciences; it would be helpful if some of these projects were in fields remote from hospitals. There are a dozen or more centres of social research in Britain to which, in the first instance, these potential hospital analysts could be attached. The training which they (and others to follow them) would receive should be looked upon as a normal part of their present professional education and would not be intended to deflect them into a wholly new career; they would merely supply the hospital service with a nucleus of senior staff capable of participating, from time to time, in projects of operational research and social analysis. After having received formal training in analytical methods and having gained research experience from two years or so of organized fieldwork, they would return to their particular professions. Apart from the benefit to their own substantive employment that they would gain from such training, the hospital service would have, within its own ranks, a corps of qualified advisers who could be seconded to help with the identification, analysis, and treatment of the social problems of particular hospitals anywhere in the country. For our experience is beginning to show that a true perception of the communication problems of a particular hospital will rarely be gained by persons, whether professional or lay, emotionally or economically involved in the affairs of that same hospital. Nor is it likely that the professional staff, between whom communication is poor or has broken down, will ever accept any diagnosis of their troubles from the lay outsider. What is needed is that some outside commission, containing members of the medical and nursing professions, should be invited to help the socially sick hospital to perceive, to understand, and to treat its own troubles.

OTHER PRACTICAL CONSIDERATIONS

The hospital service is now endowed with a number of centres of education and research, such as those established by the King Edward's Hospital Fund and the Nursing Studies Unit at the University of Edinburgh. The Nuffield Provincial Hospitals Trust, although it does not support any institutions like these, has given very powerful backing to a wide range of research into hospital problems, including the work of the present writer. There are also many professional associations, like that of the hospital matrons, as well as the Royal College of Nursing, which are interested in questions of hospital morale and efficiency. All of these in their own way can advance the study of hospital communications. What, to the writer seems most necessary is the development of the concept of self-awareness or social sensitivity. When a profession has been taught for generations that it must not become emotionally involved in those with whom it deals it is perhaps natural that its members should be slow to perceive the effects that they have upon those subordinate to them, or even, indeed, upon their colleagues.

The university medical school must contrive not only to fortify the medical student against the terrifying responsibility that he will be called upon to carry; it must make him aware that he is but one member, even if the most important one, of a hospital team that is dependent upon him, not only for its clinical success but also for its self-respect. The education of senior admistrative nursing staff must also bring out more clearly the imperative need for the matron and the sister to adopt a more supportive and a less directive role than at present. A significant volume of young talent is leaving the nursing profession on account of the unrealistic and insensitive attitudes of those in command of it. If, since these are educational responsibilities, the following questions are put by those in charge of education, "What does this mean in practice? What are we to teach?", let them be referred to some of the researches mentioned in this essay. Let them, for example, ask themselves why it is that over half the ward sisters in a representative sample of British hospitals believe that their matrons are no longer in touch with ward problems; or why over three-quarters of them believe that their doctors should be more co-operative in choosing times for their ward visits. We do not know the answers to these questions. All we can conclude is that the recovery of the patients and the morale of the staff are tied up with them.

NOTES

[1] It may be suggested that these differences can be explained by the differing demands for hospital beds in different areas. No such effect has been found; indeed, some hospitals with very long waiting lists (above 1,000 surgical patients) may have exceptionally long mean periods of patient stay. This appears to be a simple consequence of a queueing situation with a low service rate.

[2] The five hospitals of *Tables 3 and 4* were all in the homogeneous culture of industrial Lancashire; the fifteen hospitals of *Table 1* were drawn from the whole of the industrial North and Midlands. It is to be expected that the residential variances of the data of *Table 1* would be relatively greater than those of *Tables 3 and 4* together.

[3] Revans, R. W. "The measurment of supervisory attitudes." Paper presented at the meeting of the Manchester Statistical Society, January 1961.

[4] Macguire, G. M. *From Student to Nurse: The Induction Period.* Oxford Area Nurse Training Committee, Oxford Regional Hospital Board, England. 1961.

[5] Barnes, E. *People in Hospital.* London: Macmillan, 1961.

[6] McGhee, A. *The Patients' Attitude to Nursing Care.* London: E. W. Livingstone. 1961.

[7] Tannenbaum, R., I. R. Wechsler and F. Massarik. *Leadership and organization.* New York: McGraw-Hill. 1961.

[8] Lickert, R. *New patterns in mangement.* New York: McGraw-Hill. 1961.

[9] Clark, D. H. *Administrative Therapy.* London: Tavistock Publications; Philadelphia: Lippincott. 1964.

[10] Woodward, J. *Nursing Mirror*, 11, 18, and 25. Dec. 1959.

[11] Howland, D. *et al. The Development of a Methodology for the Evaluation of Patient Care.* Engineering Experiment Station, Ohio State University, 1960.

[12] The study and construction of learning mechanisms shows that inputs about outputs (or knowledge of one's results form a cardinal link in the learning process. There must also be some desire or perceived utility in the person wishing to learn; it is possible to build into a learning mechanism certain "penalties" that the mechanism "learns" to avoid. The "penalty-avoidance" circuit of the human being may also need rearrangement at an intellectual level; he must perceive that certain types of behaviour (e.g. disparaging a clinical suggestion from a sister as an encroachment upon his professional

authority) are contrary to his wider interests as well as to those of the patient and the hospital. Unless he does so he will have no desire to learn, that is, no motivation to change his present behaviour.

13 The relations between the senior professional staff of the hospital and its management committee appointed by the Regional Board deserve closer study than they so far seem to have received. What is needed is not some legalistic appraisal of the terms of reference of Boards, Hospital Management Committees, and their retinues of sub-committees, but an analysis of the real distribution of power and responsibility among them and their principal officers. In particular, a good deal of thought could well be given to the powers and duties of matrons, especially in relation to nursing sub-committees, hospital secretaries, and other senior members of the nursing administration.

ABOUT THE AUTHOR

R. W. Revans gained his B.Sc. from University College London and his Ph.D. from Emmanuel College, Cambridge. From 1935-45 he was Deputy Chief Education Officer for Essex County Council, and from 1945-50 he was Director of Education, firstly for the Mining Association of Great Britain, and later for the National Coal Board. From 1955-65 he was Professor of Industrial Administration at the University of Manchester. Since then he has been Senior Research Fellow at the European Association of Management Training Centres, Brussels, Belgium. He represented Great Britain in the Olympic Games of 1928, and was holder of the Cambridge undergraduate longjump record from 1929-62.

A Black Ghetto's Research on a University

Russell L. Ackoff

"The worst thing that can happen to operations research is that our conception of what it ought to be becomes equivalent to our conception of what it is." With this unusual but commendable statement, Ackoff begins the startling story of how operations researchers were used by Black ghetto leaders in Philadelphia. Departing radically from the structured and formula-laden style associated with O.R. literature, he makes the point that a more humble, sympathetic and supportive role by operations researchers in interaction with a spirit of self-help by the "subjects" is likely to lead to outstanding accomplishment. He argues that more of the same approach would be beneficial in other management contexts also.

In reading this paper it is not far-fetched to transpose the discussion to the relationship between operations researchers and librarians.

The worst thing that can happen to operations research is that our conception of what it ought to be becomes equivalent to our conception of what it is. In a changing world, even equilibrium must be dynamic.

OR has been dynamic. It has made considerable progress in the last two decades, most of it technical. Continued technical progress will be necessary but not sufficient if OR is to thrive, not merely survive. To thrive, OR will have to increase its ability to deal with critical social problems and expand its relevance to strategic decision making in private, as well as public, domains. The frontiers of the Seventies, it seems to me, ought to be new contexts for OR's application, or at least more systematic and comprehensive exploration of areas whose boundaries may have been crossed, but which have not yet been adequately settled.

Among other things, it is in such explorations that we are most likely to find critical shortages and inadequacies of our techniques. Thus such exploration should be a major stimulus to continued technical development. But more important is the fact that such exploration is likely to produce an enlargement of our concept, methodology, and philosophy of OR that will increase its relevance and potency.

This is a story about such an exploration. From a technical point of view it is uninteresting; but from a conceptual and philosophical point of view I have found it to be one of the most rewarding efforts with which I have been involved.

First the story; then I will reflect on its significance.

THE STORY

The problems associated with the black ghettos in urban America are familiar to all. Perhaps less familiar are the numerous unsuccessful attempts that have been made by most urban universities in the United States to contribute toward their solution. It was exposure to some of these failures that led Professors Robert B. Mitchell (City Planning), William Gomberg (Industrial Relations), and me in 1967 to engage in a series of discussions that in turn led to the development of what we believed to be an untried approach to university aid to the ghetto.

This approach was based on a few simple assumptions. First, we assumed that inhabitants

SOURCE: Reprinted from *Operations Research* 18 (September - October 1970) pp. 761-771, by permission of the author and publishers.

of the black ghettos should be given an opportunity to solve their own problems in their own way; that they will not, and should not accept "White solutions" because whites have demonstrated no particular competence in solving the blacks' problems. Furthermore, we believed that blacks could learn more from their own failures than they could from white successes. Thus, we concluded that the best the white community can do to help the black community is to enable it to solve its problems in the way it, the black community, wants to. Our task, then, was to try to make the resources of the Management Science Center and, more generally, those of our University, available to the black community to use as *it, not we,* saw fit.

Our approach required receipt of a request for aid from a black ghetto. Fortunately, in February of 1968, just after coming to this conclusion, a modest request for drafting assistance came to us from Forrest Adams, a black planner employed by the newly formed Mantua Community Planners (MCP), which was a coalition of the five most active organizations in the neighborhood just to the north of our University.

Mantua covers about eighty city blocks and has a population of approximately 22,000, 98 per cent of whom are black. By almost any standard, it is a critical poverty area. Almost 25 per cent of its housing units are overcrowded, and more than 50 per cent of them are in substandard condition. Its male unemployment rate falls between 15 and 20 per cent, more than three times higher than the rate in Philadelphia as a whole. Thirty-seven per cent of its families earn less than $3000 per year. The educational level is very low: more than a third of Mantua's residents who are over 25 years old have had less than eight years of education. Nearly 40 per cent of its minors receive some type of public assistance, more than six times the city's rate. Sixteen per cent of its population from 7 to 17 years old were arrested in 1964, nine times the rate in the city as a whole. Its adult crime rate was more than twice that of the remainder of the city.

The disadvantaged and underdeveloped state of Mantua is obvious.

The three professors arranged for a meeting with Forrest Adams and Herman Wrice, President of a group called the Young Great Society (YGS). Mr. Wrice was the most prominent of the emerging leaders in the community.

At that meeting we offered to employ any three people from the community selected by Mr. Adams and Mr. Wrice to work on the development of their community in any way that those so employed saw fit. The three were selected within a day. They were Andy Jenkins, President of the Mantua Community Planners and Vice-President and co-founder with Herman Wrice of the Young Great Society, Richard Hart, and Mrs. Doris Hamilton, Treasurer of MCP. A fourth employee on the staff of YGS was added a short while later. Those employed were given office space (which they never used), secretarial aid (which they used occasionally), and a graduate student to serve as an assistant (whom they used extensively). It was made clear to the Mantua team members that the faculty involved would volunteer nothing but were available to help them as they saw fit. They were told that they would be completely self-controlling, even with respect to hours, location, and content of their work. They had no need to come to the University except to pick up their pay checks.

Funds for support of this activity were obtained from the Anheuser-Busch Charitable Trust, which enthusiastically supported the concept and the effort based on it. But the initial grant was small. In order to stretch it to cover nine months of work, the three faculty members involved provided their services at no cost. This turned out to be a blessing in disguise. Subsequently, other faculty members, none of whose time could be bought for participation in "paying projects," were willing to give some of it to this effort.

The original three on the Mantua team were hired on a Friday. They asked us to meet with them on the following Monday. At that time they presented for comment a program for their activities that they had developed over the weekend, and they proposed regular weekly meetings with us in order to review their progress and discuss their problems. Before I review that progress, let me cite a few important events that occured subsequently.

Within a few months it became apparent that in order to meet and coordinate all the requests for aid that were coming to us from the team, and all the people from the University who became involved in providing the aid, a full-time senior member of our staff was required. Marvin Rees took on this job. More of the successes and fewer of the failures of this project are due to him than to any other member of the University.

At the end of about the sixth month of the effort, the Mantua team and the University group collaboratively prepared a proposal for continued support of their joint effort. The proposal was submitted both to the Anheuser-Busch Charitable Trust and to the Ford Foundation. It was the Mantua team's decision that any additional funds that might be obtained continue to come to it through the University. Much to our delight, each of the foundations came through with $50,000 per year for each of the next two years.

Since the project began in February of 1968, the Young Great Society and the Mantua Community Planners have grown considerably in size and strength. They and their leaders, Herman Wrice and Andy Jenkins, are by far the most significant development forces in Mantua. Herman Wrice has attained prominence not only in Philadelphia but at the state and national levels as well.

Let me review the part of what Mantuans have done for themselves in which we have been of some help.

YGS has set up nine manufacturing firms that grossed a little more than $1.5 million in 1969 and employed about 125 people from the community. The most successful of these firms makes electronic circuit boards and is supplying such companies as IBM, General Electric, and Leeds and Northrup. These nine firms and several others are being brought together physically and spiritually in an industrial complex managed by the Mantua Industrial Development Corporation, a subsidiary of YGS. The facilities just acquired for this complex will also serve as a hot-house for new business enterprises and will provide a wide variety of types of service and assistance to the businesses that it nurtures.

With University aid, MCP and YGS have been instrumental in obtaining loans from banks for the establishment and operation of a number of small businesses in Mantua and in providing these enterprises with needed technical and managerial assistance. Much of the latter has been provided by Wharton graduate students.

Both MCP and YGS provide employment services and have placed several hundred Mantuans in the last two years. Furthermore, these two organizations themselves employ about 330 people in activities that they manage.

Together they solicited and brought about $600,000 for development programs into the community last year.

MCP established the Mantua Community Federal Credit Union which Mantuans can join for 25¢ and have savings accounts that permit deposits with no lower limit, and from which they can obtain loans at relatively low interest rates.

YGS and MCP operate an Architectural and Planning Center and a Joint Workshop that are staffed by University faculty and students as well as by members of the community. The Center and Workshop have produced neighborhood development plans to which about $6 million has already been pledged. The Center has also planned the renovation and rehabilitation of more than thirty houses in Mantua in 1969 and about 120 in 1970. The reconstruction work has been done by local contractors using indigenous labor, most of which was trained on the job. The Center has also done the architectural planning required for the many facilities used in the many activities of the two sponsoring organizations.

We recently obtained from a major oil company a contract for the Architectural and Planning Center to design a community service station. The uniqueness and imaginativeness of the resulting design led to a subsequent contract for preparation of detailed working drawings and specifications for the station. Steps are now being taken to build a prototype in Mantua, one that will be operated by the community. This station will include an auto-, motorcycle-, and bicycle-parts store, a do-it-yourself repair and maintenance facility, a training center, recreational facilities, and offices for rent.

Plans for the community are frequently reviewed at open meetings. Attendance at these meetings has grown constantly. Block groups have been organized to help develop enlightened public opinion on issues of importance to the neighborhood. This development has been enhanced by a weekly hour-long broadcast by MCP over one of the city's radio stations. YGS has successfully launched two weekly newspapers that are distributed and widely read beyond Mantua. Both yield a profit derived from advertising income. In addition, YGS recently initiated a weekly newsletter from which I shall reproduce a selection below.

Their educational program is extensive. A school for 150 children in their fifth to eighth grades was opened in September 1968. This *mini-school*, as it is called, is completely controlled by a neighborhood board that selects its own teachers and designed its own curricula. It is supported by both the city's Board of Education and a grant from the Rockefeller Foundation. The school is characterized by innovative pedagogy and relevance of content for disadvantaged children. Unfortunately, the school's building was recently destroyed by fire and hence it is currently operating in temporary quarters. Three new scattered mini-schools are being planned. Eventually there will be a network of them covering the community.

This coming September the Benjamin Banneker Urban Center will open in Mantua. It will be a school with no entrance, only exit requirements, directing its major effort to rehabilitation and prevention of dropouts. It will begin with the seventh grade and add a year each year until it provides an undergraduate college degree.

A group of faculty volunteers from the Wharton School, together with MCP, YGS, and black groups from neighborhoods other than Mantua conduct an evening program in business education at the University. This program is open to the disadvantaged of the entire metropolitan area. It is now in its second year and has more than a hundred students enrolled in it. Several of those who attended the first semester were given scholarships in the regular day-time degree program of our college. These evening students are also provided with counselling and employment services.

Scholarships to private schools in the suburbs have been obtained for several children from Mantua. Tutorial programs for children in local public schools and programs for orienting and assisting new teachers in these schools are provided.

The most recent and perhaps most exciting educational project has been the Urban Leadership Training Program. The following description of this program was written by Ronald E. Thompson, one of its members, for the *Mantua Community Newsletter* of April 1970.

On February 9 started the greatest event that ever happened in urban history. The event I'm talking about is the starting of the Urban Leadership Training Pro-

gram. The program started with 21 gang leaders from the Mantua community. The Young Great Society and Mantua Community Planners are affiliated with the program. YGS funds the program. The 21 leaders were picked from different corners which consist of 36th Street, 39th Street, Lancaster Avenue, 41st Street, and 42nd Street.

A few months ago, before the program started, these corners were at war with each other. Many times before the start of ULT, social workers tried to gather the corners together, but the problem that would result would be more conflict between the young men. As always, somebody would end up getting hurt.

So far the program is doing very good. The great thing about the program is that the young men have unity among each other. You know yourself that it is good because without unity you do not have anything.

The University of Pennsylvania provides space for the young men. Members of the University faculty and community workers of various fields volunteer to teach the young men different courses. Some of the courses the young men are taking consist of criminology, sociology, black studies, community health services, community planning, housing rehabilitation, radio and TV, and communications. The purpose of these courses is to prepare for future black leadership in all fields.

After this program is ended, the program will be repeated with 21 more black brothers.

The ULT brothers are working on several projects. One of these is the Leader Movie project. The Leader Movie, which is located at 41st Street and Lancaster Avenue, has been closed for some time. Police Commissioner Frank Rizzo wants the movie to be made into a PAL (Police Athletic League) building but we know it would just result in a conflict between the little kids. I hope that with the help of the community we could fight Rizzo mentally. The ULT brothers would like to own the Leader and turn it into a place where the younger kids in the community could have something to do besides training to fight one another.

Urban Leadership Training is turning out to be a community organization to fight the problems of the ghetto area of Mantua.

The young men do other kinds of field work. Recently the ULT brothers did a housing survey of the Mantua area for the Architecture and Planning Center of YGS. The young men also take trips in various parts of the US. One trip was taken in the Harlem area of New York where the young men took surveys and analyzed the ghetto neighborhood problems there and compared them with the problems in Mantua. We found out that the way they are living in Harlem is the same identical way we're living.

The program is the first I have known to ever understand gang problems.

I used to be affiliated with one of the gangs before I went into the service. I have been home from the service since January. I was in Vietnam. I compare the fighting in Vietnam with the fighting in the streets and find out it is almost the same. The only thing is that in the streets you are fighting your own brother.

The brothers are not fighting now. That is why the program might be the greatest event in urban history.

Physical and mental health services have been initiated within the community. These include two medical centers, a mobile clinic that goes to the people, and a drug-addiction treatment center. The Department of Community Medicine of our University and members of the community are now actively engaged in developing more extensive health services that they have collaboratively designed for Mantua.

MCP arranged for the City's Department of Recreation to convert two city-owned parking lots into recreational areas. MCP sponsors a basketball league that uses these facilities. They are also used for outdoor shows, dances, food sales, raffles, and other community activities. MCP has held a number of outings for neighborhood children; the most recent was attended by more than 800 children. Use of the University's indoor swimming pool by neighborhood children was arranged for the summer. MCP sponsors dramatic, music, and dance classes in the community. Last year the students of the dance put on an evening program in the University's auditorium that was exciting in conception and professional in execution. It also made a profit.

I could go on and mention the recently opened Day Care Center, the Nursery School, the free legal, social, and welfare services, and many others, but I think I have gone far enough to provide a picture of what has been and is happening. Those from the community that we support in turn support a very large number of others, all of whom are working on community development. Our own services continue to be available to any individual or group in the community that asks for them. At times we have had as many as thirty members of the University's faculty and student body involved in such support.

Initially we had to hide the fact that we were supporting the members of the Mantua team lest they be rejected by their community as pawns of the University or as "Uncle Toms." But by their behaviour and accomplishments they have established their independence of our influence and can now openly acknowledge our support, and even use it to their advantage. Our relationship is now taken for granted in the neighborhood. The friendships we have formed with Mantuans extend beyond the boundaries of the project and have helped integrate us into their community.

We have learned much more about the nature of the ghetto by being involved in it under the direction of its members than we could have learned by any traditional type of research. More important is the fact that our knowledge and understanding of the ghetto is now acknowledged by its leaders. I know of no other way by which such a state could have been brought about. One consequence of it is that, whereas we were initially asked to help only on problems involving external relations, for some time now we have also been deeply involved in problems internal to the ghetto. A second consequence is that our special knowledge of, and relation to, the ghetto is acknowledged by our University's administration. Hence we are asked as advisors on University-community relations and have helped design and operate new functions and units within the University that are concerned with these relations.

THE IMPLICATIONS

It is easy to become absorbed by the humanistic aspects of this effort, but I believe the scientific and managerial implications of it are also important. Let me consider a few of these.

First, note that we, the researchers, designed a relation with the "subjects" in which the subjects conducted research on us. It was the community members' task to find out how to use the University and our Center effectively, and, by so doing, to solve the researchers' problem of determining how to be useful. Not only would we have been rejected by the community if we had tried to do research on it, but even if we had not been rejected, we would not have had such access to it as we have had.

Little of what we have done is OR, or even research in the conventional sense. But we have never rejected a request for aid because it did not involve research or because it required action that was beneath our dignity. In addition to such activities as chauffering, acquiring empty oil drums and pond water for a fish tank, we have conducted research, for example, to determine the cost of racial segregation to the whites in the Philadelphia area and we have done economic-development and land-use planning for the neighborhood.

At first glance, this relation of researcher to researched may seem to be relevant only to the specific type of situation involved in this particular project. But is it? Although universities have had some success in serving governmental and industrial organizations, they have not been nearly as successful as many pretend. I suspect the reasons for their lack of success are related to my remarks about the ghetto.

We in OR do not know government and industry as well as we think we do, and administrators and managers know this. Therefore, they tend to use us in restricted and highly structured ways, on specific problems on which we have propagandized them into believing that we have some competence. But much of this use of our services is only token. For example, I recently reviewed the work of a management science group in one of this nation's largest corporations. Although its fifteen professionals have been carrying out studies for more than a decade, not one had been implemented. Nevertheless this group insisted on and had complete control over the projects it undertook.

Perhaps we should not tell administrators and managers how to use us, but rather involve them in systematic efforts to find out what we can best do and how they can best use us. This may well change our conception of our skills, but in return we may be given the opportunity to become a more integrated part of organizational decision making, planning, and development.

Secondly, the types of planning problems in which we have been traditionally engaged involve organizations that already have enough resources at their command to attain further growth and development. Hence, allocation of resources, rather than generation of new resources, preoccupies our planning efforts. In ghettos (and in most underdeveloped countries) this is not the case. Few resources are available. Hence, planning in the ghetto is very sensitive to potential sources of resources and to the uses for which they can be obtained. This requires development of plans that are much more integrated with those of the larger system of which it is a part than is usually the case in most governmental and industrial planning. I have never seen planners as sensitive to, and aware of, the plans made by the larger units of which they are a part, as I have seen in the ghetto. Ghetto leaders insist on knowing what is going on "up there" and they often understand the implications of higher-level plans better than do those who prepare them. How can we reproduce this state within government and industry?

The ghetto cannot use the annual budget as an instrument of or subsitute for planning because it never knows what resources will be available to it over even short planning periods. Hence its planning must be *continuous* and *adaptive*. Its long-range plans cannot be build up out of arbitrary fiscal blocks. Furthermore, because plans cannot be imposed on a black ghetto from above, they must be supported from below. Thus its planning must also be *participative*.

Planning in government and industry is seldom continuous, adaptive, or participative. But shouldn't it be? The pervasive preoccupation of managers and administrators with making a good showing in the current fiscal year leads to an imbalance of concern with short- and long-range performance, in favor of the short. Where planning is continuous, concerned with both the long and short of the future, and adaptive, this imbalance does not occur. Promotions do not motivate ghetto leaders because there is not a hierarchical structure in which to advance; they are motivated by a desire to increase the scope and importance of their jobs, and this is largely under the control of the individual involved. He is not bound by charters and job descriptions. He truly "manages by objectives." Might not a little more of this in government and industry be desirable?

We have tended to build our institutions in such a way as to minimize errors of commission, but in doing so we have increased the frequency of errors of omission. The emerging structure of the ghetto has reversed this state. Ghetto leaders are more concerned with not doing something that should be done than with doing something that does not need to be done. This orientation, it seems to me, is more likely to yield progressive development than is the converse orientation of most of our public and private institutions.

The ghetto is not a highly structured system, let alone a hierarchical one. Hence its leaders can only survive by effectively serving both their constituents and the larger community that contains them. Without support of the larger community, ghetto leaders cannot get the resources and programs that they require to serve their constituents. Without serving their constituents they cannot retain any followers. Hence only effective leaders can survive. This is not true in either government or industry, where Peter's Law — everyone rises to his level of incompetence — seems to hold almost universally.

The ghetto leader has neither rank nor authority vested in him from above. Therefore, he cannot use these to get others to do what they do not want to do. He must know what his followers want, what they can be persuaded to do, and how he can persuade them to do it. If these skills were available to those who currently direct others by virtue of rank and authority vested in them, imagine how much more effective they would be.

I know of no better way to develop such skills than by the democratic process of giving collective control over an authority to those who are individually controlled by that authority. Such control can even be built into bureaucracies by use of participative-management schemes. Such schemes have been suggested by many but tried by few.

We are witnessing an almost world-wide pressure for participative democracy, in public affairs and in universities. Can business, industry, and governmental agencies be far behind? I do not think so. Therefore, current leaders in these institutions would do well to study and gain understanding of the successful ghetto leader. They too may have to convert from practicing the art of management to practicing the art of leadership.

Finally, let me deal with the reluctance of the ghetto, like governments and industries, to change and to exploit the few resources that are available to them. Ghettos do not push their leaders; they are pulled by them. Ghettos have to be led into internal revolutions. In Mantua we have observed the development of an effective way of doing so. The motto of the Mantua Community Planners is "*plan or be planned for.*" This recognizes an important fact that is both obvious and ignored: it is not true that if nothing is done, nothing will happen. A great deal will happen and most of it will be undesirable. Ghetto leaders know that most current trends in the larger community that includes their neighborhood are detrimental to their neighborhood's interests. These trends are the subject of their constant study and analysis. They educate their constituents to an awareness of these trends and their consequences. Thus, the effective ghetto leader has a knowledge of and concern with his environment that few governmental or industrial leaders have. The latter tend to take their environment for granted and feel that by perceiving changes in it and adapting to them, their organizations can at least survive and may even grow. Hence they take little responsibility for what happens in their environment. Not so in the ghetto. Its leaders cannot afford to let the environment take its own course. However limited his effect on the larger environment may be, the ghetto leader uses all his power to push it in a direction that is compatible with his aspirations for his neighborhood. He believes in active intervention in the larger community and its future because he knows that his neighborhood cannot thrive unless the larger community thrives. He not only knows this, but he acts on it. Can we say the same about leaders of other types of institution?

Operations researchers also have a great deal to learn from effective ghetto leaders. They should develop the same attitude toward OR as these leaders have toward their communities. They should not be willing to let OR develop only in response to changing external conditions. They should want to help create a world in which the capabilities of OR are considerably extended but in which the need for OR is diminished. Like the ghetto leader whose objective it is ultimately to dissolve the ghetto by having it absorbed into the main current of the culture of which it is a part, so OR's objective should be the dissolution of OR as an autonomous and segregated activity by having it absorbed into every aspect of the organizational life of which it is a part.

AUTHOR'S NOTE

This paper is based on an address to the Philadelphia Section of the Operations Research Society of America given on June 5, 1970.

ABOUT THE AUTHOR

Russell Lincoln Ackoff is a leading figure internationally in Operations Research of which he can be regarded as one of the founders.

He graduated with a bachelor's degree in architecture at the University of Pennsylvania and then switched to philosophy with a Ph.D. from the same University in 1947. In the same year he became an Assistant Professor of Mathematics and Philosophy at Wayne State University. 1952 saw Ackoff as Director of the Operations Research Group at Case Institute of Technology, which later transferred to the Wharton School of Finance and Commerce at the University of Pennsylvania.

Ackoff has been very active as an advisor to numerous companies and public agencies. He is past president of the Operations Research Society of America, 1956-57, a past Vice-President of the Institute of Management Sciences and a Fellow of the American Statistical Association.

He has a superior ability in presenting the concepts of operations research in non-mathematical terms. He is a popular lecturer and his books such as Scientific Method: Optimizing Applied Research Decisions *(1962).* A Manager's Guide to Operations Research(1963), Fundamentals of Operations Research *(1968) and* A Concept of Corporate Planning *(1970) reveal a powerful combination of lucid analysis and an ever-evolving quest for insight and improvement.*

VII

AN OVERVIEW

Operational Research

A. Graham Mackenzie and Michael K. Buckland

It was the late 1960's which saw the first substantial development of library O.R. It has been largely an alien activity, performed by non-librarians. The goal of helping librarians with their problems has sometimes been modified by other motivations. This and the applied science approach have tended to create severe problems of communication, which provided the raison d'etre for this Reader.

The following review was written in 1971 but still provides a reasonably up-to-date overview.

APOLOGIA

In attempting to write this review of operational research in libraries we immediately came face to face with two serious difficulties: the first was to find sufficient British work to tell a coherent story, and the second was to judge the level at which to treat a subject which is new to many of our professional colleagues and at the same time not easy to grasp. A selective, but reasonably comprehensive, bibliography on this and related topics, which was compiled in the summer of 1969[12] contained 280 items; 50 of these originated or were published in Britain, but only 29 were dated 1966 or later, and even of these some were marginal to our subject. We have therefore had to include a discussion of some of the more important American work in this field in order to present a balanced account of the state of the art.

Operational research (usually referred to as OR) is a relatively new term; it dates from about 1941, and can best be explained for our purposes by three quotations:

> OR is the application of scientific methods, techniques and tools to problems involving the operations of a system so as to provide those in control of the system with optimum solutions to the problems.[15]

> OR can be considered as being:
> (1) the application of scientific method
> (2) by interdisciplinary teams
> (3) to problems involving the control of organized (man-machine systems so as to provide solutions which best serve the purposes of the organization as a whole.[1]

> The basis of all scientific work is experimentation. Experimentation is just what apparently cannot be done with administrative systems . . . OR does not experiment with the system itself, it experiments with a model of the system.[19]

These explanations are reasonably clear, but OR work, and particularly model-building, of necessity deals in symbols, signs, equations and mathematical techniques; the average librarian (and the senior author is no exception) finds that these are somewhat disconcerting, and that considerable knowledge and effort is required to understand them properly. Hence we shall not attempt to do more than summarize the findings of studies; those readers who have the inclination or the skills to go further must refer to the original publications for details.

Note that although "systems analysis" is sometimes used as if it were synonymous with OR, it is more commonly used to describe the preliminary design work for computerized data processing, which is dealt with elsewhere.

SETTING THE SCENE

During the period 1966-70 OR became a significant aspect of librarianship. Up until then little had been published, and those who had used similar techniques had probably not

SOURCE: Reprinted from *British Librarianship and Information Science 1966-1970* edited by H. A. Whatley (London: Library Association 1972) pp. 224-231, by permission of the authors and publishers.

thought of them in these terms. A striking early example was the planning of the National Lending Library for Science and Technology in the mid-1950s by Urquhart and his colleagues, but so far as we know, the term was not explicitly mentioned in any of their published work at that time; however, those who followed could easily recognize, and be inspired by, their example. By the end of 1970 several man-years of effort had resulted in two books[31, 34], a number of substantial research reports, an important research seminar[27], and numerous articles. Almost all the work was based on universities or university libraries — there is a real distinction — and a considerable amount of it was British.

OR is based on applying a scientific approach to practical problems; it normally operates in four distinct stages:

1. Description of the system being considered, especially by means of mathematical models and computer simulations;
2. Measurement, using objective data whenever these can be obtained;
3. Evaluation; the presentation of relevant information to the system manager (here, the librarian) to aid him in making decisions between different courses of action;
4. Operational control, assisting in the development of ways and means of achieving the objectives aimed for over a period of time.

From 1966 to 1970 research was heavily concentrated on those aspects of library management which lend themselves more easily to quantification. Some real progress was made in clarifying various facets of what can be termed library stock control: collection size, hierarchical relationships in library systems, policies for lending and duplication, and shelving arrangements. Two projects grappled seriously with the comparative evaluation of library services, while others tried to define measures of performance. It is also noteworthy that the two main British projects both began to turn towards the equally important, but more intractable, problem of modelling user behaviour.

COLLECTION SIZE

Bradford's Law of scattering,[3] having been regarded as a statistical quirk for thirty years, became a topic of intense interest during this period. This was partly because of its intriguing theoretical implications, but also because Bradford had been concerned with the way in which the literature of a given subject is scattered over numerous journals: a few contain much relevant literature, but as each more "distant" journal is examined its pages contribute less and less of relevance. It came to be recognized that Bradford's Law of scattering was, in effect, a law of diminishing returns with respect to the growth of collection size; it is therefore highly relevant to the planning of libraries, especially when related to the concept of obsolescence, which is a law of diminishing returns with respect to the length of time a document is retained in the collection. Cole[16] had perceived this much earlier, but little else was published until 1968.

The most detailed treatment of scattering, obsolescence and the usefulness of a collection is by Buckland and Woodburn[11], who use data collected by Cole to explore and illustrate the likely financial and operational consequences of a variety of different acquisition, binding and discarding policies. This topic has also been lucidly treated by Brookes[5] and is sometimes referred to as the "p%" (or "90%") library. Bradford's Law (also referred to as the Bradford distribution and the Bradford-Zipf distribution) has been variously formulated by different researchers; this is a technical matter which has been treated thoroughly by Fairthorne[20]. Bradford's law has been perceived to be of practical importance in library planning (e.g.[4,9]), though the analyses based on it will remain incomplete until more is known about users' reactions to differing degrees of incompleteness of collection size. Brookes' formulation is comparatively easy to handle, and he has argued plausibly that Bradford's Law can also be used operationally to estimate the completeness of a "comprehensive" bibliography.[4] (See Section IV: 1.)

An extension of the "p%" library problem is that of relating a number of libraries to one another in a hierarchical structure. Woodburn[39] presented a model which clarified the problem but which "relied on data which would never be available." Subsequently Brookes has pointed out that the elusive data (on the pattern of demand for books) can reasonably be presumed to conform to the Bradford-Zipf distribution, and has analysed the viability of branch libraries on this basis.[67]

Williams[38] compared the cost of acquiring, storing, and servicing journals with the cost of borrowing or photocopying them when sought. The findings suggest that large libraries are paying heavily for the advantage of having extensive collections of little-used material on the premises.

LOAN AND DUPLICATION POLICIES

The long-standing lack of any rigorous examination of the effects of libraries' widely varying policies on duplication and (especially) on loan periods was ended by no less than four treatments of the topic. One of these — a major contribution — was Morse's pioneering treatise,[31] based on data gathered in the libraries of MIT over a number of years. The first half of the book is devoted to a study, in considerable depth, of OR techniques suitable for use in libraries; as the author himself admits, this is hard reading for the innumerate, but essential if the arguments are to be followed into the second part, which is addressed to the basic problem of librarians — how to get the right book to the right reader at the right time. Efficient circulation, and the estimation of future demand, are the keys to good service, and Morse provides at least some lines of approach to the problem. In brief he gives a lucid introduction to probability as it applies to library operations. He relies very heavily on queuing theory, and makes assumptions of random arrivals of demands for books, and of random return of books on loan, without adducing evidence for either — as reviewers have noted (e.g. Meyer[30]).

Meanwhile Buckland and Woodburn[8] used a similar approach to duplication in the context of a reserve (short-loan) collection, and to exploring the likely loss of immediate availability if a reference library were to permit borrowing. A somewhat naive paper by Goyal[22] describes the relevance of queuing theory to serials control and, much earlier, its use in the planning of a centralized National Lending Library had been reported by Urquhart and Bunn.[37]

At Lancaster, when attention was turned from the problems of a reserve collection to the much more complex problems of the use of a general open-access collection, queuing theory was abandoned in favour of using a computer to simulate borrowing empirically; this was considered more appropriate for operational analyses of the complexities of an actual library — as well as being easier for the non-numerate to understand. This work forms an interesting case-study in that the consideration of first principles, followed by data collection and simulation, led to recommendations which were implemented[12] — as is more likely to happen if the library is itself carrying out the investigation. In particular the relationships were clarfied between official loan periods, the probability of renewal, and the length of time books are kept out. "The librarian has, in his ability to determine official loan periods, a powerful and precise control mechanism for influencing the availability of the books in his library". The "variable" loan policy adopted was that the books most in demand (about 10 per cent of monograph stock) should be subject to a shorter loan period of one week, while lightly-used material could be retained until the end of a term. This policy was designed to increase "Satisfaction level" (the chance that readers will find the books they seek) and reduce "Collection bias" (the tendency for the more heavily used books to be absent from the shelves, thus distorting the choice available). Implementation of the system was followed by a very substantial increase in borrowing.[36]

Trueswell published a number of papers (e.g.[35]) on the distribution of demand over books in a library, and the classic study by Fussler and Simon on the prediction of future use of books was belatedly re-issued.[21]

SHELVING AND STACK ORGANISATION

The largest centre of library OR activity during this period was that led by Leimkuhler at Purdue. This investigated shelving arrangements in considerable detail: one conclusion was that shelving books by height in two sequences could make considerable economies in space, but that the marginal benefit of additional sequences diminished rapidly after three or four. Leimkuhler also reformulated the Bradford distribution — thereby internationalizing what has been largely a British interest — and applied it to hierarchical stack arrangements, e.g. a "core" working collection and a stack of less used material constitutes a two-level hierarchy.[26] This has some affinities with the library hierarchies explored by Woodburn and, more especially, Brookes (as noted above). An interesting analysis leading to a more economical arrangement of stacks was reported at Manchester Public Library.[17] A similar approach to the same problem was presented quite differently (although perhaps less realistically) by Booth.[2]

Other logistical aspects examined during this period included a collection of studies, with a cost-accounting emphasis, in a book edited by Burkhalter.[13] This was the result of a series of investigations conducted by graduate students in the University of Michigan Library: the studies range from trivial to far-reaching, from centralized book labelling to the effective utilisation of space. They are not intended as universally-applicable solutions, but rather as examples of how to apply to libraries the basic principles of cost-benefit studies; nevertheless they are well worth reading for this purpose alone.

Buckland[10] compared regional with centralized union catalogues, and argued that the latter should provide a faster and a more economical service. Dougherty and Heinritz published a book inappropriately entitled *Scientific management of library operations*[18] which is mainly concerned with an O & M study of a circulation system. However, the book contains useful notes on calculating labour costs.

EVALUATION OF LIBRARIES

Researchers at the University of Durham mounted PEBUL (Project for Evaluating the Benefits from University Libraries), a major three-year study of the role of the library in its university. As in the case of the early Lancaster work, to which it was complementary, this project was supported by OSTI, and gave rise to a number of papers performing the function of *haute vulgarisation* (e.g.[14,24]); however, the final project report[25] is particularly worthy of attention. It sets out, with a mass of supporting data, the investigators' conviction that a quantitative value can be placed on a library service by working backwards from decisions (e.g. on the level of financial support) which have already been made by the university, using a technique known as inverse linear programming. In the course of the project much information was gathered on the way in which libraries are used, and on the relative priorities which various groups of users assign to different actual or potential aspects of the service. In spite of certain reservations which may be held about the basic premise (for in the current state of our universities who would claim that past decisions necessarily represent the desired optimum?) it is obvious that the PEBUL team have cast a considerable amount of light on a subject never before studied in depth, and it is unfortunate that their work was not continued after 1969.

A second study based on MIT libraries was that by Raffel and Shisko[34] who adopted a Planning — Programming — Budgeting — System (PPBS) approach. This technique, also called Program Budgeting and Output Budgeting, involves the explicit formulation of objectives ("programs"). For MIT libraries three were specified: (i) The support of a general research collection; (ii) the provision of required reading for courses; (iii) the library's own R & I activities. The next step was to relate all library activities and services to these objectives; the effect of possible changes in library provision is then examined, and planning decisions are taken accordingly. This study is noteworthy for the attempt to ascertain the values which users assigned to different services. Hamburg[23] also recommends this approach.

Because OR normally involves the explicit definition of objectives, such studies often include discussions of objectives and of measures of performance. The most used measure during this period was, in one guise or another, the probability that a reader would find what he was looking for. Variously described as immediate availability, reader failure, satisfaction level and user frustration, this is very useful is assessing how satisfactory some aspects of library provision are — but it is not an overall objective. It is usually stated in terms of *immediate* satisfaction, but it can be extended to include delayed satisfaction, as in Orr's Document Delivery Test.[33] Another approach advocated by Meier[29] and Hamburg[23] uses the amount of time spent by a reader in using documents.

BEHAVIOURAL ASPECTS

Much early work treated the user as a "black box" — merely a source of systematic or random stimuli applied to the library being studied. More recently workers at Purdue (e.g.[32]) examined the library's power to influence users before they express their demands, and governing bodies ("funders") before they make crucial decisions; this approach heralds a new phase of OR in libraries, involving a greater concentration on factors affecting users' behaviour and on the examination of policy-making processes.

WORK IN PROGRESS

Quantitative approaches to library management (with greater or less emphasis on models of the user and the system) are actively in progress in a number of centres in Britain; much of this work is not yet published, but details are beginning to circulate on the grapevine. The foundation by OSTI of the Cambridge Library Management Research Unit in 1969 should be noted; this is largely concerned with the collection of information for effective management, the establishment of labour costs for operations, and the investigation of failure by readers to find books.

The National Libraries ADP Study, based on the University Library at Bath, has as its *raison d'etre* a study of the extent to which computers could be used in a national library system; although this is not basically an OR problem the data collection, quantification and evaluation involved will certainly interest others than those directly concerned with computers.

The Library Research Unit at the University of Lancaster (the only permanent research team in the country which is based on a university library) is engaged on two projects: one, funded by the Council on Library Resources, is a study in depth of the interactions between libraries and their users; the second is a feasibility study for OSTI on the production of a management game (to be used in the education of libraries and information officers) from

models of libraries and their users. In addition Wolfe, at the University of Edinburgh, has been directing research into the economic analysis of various library problems.

ENVOI

In the period 1966-70 OR became a significant and growing part of librarianship. Martyn and Vickery[28] have described some serious difficulties in applying these techniques, but nevertheless researchers at a number of centres have made considerable progress in elucidating certain murky areas. Present trends are likely to continue: theoretical analyses and practical applications of the Bradford-Zipf distribution; a concentration on devising several intermediate measures of library performance, rather than one single quantifiable goal; and an emphasis on the logistics of book provision, which seems to offer large and immediate practical benefits for a comparatively small outlay. The study and simulation of user behaviour will assume greater importance. A major problem here is data collection; but as computer-aided procedures grow more common in libraries, the provision of management information will plug this gap, if those introducing such procedures realize its importance at the design stage.

FURTHER READING

Those wishing to explore this aspect of librarianship are recommended to start with the proceedings of the seminar of *Planning library services*[27] and then to try the larger reports on the leading projects according to taste, e.g. Durham[25] which concentrates on library use and the evaluation of different services; Lancaster[12] which examines decisions which a university librarian has to take; and MIT by Morse[31] which is rather mathematical, and by Raffel and Shishko[34] which adopts a PPBS approach. *The Journal of Documentation* contains a number of relevant articles and reviews from 1967 onwards.

354   A. GRAHAM MACKENZIE AND MICHAEL K. BUCKLAND

REFERENCES

[1] Ackoff, R. L., and Sasieni, M. W. Fundamentals of operations research. Wiley, 1948.
[2] Booth, A. D. On the geometry of libraries. *J. Docum.*, 25 (1) 1969, 28-40.
[3] Bradford, S. C. Documentation. Lockwood, 1948.
[4] Brookes, B. C. Bradford's law and the bibliography of science. *Nature*, 224, Dec. 6, 1969, 953-956.
[5] Brookes, B. C. The derivation and application of the Bradford-Zipf distribution. *J. Docum.*, 24 (4) 1968, 247-265; 25 (1) 1969, 58-60.
[6] Brookes, B. C. The design of cost-effective hierarchical information systems. *Inf. Stor. Retr.*, 6 (2) June 1970, 127-136.
[7] Brookes, B. C. The viability of branch libraries. *J. Librarianship*, 2 (1) Jan. 1970, 14-21.
[8] Buckland, M. K. and Woodburn, I. An analytical study of library book duplication and availability. *Inf. Stor. Retr.*, 5 (1) 1969, 69-79. (An earlier version was published as University of Lancaster Library, Occasional Paper 2, 1968.)
[9] Buckland, M. K., and Hindle A. Library Zipf. *J. Docum.*, 25 (1) 1969, 52-57.
[10] Buckland, M. K. Quantitative evaluation of regional union catalogues. *J. Docum.*, 23 (1) 1967, 20-27.
[11] Buckland, M. K., and Woodburn, I. Some implications for library management of scattering and obsolescence. University of Lancaster Library, Occasional Paper 1, 1968.
[12] Buckland, M. K. *and others*. Systems analysis of a university library. University of Lancaster Library, Occasional Paper 4, 1969.
[13] Burkhalter, B. R. Case studies in library systems analysis. Scarecrow Pr., 1968.
[14] Burnett, D. Economics and the university library. *Universities Q.*, 24 (4) 1970, 440-452.
[15] Churchman, C. W., *and others*. Introductions to operations research. Wiley, 1957.
[16] Cole, P. F. Journal usage versus age of journal. *J. Docum.*, 19 (1) 1963, 1-11.
[17] Colley, D. I. The storage and retrieval of stack material. *Libr. Ass. Rec.*, 67 (2) Feb. 1965, 37-42, 59.
[18] Dougherty, R. M., and Heinritz, F. J. Scientific management of library operations. Scarecrow Pr., 1966.
[19] Duckworth, W. E. Guide to operational research. 2nd ed. Methuen, 1965.
[20] Fairthorne, R. A. Empirical hyperbolic distributions (Bradford-Zipf-Mandelbrot) for bibliometric description and prediction. *J. Docum.*, 25 (4) 1969, 319-343.
[21] Fussler, H. H., and Simon, J. L. Patterns in the use of books in large research libraries. University of Chicago Pr., 1969.
[22] Goyal, S. K. Application of OR to the problem of determining an appropriate loan period for periodicals. *Libri*, 20 (1-2) 1970, 94-100.
[23] Hamburg, M., *and others*. A systems analysis of the library and information science statistical data system: the research investigation. Interim Report. University of Pennsyvania, 1970. 2v.
[24] Hawgood, J. Evaluating the benefits from university libraries. *In* Research into library services in higher education. Papers presented at a conference held at the University of London, 1967. Society for Research into Higher Education, 1968.
[25] Hawgood, J., and Morley, R. Project for evaluating the benefits of university libraries. Final report. University of Durham, 1969.
[26] Leimkuhler, F. F. A literature search and file organization model. *Am. Docum.*, 19 (2) 1968, 131-136.
[27] Mackenzie, A. G., and Stuart, I. M. *eds*. Planning library services: proceedings of a research seminar. University of Lancaster Library, Occasional Paper 3, 1969.
[28] Martyn, J., and Vickery, B. C. The complexity of the modelling of information systems. *J. Docum.*, 26 (3) 1970, 204-220.
[29] Meier, R. L. Efficiency criteria for the operation of large libraries. *Libr. Q.*, 31 (3) 1961, 215-234.
[30] Meyer, K. H. F. Die Untersuchung uber "library effectiveness" am MIT. *Nachr. Dokum.* 21 (5) 1970, 195-200.
[31] Morse, P. M. Library effectiveness: a systems approach. M. I. T. Press, 1968.
[32] Nance, R. E. Strategic simulation of a library/user/funder system. Ph. D. Thesis, Purdue, 1968. (University Microfilms o/no. 69-2963.)
[33] Orr, R. H. *and others*. Development of methodologic tools for planning and managing library services. II. Measuring a library's capability for providing documents. *Bull. Med. Lib. Ass.* 56 (3) 1968, 241-267.
[34] Raffel, J. A., and Shishko, R. Systematic analysis of university libraries: an application of cost-benefit analysis to the MIT libraries. M. I. T. Press, 1969.
[35] Trueswell, R. W. Determining the optimal number of volumes for a library's core collection. *Libri*, 16 (1) 1966, 49-60.
[36] University of Lancaster. Report of the Librarian for 1969-70.
[37] Urquhart, D. J., and Bunn, R. M. A national loan period for scientific serials. *J. Docum.*, 15 (1) 1959, 21-37.
[38] Williams, G., *and others*. Library cost models: owning versus borrowing serial publications. (ED 026 106.) 1968.
[39] Woodburn, I. A mathematical model of a hierarchical library structure, *In*, Mackenzie, A. G., and Stuart, I. M. *op. cit.*

ABOUT THE AUTHORS

A. Graham Mackenzie: See page 66.

Michael K. Buckland: See page 28.

A Bibliography on Operations Research in Libraries

Michael K. Buckland and Donald H. Kraft

PREFACE

The purpose of this Reader is to present a selection of writings designed to instil an understanding of the nature and scope of operations research in libraries. It is hoped that many of those who peruse these articles and chapters will continue to be interested in this approach to library problems.

In order to facilitate further explorations, the following bibliography has been specially prepared in order to complement the readings themselves. Nobody should launch into a reading spree and attempt to wade through all the items in the bibliography. It should, instead, be regarded as a display from which the reader can select the individual items which are of particular interest.

The quantity of writings on library operations research is larger than is commonly realised. This may be because the items are rarely labelled as operations research and are sometimes obscurely published. It has been difficult for the compilers to define and adhere to a satisfactory definition of scope. The approach has been to include examples of quantitative approaches to problem-solving in libraries, especially when this involves, explicitly or implicitly, the use of a model. Other items generally represent topics which overlap with library operations research. A good example is bibliometrics which has a substantial literature, but which is often purely descriptive and not problem-oriented in any serious way. Therefore, only a selection of items from the literature of bibliometrics has been included. These can serve as samples and, if more are needed, reference should be made to biblio-graphies on that topic, such as Pritchard's extensive list. Similarly, few items have been included from the literatures on user-studies, cost-accounting, library administration, and so on.

This bibliography was a collaborative venture and was compiled in the following manner: Buckland had been accumulating references for a few years. This accumulation was believed to be rather comprehensive up to about 1970 but much less so for subsequent years. Kraft, in teaching operations research to library science students, had also been collecting references and undertook to update and edit the material assembled by Buckland.

A special acknowledgement is due to Professor Vladimir Slamecka, Director of the School of Information and Computer Sciences at Georgia Institute of Technology. Professor Slamecka prepared "A Selective Bibliography on Library Operations Research" for the Chicago Graduate Library School Conference on "Operations Research: Implications for Libraries" in 1971 and graciously gave the compilers permission to cannibalise his listing into the present bibliography. Also, the help of Mr. Dennis McDonald, a doctoral student in the College of Library and Information Services, University of Maryland, and Ms. Linda Kip, a masters student in the School of Librarianship, University of California, Berkeley, is acknowledged. In addition, bibliographies from the data bases of the National Technical Information Service (NTIS), the Goddard Space Center of the National Aeronautics and Space Administration (NASA), and the Educational Resources Information Center (ERIC) were used.

Ackerman, J. "Statistical Measures Required for Library Management Decision-Making Under a Planning-Programming-Budgeting System (PPBS)," M.B.A. thesis, University of Pennsylvania, Philadelphia, 1969.

Ackoff, R. L. "The Role of Recorded Information in the Decision Making Processes: Operational Research Approach." In Shera, J. H., A. Kent and J. W. Perry (Eds.), *Documentation in Action*,

New York: Reinhold Publishing Co., 1956.

Ackoff, R. L. and others. *The SCATT Report: A Tentative Idealized Design of a National Scientific Communication and Technology Transfer System.* University of Pennsylvania, the Wharton School, 1975.

Adkins, S. "Planning and Control — the Key to Better Management Information," in Blood, J., Jr. (Ed.), *Management Science in Planning and Control*, TAPPI, New York, 1969.

Afanasev, E. V. "Nauchno-Tekhnicheskaia Informatsiia Y Podgotoke I Priniatii Upravlencheskikh Reshevii" (Scientific and Technical Information in Preliminary and Final Management Decision Making), *Nauchno Tekhnicheskaia Informatsiia*, Seriial, 1973, pp. 14-20.

Agee, M. H. "Management Decision Making," Second Annual Library Management Workshop, Carol M. Newman Library and Department of Industrial Engineering and Operations Research, Virginia Polytechnic Institute and State University, Blacksburg, Virginia, 1972.

Agee, M. H. "A Rationale for Decision Making — A Tutorial," in Rudolph, G. A. (Ed.), *The Academic Community Looks at Library Management*, Carol M. Newman Library and Department of Industrial Engineering and Operations Research, Virginia Polytechnic Institute and State University, Blacksburg, Virginia, 1971.

Allen, A. H. "Systems to Manage the Industrial Library," *J. Systems Management*, vol. 23 no. 6, June 1972, pp. 24-27.

Allen, T. J. *Managing the flow of scientific and technological information.* Cambridge, Mass.: Massachusetts Institute of Technology, 1966. (NTIS PB 174 440)

Allen, T. J. and P. G. Gerstberger. *Criteria for selection of an information source.* Cambridge, Mass.: Massachusetts Institute of Technology, Alfred P. Sloane School of Management, Sept. 1967. (NTIS PB 176 899)

American Library Association. *Library Statistics: A Handbook of Concepts, Definitions, and Terminology*, Williams, Joel (ed.), Chicago, 1966.

Andrews, T. "The Role of Departmental Libraries in Operations Research Studies in a University Library." *Special Libraries*, Vol. 59, 1968, pp. 519-24 and pp. 638-44.

Applegate, H. C. "The Cost Effectiveness of Field Pickup of Long Overdue Items at the Glendale Public Library." Glendale, Calif.: Glendale Public Library, 1974.

Argyris, Chris. "Management Information Systems: the Challenge to Rationality and Emotionality," *Management Science*, 17:B275-B292 (February 1971).

Arms, W. Y. "Operational Research in Libraries" in *Studies in Library Management*, Vol. 2 by C. Bingley; Shoestring, 1975, pp. 76-91.

Arora, S. R. and R. N. Paul. "Acquisition of Library Materials: A Quantitative Approach," in J. B. Narth, ed., *Proceedings of the Thirty-second Annual Meeting of the American Society for Information Science, San Francisco, October 1-4, 1969. Vol. 6: Cooperating Information Societies*, Westport, Conn., and London: Greenwood Publishing Corp., 1969.

Arsenault, J. R., J. F. Numamaker, Jr., A. B. Whinston. "Models for the design of data organization," paper presented at 39th National Operations Research Society of America (ORSA), May 1971.

Arthur Andersen Co. *Research Study of the Criteria and Procedures for Evaluating Scientific Information Retrieval Systems.* Washington, D. C.: National Science Foundation, OSIS, 1962. (NTIS PB 273115)

Ashmole, R. F., D. E. Smith, and B. T. Smith. "Cost Effectiveness of Current Awareness Sources in the Pharmaceutical Industry," *Journal of the American Society for Information Science*, vol. 24, 1973, pp. 29-39.

Ashmole, R. F., D. E. Smith, and B. T. Stern. "Cost Effectiveness of Current Awareness Sources in the Pharmaceutical Industry" *Journal of the American Society for Information Science*, Jan.-Feb. 1973, pp. 29-39.

Auret, H. E. "Optimalisering van die bedryfskapasiteit van 'n bepaalde biblioteek," *South African Libraries*, vol. 36, April, 1969, pp. 142-151.

Avramescu, A. "Probabilistic Criteria for the Objective Design of Descriptor Languages," *Journal of the American Society for Information Science*, vol. 22, 1971, pp. 85-95.

Axford, H. "An Approach to Performance Budgeting at the Florida Atlantic University Library," *College and Research Libraries*, 32:87-104 (March 1971).

Axford, H. W. "Performance Measurement Revisited", *College and Research Libraries*, vol. 34, 1973, pp. 249-257.

Axford, H. W., ed. *Proceedings of the Larc Computer-Based Unit Cost Studies Institute.* Held Sept. 16-17, 1971, at the Joe C. Thompson Conference Center, The University of Texas, Austin. Tempe, Ariz.: Larc Association, 1972.

Axford, H. W. (Ed.) *Proceedings of the Larc Institute on Library Operations Research.* Tempe, Ariz.: Larc, 1973.

Ayres, H. T., R. C. Norris, and R. S. Robinson, "An Investigation of Missing Books in the M.I.T. Science Library," Term Report, M.I.T. Libraries, Cambridge, Mass., 1962.

Baaske, J., D. L. Tollver, J. Westerberg. "Overdue Policies: A Comparison of Alternatives," *College and Research Libraries*, vol. 35, 1974, pp. 354-359.

Baker, G. G. "Information Access Methods for Microfilm Systems," *Microdoc*, vol. 13, 1974, pp. 100-112.

Baker, J. D. *Quantitative Modeling of Human Performance in Information Systems. Technical Research Note 232.* Report No.: BESRL-TRN-232. Arlington, Va.: Army Behaviorial Science Research Labs, 1974.

Baker, R. "A Descriptive Model of Library/User/Funder Behavior in a University Environment", *Drexel Library Bulletin*, vol. 4:1968, pp. 16-30.

Baker, N. R. "Optimal user search sequences and implications for information systems operation," *American Documentation*, vol. 20, 1969, pp. 203-12.

Baker, N. R. "Quantitative models of servicer/user/funder behavior in service organizations." Paper presented at the Fourteenth International Meeting of TIMS, Mexico City, 1967, and *Drexel Library Quarterly*, vol. 4, 1968.

Baker, N. R. "Scientific information and innovation in research organizations," paper presented at the 38th National Operations Research Society of America, Detroit, Michigan, October, 1970.

Baker, Norman R. and R. E. Nance. "Organizational Analyses and Simulation Studies of University Libraries: A Methodological Overview," *Information Storage and Retrieval*, vol. 5, pp. 153-168.

Baker, N. R. and R. E. Nance. "The Use of Simulation in Studying Information Storage and Retrieval Systems," *American Documentation*, vol. 19, 1968, pp. 363-70.

Banghardt, F. W. *Educational Systems Analysis.* New York: Macmillan Co., 1969.

Barkey, Patrick. "Patterns of Student Use of a College Library," *College and Research Libraries*, vol. 26 no. 2, March 1965, pp. 115-118.

Barnikol, I. "Analyse der Berutzungsfrequenz der Universitäts- und Landes -bibliothek Sachsen-Arhalt in Halle/Saale" [Analysis of the frequency of use at the University and State Library of Sachsen-Arhalt, Halle/Saale], *Zentralblatt für Bibliothekswesen*, vol. 85, 1971, pp. 1-17.

Basile, V. A. and R. W. Smith. "Evolving the 90% pharmaceutical library," *Special Libraries*, vol. 61, 1970, pp. 81-86.

Batteke, J. P. H. and J. I. Viorst. "The Economics of Information: A Macro-Approach", American Society for Information Science Proceedings, Fall, 1973.

Baumol, W. J. and Marcus, M. *Economics of academic libraries.* Washington, D.C.: American Council on Education, 1973.

Beasley, K. E. "A Theoretical Framework for Public Library Measurement," in Goldhor, Herbert (ed.), *Research Methods in Librarianship: Measurement and Evaluation*, pp. 2-14, University of Illinois Graduate School of Library Science, Evanston, Ill., 1968.

Beaver, B. *A statistical study of scientific and technical journals*, Yale Univ., Connecticut, 1964, NTIS PB 167 672.

Beckman, Margaret. *Derivation of a simulation model of a university library system*. Guelph University. Library Administration. Guelph, Ontario, Canada. 1968. 28 p.

Beckman, M. and N. A. Brown. "The Role of the Librarian in Management," *Special Libraries*, vol. 66, 1975, pp. 19-26.

Beeler, M. G. F., A. Reisman, J. Herling, and B. V. Dean. "A Multi-Library System Distribution Network Design," paper presented at TIMS 20th International Meeting, Tel Aviv, Israel, 1973.

Bell, Karl Heinrich and E. Kabos. "Problems der Anwendung Wissenschaftlicher methoden in der Planungs- und Leitungstätigkeit Wissenschaftlicher Bibliotheken," *Zentralblatt fur Bibliothekswesen*, vol. 84, 1970, pp. 705-720, vol. 85, 1971, pp. 129-147.

Berg, S. "An Economic Analysis of the Demand for Scientific Journals," *Journal of the American Society for Information Science*, vol. 23, 1972, pp. 23-9.

Berg, S. V. *Structure, Behavior and Performance in the Scientific Journal Market*, unpublished doctoral dissertation, Yale University, 1970.

Berg, S. V. and D. Campion. "Toward a Model of Journal Economics in the Language Sciences", Center for Applied Linguistics, Washington, D. C., 1971; NTIS PB 206 498. (Appendix by L. Okreglak).

Bergen, D. P. "Implications of general systems theory for librarianship and higher education," *College and Research Libraries*, vol. 27, 1966, pp. 258-388.

Bhat, V. N., R. E. Nance, and R. R. Korfhage. "Information Networks: A Probabilistic Model for Hierarchical Transfer." Technical Report CP710023, Computer Science/Operations Research Center, Southern Methodist University, Dallas, Texas, 1971.

Biles, W. E., C. B. Estes, R. O. Hoffman, D. H. Kraft, and J. J. Talavage. "The Industrial Engineer in Environmental Information Systems," (scheduled for presentation at First Annual Systems Engineering Conference, American Institute of Industrial Engineers, New York, New York, November, 1973.)

Black, S. W. "Library Economics." *Libraries at Large: Appendixes*, Appendix F-2, pp. 590-596.

Blande & Holt. "Cost-Performance Analysis of TWX Mediated Interlibrary Loan in Medium Sized Libraries." *Med. Lib. Assn. Ba.*, vol. 59, 1971.

Blunt, C. R., *et al.* "A General Model for Simulating Information Storage and Retrieval Systems," Report No. 352.14-R2, Herb-Singer, State College, Pa., 1966, NTIS AD 636435.

Bolles, S. W. "The use of flow charts in the analysis of library operations," *Special Libraries*, vol. 58, 1967, 95-98.

Bommer, M. R. W. *The Development of a Management System for Effective Decision-Making in a University Library*, 1972. University Microfilms O.-No. 72-17328.

Bommer, R. W. "Operations Research in Libraries: A Critical Assessment," *JASIS*, vol. 26, 1975, pp. 137-139.

Bonini, C. P. *Simulation of information and decision systems in the firm*, New York, Prentice-Hall. 1963.

Bookstein, A. "The Anomalous Behavior of Precision in the Swets Model and Its Resolution", *Journal of Documentation*, vol. 30, 1974, pp. 374-80.

Bookstein, A. "Comments on the Morse-Chen Discussion of Noncirculating Books" *Library Quarterly*, vol. 45, 1975, pp. 195-198.

Bookstein, A. "A Hybrid Access Method for Bibliographic Records," *Journal of Library Automation*, vol. 7, 1974, pp. 97-104.

Bookstein, A. "Implications for Library Education," *Library Quarterly*, vol. 42, 1972, pp. 140-51.

Bookstein, A. "Models for Shelf Reading," *Library Quarterly*, vol. 43 no. 2, April 1973, pp. 126-137.

Bookstein, A. "Probabilistic Models for Automatic Indexing", *Journal of the American Society for Information Science*, vol. 25, 1974, pp. 312-8.

Bookstein, A. "Queueing Theory and Congestion of the Library Catalog," *Library Quarterly*, vol. 42, July, 1972.

Bookstein, A. "When the Most 'Pertinent' Documents Should Not Be Retrieved — An Analysis of the Swets Model", unpublished paper, Graduate Library School, University of Chicago, Chicago, Illinois, 1975.

Bookstein, A. and W. S. Cooper, "Model for an Information Retrieval System", unpublished paper, Graduate Library School, University of Chicago, Chicago, Illinois, 1975.

Bookstein, A. and D. H. Kraft. "Operations Research Applied to Document Indexing and Retrieval Decisions", paper presented at ORSA/TIMS Joint Meeting, Las Vegas, Nevada, 1975.

Bookstein, A. and D. R. Swanson. "A Decision Theoretic Foundation for Indexing", unpublished paper, Graduate Library School, University of Chicago, Chicago, Illinois, 1974.

Bookstein, A. and D. R. Swanson. "A stochastic shelfreading model," *Library Quarterly*, vol. 43 no. 2, April 1973, pp. 138-161.

Booth, A. D. "On the Geometry of Libraries," *Journal of Documentation*, vol. 25, 1969, pp. 28-40.

Borbash, S. R., Jr. "Document Retrieval Systems Using Pattern Recognition and Mathematical Programming Techniques," Unpublished doctoral dissertation, University of Pittsburgh, 1970.

Bose, A. *An Information System Design Methodology Based on PERT/CPM Networking and Optimization Techniques*, unpublished doctoral dissertation, University of Pittsburgh, 1970.

Bose, H. "Towards a Unified Documentation System, *Annals of Library Science and Documentation*, vol. 20, 1973, pp. 98-104.

Boulding, K. E. "The Economics of Knowledge and the Knowledge of Economics," American Economics Review, vol. 56, 1966, pp. 1-13.

Bourne, C. P. "Some user requirements stated quantitatively in terms of the 90% library," In: Kent, A. and O. Taulbee, (Eds.), *Electronic information handling*, Washington, D. C., Spartan Books, 1965, pp. 93-110.

Bourne, C. and G. Densmore. *A Cost Analysis and Utilization Study of the Stanford University Library System*, Menlo Park, Calif.: Stanford Research Institute, 1969.

Bourne, C. P. and D. F. Ford. "Cost analysis and simulation procedures for the evaluation of large information systems," *American Documentation*, vol. 15, 1964, pp. 142-149.

Bourne, C. P. *et al. Requirements, criteria and measures of performance of information storage and retrieval systems*, Washington, D. C., National Science Foundation, 1961, NTIS AD 270 942.

Bourne, C. P. and D. Gregor. *Methodology and Background Information to Assist the Planning of Serials Cancellations and Cooperative Serials Collection in the Health Sciences*. Berkeley, Calif. Institute of Library Research, University of Calif., 1975.

Bourne, C. P. and J. Robinson. *SDI Citation Checking as a Measure of the Performance of Library Document Delivery Systems*. Berkeley, California, Institute of Library Research, 1973.

Bradford, S. C. "Sources of information on specific subjects." *Engineering* 137 (3550) Jan. 26, 1934, 85-86.

Bradford, S. C. *Documentation*, Crosby Lockwood and Son, Ltd., London, 1948.

Braude, R. M. and N. Holt. "Cost Performance Analysis of TWX Mediated Interlibrary Loans in a Medium-sized Center Library," *Bulletin of the Medical Library Association*, vol. 59, 1971, pp. 65-70.

Bres, E., D. Cole, J. Hilt, R. Lyders, K. Russell. "Formula Allocation to Institutional Users of

Total Cost of a Medical Library: A Constrainsel Regression Approach" paper presented at ORSA/TIMS Joint Meeting at Las Vegas, Nevada, 1975.

Brett, V. M., *et al. The academic library: a systems view.* (University of Lancaster Library Occasional Papers, No. 8). Lancaster, England: University Library. (Forthcoming) ISBN 0 901699 233.

Brittain, J. M. and M. B. Line. "Sources of citations and references for analysis purposes: a comparative assessment." *Journal of Documentation 29, March 1973, 72-80.*

Brockis, G. J. and P. F. Cole. "Evaluating the technical information function." *Chemistry in Britain 3*, October 1967, 421-423.

Bromberg, Erik. Simplified PPBS for the librarian. Paper prepared for the Dollar Decision Pre-Conference Institute, sponsored by the Library Administration Division of the American Library Association at Dallas, Texas. 17-19 June 1971. 13 p. (ED 047 751).

Brookes, B. C. "Bradford's Law and the Bibliography of Science," *Nature*, vol. 224, December, 1969, pp. 953-55.

Brookes, B. C. "The Complete Bradford-Zipf 'Bibliograph'," *Journal of Documentation*, vol. 25, 1969, pp. 58-60.

Brookes, B. C. "The Derivation and Application of the Bradford-Zipf Distribution," *Journal of Documentation*, vol. 24, 1968, pp. 247-65 and vol. 25, 1969, pp. 58-60.

Brookes, B. C. "The Design of Hierarchical Information Systems," *Information Storage and Retrieval*, vol. 6, 1970, pp. 127-136.

Brookes, B. C. "The Generalyzed Law of Scatter and Its Application to Libraries and Library Systems," paper presented at ORSA/TIMS Joint Meeting, Las Vegas, Nevada, 1975.

Brookes, B. C. "The Growth, Utility, and Obsolescence of Scientific Periodical Literature," *Journal of Documentation*, vol. 26, 1970, pp. 283-94.

Brookes, B. C. "The Measures of Information Retrieval Effectiveness Proposed by Swets", *Journal of Documentation*, vol. 24, 1968, pp. 41-54.

Brookes, B. C. "Obsolescence of Special Library Periodicals: Sampling Errors and 'Utility Contours'," *Journal of the American Society for Information Science*, vol. 21, 1970, pp. 320-9.

Brookes, B. C. "On the Inverse Relationship of Recall and Precision", *Journal of Documentation*, vol. 28, 1972, pp. 345-7.

Brookes, B. C. "Optimum P% Library of Scientific Periodicals," *Nature*, vol. 232, 1971, pp. 458-61.

Brookes, B. C. "Photocopies vs. Periodicals Cost Effectiveness in the Special Library," *Journal of Documentation*, vol. 26, March, 1970, pp. 22-29.

Brookes, B. C. "The Shannon Model of IR Systems", *Journal of Documentation*, vol. 28, 1972, pp. 160-2.

Brookes, B. C. "Statistical Distribution in Documentation and Library Planning," in Mackenzie, A. G. and I. M. Stuart (Eds.), "Proceedings of a Research Seminar held at the University of Lancaster, 9-11 July, 1969," University of Lancaster Library, Lancaster, England.

Brookes, B. C. "The Viability of Branch Libraries," *Journal of Librarianship*, vol. 2, 1970.

Brophy, P. and M. K. Buckland. "Simulation in Education for library and Information Service Administration, *Information Scientist*, vol. 6, 1972, pp. 93-100.

Brophy, P., G. Ford, A. Hindle, and A. G. Mackenzie. "A Library Management Game: A Report on a Research Project," University of Lancaster Library Occasional Paper, No. 7, Lancaster, England, 1972.

Bruce, D. R. "A Markov Model to Study the Loan Dynamics at a Reserve-Loan Desk in a lending Library" *Library Quarterly*, vol. 45, 1975, pp. 161-78.

Bruce, D. R. "Measure and Standard in the University Library," *Canadian Library Journal*, vol.

31, 1974, pp. 28-30.

Buchanan, A. L., *et al.* "A General Simulation Model for Information Systems", RAND Corp., Santa Monica, California, 1969; NTIS AD 690 839.

Buckland, L. F., *et al. Survey of Automated Library Systems, Phase 1.* Maynard, Mass.: Inforonics, Inc., 1973.

Buckland, M. K. "Are Scattering and Obsolescence related?" *Journal of Documentation*, vol. 28, 1972, pp. 242-246.

Buckland, M. K. *Book Availability and The Library User.* New York: Pergamon Press, 1975.

Buckland, M. K. *Library Stock Control*, unpublished doctoral thesis, Sheffield University, England, 1973. Revised as *Book Availability and the Library User*, Pergamon Press.

Buckland, M. K. "Library systems and management studies at Lancaster University," In: *A World of Information Proceedings of the 35th Annual Meeting of the American Society for Information Science, Washington, D.C., October 1972.* Washington, D. C., ASIS and Westport, Conn., Greenwood. 1973.

Buckland, M. K. "Management of Libraries and Information Centers." (In *Annual Review of Information Science and Technology*, vol. 9, 1974. ASIS, Washington, D.C.), pp. 335-379.

Buckland, M. K. "An Operations Research Study of a Variable Loan and Duplication Policy at the University of Lancaster," *Library Quarterly*, vol. 42, 1972, pp. 97-106.

Buckland, M. K. "Progress in the Application of Operations Research in Libraries," paper presented at ORSA/TIMS Joint Meeting, Las Vegas, Nevada, 1975.

Buckland, M. K. "The Quantitative Evaluation of Regional Union Catalogs," *Journal of Documentation*, vol. 23, 1967, pp. 20-7.

Buckland, M. K. "Sources of Information for Operational Research Studies," *Operational Research Quarterly*, vol. 18, 1967, pp. 297-313.

Buckland, M. K. and A. Hindle. "The Case for Library Management Games," *Journal of Education for Librarianship*, vol. 21, 1971, pp. 92-103.

Buckland, M. K. and A. Hindle. "Library Zipf: Zipf's Law in Libraries and Information Science," *Journal of Documentation*, vol. 25, 1969, pp. 52-57.

Buckland, M. K. and A. Hindle. "Loan Policies, Duplication and Availability." In: Mackenzie, A. G. and I.M. Stuart (Eds.) *Planning Library Services: Proceedings of a Research Seminar Held at the University of Lancaster*, 9-11 July, 1969, University of Lancaster Library, Lancaster, England.

Buckland, M. K., A. Hindle, A. G. Mackenzie, and I. Woodburn. "Systems Analyses of a University Library: Final Report on a Research Project," University of Lancaster Library, Lancaster, England, 1970.

Buckland, M. K. and D. Tolliver. "Library Systems Engineering: An Introduction," in *Proceedings of the International Systems Engineering Symposium Purdue, 1972.* West Lafayette, Indiana, Purdue University, 1972. Vol. 2.

Buckland, M. K. and I. Woodburn. "An Analytical Approach to Duplication and Availability," University of Lancaster Library Occasional Paper No. 2, 1968, ERIC report ED 022 516. Reprinted by editorial request in: *Information Storage and Retrieval*, vol. 5, 1969, pp. 69-79, and Saracevic, T. (Ed.), *Introduction to Information Science*, New York, Bowker, 1971.

Buckland, M. K. and J. Woodburn. "Some Implications for Library Management of Scattering and Obsolescence," University of Lancaster Library Occasional Paper No. 1, 1968, ERIC report ED 022 502.

Bundy, M. L. "Decision making in libraries," *Illinois libraries*, vol. 43, 1961, pp. 780-93.

Bundy, M. L. and P. Wasserman (Eds.), *Reader in research methods for librarianship*, NCR Microcard, Washington, D. C., 1970.

Burgess, T. K. "A Cost Effectiveness Model for Comparing Various Circulation Systems," *Journal of Library Automation*, vol. 6, 1973, pp. 75-86.

Burkhalter, B. R. (Ed.) *Case Studies in Systems Analysis in a University Library*. Metuchen, N. J., Scarecrow Press, 1968.

Burkhalter, Barton R. and L. Hoag. "Another look at manual sorting and filing: backwards and forwards," *Library Resources and Technical Services*, vol. 14, 1970, pp. 445-454.

Burness, C. G. "Defining library objectives," Paper presented at an Institute on Program Planning and Budgeting Systems for Libraries at Wayne State University. Department of Library Science. Detroit, Michigan. 1968, ERIC ED 045 116.

Burns, R. W., Jr. A generalized methodology for library systems analysis. *College and Research Libraries*, vol. 32, 1971, pp. 295-303.

Burns, R. W., Jr. and J. T. Gladden. "Suggested Patterns for the Accumulation of Statistical Cost Information by a University Circulation Department," *American Society for Information Science Proceedings*, Fall, 1973.

Burton, R. E. and R. W. Kebler. "The 'half-life' of some scientific and technical literatures," *American Documentation*, vol. 11, 1960, pp. 18-22.

Bush, G. C., M. L. Ernst, and B. Schaffer. "M.I.T. Library operations," In: Fundamental investigations methods of operations research. Interim Technical Report No. 2, M.I.T., Cambridge, Mass., 1954.

Bush, G. C., H. P. Galliher, and P. M. Morse. "Attendance and Use of the Science Library at M.I.T.," *American Documentation*, vol. 7, 1956, pp. 87-100.

California State University and Colleges. *Report on a Cost Study of Specific Technical Processing Activities of the California State University and College Libraries*. Los Angeles: Office of the Chancellor, Calif. State University and Colleges, 1973.

Cammack, F. and D. Mann. "Institutional implications of an automated circulations study." *College and Research Libraries* 28, March 1967, pp. 129-132.

Campbell, W. R. "Feedback from the user: *sine qua non*," in Howerton, P. W. (Ed.), *Information Handling: First Principles*, Washington, Spartan Books, 1963.

Caras, G. "Computer Simulation of a Small Information System," *American Documentation*, April, 1968, pp. 120-22.

Carter, C. F. "The Allocation of Resources in Higher Education," in Mackenzie, A. G. and I. M. Stuart. (Eds.), "Proceedings of a Research Seminar held at the University of Lancaster, 9-11 July, 1969, University of Lancaster Library, Lancaster, England.

Carter, R. C. "Systems Analysis as a Prelude to Library Automation," *Library Trends*, vol. 21, 1973, pp. 505-521.

Case Institute of Technology. O. R. Group, *Measurement of value of recorded scientific information*, Cleveland, Ohio, 1961, NTIS AD 260 734.

Case Institute of Technology. O. R. Group, *An operations research study of the dissemination and use of recorded scientific knowledge*. Cleveland, Ohio, 1960, NTIS PB 171 503.

Case Institute of Technology. O. R. Group, *An operations research study of the scientific activity of chemists*, Cleveland, Ohio, 1958. PB 166 798.

Cezairliyan, A. O., P. S. Lykoudis, and Y. S. Touloukian. *Analytical and experimental study of a method for literature search in abstracting journals*, Lafayette, Indiana, Purdue University. 1959, NTIS PB 171 478.

Cezairliyan, A. O., P. S. Lykoudis, and Y. S. Touloukian. "A new method for the search of scientific literature through abstracting journals," *Journal of Chemical Documentation,* vol. 2, 1962, pp. 86-92.

Chamis, A. Y. "The design of information systems: the use of systems analysis," *Special Libraries*, vol. 60, 1969, pp. 21-31.

Chapman, E. A. "Planning for Systems Study and Systems Development," *Library Trends*, vol. 21, 1973, pp. 479-492.

Chapman, E. A. and P. L. St. Pierre. *Systems analysis and design as related to library operations,*

Troy, N. Y., Rensselaer Libraries, 1966.

Chapman, E. A., P. L. St. Pierre and J. Lubans, Jr. *Library Systems Analysis Guidelines*, Wiley, New York, 1970.

Chapman, R. L. "The case for information system simulation," In: Spiegel, J. and D. E. Walker, (Eds), *Congress on the Information System Sciences*, no. 2, Washington, D. C., Spartan Books, 1965.

Charnes, A. *et al. LP II — A Goal Programming Model for Media*, 1967, ERIC ED 019884.

Chen, C. *Applications & Operations Research Models to Libraries: A Case Study of the Use of Monographs in the Francis A. Countway Library of Medicine, Harvard University*. MIT Press, (Forthcoming)

Chicago, University of Graduate Library School. *Operations Research: Implications for Libraries*, 35th Annual Conference Aug. 24, 1971, ed. by D. R. Swanson and A. Bookstein. Chicago: University of Chicago Press, 1972.

Chodrow, M., *et al. Information service system modelling. Analytical tools for management evaluation*. Wakefield, Mass,. Information Dynamics Corporation, 1963, NRS PB 109 596.

Churchman, C. W. "Operations Research Prospects for Libraries," *Library Quarterly*, vol. 42, 1972, pp. 6-14.

Churchman, C. W. *Operations Research, Prospects for Libraries: the realities and ideals or Strategies for O. R. in Libraries*. Internal Working Paper No. 5, University of California, Berkeley, Space Sciences Laboratory, August 1971.

Churchman. C. W. *The Systems Approach*, Delacorte Press, New York, 1968.

Cigler, I. K. "Simulation method applied in designing an information system," *Information Storage and Retrieval*, vol. 6, 1970, pp. 307-312.

Clapp, V. and R. Jordan. *Quantitative Criteria for Adequacy for Library Holdings*, Washington, D. C.: Council on Library Resources, 1965.

Clements, D. W. C. "Costing of Library Systems" *ASLIB Proceedings*, vol. 27, 1975, pp. 98-111.

Cleverdon, C. W. "User Evaluation of Information Retrieval Systems, *Journal of Documentation*, vol. 30, 1974, pp. 170-180.

Clinton, M. "Study of the effect of fines on circulation," *Canadian Library J.*, May-June 1972, pp. 248-252.

Cole, P. F. "Analysis of reference question records as a guide to the information requirements of scientists," *Journal of Documentation*, vol. 14, 1958, pp. 197-207.

Cole, P. F. "Journal Usage versus Age of Journal," *Journal of Documentation*, vol. 19, 1963, pp. 1-11.

Cole, P. F. "A New Look at Reference Scattering," *Journal of Documentation,* vol. 18, 1962, pp. 58-64.

Columbia University Libraries, *A description of a project to study the research library as an economic system*. Columbia University Library, New York City, 1964.

Converse, W. R. M. and O. R. Standers. "Rationalizing the Collections Policy: A Computerized Approach," paper presented at the 3rd Canadian Conference on Information Science, Quebec, May 7-9, 1975.

Cooney, S. "Criteria for a User-Oriented Cost-effective Information Service," *Special Libraries*, vol. 65, 1974, pp. 517-526.

Cooper, A., A. K. Jain, and S. R. Polucki. "In Library Usage of Journals in a Large Industrial Technical Library," paper presented at ORSA/TIMS Joint Meeting, Las Vegas, Nevada, 1975.

Cooper, M. D. "Cost-Effectiveness Analysis and Cost-Benefit Analysis of Information Services," a tutorial presented by the Special Interest Group on Cost, Budgeting, and Economics of the American Society for Information Science, National Meeting, Washington, D. C., November, 1972.

Cooper, M. D. "A Cost Model for Evaluating Information Retrieval Systems," *Journal of the*

American Society for Information Science, vol. 23, 1972, pp. 306-12.

Cooper, M. D. "The Economics of Information", in Cuadra, C. (Ed.), *Annual Review of Information Science and Technology*, vol. 8, American Society for Information Science, Washington, D. C., 1973.

Cooper, M. D. *Evaluation of Information Retrieval Systems: a simulation and cost approach.* Ph.D. Thesis, University of California, Berkeley, School of Librarianship, May 1971.

Cooper, M. and H. W. Cooper. "Interpreting results of statistical studies," *College and Research Libraries*, vol. 28, 1967, pp. 266-268.

Cooper, M. D. and J. Wolthauser. *Misplacement of Books on Library Shelves: A Mathematical Model.* University of California, Berkeley, School of Librarianship, 1975.

Cooper, W. S., "Expected Search Length: A Simple Measure of Retrieval Effectiveness Based on the Weak Ordering Action of Retrieval Systems", vol. 19, 1968, pp. 30-41.

Cooper, W. S., "On Designing Design Equations for Information Retrieval Systems", *Journal of the American Society for Information Science*, vol. 21, 1970, pp. 385-95.

Cooper, W. S., "On Selecting a Measure of Retrieval Effectiveness Part I, The Subjective Philosophy of Evaluation, Part II, Implementation of the Philosophy", *Journal of the American Society for Information Science*, vol. 24, 1972, pp. 87-100, 413-24.

Cooper, W. S., D. T. Thompson, and K. R. Weeks. *The Duplication of Monograph Holdings in the University of California Library System.* Berkeley, Calif. Institute of Library Research, University of Calif., 1974.

Cor, J. F. and F. L. Bellomy. "Determining Requirements for a New System," *Library Trends*, vol. 21, 1973, pp. 533-552.

Coughlin, R. E., F. Taieb, and B. H. Stevens. *Urban Analysis for Regional Library System Planning*, Greenwood Pub. Co., Connecticut, 1972.

Covill, G. W. "Librarian + Systems Analyst = Teamwork?," *Special Libraries*, vol. 58, 1967, pp. 99-101.

Cox, J. G. *Optimum Storage of Library Materials*, unpublished doctoral thesis, Purdue University, Lafayette, Indiana, 1964.

Craig, R. J. "Organization Design," Second Annual Library Management Workshop, Carol M. Newman Library and Department of Industrial Engineering and Operations Research, Virginia Polytechnic Institute and State University, Blacksburg, Virginia, 1972.

Daiute, R. J. and K. A. Gorman. *Library Operations Research.* Dobbs Ferry, N. Y., Oceana Publications, 1974.

Dalziel, C. F. "Evaluation of periodicals for electrical engineers," *Library Quarterly*, VII, July 1937, pp. 254-372.

Damirchi, A. *Problems in Operations research - M.I.T. Science Library*, unpublished master's thesis, Massachusetts Institute of Technology, Cambridge, Mass., 1957.

Dammers, H. F. "Economics of Computer-based Information Systems: A Review." *Journal of Documentation*, vol. 31, 1975, pp. 38-45.

Dammers, H. F. "The Library/Information Service in an Industrial Research Establishment: Planning and Prospects," in Mackenzie, A. G. and I. M. Stuart (Eds.), "Proceedings of a Research Seminar held at the University of Lancaster, 9-11, July, 1969," University of Lancaster Library, Lancaster, England.

Dammers, H. F. "SDI: Some Economic and Organizational Aspects," *ASLIB Proceedings*, vol. 23, 1971.

Dammers, H. F. "Some quantitative relationships concerning information handling in research establishments," *Noti di bibliografia o di documentatione scientifica*, vol. 7, 1961, pp. 271-282.

Dawson, C., E. E. Aldrin, and E. P. Gould, "Increasing the Effectiveness of the M.I.T. Science Library by the Use of Circulation Statistics," Term Report, M.I.T. Libraries, Cambridge, Mass., 1962

Debons, A. and K. L. Montgomery, "Design and Evaluation of Information Systems," *Annual Review of Information Science and Technology*, vol. 9, 1974, pp. 25-55.

De Hart, F. E. Media Service as a Disciplinary Application of General Systems Science. 1974, ERIC ED 102911.

Dei Rossi, J. A., G. F. Mills, and G. C. Sumner. "A Telephone-Access Biomedical Information Center", *Operations Research*, vol. 20, 1972, pp. 643-67.

Dennis, D. and P. A. Stockton. "Automated Library Circulation System Boosts Service Control at American University," *Special Libraries*, vol. 65, 1974, pp. 512-515.

De Pew, J. N. "An Acquisition Reason Model for Academic Libraries", JASIS, vol. 26, 75, pp. 237-46.

Deprospo, E. R. and H. Voos. "The Library Researcher and Policymaker: An Observation Here, A Speculation There: And Comments on Research in the Information Sciences." Chicago, Ill.: Library Research Round Table, American Library Association, 1972.

Deutsch, D. and D. H. Kraft, "A Study of an Information Retrieval Performance Measure: Expected Search Length as a Function of File Size and Organization", paper presented at the ORSA/TIMS Joint Meeting, Boston, 1974.

Dillehay, B. H. *et al.* "Determining tomorrow's needs through today's requests: an automated approach to interlibrary loans." *Special Libraries 61,* May-June 1970, 238-243.

Dillon. M. "The Impact of Automation on the Content of Libraries and Information Centers," *College and Research Libraries*, vol. 34, pp. 418-425.

Dinka, Tesfaya and Davut Okutcu. *An Analysis of Book Storage and Transportation Requirements of the Five Associated University Libraries.* Syracuse, N. Y.: Five Associated University Libraries, 1970, ERIC ED 049 767.

Dolby, J. T. and H. L. Resnikoff. "On the Multiplicative Structure of Information Storage and Access Systems", *Interfaces*, vol. 1, 1971, pp. 23-30.

Dougherty, R. M. "Is work simplification alive & well someplace?" *American Libraries*, vol. 1, 1970, pp. 969-971.

Dougherty, R. M. "Cost analysis studies in libraries: is there a basis for comparison?" *Library Resources & Technical Services*, vol. 13, 1969, pp. 136-141.

Dougherty, R. and F. Heinritz. *Scientific Management of Library Operations*, Scarecrow Press, New Jersey, 1966.

Drickamer, J. "Analytic program budgeting - Rhode Island librarians take the plunge," *NFLA Newsletter*, vol. 3, 1971, pp. 22-24.

Drott, M. C. "Random Sampling: A Tool for Library Research," *College and Research Libraries,* 1969, pp. 119-25.

Duchesne, R. M. "Analysis of Cost and Performance," *Library Trends*, vol. 21, no. 4, April 1973, pp. 587-603.

Duchesne, R. M. "Library management information from computer-aided library systems," In: Mackenzie, A. G. and I. M. Stuart (Eds.), "Planning Library Services. Proceedings of a Research Seminar held at the University of Lancaster 9-11 July 1969," University of Lancaster Library, Lancaster, England. 1969.

Duggan. M. "Library Network Analysis and Planning (LIB-NAT)," *Journal of Library Automation*, vol. 2, 1969, pp. 157-175.

Dumont, P. E. "A Library Management Information System", *American Society for Information Science Proceedings*, Fall, 1973.

Dunn, O. C., D. L. Tolliver, and M. A. Drake. *The Past and Likely Future of 58 Research Libraries, 1951-1980: A Statistical Study of Growth and Change,* Ninth issue, 1971-72, Purdue University Libraries, Lafayette, Indiana, 1973.

University of Durham. "Project for evaluating the benefits from university libraries. Final report,

"University of Durham, Computer Unit, Durham, England, 1969.

Dym, E. D. and D. L. Shirey. "A Statistical decision model for periodical selection for a specialized information center," *Journal of the American Society for Information Sciences*, vol. 24, 1973, pp. 110-119.

Dynin, I. M. "Analiz informatsionnykh sistem na osnove teorii avtomaticheskogo upravleniya" [The analysis of information systems on the basis of automatic control theory]. *Nauchno-Teknickeskaya Informatsiya*, 2d ser., 1969, pp. 29-34.

Economics of Scientific Publications *Proceedings* of a Workshop, Sponsored by the Council of Biological Editors held at Bethesada, Md., 23 May 1973. Ed. by the CBF Committee on Economics of Publications R. A. Day (Chairman) *et al.* Washington, D. C., Council of Biological Editors, 1973.

Ellsworth, Ralph E. *The Economics of Book Storage in College and University Libraries*, Metuchen, N. J.: Scarecrow Press, 1969.

Elman, S. A. "Cost Comparison of Manual and On-line Computerized Literature Searching." *Special Libraries*, vol. 66, 1975, pp. 12-18.

Elstein, H. and F. R. Hartz. "Role of Scientific Management in the Library/ Media Center," *Illinois Libraries*, vol. 56, 1974, pp. 227-233.

Elton, M. C. J. and R. H. Orr. *Document Delivery Service in a Hierarchical System of Libraries. An Operational Research Study of the Problems of Management and Design.* Final Report of a Feasibility Study February-August, 1973, Report to OSTI on Project SI/6/053. London: Communications Studies Group. Joint Unit for Planning Research, University College London, 1973.

Elton, M. and B. Vickery, "The Scope for Operational Research in the Library and Information Field", *Aslib Proceedings*, vol. 25, 1973, pp. 305-19.

Emery, J. C. *Cost/Benefit Analysis of Information Systems*, Society for Management Information Systems, Chicago, 1971.

Ernst, M. L. "Evaluation of performance of large information retrieval systems." In: *2nd Congress on the Information System Sciences*, Mitre Corp., 1966.

Ernst, M. L., M. P. McDonough, and H. Saxenian. "M.I.T. library operation," In: Fundamental investigations in methods of operations research. Interim technical report no. 1, July 1, 1953 through March 31, 1954.

Ernst, M. L. and B. Shaffer. *A survey of circulation characteristics of some general library books*, M.I.T. Press, Cambridge, Mass., 1954.

Etnyre, V. A. "A Case Study of Improper Conclusions Drawn from an Insufficient Analysis of Information Costs and Benefits," *American Society for Information Science Proceedings*, Fall, 1973.

Etnyre, V. A. "The Use of Indirect Methods to Determine Difficult Measures of Costs and Benefits in Information Systems", *American Society for Information Science Proceedings*, Fall, 1973.

Evans, E., H. Borko, and P. Ferguson. "A Review of the Criteria Used to Measure Library Effectiveness," *Bull. Med. Lib. Ass.*, vol. 60 no. 1, Jan. 1972, pp. 102-110.

Fairthorne, R. A. "Progress in Documentation: Emprical Hyperbole Distributions (Bradford-Zipf-Mandelbrot) for Bibliometric Description and Prediction," *Journal of Documentation*, vol. 25, 1969, pp. 319-43.

Fairthorne, R. A. "Algebraic representation of storage and retrieval languages," In: Fairthorne, R. A., *Towards information retrieval*, Conn., Archon, 1968.

Fancher, M. G., J. Herling, B. U. Dean, and A. Reisman. "A Multi-Library System Distribution Network Design," paper presented at the XX International Meeting, The Institute of Management Sciences, Tel Aviv, Israel, June, 1973.

Farradane, J. E. L. "Evaluation of Information Retrieval Systems," *Journal of Documentation*, vol. 30, 1974, pp. 195-209.

Fasana, P. J. "Systems Analysis," *Library Trends*, vol. 21, 1973, pp. 465-478.

Fayollat, J. "On-line Serials Control System in a Large Biomedical Library; Part III: Comparison of On-line and Batch Operations and Cost Analysis," Journal of the American Society for Information Science, vol. 24, 1973, pp. 80-86.

Fazar, W. "The importance of PPB to libraries," Paper presented at an Institute on Program Planning and Budgeting Systems for Libraries at Wayne State University, Department of Library Science, Detroit, Michigan, 1968. ERIC ED 045 114.

Fields, D. C. "Library Management by Objectives: The Humane Way," College and Research Libraries, vol. 35, 1974, pp. 344-349.

Fletcher, J. "A view of the literature of economics," Journal of Documentation, vol. 28, 1972, pp. 283-295.

Flood, M. M. "The systems approach to library planning," Library Quarterly, vol. 34, 1964, pp. 326-338.

Flowerdew, A. D. J. and C. M. F. Whitehead. Cost-effectiveness and Cost/Benefit Analysis in Information Science. Unpublished manuscript. London School of Economics.

Ford, G. Library Automation: Guidelines to Costing. Report No.: OSTI-5153. England: British Library Lending Division, 1973.

Ford, M. G. "Data Collection and Feedback," in Mackenzie, A. G. and I. M. Stuart (Eds.), "Proceedings of a Research Seminar held at the University of Lancaster, 9-11 July, 1969," University of Lancaster Library, Lancaster, England.

Ford, M. G. "Research in user behavior in university libraries." Journal of Documentation, vol. 29 no. 1, March 1973, pp. 85-106.

Foskett, D. J. "General Systems Theory and the Organisation of Libraries," in Studies in Library Management, vol. 2 by C. Bingley, Shoe String, 1974, pp. 10-24.

Fox, A. S. "The Amenability of a cataloging Process to Simulation by Automatic Techniques" Ann Arbor, University Microfilms, 1974.

Friis, T. "The use of citation analysis as a research technique and its implications for libraries," South African Libraries, vol. 23, 1955, pp. 12-13.

Fussler, H. H. and J. L. Simon. Patterns in the Use of Books in a Large Research Library, University of Chicago Library, 1961. Reprinted by Chicago University Press, 1969.

General Electric Co. Defense systems Dept., Information systems operations, Improving information flow in a university library, Washington, D. C. General Electric Co., 1961.

Gherman, P. "Organizational Change: The Centralization of a Divisonal Circulation System." Technical Paper Number Five. Detroit, Mich.: Wayne State University Libraries, 1973.

Gilchrist, A. "Consultancy, Systems Theory and the Organisation of Libraries," in Studies in Library Management, vol. 2, ed. by C. Bingley, Shoe String, 1975, pp. 26-52.

Gilchrist, A. "Cost effectiveness" Aslib Proceedings, vol. 23, 1971, pp. 455-62.

Gilchrist, A. "Further comments on the terminology of the analysis of library systems," Aslib proceedings, vol. 20, 1968, pp. 408-412.

Glater, N. "Linear programming for libraries," Chemical and Engineering News, vol. 35, 1957, pp. 142-143.

Glover, F. and D. Klingman. "Mathematical Programming Models and Methods for the Journal Selection Problem," Library Quarterly, vol. 42, 1972, pp. 43-58.

Goddard, H. "An Economic Analysis of Library Benefits," Library Quarterly, vol. 41, 1971, pp. 244-55.

Goffman, W. "An Epidemic Process in an Open Population," Nature, vol. 205, pp. 831-832.

Goffman, W. "A General Theory of Communication," in Saracevic, T. (Ed.), Introduction to Information Science, R. R. Bowker Co., New York, 1970.

Goffman, W. "A Mathematical Method for Analyzing the Growth of a Scientific Discipline," Journal of the Association for Computing Machinery, vol. 18, 1971, pp. 173-185.

Goffman, W. "A Mathematical Approach to the Spread of Scientific Ideas," *Nature*, vol. 212, 1966, pp. 449-542.

Goffman, W., "A Searching Procedure for Information Retrieval", *Information Storage and Retrieval*, vol. 2, 1964, pp. 73-8.

Goffman, W. "Stability of Epidemic Processes," *Nature*, vol. 210, 1966, pp. 786-7.

Goffman, W. and T. Morris. "Bradford's Law and Library Acquisitions," *Nature*, vol. 226, June 6, 1970, pp. 922-923.

Goffman, W., T. G. Morris, J. Schultz, and T. Harari. "A Self-Organization Library," paper presented at the XX International Meeting, The Institute of Management Sciences, Tel Aviv, Israel, June, 1973.

Goffman, W. and V. A. Newill. "Communication and Epidemic Processes," *Proc. of the Royal Society*, vol. 298A, 1967, pp. 316-34.

Goffman, W. and V. A. Newill. "Generalizations of Epidemic Theory; and Application to the Transmission of Ideas," *Nature*, vol. 204, 1964, pp. 225-228.

Goffman, W., and K. S. Warren. "Dispersion of Papers among Journals Based on a Mathematical Analysis of Two Diverse Medical Literatures." *Nature*, 1969, pp. 1205-7.

Goldhor, H. (Ed.), *Research Methods in Librarianship: Measurement and Evaluation,* University of Illinois, Graduate Library School, Illini Union Bookstore, Champaign, Illinois, 1968.

Good, I. J. "The Decision Theory Approach to the Evaluation of Information Retrieval Systems", *Information Storage and Retrieval*, vol. 7, 1971, pp. 217-40.

Goodman, A. F., *et al.* "DOD User's Needs Study Phase II Scientific and Technical Information within the Defense Industries, Vol. III A. Frequency Distributions and Correlation, B. Relationship and Comparison," NTIS AD 649 284.

Gotsick, P. *Community Survey Guide for Assessment of Community Information and Service Needs. Public Library Training Institutes Library Service Guide Number Two.* Morehead, Ky.: Appalachian Adult Education Center, Morehead State University, 1974.

Goyal, S. K. "Allocation of Library Funds to Different Departments of a University — An Operational Research Approach," *College and Research Libraries*, vol. 34, 1973, pp. 219-22.

Goyal, S. K. "Application of Operational Research to Problems of Determining Appropriate Loan Periods for Periodicals," *Libri International*, vol. 20, 1970, pp. 94-100.

Goyal, S. K. "A systematic method for reducing over-ordering copies of books." *Library Resources and Technical Services 16,* Winter 1972, 26-32.

Grant, R. S. "Predicting the need for multiple copies of books." *Journal of Library Automation 4,* 1971, pp. 64-71.

Green, N. and C. B. Millham, "A Computer Simulation Model and Systems Analysis for Extending Library Services in the State of Washington", paper presented at ORSA/TIMS Joint Meeting, Las Vegas, Nevada, 1975.

Greenberg, H. J. and D. H. Kraft, "On Computing a Buy/Copy Policy using the Pitt-Kraft Model," working paper, Computer Science, Virginia Polytechnic Institute and State University, Extension Division Area Office, 11440 Isaac Newton Square North, Reston, Virginia, 1975.

Grier, M. E., D. D. McDonald, T. Norcio, N. Roderer, D. Seabrook, L. B. Heilprin, D. H. Kraft, and S. Bjorge. "Inconsistencies in the National Technical Information Service *Frequency List of Terms July 1969 - January 1972*," Final Report, School of Library and Information Services, University of Maryland, College Park, Maryland, 1973.

Griffin. H. L. "Implementing the New System: Conversion, Training, and Scheduling," *Library Trends*, vol. 21, 1973, pp. 565-574.

Grinstein, L. S. "Operations Research: A Lay Approach," *Mathematics Teacher*, vol. 64, pp. 167-71.

Groh, Kamil. Za jednothy system vedeckomeodickeho rizeni knihoven" [Towards a unified system of scientific-methodiological management of libraries]. *Knihovnik*, vol. 12, 1967, pp. 101-5.

Groos, O. V. "Less-used titles and volumes of science journals: two preliminary notes." *Library Resources and Technical Services 10*, Summer 1966, 289-290.

Gryaznov, N. I. and Z. N. Zolotareva. "Analysis of the Task of Determining the Optimal Number of Duplicate Books in an Automated Library. Nauchno-Tekni-Cheskaya Informatsiya, Series 2, No. 3, pp. 10-15, 1973. In *Automatic Documentation and Mathematical Linguistics* 7:1, pp. 55-65.

Gupta, S. M. and A. Ravindran. "Optimal Storage of Books by Size: An Operations Research Approach." *Journal of the American Society for Information Science*, vol. 25, 1974, pp. 354-357.

Gurk, H. M. and J. Minker. "Design and simulation of an information processing system," *Journal of the Association of Computing Machinery*, vol. 8, 1961, pp. 260-270.

Gurk, H. M. and J. Minker. "Storage Requirements for Information Handling Centers," *Journal of the Association for Computing Machinery*, vol. 17, 1970.

Guy, L. C. "Simulated management," *Library Journal*, vol. 94, 1969, pp. 37-41.

Haas, W. J. "Description of a project to study the research library as an economic system," In: Association of Research Libraries, *Minutes of the 63rd meeting, January 26, 1964, Chicago*. Washington, D. C., ASL, 194?

Haas, W. J. "Computer Simulation at the Columbia University Libraries," in Goldhor, H. (ed.), *Clinic on Library Applications of Data Processing 1964 Proceedings*, Union Bookstore, University of Illinois, Champaign, Illinois, 1965.

Haight, F. A. "Some statistical problems in connection with word association data," *Journal of Mathematical Psychology*, vol. 3, 1966.

Halbert, Michael and Russell Ackoff. *An operations research study of the dissemination of scientific information*. Cleveland, Ohio: Case Institute of Technology O. R. Group. Available from the Library of Congress as PB 144 328.

Hamburg, M., C. Clelland, R. W. Bommer, L. E. Ramist, and J. Ackerman, "A Systems of the Library and Information Science Statistical Data System: the Preliminary Study," *Interim Report*, July 1969, University of Pennsylvania.

Hamburg, M., R. C. Clelland, M. R. W. Bommer, L. E. Ramist, and R. M. Whitfield. *Library Planning and Decision-making Systems*. Cambridge, Mass. MIT Press, 1974.

Hamburg, M., R. C. Clelland, M. R. W. Bommer, L. E. Ramist, and R. M. Whitfield, "A Systems Analysis of the Library and Information Science Data System: The Research Investigation," interim report to the U. S. Office of Education, University of Pennsylvania, Philadelphia, 1970.

Hamburg, Morris, L. E. Ramist, and M. R. W. Bommer. "The development of a statistical information system for university and large public libraries," Paper presented at the 39th National Operations Research Society of American Meeting, Dallas, Texas. 1971.

Hamburg, M., L. E. Ramist, and M. R. W. Bommer. "Library Objectives and Performance Measures and Their Use in Decision Making," *Library Quarterly*, vol. 42, 1972, pp. 107-28.

Hamelman, P. W. and E. M. Mazze. "Of Models and Scientific Markets," *IEEE Transactions on Professional Communication*, vol. PC-16, 1973, pp. 120-125, 177-178.

Hamelman, P. W. and E. M. Mazze. "Toward a Cost/Utility Model for Social Science Periodicals," in Rudolph, G. A. (Ed.), *The Academic Library Looks at Library Management*, Carol M. Newman Library and Department of Industrial Engineering and Operations Research, Virginia Polytechnic Institute and State University, Blacksburg, Virginia, 1971.

Hamlin, R. J. "Controlling book circulation in a university library," In: Fundamental investigations in methods of O. R. Interim technical Report 3, December 1st 1954 through August 31, 1955.

Harter, S. P. "A Probabilistic Approach to Automatic Indexing Part I. On the Distribution of Specialty Words in a Technical Literature", *Journal of the American Society for Information Science*, vol. 26, 1975, pp. 197-206.

Hassel, P. H. *An Analytical Design Framework for Academic Library System Formulation*, unpublished doctoral thesis, Purdue University, Lafayette, Indiana, 1968.

Hawgood, J. "Assessing the benefits of library innovations." In: N. S. M. Cox and M. W. Grose (Eds.) *Organisation and handling of bibliographic records by computer.* Newcastle-upon-Tyne: Oriel Press, 1967. Pp. 69-71.

Hawgood, J. "Benefits and Management Information in the British Library," *Proceedings of the IBI/ICC. World Conference in Informatics in Government*, Florence, 1972.

Hawgood, J. "Measuring Effectiveness of Uncharged Services," paper presented at the XX International Meeting, The Institute of Management Sciences, Tel Aviv, Israel, June, 1973.

Hayes, R. M. "Library systems analysis," In: Harvey, J. (Ed.), *Data processing in public and university libraries*, Washington, D. C., Spartan Books, 1966, pp 5-20.

Hayes, R. M. "The development of a methodology for system design and its role in the library education," *Library Quarterly*, vol. 34, 1964, pp. 339-351.

Hayes, R. M. and J. Becker, *Handbook of Data Processing for Libraries*, 2nd ed. Los Angeles: Melville Publishing Co., 1974.

Hayes, R. M., and K. D. Reilly, "The Effect of Response Time Upon Utilization of an Information Retrieval System: a Simulation," paper presented to ORSA Annual Meeting, June 1967.

Heilprin, L. B. "The Economics of 'On Demand' Library Copying," in Tate, V. D. (Ed.), *Proceedings of the Eleventh Annual Meeting and Convention*, The National Microfilm Association, Annapolis, Maryland, 1962.

Heine, M. H. "Design Equations for Retrieval Systems Based on the Swets Model", *Journal of the American Society for Information Science*, vol. 25, 1974, pp. 183-98.

Heine, M. H., "Distance Between Sets as an Objective Measure of Retrieval Effectiveness" *Information Storage and Retrieval, vol. 9, 1973*, pp. 181-98.

Heine. M. H., "The Inverse Relationship of Precision and Recall in Terms of the Swets Model", *Journal of Documentation*, vol. 29, 1973, pp. 81-4.

Heinritz, F. J. "Analysis and Evaluation of Current Library Procedures," *Library Trends*, vol. 21, 1973, pp. 522-532.

Heinritz, F. J. "Optimum Allocation of Technical Services Personnel," *Library Resources and Technical Services*, vol. 3, 1969, pp. 99-101.

Heinritz, F. J. "Quantitative Management in Libraries." *College and Research Libraries*, vol. 31, 1970, pp. 232-38.

Heinritz, F. J. and J. C. Hsiao. "Optimum distribution of centrally processed material," *Library Resources and Technical Services*, vol. 13, 1969, pp. 205-708.

Heinze, H. "Quantitative Analyse der optinalen Beding ungen für die Information aus der Fach literatur in grösseren Unternehnen," *Nachrichten für Dokumentation*, vol. 18, pp. 236-242.

Hendricks, D. D. *Comparative costs of book processing in a processing centre and in five individual libraries*, unpublished doctoral dissertation, Illinois State Library, 1961.

Herner, S. "Operations research and the technical information program," In: Singer, T.E.R. (Ed.), *Information and communication practice in industry*, N. Y., Reinhold Publishing Corporation, 1958.

Herner, S. "A Pilot Study of the Use of the Stacks of the Library of Congress," unpublished, Herner and Co., Washington, D. C., 1960.

Herner, S. "System design, evaluation and costing," *Special Libraries*, vol. 58, 1967, pp. 576-581.

Hieber, C. E. *An analysis of questions and answers in libraries*, Studies in the man-system interface in libraries, Lehigh University, Center for the Information Sciences, Bethlehem, Pa., 1966.

Hillier, J. "Measuring the value of information services," *Journal of Chemical Documentation*, vol. 2, 1962, pp. 31-34.

Hindle, A. "Models and measures for non-profit making services," In: Mackenzie, A. Graham, and I. M. Stuart, (Eds), "Planning Library Services: Proceedings of a Research Seminar held at the

University of Lancaster 9-11 July 1969," University of Lancaster Library, Lancaster, England, 1969.

Hindle, A. and M. K. Buckland. "Towards An Adaptive Loan and Duplication Policy for a University Library," *O. R. Quarterly*. (Forthcoming).

Hoadley, I. B. and A. S. Clark, (Eds.) *Quantitative Methods in Librarianship*: Standards, Research, Management, Greenwood Press, Conn., 1972.

Hoffman, W. "Data processing applied to library budgets," Paper presented at an institute on Program Planning and Budgeting Systems for Libraries at Wayne State University. Department of Library Science, Detroit, Michigan, 1968. ERIC ED 045 122.

Hogg, F. N. "Cost-benefit analysis: the cost of the public library service in relation to value given," In: Library Association, *Proceedings of the Public Library Conference*, Dublin, 1967, London, 1967.

Holt, C. C. and W. E. Schrank. "Growth of the professional literature in economics and other fields and some implications," *American Documentation*, vol. 19, 1968, pp. 18-26.

Hoos, Ida R., "Information Systems and Public Planning," *Management Science*, 17:B658-671 (1971).

Houghton, B. "Cut-back on periodicals," *New Library World*, vol. 73 no. 860, Feb. 1972, p. 210.

Houghton, B. "Zipf!" *New Library World*, vol. 73, no. 857, Nov. 1971, p. 130.

Howard, E. N. "Toward PPBS in the Public Library," *American Libraries*, April 1971, pp. 386-93.

Hu, Teh-Wei, *et al. A Benefit Cost Analysis of Alternative Library Delivery Systems*. Contributions in Librarianship and Information Science No. 13. Westport, Conn.: Greenwood Press, 1975.

Humphrey, John A. *et al.* Library Cooperation in Metropolitan Baltimore: A New Approach to Determining Library Locations and Services. Baltimore: Librarian's Technical Steering Committee, Baltimore Metropolitan Area Library Study and Regional Planning Council, March 1970, rev. July 1970. (PB 194173).

Hyslop, M. R. "The Economics of Information Systems - Observations on Development Costs and Nature of the Market" in American Society for Information Science Annual Meeting, 31st, *Round-up Vol. 5*, Columbus, Ohio, Greenwood Publishing, 1968.

Institute for Operational Research, "The scope for OR in the library and information field", OSTI report 5136, also available from the National Lending Library, England, 1972.

Ivengar, T. K. S. "Circulation records in academic libraries. Data needed to assess the performance," *IASLIC Bull.* vol. 14, 1969, pp. 90-96.

Jahoda, G. "Reference Question Analysis and Search Strategy Development by Man and Machine," *Journal of the American Society for Information Science*, vol. 25, 1974, pp. 139-144.

Jain, A. K. "Document usage sampling and storage decision rules," Paper presented at the National Operations Research Society of America Meeting, Detroit, Michigan. 1970.

Jain, A. K. "Sampling and Data Collection Methods for a Book-Use Study," *Library Quarterly*, vol. 39, July, 1969, pp. 245-52.

Jain, A. K. "Sampling and Short-Period Usage in the Purdue Library," *College and Research Libraries*, vol. 27, 1966, pp. 211-18.

Jain, A. K. "Sampling In-Library Book Use," *Journal of the American Society for Information Science*, vol. 23, 1972, pp. 150-5.

Jain, A. K. *A Statistical Study of Book Use*, unpublished doctoral dissertation, Purdue University, Lafayette, Indiana, (NTIS PB 176 525), 1967.

Jain, A. K. and L. C. De Weese. *Report on a Statistical Study of Book Use Supplemented with a Bibliography of Library Use Studies*, 1967, ERIC ED 018244.

Jain, A. K. and F. F. Leimkuhler. "A Statistical Model of Book Use," *Journal of the American Statistical Association*, vol. 64, 1969, pp. 1211-24.

Jain, A., F. F. Leimkuhler, and V. L. Anderson. "A Statistical Model Usage and Its Application to the Book Storage Problem," *Journal of the American Statistical Association*, vol. 64, December, 1969, pp. 1211-24.

Jardine, N. and C. J. Van Rijsbergen, "The Use of Hierarchical Clustering in Information Retrieval", *Information Storage and Retrieval*, vol. 7, 1971, pp. 217-40.

Jeffrey, D. R. and R. Shisko *Systematic Analysis of University Libraries: An Application of Cost-Benefit Analysis to the M.I.T. Libraries*, Cambridge, Mass.: MIT Press, 1969.

Jenkins, H. R. "The ABC's of PPB." *Library Journal*, vol. 96, 1971, pp. 3089-3903.

Jennings, M. A., "Optimizating Library Automation with a Central Dynamic Store," *College and Research Libraries, 30:397-404* (1969).

Jestes, E. C. "An Example of Systems Analysis: Locating a Book in a Reference Room." *Special Libraries*, vol. 59, 1968, pp. 722-28.

Johns Hopkins University, *Operations Research and Systems Engineering Study of a University Library. Progress Report*, by R. H. Roy (and others), Baltimore, Md., 1965, available from Clearinghouse for Federal Scientific and Technical Information, Springfield, Va., document number PB-168-187.

Johnson, E. R. "Applying 'Management by Objectives' to the University Library," *College and Research Libraries*, vol. 34, 1973, pp. 436-439.

Jones, A. "Criteria for the Evaluation of Public Library Services," *J. of Librarianship*, 2:228-245 (1970).

Kaser, D. "Evaluation of Administrative Services," *Library Trends*, vol. 22, 1974, pp. 257-264.

Kendall, M. G. "The bibliography of Operational Research," *Operational Research Quarterly*, vol. 11, 1960, pp. 31-36.

Kendall, M. G. "Natural law in the social sciences," *Journal of the Royal Statistical Society*, Series A, vol. 124, 1961, pp. 1-18.

Kilgour, F. G. "Recorded Use of Books in the Yale Medical Library." *American Documentation*, vol. 12, 1969, pp. 266-69.

Kilgour, F. G. "Use of Medical and Biological Journals in the Yale Medical Library." *Bulletin of the Medical Library Association*, vol. 50, 1962, pp. 429-49.

King, D. W. "Cost effectiveness of information transfer systems," Paper presented at the 39th National Operations Research Society of America Meeting, Dallas, Texas, 1971.

King, D. W. "Experimentation, modeling and analysis to establish a new pricing policy at the Clearinghouse for Federal Scientific and Technical Information," American Society for Information Science, *Proceedings, 5th Annual Meeting*, Oct. 20-24, 1968, Columbus, Ohio.

King, D. W. and Bryant, E. C. *The Evaluation of Information Services and Products*, Washington, D. C., Information Resources Press, 1971, p. 306.

King, D. W. and N. W. Caldwell, *Cost-Effectiveness of Retrospective Search Systems*. Washington, D. C., American Psychological Association, 1971.

Kissel, G. "Einfuhrung in Die Systemforschung und Darstellung von Ansatzen zur Systemanalyse und Gestaltung im Bibliothekswesen" (Introduction to Systems Research and the Presentation of Methods for Systems Analysis and Formulation in Librarianship). In *Bibliotheksorganisation methoden Der Analyse und Gestaltung: Referate Des Fortbildungsseminars, Koln, Nov., 1972* (Library Organization-methods of Analysis and Formulation: Lectures from the Further Education Seminar, Cologne, Nov., 1972), ed. by W. Krieg, Cologne, Greven Verlar, 1973, pp. 1-20.

Kochen, M. "Directory Design for Networks of Information and Referral Centers," *Library Quarterly*, vol. 42, 1972, pp. 59-83.

Kochen, M. "Referential consulting networks," Paper presented at the National Operations Research Society of America Meeting, Detroit, Michigan, 1970. ERIC ED 027 923.

Kochen, M., "Switching Centers for Inquiry Referral," in Becker, Joseph, *Interlibrary Communications and Information Networks*, pp. 132-139, American Library Association, Chicago, 1971.

Kochen, M. and D. Cason, Jr. "A Cost-Benefit Analysis of an Information System to Help People Plan Their Families", *American Society for Information Science Proceedings*, Fall, 1973.

Kochen, M. and B. Segur. "Effects of Catalog Volume at the Library of Congress on the Total Catalog Costs of American Research Libraries," *Journal of the American Society for Information Science*, vol. 21, 1970, pp. 133-9.

Koehler, D. W. and B. N. Shrut. *Evaluation of a Computer-Based Cataloging Support System for Use by the Cornell University Libraries*. Ithaca, N. Y.: Graduate School, Cornell University, 1973.

Koningova, M. "Mathematical and Statistical Methods of Noise Evaluation in a Retrieval System", *Information Storage and Retrieval*, vol. 6, 1971, pp. 437-44.

Korfhage, R. R. "Graphical data systems for library retrieval," Paper presented at the National Operations Research Society of America Meeting, Detroit, Michigan, 1970.

Korfhage, R. R. "A note on a relevance estimate and its improvement," *Communications of the ACM*, vol. 11, 1968, p. 756.

Korfhage, R. R. and J. S. Aronofsky, "Telecommunications in Library Networks," paper presented at ORSA/TIMS Joint Meeting, Las Vegas, Nevada, 1975.

Korfhage, R. R., V. N. Bhat, and R. E. Nance. "Graph Models for Library Networks," Technical Report CP710013, Computer Science/Operations Research Center, Southern Methodist University, Dallas, Texas, 1971.

Korfhage, R. R., V. N. Bhat, and R. E. Nance. "Graph Models for Library Information Networks," *Library Quarterly*, vol. 42, 1972, pp. 31-42.

Korfhage, R. R. and T. G. DeLutis. "A Basis for Time and Cost Evaluation of Information Systems," Purdue University School of Industrial Engineering Memorandum Series, No. 69-6, Lafayette, Indiana, 1969.

Kováts, Z. "Management Problems in University Libraries," *IATUL Proceedings*, vol. 7, 1974, pp. 88-96.

Kozachkov, L. S. and L. A. Khursin. "Osnovnoe veroyatnostnoe raspredelenie v sistemakh informatsionnykh potokov [The basic probability distribution in information flow system]," *Nauchno-Technicheskaya Informatsiya*, Ser. 2, 1968, pp. 3-12.

Kozumplik, W. A. Time and motion study of library operations," *Special Libraries*, vol. 58, 1967, pp. 585-588.

Kraft, D. H. "A Comment on the Morse-Elston Model of Probabilistic Obsolescence," *Operations Research*, vol. 18, November-December, 1970, pp. 1228-1233.

Kraft, D. H., "A Decision Theory View of the Information Retrieval Situation: An Operations Research Approach", *Journal of the American Society for Information Science*, vol. 24, 1973, pp. 368-76.

Kraft, D. H. *The Journal Selection Problem in a University Library System*, unpublished doctoral dissertation, Purdue University, Lafayette, Indiana, 1971.

Kraft, D. H. and A. Bookstein, "Evaluation of Information Systems: A Decision Theory Approach", working paper, School of Librarianship, University of California, Berkeley, 1975.

Kraft, D. H. and T. W. Hill, Jr. "A Journal Selection Model and Its Implications for Librarians," *Information Storage and Retrieval*, vol. 9, 1973, pp. 1-11.

Kraft, D. H. and T. W. Hill, Jr. "The Journal Selection Problem in a University Library System," an invited paper presented at the 38th National Meeting of the Operations Research Society of America, Detroit, Michigan, October, 1970, *Management Science*, vol. 19, 1973, pp. 613-626.

Kraft, D. H. and T. W. Hill, Jr. "A Lagrangian Formulation of the Journal Selection Model," paper presented at the 39th Annual Meeting, Operations Research Society of America, Dallas, Texas, 1971.

Kraft, D. H. and T. W. Hill, Jr. "A Mathematical Model of the Information Center Location Problem and Its Implications for Decision Makers," working paper, School of Library and Information Services, University of Maryland, College Park, Maryland, 1971.

Kraft, D. H. and T. W. Hill, Jr. "Models of Journal Productivity: Ways of Measuring Journal Worth for the Journal Selection Decision," working paper, School of Library and Information Services, University of Maryland, College Park, Maryland, 1972.

Kraft, D. H. and J. W. Liesener. "An Application of a Cost-Benefit Approach to Program Planning: School Media Programs," *American Society for Information Science Proceedings*, Fall, 1973.

Kraft, D. H. and D. McDonald. "Library Operations Research: A Tutorial," Proceedings of the LARC Institute on Library Operations Research, Washington, D. C., 1973.

Kraft, D. H. and R. A. Polaesek, "Biomedical Literature Dynamics", *Methods of Information in Medicine*, vol. 13, 1974, pp. 242-8.

Kraft, D. H., R. A. Polaesek, L. Soergel, K. Burns, and A. Klair, "Journal Selection Decisions: A Biomedical Library Operations Research Model. I. The Framework," working paper, School of Librarianship, University of California, Berkeley, 1975.

Krevitt, B. I. and Griffith, B. C. "Evaluation of Information Systems: A Bibliography, 1967-1972" *Information, Part 2,* vol. 2, 1973.

Kriebel, C. H. *A resume of mathematical research on information systems*, Graduate School of Industrial Administration, Carnegie Tech., Pittsburgh, Pennsylvania, 1965, NTIS AD 616 113.

Kuehl, P. G. "Marketing Perspectives for "ERIC-like" Information Systems," *Journal of the American Society for Information Science*, vol. 23, 1972, pp. 359-64.

Kujpers, J. R. "Literature citation counting," *Science*, vol. 133, 1961, p. 1138.

Kurmey, W. J. "Management Implications of Mechanization." In C.A.C.U.L. Workshop on Library Automation. *Automation in Libraries*. Ottawa: Canadian Association of College Libraries, 1967.

Ladd, B. "Statistics in Planning for National Information Services." Paper presented at the General Council Meeting of the International Federation of Library Associations, 40th, Washington, D. C., November, 1974.

Ladendorf, J. "Information Service Evaluation. The Gap Between the Ideal and the Possible," *Special Libraries*, vol. 64, 1973, pp. 273-279.

Lamar, M. "Automated Cataloging Procedures in the Branch Libraries," *LARC Reports*, vol. 3, 1970, pp. 39-52.

Lamberton, D. M. (Ed.) *Economics of Information and Knowledge: Selected Readings*, Penquin Books, Baltimore, Md., 1971.

Lamkin, B. E. "Decision-making Tools for Improved Library Operations." *Special Libraries*, vol. 56, 1965, pp. 642-46.

University of Lancaster Library Research Unit. "Simulation Kit No. 1. A Library Management Game (Loan and Duplication Policies)," University of Lancaster, Lancaster, England, 1973.

Lancaster, F. W. "The Cost-Effectiveness Analysis of Information Retrieval and Dissemination Systems." *Journal of the American Society for Information Science*, vol. 22, 1971, pp. 12-27.

Lancaster, F. W. "The Cost-effectiveness of Information Retrieval and Dissemination Systems," *Journal of the American Society for Information Science*, vol. 22, no. 1, Jan.-Feb. 1971, pp. 12-27.

Lancaster, F. W. ed. "Systems Design and Analysis for Libraries," *Library Trends*, April 1973, pp. 463-603.

Lancaster, F. W. and W. D. Climenson. "Evaluating the Economic Efficiency of a Document Retrieval System." *Journal of Documentation*, vol. 24, 1968, pp. 16-36.

Lance, D. O. "Study of the decision-making procedures for the acquisition of science library materials and the relation of these procedures to the requirements of college and university library patrons," American Library Association, Chicago, Illinois, 1967. ERIC ED 047 712.

Lazorick, G. J. *Demand models for books in library circulation systems*. Ph.D. thesis. SUNY Buffalo, 1970. ERIC ED 061 980.

Lazorick, G. J. and T. L. Minder. "A least cost searching sequence," *College and Research Libraries*, vol. 25, 1964, pp. 126-128.

Lee, D. R. and J. R. Buck. "An Evaluation of Selected Parameters at the Microform Reading Man-Machine Interface," Purdue University School of Industrial Engineering. Memorandum Series, N. 72-3, Lafayette, Indiana, 1972.

Lee, Sul H. Planning-Programming-Budgeting System (PPBS): Implications for Library Management, ed. and with an Introduction by Sul H. Lee. Ann Arbor, Mich.: Published for the Eastern Michigan University Library, Ypsilanti, Mich. The Pierian Press, 1973.

Leffler, W. L. "A statistical method for circulation analysis," *College and Research Libraries*, vol. 25, 1964, pp. 438-490.

Leimkuhler, F. F. "The Bradford Distribution," *Journal of Documentation*, vol. 23, 1967, pp. 197-207.

Leimkuhler, F. F. "Large Scale Library Systems," *Library Trends*, vol. 21 no. 4, April, 1973, pp. 575-586.

Leimkuhler, F. F. "Library Operations Research," *Engineering Education*, January, 1970, pp. 363-5.

Leimkuhler, F. F. "Library Operations Research: A Process of Discovery and Justification," *Library Quarterly*, vol. 42, 1972, pp. 84-96.

Leimkuhler, F. F. "A literature search and File Organizational Model," *American Documentation*, vol. 19, 1968, pp. 131-6.

Leimkuhler, F. F. "A Literature Search Model," 1967, NTIS PB 174 390.

Leimkuhler, F. F. "Mathematical Models for Library Systems Analysis," *Drexel Library Quarterly*, vol. 4, 1967, pp. 185-96.

Leimkuhler, F. F. "On Information Storage Models," Purdue University School of Industrial Engineering Memorandum Series, No. 69-5, Lafayette, Indiana, 1969, also in Mackenzie, A. G. and I. M. Stuart (Eds.), Proceedings of a Research Seminar Held at the University of Lancaster, 9-11 July, 1969, University of Lancaster Library, Lancaster, England.

Leimkuhler, F. F. "Operations Research and Information Science - A Common Cause," *Journal of the American Society for Information Science*, vol. 24, 1973, pp. 3-8.

Leimkuhler, F. F. "Operations Research in the Purdue Libraries." In Andrews, T. (Ed.), *Automation in the Library — When, Where, and How*, Lafayette, Ind.: Purdue University, 1964.

Leimkuhler, F. F. "Operations Research, Librarianship, and Information Science," in Rudolph, G. A. (Ed.), *The Academic Community Looks at Library Management*, Carol M. Newman Library and Department of Industrial and Operations Research, Virginia Polytechnic Institute and State University, Blacksburg, Virginia, 1971.

Leimkuhler, F. F., "Optimal Size of a Journal Collection", paper presented at ORSA/TIMS Joint Meeting, Las Vegas, Nevada, 1975.

Leimkuhler, F. F. "Planning University Library Services: An Overview." In *Planning Library Services: Proceedings of a Research Seminar Held at the University of Lancaster, 9-11 July 1969*, edited by A. G. Mackenzie and I. M. Stuart. Lancaster: University of Lancaster Library, 1969.

Leimkuhler, F. F. "Storage Policies for Information Systems," Purdue University School of Industrial Engineering, Memorandum Series, No. 69-8, Lafayette, Indiana, 1969, also in Mackenzie, A. G. and I. M. Stuart (Eds.), "Planning Library Services Proceedings of a Conference Held at the University of Lancaster, 9-11 July, 1969," University of Lancaster Library, Lancaster, England.

Leimkuhler, F. F. Systems Analysis in University Libraries," *College and Research Libraries*, vol. 27, 1966.

Leimkuhler, F. F. and A. Billingsly. "Library and Information Center Management," in Cuadra, C. (ed.), *Annual Review of Information Science and Technology*, vol. 7, 1972.

Leimkuhler, F. F. and M. D. Cooper. "Cost accounting and analysis for university libraries," University of California, Office of the Vice President - Planning and Analysis, Berkeley, California, 1970, ERIC ED 040 728.

Leimkuhler, F. F. and M. D. Cooper. "Cost Accounting and Analysis for University Libraries," *College and Research Libraries*, vol. 32, 1971, pp. 449-64.

Leimkuhler, F. F. and M. D. Cooper. *Analytical Planning for University Libraries*, University of California Press, Berkeley, 1970.

Leimkuhler, F. F. and M. D. Cooper. "Analytical Models for Library Planning," *Journal of the American Society for Information Science*, vol. 22, November-December, 1971.

Leimkuhler, F. F. and J. G. Cox. "Compact Book Storage in Libraries," *Operations Research*, vol. 12, 1964, pp. 419-27.

Leimkuhler, F. F. and M. Morelock. "Library Operations Research and Systems Engineering Studies." *College and Research Libraries*, vol. 25, 1964, pp. 501-3.

Levine, E. H. "Effect of Instantaneous Retrieval on Indexing Criteria," *Journal of the American Society for Information Science*, vol. 25, 1974, pp. 199-200.

Levine, J. M. and R. E. Brahlek. "Parameters of Information-Seeking Behavior" Report No. AFOSR-TR-72-2465. Silver Spring, Md.: Amercian Institutes for Research in the Behavioral Sciences, 1972.

Levy, B. and W. H. Werner. "Multiple Test of ABC Method Part III Mathematical Model," Army Technical Library Improvement Studies (ATLIS) Report No. 18, 1967, NTIS AD 658 668.

Lewis, S. G. An Information System for A District School Administrator. Operation PEP, 1970.

Line, M. B. "The ability of a university library to provide books wanted by researchers," *J. Librarianship*, vol. 5 no. 1, Jan. 1973, pp. 37-51.

Line M. B. "The 'Half-Life' of Periodical Literature: Apparent and Real Obsolescence," *Journal of Documentation*, vol. 26, 1970, pp. 46-54.

Line, M. B., A. Sandison, and J. Macgregor. *Patterns of citations to articles within journals: a preliminary test of scatter, concentration and obsolescence.* Bath, England: University Library, 1972. (BATH/LIB/2)

Lipetz, Ben-Ami. "Catalog Use in a Large Library," *Library Quarterly*, vol. 42, 1972, pp. 129-39.

Lister, W. C. *Least Cost Decision Rules for the Selection of Library Materials for Compact Storage*, 1967, unpublished doctoral dissertation, Purdue University, Lafayette, Indiana (ERIC ED 027 916), 1967.

Liston, D. M. and M. L. Schoene. "A Systems Approach to the Design of Information Systems," *Journal of the American Society for Information Science*, vol. 22, 1971, pp. 115-22.

Arthur D. Little, Inc. *Centralization and documentation*, NTIS PB 181 548 and PB 181 548-A.

Llinas, J., E. T. O'Neill. "The Effect of cyclic demand on book availability," *American Society for Information Science. Proceedings, Fall 1973.*

Longsworth, A. "Public Library Services," in Mackenzie, A. G. and I. M. Stuart (eds.) "Proceedings of a Research Seminar held at the University of Lancaster, 9-11 July, 1969," University of Lancaster Library, Lancaster, England.

Lotka, A. J. "The frequency distribution of scientific productivity," *Journal of the Washington Academy of Sciences*, vol. 16, 1926, pp. 317-323.

Lourey, E. D. "Systems Design for a Mini-Computer-Based Library of Data Processing, 1974, University of Illinois. *Proceedings*, University of Illinois, Graduate School of Library Science, 1974, pp. 181-190.

Lubans, J. "Non-Use of an academic Library," *College and Research Libraries*, vol. 32 no. 5, 1971.

Lubans, J., Jr., "Systems Analysis, Machineable Circulation Data and Library Users and Non-

Users," paper presented at American Society for Engineering Education Meeting, June, 1971.

Lubans, J., Jr., *et al. A Study with Computer-Based Circulation Data of the Non-use and Use of a Large Academic Library. Final Report.* Boulder, Col.: University of Colorado Libraries, 1973.

Lucas, H. C., Jr., "The Practical Application of Information Systems Research Paper presented at ORSA/TIMS Joint Meeting at Las Vegas, Nevada, 1975.

Luckham, B.L.G. "The distribution of public library members in Southampton by distance of residence from library promises," *Research in Librarianship*, vol. 1, 1967, pp. 169-170.

Lutterbeck, E. Dokumentation und Information; Auf dem Wegins Informationszeitalter; 27 Fachleute Berichten uber Probleme und Methoden, uber den Gegenwartigen Stand und Zukunftige Entwicklungen (Documentation and Information; On the Way into the Information Age; 27 Experts Report on Problems and Methods, Current Position and Future Growth) Frankfur Am Main, Unschau Verlag, 1971.

Lutz, R. P. "Costing Information Services", *Bulletin of the Medical Library Association*, vol. 59, 1971, pp. 254-61.

Lynch, B. P. *Library Technology: A Comparison of the Work of Functional Departments in Academic Libraries.* Ph.D. Thesis. Madison, Wis.: Univerisity of Wisconsin, 1974.

McAllister, C., and J. M. Bell. "Human Factors in the Design of an Interactive Library System," *Journal of the American Society for Information Science*, vol. 22, 1971, pp. 96-104.

McClelland, W. C. "Management in a Service Environment," *ASLIB Proceedings*, vol. 25, March, 1973, pp. 93-99.

McDonald, D. and D. H. Kraft, "Library Operations Research: Its Past and Our Future", in Hammer, D. (Ed.), *Accomplishment in Information Science*, Scarecrow Press, to be published in 1975.

McGrath, W. "The significance of books use according to classified profile of academic depart ment," *College and Research Libraries*, vol. 33, 1973, pp. 212-219.

McGrath, W. E. and Barber, G. R. "An Allocation Formula Derived from a Factor Analysis of Academic Departments." *College and Research Libraries*, vol. 30, 1969, pp. 51-62.

Machlup, F. *The Production and Distribution of Knowledge in the United States.* Princeton, N. J. Princeton University Press, 1962.

McInnis, R. Marvin. "The formula approach to library size: an empirical study of its efficiency in evaluating research libraries." *Coll. & Res. Lib.*, vol. 33 no. 3, May 1972, pp. 190-198.

McKenney, James L. "Guidelines for simulation model development." In: Walker, Donald E. (ed.), *Information systems science and technology.* 1967. Washington, Umpson Book Co., pp. 169-173.

Mackenzie, A. G. "Bibliotheconomics; or Library Science Revised," *An Leabharlann.*

Mackenzie, A. G. "Library Research at the University of Lancaster," *Libr. Ass. Rec.*, vol. 73, 1971.

Mackenzie, A. G. "Systems Analysis as a Decision-Making Tool for the Library Manager," *Library Trends*, vol. 21 no. 4, April 1973, pp. 493-504.

Mackenzie, A. G. "Systems Analysis of a University Library." In Foskett, D. J., A. Reuck, and H. Coglans, (Eds.), *Library Systems and Information Services: Proceedings of the Second Anglo-Czech Conference of Information Specialists*, London: Crosby Lockwood, 1970.

Mackenzie, A. G. "Systems Analysis of a University Library." *Program*, vol. 2, 1968, pp. 7-14.

Mackenzie, A. G. and M. K. Buckland. "Operational Research," *In*: Whatley, A. H., (ed.), *British Librarianship and Information Science*, 1966-1970. London, Library Association, 1972.

Mackenzie, A. G. and I. M. Stuart (eds.), "Planning Library Services: Proceedings of a Research Seminar held at the University of Lancaster, 9-11 July, 1969," Occasional Paper No. 3, University of Lancaster Library, Lancaster, England, 1969.

MacLachlan, J. *A Plan for a Publication Network for Rapid Dissemination of Technical Infor-*

mation. Berkeley, Calif.: Office of the President, University of California, 1973.

Magson, M. S. "Techniques for the Measurement of Cost-Benefit in Information Centres," *ASLIB Proceedings*, vol. 25, 1973, pp. 164-185.

Maidment, W. R. "Management information from housekeeping routines," *Journal of Documentation*, vol. 27, 1971, pp. 37-42.

Maidment, W. R., "Progress in Documentation: Management Information from Housekeeping Routines," *J. of Documentation*, 27:37-42 (1971).

Maizell, R. E. "Standards for measuring effectiveness of technical library performance," *I.R.E. Transactions on Engineering Management*, vol. EM-7, 1960, pp. 67-72.

Mandelbrot, B. "An informational theory of the structure of language based upon the theory of the statistical matching of messages and coding," In: Jackson, W. [ed.], "Communication theory," paper presented at A Symposium on Applications of Communication theory, London, Butterworths, 1952.

Mandelbrot, B. "A Note on a Class of Skew Distribution Functions: Analysis and Critique of a Paper by H. A. Simon," *Information and Control*, 2:90-99 (1959).

Mandelbrot, B. "Simple games of strategy occurring in communication through natural languages," *Transactions of the I.R.E. Professional Group on Information Theory*, vol. PGIT-3, 1954, pp. 124-137.

Mann, S. H. "Least-Cost Decision Rules for Dynamic Library Management," *Information Storage and Retrieval*, vol. 7, 1971, pp. 111-21.

Mann, S. H. *Optimal library size.* Pennsylvania State University. College of Human Development. University Park, Pennsylvania.

Mantell, L. H. "On laws of special abilities and the production of scientific literature," *American Documentation,* vol. 17, 1966, pp. 8-16.

Marchant, M. P., "The Effects of the Decision Making Process and Related Organizational Factors on Alternative Measures of Performance in University Libraries," Ph.D. dissertation, University of Michigan, Ann Arbor, 1970.

Maron, M. E. and J. L. Kuhns. "On relevance, probabilistic indexing, and information retrieval," *Journal of the Association for Computing Machinery*, vol. 7, 1960.

Martin, J. "Flexible Data Base Management System Expidites Library Planning and Control," *Special Libraries*, vol. 65, 1974, pp. 110-115.

Martyn, J. "Cost Effectiveness in Library Management." *Aslib Electronic Group Newsletter*, no. 40, 1969, pp. 3-9.

Martyn, J. and B. C. Vickery. "The Complexity of the Modeling of Information Systems," *Journal of Documentation*, vol. 26, 1970, pp. 204-20.

Mason, D. "Management Techniques Applied to the Operation of Information Services," *ASLIB Proceedings*, vol. 25, 1973, pp. 445-458.

Mason, D. "Programmed Budgeting and Cost Effectiveness," *Aslib Proceedings*, vol. 25, no. 3, March 1973, pp. 100-110.

Matarazzo, T. M. "Scientific Journals: Page or Price Explosion?" *Special Libraries.*

Mathematica, "On The Economics of Library Operation," prepared for National Advisory mission on Libraries, Princeton, 1967, incorporated into Knight, Douglas M., and E. Shepley Nourse (eds.), *Libraries at Large: Tradition, Innovation and the National Interest*, pp. 168-227, 590-596, R. R. Bowker, New York, 1969.

Mathematica, *On Library Statistics*, Princeton, 1967.

Mavor, A. S. and W. S. Vaughn, Jr. Development and Implementation of a Curriculum-Based Information Support System for Hamline University. St. Paul, Minn.: Hamline University and Landover, Md.: Whittenburg, Vaughan Associates, Inc., 1974.

Meier, R. L. "Information input overload: features of growth in communications - orientated institutions," In: Massarik, F. and P. Ratoosh, (eds.), *Mathematical explorations in behavioral sciences*, Homewood, Ill., Irwin, 1965.

Meier, R. L. "Efficiency criteria for the operation of large libraries," *Library Quarterly*, vol. 31, 1961, pp. 215-234.

Merchant, H. D. and M. W. Sasieni. "Centralization or Decentralization of Case's Library Facilities." Paper presented at Fourteenth National Meeting of the Operations Research Society of America, Saint Louis, Mo., 1958.

Meyer, Robert S. and G. N. Rostvold. "The library and the economic community: a market analysis of information needs of business and industry in the communities of Pasadena and Pomona, California," Pasadena Public Library. Pasadena, California, May 1969. ERIC ED 046 424.

Michael, M. E. and A. P. Young. *Planning and Evaluating Library System Services in Illinois*. Urbana, Ill.: Illinois University, Library Research Center, 1974.

Mikhailov, A. I. *et al* (eds.). On theoretical foundations of informatics," FID 435, Moscow, All-Union Inst. for Sci. & Tech. Inf., 1969.

Miller, E. P. "An Effectiveness Measure for Information Center Operations", *American Society for Information Science Proceedings*, Fall, 1973.

Miller, Edward P. and R. P. Lutz. "A unique program in library education," *Special Libraries*, vol. 62, 1971, pp. 353-356.

Minder, T. "Application of Systems Analysis in Designing a New System," *Library Trends*, vol. 21, 1973, pp. 553-564.

Minder, T. "Library systems analyst - a job description," *College and Research Libraries*, vol. 27, 1966, pp. 271-276.

Minker, J. "A Stochastic Model of an Information Center," Computer Science Center, University of Maryland, College Park, Md., 1969.

Mittler, E. "Moderne Bibliothekoplanung." (Modern Library Planning) *Zeitschnift fur Bibliothekswesen and Bibliographic* 19 (4/5) 1972, 260-284.

Mjøsund, A. *An optimal literature search and methods of estimating the probability parameter*, unpublished doctoral dissertation, Johns Hopkins University, Baltimore, Md., 1967.

Mlynarczyk, F., Jr. "Measuring library costs," Paper presented at an Institute on Program Planning and Budgeting systems for Libraries at Wayne State University. Department of Library Science, Detroit, Michigan, 1968. ERIC ED 045 120.

Moore, E. Systems analysis: an overview, *Special Libraries*, vol. 58, 1967, pp. 87-90.

Morehead State University, Appalachian Adult Education Center. *The Interrelating of Library and Basic Education Services for Disadvantaged Adults: A Demonstration of Four Alternative Working Models*. Annual Report: Vol. 2, Washington, D. C.: Bureau of Libraries and Learning Resources, 1973.

Morelock, M. and F. F. Leimkuhler. "Library Operations Research and Systems Engineering Studies," *College and Research Libraries*, vol. 25, November 1964, pp. 501-3.

Moriarty, J. ,H., "Measurement and Evaluation in College and University Library Studies: Library Research at Purdue University," in Goldhor, Herbert (ed.), *Research Methods in Librarianship: Measurement and Evaluation*, University of Illinois, Urbana, Ill., 1968.

Morley, R. M. "Maximising the Benefit from Library Resources," in Mackenzie, A. G. and I. M. Stuart (eds.) *Proceedings of a Research Seminar Held at the University of Lancaster, England, July, 1969.*

Morris, W. T. "On the Art of Modeling," *Management Science*, August, 1967.

Morse, P. M. *Library Effectiveness: A Systems Approach*, M.I.T. Press, Cambridge, Mass., 1968.

Morse, P. M. "Measures of Library Effectiveness," *Library Quarterly*, vol. 42, 1972, pp. 15-30.

Morse, P. M. "On browsing: the use of search theory in the search for information," Paper presented at the 39th National Operations Research Society of American Meeting, Dallas, Texas,

1971. NTIS AS 702 920.

Morse, P. M. "On Browsing - The Use of Search Theory in the Search for Information," NTIS N70-31459 and AD 702920.

Morse, P. M. "On the Prediction of Library Use," in Overhage, C.F.J. and R. J. Haram (eds.), *Intrex: Report of a Planning Conference on Information Transfer Experiments*, M.I.T. Press, Cambridge, Mass., 1965.

Morse, P. M. "Optimal Linear Ordering of Information Items", *Operations Research*, vol. 20, 1972, pp. 741-51.

Morse, P. M. "Probabilistic models for library operations," in Association of Research Libraries, *Minutes of the 63rd meeting, 1964, Chicago*. Washington, D. C., The Association, 1964, pp. 9-19.

Morse, P. M. "Search Theory and Browsing," *Library Quarterly*, vol. 40, 1970, pp. 391-408.

Morse, P. M. & Chung-Chich Chev. Using Circulation Desk Data to Obtain Unbiased Estimates of Book Use. *Library Quarterly*, vol. 45, 1975, pp. 179-194.

Morse, P. M. and C. Elston. "A Probabilistic Model for Obsolescence," *Operations Research,* vol. 17, 1969.

Mosley, I. *Cost-Effectiveness Analysis of the Automation of a Circulation System*. Master's Thesis, University of Sheffield, England, 1974.

Mudge, I. G. "Present day economics in cataloging," In: Rowland, A. R. (ed.), Reference services Contributions to library literature, Hamden, Connecticut, Shoe String Press, 1964.

Müller, P. H. "Die Bedeutung der Bedienungstheorie im Bibliothekswesen" [The impact of queuing theory on librarianship]. *Technische Universität Dresden Wissenschaftliche Zeitschrift*, vol. 16, 1967, pp. 1633-36.

Muller, R. H. "Economics of Compact Book Shelving." *Library Trends*, vol. 13, 1965, pp. 433-47.

Muller, R. H. *et al.* "Research approach to university library problems," *College and Research Libraries*, vol. 24, 1963, pp. 199-203.

Mullick, S. K. *Optimal design of a stochastic system with dominating fixed costs*, unpublished doctoral dissertation, Johns Hopkins University. Baltimore, Maryland, 1965.

Mullick, S. K., "Optimal Design of a Stochastic System with Dominating Fixed Costs," *Journal of Financial and Quarterly Analysis*, 1:55-74 (1966).

Mullick, S. K. "Optimal Design of a Stochastic System with Dominating Fixed Costs." Paper presented at TIMS, the Institute of Management Sciences, National Meeting, Dallas, Tex., February 16, 1966.

Nance, R. E. "An Analytical Model of a Library Network," *Journal of the American Society for Information Science*, vol. 21, January 1970, pp. 58-66.

Nance, R. E. "Algorithmic structures for the solution of library network problems," Paper presented at the National Operations Research Society of America Meeting, Detroit, Michigan, 1970.

Nance, R. E. *Strategic Simulation of a Library/User/Funder System*, unpublished doctoral dissertation, Purdue University, Lafayette, Indiana, 1969.

Nance, R. E. "Systems Analysis and the Study of Information Systems." In *American Documentation Institute Proceedings*, Washington, D. C.: Thompson Book Co., 1967.

Nance, R. E. and N. R. Baker. "Library Policy Structure: An Industrial Dynamics Study," *Simulation*, September, 1971.

Nance, R. E. and N. R. Baker. "The Use of Simulation in Studying Information Storage and Retrieval," *American Documentation*, vol. 19, 1968, pp. 363-70.

Nance, R. E., R. R. Korfhage, and V. N. Bhat. "Information Networks: Definition and Message Transfer Models," Technical Report CP-710011, Computer Science/Operations Research Center, Southern Methodist University, Dallas, Texas, 1971.

Nance, R. E., W. K. Wickham, and M. Duggan. "A Computer System for Effective Management of a Medical Library Network: An Overview," Technical Report CP71005, Computer Science/Operations Research Center, Southern Methodist University, Dallas, Texas, 1971.

Naranan, S. "Bradford's Law of science bibliography - an interpretation," *Nature*, vol. 227, 1970, pp. 631-632.

Naranan, S. "Power law relations in science bibliography - a self-consistent interpretation," *Journal of Documentation*, vol. 27, 1971, pp. 83-97.

National Advisory Commission on Libraries, *On the Economics of Library Operation*, Princeton, N. J.: Mathematica, 1967.

Neelameghan, A. "Systems Approach to the Study of the Attributes of the Universe of Subjects" *Library Science with a Slant to Documentation*, vol. 9, 1972, pp. 445-472.

Neelameghan, A. *et al.* "Planning of Library and Documentation Systems: A Model Plan for Central and Regional Units of a System," *Library Science with a Slant to Documentation*, vol. 10, 1973, pp. 529-582.

Nelson, J. B. "Work Measurement," Second Annual Library Management Workshop, Carol M. Newman Library and Department of Industrial Engineering and Operations Research, Virginia Polytechnic Institute and State University, Blacksburg, Virginia, 1972.

Neuman, K. and H. Riedel. "Über die Modellierung von Struktur and Informationsfluss des betrieblichen Informations-system Wissenschaft und Technik mit Hilfe einer Kreisdarstellung" [Modeling the structure and information flow of an industrial information system using a circular flow diagram]. *Informatik* 16 (1969): 32-36.

Newfield, J. W. "A Model for Evaluating Document Based Educational Information Systems," Paper presented at the Annual Meeting of the Urban Regional Information Systems Association, Montreal, Quebec, August 1974.

Newhouse, Joseph P. *Libraries and the Other Triangle under the Demand Curve*. Santa Monica, Calif.: RAND Corp., 1970, NTIS AD 701 187.

Newhouse, J. P. and A. J. Alexander. "An Economic Analysis of Public Library Service", RAND Corp., Santa Monica, Calif., 1972.

Niland, P. "Developing standards for library expenditure," *Management Science*, vol. 13, 1967, pp. B797-B808.

Nistor, E. and E. Roman. "Despre conducerea stintifica a unitatilor de documentare" [Scientific management of documentation units]. *Probleme de informare si documentare 3* (February 1969): 80-87.

Nozik, B. S., "A Stochastic Model to Predict Demand for Library Services," unpublished doctoral dissertation, University of California, Berkeley, 1974.

Nussbaum, H. "Operations research applied to libraries," Paper presented at an Institute on Program Planning and Budgeting Systems for Libraries at Wayne State University. Department of Library Science, Detroit, Michigan, 1968, ERIC ED 045 121.

Oh, Tai Keun. New dimensions of management theory," *College and Research Libraries*, vol. 27, 1966, pp. 431-438.

Ohlman, H. "The activity spectrum: a tool for analyzing information systems," in: Heilprin, L. B., *et al* (eds.), *Proceedings of the Symposium on Education for Information Services*, London, Macmillan, 1965.

Oliver, M. R. "The effect of growth on the obsolescence of semi-conductor physics literature," *Journal of Documentation*, vol. 27, 1971, pp. 11-17.

Olson, E. E. "Quantitative Approaches to Assessment of Library Service Functions." In Ramey, J. A., (ed.), *Impact of Mechanization on Libraries: Fifth Annual Colloquium on Information Retrieval*, Philadelphia: Information Interscience, Inc., 1968.

Olson, E. E., J. W. Liesener, and D. H. Kraft. "An Educational Model for Library Problem-Solving: Teaming Librarians, Students, and Faculty," *Special Libraries*, vol. 63, 1972, pp. 231-4.

Olsen, H. A. *The economics of information: bibliography and commenting on the literature*. Washington, ERIC Clearinghouse on Library and Information Sciences, 1971, and *Information*

Part 2 Reports and Bibliography, vol. 1, 1972.

Olsen, H. A. "Tutorial: The Economics of Information", presented by the Special Interest Group on Costs, Budgeting, and Economics, American Society for Information Science, National Meeting, Los Angeles, 1973.

O'Neill, E. T. "Distribution of Library Resources", *American Society for Information Science Proceedings*, Fall, 1973.

O'Neill, E. T., "The Effect of Demand Level on the Optimal Size of Journal Collections" paper presented at ORSA/TIMS Joint Meeting, Las Vegas, Nevada, 1975.

O'Neill, E. T. *Journal Usage Patterns and Their Implications in the Planning of Library Systems*, unpublished doctoral thesis, Purdue University, Lafayette, Indiana, 1971.

O'Neill, E. T. "Limitations of the Bradford Distribution," American Society for Information Science Proceedings, Fall, 1973.

O'Neill, E. T. "A Model of Statistical Sampling of Collections," Presented to the Spring Conference of the College and University Libraries and the Resources and Technical Services Sections of the New York Library Association at Hofstra University, Hempstead, New York, April 1971.

O'Neill, E. T. "Sampling University Library Collections," *College and Research Libraries*, vol. 27, 1964, pp. 450-4.

O'Neill, E. T. *Sampling University Library Collections*, unpublished Master's thesis, Purdue University School of Industrial Engineering, Lafayette, Indiana, 1966.

O'Neill, E. T. "A Survey of Library Resources in Western New York," Western New York Library Resources Council, Buffalo, New York, 1972.

Orr, R. H. "Measuring the Goodness of Library Services: A General Framework for Considering Quantitative Measures," *Journal of Documentation*, vol. 29, 1973, pp. 315-332.

Orr, R. H., V. M. Pings, I. H. Pizer, and E. E. Olson. "Development of Methodologic Tools for Planning and Managing Library Services. I. Project Goals and Approach, II. Measuring a Library's Capability for Providing Documents, III. Standardized Inventories of Library Services," *Bulletin of the Medical Library Association*, vol. 56, 1968, pp. 235-267 and 380-403.

Palmer, D. "Measuring library output," Paper presented at an Institute on Program Planning and Budgeting Systems for Libraries at Wayne State University, Department of Library Science, Detroit, Michigan, 1968, ERIC ED 045 118.

Palmour, V. E., E. C. Bryant, N. W. Caldwell, L. M. Gray (Comps.). *A Study of the Characteristics, Costs, and Magnitude of Interlibrary Loans in Academic Libraries*, Greenwood Publishing Co., Westport, Conn., 1972.

Palmour, V. E. and L. M. Gray. "Costs and Effectiveness of Interlibrary Loan and Reference Activities of Resource Libraries in Illinois," Illinois State Library, Springfield, Illinois, 1972.

Palmour, V. E., E. E. Olson, N. K. Roderer. *Methods of Financing Interlibrary Loan Services*. Washington, D. C., Association of Research Libraries, 1974.

Palmour, Vernon E., and R. Wiederkehr, "A Decision Model for Library Policies on Serial Publications," paper presented at XVII International Conference of The Institute of Management Sciences, London, July 1970.

Papier, L. "Sources of Criteria for Intermediate Evaluation of Information Retrieval and Dissemination Systems, *Management Informatics*, vol. 2, 1973, pp. 71-4.

Parker, E. B., and W. J. Paisley, "Predicting Library Circulation from Community Characteristics," *Public Opinion Quarterly*, 29:39-53 (1965).

Parker, E. B., W. I. Paisley, and R. Garrett. *Bibliographic citations as unobtrusive measures of scientific communication*, Stanford University, Institute for Communication Research, Palo Alto, California, 1967.

Parker, T. E. "The Missing Stream: Operations Management in Libraries," *Library Journal*, vol. 94, 1969, pp. 42-3.

Patterson, G. W. "Waiting-line theory applied to purchasing of library books," In: Fundamental investigations in methods of operations research, Interim Technical Report No. 3, 1955.

Penner, R. J. "Measuring a Library's Capability . . . ", *Journal of Education for Librarianship*, vol. 13, 1972, pp. 17-30.

Pings, Vern M. "Development of Quantitative Assessment of Medical Libraries." *College and Research Libraries*, vol. 29, 1968, pp. 273-80.

Pings, V. M. "Monitoring and Measuring Document Delivery Services," 1969, ERIC ED 035 423.

Pinzelik, B. and D. L. Tolliver. *Statistical collection simplified within the General Library.* West Lafayette, Ind.: Purdue University, Libraries and Audio-Visual Center, 1972. (IMRU-02-72).

Pitt, W. B., D. H. Kraft and L. B. Heilprin. "Buy or Copy? A Library Operations Research Model," paper presented at the XX International Meeting of the Institute of Management Sciences, Tel Aviv, Israel, June 1973. *Information Storage and Retrieval*, vol. 10, 1974, pp. 331-41.

Pizer, I. H. and A. M. Cain. "Objective tests of library performance," *Special Libraries*, vol. 59, 1968, pp. 704-711.

Poage, S. T. "Work sampling in library administration," *Library Quarterly*, vol. 30, 1960, pp. 213-218.

Poole F. G. "Performance standards and specifications in the library economy," *Library Trends*, vol. 11, 1963, pp. 436-444.

Popovitch, J. D. "Compact Book Storage," unpublished paper for Master's degree work, Purdue University School of Industrial Engineering, Lafayette, Indiana, 1965.

Pratt, A. D. "Libraries, Economics, and Information: Recent Trends in Information Science Literature." *College and Research Libraries News*, vol. 36, pp. 33-38.

Pratt, A. D. "Objectives and performance evaluation of information systems" In: American Society for Information Science. *Information Transfer; proceedings of the annual meeting*, 1968, New York, Greenwood, 1968.

Pratt, L. "Analysis of library systems: a bibliography," *Special Libraries*, vol. 55, 1964, pp. 688-695.

Price, D. J. de S. "Citation measures of hard science, soft science, technology and nonscience." In: C. E. Nelson and D. K. Pollock, *Communication amongst scientists and technologists*. Lexington, Mass.: Health, 1970. Pp. 3-22.

Price, D. J. de S. "Masurari da referiate bibliografica (citate) in domeniul stiintelor dans structurate, al stiintelor slab structurate, al technicii si al stiintelor nestructurate. [Citation measures of hard science, soft science, technology and non-science]." *Studii si Ceretari de Documentare*, vol. 12, 1970, pp. 205-221.

Price, D. S. "Collecting and Reporting Real Costs of Information Systems", tutorial presented at the American Society for Information Science Annual Meeting, 1971.

Price, D. S. "Rational Cost Information: Necessary and Obtainable," *Special Libraries*, vol. 65, 1974, pp. 49-57.

Pritchard, A. *Statistical bibliography: an interim bibliography*, Report SABS-5, North-Western Polytecnic, School of Librarianship, London, England, 1969.

Quatman, G. L. *The cost of providing library services to groups in the Purdue University Community*, Lafayette, Ind., Purdue University Libraries, 1962.

Radford, N. A. "The problems of academic library statistics," *Library Quarterly*, vol. 38, 1968, pp. 231-248.

Raffel, J. "From Economic to Political Analysis of Library Decision Making." *College and Research Libraries*, vol. 30, 1974, pp. 412-423.

Raffel, J. and R. Shisko. "Centralization vs. Decentralization: A Location Analysis Approach for Librarians," *Special Libraries*, March, 1972, pp. 135-43.

Raffel, J. A. and R. Shisko. *Systematic Analysis of University Libraries: An Application of Cost-Benefit Analysis to the M. I. T. Libraries*, M.I.T. Press, Cambridge, Mass., 1969.

Raffel, L. J. *Compact Book Storage*, unpublished Master's thesis, Purdue University School of Industrial Engineering, Lafayette, Indiana, 1965.

Raisig, L. J. "Mathematical Evaluation of the Scientific Serial," *Science*, vol. 131, May 13, 1960, pp. 1417-19.

Ravindran, A. "On Compact Storage in Libraries," Purdue University School of Industrial Engineering Research Memorandum No. 70-14, Lafayette, Indiana, 1970.

Redmond, D. A. "Optimum size: the special library viewpoint," *Sci-Tech News*, vol. 20, 1964, pp. 40-42.

Rees, A. M. "Criteria for the operation of libraries and information retrieval systems," *Special Libraries*, vol. 57, 1966, pp. 641-642.

Reichard, E. W., and T. J. Orsagh. "Holdings and Expenditures of U. S. Academic Libraries: An Evaluative Technique." *College and Research Libraries*, vol. 27, 1966, pp. 478-87.

Reisman, A. *An Operations Research Study and Design of an Optimal Distribution Network for Selected Public, Academic and Special Libraries in Greater Cleveland:* Technical Report. The Task Force, LSCA Title III Distribution Project, Cleveland, Ohio, 1972.

Reisman, A., *et al.* "Timeliness of Library Materials Delivery: A Set of Priorities," *Socio-Economic Planning Sciences*, vol. 6, 1972, pp. 145-152.

Resnikoff, H. L., and J. Dolby, *Access: a Study of Information Storage and Retrieval with Emphasis on Library Information Systems*, U. S. Office of Education, Washington, D. C., 1971 available from ERIC Document Reproduction Service, Bethesda, Md., document number ED-050-773. To be published by Melville Publishing Co., Los Angeles.

Resnikoff, H. L. and J. Dolby. "Economic Accumulation of Book Indexes and Information Theory," American Society for Information Science Proceedings, Fall, 1973.

"Review of Budgeting Techniques in Academic and Research Libraries." *ARL Management Supplement* vol. 1, No. 2, 1973.

"Review of the Formulation and Use Objectives in Academic and Research Libraries," *ARL Management Supplement*, vol. 2, no. 1, 1974.

Reynolds, Rose, comp. *A selective bibliography on measurement in library and information services*, London, Aslib, 1970.

Ricking, M. and R. E. Booth, "Personnel Utilization in Libraries: A Systems Approach," prepared for the Ill. Library Task Analysis Project, ALA, 1974.

Robertson, S. E., "Explicit and Implicit Variables in Information Retrieval (IR) Systems", *Journal of the American Society for Information Science*, vol. 26, 1975, pp. 214-22.

Robertson, S. E., "The Parametric Description of Retrieval Tests Part II: Overall Measures", *Journal of Documentation*, vol. 25, 1969, pp. 93-107.

Robertson, S. E., R. Reynolds, and A. P. Wilkin. "Standard Costing for Information Systems: Background to a Current-Study", *ASLIB Proceedings*, vol. 22, 1970, pp. 452-7.

Roessler, D. Systemtheorie und Anwendungsmoglichkeitender Systemanalyse im Bibliothekswesen (System Theory and Possibilities of Application of System Analysis in Libraries). Verband der Bibliotheken des Landes Nordrhen-Westfalen Miiteilungsblatt, Vol. 22, 1972, pp. 184-192.

Rohlf, R. H. "Library management aid," *Library Journal*, vol. 79, 1954, pp. 1860-1862.

Rosenberg, V. *The application of psychometric techniques to determine the attitudes of individuals toward information seeking.* (Studies in the man-system interface in libraries, 2.) Bethlehem. Pa., Lehigh University, Center for the Information Sciences, 1966. Reprinted in: P. Brophy, M. K. Buckland and A. Hindle (Eds.) *Reader in operations research for libraries.* Washington, D. C.: NCR Microcard Editions. (Forthcoming)

Rosenberg, V. "Scientific Premises of Information Science," *Journal of the American Society for Information Science,* vol. 25, 1974, pp. 263-269.

Rosenberg, V. "A Study of Statistical Measures in Predicting Terms Used to Index Documents,"

Journal of the American Society for Information Science, vol. 22, 1971, pp. 41-50.

Ross, J. and J. Brooks. "Costing Manual and Computerized Library Circulation Systems", *Program: News of Computers in Libraries*, vol. 6, 1972, pp. 217-27.

Rothenberg, D. H. "An Efficiency Model and Performance Function for an Information Retrieval System," 1968, ERIC ED 023 433.

Rothkopf, M. "The Future Circulation Rate of a Book, and an Application of Queuing Theory to Library Problems," Course Term Report, M.I.T. Libraries, Cambridge, Mass., 1962.

Rothkopf, M. *Two Phases of an Operations Research Study of M.I.T.'s Science Library*, Report, M.I.T., Cambridge, Mass., 1962.

Rothstein, S. "Measurement and evaluation of reference service," *Library Trends*, vol. 12, 1964, pp. 456-472.

Rouse, W. B. (Ed.) *Applications of Operations Research Techniques in Tufts University Libraries*. Medford, Mass.: College of Engineering, Tufts University, 1973.

Rouse, W. B. "Circulation Dynamics. A Planning Model." *Journal of the American Society for Information Science*, Vol. 25, 1975, pp. 358-363.

Rouse, W. B. "A Library Network Model", paper presented at ORSA/TIMS Joint Meeting, Las Vegas, Nevada, 1975.

Rouse, W. B. "Optimal Selection of Acquisition Sources," *Journal of the American Society for Information Science*, vol. 25, 1974, pp. 227-231.

Rouse, W. B. "Optimal Staffing of Service Desks." Working copy from Assistant Professor in the Department of Mechanical and Industrial Engineering and Research and Research Assistant Professor in the Coordinated Science Laboratory. University of Illinois at Urbana-Champaign, Urbana, Ill., 61801.

Rouse, W. B., ed. *Quantitative Approaches to the Management of Information/Document Retrieval at the University of Illinois*, working copy, department of Mechanical and Industrial Engineering and Graduate School of Library Science, University of Illinois at Urbana-Champaign, June 1975.

Rouse, W. B., J. L. Divilbiss, and S. H. Rouse. *A Mathematical Model of the Illinois Interlibrary Loan Network*. Urbana, Ill., University of Illinois, 1975.

Rouse, W. B., J. L. Divilbiss, and S. H. Rouse. *A Mathematical Model of the Illinois Interlibrary Loan Network: Report no. 2*. Coordinated Science Laboratory. Urbana, Illinois. University of Illinois, 1975.

Rouse, W. B. and S. H. Rouse. *Illinet, Interlibrary Loan and Information Network Model User's Manual*. Coordinated Science Laboratory. Urbana, Ill. University of Illinois, 1975.

Rouse, W. B. and S. H. Rouse. "Use of a Librarian/Consultant Team to Study Library Operations," *College and Research Libraries*, vol. 34, 1973, pp. 242-248.

Rublev, Yu V., Ukhamed'Yarov, R., A. M. d Karpenko, V. N. Chastotnyi printsip organizatsii pamyati informatslonnopoiskovgkh sisyen. [The organization of a retrieval system memory based on call-frequence principle]. *Nauchnotechnichiskaya Informatsiya*, Ser. 2, 1968, no. 3, 28-32.

Rudolph, G. A. (ed.). *The Academic Community Looks at Library Management*, proceedings of a conference, Carol M. Newman Library and Department of Industrial Engineering and Operations Research, Virginia Polytechnic Institute and State University, Blacksburg, Virginia, 1971.

Ruecking, F. "Selecting a circulation-control system: a mathematical approach," *College and Research Libraries*, vol. 25, 1964, pp. 385-390.

Rush, B., S. Steinberg, and D. H. Kraft. "Jounral Disposition Decision Policies," *Journal of the American Society for Information Science*, vol. 25, 1974, pp. 213-7.

Rzasa, P. V. *The Development of Measures of Effectiveness for a University Library*, unpublished Master's theses, School of Industrial Engineering, Purdue University, Lafayette, Indiana, 1969.

Rzasa, P. V. and N. R. Baker. "Measures of Effectiveness for a University Library," *Journal of the American Society for Information Science*, July-August, 1972, pp. 248-53.

Rzasa, P. V. and J. H. Moriarity. "The Types and Needs of Academic Library Users: A Case Study of 6568 Responses," *College and Research Libraries*, 1970, pp. 403-9.

Sackman, H. and B. W. Boehm, (Eds.). *Planning Community Information Utilities*. Montvale, N. J.: American Federation of Information Processing Societies, 1972.

Sakura, Shigeki and Miyok Vehara. Tsushinko Riron'o oyoshila Zasshino jufuku konyu Busu Ketteiho. [A method to establish the duplication of journals by the traffic theory]. In: *Proceedings of the 4th National Convention for the Study of Information and Documentation*, 15-17 November 1967, Tokyo, 1968. Tokyo, Japan Information Center for Science and Technology, pp. 23-28. In Japanese.

Salton, G. *Dynamic Information and Library Processing*, Englewood Cliffs, N.J.: Prentice Hall, 1975.

Sammon, J. W., Jr. "Some Mathematics of Information Storage and Retrieval," 1968, ERIC ED 026 084.

Sandison, S. "Library Optimum," *Nature*, vol. 234, December 10, 1971, pp. 368-369.

Sandison, S. "The Use of Older Literature and Obsolescence," *Journal of Documentation*, vol. 27, 1971, pp. 184-199.

Saracevic, Tefko (ed.), *Introduction to Information Science*, New York, Bowker, 1970.

Saracevic, T. *et al.* "An Inquiry into Testing of Information Retrieval Systems Part I: Objectives, Methodology, Design, and Controls; Comparative Systems Laboratory Final Report," 1968, ERIC ED 023 421 and Part II: Analysis of Results," 1968, ERIC ED 027 042.

Saxena, S. K. "Compact Storage of Books in Open-Shelf Libraries Where Book Height Follows a Compound Type of Truncated Double Exponential Distribution." *Opsearch*, vol. 3, 1967, pp. 157-67.

Sayer, J. S. "The economics of a national information system," In: Rubinoff, M. (ed.), *Toward a national information system*. 2nd Annual National Colloquium on Information retrieval, Washington, D. C., Spartan Books, 1965.

Schofield, J. L., A. Cooper and D. H. Waters. "Evaluation of an Academic Library's Stock Effectiveness." *Journal of Librarianship* 7 (3) July 1975, 207-227.

Schultz, C. K., "Cost-Effectiveness as a Guide in Developing Indexing Rules," *Information Storage and Retrieval*, 6:335-340 (1970).

Schwuchow, W. "Fundamental Aspects of the Financing of Information Centres" *Information Storage and Retrieval*, vol. 9, 1973, pp. 569-575.

Second Annual Library Management Workshop, Virginia Polytechnic Institute and State University, Blacksburg, Virginia, 1972.

Senko, M. E. "Modeling of information systems," Paper presented at the National Operations Research Society of America Meeting, Detroit, Michigan, 1970.

Seymour, C. A. "Weeding the Collection: A Review of Research on Identifying Obsolete Stock," *Libri*, vol. 22, 1972, pp. 137-48, and pp. 183-9.

Shapiro, E. L. "O Metodike Podgotovki Potrebitelei Informatsiia" (Systems Approach to Information User Training) *Nauchno-Tekhnicheskaia Informatsiia*, seriia 1, 1972, pp. 13-16.

Shaw, R. R. "Scientific Management in the Library," *Wilson Library Bulletin*, vol. 21, January, 1947, pp. 349-52.

Shaw, R. R. (ed.), "Scientific Management in Libraries." *Library Trends*, vol. 2, 1954, pp. 359-60.

Shaw, W. M. "Computer Simulation of the Circulation Subsystem of a Library." *Journal of the American Society for Information Science* 26 (5) September-October, 1975, 271-279.

Shisko, R. and J. A. Raffel. "Centralization Versus Decentralization: A Location Analysis

Approach for Librarians, RAND Corp., Santa Monica, Calif., 1971; ERIC ED 060 856.

Silver, E. A., "Quantitative Appraisal of the M.I.T. Science Library Mezzanine Books, with an Application to the Problem of Limited Shelf Space," Term Report, M.I.T. Libraries, Cambridge, Mass., 1962.

Simmons, P. "Collection development and the computer; a case study in the analysis of machine readable loan records and their application to book selection," University of British Columbia, 1971.

Simmons, P. "Improving collections through computer analysis of circulation records in a university library." In: *American Society for Information Science. Proceedings,* 7, 1970. Washington, D. C.: ASIS, 1970. Pp. 59-63.

Simmons, P. "Reserve collections: some computer assistance for the perennial problems." *Canadian Library Journal 29*, March-April 1972, 82-87.

Simms, D. M. "What is a systems analyst?" *Special Libraries*, vol. 59, 1968, pp. 718-21.

Simon, H. A., "On a Class of Skew Distribution Functions," *Biometrika*, 42:425-440 (1955), reprinted in Simon, Herbert A., *Models of Man: Social and Rational*, pp. 145-164, John Wiley & Sons, New York, 1957.

Simon, J. L. *Economics of book storage plans for a large university library*, unpublished doctoral thesis, University of Chicago, 1961.

Simon, J. L. "How Many Books Should be Stored Where? An Economic Analysis," *College and Research Libraries*, 1967, pp. 92-103.

Sinha, B. K., *Operations Research in Controlled Acquisition and Weeding of Library Collections*, Ph.D. dissertation in Operations Research, University of Pennsylvania, Philadelphia, 1971.

Slamecka, V. "A Selective Bibliography on Library Operations Research," *Library Quarterly*, vol. 42, 1972, pp. 152-8.

Slater, F. (ed.), *Cost Reduction for Special Libraries and Information Centers*, American Society for Information Science, Washington, D. C., 1973.

Slingerland, F. W. and V. Srinivasan. "A Mathematical Model of an Information System," American Society for Information Science Proceedings, Fall, 1973.

Slote, S. "Identifying Useful Core Collections: A Study of Weeding Fiction in Public Libraries," *Library Quarterly*, vol. 41, January, 1971, pp. 25-34.

Slote, S. *The predictive value of past-use pattern of adult fiction in public libraries.* Ph.D. thesis, Rutgers University, January 1969.

Slote, S. J. *Weeding Library Collections.* Littleton, Colo., Libraries Unlimited, 1975.

Smith, D. A. *Operational Research in Libraries*, unpublished study for Postgraduate Diploma in Librarianship, University of Sheffield, England, 1967.

Snowball, G. J. "Integrated Management of Libraries and Collection Development." Ottawa: Canadian Association of College and University Libraries, 1973.

Snowball, G. J. "Survey of social sciences and humanities monograph circulation by random sampling of the stack," *Canadian Library Journal*, vol. 28, 1971, pp. 352-361.

Solomon, S. L. Determination of Satisfactory Scale for Data Processing Facilities, *Journal of the American Society for Information Science*, vol. 25, 1974, pp. 151-155.

Sparks, D., M. M. Chodrow, and G. M. Walsh. "A Methodology for the Analysis of Information Systems," 1965, NTIS PB 168 264, ERIC ED 030 438, ED 039 439.

Spencer, M. "Projecting program cost over an adequate time horizon," Paper presented at an Institute on Program Planning and Budgeting Systems for Libraries at Wayne State University. Department of Library Science, Detroit, Michigan, 1968, ERIC ED 045 119.

Spyers-Duran, P. *Proposed Model Budget Analysis System and Quantitative Standards for the Libraries of Nebraska State Colleges.* Lincoln, Neb.: Libraries, Nebraska State Colleges, 1973.

Standera, O. R. "Costs and Effectiveness in the Evolution of an Information System: A Case

Study," *Journal of the American Society for Information Science*, vol. 25. 1974, pp. 203-207.

Stegemann, H. "Kostenrechnung Einer Datenbank für Unfragen", *Nachrichten für Dokumentation*, vol. 23, 1972, pp. 69-79.

Stephens, Irving E. "Computer simulation of library operations: an evaluation of an administrative tool," *Special Libraries*, vol. 61, no. 6, July/August, 1970, pp. 280-287.

Stigler, G. J. "The Economics of Information", *Journal of Political Economy*, vol. 69, 1961, pp. 212-25.

Stitelman, Leonard. Cost utility analysis applied to library budgeting. Paper presented at an Institute on Program Planning and Budgeting Systems for Libraries at Wayne State University, Department of Library Science, Detroit, Michigan, 1968, ERIC ED 045 126.

Stock, K. F. *Grundlagen and Praxis der Bibliotheksstatistik*. (Bases and Practice of Library Statistics). Pullach bei Munchen, Verlag Dokumentation, 1974.

Sturtz, C. "The difference between conventional budgeting and PPB," Paper presented at an Institute on Program Planning and Budgeting Systems for Libraries at Wayne University, Department of Library Science, Detroit, Michigan, 1968, ERIC ED 045 115.

Swank, R. C. "The cost of keeping books," In: Williams, E. E. (ed.), *Problems and prospects of the research library*, New Brunswick, N. J., Scarecrow Press, 1955.

Swanson, D. R. "Education for library planning," Canadian Library Association Occasional Papers, No. 62, Ottawa, 1965.

Swanson, D. R. "Education for systems planning," In: *International Federation for Documentation, Proceedings of the 1965 congress*, Washington, D. C., Spartan, 1965.

Swanson, R. W. *System Analysis + Work Study = Library Accountability*. Denver: S.E. Metropolitan Board of Cooperative Service, 1974.

Swets, J. A., "Effectiveness of Information Retrieval Methods", *American Documentation*, vol. 20, 1969, pp. 72-89.

Swets, J. A., "Information Retrieval Systems", *Science*, vol. 241, 1963, pp. 245-50.

Taylor, David W. *et al. An operations research study of the pacific northwest bibliographic center:final report*. Olympia, Washington: Washington State Library, June 1972, ERIC ED 065 127.

Taylor, R. S. (Ed.) Economics of Information Dissemination. A Symposium. Syracuse, N.Y.: Syracuse University, School of Library Science.

Thomas, P. A., *Procedural Models for Use of Bibliographic Records in Libraries*, Aslib, London, 1970.

Thomas, P. A. "Task analysis of library operations," Aslib occasional publication no. 8, Aslib, London, England, 1971.

Thomas, P. A. "Tasks and the Analysis of Library Systems," *Aslib Proceedings*, vol. 22, 1970, pp. 336-43.

Thomas, P. A. and S. E. Robertson. Computer Simulation Model of Library Operations *Journal of Documentation*, vol. 31, 1975, pp. 1-18.

Thompson, F. L. "The Dynamics of Information", *Engineering and Science*, vol. 36, 1972, pp. 4-7, 27-9.

Thorne, R. G. "The efficiency of subject catalogues and the cost of information searches," *Journal of Documentation*, vol. 11, 1955, pp. 130-148.

Tolliver, D. L. and T. R. Lied. "Determining a Cost Effective Sampling Technique which will provide Estimates of the Number of Patrons Utilizing the Purdue General Library during the Fall Semester of 1973." Lafayette, Ind.: Instructional Media Research Unit, Purdue University, 1973.

Travis, I., "Design Equations: Vehicles for Research into the Factors Affecting Bibliographic Reference Retrieval System Performance", unpublished doctoral dissertation, University of California, Berkeley, School of Librarianship, 1974. Also, an unpublished paper, College of Library and Information Services, University of Maryland, College Park, Maryland, 1975.

Trueswell, R. W. "User Behavior Patterns and Requirements and Their Effect on the Possible Applications of Data Processing and Computer Techniques in a University Library," unpublished doctoral dissertation, Northwestern University, Evanston, Illinois, 1964.

Trueswell, R. "A Quantitative Measure of User Circulation and Its Possible Effect on Stack Thinning and Multiple Copy Determination," *American Documentation*, vol. 16, January, 1965, pp. 20-5.

Trueswell, R. "Two characteristics of Circulation," *College and Research Libraries*, vol. 25, 1964, pp. 285-91.

Trueswell, R. C. "Some Circulation Data from a Research Library," *College and Research Libraries*, 1968, pp. 453-5.

Trueswell, R. L. "Some Behavioral Patterns of Library Users: The 80/20 Rule," *Wilson Library Bulletin*, vol. 43, 1969, pp. 458-61.

Trueswell, R. W. "Article Use and Its Relationship to Individual User Satisfaction," *College and Research Libraries*, vol. 31, 1970, pp. 239-43.

Trueswell, R. W. "Determining the Optimum Number of Volumes for a Library's Holdings," Paper presented at the 1964 National Joint Meeting of the Institute of Management Sciences and Operations Research Society of America, Minneapolis, Minn., October, 1964.

Trueswell, R. W. "User Circulation Satisfaction vs. Size of Holdings at Three Academic Libraries," *College and Research Libraries*, vol. 30, 1969, pp. 204-13.

Tudor, D. "Planning-programming-budgeting systems," Revised ed. Council of Planning Librarians, Monticello, Illinois, 1972.

Turner, W. C. "Operations and Process Analysis," Second Annual Library Management Workshop, Carol M. Newman Library and Department of Industrial Engineering and Operations Research, Virginia Polytechnic Institute and State University, Blacksburg, Virginia, 1972.

Urquhart, D. J. "National Libraries," in Mackenzie, A. G. and I. M. Stuart (eds.), "Proceedings of a Research Seminar held at the University of Lancaster, 9-11 July, 1969," University of Lancaster Library, Lancaster, England.

Urquhart, D. J. and R. M. Bunn. "A national loan policy for scientific serials," *Journal of Documentation*, vol. 15, 1959, pp. 21-37.

Urquhart, J. A. and Schofield, J. L. "Measuring readers' failure at the shelf." *Journal of Documentation 27,* December 1971, 273-286. Vol. 28, 1972, 233-241. Schofield follow up paper.

Vakhabov, V. K. Nekotorye resultaty staticheskikh issledovaniy deskrystornogo yazyka [Some findings of statistical studies of a descriptor language], *Nauchno-technickeskaya Informatsiya*, Ser. 2, 1970, no. 4, 2327-31.

Van Cott, H. P. and R. G. Kinkade. "Human simulation applied to the functional design of information systems," *Human Factors*, vol. 10, 1968, pp. 211-216.

Van Loo, W. "Decision Criteria and Evaluation Models for Information Retrieval Models for Information Retrieval Systems," in Kochen, M. (ed.), *Integrative Mechanicsm in Literature Growth*, Final Report, Ann Arbor, Michigan, 1970.

Van Rijsbergen, C. J. "Foundations of Evaluation", *Journal of Documentation,* vol. 30, 1974, pp. 365-73.

Van Rijsbergen, C. J. "Further Experiments with Hierarchic Clustering in Document Retrieval," *Information Storage and Retrieval*, vol. 10, 1974, pp. 1-14.

Vaughn, B. W. "Network Analysis Applied to the Choice of A-V Aids," *Visual Education*, April, 1971, pp. 22-3.

Veaner, A. B. "Institutional Political and Fiscal Factors in the Development of Library Automation, 1967-71," *Journal of Library Automation*, vol. 7, 1974.

Veazie, W. H., Jr. and T. F. Connally. "The Marketing of Information Analysis Center Products and Services," ERIC/CLIS and ASIS-SIG/IAC, Washington, D. C., 1971.

Verhoeff, J., W. Goffman, and J. Belzer, "Inefficiency of the Use of Boolean Function for Information Retrieval Systems", *Communications of the Association for Computing Machinery*, vol. 4, 1961, pp. 557-8.

Vickery, B. C. "Bradford's law of scattering," *Journal of Documentation*, vol. 4, 1948, pp. 198-203.

Vickery, B. C. "Indicators of the use of periodicals, *Journal of Librarianship*, vol. I, 1969, pp. 170-182.

Vickery, B. C. "Library Management Research: What Next?" in Mackenzie, A. G. and I. M. Stuart (eds.), "Proceedings of a Research Seminar held at the University of Lancaster, 9-11 July, 1969," University of Lancaster Library, Lancaster, England.

Vickery, B. C. "Periodical sets - what should you buy?" *Aslib Proceedings*, 5, 1953, pp. 69-74.

Vickery, B. C. "Statistics of Scientific and Technical Articles," *Journal of Documentation*, vol. 26, 1970, pp. 53-54.

Vickery, B. C. "The use of scientific literature," *Library Association Record*, vol. 63, 1961, pp. 263-269.

Wanga, J. and M. A. Henderson. "Evaluation Study of NCEC Information Analysis Products: Final Report, Volume 1: Description of Study Methodology and Findings, Volume 2: Individual Document Evaluation Profiles", System Development Corporation, Falls Church, Virginia, 1972.

Way, K. "All the red-legged partridges; or 99.5% retrieval of scientific information," *Physics today*, vol. 13, 1965.

Weber, D. C. "Criteria for evaluating a college library." *Association of American Colleges Bulletin 43*, 1957, 629-635.

Webster, D. "Library Policies: Analysis, Formulation and Use in Academic Institutions," OMS Occasional Paper No. 2, Association for Research Libraries University Library Management Studies Office, Washington, D.C., November, 1972.

Webster, D. "Organization and Staffing of the Libraries of Columbia University: A Summary of the Case Study sponsored by the ARL in cooperation with the American Council on Education under a grant from the Council of Library Resources," Association of Research Libraries, Office of University Library Management Studies, Washington, D.C., 1972. ERIC ED 061 948.

Webster, D. "Planning Aids for the University Library," OMS Occasional Paper No. 1, Association for Research Libraries, University Library Management Studies Office, Washington, D.C., December 1971.

Wedgeworth, R. "Budgeting for School Media Centers," *School Libraries*, Spring 1971, pp. 29-36.

Weed, K. K. "A tool for management evaluation of library services," *Special Libraries*, vol. 48, 1957, pp. 378-382.

Weeks, K. *Determination of Pre-Acquisition Predictors of Book Use: Final Report.* Berkeley, California, Institute of Library Research, 1973.

Weinberg, C. B. "The University Library: Analysis and Proposals," *Management Science*, vol. 21, 1974, pp. 130-140.

Weisman, H. M. *Information Systems Services and Centers.* Wiley, 1972.

Weiss, P. "Knowledge: A Growth Process," in Kochen, M. (ed.), *The Growth of Knowledge*, New York: John Wiley & Sons, Inc., 1967.

Welch, H. M. "Technical service costs, statistics and standards," *Library Resources and Technical Services*, vol. 11, 1967, pp. 436-442.

Wessel, C. J. "Criteria for evaluating technical library effectiveness," *Aslib Proceedings*, vol. 20, 1968, pp. 433-481.

Wessel, C. J. *Criteria for evaluating the effectiveness of library operations and services: Phase 1: Literature search and state of the art*, (ATLIS report, 10), Washington, D. C., John I. Thompson & Co., 1967, NTIS AD 649 468.

Westat Research, Inc. *A Study of the Characteristics, Costs and Magnitude of Interlibrary Loans in Academic Libraries*, report to Association for Research Libraries, Greenwood Publishing Co., Conn., 1972.

White, J. A. "Operations Research in Library Management," in Rudolph, G. A. (ed.), *The Academic Community Looks at Library Management*, Carol M. Newman Library and Department of Industrial Engineering and Operations Research, Virginia Polytechnic Institute and State University, Blacksburg, Virginia, 1971.

Whitfield, R. M., "Allocation of Funds for Libraries at the State Level," paper presented at ORSA/TIMS Joint Meeting, Las Vegas, Nevada, 1975.

Whitfield, R. M. The Efficient Allocation of Resources by the State to Systems of Public Libraries. Supplement to final report. Philadelphia: Graduate School of Arts and Sciences, Pennsylvania University, 1974.

Wilkin, A. P., R. Reynolds, and S. E. Robertson. "Standard Times for Information Systems: A Method for Data Collection and Analysis," *Journal of Documentation*, vol. 28, 1972, pp. 131-50.

Wilkinson, E. A. "The Ambiguity of Bradford's Law," *Journal of Documentation*, vol. 28, June, 1972, pp. 122-130.

Williams, G., E. C. Bryant, R. R. V. Wiederkehr, and V. E. Palmour. "Library Cost Models: Owning Versus Borrowing Serial Publications," report, Center for Research Libraries, Chicago, 1968 NTIS PB 182 304.

Wills, G. and C. Oldman. *A Longitudinal Study of the Costs and Benefits of Selected Library Services: Initial Exploration and Framework*. Working Discussion Document No. 74/6-1. Cranfield, England: School of Management, Cranfied Institute of Technology, 1974.

Wilson, P. C. *Two Kinds of Power: an essay on bibliographic control*, University of California Press, Berkeley, 1968.

Windsor, D. A. "Rational Selection of Primary Journals for a Biomedical Research Library: The Use of Secondary Journal Citations," *Special Libraries*, vol. 64, 1973, pp. 446-451.

Wolfe, J. N. "An Introduction to the Study of Cost Effectiveness in Information Systems," NTIS N70-12062.

Wolfe, J. N. and T. M. Aitchison, *et al. The Economics of Technical Information Systems*. New York, Praeger, 1974.

Wood, D. N. "User studies: a review of the literature from 1960 to 1970." *Aslib proceedings 23,* January 1971, 11-23.

Wood, M. S. and R. S. Seeds. "Development of SDI Services from a Manual Current Awareness Service to SDI Line." *Medical Library Association Bulletin,* vol. 62, 1974, pp. 374-384.

Woodburn, I. "A mathematical model of a hierarchical library system," In Mackenzie, A. G. and I. M. Stuart (eds.) "Planning Library Services; Proceedings of a Research Seminar held at the University of Lancaster 9-11 July 1969," University of Lancaster Library. Lancaster, England, 1969.

Woodruff, E. "Work measurement applied to libraries," *Special Libraries,* vol. 48, 1957, pp. 139-144.

Yenawine, W. S. (ed.), *Library evaluation*, Syracuse, N.Y., Syracuse University Press, 1959.

Yerkey, A. N. "Models of Index Searching and Retrieval Effectiveness of Keyword-in-Context Indexes," *Journal of the American Society for Information Science*, vol. 24, 1973, pp. 282-286.

Zais, H. W., "The Pricing of Information: A Model for Selective Dissemination of Information Services," unpublished doctoral dissertation, University of California, Berkeley, 1975.

Zannetos, Z. S. and M. R. Sertel. *Computerized Management Information Systems and Organizational Structures*. Cambridge, Mass.: Alfred Sloan School of Management, M.I.T., 1970.

Zipf, G. K. *Human behavior and the principle of least effort; an introduction to human ecology.* New York: Hafner, 1965.

Zunde, P. and V. Slamecka, "Distribution of Indexing Terms for Maximum Efficiency of Information Transmission", *American Documentation*, vol. 18, 1967, pp. 245-50.

ABOUT THE AUTHORS

D. H. Kraft graduated B.S., M.S. and Ph.D. in Industrial Engineering at Purdue University. His doctoral dissertation was concerned with the application of O.R. techniques to journal selection problems. After Purdue he moved to the University of Maryland at College Park as Assistant Professor in the College of Library and Information Services and in 1975-76 is Visiting Professor at the School of Librarianship at the University of California at Berkeley. Professor Kraft has published several papers on the application of O.R. to libraries, some of them on journal selection problems but others on a variety of other aspects of bibliometrics and indexing.

Michael K. Buckland: See page 28.